Web Dev with an AI Sidekick

Master the foundations of web development with hands-on AI-assisted learning for absolute beginners

Mark J. Price

Web Dev with an AI Sidekick

Portfolio Director: Ashwin Nair
Relationship Lead: Nitin Nainani
Project Manager: Ruvika Rao
Content Engineer: Adrija Mitra
Technical Editor: Arjun Varma
Indexer: Tejal Soni
Proofreader: Adrija Mitra
Production Designer: Deepak Chavan
Growth Lead: Priyadarshini Sharma

First published: May 2026

Production reference: 1210526

Published by Packt Publishing Ltd.
Grosvenor House
11 St Paul's Square
Birmingham
B3 1RB, UK.

ISBN 978-1-80611-125-1
`www.packtpub.com`

Foreword

Computer Science as a subject never stands still. Teaching it can often feel like trying to keep pace with a discipline that is constantly reinventing itself. In recent years, the rapid emergence of artificial intelligence has accelerated this challenge even further. AI has, in many respects, made teaching computer science both easier and more difficult than ever before. Easier, due to the tools available to teachers and students being extraordinarily powerful. More difficult, because those same tools can obscure the very fundamentals we are trying to teach.

In the classroom, it is not enough to simply introduce students to programming languages and frameworks. We must help them navigate an ecosystem where AI-assisted development is commonplace. Students will experiment with code-generating tools and lean on these when the going gets tough. They may rely on them to produce working solutions before they fully understand variables, program flow, or the techniques used. While this can accelerate progress, it often leaves students unable to explain why their code works. As educators, our responsibility is to ensure students do not mistake correct output for genuine understanding.

Mark Price's .NET books have been a popular addition to Greenhead College's programming book library. His books are structured in a way that respects the learner's journey, carefully scaffolding concepts while still engaging with modern, real-world development practices. Clear explanations, well-chosen examples, and a strong emphasis on building understanding step by step have made his books some of the most reliable resources I have used in both introductory and intermediate programming courses. They have proven particularly effective in supporting students through substantial coursework projects, where confidence and clarity matter just as much as technical correctness.

With the rise of AI-assisted development, the landscape is shifting again. The question is no longer should students use AI tools, but how can they use them responsibly and effectively. This is why a book like *Web Dev with an AI Sidekick* feels so timely. Rather than ignoring AI or treating it as a shortcut, the book directly addresses the tension educators now face: how to embrace these tools while ensuring they enhance learning instead of replacing it.

My expectation for this book is that it will bring the same strengths that have defined Mark Price's previous work. If AI is approached with the same measured and thoughtful mindset that he has applied to frameworks and languages throughout his writing, this book will help students develop not only functional solutions, but real understanding. That balance, between capability and comprehension, is exactly what educators and learners need in this new era of software development.

Stephen Wood

Head of Computer Science at Greenhead College

Contributors

About the author

Mark J. Price has over 30 years of experience teaching programming and technical subjects to a wide range of learners. He has worked extensively with students at different stages, from school-age learners and apprentices to experienced professionals, helping them build practical skills and confidence in technology.

Alongside his work in software development, Mark has taught mathematics and computing, with a focus on making complex ideas clear and approachable. His teaching style emphasizes understanding how systems work, rather than memorizing syntax, so that learners can apply their knowledge in real situations.

Mark holds a BSc in Computer Science and has spent much of his career developing courses, writing books, and supporting learners as they move from foundational concepts to building complete, working projects.

Thank you to all my readers. Your support means I get to write these books and celebrate your successes. Special thanks to the readers who give me actionable feedback via my GitHub repository and email, and who interact with me and the book communities on Discord. You help make my books even better with every edition.

About the reviewers

Sunil Raj Thota is a software engineer specializing in web development, AI applications, and agentic AI systems. He currently works on the Agentic AI Foundation team at Amazon, building intelligent agent-driven solutions. Previously, he contributed to Amazon QuickSight and held roles at Yahoo Inc., where he enhanced user engagement across Yahoo and AOL Mail products. Sunil has also worked as a Research Assistant at Northeastern University and as a Senior Software Engineer at MOURI Tech, leading web optimization and deployment projects. He co-founded ISF Technologies, championing user-centric design and agile methodologies. He holds a Master's in Analytics from Northeastern University.

David Guida is a Montreal-based software engineer and architect with nearly 20 years of experience building robust, distributed systems. He has spent his career untangling the complexities of modern software design and has a deep-seated passion for mentoring developers as they master architecture and scale. Currently, he's at Microsoft working on some very cool projects, and when he's not busy coding, blogging, or hunting for his next favorite book, you can usually find him in the kitchen baking cakes.

Jo Van Eyck is an experienced software engineer and technical coach based in Belgium. He helps teams ship software they're proud of.

He writes articles and publishes videos about whatever is currently rewiring his thinking, which lately means AI-assisted coding, the changing shape of the engineering role, and how to best prepare for this transition.

Table of Contents

Chapter 3: CSS – Styling Your Web Pages 85

Chapter 5: JavaScript – Making Web Pages Interactive 165

Chapter 6: TypeScript – Safer JavaScript 211

Chapter 9: Django – Web Development on the Backend 369

Chapter 10: Bash/Shell – Command-Line Skills for Developers 429

Chapter 12: Unit, Integration, and End-to-End Testing 503

Chapter 14: Adding Project Features Using Spec-Driven Development 595

Preface

Web Dev with an AI Sidekick reinvents how beginners learn to code by harnessing the power of interactive AI. This comprehensive guide transforms the static textbook experience into a two-way conversation with your AI coding partner. Instead of just reading about code, you'll prompt an AI to explain concepts, generate examples, and help you solve problems on the fly. It's like having a tutor available 24/7.

The result is a highly engaging learning journey that adapts to your questions and needs. You can ask the "dumb" questions without fear, get instant clarifications, and receive step-by-step guidance tailored to your pace. It's an engaging way to learn programming fast, making coding more accessible and rewarding. By leveraging AI models such as OpenAI's ChatGPT, Google's Gemini, and others, the book turns the latest AI technology into your personal coding mentor and collaborator.

Who this book is for

This book is for complete beginners who are curious about web development and excited about what's possible using AI to both learn programming skills and build complete projects. This book is ideal for:

- Students exploring coding for the first time
- Career changers entering the technology field and needing a friendly entry point
- Self-taught learners who feel overwhelmed by traditional textbooks or video courses
- Creatives, designers, or writers who want to build interactive web projects
- Hobbyists or entrepreneurs with app ideas but no formal training
- Anyone fascinated by AI and wondering how it can help them learn to code

It especially appeals to people who prefer hands-on, practical learning and value being able to ask questions in natural language while coding.

What prerequisites do you need?

None. The book assumes zero prior experience in programming, web development, or using AI tools. If you can open a browser and follow instructions, you're ready. The early chapters walk through every step, including how to sign up for ChatGPT, install VS Code with various extensions like GitHub Copilot, and even how to talk to an AI effectively. Later, the book explains how web pages are structured and styled, how to draw graphics, what a variable is, what a loop is, and even how to host your finished web projects. It builds up from nothing to a complete website.

Why should you buy this book?

This book teaches modern web development faster, more enjoyably, and more interactively than any traditional book.

It introduces a fun and friendly way to learn by using AI tools as a tutor, debugger, and coding assistant.

It's tailored for beginners like you, removing jargon and gatekeeping.

It covers everything in one book: frontend, backend, databases, deployment, and development tools.

It delivers real-world results. You will build and deploy a fully functional web app.

It keeps you up-to-date by teaching you how to learn continuously with AI. It's not just a reference book about specific syntax.

It's future-proof because you gain both web development skills and fluency with AI-assisted development, a major advantage in today's job market.

What this book covers

Let's briefly review what you can expect in this book.

Part 1: Frontend Web Development

Part 1 introduces the main technologies used to build the visible parts of a web page in dedicated chapters, each structured for interactive learning. You'll start with the building blocks of the Web: HTML and CSS with SVG for graphics, then progress to JavaScript and its typed superset TypeScript.

Every chapter introduces core concepts in a friendly way and immediately invites you to put them into practice by chatting with an AI. For example, when learning HTML, you'll ask the AI to generate a simple web page structure and then tweak it through prompts. This way, you get to experience firsthand that HTML defines the meaning and structure.

In the CSS chapter, you will style the page and see how CSS controls layout, colors, spacing, and typography, reinforcing that CSS describes how elements should be rendered on screen, on paper, or on other media.

JavaScript brings your web pages to life as you collaborate with the AI to make your pages interactive, reflecting JavaScript's role as a core web language, and TypeScript is introduced as an extension that adds static types to JavaScript for safer coding.

Each chapter includes exercises where you ask an AI tool to explain, revise, or debug small examples. Each chapter wraps up with a quiz to solidify your knowledge, and a curated list of official documentation links for further reference, encouraging you to consult authoritative sources as part of your learning.

Part 2: Backend Web Development

We then cover all the essential backend web development technologies, again in dedicated chapters, each structured for interactive learning. You'll explore database interactions with SQL, dive into programming with Python, master web frameworks with Django, and get comfortable with command line scripting for automation with Bash.

By the end of *Part 1* and *Part 2*, you will have a solid grasp of the entire web stack, from frontend to backend, all gained through hands-on, interactive practice with an AI chatbot by your side.

Part 3: Survey Project

Now armed with the fundamentals, you'll embark on an exciting capstone project: developing a survey creation web application using Django, modern web technologies, and your AI assistant at every step. This part of the book is a project-based tutorial split into several chapters that mirror a real development workflow.

In the planning phase, you'll design the app's features and data models in Django with the AI helping brainstorm model fields and relationships. We'll set up a professional development environment using Docker containers to run Django and a database locally, ensuring that everyone can follow along with the same setup.

The book provides detailed instructions for using either OpenAI Codex or Anthropic Claude Code, cutting-edge AI-powered coding environments, to build the project. We'll show how Codex or Claude Code seamlessly integrates AI into the coding workflow, so you can write code using instructions and use the AI to draft code while you review, test, and revise it. Through this AI-enhanced process, you'll implement all the key features of the survey app:

- Creating surveys with multiple question types (text, multiple-choice, ratings, and so on.)
- Letting users submit responses.
- Building an admin interface for managing surveys.
- Displaying results in dynamic tables and charts.

Along the way, you'll practice AI-assisted debugging and testing: for instance, writing unit tests for your Django views.

We emphasize effective prompt techniques to get useful output from the AI, and also caution about AI quirks and how to verify and correct AI-generated solutions.

The project chapters also highlight collaboration between tools. For example, using Git version control with GitHub or locally to manage changes suggested by the AI, and using Docker for local live testing.

In the final project chapter, we guide you through deploying the finished app to a production environment. Throughout deployment, the AI copilot can assist with tasks like writing Dockerfiles or `.gitignore` files.

By the end of *Part 3*, you will have built a full-stack web application and practiced using AI tools during planning, coding, testing, and deployment. This is a portfolio-worthy project that reinforces everything you learned in *Part 1* and *Part 2* and teaches you how those pieces interconnect in a real app.

More importantly, you will have experienced a new paradigm of building software: coding with an AI partner.

AI-interactive philosophy

Unique to this book is its AI-interactive philosophy. The content stays fresh and up-to-date because instead of relying on pre-written text alone, it leverages real-time AI models that are continually improving. Whenever a new API emerges or a language update happens, your AI copilot can fill you in making this a book that grows with the technology.

We also stress good habits, like cross-checking AI outputs against official documentation. Each chapter directs you to the primary sources, like the official Python docs and Django's docs, so you learn to verify and deepen your knowledge beyond what the AI provides.

The tone and content of this book is tailored for complete beginners and written in plain, friendly US English. Complex topics are broken down into manageable, conversational exchanges with the AI, making the learning experience feel more like a guided dialogue than a lecture.

The book is about learning a new way to code, one where you ask the AI to teach you concepts and why things work and then apply that knowledge creatively.

Whether you're a student, a professional looking to switch careers, or just tech-curious, *Web Dev with an AI Sidekick* will fast-track your journey from novice to confident web developer.

By the final page, you'll not only have a functioning web app deployed online, but also the know-how to keep learning any new technology with the help of your AI sidekick.

Our principles for using AI-generated content

This book was written by Mark J. Price. Generative AI tools such as ChatGPT, Gemini, and Claude were used to help explore ideas, troubleshoot code, and generate examples during development. This thoughtful use of AI reflects the book's core philosophy that learning to code can be more intuitive, responsive, and engaging when guided by interactive AI.

The purpose behind incorporating AI in the writing process was to offer readers more examples across a wider range of programming languages, cover solutions in greater depth, and address new scenarios more quickly.

All the instructional content in this book were developed, reviewed, and tested by the author and Packt's editorial team. Packt does not publish AI-generated content as a substitute for expert authorship.

To get the most out of this book

- To complete *Part 1* and *Part 2* of this book, you will need access to an AI chatbot like OpenAI ChatGPT, Anthropic Claude, or Google Gemini. You can use a free account, although a paid account will let you access more capable models.
- To complete *Part 3* of this book, you will need an AI-enhanced IDE like VS Code with GitHub Copilot and CLI tools like OpenAI Codex or Claude Code.

Download the example code files

The code for the book is hosted on GitHub at `https://github.com/markjprice/web-dev-ai`.

We also have other code bundles from our rich catalog of books and videos available at `https://github.com/PacktPublishing`. Check them out!

Conventions used

There are a number of text conventions used throughout this book.

`CodeInText`: Indicates code words in text, database table names, folder names, filenames, file extensions, pathnames, dummy URLs, user input, and Twitter handles. For example: "Change the `<h1>` and `<title>` text to something else."

A block of code is set as follows:

```
<p>
  HTML tells the browser what each piece of content <em>is</em>.
  Styling comes later (that's CSS), and interactivity comes later (that's 
JavaScript).
</p>
```

When we wish to draw your attention to a particular part of a code block, the relevant lines or items are set in bold:

```
<h2>Useful link</h2>
<p>
  Here's a link to learn more about HTML:
  <a href="https://developer.mozilla.org/en-US/docs/Web/HTML">MDN Web 
Docs: HTML</a>.
</p>
```

Any command-line input or output is written as follows:

```
code --install-extension ms-vscode.live-server
```

Bold: Indicates a new term, an important word, or words that you see on the screen. For instance, words in menus or dialog boxes appear in the text like this. For example: "In VS Code, click the **Extensions** icon or navigate to **View** | **Extensions**."

Get in touch

Feedback from our readers is always welcome.

General feedback: If you have questions about any aspect of this book or have any general feedback, please email us at `customercare@packt.com` and mention the book's title in the subject of your message.

Errata: Although we have taken every care to ensure the accuracy of our content, mistakes do happen. If you have found a mistake in this book, we would be grateful if you reported this to us. Please visit `http://www.packt.com/submit-errata`, click **Submit Errata**, and fill in the form.

Piracy: If you come across any illegal copies of our works in any form on the internet, we would be grateful if you would provide us with the location address or website name. Please contact us at `copyright@packt.com` with a link to the material.

If you are interested in becoming an author: If there is a topic that you have expertise in and you are interested in either writing or contributing to a book, please visit `http://authors.packt.com/`.

Free benefits with your book

This book comes with free benefits to support your learning. Activate them now for instant access (see the *How to Unlock* section for instructions).

Here's a quick overview of what you can instantly unlock with your purchase:

1

Introduction to Web Development with an AI Sidekick

This chapter explains how to use this book and set up your AI-assisted learning environment. You will be introduced to the concept of learning with an AI partner. I guide you through choosing and configuring an AI tool, share tips for effective prompting, like asking the AI to explain before coding, and outline the structure of the book.

By the end of this chapter, you will know how to learn with AI tools and have a practical setup for trying the examples yourself.

In this chapter, we will cover the following topics:

- Breaking down the chapters in this book
- Setting up your web development environment
- Learning with an AI chatbot as your coach
- Coding with an AI assistant as your coworker
- Pros and cons of AI tools

Your purchase includes a free PDF copy + exclusive extras

Your purchase includes a DRM-free PDF copy of this book, 7-day trial to the Packt+ library (no credit card required), and additional exclusive extras. See the *Free benefits with your book* section in the *Preface* to unlock them instantly and maximize your learning.

Breaking down the chapters of this book

Let's start by breaking down what you will learn in the rest of the chapters of this book. After this first chapter, the book is divided into three major parts:

1. **Frontend Web Development**: Learn the technologies for developing what the user experiences in their web browser: HTML, CSS, SVG, JavaScript, and TypeScript.
2. **Backend Web Development**: Learn the technologies for developing the parts of a website that run on the web server: a SQL database, Python, Django, and Bash, aka shell scripting for automating developer tasks.
3. **Survey Project**: Build and then optionally deploy a complete website for creating, taking, and analyzing surveys and polls.

Frontend Web Development

Chapter 2, HTML – Structuring Your Web Pages, covers the basics of HTML (HyperText Markup Language). You'll use the AI to generate a simple page and, in doing so, learn about elements, tags, and attributes. You'll learn about HTML's role in defining web content structure (from headings to links and images). You will create a contact form, introducing form elements.

Chapter 3, CSS – Styling Your Web Pages, shows you how to control presentation and layout. You will get the AI to explain selectors, properties, and values. You will apply styles to your web page from *Chapter 2, HTML – Structuring Your Web Pages.* You will learn about responsive design and making mobile-friendly web pages using CSS media queries.

Chapter 4, SVG – Drawing Scalable Graphics, introduces SVG as a way to generate graphics with code, which will be useful for charting survey results. AI will explain that SVG is an XML-based markup language for 2D graphics and how it differs from canvas/bitmaps. Through AI-guided examples, you create basic shapes (circle, rectangle, line) in SVG and embed them in HTML.

Chapter 5, JavaScript – Making Web Pages Interactive, covers fundamental JavaScript concepts like variables, functions, events, and the DOM. We start by describing what JavaScript is (a lightweight, interpreted language that runs in browsers) and where to include `<script>` blocks in HTML.

Chapter 6, TypeScript – Safer JavaScript, introduces TypeScript as a superset of JavaScript that adds static types and explains why they are useful.

Backend Web Development

Chapter 7, SQL – Managing Data, demystifies SQL (using SQLite and a simple database for practice). The AI explains what a database is and how SQL is used to query data. You will practice basic SQL commands through AI prompts: `SELECT` statements, filtering (`WHERE`), and sorting (`ORDER BY`). The AI can generate a sample dataset (like a `users` table) and challenge you with queries ("How would you get all users who signed up this month?").

Chapter 8, Python – Programming on the Backend, covers fundamental Python syntax and concepts, preparing readers for backend web development. You'll install Python and then learn coding for Python basics like variables, loops, and functions. You will ask the AI to explain code line by line, reinforcing understanding.

Chapter 9, Django – Web Development on the Backend, focuses on Django, Python's most commonly-used web framework. Your AI will explain how Django works with its **MVT (Model-View-Template)** pattern, which is related to but distinct from the traditional **MVC (Model-View-Controller)** pattern, and why it's used for rapid web development. With AI guidance, you start a Django project (the book provides step-by-step instructions, and the AI can help troubleshoot). You'll create a new Django project, which lays the groundwork for the full project in the *Survey Project* part of the book. The AI helps you write a simple view and a template. You learn how Django serves HTML and how to use template variables.

Chapter 10, Bash/Shell – Command-Line Skills for Developers, briefly steps aside from web programming to teach Bash/Shell usage, since many development tasks involve the command line, especially to automate deployments. You will practice common commands (`ls`, `cd`, `mkdir`, `rm`, etc.) by having the AI describe what each does and trying them in a terminal or emulator. The AI will walk you through creating a small Bash/Shell script to automate a task like backing up a file or starting your Django server.

Survey Project

Chapter 11, Setting Up Your Project Environment, kicks off the TallyApp survey project and configures tools. You will see an overview of the survey app you'll build and its features, like creating surveys, taking surveys, and viewing results. Step-by-step instructions (with screenshots or code snippets) for setting up VS Code with GitHub Copilot are provided. You will be introduced to a Docker-based development environment and how to place code under version control using Git.

Chapter 12, Unit, Integration, and End-to-End Testing, teaches you how to design and implement a layered testing strategy for TallyApp, write meaningful unit and integration tests in Django, automate real browser interactions with end-to-end tests using Playwright, and use AI tools to generate tests automatically.

Chapter 13, Specifying and Building the Initial Project, defines a clear project brief for TallyApp, translates that into an actionable development plan, guides you to scaffold a Django 6 project with appropriate apps and models, and implements core authentication and survey functionality.

Chapter 14, Adding Project Features Using Spec-Driven Development, covers how to implement a structured feature specification, use an AI coding assistant to implement it inside an existing Django project, and verify that the implementation satisfies clearly defined acceptance criteria.

Chapter 15, Deploying to Public Servers, reviews options for deploying TallyApp to a server connected to the wider internet so that members of the public can use the website. You will deploy TallyApp to a publicly accessible server, understand how requests flow through a production Django stack, know how to preserve and back up user data across deployments, and know what has to change as traffic and expectations increase.

Epilogue, reviews the next steps on your web development learning journey.

Appendix, contains answers to questions at the end of each chapter.

Why these languages and skills?

You might wonder why I've chosen to cover these specific languages, frameworks, and skills. One major reason is that Stack Overflow conducts a survey of thousands of developers every year and one question they ask is: *Which programming, scripting, and markup languages have you done extensive development work in over the past year?*

The 31,771 responses to this question in the 2025 survey revealed the top six languages that developers reported using extensively over the past year are JavaScript, HTML/CSS, SQL, Python, Bash/Shell, and TypeScript, as shown in *Figure 1.1*:

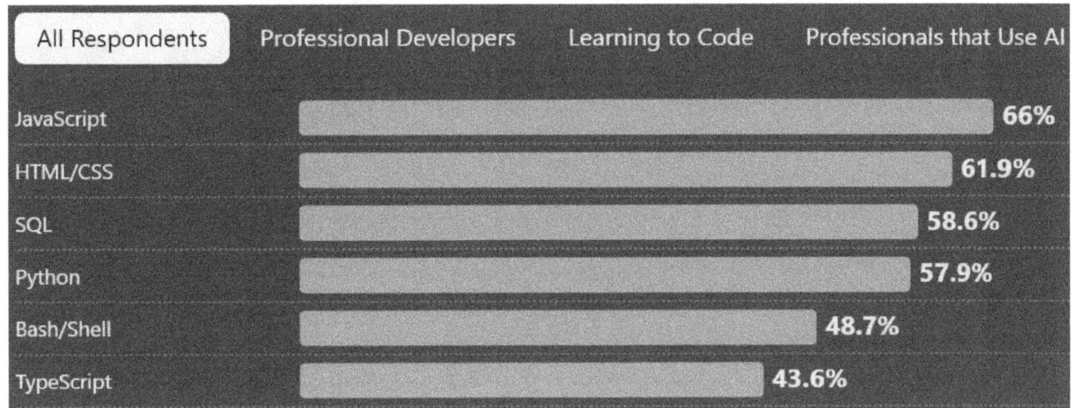

Figure 1.1: 2025 survey of the most extensively used programming languages

You can see these results in the survey at the following link: `https://survey.stackoverflow.co/2025/technology#most-popular-technologies-language`

These results make sense when you realize that all those languages are needed to do web development, and most programming work these days is web development. All that's missing in the top six are SVG for drawing scalable vector graphics, and Django which is the most popular web development framework for Python. I even briefly considered naming the book, *Top Six Programming Languages*, but ultimately decided that web development is a better connecting theme for a book that covers all those languages.

You can see a summary of what roles each of the languages and frameworks play in web development in *Figure 1.2*:

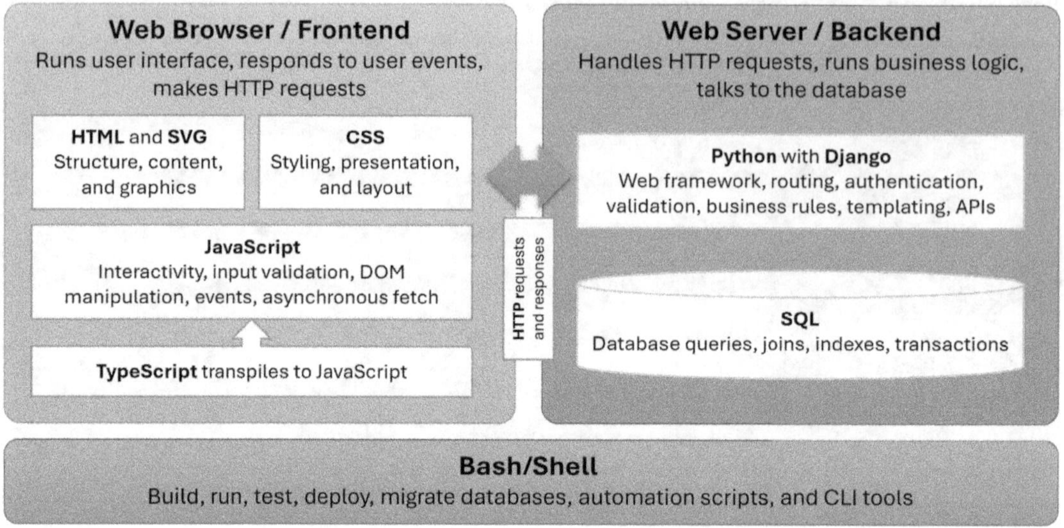

Figure 1.2: Language, framework, and tool roles in web development

How to use this book

Technical books are not meant to be read in a strictly linear way. Unlike a novel, you are free to move around based on your interests, your goals, and your existing experience. Some readers will feel an immediate pull toward building a complete project and may be tempted to jump ahead to the later chapters where that work comes together.

That instinct is understandable, and I encourage you to explore. However, if you do, you will quickly encounter the practical reality that web development draws on multiple layers of knowledge. Concepts that may seem slow or isolated in earlier chapters become important to understand when combined in a real application. The structure of this book reflects that progression.

As you've seen in the chapter breakdown, the first two parts of the book focus on learning individual technologies one at a time. This is deliberate. Each language, framework, and tool is introduced in isolation so you can understand its role, its strengths, and how it behaves without unnecessary complexity. Trying to learn everything at once often leads to confusion and shallow understanding. Learning one tool at a time makes the later project less confusing.

The final part of the book brings these elements together into a complete project. This is where the earlier investment pays off. Instead of copying and pasting code without context, you will be more likely to understand what you are building and why it works the way it does.

It is also important to recognize that a book is only one part of the learning process. Real progress comes from a combination of reading, hands-on practice, experimentation, and exposure to different perspectives. It would be impossible to write a single book that teaches everything about web development. And most readers learn more thoroughly from a variety of instructional techniques. Videos, documentation, and community discussions all play a role. Most importantly, your own persistence and curiosity will determine how far you go.

Learning to build software is a long-term effort. It requires time, repetition, and patience. This book is designed to give you structure so that your time is well spent. Instead of piecing together dozens of free but disconnected tutorials and articles, you are following a coherent path where each chapter builds on the last.

Approach the material in a way that works for you, but understand why the book is organized this way. If you take the time to build a solid foundation, the later stages will feel far more rewarding and far less frustrating.

> Files for the code in the book are available in the book's GitHub repository: `https://github.com/markjprice/web-dev-ai/tree/main/Code`. If you have a complaint about this book, then please contact me before writing a negative review on Amazon. Authors cannot respond to Amazon reviews, so I cannot contact you directly to resolve the problem and help you, or listen to your feedback and try to do better in the next edition. Please ask a question on the Discord channel for this book at `https://discord.gg/rdEsrVbbC` or raise an issue in the book's GitHub repository: `https://github.com/markjprice/web-dev-ai/issues`.

Making good use of the GitHub repository for this book

I created a GitHub repository for this book, and I use it for the following:

- To store the solution code for the book that can be maintained after the print publication date
- To provide extra materials that extend the book, like errata fixes, small improvements, lists of useful links, and optional sections about topics that cannot fit in the printed book
- To provide readers with a place to contact me regarding any issues with the book
- To make it easier to enter commands at the command prompt or terminal, I list all commands that can be easily copied and pasted: `https://github.com/markjprice/web-dev-ai/blob/main/docs/commandlines.md`

Before attempting any coding task, I strongly recommend that you all review the errata, improvements, post-publication changes, and common errors pages. You can find them at the following link: `https://github.com/markjprice/web-dev-ai/blob/main/docs/errata/README.md`.

Raising issues with the book

If you get stuck following any of the instructions in this book, or if you spot a mistake in the text or the code in the solutions, please raise an issue in the GitHub repository:

1. Use your favorite browser to navigate to the following link: `https://github.com/markjprice/web-dev-ai/issues`.
2. Click **New Issue**.
3. Enter as much detail as possible that will help me diagnose the issue. For example:
    - The specific section title, page number, and step number
    - As much of your code and configuration as you feel is relevant and necessary
    - A description of the expected behavior and the behavior experienced
    - Screenshots (you can drag and drop image files into the Issue box)

I cannot always respond immediately to issues. But I want all my readers to find success with my book, so if I can help you (and others) without too much trouble, then I will gladly do so.

Giving me feedback

If you'd like to give me more general feedback about the book, email me at `markjprice@gmail.com` or ask a question in the book channel on Discord. You can provide the feedback anonymously, or if you would like a response from me, you can supply an email address. I will only use this email address to answer your feedback.

Please join me and your fellow readers on Discord using this invitation: `https://discord.gg/rdEsrVbbC`. I love to hear from my readers about what they like about my book, as well as suggestions for improvements and how they are working with their AI sidekick, so don't be shy. Please get in touch!

Thank you in advance for your thoughtful and constructive feedback. Learn how to write a good question or raise an issue: `https://github.com/markjprice/markjprice/blob/main/articles/issues.md`.

Shared content across all my books

I use my personal GitHub repository to store shared content that is relevant to all my books. Useful sections include the following:

- FAQs: `https://github.com/markjprice/markjprice/blob/main/FAQs.md`
- Articles: `https://github.com/markjprice/markjprice/blob/main/articles/README.md`

Now that you know what to expect from the rest of the chapters in this book, let's set up your development environment. Although we won't start building a full project until the *Survey Project* part of this book, during all the language-learning chapters you will want to write snippets of code and see them run for real.

Setting up your web development environment

Before you start programming, you'll need a code editor for multiple languages including, HTML, CSS, JavaScript, TypeScript, SQL, and Python, either from Microsoft or a third party. I recommend VS Code because it supports extensions for all common languages and runs cross-platform on Windows, Mac, and Linux.

VS Code is by far the most popular code editor or IDE across all developers with over 75% of professional developers selecting it in a Stack Overflow 2025 survey, which you can read at the following link: `https://survey.stackoverflow.co/2025/technology/#1-dev-id-es`.

Downloading and installing VS Code

Let's now download and install VS Code and some useful extensions:

1. Download and install either the Stable build or the Insiders edition of VS Code from the following link: `https://code.visualstudio.com/download`, as shown in *Figure 1.3*:

If you need more help installing VS Code, you can read the official setup guide at the following link: `https://code.visualstudio.com/docs/setup/setup-overview`.

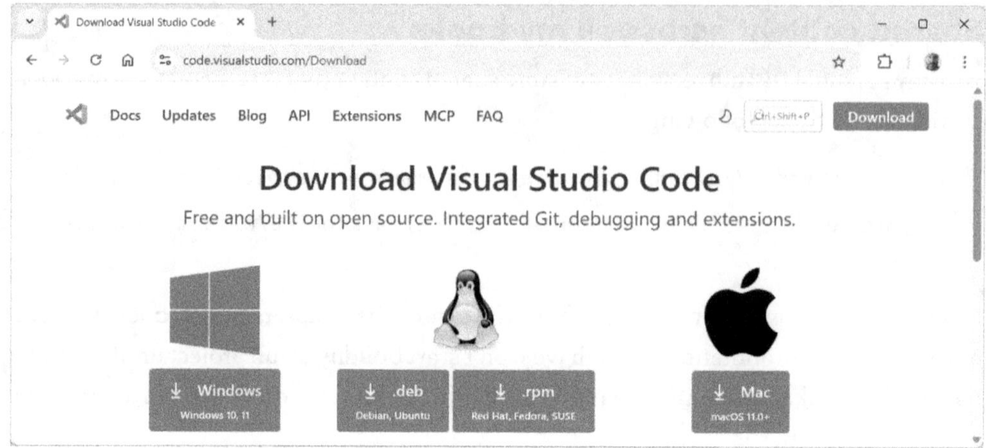

Figure 1.3: VS Code download web page for Windows, Linux, and Mac

2. To install the VS Code extensions with a user interface, you must first launch the VS Code application.
3. In VS Code, click the **Extensions** icon or navigate to **View | Extensions.**
4. Enter `Live Preview` in the search box.
5. Select the **Live Preview** extension and confirm that it is the correct one, as shown in *Figure 1.4*:
    - **Identifier:** `ms-vscode.live-server`
    - **Version: 0.4.16 or later**
    - **Publisher:** Microsoft
    - **Downloads:** more than 11 million

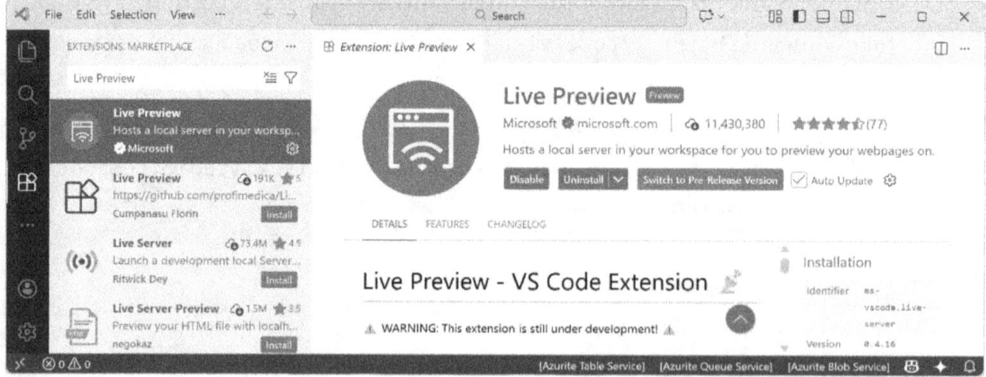

Figure 1.4: Installing the Live Preview extension published by Microsoft

6. Click **Install** and wait for it to download and install.

VS Code has built-in support for editing HTML, CSS, JavaScript, and TypeScript, but other languages can be supported by installing more extensions.

Installing other extensions

In later chapters of this book, you will use more VS Code extensions. If you want to install them now, all the extensions that we will use are shown in *Table 1.1*:

Extension name and identifier	**Description**
Live Preview `ms-vscode.live-server`	Hosts a local server in your workspace for you to preview your web pages.
Markdown All in One `yzhang.markdown-all-in-one`	All you need for Markdown (keyboard shortcuts, table of contents, auto preview, and more).
SQLite `alexcvzz.vscode-sqlite`	Explore and query SQLite databases.
Python `ms-python.python`	Rich support for the Python language (for all actively supported Python versions), providing access points for extensions to work with and offer support for IntelliSense (Pylance), debugging (Python Debugger), formatting, linting, code navigation, refactoring, and so on.
Django `batisteo.vscode-django`	Beautiful syntax and scoped snippets for perfectionists with deadlines
GitHub Copilot `github.copilot`	AI peer programming tool that helps you write code faster and smarter.
Claude Code for VS Code `anthropic.claude-code`	Claude autonomously explores your codebase, reads and writes code, and runs Terminal commands with your permission.
Gemini Code Assist `google.geminicodeassist`	AI-assisted development powered by Gemini.
Playwright Test for VSCode `ms-playwright.playwright`	Run Playwright Test tests in VS Code.

Table 1.1: VS Code extensions for web development

You can install a VS Code extension at the command prompt or terminal, as shown in *Table 1.2*:

Command	**Description**
`code --list-extensions`	List installed extensions
`code --install-extension <extension-id>`	Install the specified extension
`code --uninstall-extension <extension-id>`	Uninstall the specified extension

Table 1.2: Managing VS Code extensions at the command prompt

For example, to install the **Live Preview** extension, enter the following in the command prompt:

```
code --install-extension ms-vscode.live-server
```

I have created PowerShell scripts to install and uninstall the VS Code extensions in the preceding table. You can find them at the following link: `https://github.com/markjprice/web-dev-ai/tree/main/scripts/extension-scripts/`. PowerShell scripts are cross-platform, as you can read about at the following link: `https://learn.microsoft.com/en-us/powershell/scripting/overview`.

Understanding VS Code versions

Microsoft releases a new feature version of VS Code (almost) every month and bug-fix versions more frequently. For example:

- Version 1.109.0, January 2026 feature release
- Version 1.109.1, January 2026 bug-fix release

The version used in this book is 1.112.0, the April 2026 feature release, but the version of VS Code is less important than the versions of the extensions that you install. Make sure to keep all your extensions up to date.

Keyboard shortcuts for VS Code

If you want to customize your keyboard shortcuts for VS Code, then you can, as shown at the following link: `https://code.visualstudio.com/docs/getstarted/keybindings`.

I recommend that you download a PDF of VS Code keyboard shortcuts for your operating system from the following list:

- Windows: `https://code.visualstudio.com/shortcuts/keyboard-shortcuts-windows.pdf`
- macOS: `https://code.visualstudio.com/shortcuts/keyboard-shortcuts-macos.pdf`
- Linux: `https://code.visualstudio.com/shortcuts/keyboard-shortcuts-linux.pdf`

Now that you have set up your development environment, let's dive into how to get the best out of an AI chatbot when you want it to act as your coach for learning web development.

Learning with an AI chatbot as your coach

AI chatbots like ChatGPT can be useful learning tools when you use them well.

This section compares three chatbots that are commonly used for learning web development.

Good practice: If you are new to web development or unsure which tools to choose, use the following setup. This is the simplest path through the book, and what the examples assume:

- **Chatbot**: ChatGPT (free or Plus at $20 USD per month)
- **Code editor or IDE**: VS Code (free)
- **IDE-integrated coding assistant**: GitHub Copilot (individual plans like Copilot Free and Copilot Pro include GitHub AI Credits allowances that vary by plan)
- **Command-line coding assistant**: OpenAI Codex (because it's currently included with ChatGPT Plus)

You can complete this entire book using just these tools. Other options like Claude or Gemini are excellent, and you are encouraged to explore them later. But switching tools too early can feel overwhelming and slow down your learning. Start simple, build confidence, and then experiment.

Now let's compare chatbots: OpenAI's ChatGPT, Anthropic's Claude, and Google's Gemini.

OpenAI's ChatGPT

ChatGPT is particularly useful for explanations, debugging help, and iterative back-and-forth while you learn. When you're stuck on HTML semantics, JavaScript quirks, or Django data model logic, a well-structured prompt will usually produce a useful explanation.

Free vs paid subscriptions:

- **Free**: The free version works well for conversational learning but does not include access to Codex coding agent.
- **Go ($8 USD per month)**: Expanded access with more messages, uploads, image creation, and longer memory.
- **Plus ($20 USD per month)**: Access to advanced GPT family models, which are generally better at reasoning, code generation, and maintaining context across longer sessions. Access to Codex coding agent, projects, and custom GPTs. This is my recommendation if you want more capability without committing to a high monthly cost.
- **Pro ($100 USD per month)**: 5x more usage than Plus with the Frontier Pro model, maximum access to Codex and deep research, and unlimited and faster image creation.
- **Business ($20 USD per month per seat) / Enterprise**: Best for corporate teams because it requires 2+ seats billed annually. OpenAI promises that your data will never be used for training their models.

ChatGPT pricing information can be found at the following link: `https://chatgpt.com/pricing/`

All major AI providers offer a range of models that trade speed and cost for capability. While the names differ, the pattern is consistent. OpenAI names its faster, less-thinking models `mini`. For example, `GPT-5 mini`. Google names its Gemini faster, less-thinking models Flash, and its deeper thinking models Ultra.

The current version of the GPT model at the time of writing is 5.5, released on April 23, 2026. You can learn about GPT-5.5 at the following link: `https://openai.com/index/introducing-gpt-5-5/`. OpenAI released version 5.4 on March 5, so improvements happen fast. Check OpenAI's releases page for the latest: `https://openai.com/research/index/release/`

How to set it up for success:

- Start each session with context by mentioning your stack (HTML, JavaScript, Django, and so on) and your exact goal.
- Include instructions like "show clear examples" and "explain line by line."
- Upload smaller files when you want the bot to read and comment on your code.
- If you upgrade, explore Custom GPTs via the GPT Store to create a tailored tutor that knows specific development technologies deeply.

You can sign up for ChatGPT at the following link: `https://chatgpt.com/`

Anthropic's Claude

Claude is particularly good at reasoning, explanations, and working with long documents.

Claude is often the main alternative people try when they want stronger long-form explanations. It's widely used by developers, writers, lawyers, and researchers who care about clarity and depth rather than flashy features.

Why people like Claude:

- Very strong at explaining complex ideas calmly and clearly
- A very large context window. You can paste entire files, articles, or chapters
- Less likely to produce confident but incorrect explanations

Downsides:

- Slightly more conservative (meaning behaviorally cautious, not politically conservative)

Anthropic designed Claude around *constitutional AI*, a system of explicit ethical principles that guide its responses. This makes it structurally more cautious than models trained mainly on user feedback. You can read more about this aspect of Claude at the following link: `https://deeperinsights.com/ai-review/claude-ai-features-uses-comparison-to-chatgpt/`

- Code output is good, but tends to be more cautious and incremental than ChatGPT when prototyping
- If you prefer a more measured, explanatory style, Claude is a good choice

Anthropic offers several versions of Claude, commonly referred to as Haiku, Sonnet, and Opus. These are not completely different systems; they are different trade-offs between speed, cost, and capability.

A simple way to think about them is:

- Haiku for speed
- Sonnet for everyday work
- Opus for the hardest problems

Most beginners should start with Sonnet and only switch when they have a clear reason. If the task is simple or repetitive, try Haiku. If the task is complex, unclear, or keeps failing, move up to Opus.

Do not treat model choice as a permanent decision. Pick the model that suits the job.

You can sign up for Claude at the following link: `https://claude.ai/`

Google's Gemini

Gemini has improved since its initial release and is now competitive with ChatGPT and Claude for many web development tasks.

Why do people like it:

- Strong multimodal support. Text, images, documents, screenshots
- Good JavaScript and web-related answers

Downsides:

- Responses can sometimes feel generic
- Still uneven on deep backend or framework-specific questions

You can sign up for Gemini at the following link: `https://gemini.google.com/`

Which chatbot to choose?

If you want to choose your preferred chatbot, then I recommend comparing them for a month each to see which you get on with best. Each has a distinct personality that suits different people.

Now that we've reviewed the three main chatbots, you can decide which you'd prefer to use to learn about all the languages that we will cover in the *Frontend Web Development* and *Backend Web Development* parts of this book. You could even choose another chatbot that I haven't covered if you wish or use multiple chatbots simultaneously and compare their results. This can be a useful way to learn, seeing what each chatbot chooses to include in their responses. If multiple chatbots emphasize the same information, then you can be more reassured that they are giving accurate responses.

Early in your learning, consistency matters more than optimization. Using one simple, widely supported setup will help you focus on concepts instead of tools. Do not waste the first week comparing tools. Pick one setup and start learning. Tools will change quickly, but the way you think about systems and code will last. Regardless of which chatbot(s) you choose to use as your learning coach, let's now look at some important points that apply to all AI chatbots.

Getting the most from the book's suggested prompts

Throughout this book, you will see suggested prompts that you can copy and paste into chatbots like ChatGPT, Gemini, and Claude. These prompts are designed to give you a starting point for exploring a topic further, but how you use them matters as much as the prompt itself.

For example, here's the first suggested prompt for this chapter:

Prompt: Please give me a checklist to evaluate whether an AI response actually helped me learn web development.

In the book's GitHub repository, I have created pages with all the suggested prompts for each chapter. For example, you can find the suggested prompts for this chapter at the following link:

`https://github.com/markjprice/web-dev-ai/blob/main/prompts/ch01-intro/readme.md`

While writing this book in Spring 2026, I used Gemini with a Pro subscription and its **Fast** model to answer each of the optional prompts, as shown in *Figure 1.5*:

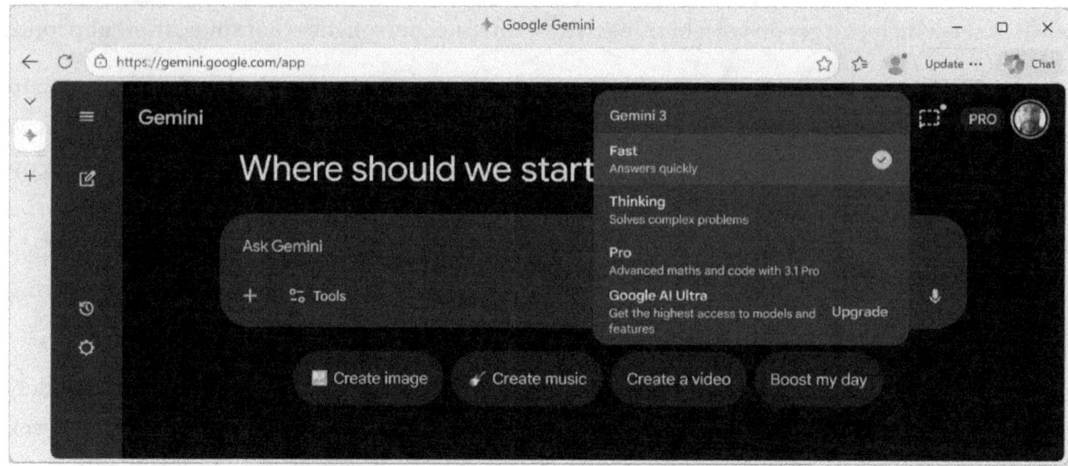

Figure 1.5: Configuring Gemini Pro to use fast responses

Although you can view those Gemini Pro responses in the book's GitHub repository, I strongly recommend that you enter the same (or similar) prompts into your preferred AI chatbot. Models improve all the time, and it can be interesting to see the differences in responses based on pricing, model, and thinking time.

Use a baseline custom instruction

A practical technique is to define a baseline instruction that is always applied to your prompts. This is sometimes called a custom instruction, system prompt, or profile context, depending on the tool.

Instead of repeating the same guidance every time, you configure the AI once with instructions like:

```
You are helping me learn web development. I am reading a book titled *Web
Dev with an AI Sidekick*.

[about_me]

- Use clear, beginner-friendly explanations
- Prefer simple, maintainable solutions over complex ones
- When writing code, include comments to explain "why"
- Assume I am using SQLite unless told otherwise
- Use good practices for security and performance but don't overcomplicate
while I am learning the basics
```

`[about_me]` must be replaced with relevant information about you. For example, if you are a student, you might write:

```
I have done some basic HTML and CSS before, but I have never written any
programming languages. I am 16 years old and a high-school student in the
USA. I want to pursue a software development role in the future.
```

Or if you are a career-switcher, you might write:

```
I am a building contractor who wants to change careers. I know very little
about programming, but I have heard that AI can help me build websites by
vibe coding. I am eager and willing to study hard to learn something new.
```

Or if you are a technologist in a different area, you might write:

```
I am a .NET backend developer with five years of experience. I am bored
with my current position, and there aren't many .NET job opportunities
near me. I want to switch to full stack web development with an emphasis
on frontend user interface design.
```

Once set, every prompt you send will automatically include this context.

How to configure this in common tools

Each platform provides a slightly different way to do this:

- **ChatGPT**: Use **Custom Instructions** in settings. You can define how the assistant should behave and what it should know about you.
- **Gemini**: Use saved prompts or context features (in supported environments) to establish consistent instructions.
- **Claude**: Use **Projects** or conversation setup instructions to define persistent context for a session or workspace.

The names differ, but the idea is the same: set your expectations once, reuse them everywhere.

AI magnifies whatever habits you already have

AI does not make you good at web development. It makes you more of whatever you already are:

- If you understand fundamentals, AI multiplies your output
- If you hand-wave fundamentals, AI multiplies your confusion

For example: AI can generate code, but it cannot know whether that code matches how you think the code should work unless you do.

For example, let's take HTML. If you already think in terms of document structure, accessibility, and semantic meaning, then AI can speed you up dramatically.

You could enter the following prompt:

```
Generate a semantic HTML layout for a blog page with header, nav, main
content, and aside.
```

When you review the response from the AI, you immediately understand:

- Why `<main>` exists
- Why `<article>` vs `<section>` matters
- Where the mistakes are

You'll correct any mistakes that the AI has made in seconds.

But if you don't understand semantics, AI will happily produce something that looks right but is structurally wrong. You won't notice missing landmarks, broken accessibility, or misuse of headings. You ship fragile markup and never know why things feel off later. AI didn't cause this problem but it did amplify it.

If you copy CSS generated by an AI until it looks right, you'll end up with styling that works only by accident. Worse, AI will make it faster to reach that broken state.

When debugging, if you already read error messages, form hypotheses, and isolate variables, then AI becomes a debugging partner. You can say:

```
Here's the error message. What's the most likely cause and how do I
confirm it?
```

You learn faster because you see the reasoning.

But if you don't already know the basic tenets of debugging skills, then AI lets you thrash faster by changing five things at once, you end up pasting fixes blindly, and even creating new bugs! You feel busy, but you're not learning.

Prompt: Please compare learning web development with AI vs without AI. What skills improve and what skills degrade?

Your learning style

If you naturally ask:

- Why this pattern?
- Why not another?
- What breaks if I change this?

AI can be patient and available whenever you need to ask another question.

But if your instinct is, *Just give me the solution*, then AI will happily comply, but you'll finish projects without understanding them. Do not let the tool do your thinking for you.

You need to use AI as an explainer, a reviewer, a sparring partner in decision making, or a debugger, not as the primary author, architect, or decision maker.

Some good phrases to frequently use in your chats with the AI:

- Please show me minimal examples.
- What are two alternative approaches?
- What assumptions am I making?

Prompt: Please explain why AI is described as a multiplier of existing skills with concrete examples in web development.

Configuring an AI chatbot for learning

If you want a free AI chatbot to genuinely help you learn web development (instead of just spitting out code you don't understand), you need to configure it in three ways:

- How you start each chat (your learning contract)
- How you ask questions (prompt patterns)
- How you verify and practice (so you don't get tricked by confident nonsense)

Below is a setup that works well with ChatGPT, Gemini, and Claude.

Create a reusable learning contract message

At the start of a new chat, paste something like the following learning contract and tweak it to your taste.

Learning contract (paste this at the top of the chat):

```
You are my web dev tutor for HTML, CSS, JavaScript, SQL, Python and
Django. Teach me like a beginner who wants to become competent, not like
someone who wants a quick copy-paste. Prefer short steps with checkpoints.

When giving code, also explain:
- what the code does
- why this approach is used
- common mistakes

Ask me 1–3 quick questions if needed (but do not stall). Always provide a
tiny exercise after explaining a concept.

When I paste an error, help me debug by:
- explaining likely causes
- telling me exactly what to check
- giving the minimal fix first
```

If your chatbot supports *custom instructions* or *memory*, put the same content there so you don't have to repeat it. If it doesn't, keep it in a note and paste it into each new chat.

Pick a track so the bot teaches coherently

Free chatbots can be amazing, but they'll happily jump around unless you set a structure. Pick one learning track and stick with it for a few sessions:

- HTML semantics and structure
- CSS layout and styling
- JavaScript fundamentals
- SQL basics using SQLite
- Django basics
- Deployment concepts and scripting with Bash

Tell the chatbot:

```
Use this track. If I ask something beyond the scope of my current track,
briefly answer but then guide me back to the track.
```

Use prompt templates that force real learning

Prompt patterns that make it more likely that the model will explain instead of dumping code on you are shown in *Table 1.3*:

Template	Example
Explain, then quiz me	Teach me [topic] like I'm new. Use a simple example. After each section, ask me a quick question to check understanding. Don't move on until I answer.
Socratic debugging	I'm getting this error in [language/framework]. Ask me the most important questions first, one at a time, and explain what each answer would imply. Here's the traceback: [traceback].
Minimal code with "why"	Show the smallest possible example of [feature] that handles [functionality]. Explain each line. Then give me one small change to implement.
Make me practice	Give me a 20-minute exercise: [task]. Provide requirements and hints only. Don't give the solution unless I ask. For example, build a Django page that lists products from SQLite, with a search box using `GET` parameters.
Compare options	Explain three ways to structure a [language/framework] project using [feature]. Give pros/cons and when to choose each. For example, function views vs class views, apps layout.

Table 1.3: Prompt templates for learning

Make the bot work inside your actual project

You'll get dramatically better help if you feed it the right context. This will become easier once we use an AI tool integrated into your code editor or IDE, but you can also manually provide context even when using a separate AI chatbot.

Try to provide:

- Your goal ("I want a page that lists blog posts")
- Your current code (the smallest relevant piece)
- The error message/traceback
- Your file names and where the code lives (`views.py`, `urls.py`, template path)

This prevents the chatbot from guessing your setup.

Put guardrails on code generation

Many readers skip this step, but it makes a real difference.

Add these rules to your chat:

```
You must follow these rules when your response includes code:
- Do not generate more than about 40 lines of code at once unless I ask.
- Prefer incremental changes with diffs.
- If you propose a change, show it as: what to delete, what to add.
- Tell me the one most likely issue first.
```

This keeps the experience interactive and reduces the chance that you end up with a Frankenstein project.

Use AI as a tutor, not a compiler

AI should not be used as a tool that replaces your own implementation work. A solid routine that should become a habit for you is to use the four-step learning loop, as shown in *Figure 1.6*:

1. Ask for explanation + tiny example
2. Implement it yourself (even if it's slow)
3. Paste your attempt and ask for feedback
4. Do a small variation ("Now add validation," "Now add search," and so on)

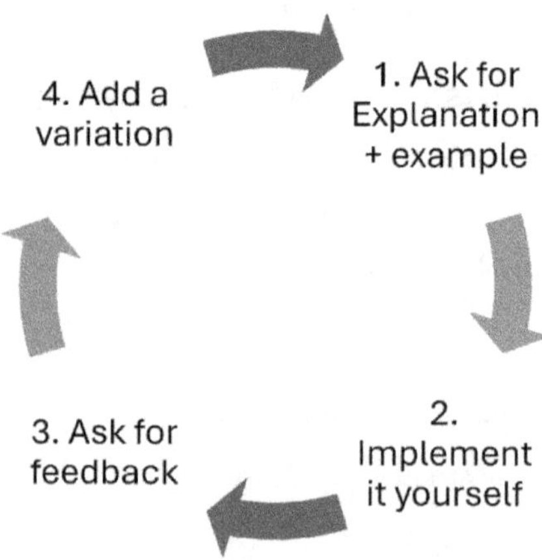

Figure 1.6: The AI learning loop

Tell the chatbot explicitly:

```
Don't write the final solution. Coach me through implementing it.
```

Verification habits

Chatbots (especially free ones) will be wrong sometimes so you can encourage the AI to check themselves with the following prompts:

- `List the assumptions you made about my project structure.`
- `What are 3 ways this could fail and how would I detect each?`
- `What's the simplest alternative approach?`

If you want extra safety, cross-check tricky answers by asking a second chatbot the same question. When they disagree, that's your cue to test carefully.

You've now picked one or more AI chatbots as your learning coaches and seen how to get the best mentoring experience out of them. Let's now turn our attention to actively coding, rather than learning concepts.

Coding with an AI assistant as your coworker

Although chatbots are great for learning, when building a complete web development project, you need a more specialized tool that works inside your code editor or IDE and can help with multi-step coding tasks (aka agentically, a horrible marketing word that I hope dates fast). The goal of this section is to understand the pros and cons of various AI tools that integrate with your coding tools.

Good practice: If you follow only one setup for a code editor or IDE with an integrated coding assistant in this book, use VS Code with GitHub Copilot. This combination is widely used, integrates cleanly with the workflows we will build, and provides the least friction for beginners.

Before we look at specific tools, there is an important factor to consider about their relationship to AI models.

Understanding the tool–model relationship

When you start using AI coding assistants, it is easy to think of each tool as a single, fixed system. For example, you might assume that GitHub Copilot is one AI, in the same way that ChatGPT or Claude feels like a single product.

In reality, tools like Copilot are better understood as interfaces to multiple underlying models.

This means that when you use a tool like GitHub Copilot in a code editor or IDE like VS Code, you are not always talking to one specific AI system. Instead, the tool can route your request to different models depending on the task, the feature you are using, or your subscription level.

AI tools are built in layers:

- The editor or interface (for example, VS Code with Copilot)
- The integration layer that connects your editor to AI services
- One or more underlying models that actually generate responses

In some cases, this includes models from different providers.

For example, inside Copilot you might:

- Get inline code completions from one model
- Use chat features powered by another model
- Select or be routed to models such as OpenAI's GPT-5.5 or Anthropic's Claude Sonnet

So even though you are using Copilot, the actual intelligence behind a response might come from a completely different system.

This affects how you choose tools:

1. First, tool choice and model choice are not the same thing. You might prefer working in Copilot because it integrates with your editor, but still want to use a specific model like Claude Opus for certain tasks.
2. Second, results can vary even within the same tool. If Copilot switches models or you change settings, you may see different styles of responses, levels of detail, or coding approaches.
3. Third, you can combine strengths. For example:
    - Use Copilot for fast inline suggestions while coding
    - Use a Claude-powered chat for deeper explanations
    - Use a stronger model for complex debugging or design decisions

Do not think in terms of which single AI should I use. Instead, think about:

- Which tool fits your workflow (for example, VS Code with Copilot)?
- Which model is best for the current task (for example, Claude Opus with high thinking level for reviewing the architecture of a complex project, or GPT-5 mini with fast thinking for writing dozens of unit tests)?

As AI tools evolve, this separation will become more important. The developers who get the most value are not the ones who pick a single tool and stick to it. They are the ones who understand what is happening underneath and choose the right combination for the job.

The importance of a great harness

A coding assistant or agent is composed of a model and a harness:

- The model is the raw intelligence
- The harness is everything that makes it usable

An **agent harness** is the software infrastructure surrounding a model that manages tool execution, memory, state persistence, and verification. The harness is the complete software infrastructure wrapping a model, including the orchestration loop, tools, memory, context management, state persistence, error handling, and guardrails.

A **coding harness** is the software scaffold around a model that helps it write and edit code effectively. Codex and Claude Code can be considered coding harnesses.

The harness provides six core capabilities:

1. **Orchestration loop**: The harness turns one-shot responses into a loop: call model, take action, observe result, repeat.
2. **Tool use**: The harness connects the model to tools that provide access to the file system, terminal, tests, and APIs. Without these tools, the model can only describe code. With it, the system can change code.
3. **Context management**: A raw model has a limited context window. The harness decides which files to include, how to summarize, and what to exclude..
4. **Memory and state**: LLMs are stateless by default. The harness adds session memory and persistence across runs.
5. **Execution environment**: Codex and similar tools run in real environments that is part of the harness, like a sandbox, runtime, and execution logs.
6. **Guardrails and control**: The harness enforces permissions and safety constraints.

A raw model is like a processor on its own, capable of computation but disconnected from everything else. The harness is what surrounds it with memory, storage, and input/output, turning it into a complete system that can actually do useful work.

If you want the best coding assistant, you need to think about two aspects:

- Your model choice affects the balance of responsiveness with smarter reasoning
- Your harness is important to getting work done

The biggest improvements in coding assistants are coming from the harness, not the model. To summarize, a harness is the system around an AI model that gives it tools, memory, and a workflow, turning it from a text generator into something that can complete real tasks.

Now let's review some of the most popular coding assistants that can integrate with your preferred code editor or IDE (and model).

GitHub Copilot

For hands-on learning, GitHub Copilot is the option I would start with because it sits in your code editor or IDE (VS Code, Visual Studio, JetBrains, and so on) and suggests code completions, templates, and entire functions as you type.

GitHub Copilot is very different from the "Copilots" that are integrated into Windows, Office, and every other Microsoft product these days. Please don't be put off by its branding.

Copilot is best for learning by coding, not chatting. Copilot doesn't replace your preferred chatbot. It reduces the need to repeatedly search for common code patterns. It is widely used by developers because it works while you type and has access to your whole project context.

Strengths:

- Excellent code autocomplete
- Works inside your code editor or IDE
- Uses your project context to improve suggestions

Weakness:

- Poor for conceptual learning unless paired with a chatbot

Free vs paid plans for in:

- **Free / Student:** Includes up to 2,000 inline suggestions in IDEs per month and up to 50 premium requests per month, giving you a limited taste of Copilot's capabilities. Students get unlimited completions in IDEs and up to 300 premium requests per month.

- **Paid**: Copilot Pro (1,000 AI credits per month for $10 USD) / Pro+ (3,900 AI credits per month for $39 USD), unlocking more completions and integrations.
- **Business / Enterprise**: $19 USD per user per month (with the option to purchase additional premium requests at $0.04 USD per request), $39 USD per user per month (GitHub Enterprise Cloud only).

You can learn about GitHub Copilot's usage-based billing at the following link: `https://docs.github.com/en/copilot/concepts/billing/usage-based-billing-for-individuals`

Sign up for GitHub Copilot at the following link: `https://github.com/features//copilot`

How to set it up for success:

- Install the Copilot plugin in your editor
- Start by coding the bare minimum and ask Copilot to suggest snippets like HTML layout, JavaScript functions, and REST views in Django
- When something is suggested, ask "why this pattern?" in Copilot Chat. That shifts you from being a copy-paste monkey to having a deeper understanding

Google's Gemini Code Assist

Google offers an AI coding assistant that gives generous free assistance (many completions per month) and is integrated with major editors like VS Code. It can be useful for prototyping HTML and JavaScript or debugging Django views because the bot understands the context of your changes and suggests larger blocks of code, not just individual lines.

Gemini Code Assist is a tool that you may want to explore later, once you are comfortable with the basic concepts of using VS Code and GitHub Copilot.

Free vs Paid:

- Free: Individual tier gives lots of completions monthly
- Paid/Standard: Adds deeper integrations and metrics

How to set it up for success:

- Install the Gemini Code Assist extension in your editor of choice
- Use natural language prompts while coding ("Create a responsive navbar in HTML + CSS + JavaScript")
- For Django, work in the shell and ask for model definitions, migrations, and admin customizations interactively

You can sign up for Gemini Code Assist at the following link: `https://codeassist.google/`

AI coding tool costs and capabilities

By the first half of 2026, AI coding tools have become a normal part of many developer workflows, but their cost, limits, and reliability are still evolving.

In *The Pragmatic Engineer*'s March 2026 survey, 95% of respondents said they use AI tools at least weekly, 55% said they regularly use AI agents, and Claude Code was both the most-used and most-loved tool in that survey.

Jellyfish's latest engineering study says more than half of companies in its dataset use AI coding tools consistently, 64% generate a majority of their code with AI assistance, and higher-adoption teams are seeing about 2x the **pull request** (**PR**) throughput of low adopters.

You can read more about these studies and surveys at the following links: https://newsletter.pragmaticengineer.com/p/ai-tooling-2026 and https://jellyfish.co/newsroom/jellyfish-reveals-ais-real-impact-on-engineering-teams/

But that does not mean developers are serene about it. The mood on Reddit, Hacker News, and other public channels is more like: *this is unbelievably useful, slightly addictive, and constantly threatening to waste time or money if you use it badly.*

Developers describe Claude Code, Codex, and Copilot as useful for end-to-end feature implementation, repo-wide refactors, planning, code review, and running multiple competing agents at once to compare outputs.

Reuters reported in late March 2026 that Codex now has more than 2 million weekly active users, after a 3x increase in users and 5x increase in usage in the first quarter of 2026: `https://www.reuters.`

com/technology/openai-buy-python-toolmaker-astral-take-anthropic-2026-03-19/

Token and quota burn

A common complaint is unclear cost and usage limits, especially token burn and quota burn. On r/codex, multiple March 2026 posts complain that weekly usage disappears much faster than expected, with people reporting things like *takes 10% of my weekly limit per task, 75% of my weekly limit from like 3 days of using it*, and screenshots showing almost exhausted limits after only a couple of days of normal work. Other posts say token burn suddenly spiked in mid-March without an obvious change in process.

GitHub Copilot users are complaining about the same thing in a different form. Since Copilot mixes unlimited completions with capped premium requests, the argument is less about raw tokens and more about which models chew through premium allowance too quickly. In March 2026 discussions, users complained that Claude Opus inside Copilot was consuming premium requests much faster than expected, and others reported higher token usage after recent updates.

Prompt: Please explain token usage in simple terms with a real example of a coding session. What causes high token usage in AI coding tools and how can I reduce it?

A practical approach to token usage

A practical approach is to use tiering instead of picking the "smartest" model and using it for everything. Use a cheaper or capped tool for broad exploration, boilerplate, and repetitive edits. Escalate to the expensive frontier model only for architecture, tricky debugging, or large refactors.

You can see that pattern directly in public discussion. One Reddit user says they *plan with Claude initially and review with Codex*, others recommend sticking to Sonnet or Haiku for normal work and saving Opus for tougher tasks, and Copilot users talk about using cheaper models for iterative back-and-forth because premium models burn quota too fast.

Good practice: Use a cheap model to search, summarize, lint, scaffold, and rewrite. Use a premium model for hard reasoning. Use a separate reviewer model to check the work of your primary model. The developers getting wrecked on cost are often the ones running frontier models on `xhigh` thinking levels for tasks that should have been handled by a cheaper pass first.

Prompt: Please design a low-cost workflow using free and paid AI tools for a beginner.

Pricing and choosing between plans

What the public chatter suggests is this rough pattern: newbies and students are mostly using free tiers and educational entitlements; working individual developers go for the $10 to $20 range plans; and the $100 to $200 plans are mainly justified by heavy users who are doing hours of daily agentic coding and believe they are getting far more than the list price back in value.

You can read a typical discussion about the best value-for-money combination of AI subscriptions at the following link: `https://www.reddit.com/r/ClaudeCode/comments/1rp294g/the_best_value_for_money_combination_of_ai/`

Comparing developers' opinions about AI tools

Anthropic's Claude Code is praised as the strongest pure coding agent experience by a lot of power users, especially in smaller teams, and *The Pragmatic Engineer*'s survey that I linked to earlier says it is currently the most loved tool.

OpenAI's Codex is praised for feeling more direct and engineering-oriented, but `r/codex` in April 2026 was full of anxiety about unpredictable quota burn. OpenAI's own positioning is that Codex is included inside paid ChatGPT tiers, which makes it appealing to people who already live in that ecosystem.

GitHub Copilot is still the safe default choice of coding assistant. It is cheaper than most paid competitors for individuals, deeply integrated into mainstream IDEs, and much more natural for enterprise procurement. *The Pragmatic Engineer* survey says larger enterprises still skew toward Copilot, so if you work for a corporation, it is the most likely tool that you will be expected to use. But the knock against it is that it no longer feels as cutting-edge or as loved by power users as Claude Code.

Good practice: If a vendor changes limits, prices, or defaults in a way users hate, developers often switch tools quickly. So, in many ways, it doesn't matter much for beginners which one you pick to get started because you might switch between providers many times in a few months! So, pick a plan that you can pay for month-to-month and cancel at will.

Mixing models and prompting styles

Some developers use multiple models against the same task, use one model for planning and another for implementation, or keep a cheap general assistant plus one premium coding specialist. Effective use depends on knowing when to stop, when to simplify by trimming context, or when to switch tools, not on the person using the best-benchmarked model.

Some developers also adjust how they prompt and interact with models, even to the point of applying psychology that is usually only applied to fellow humans, as in the following link: `https://news.ycombinator.com/item?id=47357042`

I recommend you start with one simple, low-cost tool, and one premium specialist, not five subscriptions. Copilot Free or Pro is the entry point combined with ChatGPT Plus with Codex or Claude Pro. The $200 plans only make sense once you are clearly running into limits every week and can point to actual throughput gains. Higher-cost plans are usually only worthwhile for heavy daily use, but a beginner who jumps straight there is usually paying tuition for confusion.

AI agents and multi-agent workflows

You have already seen how AI assistants can help you write code, explain concepts, and guide your learning. AI agents build on that idea, but the difference is that an AI agent is not responding to a single prompt. It is trying to complete a task over multiple steps, and the agent is taking more initiative. Instead of waiting for your next prompt, it may:

- Break a task into smaller steps
- Modify multiple files
- Run commands or tests
- Revise its approach based on what happens

Where things become even more interesting is when multiple agents are involved.

Some tools use a coordinating agent that manages a group of smaller, specialized agents. Each of these subagents focuses on a specific type of work.

For example, a system might include:

- A planning agent that decides what needs to be done
- A coding agent that writes or edits code
- A testing agent that runs tests and reports failures
- A review agent that checks for mistakes or improvements

The coordinating agent assigns tasks to these subagents, collects their results, and decides what to do next. This creates a routine that is closer to a small team than a single assistant.

This approach can be very effective. Different agents can focus on what they do best, and the system can iterate more quickly across multiple steps. The agents often have different capabilities or thinking levels, or may even be from different companies. For example, some advanced developers have found that OpenAI's Codex at very high thinking level is best for planning, and then they hand off the implementation to Claude Code Sonnet, or a local model like Qwen3-Coder-Next or DeepSeek Coder. In *Chapter 11, Setting Up Your Project Environment*, I cover local models in more detail.

Why agents matter

At first glance, multi-agent systems sound like a clear upgrade. In many cases, they are. They can handle larger, more complex tasks, work across multiple files and layers of a project, and catch issues earlier through built-in review or testing steps.

But there is a cost that is easy to overlook.

Every time an agent performs a step, it sends and receives data. In a multi-agent system, this happens multiple times per task, and often between several agents. This has a direct impact on token usage. If multiple agents are communicating with each other, the same context may be passed around several times. This can increase token usage quickly, even for tasks that seem small.

This is why developers often notice that agent-based tools feel more expensive or burn through quota faster than simple chat-based tools.

For learning, it is important to use these tools with some discipline.

If you rely on a multi-agent system to build large features from scratch, it may produce working code, but you risk paying for a lot of computation that does not actually help you learn.

A better approach is to:

- Use smaller, focused tasks rather than large open-ended goals
- Limit how much the agent is allowed to do in one go
- Review each step instead of accepting everything automatically
- Be aware that more automation usually means higher token usage

As you gain experience, you can start to take advantage of multi-agent workflows for more complex tasks. At that point, the trade-offs between speed, cost, and understanding will become clearer.

We will look at AI agents in more detail in the third part of this book when we build a real-world project. For now, let's review some practical tips for working with AI.

Prompt: When should I switch from chatbot to IDE-integrated assistant?

Practical tips for collaborating with any AI

Here's how to make these tools actual teachers instead of glorified code generators.

- **State your learning goal up front**: Instead of "write me a Django view", ask "teach me how Django views handle GET vs POST with examples." That forces the AI to explain, not just produce an end result.
- **Ask for step-by-step explanations**: Always include phrasing like "explain line by line and why it matters."
- **Iterate with small prompts**: Instead of huge requests, break things down into smaller steps. You can always use follow-ups like "now expand on this" when you want to go deeper.
- **Use editor integration for practice**: Chatbots inside editors like Copilot, Gemini, and DeepSeek make learning contextual from the active project and its code files. You're not just learning abstract theory, the chatbot is applying it to your current code.
- **Validate with multiple sources.** For tricky concepts, ask two assistants (for example, ChatGPT and Claude) and compare answers. Discrepancies often reveal subtle nuances you'd miss otherwise.

A useful prompt is the following:

```
Act as a strategic advisor. Based on my goal below, recommend ONE best
option and explain why it is superior to alternatives. Then, list two
backup options and specify exactly when I should choose them instead. My
goal is [Insert your goal here]
```

Anthropic has useful prompt guidance on their website that also applies to most models, found at the following link: `https://platform.claude.com/docs/en/build-with-claude/prompt-engineering/claude-prompting-best-practices`

Now let's review some key information about using AI tools and how AI has changed the role of software developers.

Pros and cons of AI tools

Many people claim that human developers will soon be obsolete because AI will write software autonomously and make coders unnecessary. But I am unconvinced that we have entered anything resembling a post-developer world.

Companies are increasingly using AI tools

It is true that companies are increasingly adopting AI tools. For example, an article in Forbes reported that AI writes over 25% of the code committed at Google. But human developers remain deeply involved in the process, guiding AI, reviewing its output, editing the code, and shaping it into a coherent product. AI is a tool controlled by humans, not a replacement for humans.

Human + AI = success

While AI tools like GitHub Copilot can produce impressive results in well-defined tasks, they still require a human hand on the tiller. To mix my metaphors, using AI in development is like flying a plane with cruise control: the aircraft goes where you point it, but without constant guidance and corrections from a skilled pilot, it could drift off course, and critical steps in the flight like landing and takeoff should be done entirely under human control.

As a software developer using AI tools, if you do not understand the code being generated, you won't know when or how to correct it. This limitation is central to why the idea that we are entering a post-human programmer world is exaggerated.

Limits of AI

There are plenty of tasks where current large language models struggle. Some of the most hyped tools have failed in real testing contexts. You might find that your AI tool can only complete a subset of assignments satisfactorily and you ultimately spend more time working around its mistakes than you would have writing the code yourself.

These results suggest that AI in its current form is good at well-scoped, repetitive tasks, but poor at open-ended or complex development problems without significant human intervention.

There has also been interesting recent research suggesting a gap between perceived and actual productivity gains from AI assistance. A 2025 randomized controlled trial by the nonprofit research group **METR (Model Evaluation & Threat Research)** reported that developers using AI tools actually took longer to complete tasks compared to those who did not use AI, even while they felt like they were faster. This speaks to the psychological allure of AI promises versus the messy reality of real engineering work.

Researchers found developers spent extra time prompting the AI, reviewing suggestions, correcting errors, and integrating generated code.

In other words: less typing, more verification. Developers had to verify and correct AI suggestions that were often only broadly accurate.

The key paper is *Measuring the Impact of Early-2025 AI on Experienced Open-Source Developer Productivity* by researchers at METR. The main finding was that developers using AI tools took 19% longer to complete tasks than those who did not. Yet they believed AI made them faster by about 20–24%. You can read more at the following link: `https://metr.org/blog/2025-07-10-early-2025-ai-experienced-os-dev-study/`

This study does *not* mean AI always slows developers down. It applies mainly to experienced developers with familiar codebases and complex real-world tasks.

Other studies show the opposite.

For example, GitHub Copilot users completed tasks 55.8% faster in controlled experiments. You can read *The Impact of AI on Developer Productivity: Evidence from GitHub Copilot* paper at the following link: `https://arxiv.org/abs/2302.06590`

Google engineers were about 21% faster in an enterprise trial that you can read about at the following link: `https://arxiv.org/abs/2410.12944`

So the reality of AI-enhanced coding in the current era is messy.

How AI impacts junior and senior developers differently

This is one of the most revealing things about AI and software development. It looks paradoxical at first, but it actually makes perfect sense once you unpack how juniors and seniors think.

The core idea in one sentence is that AI tends to be most helpful for junior developers because it reduces the friction of writing code and helps close common knowledge gaps. For senior developers, however, the benefits can be less consistent, since AI can sometimes interrupt deeper, expert-level thinking.

Junior developers often struggle with things like syntax, boilerplate, unfamiliar APIs and libraries, patterns they have not encountered yet, and even the basic question of what code to write in the first place. Their cognitive load is often highest at the mechanical level, and AI works well as a powerful autocomplete tool and an on-demand tutor. As a result, using AI to learn and write code can lead to major productivity gains.

Senior developers, on the other hand, typically spend more mental effort on higher-level concerns such as architecture decisions, trade-offs, system constraints, legacy code behavior, performance, scalability, security, and subtle bugs. Their cognitive load is more conceptual than mechanical, and they usually already know how to write code quickly.

In these cases, AI may fill fewer gaps. It can also introduce noise, generic advice, or context-missing suggestions that appear plausible but do not hold up in a specific system. This can increase review time, create distractions, and in some situations slow progress rather than speeding it up.

Prompt: Please explain why AI helps junior developers more than senior developers. And what skills should a junior developer focus on to become a senior-level thinker early?

AI shifts work from writing code to judging code

Historically, junior developers spent more time learning how to write code, while senior developers spent more time deciding what code should exist in the first place. AI is pushing more of the profession in that direction. Writing code is becoming less important as a standalone skill. Understanding systems, architecture, trade-offs, and behavior is becoming more important.

In practical terms, the value of a developer is shifting away from typing code and toward thinking clearly about what should be built, how it should behave, and how to recognize when an AI-generated solution is wrong, brittle, insecure, or simply a bad fit.

That is one of the main reasons this book is structured the way it is. Before you build the larger project later in the book, you first spend time learning the individual languages, frameworks, tools, and concepts. This book is not trying to turn you into a human syntax machine. It is trying to help you build the judgment needed to direct AI well, review its work intelligently, and make sound engineering decisions.

This is why, although AI can accelerate your learning experience for web development, ultimately you do still need to learn HTML, CSS, JavaScript, SQL, Python, and so on, so that you can then apply your human judgment to the code your AI assistant writes for you when building a complete project.

Developer job market

Even factual sources of evidence like the job market, where the idea that AI is the main cause of employment challenges for developers is prevalent, can be misleading. While layoffs and hiring slowdowns are real, they are likely caused by broader macroeconomic factors, such as high interest rates and investment contractions, rather than a sudden lack of need for human developers. Some companies may hold back hiring because of myths about imminent AI takeover, but I believe this narrative is hurting growth more than actual automation is.

Two things have remained true since ChatGPT burst into society's consciousness in November 2023: companies still need human developers, and AI evangelists continue to claim that developers will be obsolete any week now.

Neither of these points seems likely to change soon. Once companies fully recognize that AI functions best as an enhancer of human capability and not a replacement, they will resume more vigorous hiring. Rather than fearing the machines, aspiring developers should see this era as one where skilled developers using AI well can get more done than developers who ignore it or trust it blindly.

It's all about you

I'll end this discussion with a cautionary note for you, my reader. How learners and early-career developers like you integrate AI into your education and eventually into your daily development lives is important. If you rely too heavily on AI's output without understanding it, you risk building brittle knowledge that fails when AI inevitably stumbles.

Conversely, when used as a tutor or assistant that helps explain errors, clarify concepts, and guide exploration, AI can be a useful learning aid. I wrote this book to help you use these new AI tools to help you learn faster, but you still do need to work hard at it.

Warning!

AI decreases critical thinking capability through a process called cognitive offloading. It is fine to rely on an AI for relatively simple tasks but don't allow AI to take over your judgment.

Prompt: What is cognitive offloading in learning, and how does it apply to AI coding assistants?

No one knows how AI models will evolve, and the world still needs people who understand how to build software. Rather than getting discouraged by hype or fear, I recommend that you use AI, but do not outsource your judgment to it. The world still needs people who understand how software works because AI tools still do not really have that understanding.

Practice, references, and resources

In this section, you will be tested on what you've learned in this chapter and provided with useful links to reference materials and resources.

Studying with NotebookLM

Google's **NotebookLM** is a useful tool for learning because it grounds AI responses in sources that you control. Instead of asking general questions and getting answers based on a model's broad training, you upload your own material such as book chapters, documentation, or notes, and the AI works only within that context. This makes NotebookLM particularly effective for studying, since you can treat it as a focused tutor for a specific topic.

A practical routine is to upload a chapter or set of notes, then ask questions like *summarize this section*, *explain this concept in simpler terms*, or *quiz me on the key ideas*.

You can also ask it to compare sections, generate examples, or identify gaps in your understanding. Because every response is tied back to your source material, it reduces the risk of irrelevant or incorrect explanations and helps reinforce what you are actually trying to learn, rather than sending you off into unrelated topics.

Check your understanding

Answer the following questions about the topics we covered in this chapter:

1. What does it mean to say that AI is a multiplier rather than a replacement?
2. Why is it important to ask AI for explanations instead of just code?
3. What is a learning contract, and why does it help?
4. Name two prompt patterns that improve learning outcomes
5. Why should you limit the amount of code an AI generates at once?
6. What is the main risk of relying too heavily on AI-generated code?
7. Describe the difference between chatbots and IDE-integrated AI tools.
8. What is token or quota usage, and why does it matter?
9. What is the recommended approach to using cheap vs premium AI models?
10. Why can AI sometimes slow down experienced developers?

Answers are found in the GitHub repository for this book at the following link:

`https://github.com/markjprice/web-dev-ai/blob/main/docs/Appendix-A.pdf`

Links

Links for prompting and learning with AI:

- Anthropic prompt engineering guide: `https://docs.anthropic.com/en/docs/build-with-claude/prompt-engineering/overview`
- OpenAI prompting guide: `https://platform.openai.com/docs/guides/prompt-engineering`
- Learn Prompting: `https://learnprompting.org/`

Reddit communities for developer public discussions:

- OpenAI Codex: `https://www.reddit.com/r/codex/`
- Anthropic Claude: `https://www.reddit.com/r/ClaudeAI/`
- GitHub Copilot: `https://www.reddit.com/r/GithubCopilot/`

Summary

In this chapter, you learned the following:

- AI tools can significantly accelerate learning, but only when used as a tutor rather than a code generator
- Effective learning with AI depends on asking for explanations, not just solutions
- A structured approach such as the learning loop leads to deeper understanding
- Prompt quality directly affects learning outcomes
- Chatbots are best for explanations and learning, while tools like Copilot are best for hands-on coding
- AI amplifies both good and bad habits, making strong web development fundamentals important when a human and AI are working together
- Token usage and cost can quickly become an issue without a deliberate process, so a tiered approach using cheap models for simple tasks and premium models for complex reasoning is most efficient
- Developers often combine multiple AI tools rather than relying on a single one

- Human judgment still matters because AI does not replace developer judgment; it shifts the role from writing code to evaluating and refining it

In the next chapter, you will learn about HTML, a markup language used to provide structure to the content on a web page.

Learn more on Discord

To join the Discord community for this book – where you can share feedback, ask questions to the author, and learn about new releases – follow this QR code:

`https://discord.gg/rdEsrVbbC`

Part 1

Frontend Web Development

In this first part of the book, you'll focus on what the user sees and interacts with in a web application. You begin with HTML and CSS to understand structure and styling, use SVG for graphics, and move into JavaScript and TypeScript to add behavior. You do not need to master every detail yet. The aim is to make frontend code readable and less intimidating.

Along the way, you learn how browsers interpret and render pages, how styling and layout decisions affect usability, and how small pieces of logic shape the user experience. By the end of this part, you should be able to build and adjust simple web user interfaces and understand how frontend technologies connect to the rest of the system.

This part of the book includes the following chapters:

- *Chapter 2, HTML – Structuring Your Web Pages*
- *Chapter 3, CSS – Styling Your Web Pages*
- *Chapter 4, SVG – Drawing Scalable Graphics*
- *Chapter 5, JavaScript – Making Web Pages Interactive*
- *Chapter 6, TypeScript – Safer JavaScript*

2

HTML – Structuring Your Web Pages

This chapter covers the basics of **HTML (HyperText Markup Language)**. You'll learn the key concepts about HTML and then use the AI to generate a simple page, and in doing so, learn about elements, tags, and attributes.

By the end of this chapter, you will be able to read, write, and understand HTML as a structured description of a web page, and confidently build simple, meaningful pages that form a solid foundation for everything that comes next.

In this chapter, we will cover the following topics:

- What is HTML?
- Building a basic web page
- Working with forms and inputs
- AI exercises
- Other markup languages

Suggested chatbot prompts with example responses for this chapter can be found at the following link: `https://github.com/markjprice/web-dev-ai/blob/main/prompts/ch02-html/readme.md`

What is HTML?

HTML stands for HyperText Markup Language. That sounds scary, but the idea is simple.

HTML is not a programming language:

- It does not make decisions
- It does not run logic
- It does not calculate anything

HTML describes the structure and meaning of content on a web page.

HTML is the page's structure. It defines:

- What text is a heading
- What text is a paragraph
- What counts as a list
- Where do links point?
- Which images belong on the page?
- How tabular data is organized

CSS makes things look good. You will learn about CSS in *Chapter 3, CSS – Styling Your Web Pages*. For this chapter, ignore how things look and focus on what they are and how they are structured.

JavaScript makes things interactive. The web pages that you create in this chapter will be static. In *Chapter 5, JavaScript – Making Web Pages Interactive*, you will write JavaScript code to make them come alive.

HTML decides what things are. Without HTML, the web would just be a stream of unstructured text.

HTML is made of elements

HTML is built from **tags** to form **elements**. A tag is the actual markup syntax enclosed in angle brackets, such as `<p>` or `</p>`, which tells the browser how to interpret content. An element, on the other hand, is the complete structure that includes the opening tag, the content, and the closing tag.

For example, `<p>Hello</p>` is a paragraph element, made up of the opening `<p>` tag, the text `Hello`, and the closing `</p>` tag. Tags are the building blocks, while elements are the full constructs created from those tags.

Most elements look like this:

```
<p>This is a paragraph.</p>
```

- `<p>` means *start a new paragraph*
- `</p>` means *end of the paragraph*
- Everything in between is the content of the paragraph

In HTML, **attributes** provide additional information about an element and are placed inside the opening tag. They usually come in name–value pairs, such as `class="intro"` or `href="https://example.com"`, and they modify how the element behaves or is displayed.

For example, in `<a href="https://example.com">Visit</a>`, the `href` attribute tells the browser where the link should go. While the element defines the structure and meaning, attributes refine or configure that element's behavior.

Two attributes appear constantly in HTML: `id` and `class`. An `id` identifies one unique element on a page. A `class` labels one or more elements as belonging to the same group. Later, CSS and JavaScript will use these heavily. For now, the important `id` idea is simple: `id` is for one specific element, while `class` can be shared.

Some elements are **void elements**, like `<img>` or `<br>`, which do not have closing tags or inner content. Others are **container elements**, such as `<div>` or `<section>`, which wrap content and can include other elements inside them.

A `<div>` is a generic container element with no inherent meaning. It's useful for grouping content for styling, but it should not replace semantic elements like `<section>`, `<nav>`, or `<p>` when those are more appropriate.

It is also important to know that elements can be nested, meaning one element can sit inside another to create a hierarchy. Proper nesting is important because incorrect structure can lead to unexpected rendering or accessibility issues.

Good practice: Accessibility in web development means designing and structuring content so that it can be used by everyone, including people with disabilities such as visual, hearing, motor, or cognitive impairments. This includes using proper HTML structure, meaningful text alternatives like `alt` attributes for images, and clear navigation so assistive technologies such as screen readers can interpret the page correctly.

Another key idea is the distinction between **block-level elements** and **inline elements**. Block-level elements, like `<p>` and `<h1>`, typically start on a new line and take up the full width available, while inline elements, like `<span>` or `<a>`, flow within text without breaking the layout.

Modern HTML emphasizes semantic elements, such as `<article>`, `<nav>`, and `<footer>`, which describe the meaning of content rather than just its appearance. Using these correctly improves accessibility, search engine understanding, and overall code clarity.

You will reuse these ideas throughout the chapter.

Prompt: Please explain the difference between semantic HTML and non-semantic HTML with real-world examples and why it matters for accessibility.

Comments in HTML

HTML comments let you leave notes in the source code that are not shown on the page. They look like this:

```
<!-- This is a comment -->
```

Comments are useful for reminders, temporary notes, or explaining examples in teaching code. They are not a way to hide sensitive information, because anyone can still view the page source.

The basic structure of a web page

Every HTML page follows the same overall pattern:

```
<!DOCTYPE html>
<html>
  <head>
    <title>My first page</title>
  </head>
  <body>
    <h1>Hello world</h1>
    <p>This is my first web page.</p>
  </body>
</html>
```

Each part has a distinct role:

- <!DOCTYPE html> tells the browser *this is modern HTML*, meaning standards-based HTML, specifically HTML5. If you omit it, browsers may fall back to **quirks mode**, which emulates legacy behavior from the early web to maintain compatibility with very old pages. That can lead to inconsistent layout, especially with CSS.
- <html> wraps the entire document.
- <head> contains metadata like the title, character encoding, and links to CSS for applying styles.
- <body> contains everything the user can see.

Nothing visible on the page goes outside <body>. The page title is defined in <head> and usually appears in the browser tab.

Prompt: Please show me examples of good and bad HTML structure and explain what makes one better than the other.

Try it out!

Use your favorite text editor to create a file named myfirstpage.html. Copy the previous HTML into the file and save it. Then open the file in your preferred web browser. Compare the file in your text editor and browser side-by-side, as shown in *Figure 2.1*:

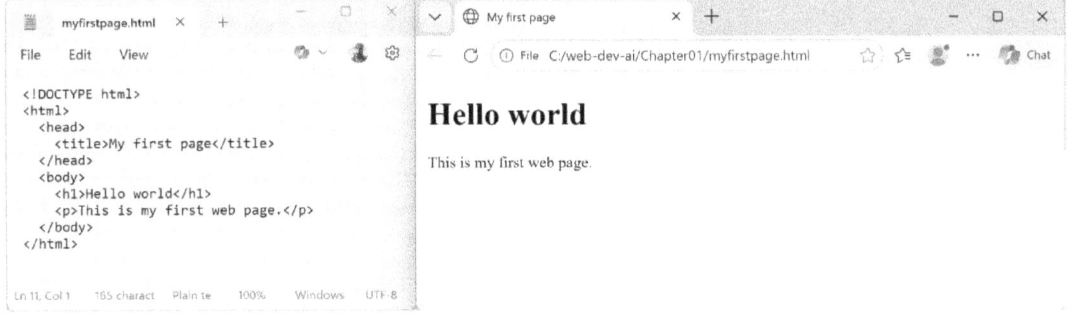

Figure 2.1: Comparing the source code for a web page to its visual look using Notepad and Microsoft Edge on Windows

Instead of a plain text editor and a web browser, you can also try out your work using VS Code and its Live Preview extension, as shown in *Figure 2.2* and *Figure 2.3*:

Figure 2.2: Click the Show Preview button to see a Live Preview of a web page

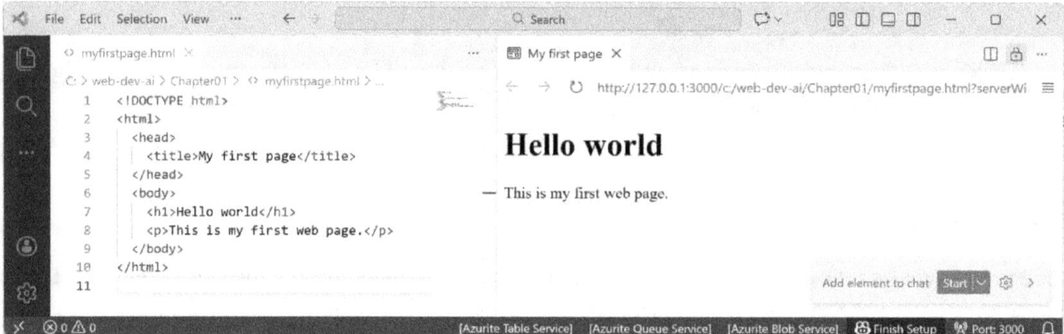

Figure 2.3: Comparing the source code for a web page to its visual look using VS Code

For the rest of this book, I recommend using VS Code with Live Preview, since it gives immediate feedback as you work and matches the workflow used in later chapters.

Prompt: Please show me the HTML for a basic web page with examples of headings, paragraphs, and lists, so that I can learn about how web pages are structured, with an explanation of all the elements.

Headings give content hierarchy

Headings define document structure. Their visual size is a styling decision. The font family and font size for each heading level will be applied using CSS later and do not have to match the level number!

HTML has six heading levels:

```
<h1>Main page title</h1>
<h2>Section title</h2>
<h3>Subsection title</h3>
<h4>Sub-subsection title</h4>
<h5>Sub-sub-subsection title</h5>
<h6>Sub-sub-sub-subsection title</h6>
```

Key beginner rule:

- `<h1>` is the most important heading on the page
- `<h2>` is a section inside that page
- `<h3>` is a subsection inside an `<h2>`

Treat headings as part of the page outline, not as a way to pick a bigger font.

Search engines, screen readers, and accessibility tools rely heavily on correct heading structure. Using headings purely for visual effect is one of the most common beginner mistakes.

Paragraphs hold readable text

Normal text belongs in paragraphs:

```
<p>This is a paragraph of text.</p>
```

Browsers automatically add spacing between paragraphs.

You do not press *Enter* repeatedly like in Word. In fact, extra whitespace characters like carriage returns, tabs, and spaces are ignored when rendering HTML in a browser!

HTML is about meaning, not layout.

Links connect the web

Links are what connect pages into the web:

```
<a href="https://example.com">Visit Example Website</a>
```

`Here:`

- `<a>` stands for *anchor*
- `href` is the destination
- The text between the tags is what users click on

Links can point to:

- Other websites
- Other pages on the same site
- Sections within the same page

Without links, HTML pages are just isolated documents.

Images add visual content

Images are embedded using the `<img>` element:

```
<img src="photo.jpg" alt="A photo of a cat">
```

Note the following about the preceding code:

- `<img>` has no closing tag
- `src` is the image file location
- `alt` describes the image in words

`<img>` is a void element, which means it has no closing tag because it doesn't wrap any other content or contain nested elements. Other void elements you'll encounter include `<br>` (line break), `<hr>` (horizontal rule), and `<input>` for forms. While `<img>` does not need a closing tag, it does need certain attributes to be considered well-formed and accessible, like `src` and `alt`.

The `alt` text is important because it carries meaning when the image cannot. Screen readers rely on it. Search engines read it. If the image fails to load, the text still communicates meaning.

HTML treats images as content, not decoration. Decorative images, such as using emojis as custom bullets in lists, are usually handled in CSS.

Prompt: Please show me how to write accessible HTML for images, links, and forms.

Lists group related items

HTML supports two main list types.

Unordered lists use the `<ul>` tag:

```
<ul>
  <li>Milk</li>
  <li>Bread</li>
  <li>Eggs</li>
</ul>
```

This means a list in which order does not matter.

Ordered lists use the `<ol>` tag:

```
<ol>
  <li>Preheat the oven</li>
  <li>Mix ingredients</li>
  <li>Bake for 30 minutes</li>
</ol>
```

This means *steps in a specific sequence.*

Each **list item** lives inside `<li>`.

Tables structure data, not layout

Tables are for data, not page layout:

```
<table>
  <tr>
    <th>Name</th>
    <th>Age</th>
  </tr>
  <tr>
    <td>Alex</td>
    <td>32</td>
  </tr>
</table>
```

Conceptually:

- `<table>` wraps the data
- `<tr>` is a **table row**
- `<th>` is a **table header** cell
- `<td>` is a **table data** cell

Tables are best when showing:

- Prices
- Schedules
- Statistics
- Comparisons

Using tables to position content for layout is an outdated practice and causes accessibility problems.

HTML elements nest inside one another

HTML elements form a tree structure.

Example:

```
<body>
  <section>
    <h2>About me</h2>
    <p>I write books.</p>
  </section>
</body>
```

Here:

- `<section>` lives inside `<body>`
- `<h2>` and `<p>` live inside `<section>`

This nesting is how browsers understand relationships between content.

Prompt: Please give me examples of incorrectly nested HTML and explain why they break things.

Using <div> as a generic container

Sometimes you need to group several pieces of content together without adding any specific meaning. That is what the `<div>` element is for.

A `<div>` is a generic block-level container. It does not tell the browser or a screen reader what the content means. It simply groups content together.

For example:

```
<div>
  <h2>About this book</h2>
  <p>This book teaches web development with AI as a learning partner.</p>
</div>
```

This can be useful when you want to style or script a group of elements later with CSS or JavaScript.

But `<div>` should not be your first choice when a semantic element fits better. If the content is a section of the page, use `<section>`. If it is navigation, use `<nav>`. If it is a paragraph, use `<p>`. If it is the page footer, use `<footer>`.

A good beginner rule is this: use `<div>` when you need a container, not when you need meaning. A page full of `<div>` elements can still work, but it tells humans and tools much less about the structure of the content. Semantic elements make your HTML easier to read, easier to maintain, and more accessible.

Prompt: Please show me three examples where `<div>` is appropriate and three where a semantic element would be better.

HTML describes meaning, not appearance

For beginners, this distinction makes the rest of the web technology stack easier to understand.

HTML answers questions like:

- Is this a heading?
- Is this a paragraph?
- Is this navigation?
- Is this a list of items?
- Is this tabular data?

HTML does not answer:

- Should this be blue?
- Should this be centered?
- Should this animate?

That separation is deliberate. It keeps the web flexible, accessible, and device-independent.

Good practice: Do not try to memorize every HTML tag. Start by asking what each piece of content is. Is it the main heading? A paragraph? A navigation link? A list of steps? A table of data? Once you can answer those questions, the tags become easier to choose, and AI-generated HTML becomes easier to review.

Prompt: What are ARIA attributes and when should beginners care about them?

What good structure gives you

When HTML is written properly:

- Browsers can display it correctly on any screen size
- Search engines understand the content
- Screen readers can navigate the page
- CSS and JavaScript become easier to apply later

A page can look fine in a browser while still having poor structure or accessibility.

Well-structured HTML is easier to maintain. Bad HTML creates maintenance problems almost immediately.

Prompt: How do search engines use HTML structure to understand a page?

HTML DOM (document object model)

The HTML **DOM** (**Document Object Model**) is how the browser represents an HTML page internally after it has been loaded. Instead of thinking of your page as plain text, the browser turns it into a tree of objects that it can understand, manipulate, and render.

Let's see how it works with a simple HTML example:

```
<!DOCTYPE html>
<html>
  <head>
    <title>My Page</title>
  </head>
  <body>
    <h1>Hello</h1>
    <p>This is a paragraph.</p>
  </body>
</html>
```

When the browser reads the preceding code, it does not keep it as raw text. It parses the HTML and builds a tree structure, where each element becomes a node:

```
Document
 └── html
      ├── head
      │    └── title
      │         └── "My Page"
      └── body
           ├── h1
           │    └── "Hello"
           └── p
                └── "This is a paragraph."
```

Here is how to think about this:

- `Document` is the root of everything
- Each HTML element becomes a node in the tree
- Elements can have child nodes (like `<body>` containing `<h1>` and `<p>`)
- Text inside elements also becomes nodes

This structure reflects the nesting you write in HTML. If you nest elements incorrectly, the DOM will also be incorrect, which can lead to confusing behavior.

What the browser actually does (step by step):

1. It downloads the HTML file
2. It reads it from top to bottom
3. It parses each tag and creates nodes
4. It builds the DOM tree in memory
5. It uses that tree to render the page

The DOM is not just for display. CSS uses the DOM to decide what to style, and JavaScript uses the DOM to read and change the page dynamically after the page is initially rendered. For example, JavaScript can do things like:

- Change text inside `<h1>`
- Add new elements
- Remove elements
- Respond to user actions

HTML is the source document. The DOM is the browser's live tree built from that document. Once the page is loaded, the browser works with the DOM, not your original HTML file. The DOM is the browser's internal representation of your HTML as a tree of objects. If your HTML structure is clean and logical, the DOM will be easy to work with. This is why logical thinking about structure matters more than raw typing speed.

The beginner takeaway

If you remember only one thing from this chapter, it should be this:

HTML is about what content is, not how it looks.

Once you understand that distinction, HTML, CSS, and JavaScript make more sense as separate tools.

Prompt: Please show me 10 common beginner HTML mistakes and how to fix them.

Enough theory, let's do something practical and build a more complete web page.

Building a basic web page

In this section, you're going to make a tiny *about me* page, then watch it update instantly as you edit it.

Build a web page in VS code and preview it live

Create a project folder:

1. Make a new folder on your computer called `about-me-webpage`
2. Inside it, create another folder called `images`

Your folder structure will look like this:

```
about-me-webpage/
  images/
```

Open the `about-me-webpage` folder in VS Code:

1. Open VS Code.
2. Go to **File** | Open Folder...
3. Choose `about-me-webpage`.

Opening the folder (not just a single file) is important because live preview tools behave better when VS Code knows what your project root is.

4. If you see a warning about trusting the authors of files in this folder, check the box and click the **Yes, I trust the authors** button, as shown in *Figure 2.4*:

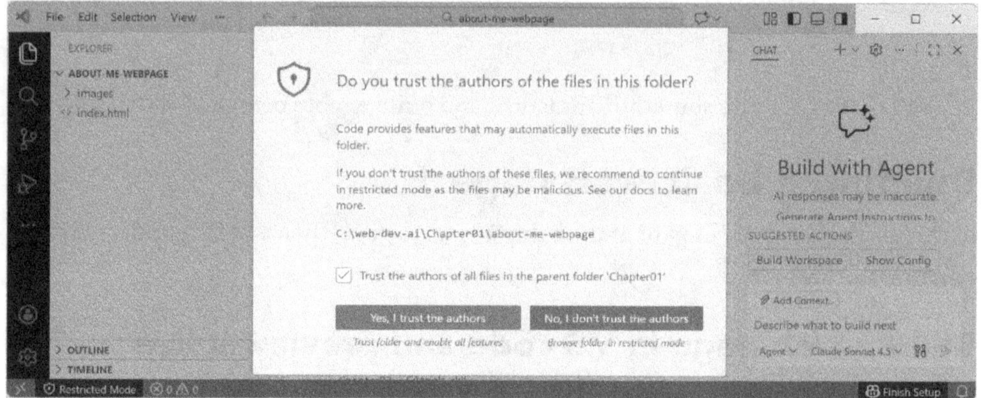

Figure 2.4: Trusting the authors of files in this folder in VS Code

5. In VS Code Explorer (left side), click **New File**, and name it `index.html`, as shown in *Figure 2.5*:

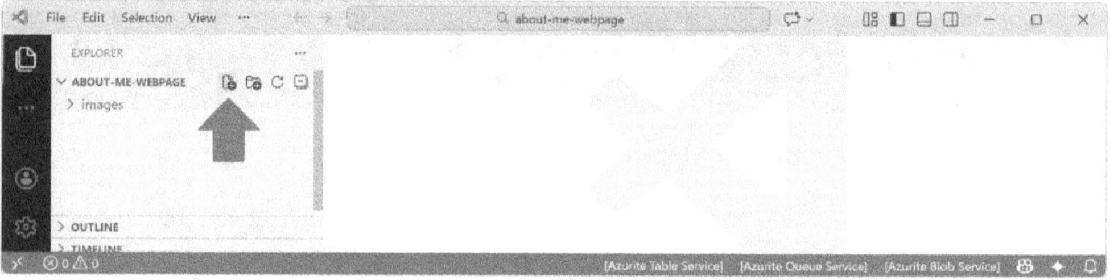

Figure 2.5: VS Code Explorer and its New File button

6. Add the following HTML to the empty file (this example includes everything you've learned with important elements highlighted). Paste this into `index.html`:

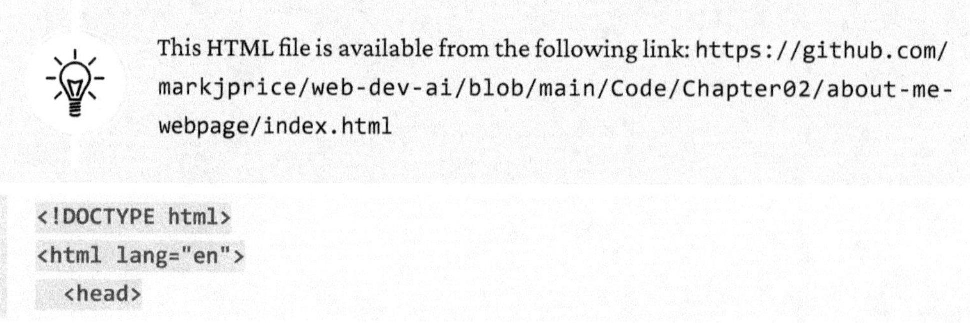

This HTML file is available from the following link: `https://github.com/markjprice/web-dev-ai/blob/main/Code/Chapter02/about-me-webpage/index.html`

```
<!DOCTYPE html>
<html lang="en">
  <head>
```

```
    <meta charset="utf-8">
    <meta name="viewport"
          content="width=device-width, initial-scale=1.0">
    <title>Mark's First Web Page</title>
  </head>

  <body>
    <h1>Mark's First Web Page</h1>

    <p>
      Welcome! This page is a simple example of HTML structure:
headings, paragraphs, links, images, lists, and a table.
    </p>

    <h2>About this page</h2>
    <p>
      HTML tells the browser what each piece of content <em>is</em>.
      Styling comes later (that's CSS), and interactivity comes
later (that's JavaScript).
    </p>

    <h2>Useful link</h2>
    <p>
      Here's a link to learn more about HTML:
      <a href="https://developer.mozilla.org/en-US/docs/Web/
HTML">MDN Web Docs: HTML</a>.
    </p>

    <h2>Image</h2>
    <p>
      Below is an image. You can use a web image URL, or a local
image file.
      The <strong>alt</strong> text describes the image for screen
readers and when the image can't load.
    </p>

    <!-- Option A: Use a local image -->
```

```
    <!-- Save an image as images/profile.jpg and use this: -->
    <!-- <img src="images/profile.jpg" alt="A friendly profile
photo"> -->

    <!-- Option B: Use a placeholder image from the web -->
    <img
      src="https://via.placeholder.com/640x240.
png?text=My+First+Image"
      alt="A placeholder banner that says My First Image"
    >

    <h2>Lists</h2>
    <p>Unordered list (a list where the order doesn't matter):</p>
    <ul>
      <li>Headings organize the page</li>
      <li>Paragraphs hold normal text</li>
      <li>Links connect pages together</li>
    </ul>

    <p>Ordered list (a list of steps):</p>
    <ol>
      <li>Create a folder for your project</li>
      <li>Add an <code>index.html</code> file</li>
      <li>Open it with Live Preview</li>
    </ol>

    <h2>Table</h2>
    <p>
      Tables are for data. Here's a tiny "learning plan" table:
    </p>

    <table>
      <thead>
        <tr>
          <th>Topic</th>
          <th>What you'll practice</th>
          <th>Time (minutes)</th>
        </tr>
```

```
      </thead>
      <tbody>
        <tr>
          <td>Headings</td>
          <td>Page outline and sections</td>
          <td>10</td>
        </tr>
        <tr>
          <td>Links</td>
          <td>Link to another page</td>
          <td>10</td>
        </tr>
        <tr>
          <td>Images</td>
          <td>Add alt text</td>
          <td>10</td>
        </tr>
      </tbody>
    </table>

    <h2>Next idea</h2>
    <p>
      Try editing the text above and watch the preview update
instantly.
      When you're ready, you can add CSS to make it look nicer.
    </p>
  </body>
</html>
```

Note the following about the preceding code:

- Document structure: `<!DOCTYPE html>`, `<html>`, `<head>`, `<title>`, `<body>`
- Headings: `<h1>`, `<h2>`
- Paragraphs: `<p>`
- Links: `<a href="...">`
- Images: `<img src="..." alt="...">`

If you see a broken image icon instead of the picture, it may be because the external image service is temporarily unavailable. Your HTML is still correct. Try switching to Option A which uses a local image file by saving any image to the correct path and filename `images/profile.jpg` and uncomment the local `<img>` element.

- Lists: `<ul>` + `<li>`, and `<ol>` + `<li>`
- Tables: `<table>`, `<thead>`, `<tbody>`, `<tr>`, `<th>`, `<td>`

Good practice: The viewport `meta` tag is considered an standard part of any HTML document and is required for pages to render correctly on mobile devices. Without it, mobile browsers will render the page at a desktop-width viewport and then scale it down, making text unreadable. Tables should be divided into a heading row (a `<thead>` with a `<tr>` element and nested `<th>` header column elements) and data rows (a `<tbody>` with one or more `<tr>` elements with nested `<td>` datum column elements).

Generating bitmap images for web pages

Up to this point, you have been working with image files that already exist. In real projects, you often need images before you have a designer, a photo library, or final assets.

Image generation tools are useful for this purpose especially as placeholders.

Tools such as Google's Nano Banana and ChatGPT Images can generate bitmap images from text descriptions. You can use them to create:

- Placeholder images while building your layout
- Hero images for landing pages
- Illustrations for blog posts or product pages
- Simple icons or visual accents

This gives you something to design around before the final artwork exists.

On April 21, 2026, OpenAI announced ChatGPT Images 2.0 with many improvements: `https://openai.com/index/introducing-chatgpt-images-2-0/`

The images generated by these tools are usually bitmap images, meaning they are made of pixels.

Common bitmap formats include:

- JPEG is good for photos
- PNG is good for transparency and sharp edges
- WebP is a format with good compression

When you are building a page layout, you often just need something that looks reasonable.

For example, you might prompt an image generator with:

```
Please create a simple hero image with a soft blue gradient background,
abstract shapes, clean and minimal, suitable for a tech website.
```

The result does not need to be perfect. It just needs to fill the space to give the page visual structure and help you think about layout and spacing. This is much better than leaving empty space or using a broken image link.

A hero image is the large visual at the top of a page. It sets the tone for everything that follows.

For example, for a survey app landing page, you might generate something like:

```
Please create a web app hero image showing a dashboard with charts and
polls, clean UI, light background, friendly colors, no text.
```

A few practical tips for hero images:

- Avoid putting important text in the image itself; use real HTML text instead
- Keep the composition simple, so it works at different screen sizes
- Prefer wide, horizontal images for hero sections

Generated images are useful but remember that generated images can sometimes include visual artifacts or odd details. Look at them critically before using them.

Bitmap images are not always the best choice. For diagrams, icons, and anything that needs to scale cleanly or animate, vector graphics are usually better.

In *Chapter 4, Drawing Scalable Graphics*, you will learn about SVG, which is better than bitmaps for diagrams, charts, icons, animations, and dynamic graphics that change with data. In this book's survey project, SVG will be especially useful for rendering charts and visualizing results.

Use generated images to support the page, not to distract from it. A useful image fits the content, the layout, and the purpose of the page.

Try these quick edits to prove it's live

While the preview is open:

- Change the `<h1>` and `<title>` text to something else
- Add a new list item: `<li>I can preview changes instantly</li>`
- Edit the table by changing a time value from 10 to 15

You've created a basic web page and used lots of different HTML elements. You could create a full website with read-only content but it would be static. One of the most common ways to make a website interactive is to provide forms for a visitor to fill in and then submit. These could be login forms for authenticating a visitor, or forms to create or edit data.

Let's look at how you can create web pages with forms and various input elements.

Working with forms and inputs

So far, your page has been *read-only*. Forms are how a user types information into a page and sends it somewhere, like a contact form, login screen, newsletter signup, checkout, and so on.

At the center of this is the `<form>` element, which wraps your input controls (text boxes, drop-downs, buttons) and defines how the browser should submit the data.

In this section, you're going to:

1. Create a new page called `contact.html` with a contact form
2. Link to it from your `index.html` **About Me** page

Create contact.html

In VS Code, create a new file in the same folder as `index.html`: `contact.html`.

Paste this in:

This HTML file is available from the following link: `https://github.com/markjprice/web-dev-ai/blob/main/Code/Chapter02/about-me-webpage/contact.html`

```
<!DOCTYPE html>
<html lang="en">
  <head>
```

```
    <meta charset="utf-8">
    <title>Contact Me</title>
  </head>

  <body>
    <h1>Contact Me</h1>

    <p>
      Use this form to send me a message. For now, it doesn't actually
send email.
      It demonstrates how forms collect data and submit it to a server.
    </p>

    <form action="/contact" method="post">
      <h2>Your details</h2>

      <p>
        <label for="fullName">Full name</label><br>
        <input type="text" id="fullName" name="fullName" required>
      </p>

      <p>
        <label for="email">Email address</label><br>
        <input type="email" id="email" name="email" required>
      </p>

      <p>
        <label for="phone">Phone (optional)</label><br>
        <input type="tel" id="phone" name="phone">
      </p>

      <h2>Your message</h2>

      <p>
        <label for="topic">Topic</label><br>
        <select id="topic" name="topic">
          <option value="question">Question</option>
```

```
          <option value="feedback">Feedback</option>
          <option value="business">Business inquiry</option>
        </select>
      </p>

      <p>
        <label for="message">Message</label><br>
        <textarea id="message" name="message" rows="6" cols="40"
required></textarea>
      </p>

      <h2>Preferences</h2>

      <p>
        Preferred contact method:
        <br>
        <input type="radio" id="contactEmail" name="preferredContact"
value="email" checked>
        <label for="contactEmail">Email</label>

        <br>

        <input type="radio" id="contactPhone" name="preferredContact"
value="phone">
        <label for="contactPhone">Phone</label>
      </p>

      <p>
        <input type="checkbox" id="newsletter" name="newsletter"
value="yes">
        <label for="newsletter">Send me occasional updates</label>
      </p>

      <p>
        <button type="submit">Send message</button>
        <button type="reset">Clear form</button>
      </p>
```

```
    </form>

    <p>
      <a href="index.html">Back to About Me</a>
    </p>
  </body>
</html>
```

A few things to notice:

- The `<form>` has `action="/contact"` and `method="post"`
    - `action` is the URL the browser sends the form data to
    - `method="post"` sends the data in the request body; `get` (the default) appends it to the URL after `?`
- Every control that should be submitted has a `name="..."`. If you forget name, the value won't be included in the submitted data.
- Each text field is labeled using `<label for="...">` that matches the input's `id`. This improves both usability and accessibility.

Link to the contact form from index.html

Open your existing `index.html` and add a link somewhere sensible, for example, under your `Useful link` section or near the bottom.

For example:

```
<h2>Contact</h2>
<p>
  Want to get in touch?
  <a href="contact.html">Go to my contact form</a>.
</p>
```

Because `contact.html` is in the same folder as `index.html`, a simple **relative link** like just the HTML filename works. Alternatively, you could specify an **absolute link** using a full URL: `https://example.com/contact.html`.

An absolute link is the full address of a resource, like a web page, that works regardless of the current page's location. A relative link is a shorter address based on the current page's location. If I am in Alaska and I want to send a letter to someone in Scotland, I would need to use their full, or absolute, address. If I wanted to send a letter to someone on my street, I could hand it to a neighbor and ask them to give it to "Bob at number 23." This is their address relative to another address on the same street. To send it to someone in the same city, we might need to use their street name too. To send it to someone in the same state, we would need to include their city name as well. A resource like a web page has one absolute address, and many relative addresses depending on how close you already are to their location.

Try it out in live preview

Now we can see the results in Live Preview:

1. Open `index.html` and start **Live Preview**, as shown in *Figure 2.6*:

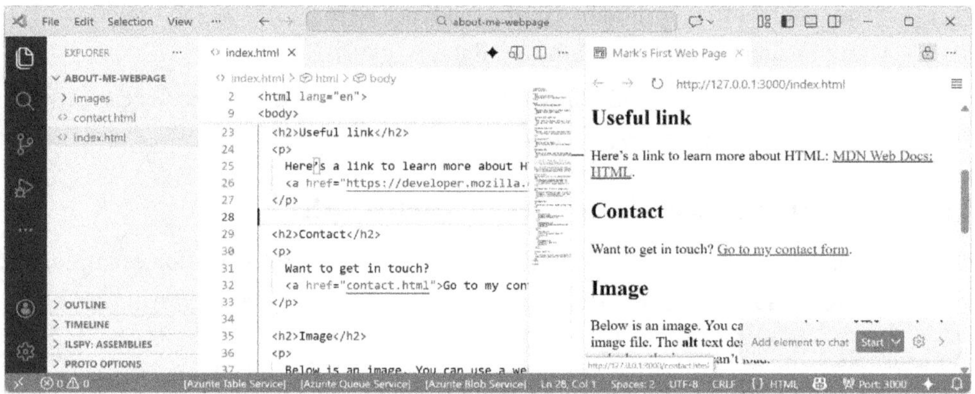

Figure 2.6: Live Preview of the link to the contact form

2. Click the **Go to my contact form** link
3. Fill in the form and click **Send message**

What you'll likely see right now:

- If you leave required fields empty, the browser will block submission and prompt you. (That's HTML's built-in validation.)
- If it does submit, you might get a `Cannot POST /contact`-style message, or a `404`, or some `not found` response, as shown in *Figure 2.7*:

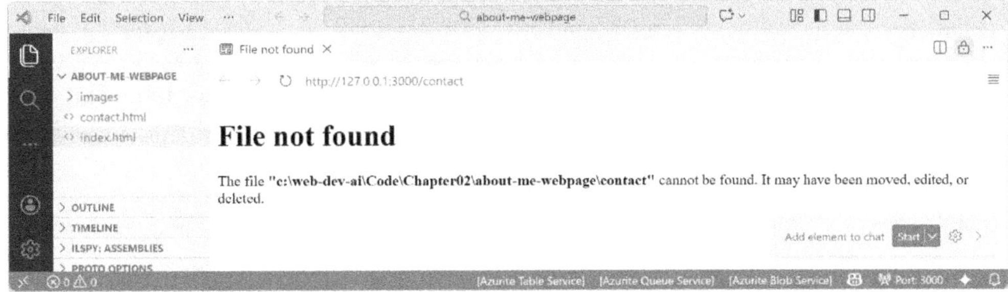

Figure 2.7: A file not found message when you do not have a server to process a form

This error appears because your browser is trying to send the form data to a server at `/contact`, but no server is running to receive it yet. This is expected at this stage because you have only built the HTML page, not the server that processes the form.

You've just hit the boundary between frontend (HTML) and backend (server code) web development. You will learn how to process form submissions in *Chapter 9, Django – Web Development on the Backend*.

A quick, practical table of common form elements

A cheat sheet you can keep nearby while learning is shown in *Table 2.1*:

Element	**Example**	**What it's for**
<form>	<form action="/contact" method="post">	Wraps inputs and defines where and how data is submitted. action and method control submission.
<label>	<label for="email"> Email </label>	Provides a human-readable label for a form control. Best practice is matching for to the input's id.
<input type="text">	<input type="text" name="fullName">	Single-line text input. Include name so it submits.
<input type="email">	<input type="email" name="email">	Email-shaped input with basic validation in many browsers.

Element	Example	What it's for
<input type="tel">	<input type="tel" name="phone">	Phone number input (often shows a phone keypad on mobile).
<textarea>	<textarea name="message"> </textarea>	Multi-line text input (great for messages).
<select> + <option>	<select> <option value="..."> ...</option> ... </select>	Dropdown list of options. Each has text inside and an optional value.
<input type="radio">	<input type="radio" name="preferredContact" value="email">	Choose one option from a group. Grouping is done by sharing the same name.
<input type="checkbox">	<input type="checkbox" name="newsletter" value="yes">	On/off option (checked or unchecked).
<button type="submit">	<button type="submit"> Send</button>	Submits the form.
<button type="reset">	<button type="reset"> Clear</button>	Resets fields to their initial values.

Table 2.1: Common form elements

You'll see lots more input types out there, but if a beginner gets comfortable with this set, they can build most basic forms.

What "posting back to the web server" means

When the user clicks the **Send** button, the browser takes all the form controls that have a `name` and sends them as an HTTP request to the URL in the action.

There are two common ways to submit the data:

- `GET` (default): the form data is appended to the URL after ? This is good for searches and filters where you want a shareable URL.
- `POST`: the form data is sent in the request body. This is common for contact forms, logins, or anything that changes server state, like a form for editing customer or order data.

On the server side (you'll do this later with Django), your web app would:

1. Receive the request at something like `/contact`
2. Read the submitted fields (name/value pairs)
3. Validate them (for real, not just browser validation)
4. Do something useful:
    - Store it in a database
    - Send an email
    - Create a support ticket
5. Return a response page (like **Thanks, message received!**)

At this stage, you're only building the HTML user interface. Server-side processing comes later.

Prompt: Please show what form data looks like when it is submitted from a browser including the difference between `GET` and `POST` with real HTTP examples.

Let's make use of your AI coach to discover some history of HTML and then practice what you've learned so far about making web pages by taking a quiz and then building more web pages.

AI exercises

Now let's use your favorite chatbot to help you learn more about HTML, first by learning about the history of HTML, then by quizzing you about HTML syntax.

History of HTML

HTML has had multiple versions over its lifetime. The current version is HTML5. Let's learn a bit about the history of HTML:

Prompt: Please show me a table of HTML versions and when they were introduced. Then describe HTML5 and show me a table of new tags that it introduced, and what they should be used for.

HTML chapter quiz

Answer the following questions without looking back at the chapter if you can.

This quiz checks whether you understand what HTML is for, not whether you can type tags from memory.

Answers are in *Appendix A*, which can be downloaded from the book's GitHub repository at the following link: `https://github.com/markjprice/web-dev-ai/blob/main/docs/Appendix-A.pdf`

Part 1: multiple choice

1. What is the main purpose of HTML?

A. To control how a web page looks

B. To add animations and interactivity

C. To describe the structure and meaning of web content

D. To process data on the server

2. Which tag should be used for the most important heading on a page?

A. `<h6>`

B. `<heading>`

C. `<title>`

D. `<h1>`

3. Which element creates a clickable link to another page?

A. `<link>`

B. `<a>`

C. `<href>`

D. `<url>`

4. What is the purpose of the alt attribute on an image?

A. To change the image size

B. To add a caption under the image

C. To describe the image in text

D. To link the image to another page

5. Which HTML element is best suited for displaying tabular data like prices or schedules?

A. `<div>`

B. `<section>`

C. `<table>`

D. `<list>`

Part 2: true or false

6. HTML decides how big text is and what color it appears on the page.

7. An HTML page can work without a <body> element.

8. Every form input that should be submitted must have a name attribute.

9. Radio buttons are used when the user should be able to select more than one option.

Part 3: spot the mistake

10. What is wrong with this HTML?

```
<img src="photo.jpg">
```

11. What is wrong with this heading structure?

```
<h1>My Website</h1>
<h4>About Me</h4>
```

12. What is wrong with this form input?

```
<input type="text" id="username">
```

Part 4: short answer

13. In your own words, explain the difference between HTML and CSS.

14. What does the <form> element do?

15. What happens when a form is submitted using method="post"?

Part 5: practical thinking (no code required)

16. Which HTML elements would you use for each of the following?

a) A page title

b) A paragraph of text

c) A navigation link

d) A list of steps in a recipe

e) A contact message box

Self-check scoring guide

14–16 correct: You've genuinely understood HTML structure. Move on.

10–13 correct: Solid understanding, but skim the chapter once more.

Below 10: Re-read slowly. HTML will click if you focus on meaning, not syntax.

Create a custom quiz

Prompt: Please quiz me about the new tags introduced with HTML5. Focus mainly on understanding the concepts rather than memorizing exact syntax.

Mini-challenge: build a "Workshop Signup" website

You are creating a small website for a one-day workshop called *Introduction to Web Development*. The site has two pages:

- A **Workshop Info** page that explains the event
- A **Signup** page where users register their interest

You are only allowed to use HTML. No CSS. No JavaScript. Focus on structure and meaning.

Page 1: workshop.html (workshop info)

Create a file called `workshop.html` that includes the document structure:

- `<!DOCTYPE html>`
- `<html>`, `<head>`, `<body>`
- A `<title>` that matches the page's purpose

The requirements for the page content are:

- Main heading: Use one `<h1>` for the workshop title.
- Introduction paragraph: Describe what the workshop is about in plain text.
- Image: Add an image banner for the workshop. Include meaningful alt text. You may use a placeholder image URL.
- Agenda section: Use a <h2> heading.
- Include an ordered list of workshop sessions (at least four items).
- What you'll learn section: Use an `<h2>` heading. Include an unordered list of skills or topics.
- Schedule table: Use an <h2> heading. Include a <table> with columns for: Time, Topic, Format (Lecture, Hands-on, Break).
- Add a link to the signup page: `<a href="signup.html">Sign up for the workshop</a>`.

Page 2: signup.html (workshop sign up)

Create a file called `signup.html` that includes the document structure:

- Proper `<head>` and `<body>`
- A clear page `<title>`

The requirements for the form are:

- Your page must include a `<form>` element with `method="post"` and a realistic action value (for example `/signup`).
- Inside the form, include:
    - Personal details like full name (text input, required) and email address (email input, required).
    - Experience level as a set of radio buttons: Beginner, Some experience, Advanced. (All radio buttons must share the same name to be a group.)

    - Topics of interest with at least three checkboxes (for example HTML, CSS, Python, JavaScript).
    - Additional notes as a `<textarea>` for comments or questions.
    - Submit button.

- Navigation with a link back to `workshop.html`.

Rules of the challenge

- Every input that should be submitted must have a name
- Every form control must have a `<label>` element
- Headings must follow a logical order
- Tables are for data only
- Do not use `<div>` to replace meaningful elements you've already learned

If you want to push a little further:

- Add `required` to appropriate inputs
- Add a `<select>` dropdown for **How did you hear about this workshop?**
- Add placeholder text to text inputs

Try submitting the form in **Live Preview** and observe what happens.

You've completed the challenge successfully if:

- Both pages open correctly in **Live Preview**
- The link from `workshop.html` to `signup.html` works
- The form enforces required fields
- Submitting the form produces a browser response (even if it errors)

A solution to this mini-challenge can be found in the book's GitHub repository at the following link: `https://github.com/markjprice/web-dev-ai/blob/main/code/chapter02/workshop-challenge/`

What this challenge checks

This exercise proves you understand that:

- HTML defines structure, not styling
- Pages connect through links
- Forms collect and submit data
- Tables communicate structured information

While HTML specializes in web content, it is just one of several markup languages, and understanding related technologies like XML and SVG helps round out how structured data and graphics are represented on the web. Let's learn about those languages next.

Other markup languages

HTML is the markup language most closely associated with the web, but it belongs to a wider family of languages that use tags to describe content. Understanding this family will help you see that HTML isn't random or magical. It's one practical solution that emerged from a longer history.

What "markup language" means

A **markup language** is a system for adding annotations to text so that a computer can understand what different parts of that text represent. In other words, markup answers questions like:

- Is this text a heading or a paragraph?
- Is this a list item or a table cell?
- Is this content data, structure, or metadata?

Markup languages do not execute logic. They describe structure and meaning. That puts HTML in the same conceptual category as languages like XAML and SVG.

HTML is a domain-specific markup language designed for one job: describing documents meant to be viewed in a web browser.

HTML is intentionally forgiving. Browsers try very hard to display something sensible even if the markup is imperfect. That design choice is one of the reasons the web spread so quickly.

XML (eXtensible Markup Language) came later and took a different approach. Where HTML is opinionated and forgiving, XML is strict about syntax, extensible (you define your own tags), and focused on data, not presentation.

An example of XML is shown in the following code:

```
<book>
  <title>Python Programming</title>
  <author>Mark</author>
  <pages>320</pages>
</book>
```

There are some key differences between XML and HTML:

- Every tag must be closed either with a closing tag (`<book>...</book>`) or as a self-closing tag (`<br />`) because, unlike HTML5, which allows unclosed void elements, XML will not allow them
- Tags must be properly nested
- There is no predefined set of tags
- XML does not define how things should look

XML is commonly used for configuration files, data interchange, document formats, and APIs (especially historically).

Prompt: Please explain why HTML is forgiving but XML is strict, with examples.

SVG: markup for graphics

SVG (**Scalable Vector Graphics**) is another markup language, but for graphics instead of documents. SVG uses tags to describe shapes, paths, text, and transformations, as shown in the following code:

```
<svg width="100" height="100">
  <circle cx="50" cy="50" r="40" />
</svg>
```

There are important things to understand about SVG:

- It is XML-based
- It describes *what the graphic is*, not how to draw pixels
- It scales cleanly at any resolution

SVG can be embedded directly inside HTML documents, which is why learning HTML structure makes SVG easier to understand later. You will learn about SVG in *Chapter 4, SVG – Drawing Scalable Graphics*.

A very short history of markup languages

HTML was not the first markup language:

1. Early document systems based on **Standard Generalized Markup Language** (**SGML**) inspired structured markup long before the web. It is the grandparent of most markup languages, including HTML, XML, and anything derived from them. SGML is a meta-language, not a markup language in the everyday sense. That means SGML does not define a fixed set of tags. Instead, it defines rules for creating your own markup languages.
2. HTML was created to describe scientific documents with links. As browsers became more powerful, and became important for commerce and industry, HTML grew features. HTML is an SGML application.
3. XML emerged to provide a strict, general-purpose markup format. XML is a simplified descendant of SGML.
4. SVG emerged to describe graphics in a resolution-independent way. SVG inherits SGML ideas via XML.
5. **XAML** (**Extensible Application Markup Language**) is a markup language created by Microsoft for defining user interfaces in desktop and cross-platform applications, rather than web pages. XAML is most commonly used with **WPF** (**Windows Presentation Foundation**), WinUI, .NET MAUI, and Avalonia.

They are not competitors. They are variations on the same idea: structured markup with meaning, applied to different domains.

Prompt: Where does XHTML fit in the history of markup languages?

Why beginners should care

HTML is not unique because it uses tags. It's unique because it uses markup to describe documents meant for the web. Other markup languages exist for other jobs.

HTML just happens to be the one that holds the web together.

SGML is not something you learn to use. It is something you learn about. It's the root of the markup family tree. Everything else makes more sense once you know where it came from.

References and resources

Let's review the official HTML documentation and references.

MDN web docs (beginners should start here)

MDN Web Docs is the best HTML documentation on the internet for learning and day-to-day reference. It is maintained by Mozilla with contributions from browser vendors and the web community.

- Homepage: `https://developer.mozilla.org/`
- HTML overview: `https://developer.mozilla.org/en-US/docs/Web/HTML`
- HTML elements reference: `https://developer.mozilla.org/en-US/docs/Web/HTML/Element`
- Forms and input elements: `https://developer.mozilla.org/en-US/docs/Learn/Forms`, `https://developer.mozilla.org/en-US/docs/Web/HTML/Element/form`, and `https://developer.mozilla.org/en-US/docs/Web/HTML/Element/input`

MDN is so good because it is written for humans, not lawyers, with uncomplicated examples, and it explains why, not just what. It is kept in sync with real browser behavior.

Good practice: If a beginner uses only one documentation site while learning HTML, it should be MDN.

W3C HTML specification (official but not beginner friendly)

The **World Wide Web Consortium** (**W3C**) publishes the official HTML specifications. This is the formal definition of how HTML works at a standards level.

- HTML specification landing page: `https://www.w3.org/TR/html/`
- Living HTML standard (WHATWG, see below): `https://html.spec.whatwg.org/`

The specification is written for browser implementers like the programmers at Microsoft, Google, and Apple, who build rendering engines. It is not written to teach HTML. It is dense, precise, and unforgiving.

This is reference material, not learning material. You don't read it cover to cover. You look things up when you need exact behavior.

WHATWG HTML living standard

Most browsers now follow the WHATWG HTML Living Standard, which evolves continuously instead of being frozen into versions.

HTML Living Standard: `https://html.spec.whatwg.org/`

For current browser behavior, this is the main specification to check.

Again, this is not beginner reading. It's for checking edge cases, resolving ambiguity, and understanding how browsers really behave.

How beginners should actually use these resources

A practical approach is to start with MDN, build a small example, and consult the specification only when needed:

- Concepts
- Examples
- Best practices

Then get your hands dirty by building something:

- Make mistakes
- Break things
- Fix them

Only then glance at the official specifications if:

- Browser behavior seems odd
- You need absolute precision
- You're curious how the machinery works

For learning HTML, use MDN Web Docs. It explains HTML the way humans think.

The W3C and WHATWG specifications define how browsers work, but they are not teaching material. Treat them as reference manuals, not tutorials.

Summary

In this chapter, you learned the following:

- HTML describes the structure and meaning of content, not how it looks
- An HTML document is built from elements, which are made of tags and content
- Attributes provide additional information that configures how elements behave
- Headings create a logical outline of a page and should reflect meaning, not appearance
- Paragraphs, lists, links, images, and tables represent different types of content
- Elements can be nested to form a hierarchical structure that browsers interpret as a tree
- Block-level elements structure layout, while inline elements flow within text
- Semantic HTML improves accessibility, search engine understanding, and maintainability
- Forms allow users to input data and submit it to a server using `GET` or `POST`
- Every form control must have a name to be included in submitted data
- HTML is forgiving and designed for documents, unlike stricter markup languages like XML
- SVG uses markup to describe scalable graphics and can be embedded in HTML
- Good HTML creates a strong starting point for CSS styling and JavaScript interactivity

In the next chapter, you will learn about CSS, a language used to provide styling and layout to the content on a web page.

Get this book's PDF version and more

Scan the QR code (or go to packtpub.com/unlock). Search for this book by name, confirm the edition, and then follow the steps on the page.

UNLOCK NOW

Note: Keep your invoice handy. Purchases made directly from Packt don't require an invoice.

3

CSS – Styling Your Web Pages

Make your pages beautiful using **Cascading Style Sheets (CSS)**. This chapter shows how CSS controls presentation and layout.

By the end of this chapter, you will have taken a plain HTML document and transformed it into a visually appealing, readable, and responsive web page. You will understand how styles are applied, how to control color and typography, how elements are positioned on the page, and how websites adapt to different screen sizes. You will also learn how to spot and fix common CSS mistakes, including using AI tools to help debug layout and styling problems when things do not look the way you expect.

In this chapter, we will cover the following topics:

- CSS basics
- Colors, fonts, and layout
- Responsive design
- AI challenge – CSS debugging
- Transforms and animation

Suggested chatbot prompts with example responses for this chapter can be found at the following link: `https://github.com/markjprice/web-dev-ai/blob/main/prompts/ch03-css/readme.md`

CSS basics

CSS exists to control presentation: HTML describes what content is, CSS describes how that content should look. Keeping those concerns separate makes web pages easier to maintain, restyle, and scale.

In *Chapter 2, HTML – Structuring Your Web Pages*, you created pages using headings, paragraphs, links, images, lists, tables, and forms. At that point, the browser decided how everything looked. Fonts followed browser defaults, spacing was basic, and everything was stacked vertically. CSS is how you take control away from the browser and make deliberate design choices.

CSS works by defining rules. Each rule says "select these elements" and "apply these styles to them". Once you understand that sentence, you understand the core of CSS.

Adding CSS to a web page

There are three ways to apply CSS to HTML. You will see all three in real projects, but only one of them is recommended for most sites. They are:

- **Inline CSS**: Style defined at the element level.
- **Internal CSS**: Style defined at the page level.
- **External CSS**: Style defined at the website level.

Let's see examples of each.

Inline CSS is written directly on an HTML element:

```
<p style="color: red;">This text is red.</p>
```

This works, but it is messy. Styles get scattered throughout your HTML, they are hard to reuse, and they are painful to maintain.

Good practice: Avoid inline CSS except when experimenting.

Internal CSS is written inside a `<style>` tag in the `<head>` section of the page:

```
<!DOCTYPE html>
<html lang="en">
<head>
  <meta charset="UTF-8">
```

```
    <title>My First CSS</title>
    <style>
      p {
        color: blue;
      }
    </style>
  </head>
  <body>
    <p>This paragraph is blue.</p>
  </body>
</html>
```

Internal CSS is easier to maintain than inline CSS, but it still ties style definitions to a single HTML file, so if you need the same styles in multiple web pages, you will have to duplicate them.

Good practice: External CSS should be your default while learning because it keeps structure and presentation separate. Later, you may see small internal styles used for performance, especially for above-the-fold CSS, but do not start there. This is because the styles are downloaded with the web page and defined in the `<head>` so styling is applied to the content immediately as it is rendered.

External CSS is written in a separate `.css` file and linked to your HTML. After downloading the web page, the browser downloads the CSS file and applies its styles to the content.

Let's see an example:

1. Create a new folder named `Chapter03`.
2. In the `Chapter03` folder, create a new folder named `StyleBasics`.
3. In the `StyleBasics` folder, download the file called `index.html` from the following link: `https://github.com/markjprice/web-dev-ai/blob/main/Code/Chapter03/StyleBasics/index.html`
4. In VS Code, open the `StyleBasics` folder.
5. In the `StyleBasics` folder, create a new file called `styles.css` and add style definitions:

    ```
    p {
      color: green;
    }
    ```

6. In `index.html`, in the `<head>` element, add a link to the CSS file:

```
<link rel="stylesheet" href="styles.css">
```

7. Live preview the page. The paragraph should now be green, as shown in *Figure 3.1*:

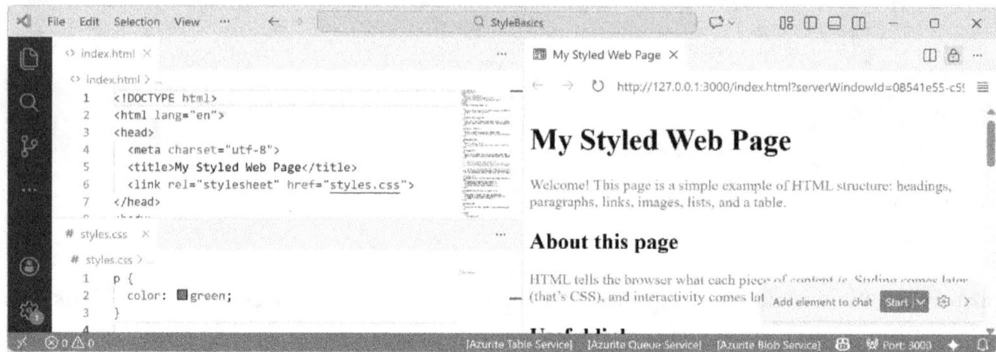

Figure 3.1: External CSS file changing the color of paragraphs to green

If nothing changes, check the filename, check the path, and make sure the `<link>` tag is inside `<head>`.

From this point on, assume all CSS lives in an external stylesheet unless explicitly stated otherwise.

Good practice: External CSS is what you should use by default. It allows you to define your styles once and reuse them throughout all the web pages in a website.

Selectors and rules

A CSS rule has two main parts: a selector and a declaration block:

```
p {
  color: navy;
  font-size: 18px;
}
```

In the preceding code:

- `p` is the selector. It tells the browser which elements to target.
- Everything inside the curly braces `{ }` is the declaration block.
- Each declaration is a property like `color` or `font-size` and a value like `navy` or `18px`, separated by a colon and ending with a semicolon.
- This rule applies navy color and 18px font size to all `<p>` elements on the page.

Try adding these rules to your stylesheet file:

```
h1 {
  color: darkslateblue;
}

p {
  color: green;
  font-size: 18px;
  line-height: 1.8;
}
```

The preceding code shows an example of element selectors. These select all elements for the same tag type. In these examples, the rules apply to all `<h1>` elements and all `<p>` elements. But what if you want to select only a subset of headings and paragraphs? We can use two other types of selector to do this.

Classes and IDs

Targeting every paragraph or heading is rarely enough. You often want to style specific elements differently. A **CSS class** can be reused across multiple elements. You can add this example to your web page and stylesheet files.

The HTML to add:

```
<h2>Example of a class selector</h2>
<p class="intro">This will be bold and 14px.</p>
<p>This is regular content.</p>
```

The CSS to add is shown in the following code:

```
.intro {
  font-size: 14px;
  font-weight: bold;
}
```

A class selector always starts with a dot like `.intro` in the preceding code.

A class or ID name is an identifier. The key rules are:

- It must not contain spaces.
- It may contain letters, digits, hyphens, and underscores.
- It must not start with a digit.
- It may start with a letter or a hyphen.
- It is case-sensitive, but relying on case differences is a bad idea.

There are practical naming conventions too:

- Use lowercase only because mixing case adds cognitive load and invites bugs.
- Use hyphens, not underscores, because hyphens are the dominant convention in CSS and match property naming like `font-size` and `background-color`.
- Name things by purpose, not appearance. For example, `.red-text` is bad, `.error-message` is good. This guideline saves trouble later.

An element's ID should be unique within the page. An ID selector should therefore only select that one element on the page and apply its style to it.

The HTML to add is shown highlighted in the following code:

```
<h1 id="main-title">My Styled Web Page</h1>
```

The CSS to add is shown in the following code:

```
#main-title {
  text-transform: uppercase;
}
```

An ID selector starts with a hash like `#main-title` in the preceding code. Use IDs sparingly. Classes scale better and are easier to reuse.

Good practice: Avoid IDs for styling because they can only be applied to one element. Even if you currently only have one element that needs a style, you probably want to apply it using a class instead. That way, if you later add another element that needs the same style, you can easily apply it.

The cascade and specificity

CSS stands for Cascading Style Sheets, and the cascade matters. When multiple rules target the same element, the browser must decide which one wins.

Consider the following CSS:

```
p {
  color: black;
}

.intro {
  color: darkgreen;
}
```

And this HTML:

```
<p class="intro">Hello world</p>
```

The element selector sets paragraphs to `black`. The class selector rule says to color any element with the class of `.intro` in `darkgreen`. Which one *wins*?

The paragraph will be colored dark green, not black, because class selectors are more *specific* than tag selectors.

Prompt: Please explain the CSS cascade with real examples showing conflicts between element, class, and ID selectors. Show me examples where CSS rules conflict and explain why one wins over another.

Specificity rules get very complicated, so let's simplify them:

- Element selectors are weakest
- Class selectors override element selectors

- ID selectors override both
- Inline styles override everything else

```
Element < Class < ID < Inline
```

Order also matters. If two rules have equal specificity, the one written later in the stylesheet wins. For example, the following CSS has two class rules:

```
.intro {
  color: darkgreen;
}

.branding {
  color: darkred;
}
```

If we have an element that has both classes applied:

```
<p class="intro branding">Hello world</p>
```

Then the `.intro` style is applied first, and then the `.branding` style is applied next, making the text color `darkred`.

To apply multiple classes to the same element then use spaces as separators. The order of the class names in the class attribute does not matter. Both `class="intro branding"` and `class="branding intro"` have the same effect.

Specificity explains many “why isn’t my CSS working?” moments.

Prompt: What is CSS specificity, and how is it calculated step by step?

The box model

Every element on a web page is a rectangular box. Understanding this is important if you want layouts that behave predictably.

As shown in *Figure 3.2*, each box consists of:

- **Element Content**: The text or image itself
- **Padding**: Space inside the element, around the content
- **Border**: A *line* around the padding
- **Margin**: Space outside the element, separating it from other elements around it

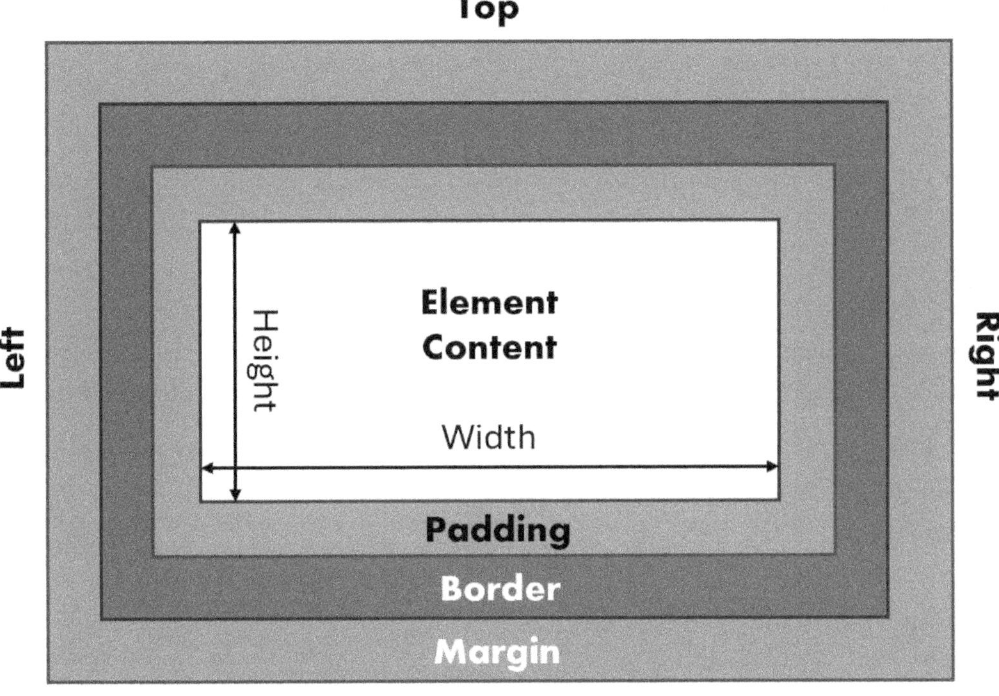

Figure 3.2: The CSS box model

Try this example CSS:

```
.card {
  width: 300px;
  padding: 16px;
  border: 5px dashed #333;
  margin: 20px;
}
```

One important detail: `width: 300px;` sets the width of the content area, not the total visible width of the box. Because this card also has `padding: 16px;` on both sides and a `5px` border on both sides, the full rendered width is `300` + `16` + `16` + `5` + `5` = `342px`, plus any outside margin. This is the default CSS box model and one of the most common beginner surprises.

Later in this chapter, you will see how `box-sizing: border-box;` changes this behavior so the declared width includes padding and border.

And here's the HTML to add:

```
<h2>Box model example</h2>
<div class="card">
  <h3>Card Title</h3>
  <p>This is a simple content card. This is a simple content card. This
is a simple content card. This is a simple content card. This is a simple
content card.</p>
</div>
```

Experiment by changing padding and margin values. Watch how the space inside and outside the element changes. You will use this idea throughout the chapter and later layout work.

`margin: 0 auto;` centers an element horizontally because of how the browser calculates margins when the element has a constrained width. This is shorthand for:

```
margin-top: 0;
margin-bottom: 0;
margin-left: auto;
margin-right: auto;
```

The vertical margins are fixed at zero, while the horizontal margins are set to `auto`. This only works if the element:

- Is a block-level element, and
- Has a width that is less than the available space

If the element already fills the entire width of its container, there is no extra space to distribute and nothing to center. When left and right margins are set to `auto`, the browser calculates how much horizontal space is left over after accounting for the element's width.

`margin: 0 auto;` does not center vertically because vertical margins do not participate in the same automatic space distribution logic. There is no concept of "split the leftover height" for margins in normal document flow.

You can think of `margin: 0 auto;` as telling the browser to split the remaining horizontal space evenly on both sides of this box.

If there is no space to split, nothing moves. That explains most common cases.

Prompt: Please explain the difference between margin, padding, and border with visual examples and common mistakes.

Add the following CSS incrementally. Do not paste it all in at once. Add a rule, refresh, observe, repeat:

```
body {
  font-family: Arial, Helvetica, sans-serif;
  background-color: #f5f5f5;
  color: #222;
}

div.container {
  max-width: 800px;
  margin: 0 auto;
  padding: 20px;
  background-color: white;
}

a {
  text-decoration: none;
  color: #0066cc;
}

a:hover {
  text-decoration: underline;
}
```

Note the following about the preceding code:

- The body selector applies to the entire page. `font-family` sets the default font stack. The browser will first try `Arial`, then `Helvetica`, and finally any generic `sans-serif` font. This is a common font stack for simple, readable text. `background-color: #f5f5f5;` gives the whole page a very light gray background. `color: #222;` sets the default text color to a very dark gray instead of pure black, which is easier on the eyes.
- The `div.container` selector targets `<div class="container">`. `max-width: 800px;` limits the width of the content to 800 pixels, even on large screens, which improves readability by preventing overly long lines. `margin: 0 auto;` means no top/bottom margin and the browser evenly distributes space so the container is horizontally centered. `padding: 20px;` adds space inside the container so content doesn't touch the edges. `background-color: white;` creates a white card effect against the light gray page background.
- The a selector (for hyperlinks) removes the default underline from links and sets a custom blue color. The `a:hover` selector applies when a pointing device hovers over a link with the mouse and adds the underline back, giving users a visual cue that the text is interactive.

Good practice: Removing the underline for links by default and adding it dynamically on hover means links are only identifiable by color when not hovered. This makes links harder to identify for users with color vision deficiencies. A more accessible approach is to keep the underline (or add another visual distinction beyond color like font weight or a `border-bottom`, or sufficient contrast between the link color and surrounding text) in the default state.

You have not learned everything in this CSS yet, and that is fine. Here, you are learning a repeatable debugging process, not memorizing fixes. You should now see how CSS changes plain HTML into a page with clearer spacing, color, and typography.

Prompt: What does the selector `a:hover` do?

The four-sides model

In CSS, many properties apply to the four sides of a box. Rather than inventing four unrelated properties, CSS uses a directional system based on top, right, bottom, and left. Once you understand this pattern, a large chunk of CSS suddenly becomes predictable instead of arbitrary.

Most layout-related CSS properties operate on the same four edges: Top, Right, Bottom, and Left. These directions always follow the same clockwise order, which matters when shorthand syntax is used.

Properties that support directional variants

The most common properties with `-top`, `-right`, `-bottom`, and `-left` forms are spacing like `margin` and `padding`.

Each has:

- `margin-top`, `margin-right`, `margin-bottom`, `margin-left`
- `padding-top`, `padding-right`, `padding-bottom`, `padding-left`
- `border-top`, `border-right`, `border-bottom`, `border-left`

Borders also have sub-properties:

- `border-top-width`, `border-top-style`, `border-top-color`
- And equivalents for the other sides

Positioning offsets (when `position` is not `static`): `top`, `right`, `bottom`, `left`.

Note the naming pattern in corner rounding:

- `border-top-left-radius`
- `border-top-right-radius`
- `border-bottom-right-radius`
- `border-bottom-left-radius`

Shorthand vs longhand

Most of these properties support shorthand notation as well as longhand.

Take margin as the canonical example. To set all four sides to `20px`:

```
margin: 20px;
```

To set top and bottom to `10px`, and left and right: `20px`:

```
margin: 10px 20px;
```

To set top to 10px, left and right to `20px`, and bottom to `30px`:

```
margin: 10px 20px 30px;
```

To set top to `10px`, right to `20px`, bottom to `30px`, and left to `40px`:

```
margin: 10px 20px 30px 40px;
```

The order is always: top → right → bottom → left

A useful mnemonic is *clockwise starting at the top.*

The same rules apply to `padding`, `border-width`, and `border-radius` (with some quirks for corners).

This model exists because the CSS box model is directional. Content sits inside `padding`, `padding` is inside `borders`, and `borders` are separated from other elements by `margins`. Every one of those layers can vary per side.

CSS chose predictability over verbosity. You can be explicit when needed, concise when you are not.

When to use longhand and shorthand property names

Use longhand property names when:

- Only one side needs adjustment
- You want to override a specific side later
- You are fixing a bug and need precision

```
margin-bottom: 24px;
```

Use shorthand property names when:

- Values are symmetrical
- You want visual grouping
- You want the code to show that these sides belong together

```
padding: 16px 24px;
```

This communicates layout intent better than four separate lines. This is clearer than rewriting an entire shorthand declaration.

What is box-sizing and why use border-box?

By default, CSS uses the content-box model to calculate the size of elements. This means that when you set a width or height, you are only defining the size of the content area. Padding and borders are then added on top of that, increasing the total size of the element:

```
.card {
  width: 300px;
  padding: 20px;
  border: 5px solid #333;
}
```

In the preceding example, the actual rendered width is not 300px. It becomes:

- 300px (content)
- 40px (left and right padding)
- 10px (left and right border)
- Total width = 350px

This often surprises beginners and is a common source of layout bugs, especially when elements overflow their containers.

The border-box alternative

The `box-sizing` property changes how the browser calculates an element's size. When set to `border-box`, the width and height include content, padding, and border:

```
.card {
  box-sizing: border-box;
  width: 300px;
  padding: 20px;
  border: 5px solid #333;
}
```

Now the total width stays exactly 300px, and the content area shrinks to make room for padding and border.

Most developers use `box-sizing: border-box` these days because it matches how people naturally think about layout:

- A box set to 300px wide actually appears as 300px wide
- Padding and borders do not unexpectedly increase size
- Layouts are easier to understand and maintain
- It reduces bugs caused by overflowing elements

This becomes especially important in responsive design, where elements must adapt to different screen sizes without breaking.

Instead of setting `box-sizing` on individual elements, developers often apply it globally:

```
*,
*::before,
*::after {
  box-sizing: border-box;
}
```

The preceding code ensures all elements, including pseudo-elements, use the same sizing model.

For most projects, using `box-sizing: border-box` from the start makes CSS behave in a more intuitive and reliable way.

How to write a CSS comment

CSS uses block comments only:

```
/* This is a CSS comment */
```

There is no single-line comment syntax in CSS. Anything outside `/* */` is treated as code. Comments can appear almost anywhere in a stylesheet:

```
body {
  color: #222; /* Main text color */
  background-color: #fff;
}
```

Comments should explain intent, not restate what the code already says. Here's an example of a pointless comment:

```
/* Set the color to blue */
color: blue;
```

Here's an example of a useful comment:

```
/* Primary link color chosen for contrast on light backgrounds */
color: #0066cc;
```

The comment explains why the value exists, not what the syntax does.

Where comments are actually helpful

Use comments to divide a stylesheet into logical sections:

```
/* =========================
   Base styles
   ========================= */
```

This is especially helpful as files grow.

Use comments for non-obvious decisions. If a value looks arbitrary, explain it:

```
/* Extra padding prevents text from touching rounded corners */
padding: 18px 22px;
```

Use comments for workarounds and hacks. If you had to fight the browser, document it:

```
/* Safari rounding bug: prevents 1px overflow on flex items */
overflow: hidden;
```

Future you will thank past you.

Do not comment obvious rules:

```
/* Center the content */
margin: 0 auto;
```

CSS comments are ignored by the browser. They do not affect rendering. In production builds, tools often remove them automatically. That means comments are for humans, not machines.

Good practice: If a comment does not reduce the time it takes another developer to understand why a rule exists, it should not be there. That includes future you.

Inheritance vs non-inherited properties

One of the reasons CSS can feel unpredictable at first is that not all properties behave the same way. Some properties are inherited from parent elements, while others are not.

Inherited properties automatically pass from a parent element to its children. These are usually related to text and readability. For example, if you set a font or text color on the <body> element in the CSS file:

```
body {
  font-family: Arial, Helvetica, sans-serif;
  color: #222;
}
```

Then most elements inside it will use those values unless explicitly overridden on the page, like <p> and <div> elements:

```
<p>This text inherits the font and color.</p>
<div>
  <p>This paragraph also inherits the same styles.</p>
</div>
```

In this case, both paragraphs inherit the `font-family` and `color` from the <body> element.

Common inherited properties include `color`, `font-family`, `font-size`, `line-height`, and `text-align`.

Non-inherited properties do not pass down automatically. These are usually related to layout and spacing. Each element must define them explicitly if needed. For example, if you set a margin or border on the <body> element in the CSS file:

```
body {
  margin: 20px;
  border: 5px solid red;
}
```

Then most elements inside it will not use those values on the page:

```
<div>
  <p>This paragraph does not inherit the margin or border.</p>
</div>
```

Even though <body> has a `margin` and `border`, the <div> and <p> inside it do not inherit those values.

Common non-inherited properties include `margin`, `padding`, `border`, `width`, `height`, and `background-color`.

If needed, you can force inheritance using the `inherit` value:

```
p {
  border: inherit;
}
```

This tells the paragraph to explicitly take the same border as its parent.

Understanding which properties inherit and which do not helps explain many confusing CSS behaviors. When something is not applying, the issue is often that you are relying on inheritance for a property that does not inherit by default.

Prompt: Please explain inheritance in CSS and which properties inherit by default.

Web Content Accessibility Guidelines (WCAG)

When writing CSS, it is important to consider not just how a website looks, but how it can be used by as many people as possible. The **Web Content Accessibility Guidelines** (**WCAG**) are an internationally recognized set of recommendations for making web content more accessible, particularly for people with disabilities.

WCAG is built around four key principles. Content should be *perceivable*, meaning users can see or hear it. It should be *operable*, so users can interact with it using a variety of input methods, including keyboards. It should be *understandable*, with clear and predictable behavior. Finally, it should be *robust*, meaning it works across different browsers, devices, and assistive technologies.

CSS plays a significant role in accessibility. For example, choosing sufficient color contrast between text and background helps users with visual impairments. Avoiding fixed font sizes allows users to scale text more easily. Ensuring that focus states (such as outlines on links and buttons) are visible supports keyboard navigation.

Accessibility is not an optional extra or a final step. It should be considered from the beginning of the design and development process. Following WCAG guidance leads to websites that are more inclusive, easier to use, and often better designed overall.

The following links will help you learn WCAG:

- Explains the *why* behind accessibility before diving into rules: `https://www.w3.org/WAI/fundamentals/accessibility-intro/`
- Quick reference: `https://www.w3.org/WAI/WCAG22/quickref/`
- Current WCAG full specifications (2.0, 2.1, 2.2) with supporting documents and explanations: `https://www.w3.org/WAI/standards-guidelines/wcag/`

In the next section, we will go deeper into colors, fonts, and layout, and start making design choices instead of relying on browser defaults.

Colors, fonts, and layout

In beginner projects, simple design choices usually work better than adding more decoration. Good design is mostly about restraint. CSS gives you enormous power, and the hardest part is knowing when to stop.

Working with color

The syntax of color in CSS is simple, but choosing colors well is harder. You set a value, the browser paints pixels. The difficulty is not syntax, it is consistency and contrast.

CSS supports several color formats, but you should focus on two, color names like `red` or `darkblue`, and hexadecimal values:

```
color: red;
color: #336699;
```

Named colors like `red` and `blue` exist mainly for quick experiments. Real projects use hexadecimal values because they are precise and predictable.

Hex colors are written as `#RRGGBB`, where each pair controls the intensity of red, green, and blue.

```
body {
  background-color: #f5f5f5;
  color: #222222;
}
```

This combination already improves readability compared to pure black on pure white, which is harsh on the eyes.

You can also use color functions:

```
color: rgb(255, 99, 71);
color: rgba(255, 99, 71, 0.5);
color: hsl(120, 60%, 50%);
color: hsla(120, 60%, 50%, 0.7);
```

Prompt: Please explain the color functions `rgb`, `rgba`, `hsl`, and `hsla`, especially how to set alpha or transparency.

A few strong rules that will save you from ugly pages:

- Do not use too many colors. Two or three core colors is plenty for most beginner projects.
- Ensure text contrast is high enough. WCAG 2.1 AA requires a minimum contrast ratio of 4.5:1 for normal text and 3:1 for large text (18pt+ or 14pt bold). Light gray text on a white background looks fashionable and reads terribly.
- Use color to communicate meaning, not decoration. Links, errors, warnings, and highlights should use color meaningfully and consistently.

Prompt: How do I check if my color contrast meets WCAG standards? What CSS techniques improve accessibility beyond color contrast?

Fonts and typography

Typography often affects readability more than color does. Poor font choices make a site feel amateur faster than almost anything else.

Start simple. System fonts are your friend:

```
body {
  font-family: Arial, Helvetica, sans-serif;
}
```

This tells the browser to use Arial if available, otherwise Helvetica, otherwise any generic sans-serif font. It loads instantly and looks clean on every platform.

browsers use a sensible default font size (typically 16px), and users may adjust this for readability. Instead of overriding it with fixed pixel values, prefer relative units such as percentages or `rem` (root `em`, explained later) so that user preferences are respected. You should usually trust the browser default font size and build on top of it, not override it. For example, either set it to `100%` or slightly larger for a home page on a marketing site:

```
html {
  font-size: 112.5%; /* ~18px equivalent */
}
```

Good practice: Setting `font-size` on body affects most text because font size is inherited by default, and most elements are inside `<body>`. You will see this a lot in code examples, and LLMs often follow that old practice. But `<body>` does not define the root font size and therefore it does not control `rem` units. To control `rem` and default `font-size`, use the `html` selector.

Line height is as important as font size. Dense text feels hostile. Slightly generous spacing feels calm and readable:

```
body {
  line-height: 1.6;
}
```

Headings should clearly contrast with body text, but not shout:

```
h1, h2, h3 {
  line-height: 1.3;
}

h1 {
  font-size: 2rem;
}

h2 {
  font-size: 1.5rem;
}
```

Good practice: Avoid setting everything in bold or uppercase. Most beginner sites look bad because they try to be dramatic with fonts instead of readable. Readability wins.

Prompt: Please explain `px` vs `%`, `em`, and `rem` with practical examples and when to use each. How do `rem` and `em` behave differently in nested elements? Please include an example to show how `em` compounds but `rem` does not.

Layout fundamentals

HTML stacks elements vertically by default. CSS layout is about controlling width, spacing, and alignment so the page has a clear structure.

Start by constraining the content width of your main content block:

```
main {
  max-width: 800px;
  margin: 0 auto;
  padding: 20px;
}
```

This single rule does several things:

- Prevents text lines from becoming too wide
- Centers the content horizontally
- Adds breathing room around the content

This pattern appears in almost every professional website.

Spacing is more important than borders and backgrounds. If you divide your main content into multiple sections, then add extra margin at the bottom of each section:

```
section {
  margin-bottom: 40px;
}
```

White space is not wasted space. It is how the eye understands structure. White space helps readers distinguish sections, hierarchy, and grouping. When you need columns, resist the urge to force things with margins. Use layout tools designed for the job.

For example, define a class style:

```
.layout {
  display: flex;
  gap: 20px;
}
```

Then apply the class style to elements like <div> elements:

```
<div class="layout">
  <aside>Sidebar content</aside>
  <main>Main content</main>
</div>
```

You will learn Flexbox properly later, but even now you can see how it produces clean, predictable layouts without hacks.

The gap property controls the space between items in a layout container, most commonly Flexbox and Grid. It exists to solve a very old and annoying problem in CSS: spacing elements evenly without hacks.

When a container uses Flexbox, gap defines the amount of space between flex items, not around the outside of the container. For example, with the following CSS:

```
.container {
  display: flex;
  gap: 20px;
}
```

In the following HTML, each item will be separated by exactly 20 pixels. You do not need margins on the children. You do not need special rules for the last item:

```
<div class="container">
  <div>One</div>
  <div>Two</div>
  <div>Three</div>
</div>
```

With Flexbox, you can set different values for row and column gaps:

```
gap: 10px 20px;
```

This sets row gap first, column gap second. With Grid, you can explicitly set `row-gap` and `column-gap`.

Prompt: Please explain how `display: flex` works and what `flex-direction`, `justify-content`, and `align-items` do, including the difference between `gap` and `margin`.

You now have enough CSS to control basic presentation and layout. Now let's look at the topic every web page must deal with: adapting to different devices, from large desktops to small screens on phones and tablets.

Responsive design

So far, everything you have styled assumes a comfortable desktop screen. These days, that assumption is wrong more often than it is right. Websites are viewed on phones, tablets, laptops, ultra-wide monitors, TVs, and everything in between. Responsive design is how you make one site adapt without breaking or forcing users to zoom and scroll sideways. Responsive design is mostly standard CSS applied with flexible sizing and layout decisions.

What responsive design actually means

Responsive design does not mean *designing for mobile* and then stretching things for desktop. It means creating layouts that respond to available space.

A responsive page:

- Adjusts layout based on screen width
- Keeps text readable at all sizes
- Avoids horizontal scrolling
- Does not rely on fixed pixel widths everywhere

If your layout only works at one screen size, it is fragile.

The viewport and why it matters

Every responsive web page starts with this line in the `<head>` section:

```
<meta name="viewport" content="width=device-width, initial-scale=1.0">
```

Without it, mobile browsers pretend they are much wider than they are and then scale the page down. The result looks tiny and broken.

With it, CSS pixels map more closely to the actual screen size. You only need to add this once, but forgetting it breaks everything that follows.

Try it out: simulate mobile devices in your browser

You do not need a physical phone to test responsive layouts. In Chrome, open **Developer Tools** (*F12*), then click the device toolbar icon or press *Ctrl* + *Shift* + *M*.

Select a device like **iPhone** or **Pixel**, then resize the viewport. Watch how your layout changes as your media queries apply.

This is the fastest way to debug responsive CSS.

Flexible layouts instead of fixed widths

The fastest way to ruin responsiveness is hard-coding widths everywhere.

For example, it is bad practice to set a fixed width:

```
main {
  width: 1200px;
}
```

It is much better to set a maximum width and let the width scale with the available width, with automatic margins and a sensible fixed padding for spacing inside content elements:

```
main {
  max-width: 1200px;
  margin: 0 auto;
  padding: 20px;
}
```

The preceding layout:

- Shrinks on small screens
- Stops growing on very large ones
- Stays centered and readable

Percentages and flexible units adapt naturally:

```
.container {
  width: 90%;
}
```

This allows content to breathe without pinning it to a specific device size.

Prompt: What are common mistakes that break responsive layouts?

Responsive typography

Text should scale with the screen, but not dramatically.

Instead of tying everything to pixels, use relative units where appropriate.

You can set a font size for the root element of the page (`<html>`) as a starting point:

```
html {
    font-size: 100%;
}
```

And then set the sizes of other page elements using relative sizes:

```
h1 {
  font-size: 2rem;
}
```

`rem` stands for *root em*. It is relative to the font size of the root element, which defaults to `16px` in most browsers. So `2rem` would be `32px` at the default size. If you change the root font size, all `rem` values scale proportionally.

There's also `em`, which is relative to the font size of the parent element, not the root. `rem` is generally preferred because it's more predictable since it always refers to the same base, regardless of nesting. This improves accessibility and keeps proportions consistent.

Line length matters more than font size. Long lines are hard to read, especially on wide screens. That is why constraining content width is part of responsive design.

Fluid font sizing with clamp()

So far, font sizes have been fixed relative to a base value. In responsive design, you can also make text scale smoothly between sizes instead of jumping at breakpoints.

CSS provides the `clamp()` function for this:

```
h1 {
  font-size: clamp(1.5rem, 2.5vw, 2.5rem);
}
```

This means:

- The font will never be smaller than `1.5rem`
- It will scale based on the viewport width (`2.5vw`)
- It will never grow larger than `2.5rem`

As the screen gets wider, the text grows gradually. On smaller screens, it shrinks, but stays readable. This approach avoids sudden jumps in size at media query breakpoints and can produce smoother, more natural typography.

Think of `clamp()` as setting boundaries: flexible within limits. You do not need to use `clamp()` as a beginner yet, but you will see it in CSS because it combines flexibility with control.

Media queries

Media queries let you apply CSS only when certain conditions are true. Most commonly, this means screen width:

```
@media (max-width: 768px) {
  body {
    background-color: #ffffff;
  }
}
```

This rule only applies when the viewport is 768 pixels wide or less, roughly tablet and phone territory.

A practical example building on your earlier layout:

```
.layout {
  display: flex;
  gap: 20px;
}

@media (max-width: 768px) {
  .layout {
```

```
        flex-direction: column;
    }
}
```

On larger screens, content sits side by side. On smaller screens, it stacks vertically. Same HTML. Same CSS file. Different behavior based on space.

Prompt: Please explain media queries with multiple breakpoints and real examples.

Mobile-first thinking

A common beginner mistake is designing for desktop first and then trying to *fix* mobile with dozens of overrides.

A better approach is mobile-first design:

- Write simple styles that work on small screens
- Add enhancements for larger screens

That often looks like this:

```
.layout {
    display: flex;
    flex-direction: column;
    gap: 20px;
}

@media (min-width: 768px) {
    .layout {
        flex-direction: row;
    }
}
```

The default works everywhere. Larger screens get more complex layouts. This approach produces cleaner CSS and fewer surprises.

Prompt: What is mobile-first design and why is it better than desktop-first?

Images and responsiveness

Images are a frequent source of layout breakage.

At minimum, every image should be constrained:

```
img {
  max-width: 100%;
  height: auto;
}
```

This prevents images from overflowing their containers and blowing up layouts on small screens.

In the next section, you will deliberately break a responsive layout and then fix it using AI-assisted debugging. That exercise matters more than memorizing syntax, because responsive bugs are inevitable, and knowing how to understand them is the real skill.

AI challenge – CSS debugging

This section uses broken CSS on purpose. You are going to work with CSS that is broken, confusing, and slightly wrong. That is not an accident. Writing CSS is easy. Understanding why CSS is not doing what you expect is the real skill.

The goal here is not to memorize fixes, but to learn a repeatable debugging process and to use AI as a source of questions and explanations, not a replacement for checking the browser yourself.

This is part of a much larger shift in software development. Writing code matters, but it matters less than it used to. What matters more is understanding how systems behave, why a layout breaks, what the browser is doing, and what outcome you actually want. In other words, the value of a developer is shifting from typing CSS rules to thinking clearly about structure, behavior, and intent.

When debugging layout issues, keep **Developer Tools** open in device mode so you can see exactly when and why your layout breaks.

The broken page

Start with this HTML. It should look familiar and simple:

You can download this HTML file from the following link: `https://github.com/markjprice/web-dev-ai/blob/main/Code/Chapter03/CssDebugging/index.html`

```
<!DOCTYPE html>
<html lang="en">
<head>
  <meta charset="UTF-8">
  <meta name="viewport" content="width=device-width, initial-scale=1.0">
  <title>CSS Debugging Challenge</title>
  <link rel="stylesheet" href="styles.css">
</head>
<body>
  <div class="layout">
    <aside class="sidebar">
      <h2>Menu</h2>
      <ul>
        <li><a href="#">Home</a></li>
        <li><a href="#">Articles</a></li>
        <li><a href="#">Contact</a></li>
      </ul>
    </aside>
    <main class="content">
      <h1>Welcome</h1>
      <p>This layout should be responsive, readable, and well spaced.</p>
      <p>On smaller screens, the sidebar should stack above the content.</
p>
    </main>
  </div>
</body>
</html>
```

CSS:

You can download this CSS file from the following link: https://github.com/markjprice/web-dev-ai/blob/main/Code/Chapter03/CssDebugging/styles.css

```
body {
  font-family: Arial, Helvetica, sans-serif;
  margin: 0;
}

.layout {
  display: flex;
}

.sidebar {
  width: 300px;
  background-color: #f0f0f0;
}

.content {
  width: 800px;
}

@media (max-width: 768px) {
  .layout {
    flex-direction: row;
  }
}
```

Open the page on a large screen and then slowly shrink the browser window.

Several things are wrong.

Do not fix anything yet.

Step 1: Describe the problem in plain English

Before touching the code, write down what you observe.

For example:

- The layout overflows on smaller screens
- The content area is wider than the screen
- The sidebar does not stack on mobile
- Horizontal scrolling appears

If you cannot describe the problem clearly, you cannot fix it. This is where beginners usually panic and start changing random values.

Do not do that.

Step 2: Ask AI the right way

Paste both the HTML and CSS into your AI tool and ask a precise question.

Bad prompt:

```
My CSS is broken, please fix it.
```

Good prompt:

```
Here is a flexbox layout with a sidebar and main content. On screens
smaller than 768px, I expect the layout to stack vertically, but it does
not. Please explain what is wrong and why.
```

AI is far more useful when you ask for explanations, not just solutions.

Step 3: Read the explanation, not just the fix

A good AI response should point out at least these issues:

1. Fixed widths (`width: 800px`) break responsiveness
2. The media query uses `flex-direction: row`, which is already the default
3. There is no spacing or width constraint on the overall layout

If the AI jumps straight to dumping corrected CSS without explanation, ask for clarification. You should be learning not copying answers.

Step 4: Apply fixes incrementally

Now fix the CSS one problem at a time.

First, remove rigid widths:

```
.sidebar {
  max-width: 300px;
  width: 100%;
}
```

Next, correct the media query to use column layout instead of row layout when the width is less than 768 pixels:

```
@media (max-width: 768px) {
  .layout {
    flex-direction: column;
  }
}
```

Then improve spacing and containment:

```
.layout {
  display: flex;
  gap: 20px;
  max-width: 1200px;
  margin: 0 auto;
  padding: 20px;
}
```

Reload the page after each change. Observe what improved and why.

Step 5: Ask "what else could go wrong?"

Now challenge the AI again.

Try prompts like:

- `What accessibility issues might this layout still have?`
- `What happens if the menu text becomes much longer?`
- `How would this behave on a very wide screen?`

AI can be good at pointing out edge cases you have not yet learned to anticipate.

Debugging CSS with browser developer tools

When CSS does not behave the way you expect, the fastest way to understand why is to use your browser's developer tools. Every browser includes built-in tools that let you inspect elements, view applied styles, and experiment with changes in real time.

You can open developer tools by right-clicking on an element and selecting **Inspect**, or by pressing *F12* or *Ctrl* + *Shift* + *I* in most browsers.

Inspecting elements and styles

The most useful panel for CSS is the **Elements** (or **Inspector**) panel. When you select an element, you see the HTML structure on one side, and you see all CSS rules applied to that element on the other.

Each rule shows:

- Which selector applied it
- Which file it came from
- Whether it is overridden (crossed out)

If a rule is crossed out, it means another rule with higher specificity or later order is overriding it.

DevTools allows you to edit CSS directly in the browser:

- Change values (for example, padding: 20px → 40px)
- Toggle properties on and off
- Add new rules

These changes are temporary, but they let you experiment instantly without switching back to your code editor.

The box model diagram

One of the most useful debugging tools is the box model diagram, usually shown in the **Styles** or **Layout** panel. It visually represents:

- Content (center)
- Padding (inner space)
- Border (outline)
- Margin (outer space)

You can see the exact values for each side (top, right, bottom, left), often color-coded.

This is extremely helpful for diagnosing layout issues such as unexpected spacing, elements that are larger than expected, and misaligned layouts. You can even hover over parts of the diagram to highlight them on the page, making it clear where space is coming from.

DevTools turns CSS from guesswork into investigation. Instead of changing random values and hoping for the best, you can see exactly what the browser is doing and adjust your styles with confidence. This is a good example of the shift in web development: the skill is not typing CSS faster, but understanding how the browser is interpreting what you wrote.

What this exercise teaches you

You just practiced several professional habits:

- Separating observation from action
- Understanding layout intent before changing code
- Using AI as a reviewer and explainer, not an oracle
- Fixing CSS by investigation, not trial and error

If you rely only on generated CSS without understanding it, your progress will be slower. Developers who use AI to explain broken CSS level up fast. These habits of investigating behavior are more valuable than raw typing speed.

Your takeaway

When CSS breaks, the browser is not being random. It is following the rules you either misunderstood or forgot. Your job is to slow down, think about the cascade and layout, and use tools, including AI, to illuminate what is actually happening.

That mindset will matter far more than any specific property you memorized in this chapter.

We've now covered the basics of styling web pages with CSS, especially colors, fonts, and layouts, learned about responsive design, and had some practice debugging common issues. Let's end this chapter with one of the most fun parts of CSS, and one that many beginners do not even know is possible: transforms and animation.

Transforms and animation

Transforms and **animation** moves CSS beyond layout into motion design. Used carefully, they add clarity and feedback. Used carelessly, they make pages feel jittery and exhausting. The goal here is control, not spectacle.

This section introduces the core ideas without turning your site into a carnival.

CSS transforms

Transforms let you visually change an element without affecting the layout around it. This point matters more than it sounds.

A transformed element:

- Moves, rotates, or scales visually
- Still occupies its original space in the document flow

That is why transforms are preferred over margins or positioning for visual effects.

The most common transform functions are shown in *Table 3.1*:

Transform function	Description
`translate()`	Move an element
`scale()`	Resize an element
`rotate()`	Rotate an element
`skew()`	Slant an element

Table 3.1: Transform functions and what they do

Let's see a code example:

```
.card {
  transform: translateX(20px);
}
```

This shifts any element styled with the `.card` class 20 pixels to the right, but other elements behave as if nothing moved.

You can combine transforms:

```
.card {
  transform: translateY(-4px) scale(1.02);
}
```

Order matters. The functions are applied left to right.

Transforms are especially cool when paired with interaction, such as hovering over an element like a button:

```
.button {
  transition: transform 0.2s ease;
}

.button:hover {
  transform: translateY(-2px);
}
```

This creates a subtle "lift" effect on hover with no layout reflow and no side effects.

Good practice: If an interaction causes the page to jump or reflow, it is probably implemented with the wrong tool.

Prompt: Why are transforms better than using `margin` or `position` for animations?

The transition property

Transitions control how CSS changes happen over time. Without them, state changes are instant:

```
.card {
  transition: background-color 0.3s ease;
}
```

Now when the background color changes, it animates smoothly.

You can transition multiple properties:

```
transition: transform 0.2s ease, box-shadow 0.2s ease;
```

Good practice: Not all properties are good candidates for transitions. It works best for: transform, opacity, box-shadow, background-color. Avoid animating layout properties like width, height, top, or left unless you know why you are doing it.

Prompt: Which CSS properties are safe to animate for performance and why?

Keyframe animations

Transitions respond to state changes. Animations run on their own timeline:

```
@keyframes fade-in {
  from {
    opacity: 0;
  }
  to {
    opacity: 1;
  }
}
```

Apply it like this:

```
.modal {
  animation: fade-in 0.3s ease;
}
```

This runs once when the element appears.

Animations can loop, reverse, pause, and change speed curves. For example:

```
.spinner {
  animation: spin 1s linear infinite;
}

@keyframes spin {
  to {
    transform: rotate(360deg);
  }
}
```

That is a full loading spinner in four lines of CSS.

Timing functions and realism

Timing functions shape how motion feels.

Common values include linear for constant speed, ease for slow start and end, ease-in for just a slow start, and ease-out for just a slow end.

Most UI interactions should use ease or ease-out. Linear motion feels mechanical. If motion feels wrong, it is usually the timing, not the distance.

Reduced motion and accessibility

Some users prefer less motion. CSS allows you to respect that:

```
@media (prefers-reduced-motion: reduce) {
  * {
    animation: none;
    transition: none;
  }
}
```

Guidelines for using motion well:

- Use motion to explain change. If something appears, disappears, or moves, animation can make it feel intentional.
- Keep durations short. Most UI animations should be between 150ms and 300ms.
- Animate fewer things. One moving element draws attention. Five is noise.
- Never animate without purpose. If removing the animation does not make the interface worse, it probably does not belong.

Animation should help the user understand what just happened. If it exists only because it looks cool, it will age badly.

Practice, references, and resources

In this section, you will be tested on what you've learned in this chapter and be provided with useful links to reference materials and resources.

Check your understanding

Answer the following questions about the topics we covered in this chapter:

1. What are the three ways to apply CSS, and which is preferred?
2. What are the two parts of a CSS rule?
3. What is the difference between a class selector and an ID selector?
4. What happens when two CSS rules have the same specificity?
5. What are the four parts of the CSS box model?
6. Why might increasing padding change the total size of an element?
7. Why is max-width preferred over width for responsive layouts?
8. What is the difference between px and rem?
9. What is a media query?
10. What is the difference between a transition and an animation?

Answers are found in the GitHub repository for this book at the following link:

`https://github.com/markjprice/web-dev-ai/blob/main/docs/Appendix-A.pdf`

Links

Use MDN for learning, examples, and an everyday reference. Use W3C specs for clarifying edge cases, settling disagreements, and understanding why CSS behaves the way it does.

MDN CSS reference

This is authoritative for practical properties, values, and syntax:

`https://developer.mozilla.org/en-US/docs/Web/CSS/Reference`

This is the page you return to again and again. Every CSS property links to the formal syntax, supported values, with examples and browser compatibility, and a direct link to the relevant W3C spec section.

If you only bookmark one CSS page, make it this one.

Core MDN CSS guides

Good for beginner-friendly explanations of CSS basics:

`https://developer.mozilla.org/en-US/docs/Learn/CSS`

Use it for understanding the box model, cascade and specificity, layout fundamentals, and responsive design.

This material follows current CSS standards rather than old browser quirks.

W3C specifications

This is the formal specification for CSS. MDN is usually better for learning, while the specification is better for precise reference. You generally do not learn CSS from specs, but they are invaluable for clarity and edge cases. For the W3C CSS Snapshot on the current state of CSS: `https://www.w3.org/TR/CSS/`

Summary

In this chapter, we learned the following:

- CSS separates presentation from structure and applies styles using rules made of selectors and declarations
- External stylesheets are the preferred way to manage and reuse styles across pages
- The cascade determines which styles apply, based on specificity and order
- Classes are reusable and preferred over IDs for styling
- Every element follows the box model: content, padding, border, and margin
- Shorthand properties follow a consistent top-right-bottom-left pattern
- Layout depends more on spacing and width constraints than decorative styles
- Relative units such as `%` and `rem` respect user settings and improve accessibility
- Responsive design uses flexible layouts, media queries, and mobile-first thinking
- Flexbox provides a modern way to build layouts without hacks
- Debugging CSS requires understanding layout rules, not trial and error
- Accessibility should be considered from the start, including contrast, scaling, and interaction states
- Transforms and transitions allow smooth visual effects without breaking layout
- Animation should be used sparingly and with purpose

In the next chapter, you will learn about SVG, a language used to provide scalable vector graphics for drawings on a web page.

Get this book's PDF version and more

Scan the QR code (or go to packtpub.com/unlock). Search for this book by name, confirm the edition, and then follow the steps on the page.

UNLOCK NOW

Note: Keep your invoice handy. Purchases made directly from Packt don't require an invoice.

[illegible]

Get this book's PDF version and more

[illegible]

[illegible]

4

SVG – Drawing Scalable Graphics

SVG (**Scalable Vector Graphics**) lets you create graphics on a web page using code, rather than drawing them as raster images made up of lots of pixels. SVG is vector-based, meaning it uses mathematical instructions that can scale up and down without losing clarity, so it stays sharp at any size. This makes SVG a good fit for icons, logos, simple illustrations, charts, and UI details.

SVG excels at anything made of shapes, lines, and simple colors. For photographs or images with millions of colors, raster formats like JPEG, PNG, or WebP are better choices. A good rule of thumb: if you could describe the image as a set of shapes, SVG is probably right. If it looks like a photograph, use a raster format.

Even better, SVG can live right inside your HTML, so you can style it with CSS, animate it, and react to clicks, hovers, and other events like any other element on the page.

By the end of this chapter, you will understand SVG fundamentals, draw some simple shapes, and build interactive and reusable SVG graphics.

In this chapter, we will cover the following topics:

- SVG fundamentals for drawing shapes
- Scaling, grouping, and styling graphics
- Custom shapes using paths
- SVG as a reusable design system
- Making SVG accessible

Suggested chatbot prompts with example responses for this chapter can be found at the following link: https://github.com/markjprice/web-dev-ai/blob/main/prompts/ch04-svg/readme.md

SVG fundamentals for drawing shapes

SVG is an HTML-friendly drawing format. You can use it in five common ways:

- **Inline SVG**: Write the SVG markup directly in your HTML. This lets CSS and JavaScript reach the SVG elements directly, which is useful for interactivity and theming:

```
<svg width="120" height="120" viewBox="0 0 100 100">
  <circle cx="50" cy="50" r="40"></circle>
</svg>
```

- **External SVG**: Link to an external file like `logo.svg`:

```
<a href="logo.svg">Go to SVG file</a>
```

- **Image element**: No CSS or JavaScript interaction with SVG internals. Simplest and safest for static graphics:

```
<img src="logo.svg" alt="Simple teal square logo"
     width="120" height="120">
```

- **Object element**: SVG is interactive but lives in its own document context:

```
<object data="logo.svg" type="image/svg+xml"
        width="120" height="120">
  Your browser does not support SVG.
</object>
```

- **CSS background**: Purely decorative with no interaction or accessibility:

```
<!DOCTYPE html>
<html lang="en">
<head>
  <meta charset="UTF-8">
  <title>CSS Background SVG</title>
  <style>
    .box {
```

```
      width: 120px;
      height: 120px;
      background-image: url("logo.svg");
      background-size: cover;
      background-repeat: no-repeat;
      border: 1px solid #ccc;
    }
  </style>
</head>
<body>

<h1>CSS Background SVG Example</h1>

<div class="box"></div>

</body>
</html>
```

In this chapter, we will start with inline SVG because it gives you the clearest view of how the SVG building blocks work.

Prompt: Please explain the difference between inline SVG and `<img>` SVG with pros, cons, and real use cases.

Let's start with the smallest useful inline SVG, as shown highlighted in the following code. Create a `Chapter04` folder, and in the folder, create an HTML page named `simple-svg.html` with the following content:

You can download this file at the following link: `https://github.com/markjprice/web-dev-ai/blob/main/Code/Chapter04/simple-svg.html`

```
<!doctype html>
<html lang="en">
  <head>
    <meta charset="utf-8" />
```

```
    <meta name="viewport"
          content="width=device-width, initial-scale=1" />
    <title>My First SVG</title>
    <style>
      /* Just to make the SVG area obvious on the page */
      .frame {
        width: 320px;
        padding: 12px;
        border: 1px solid #ccc;
      }
      svg {
        display: block;
        border: 1px dashed #999;
      }
    </style>
  </head>
  <body>
    <h1>SVG Playground</h1>
    <div class="frame">
      <svg width="300" height="120"
           xmlns="http://www.w3.org/2000/svg">
        <!-- Background rectangle -->
        <rect x="10" y="10" width="280" height="100" fill="#f2f2f2" />
      </svg>
    </div>
  </body>
</html>
```

The <svg> element is a container with its own coordinate system.

What you're seeing here is a rectangle (<rect>) drawn into a 300 by 120 *canvas,* as shown in *Figure 4.1.* The rectangle starts at (10, 10) and is 280 pixels wide and 100 pixels tall. SVG coordinates start at the top-left corner, with x increasing to the right and y increasing downwards, which will feel familiar if you've done any layout work in CSS.

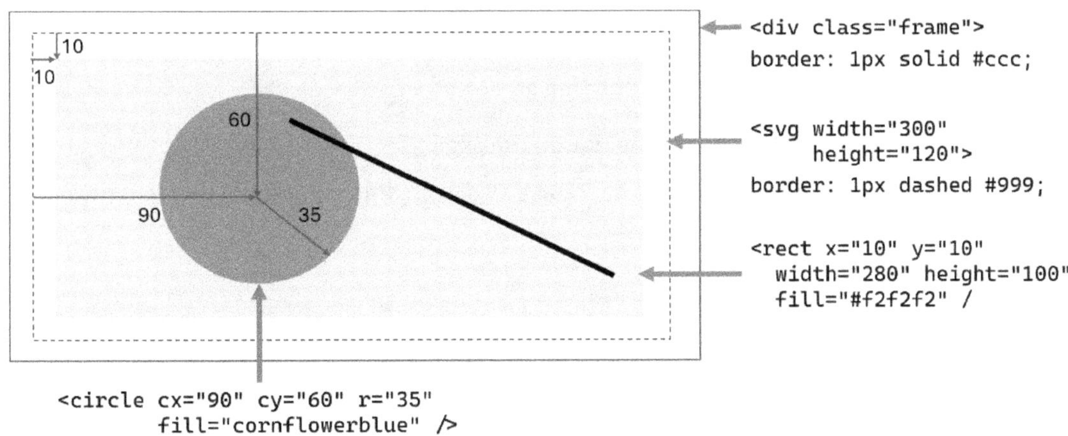

Figure 4.1: Using SVG to draw simple shapes

Prompt: Please explain how the SVG coordinate system works compared to CSS layout, with diagrams and examples.

In SVG, later elements are drawn on top of earlier ones. Add a couple more shapes to understand layering, as shown in *Figure 4.1* and shown highlighted in the following code:

```
<svg width="300" height="120"
     xmlns="http://www.w3.org/2000/svg">
  <!-- Background rectangle -->
  <rect x="10" y="10" width="280" height="100" fill="#f2f2f2" />

  <!-- Circle on top of the background -->
  <circle cx="90" cy="60" r="35" fill="cornflowerblue" />

  <!-- A line drawn on top of both -->
  <line x1="100" y1="45" x2="280" y2="95"
        stroke="black" stroke-width="4" />
</svg>
```

A few key concepts you used:

1. The `<svg>` element defines the drawing area.
   - `width` and `height` set the size on the page.
   - `xmlns="http://www.w3.org/2000/svg"` is an XML namespace that tells the browser *this is SVG markup*.

In a standalone `.svg` file, this attribute is required. However, when SVG is written inline inside an HTML5 document (with `<!DOCTYPE html>`), the `xmlns` attribute is optional because the HTML5 parser handles namespaces automatically. You'll often see it omitted in real-world inline SVG.

2. Shapes are elements.
   - `<rect>` draws rectangles.
   - `<circle>` draws circles.
   - `<line>` draws straight lines.
3. Positioning uses simple coordinates from the top-left corner (0, 0).
   - For a rectangle, you specify the top-left corner `x` and `y`.
   - For a circle, you specify the center point using `cx` and `cy`, plus the radius `r`.
   - For a line, you specify start (`x1`, `y1`) and end (`x2`, `y2`) points.
4. Color and strokes feel like CSS, but they're SVG attributes.
   - `fill` is the interior color of a shape.
   - `stroke` is the outline color.
   - `stroke-width` is the thickness of that outline.

Presentation attributes

In SVG, the properties that control how shapes are painted are collectively called **presentation attributes**. Most of them map directly to CSS properties, and in modern SVG, you should think of them as CSS first, attributes second.

Stroke properties (the outline of shapes)

`stroke` controls how the outline of a path, line, circle, and so on is drawn, for example, what color or paint is used for the outline. Possible values:

- `none`
- Any CSS color value: `black`, `red`, `#ff0000`, `rgb(255,0,0)`, `hsl(...)`
- `currentColor` (inherits from `color`)
- `url(#id)` a reference to a gradient or pattern defined in `<defs>`

For example:

```
stroke: #333;
```

`stroke-width` controls the thickness of the stroke. Stroke is centered on the path by default. Possible values:

- A number with or without units: `1`, `2.5`, `4px`
- Percentages are allowed but uncommon

For example:

```
stroke-width: 4;
```

`stroke-linecap` controls how the ends of open paths are drawn. Possible values:

- `butt` (flat end, default)
- `round`
- `square`

For example:

```
stroke-linecap: round;
```

`stroke-linejoin` controls how corners between segments are drawn. Possible values:

- `miter` (sharp corner, default)
- `round`
- `bevel`

For example:

```
stroke-linejoin: round;
```

`stroke-miterlimit` limits how sharp a miter join can be before it turns into a bevel. It applies only when `stroke-linejoin` is set to `miter`. Possible values:

- Any number greater than or equal to `1`

For example:

```
stroke-miterlimit: 4;
```

`stroke-dasharray` creates dashed lines. Possible values:

- `none`
- A list of numbers: `5, 5 10, 10 5 2 5`

Numbers alternate between dash length and gap length. For example:

```
stroke-dasharray: 8 4;
```

`stroke-opacity` controls the opacity of the stroke only. Possible values:

- Number from `0` to `1`

For example:

```
stroke-opacity: 0.6;
```

Fill properties (the interior of shapes)

These control how closed shapes are filled.

`fill` controls what paint is used inside the shape. Possible values:

- `none`
- Any CSS color value
- `currentColor`
- `url(#id)` (gradient or pattern)

Default is `black` if not specified.

For example:

```
fill: cornflowerblue;
```

`fill-opacity` sets the opacity of the fill only. Possible values:

- Number from `0` to `1`

For example:

```
fill-opacity: 0.5;
```

`fill-rule` controls how SVG decides what *inside* means for complex or self-intersecting paths. Possible values:

- `nonzero` (default)
- `evenodd`

You will encounter this mostly with icons. Example:

```
fill-rule: evenodd;
```

Shared painting and visibility properties

These affect both `fill` and `stroke`, or how the painting behaves overall.

`opacity` controls overall opacity of the element, affecting both `fill` and `stroke`. Possible values:

- Number from `0` to `1`

For example:

```
opacity: 0.8;
```

`paint-order` controls whether `fill` or `stroke` is drawn first. Possible values:

- `normal` (`fill` first, then `stroke`)
- Any combination of `fill`, `stroke`, `markers`

For example:

```
paint-order: stroke fill;
```

This is useful when you want the stroke to sit behind the fill.

Inheritance and special values

These are not SVG-only, but they matter a lot in SVG.

`currentColor` uses the element's color property as the paint value. For example:

```
svg {
  color: #0066cc;
}
```

```
path {
  stroke: currentColor;
}
```

This makes SVG icons behave like text icons.

`inherit` explicitly inherits from the parent.

Example:

```
stroke: inherit;
```

Prompt: Please provide code examples of SVG line caps and line joins embedded in HTML so I can visually understand the differences by comparing the code with the results.

Hands-on mini-task

Make a *badge* icon: a circle with a smaller circle inside it, plus a checkmark line, as shown in *Figure 4.2*:

Figure 4.2: A checkmark drawn with SVG

In the web page, add a new <svg> element and tweak the numbers until it looks right to you:

```
<svg width="180" height="180" xmlns="http://www.w3.org/2000/svg">
  <!-- Outer circle -->
  <circle cx="90" cy="90" r="70" fill="#e6f4ea"
          stroke="#1e8e3e" stroke-width="6" />

  <!-- Inner circle -->
  <circle cx="90" cy="90" r="52" fill="white" />

  <!-- Checkmark (two lines) -->
```

```
  <line x1="60" y1="95" x2="82" y2="115"
        stroke="#1e8e3e" stroke-width="10" stroke-linecap="round" />
  <line x1="82" y1="115" x2="122" y2="70" stroke="#1e8e3e"
        stroke-width="10" stroke-linecap="round" />
</svg>
```

If it doesn't look centered or balanced, change one number at a time. This is one of the best ways to build intuition for SVG coordinates.

In the next section, we will introduce `viewBox` so SVG scales cleanly, grouping with `<g>`, and styling with CSS classes so your SVG doesn't turn into a wall of attributes.

Scaling, grouping, and styling graphics

So far, you've been drawing SVG using fixed pixel sizes. That works, but it misses one of SVG's biggest strengths: scalability. The key to scalable SVG is separating the drawing's internal coordinate system from the size it appears on the page. That's what `viewBox` does.

Scaling with viewBox

The `viewBox` attribute defines an internal grid that your shapes live in. It has four numbers: `min-x`, `min-y`, `width`, and `height`. Most of the time, the first two are `0 0`.

Here's the same SVG as before, rewritten to use a `viewBox` instead of relying purely on width and height:

```
<svg viewBox="0 0 300 120" width="100%" height="auto"
     xmlns="http://www.w3.org/2000/svg">
  <rect x="10" y="10" width="280" height="100" fill="#f2f2f2" />
  <circle cx="90" cy="60" r="35" fill="cornflowerblue" />
  <line x1="160" y1="25" x2="280" y2="95"
        stroke="black" stroke-width="4" />
</svg>
```

What changed conceptually:

- `viewBox="0 0 300 120"` says *pretend this SVG is drawn on a 300 by 120 grid.*
- The browser scales that grid up or down to fit whatever size the SVG is displayed at.
- Your coordinates stay the same, but the rendered size adapts to the layout.

SVG icons stay sharp on phones, laptops, and 4K screens without needing multiple image assets. If you remember only one SVG rule, remember this: most production SVG almost always uses `viewBox`.

The `preserveAspectRatio` attribute controls what happens when the viewBox's aspect ratio doesn't match the SVG's display size. The default value, `xMidYMid meet`, scales the graphic uniformly and centers it within the available space. If you want the SVG to stretch to fill its container (ignoring aspect ratio), use `preserveAspectRatio="none"`. For most icon and illustration use cases, the default behavior is what you want. This is why most SVGs resize without extra work.

Prompt: Show how `viewBox` and `width`/`height` interact using multiple examples with resizing.

Grouping elements with <g>

As soon as your SVG has more than a couple of shapes, you'll want a way to organize them. The <g> element groups shapes together so you can move them, style them, or hide them as a unit.

Here's the badge icon again, but with logical grouping:

```
<svg viewBox="0 0 180 180" width="180"
     xmlns="http://www.w3.org/2000/svg">
  <!-- Badge background -->
  <g class="badge-base">
    <circle cx="90" cy="90" r="70" />
    <circle cx="90" cy="90" r="52" />
  </g>

  <!-- Checkmark -->
  <g class="badge-check">
    <line x1="60" y1="95" x2="82" y2="115" />
    <line x1="82" y1="115" x2="122" y2="70" />
  </g>
</svg>
```

Notice what's missing: color and stroke details, because those will move into CSS. SVG becomes much easier to maintain once you stop hard-coding styles into every element.

Styling SVG with CSS

Inline SVG can be styled using regular CSS. You can place styles in a `<style>` block, a separate CSS file, or alongside your existing site styles.

Here's how to style the grouped badge using CSS classes:

```
<style>
  svg {
    max-width: 220px;
  }

  .badge-base circle:first-child {
    fill: #e6f4ea;
    stroke: #1e8e3e;
    stroke-width: 6;
  }

  .badge-base circle:last-child {
    fill: white;
  }

  .badge-check line {
    stroke: #1e8e3e;
    stroke-width: 10;
    stroke-linecap: round;
  }
</style>
```

This should feel familiar if you've already worked through the CSS chapter. The selectors work the same way. The only difference is that properties like `fill` and `stroke` apply to SVG shapes instead of text or boxes.

Moving style into CSS gives you three advantages:

- Your SVG becomes readable markup instead of a pile of attributes.
- You can change colors for dark mode, themes, or hover states.
- Designers and developers can change the drawing and its styling separately.

Try this small experiment. Add a hover effect to the badge:

```
svg:hover .badge-base circle:first-child {
  fill: #d2eadc;
}
```

You made your SVG interactive using nothing but CSS, as shown in *Figure 4.3*:

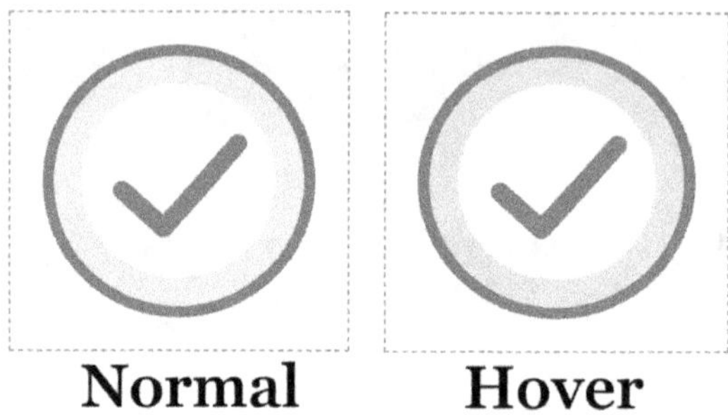

Figure 4.3: Interactive normal and hover states

Transforms on groups

One more reason <g> is useful is transforms. You can move, scale, or rotate an entire group with a single attribute, as shown highlighted in the following code:

```
<g class="badge-check" transform="rotate(-5 90 90)">
  <line x1="60" y1="95" x2="82" y2="115" />
  <line x1="82" y1="115" x2="122" y2="70" />
</g>
```

This rotates the checkmark slightly around the center of the SVG at (90, 90). Without grouping, you'd have to recalculate every coordinate manually, which is tedious and prone to error.

Now you're ready for the next step: paths (`<path>`), which is where SVG grows from combining basic shapes to illustration and iconography.

Custom shapes using paths

So far, SVG has felt friendly. Rectangles, circles, and lines get you a long way, but they can't describe arbitrary shapes. The moment you want icons, waves, blobs, arrows, or anything that looks *designed*, you end up using `<path>`. Paths give SVG its flexibility, but they are often the hardest part for beginners.

The <path> element

A `<path>` is a sequence of drawing commands stored in a single attribute called `d`. The `d` attribute is a set of instructions for an invisible pen: move here, draw a line there, draw a curve like this, close the shape (meaning draw a line back to the starting point).

Here's the smallest possible path that actually draws something, a horizontal line, as shown in *Figure 4.4* and the following code:

```
<svg viewBox="0 0 120 120" width="200"
     xmlns="http://www.w3.org/2000/svg">
  <path
    d="M 20 60 L 100 60"
    stroke="black"
    stroke-width="6"
    fill="none"
  />
</svg>
```

Figure 4.4: A horizontal line drawn using a path

Read that `d` value slowly:

- `M 20 60` means *move the pen to (20, 60)*
- `L 100 60` means *draw a line to (100, 60)*

Nothing is filled because we explicitly said `fill="none"`. Without that, SVG would try to fill the shape, which makes no sense for a single line.

Why paths look intimidating at first

Paths look intimidating because all the logic is compressed into one string. There are no named attributes like `x`, `y`, or `r`. But each command is simple on its own, and most real-world paths are built from a few command types.

The commands you'll use most often are:

- `M` move to
- `L` line to
- `C` cubic Bézier curve
- `Q` quadratic Bézier curve
- `Z` close path

Uppercase commands use absolute coordinates. Lowercase versions (`m`, `l`, `c`, `q`) use relative coordinates. For beginners, absolute coordinates are much easier to understand, so stick to uppercase while learning.

A closed shape with Z

Here's a simple house-like shape drawn with straight lines, as shown in *Figure 4.5* and the following code:

```
<svg viewBox="0 0 120 120" width="200" xmlns="http://www.w3.org/2000/svg">
  <path
    d="
      M 20 70
      L 60 30
      L 100 70
      L 100 100
      L 20 100
      Z
    "
    fill="#cfe8ff"
    stroke="#1f5fbf"
    stroke-width="4"
  />
</svg>
```

Figure 4.5: A house drawn with a path

The important new command is Z, which closes the path by drawing a line back to the starting point. Once a path is closed, fill suddenly makes sense, because the shape encloses an area.

Prompt: Give a step-by-step breakdown of how an SVG path is interpreted by the browser.

Drawing curves with paths

Straight lines are fine, but curves are where paths show their strengths. SVG uses Bézier curves, which are controlled by points that *pull* the curve into shape.

Prompt: Please explain control points in SVG curves with code examples.

Here's a smooth wave using a cubic Bézier curve (C), as shown in *Figure 4.6*:

```
<svg viewBox="0 0 300 120" width="300"
     xmlns="http://www.w3.org/2000/svg">
  <path
    d="
      M 10 60
      C 60 10, 120 110, 170 60
      C 220 10, 280 110, 330 60
    "
```

```
    fill="none"
    stroke="#6a5acd"
    stroke-width="6"
  />
</svg>
```

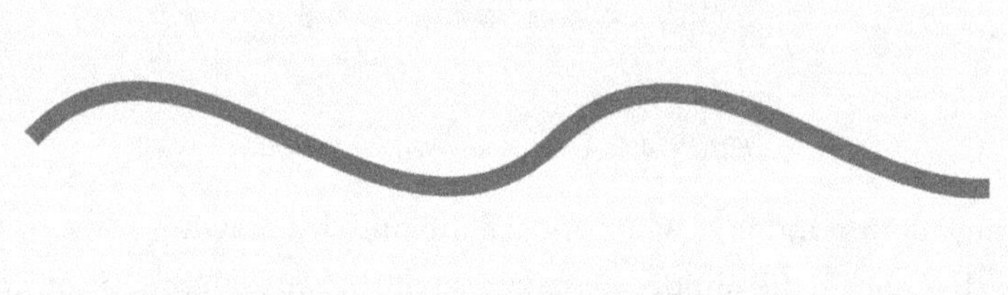

Figure 4.6: A curvy line drawn with a path

Each `C` command takes six numbers (three pairs of coordinates):

- First control point (X and Y coordinates)
- Second control point (X and Y coordinates)
- End point (X and Y coordinates)

The curve starts where the previous command ended. You don't need to understand the math to use this effectively. The useful way to think about it is that *control points pull the curve toward themselves*, as shown in *Figure 4.7*:

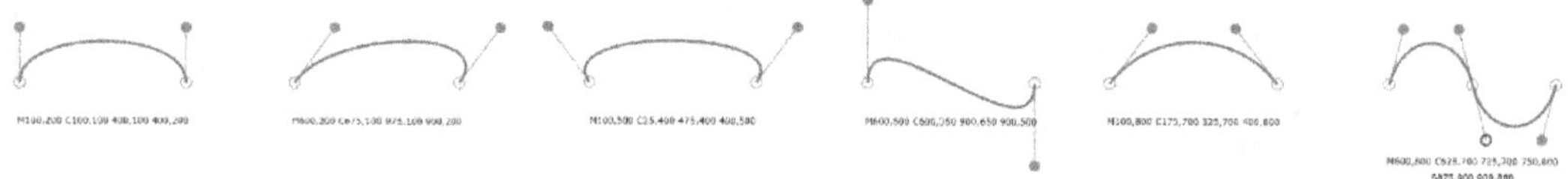

Figure 4.7: Bézier curve drawn using paths

Figure 4.7 is taken from the W3 website. I do not expect you to only look at the figure above because it is too small to be useful. View the source of the SVG and compare it to the rendered curves at the following link: `https://www.w3.org/TR/SVG/images/paths/cubic02.svg`

Prompt: Please explain cubic vs. quadratic Bézier curves in SVG with visual diagrams and interactive-style explanations.

A cool-looking blob using paths and fill

Let's make a soft blob shape, the kind often used as a background accent in web pages, as shown in *Figure 4.8*:

```
<svg viewBox="0 0 300 300" width="260"
     xmlns="http://www.w3.org/2000/svg">
  <path
    d="
      M 150 30
      C 220 20, 280 80, 260 150
      C 240 220, 180 270, 120 250
      C 60 230, 20 170, 40 110
      C 60 50, 100 40, 150 30
      Z
    "
    fill="#ffb703"
  />
</svg>
```

Figure 4.8: A blob drawn using a path

This shape is nothing more than curves stitched together and closed with Z. This is a common way to build background shapes, hero graphics, and understand how abstract illustrations are made on websites.

Icons are paths

Almost every SVG icon you've ever used is made of paths. When you copy an icon from a design tool or an icon library, you usually get one or more <path> elements.

Here's a simple heart icon drawn as a single path, as shown in the following code and *Figure 4.9*:

```
<svg viewBox="0 0 120 120" width="160"
     xmlns="http://www.w3.org/2000/svg">
  <path
    d="
      M 60 100
      C 20 70, 20 30, 50 30
      C 65 30, 60 45, 60 45
      C 60 45, 55 30, 70 30
      C 100 30, 100 70, 60 100
      Z
    "
    fill="#e63946"
  />
</svg>
```

Figure 4.9: A heart drawn using a path

This looks complex, but the key insight is this: you almost never write paths like this by hand.

SVG is a good example of the theme running through this book: the typing is not the hard part. You rarely need to memorize path commands or type long coordinate strings by hand. The useful skill is knowing what the shape represents, how it should scale, how it should respond to CSS or JavaScript, and what you can safely change when the design changes.

Designers draw them in tools like Illustrator, Figma, or Inkscape, and you paste the resulting SVG into your HTML.

AI can also help generate starting points, but developers still need to judge the result and, in many cases, may still work with designers. You can ask your chatbot to create the SVG for you. Your job as a web developer is to understand enough to style, scale, animate, and tweak them safely.

Styling and animating paths

Paths respond to the same CSS ideas you already know:

```
.icon path {
  fill: none;
  stroke: #333;
  stroke-width: 4;
}

.icon path:hover {
  stroke: #0077cc;
}
```

You can also do things that feel almost magical, like animating a path so it looks like it's being drawn. This works by animating `stroke-dasharray` and `stroke-dashoffset`, and it's one of SVG's party tricks.

Prompt: Please give a code example of animating a path so it looks like it's being drawn using `stroke-dasharray` and `stroke-dashoffset`.

Mini-tasks

Now let's practice with some quick tasks.

Take some SVG from an icon site and tweak it:

- `https://www.svgrepo.com/`
- `https://iconbuddy.com/`

Generate some new icons:

Prompt: Please create SVG source code suitable for icons in a toolbar for a web app with the following features: New File, Open File, Save File As, Close, Cut, Copy, Paste. Please provide the raw SVG source code directly in the chat instead of generating an image file.

Warning! These days, your AI will often interpret *generate an image* by using an internal image-generation tool, which produces high-resolution pixel-based files (like PNGs) rather than code. When you want the actual SVG source code that you can copy and paste into an HTML file, the best way to ensure the chatbot provides it is to specify that you want *SVG code* or *SVG markup* rather than *an image*.

Prompt: Please create a loading spinner using SVG and CSS animation.

Converting shapes into path commands

Friendly, readable elements like `<rect>` and `<circle>` are great for learning and for simple graphics. But in real-world SVG, especially icons and illustrations, almost everything ends up as `<path>`.

Why? Because `<path>` can describe any shape, while elements like `<rect>` and `<circle>` are limited. Converting basic shapes into paths helps you see how SVG represents drawings internally

Converting a rectangle into a path

Start with a simple rectangle:

```
<rect x="20" y="20" width="100" height="60" fill="skyblue" />
```

This draws a rectangle starting at `(20, 20)`.

Now let's convert it into a path step-by-step:

1. Move to the top-left corner
2. Draw lines around the edges

3. Close the shape:

```
<path
  d="
    M 20 20
    L 120 20
    L 120 80
    L 20 80
    Z
  "
  fill="skyblue"
/>
```

How those numbers were calculated:

- Top-left: `(20, 20)`
- Top-right: `(20 + 100, 20)` therefore `(120, 20)`
- Bottom-right: `(120, 80)`
- Bottom-left: `(20, 80)`

So a rectangle is four lines plus `Z`.

Rectangle with rounded corners

A `<rect>` can also have rounded corners using `rx` and `ry`:

```
<rect x="20" y="20" width="100" height="60" rx="10" fill="skyblue" />
```

To replicate this with a path, you need curves. Typically, you'd use arc commands (`A`), but here's a simplified version to show the idea:

```
<path
  d="
    M 30 20
    L 110 20
    Q 120 20 120 30
    L 120 70
    Q 120 80 110 80
    L 30 80
    Q 20 80 20 70
```

```
      L 20 30
      Q 20 20 30 20
      Z
    "
    fill="skyblue"
/>
```

This uses quadratic curves (`Q`) to round the corners. It's more verbose, but much more flexible.

Converting a circle into a path

Here's a circle:

```
<circle cx="80" cy="60" r="40" fill="tomato" />
```

To convert a circle to a path, you use arc commands (`A`):

```
<path
    d="
      M 80 60
      m -40 0
      A 40 40 0 1 0 80 100
      A 40 40 0 1 0 80 20
    "
    fill="tomato"
/>
```

Breakdown:

1. `M 80 60` means move to center
2. `m -40 0` means move left to edge of circle
3. The first `A` means draw half the circle
4. The second `A` means complete the circle

This looks complicated, and that's exactly the point: paths can describe almost any shape, but not human-friendly to write from scratch.

Why convert shapes to paths?

You are not expected to manually convert shapes like this in day-to-day work. But understanding it gives you several practical advantages.

As you saw earlier, icons from design tools are almost always `<path>` elements. Knowing how basic shapes map to paths helps you read and tweak them without guessing.

Paths unlock features that shapes don't support. You can:

- Animate parts of a shape
- Morph one shape into another
- Combine shapes into a single outline
- Apply advanced effects more easily

For example, animating a rectangle border is trivial as a path, but awkward with `<rect>`.

When everything is a path, you can combine shapes into one element, apply a single stroke or animation, and simplify complex SVG structures. That gives the browser fewer elements to track and gives you fewer places to edit later.

Tools like Figma, Illustrator, and Inkscape export everything as paths. If you don't understand paths, you're effectively copy-pasting blind.

Prompt: Please show me how to optimize an SVG file exported from Figma or Illustrator for use on the web.

Mini-task

Take this rectangle:

```
<rect x="40" y="30" width="120" height="80" />
```

Convert it into a `<path>` manually.

Then:

- Change one coordinate slightly
- Watch how the shape distorts

This small exercise will build path intuition faster than reading ten explanations. Once you're comfortable with this idea, SVG becomes much less mysterious.

Practical advice for SVG

Here's some advice that you can apply to your SVG work:

- Prefer CSS over inline attributes for `fill` and `stroke`. It keeps SVG maintainable.
- Use `currentColor` for icons whenever possible. It's the cleanest integration with the rest of the page. When you change the color of other elements on the page, especially text, then your icons will adopt that color too.
- Learn `stroke-dasharray` and `stroke-dashoffset`. They let you create animations that look far more complex than they are.

You don't need to memorize all of this. Know what exists and then look it up when needed. Or ask your AI to do what you already know is possible. Once paths make sense, the rest of SVG becomes less mysterious.

Producing the markup is rarely the main difficulty. The harder job is deciding what the graphic should communicate, how it should scale, and how it fits with the rest of the page.

Prompt: Please explain how to make SVG icons theme-aware using `currentColor` and CSS variables.

In the next section, we will cover `<defs>`, `<use>`, gradients, and patterns, which is where SVG becomes a reusable design system rather than a static drawing.

SVG as a reusable design system

Up to now, every SVG you've written has been fairly literal: shapes appear once, styles are applied directly, and the drawing is mostly static. `<defs>` lets SVG work more like a small library of reusable parts. It lets you define things once and reuse them many times.

`<defs>` itself does not render anything. It's a container for *definitions*: shapes, gradients, patterns, filters, and symbols that can be referenced elsewhere.

Defining and reusing shapes with <defs> and <use>

The simplest use of `<defs>` is to define a shape once and reuse it multiple times with `<use>`, as shown in the following code and *Figure 4.10*:

```
<svg viewBox="0 0 300 120" width="300"
     xmlns="http://www.w3.org/2000/svg">
```

```
  <defs>
    <path
      id="star"
      d="
        M 50 0
        L 61 35
        L 98 35
        L 68 57
        L 79 91
        L 50 70
        L 21 91
        L 32 57
        L 2 35
        L 39 35
        Z
      "
    />
  </defs>

  <use href="#star" x="20" y="15" fill="#f4c430" />
  <use href="#star" x="120" y="15" fill="#ff8c00" />
  <use href="#star" x="220" y="15" fill="#e63946" />
</svg>
```

Figure 4.10: Three differently colored stars that reuse the same shape

In the preceding example:

- The `star` path is defined once inside `<defs>`.
- Each `<use>` creates a copy of that path.
- You can position (x, y), fill, scale, rotate, and style each instance independently.

This is useful for icons, repeated UI elements, charts, and decorative motifs.

Warning! Modern SVG uses `href`, not `xlink:href`. You'll still see older examples online and SVG files exported from design tools using `xlink`, but you shouldn't copy those anymore. It works but is deprecated in SVG 2.

Prompt: Please show me how to build a reusable SVG icon system using `<symbol>` and `<use>`.

Gradients: paint that isn't flat

Gradients are defined in `<defs>` and referenced using `url(#id)` as a `fill` or `stroke`.

Here's an example of a linear gradient filling a rectangle, as shown in *Figure 4.11*:

```
<svg viewBox="0 0 300 120" width="300"
     xmlns="http://www.w3.org/2000/svg">
  <defs>
    <linearGradient id="sunset" x1="0%" y1="0%" x2="100%" y2="0%">
      <stop offset="0%" stop-color="#ff6a00" />
      <stop offset="50%" stop-color="#ffb703" />
      <stop offset="100%" stop-color="#ffd166" />
    </linearGradient>
  </defs>

  <rect x="20" y="20" width="260" height="80" fill="url(#sunset)" />
</svg>
```

Figure 4.11: A linear gradient filling a rectangle

Key concepts in the preceding code:

- A gradient is a named paint.
- `stop` elements define color transitions.
- Gradients can be reused across multiple shapes.

Here's an example of a radial gradient:

```
<defs>
  <radialGradient id="spotlight" cx="50%" cy="50%" r="50%">
    <stop offset="0%" stop-color="white" />
    <stop offset="100%" stop-color="#90dbf4" />
  </radialGradient>
</defs>

<circle cx="150" cy="60" r="45" fill="url(#spotlight)" />
```

Radial gradients are good for highlights, bubbles, and soft UI accents.

Patterns: repeating designs as paint

Patterns let you fill shapes with repeating graphics instead of colors or gradients. SVG patterns are often cleaner than trying to fake the same effect with background images or repeated CSS rules:.

```
<svg viewBox="0 0 300 120" width="300"
     xmlns="http://www.w3.org/2000/svg">
  <defs>
    <pattern id="diagonal-stripes" width="10" height="10"
      patternUnits="userSpaceOnUse"
      patternTransform="rotate(45)"
    >
      <rect width="10" height="10" fill="#f1faee" />
      <line x1="0" y1="0" x2="0" y2="10"
            stroke="#457b9d" stroke-width="4" />
    </pattern>
  </defs>

  <rect x="20" y="20" width="260" height="80"
        fill="url(#diagonal-stripes)" />
</svg>
```

Note the following about the preceding code:

- A pattern defines a tile.
- SVG repeats that tile automatically.
- Patterns can contain any SVG content: shapes, paths, even text.

Patterns are excellent for charts, backgrounds, accessibility-friendly fills, and subtle UI textures.

Combining <use> with gradients and patterns

Once everything is defined in `<defs>`, you can reuse them with short references:

```
<use href="#star" x="40" y="20" fill="url(#sunset)" />
<use href="#star" x="140" y="20" fill="url(#diagonal-stripes)" />
```

Change a gradient, pattern, or base shape once, and every reference updates with it.

Here's what to remember:

- `<defs>` is your library of definitions.
- IDs are used for naming and referencing.
- `<use>` is instantiation for a shape.
- `url(#id)` is referencing for paint.

That may sound grand, but it's genuinely how SVG is built in real projects.

Reusable icons with <symbol>

When building reusable SVG graphics such as icons, `<symbol>` is often a better choice than using `<defs>` with individual shapes.

A `<symbol>` element defines a reusable graphic, similar to `<defs>`, but with one important difference: it can have its own `viewBox`. This means the symbol behaves like a self-contained SVG.

For example:

```
<svg style="display: none;">
  <symbol id="icon-star" viewBox="0 0 24 24">
    <path d="M12 2l3 7h7l-5.5 4.5L18 21l-6-4-6 4 1.5-7.5L2 9h7z"/>
  </symbol>
</svg>
```

You can then reuse it anywhere using <use>:

```
<svg width="24" height="24">
  <use href="#icon-star"></use>
</svg>
```

Why <symbol> is useful:

- It allows each icon to define its own coordinate system using viewBox
- It keeps icons consistent and scalable
- It avoids repeating SVG markup across your page

Many icon systems use <symbol> together with <use> so the same icon markup does not have to be repeated. Think of <defs> as a storage container, and <symbol> as a reusable component with its own layout rules.

Prompt: Please explain how SVG filters (blur, shadow, glow) work with examples.

Making SVG accessible

SVG is part of the DOM, which means it participates in accessibility in ways that plain images do not. That's a good thing, but it also means you need to be deliberate. An SVG without accessible text is effectively invisible to screen reader users, while a poorly labeled SVG can be noisy and confusing.

The goal is simple: if the SVG conveys meaning, provide a clear text alternative. If it is purely decorative, hide it from assistive technologies.

Providing a text alternative with <title>

The <title> element is the SVG equivalent of alt text on an <img>. It should be the first child inside <svg>, so assistive technologies can find it reliably, as shown highlighted in the following code:

```
<svg viewBox="0 0 120 120"
     role="img" aria-labelledby="icon-title"
     xmlns="http://www.w3.org/2000/svg">

  <title id="icon-title">Success checkmark</title>
```

```
  <circle cx="60" cy="60" r="50" fill="#e6f4ea" />
  <path d="M 35 60 L 55 80 L 85 40" stroke="#1e8e3e"
        stroke-width="6" fill="none" />
</svg>
```

Good practice: Keep `<title>` short and descriptive, similar to `alt` text. Describe the meaning, not the shape. "Success checkmark" is better than "green circle with a tick".

Adding longer descriptions with <desc>

If the SVG contains more complex information, such as a chart or diagram, use `<desc>` for a longer explanation, as shown highlighted in the following code:

```
<svg viewBox="0 0 200 120"
     role="img" aria-labelledby="chart-title chart-desc"
     xmlns="http://www.w3.org/2000/svg">
  <title id="chart-title">Monthly sales</title>
  <desc id="chart-desc">
    Bar chart showing steady growth from January to June, with the highest
sales in June.
  </desc>

  <!-- chart shapes here -->
</svg>
```

Think of `<desc>` as the equivalent of a figure caption or summary. It gives context that wouldn't fit in a short label.

Linking text with aria-labelledby

The `<title>` and `<desc>` elements only become useful when assistive technologies are explicitly told to use them. That's what `aria-labelledby` does:

```
aria-labelledby="chart-title chart-desc"
```

Keep these details in mind:

- The value is a space-separated list of IDs.
- Order matters. The text will be read in that order.
- You can include just `<title>`, or both `<title>` and `<desc>`.

Declaring the SVG as an image with role="img"

SVG elements are not always treated as images by default, especially inline SVG. Adding `role="img"` tells assistive technologies to treat the SVG as one image:

```
<svg role="img" ...>
```

The preceding attribute ensures:

- Screen readers treat the SVG as a single image
- The label from `aria-labelledby` is announced properly

Hiding decorative SVGs

If an SVG adds no meaning and is purely decorative, it should be hidden from assistive technologies to avoid noise:

```
<svg aria-hidden="true" ...>
  <!-- decorative shapes -->
</svg>
```

Use this for:

- Background flourishes
- Divider graphics
- Icons that duplicate nearby text, for example, a trash icon next to the word *Delete*

Do not combine `aria-hidden="true"` with accessible labels. If it's hidden, it should be completely ignored.

Inline SVG vs <img> SVG

There's an important distinction:

- `<img src="icon.svg" alt="...">` uses standard HTML accessibility.
- Inline `<svg>` requires ARIA, `<title>`, and `<desc>`.

If you don't need to style or manipulate the SVG, using `<img>` is often simpler and safer. Inline SVG is more flexible but comes with more responsibility.

Good practice: If the SVG communicates something, label it clearly. If it doesn't, hide it completely. Treat `<title>` like `alt`, and `<desc>` like a caption.

Practice, references, and resources

In this section, you will be tested on what you've learned in this chapter and be provided with useful links to reference materials and resources.

Check your understanding

Answer the following questions:

1. What is the main difference between SVG and raster images?
2. Where is the origin (0,0) in an SVG coordinate system?
3. How do you position a circle compared to a rectangle?
4. What is the difference between `fill` and `stroke`?
5. What problem does `viewBox` solve?
6. What happens if the aspect ratio of the `viewBox` does not match the display size?
7. What does the `M` command do in a path?
8. What is the purpose of the `Z` command?
9. How does `<use>` help reduce duplication?
10. When should you use `aria-hidden="true"`?

Links

MDN Web Docs is the best SVG resource for humans. It explains what things are for, how they're used in real browsers, and includes examples that actually work.

SVG tutorial overview

This is the best starting point:

`https://developer.mozilla.org/en-US/docs/Web/SVG/Tutorial`

It covers what SVG is, understanding the coordinate systems, basic shapes, paths, groups, transforms, and styling. It's written assuming you're a web developer, not a graphics researcher.

SVG element reference

This is the page you'll return to constantly.

`https://developer.mozilla.org/en-US/docs/Web/SVG/Element`

Every SVG element is listed alphabetically with a clear description, supported attributes, usage notes, and browser compatibility.

If you forget how `<path>`, `<g>`, `<defs>`, or `<use>` works, this is where you look.

SVG attribute reference

SVG has many attributes that don't exist anywhere else on the web platform.

`https://developer.mozilla.org/en-US/docs/Web/SVG/Attribute`

This page explains geometry attributes like `viewBox`, `d`, `cx`, `cy`, presentation attributes like `fill`, `stroke`, `opacity`, and how attributes interact with CSS.

SVG and CSS

This page is useful when you style inline SVG with CSS:

`https://developer.mozilla.org/en-US/docs/Web/SVG/SVG_and_CSS`

It explains which SVG properties are stylable with CSS, how selectors behave with inline SVG, and the differences between presentation attributes and CSS rules.

MDN's SVG content is maintained by browser vendors and working web developers, which is why it tends to reflect reality instead of theory.

W3C SVG specification

World Wide Web Consortium publishes the official SVG specifications. These documents define how SVG is supposed to work, independent of any browser. This is best for precision and edge cases.

SVG 2 specification: `https://www.w3.org/TR/SVG2/`

This is the modern SVG specification. It defines the SVG DOM, geometry, painting, and rendering rules, and interaction with CSS, HTML, and scripting.

If something behaves oddly and MDN doesn't explain why, this document usually does.

SVG paths specification

If you're learning `<path>` properly, this is the definitive reference for path commands (M, L, C, Q, A, etc.), how curves and arcs are mathematically defined, and fill rules and stroke behavior.

`https://www.w3.org/TR/SVG/paths.html`

Summary

In this chapter, we did the following:

- Understood how SVG uses a coordinate system to draw shapes
- Created basic shapes using `<rect>`, `<circle>`, and `<line>`
- Styled SVG using presentation attributes and CSS
- Learned how `viewBox` enables scalable, resolution-independent graphics
- Grouped and transformed elements using `<g>`
- Created complex shapes using `<path>` commands
- Used Bézier curves to create smooth, expressive graphics
- Animated SVG paths using stroke dash techniques
- Built reusable graphics using `<defs>` and `<use>`
- Applied gradients and patterns for advanced visual effects
- Made SVG accessible using `<title>`, `<desc>`, and ARIA attributes

In the next chapter, you will learn about JavaScript, a language used to add interactivity to a web page.

Learn more on Discord

To join the Discord community for this book – where you can share feedback, ask questions to the author, and learn about new releases – follow this QR code:

`https://discord.gg/rdEsrVbbC`

5

JavaScript – Making Web Pages Interactive

JavaScript is what makes a web page do something. HTML gives the page structure. CSS controls its appearance. JavaScript handles behavior: responding to clicks, reading form input, updating text, and changing what the user sees without reloading the page.

In this chapter, you will learn JavaScript the practical way by building small browser examples. You will start with the basics: variables, data types, functions, conditionals, loops, and console logging. Then you will use those ideas to work with events and the DOM, which is how JavaScript reads from and writes to the page.

You will also use AI throughout the chapter, mainly for explanations, debugging help, and checking your understanding. It can help explain errors, compare approaches, and clarify what the code is doing. It should not replace your understanding. Do not paste in JavaScript and hope for the best. Learn enough browser code to judge whether a suggested answer is right, wrong, or nearly right but missing something.

By the end of the chapter, you should be comfortable reading small JavaScript programs, running them in the browser, debugging them with Developer Tools, and making straightforward DOM updates in response to user actions.

In this chapter, we will cover the following topics:

- Introducing JavaScript
- Programming basics
- DOM manipulation

The step-by-step instructions and screenshots in this chapter use Chrome on Windows, but all web browsers provide similar features.

Suggested chatbot prompts with example responses for this chapter can be found at the following link: `https://github.com/markjprice/web-dev-ai/blob/main/prompts/ch05-js/readme.md`

Introducing JavaScript

JavaScript is the language that turns a web page from a static document into something that reacts and responds to the user. HTML gives the page its structure, CSS controls how it looks, but JavaScript is what lets the page do things.

When you click a button and something changes, when a form validates your input before submitting, when content updates without a full page reload, JavaScript is involved. Without it, most pages would still behave like boring static documents.

JavaScript is a full programming language

One important thing to be clear about early is that JavaScript is a real programming language, not just a few tricks bolted onto HTML. It has variables, functions, conditionals, loops, data structures, and its own rules and quirks.

You can write tiny scripts that only react to a single button click, or you can build entire applications that rival desktop software in complexity. The same language scales from examples to large applications, which is useful but can also make it frustrating for beginners.

Running JavaScript

JavaScript usually runs in the browser, inside the JavaScript engine built into Chrome, Edge, Firefox, Safari, and other browsers. This matters because your code runs on the user's machine, not on the server.

That is why JavaScript is fast to respond to user actions and why it can directly manipulate what the user sees on the screen. But it also means that you must remember that JavaScript runs inside a *sandbox* that limits what it can do to protect the user's computer.

Prompt: What is a sandbox in IT terms? Where does the term come from? Is it an Americanism?

In later chapters, when you work with Python and Django on the server, you will see how different that programming model feels. For now, the key idea is that JavaScript lives alongside your HTML and CSS and can read, change, and react to them in real time.

Is JavaScript difficult?

JavaScript has a reputation problem. People love to complain about it. Some of that criticism is deserved, especially if you look at older JavaScript or confusing edge cases. Some of it is fair. Some of it is just habitual grumbling.

Prompt: Show me three of the most common JavaScript memes as images on Reddit.

JavaScript written in a clear, current style is much easier to work with than its reputation suggests. The real danger is not the language itself but copying code you do not understand. This is where AI can help if you use it properly.

Throughout this chapter, you will be encouraged to work with AI as a thinking aid. You can ask it to explain error messages, rephrase concepts in different ways, or show alternative solutions to the same problem. What you should not do is blindly paste in answers and move on. If you do that, it will seem to work right up until you hit a bug you cannot explain. Treat AI as help after you have tried to understand the code yourself.

Prompt: Tell me a bit about the history of JavaScript and some of the ways that it is unusual compared to other languages. For example, is it derived from Java? Its syntax looks like C, C++, Java, and C#, but how similar is it to those languages?

Using browser developer tools to find errors and bugs

It is important to understand that mistakes are part of working with JavaScript. Syntax errors, undefined variables, and logic bugs happen constantly, even to experienced developers. The browser's developer tools are your best friend here. They show error messages, let you inspect values, and let you try changes without editing your source files. AI can help explain errors and suggest fixes, but you should always tie those explanations back to what your code is actually doing.

That is enough setup. Let's build a simple page and start writing JavaScript.

Programming basics

The basics of JavaScript come down to a small set of ideas that you will reuse constantly. Once these ideas click, most JavaScript code starts to look familiar, even when it is doing new things.

Setting up a web page with code

Here's a simple starting page you can reuse for every code example in this section. It has a few elements we can select and update, as well as buttons and inputs to trigger logic.

Create a `Chapter05` folder, create a subfolder named `ProgrammingBasics`, and in it create a file named `index.html` with the following code:

You can download the source code for this web page from the following link: `https://github.com/markjprice/web-dev-ai/blob/main/Code/Chapter05/ProgrammingBasics/index.html`

```
<!doctype html>
<html lang="en-US">
<head>
  <meta charset="utf-8" />
  <meta name="viewport"
        content="width=device-width, initial-scale=1" />
  <title>JavaScript Basics Playground</title>
  <style>
    body { font-family: Arial, sans-serif; margin: 2rem; }
    .row { margin: 0.75rem 0; }
    .box { padding: 0.75rem; border: 1px solid #ccc;
           border-radius: 0.5rem; }
    button { padding: 0.5rem 0.75rem; }
```

```
    input { padding: 0.5rem; width: min(360px, 100%); }
    code { background: #f6f6f6; padding: 0.1rem 0.3rem;
           border-radius: 0.25rem; }
  </style>
</head>
<body>
  <h1>JavaScript Basics Playground</h1>

  <div class="row box">
    <p id="status">Status: Waiting for JavaScript…</p>
    <p id="message">Message: (none)</p>
    <p>Counter: <strong id="counterValue">0</strong></p>
  </div>

  <div class="row box">
    <label for="nameInput">Your name:</label><br />
    <input id="nameInput" type="text" placeholder="Type your name" />
    <button id="helloBtn" type="button">Say hello</button>
  </div>

  <div class="row box">
    <button id="incrementBtn" type="button">Increment counter</button>
    <button id="resetBtn" type="button">Reset counter</button>
  </div>

  <div class="row box">
    <p>Open Developer Tools Console to see logs.</p>
  </div>

  <!-- We'll add script files in the next few sections. -->
  <script src="code-order.js"></script>
</body>
</html>
```

Note the following about the preceding HTML file:

- It contains a paragraph element with an `id` of `status` and an initial content of: `Status: Waiting for JavaScript…`.

- It contains a paragraph element with an `id` of `message` and an initial content of: `Message: (none)`.
- It references a code file named `code-order.js`. We will create this file in the next section.

Each section below is a self-contained example. For each one, add a new script element to reference the code file for the concept you're learning, then refresh the browser and observe what changes on the page and in the console.

Execution order is top-to-bottom

The first idea is that JavaScript is executed step by step, from top to bottom. When the browser encounters JavaScript, it reads each statement in order and runs it immediately unless told otherwise. That sounds obvious, but it explains a lot of beginner confusion. If you try to use something before it exists, JavaScript will complain. Order matters.

Create a second file in the same folder as the HTML file named `code-order.js`.

In `code-order.js`, add the following code:

```
console.log("1) Script started.");

const statusElement = document.querySelector("#status");
statusElement.textContent = "Status: JavaScript is running.";

console.log("2) Updated the status paragraph.");

const messageElement = document.querySelector("#message");
messageElement.textContent = "Message: The script ran top-to-bottom.";

console.log("3) Updated the message paragraph.");

console.log("4) Script finished.");
```

The expression `document.querySelector("#status")` returns a reference to the element on the web page with the `id` of `status`. You will learn more about this and other ways of working with a page's DOM in a later section in this chapter. For now, this is all you need to know.

Prompt: How does the browser render the DOM and when does JavaScript run during page load? A common beginner mistake is trying to access DOM elements before the browser has parsed them.

Open the web page in your browser and view **Developer Tools**, as shown in *Figure 5.1*:

1. In the Chrome toolbar, click the three dots to open the main menu.
2. In the menu, click **More tools**.
3. In the submenu, click **Developer Tools** (and note the keyboard shortcut).
4. In **Developer Tools**, click the **Console** tab.

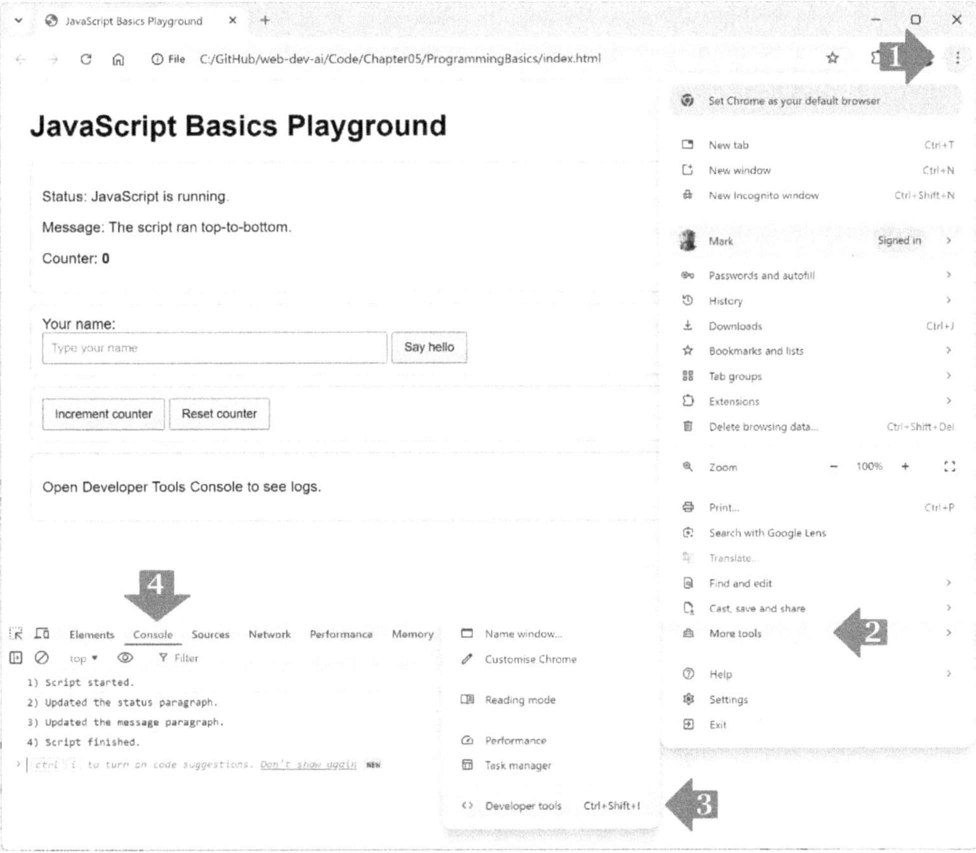

Figure 5.1: Watching console output in Developer Tools

Good practice: Instead of navigating through the menus, learn the keyboard shortcut to toggle the display of **Developer Tools** in your web browser, because you will use it all the time during web development. For Chrome on Windows, this is *Ctrl + Shift + I*.

This shows that JavaScript executes immediately upon opening the web page, in the order it's written. You will see that the status and message elements on the page have updated and that the console logs appear in sequence. If you move code statements around in `code-order.js`, the output changes. If you reference `messageElement` before it is created, you get an error.

Comments for documenting your code

Comments are notes for people reading the code, not for the browser. The JavaScript engine completely ignores them. Comments exist to explain why code is there, clarify tricky logic, and temporarily disable code while you are experimenting or debugging. Used well, comments help readers understand intent. Used badly, they add clutter or fall out of date and mislead the comment reader.

JavaScript supports two kinds of comments.

- Single-line comments start with `//`. Everything after `//` on that line is ignored. These are best for short explanations or quick notes. They are also commonly used to explain why something is done a certain way, which is often more valuable than explaining what the code does:

```
// This is a single-line comment.
let counter = 0; // This comment might explain why the variable
named counter exists and has been initialized to zero.
```

- Multi-line comments start with `/*` and end with `*/`. Everything inside is ignored, even if it spans multiple lines:

```
/*
  This is a multi-line comment.
  It can span several lines
  and is useful for longer explanations.
*/
let total = 10;
```

Multi-line comments are often used for file-level explanations or for temporarily commenting out a block of code during testing, as shown in the following code:

```
/*
function calculateTotal(price, tax) {
  return price + tax;
}
*/
```

Be careful with this technique. It is easy to forget commented-out code and leave dead logic behind.

A note about phrasing related to comments. You **comment** code by adding descriptive text above or after code statements. You **comment out** code by adding comment characters before or around statements to make them inactive. **Uncommenting** means removing the comment characters.

Comments are especially useful when the code expresses *how* something is done but not *why*. For example, the following code is obvious:

```
counter = counter + 1;
```

A comment explaining *why* might actually help:

```
// Increment the counter to track user clicks for analytics.
counter = counter + 1;
```

Avoid comments that simply repeat what the code already says. This adds clutter without adding understanding. Anyone who can read JavaScript already knows what the line does.

Comments are also useful when working with an AI sidekick. When you ask an AI to help with a function, a short comment describing the job often gives better results:

```
// Update the UI so it reflects the current counter value.
function renderCounter() {
  counterEl.textContent = String(counter);
}
```

Finally, remember that comments do not run, cannot fix bugs, and cannot replace clear naming. If you find yourself writing long comments to explain confusing code, that is usually a sign the code itself should be simplified. Good JavaScript should be clear enough that comments mostly explain why, not what or how.

Logging to the console

The browser console is the first debugging tool you should reach for when writing JavaScript. Logging data to the console lets you see what your code is doing while it runs, without changing what appears on the page. When something behaves strangely, the console is usually the first place you should look.

The most common way to write to the console is `console.log()`. You pass values into it, and the browser prints them to the console in the order they are received, as shown in the following code:

```
console.log("Hello from JavaScript");
```

When this statement runs, the text appears in the **Developer Tools Console.** It does not affect the page itself at all.

You can log variables to see their current values. This is extremely useful when you are unsure whether a variable contains what you expect:

```
let age = 42;
console.log(age);
```

The console will display 42. If it does not, you know the problem is not further down the code. That is how you narrow down where the bug is.

You can log multiple values in a single call. JavaScript will print them left to right, separated by spaces:

```
console.log(typeof age, age);
```

Here is what is happening step by step:

1. First, `typeof` age is evaluated. The `typeof` operator returns a `string` describing the type of the value stored in the variable named age, such as `"number"`, `"string"`, or `"boolean"`.
2. Second, age itself is evaluated to its current value.
3. Finally, both results are passed into `console.log`, which prints them together. In the console, you would see something like the following output:

   ```
   number 42
   ```

This pattern of logging to the console is very common because it answers two questions at once: what is the value, and what type is it?

Strings and labels are often combined with values to make logs easier to read, as shown in the following code:

```
console.log("Age:", age);
console.log("Type of age:", typeof age);
```

This is especially helpful once you have many logs and need to scan the output quickly.

There are also related console methods that are worth knowing, even if you mostly use `console.log`, as shown in the following code:

```
console.warn("This is a warning");
console.error("This is an error");
```

Warnings and errors are styled differently in the console, making them stand out. This can help when scanning large amounts of output.

A practical rule of thumb is to log early and log often while learning, then remove or reduce logs once your code works. Logging is not a sign of weakness or inexperience. It is how you make invisible program state visible.

Prompt: What are the most useful console methods besides `console.log`?

Using template literals for custom output

Template literals allow you to embed variables and expressions directly inside a `string`, instead of manually concatenating pieces together.

Inside a template literal, anything written as `${...}` is evaluated as JavaScript. The result is converted to a `string` and inserted at that position. For example, the following code:

```
let message = `Message: Title is "${pageTitle}", clicks = ${clicks}.`;
```

The preceding code statement builds a readable message by inserting variable values into a string. Let's break the statement down:

- The text is wrapped in backticks, not quotes. Backticks define a template literal.
- `Message: Title is "` is just literal text.
- `${pageTitle}` is replaced with the current value stored in the `pageTitle` variable.
- `", clicks =` is more literal text.
- `${clicks}` is replaced with the current value stored in the `clicks` variable.
- `.` is the final literal character.

If `pageTitle` is `"Playground"` and `clicks` is `1`, the final `string` that JavaScript produces is:

```
Message: Title is "Playground", clicks = 1.
```

Variables for storing data

Variables are how you store information so you can use it later. In up-to-date JavaScript, you will mostly see variables declared with `let` and `const`. A variable is a named place in your computer's memory where your program stores a value. That value might be a number, some text, a `true` or `false` value, or something more complex like an object.

Good practice: You'll encounter `var` in older JavaScript code and AI-generated snippets. `var` was the original way to declare variables, but it has confusing scoping behavior because variables declared with `var` are function-scoped, not block-scoped, which means they can leak out of `if` blocks and loops. Modern JavaScript uses `let` and `const` instead. If you see `var`, mentally replace it with `let`.

Prompt: Please explain JavaScript scope and the difference between global, function, and block scope with examples.

For example, you might store a user's name or a counter that tracks how many times a button has been clicked. `let` is used when the value is expected to change. `const` is used when the variable should always point to the same value.

Good practice: A common beginner mistake is using `const` everywhere and then being surprised when JavaScript refuses to let the value change. The rule of thumb is simple. If the value will change, use `let`. If it should not, use `const`.

This example shows how reassignment works and why a `const` variable cannot be reassigned a new value.

In `index.html`, after the existing `<script>` element, add a new `<script>` element to reference a new code file named `variables.js`, as shown highlighted in the following code:

```
<script src="code-order.js"></script>
<script src="variables.js"></script>
```

In the same folder as the HTML file, create the code file named `variables.js`, and enter the following code:

```
statusElement.textContent = "Status: Demonstrating variables.";

let clicks = 0; // This value can change.
const pageTitle = "Playground"; // This value will never change.

messageElement.textContent = `Message: Title is "${pageTitle}", clicks =
${clicks}.`;

clicks = clicks + 1;
console.log("After increment, clicks =", clicks);

messageElement.textContent = `Message: Title is "${pageTitle}", clicks =
${clicks}.`;

// Try uncommenting the next line to see the error.
// pageTitle = "New Title";
```

Note that `variables.js` uses `statusElement` and `messageElement` even though they were declared in `code-order.js`. This works because all the `<script>` tags share the same global scope. It's as if all the code were in one giant file. For now, you can think of it as one shared global scope. This is convenient for learning but becomes problematic in larger projects. In later chapters, you'll learn about JavaScript modules, which give each file its own private scope.

Refresh the web page and note the following:

- The variable named `clicks` changes from `0` to `1`.
- The variable named `pageTitle` does not change. You can still change the page title in the DOM, but the variable `pageTitle` cannot be reassigned.
- If you uncomment the last statement and refresh the page, you will see an error message in the **Console**, as shown in *Figure 5.2*:

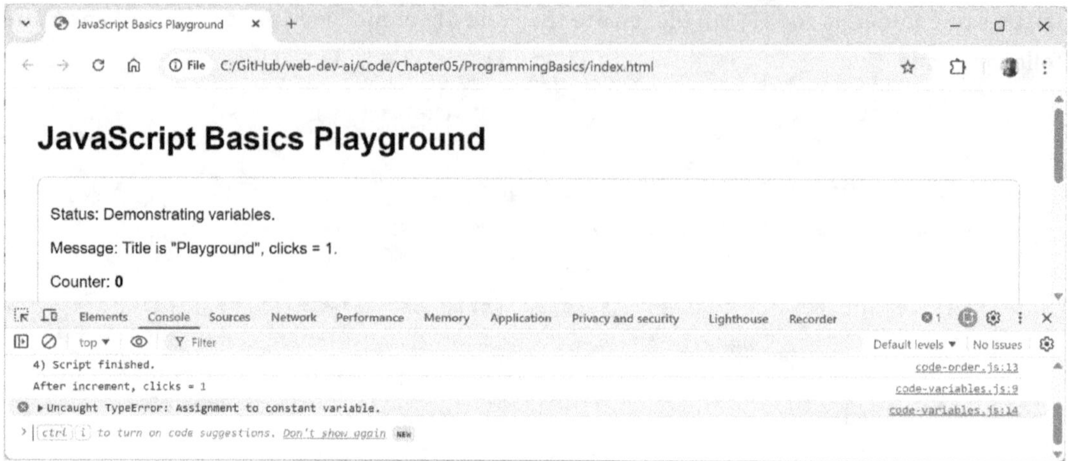

Figure 5.2: An error about assignment to a constant variable

Comment out the last statement to remove the error.

Scope is where your variables live

Scope describes where a variable can be accessed in your code. In other words, it answers the question: where does this variable exist, and who can use it?

Understanding scope helps you avoid bugs where a variable is unexpectedly missing, overwritten, or shared more widely than you intended.

There are three main kinds of scope in JavaScript that you will encounter in this chapter.

Global scope

A variable in **global scope** is accessible from anywhere in your script.

In the examples earlier, variables such as `statusElement` and `messageElement` were declared in one file and then used in another:

```
const statusElement = document.querySelector("#status");
```

Because both the `<script>` elements run on the same page, they share the same global scope. That is why `variables.js` can use variables declared in `code-order.js`.

This is convenient for small examples, but it becomes risky in larger applications because any script can change those values.

Function scope

Variables declared inside a function exist only inside that function:

```
function makeGreeting(name) {
  const message = `Hello, ${name}!`;
  return message;
}
```

In the preceding code, `message` only exists inside `makeGreeting`. If you try to use it outside the function, JavaScript will throw an error. This is useful because it keeps temporary values contained and prevents accidental interference with other parts of your code.

Block scope

Block scope applies to variables declared with `let` and `const` inside curly braces `{ }`, such as in `if` statements or loops:

```
if (true) {
  const secret = "hidden value";
  console.log(secret); // Works here
}

console.log(secret); // Error: secret is not defined
```

The `secret` variable only exists inside the `if` block.

This is one of the reasons `let` and `const` are preferred over `var`. The older `var` keyword ignores block boundaries and can lead to confusing bugs.

Scope and event handlers

Event handlers introduce another layer of scope.:

```
let counter = 0;

incrementBtn.addEventListener("click", () => {
  counter = counter + 1;
});
```

In the preceding code example:

- `counter` lives in the outer (global) scope
- The `() => { }` arrow function creates its own scope
- The function can still access `counter` because it was defined outside

This behavior is called a **closure**. You do not need to master that term yet, but it explains why event handlers can remember variables defined earlier.

Keep variables in the smallest scope that makes sense:

- Use block scope (let or const) for temporary values.
- Use function scope to organize logic.
- Use global scope sparingly, especially as your programs grow.

If a variable is accessible everywhere, it can be changed from anywhere. That is where subtle bugs start to appear.

You will soon see that some operations, such as `document.querySelector`, can return a special value called `null` when nothing is found. Mastering scope helps you understand where values come from, and understanding values like `null` helps you handle cases where something is missing.

Data types: number, string, Boolean, array, and object

JavaScript has a handful of core data types you will use all the time:

- **Numbers** are used for counts and calculations.
- **Strings** are used for text and are written inside quotes.
- **Booleans** are either `true` or `false` and are used for decisions.
- **Arrays** are ordered lists of values.
- **Objects** group related values together under named properties.

This section shows common data types and how they behave.

In `index.html`, after the existing `<script>` elements, add a new `<script>` element to reference a new code file named `data-types.js`, as shown in the following code:

```
<script src="data-types.js"></script>
```

In the same folder as the HTML file, create the code file named `data-types.js`, and enter the following code:

```
statusElement.textContent = "Status: Demonstrating data types.";

const age = 54;                         // number
const firstName = "Mark";               // string
const isMember = true;                  // boolean

messageElement.textContent = `Message: ${firstName} is ${age} years old.
Member: ${isMember}.`;

console.log(typeof age, age);
console.log(typeof firstName, firstName);
console.log(typeof isMember, isMember);

// Two types you'll use constantly:
const favoriteShows = ["Andor", "Heated Rivalry"]; // array (list)
const user = { name: "Mark", age: 42 }; // object (grouped properties)

console.log("Array example:", favoriteShows);
console.log("Object example:", user);
```

Refresh the web page and note that browsers let you expand these objects in the console to inspect their properties. This is far more informative than trying to print everything manually, as shown in *Figure 5.3*:

Figure 5.3: Logging variables with different data types to the console

Arrays and objects show up constantly when you start working with the DOM and APIs, so it is especially important to become familiar with how to log them to the console for debugging purposes.

Prompt: How do I debug JavaScript using Chrome DevTools step by step? Show me how to use breakpoints in JavaScript and why they are useful.

Functions: reusable code, parameters, return values

A **function** is a reusable block of code that performs a specific task. You define a function once, then call it whenever you need it. This keeps your code readable and avoids repetition. Functions make JavaScript reusable.

Functions can accept inputs, called parameters, and they can return results. Even when JavaScript code looks complicated, it is usually just functions calling other functions.

This example will define functions, call them, and then use return values to update the page.

In `index.html`, after the existing `<script>` elements, add a new `<script>` element to reference a new code file named `functions.js`, as shown in the following code:

```
<script src="functions.js"></script>
```

In the same folder as the HTML file, create the code file named `functions.js`, and enter the following code:

```
statusElement.textContent = "Status: Demonstrating functions.";

function makeGreeting(personName) {
  return `Hello, ${personName}!`;
}

function showMessage(text) {
  messageElement.textContent = `Message: ${text}`;
}

const greeting = makeGreeting("Captain Picard");
console.log("Greeting returned from function:", greeting);

showMessage(greeting);
```

Note the following about the preceding code:

- `makeGreeting` returns a `string` value.
- `showMessage` performs an action.

Refresh the web page and note that the message that uses a `string` value returned from a function is shown in the web page and in the console, as shown in *Figure 5.4*:

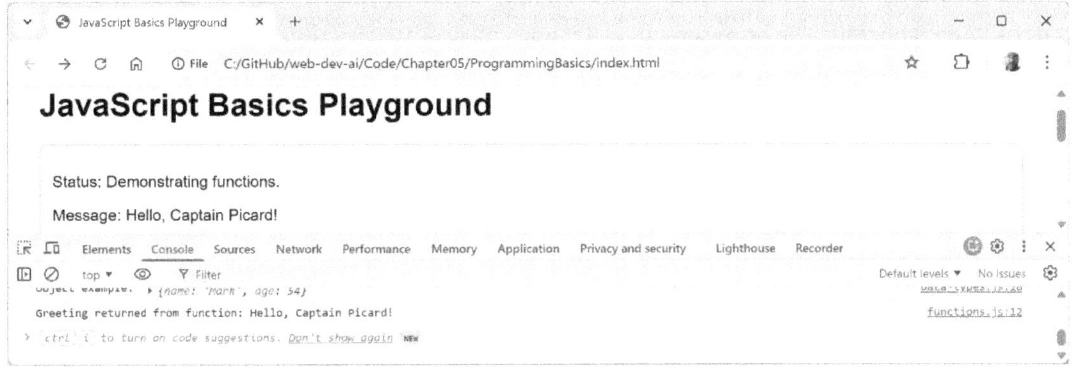

Figure 5.4: Calling a function to return a string value

Keeping functions small and clear makes later DOM code much easier to follow and debug.

Prompt: What is the call stack in JavaScript, and how does it relate to function execution?

Hooking up event handlers

`addEventListener` is a method available on DOM elements. It lets you listen for a specific event and register a function to run when that event happens. You are not running the function now. You are handing it to the browser so it can run it later.

For example:

```
incrementBtn.addEventListener("click", () => {
  counter = counter + 1;
  renderCounter();
});
```

The first argument, `"click"`, is the event type. It tells the browser which kind of event you care about. In this case, it is a mouse or a touch click on the button.

The second argument is a function. This function is called the **event handler**:

```
() => {
    counter = counter + 1;
    renderCounter();
}
```

This is an **arrow function**. It defines a small, anonymous function with no parameters. You are not calling it yourself. The browser will call it automatically every time the button is clicked.

`counter` is a variable that lives outside the function. Each click increases its value by one. Because the function runs again on every click, the value keeps increasing over time.

Typically, `renderCounter` reads the current value of counter and writes it into the DOM so the user can see the new number.

One detail matters here: timing. None of the code inside the arrow function runs until the user clicks the button. JavaScript finishes loading the page, sets up the event listener, and then waits. When the click happens, the browser calls the handler function at the right moment.

In plain English, this code means: *When the increment button is clicked, increase the counter by one and then update the display to match.*

Prompt: What is event bubbling and capturing in JavaScript? Show a simple visual explanation.

Conditionals: if / else with Booleans and comparisons

Decisions in JavaScript are made using **conditional statements**. The most common is the `if` statement. It allows your code to choose between different paths based on whether something is `true` or `false`.

For example, you might check whether a form field is empty before allowing submission. This is how JavaScript chooses one path instead of running the same code every time.

This section uses the input field and checks whether the user typed anything. It also introduces comparisons and truthiness in a beginner-friendly way.

In `index.html`, after the existing `<script>` elements, add a new `<script>` element to reference a new code file named `conditionals.js`, as shown in the following code:

```
<script src="conditionals.js"></script>
```

In the same folder as the HTML file, create the code file named `conditionals.js`, and enter the following code:

```
const nameInput = document.querySelector("#nameInput");
const helloBtn = document.querySelector("#helloBtn");

statusElement.textContent = "Status: Demonstrating conditionals.";

helloBtn.addEventListener("click", () => {
  const typedName = nameInput.value; // string (possibly empty)

  if (typedName.trim() === "") {
    messageElement.textContent =
      "Message: Please type your name first.";
  } else {
    messageElement.textContent =
      `Message: Hello, ${typedName}!`;
  }
});
```

Note the following about the preceding code:

- `trim()` removes leading or trailing whitespace so "   " counts as empty.
- `===` checks equality without type coercion, which avoids lots of confusing bugs.

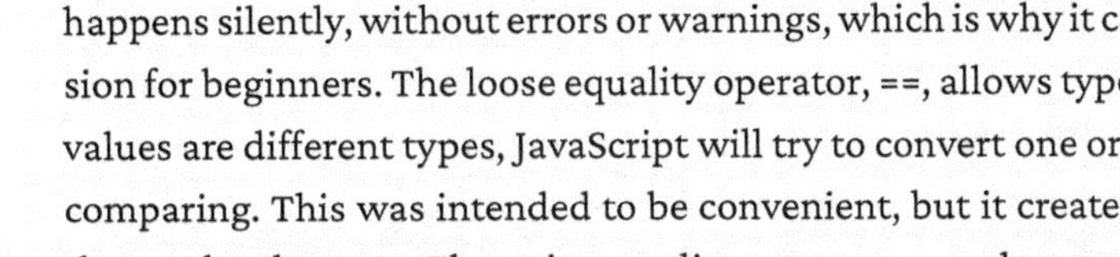

Good practice: Type coercion is JavaScript's habit of automatically converting values from one type to another when it thinks it can make an operation *work*. This usually happens silently, without errors or warnings, which is why it causes so much confusion for beginners. The loose equality operator, `==`, allows type coercion. If the two values are different types, JavaScript will try to convert one or both of them before comparing. This was intended to be convenient, but it creates surprises and bugs that are hard to spot. The strict equality operator, `===`, does not allow type coercion. Both the type and the value must match exactly for the comparison to be `true`. Use the strict equality operator for comparisons unless you have very good reasons not to.

Refresh the web page, click the **Say hello** button, and note the response. Then enter your name, click the **Say hello** button, and note the response, as shown in *Figure 5.5*:

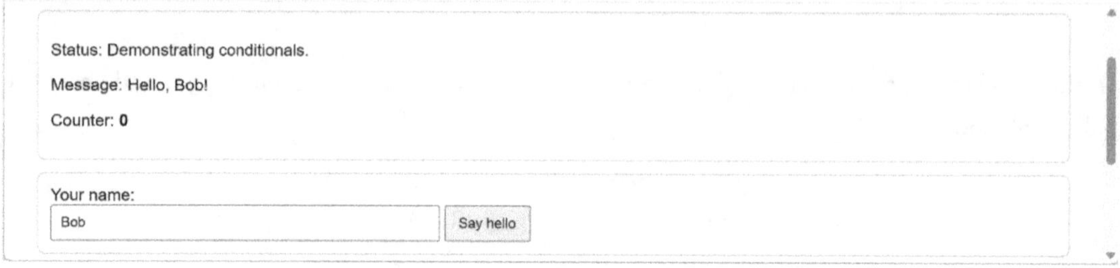

Figure 5.5: A conditional check before saying Hello to Bob

We have not added any code to change **Counter: 0** yet.

Loops: repeating work and iterating arrays

Loops allow you to repeat an action multiple times. Instead of writing the same line of code again and again, you tell JavaScript how many times to run it or to keep running until a condition changes. Loops are especially useful when working with arrays or groups of elements on a page.

This section updates the message and logs multiple times, then loops through an array.

In `index.html`, after the existing `<script>` elements, add a new `<script>` element to reference a new code file named `loops.js`, as shown in the following code:

```
<script src="loops.js"></script>
```

In the same folder as the HTML file, create the code file named `loops.js`, and enter the following code:

```
statusElement.textContent = "Status: Demonstrating loops.";

// A simple for loop counts from 1 to 5.
let output = "Counting: ";
for (let i = 1; i <= 5; i++) {
  output += i + " ";
  console.log("i is", i);
}
messageElement.textContent = "Message: " + output.trim();

// Looping through an array (list)
```

```
const languages = ["HTML", "CSS", "JavaScript", "Python"];
for (let i = 0; i < languages.length; i += 1) {
  console.log(`Language ${i}:`, languages[i]);
}
```

Note the following about the preceding code:

- The `for` loop has three parts: start (`let i = 1`), condition (`i <= 5`), and step aka increment (`i++`).
- Arrays use `length`, and indexes start at `0`.

Refresh the web page and note that the `for` loop increments from 1 to 5 and the array is iterated through all of its items, as shown in *Figure 5.6*:

Figure 5.6: Loops

Prompt: Please summarize all the conditional and loop statements in JavaScript and include code examples for each one.

Error handling

Errors are a normal part of writing JavaScript. You will see them constantly while learning, and you will still see them in production code.

So far, you have relied on the browser console to show errors. That is useful, but sometimes you also want to handle errors in your code so your program can fail gracefully instead of crashing. JavaScript provides a built-in way to do this using `try` and `catch`.

A `try` block contains code that might fail. If an error occurs, JavaScript stops running that block and jumps to the `catch` block:

```
try {
  const result = riskyOperation();
  console.log(result);
} catch (error) {
  console.error("Something went wrong:", error);
}
```

The preceding code means: try to run the `riskyOperation()` function and log the result, but if something breaks, catch the error and handle it.

As another example, you might try to find an element named `status` and change its text content to display a message to the user:

```
const element = document.querySelector("#status");

try {
  element.textContent = "Updated safely";
} catch (error) {
  console.error("Failed to update element:", error);
}
```

In the preceding code, if `element` is `null`, trying to access `textContent` would normally throw an error and stop execution. With `try` and `catch`, you can handle that situation instead of letting it crash silently or unpredictably.

That said, in this specific case, a simple `if (element)` check is usually better. Use `try` and `catch` when you cannot easily predict or prevent the error.

Throwing your own errors

You can also create errors deliberately using `throw`. This is useful when you detect an invalid situation:

```
function greet(name) {
  if (!name) {
    throw new Error("Name is required");
  }
  return `Hello, ${name}!`;
}
```

Then handle it where the function is used:

```
try {
  const message = greet("");
  console.log(message);
} catch (error) {
  console.error(error.message);
}
```

This pattern makes it clear when something is wrong and allows you to respond appropriately.

You can also add a `finally` block. This always runs, whether an error occurred or not:

```
try {
  console.log("Trying something...");
} catch (error) {
  console.error("It failed:", error);
} finally {
  console.log("This always runs");
}
```

Use `finally` for cleanup tasks, such as resetting UI state or stopping a loading indicator.

When to use error handling

A common beginner mistake is overusing `try` and `catch`.

Use it when:

- You are calling code that might fail unpredictably
- You want to prevent the entire program from stopping
- You need to recover or show a user-friendly message

Avoid it when:

- A simple conditional check would prevent the error
- You are using it to hide bugs instead of fixing them

For example, this is better:

```
if (element) {
  element.textContent = "Updated";
}
```

Than this:

```
try {
  element.textContent = "Updated";
} catch {}
```

The second version hides the problem instead of addressing it.

Good practice: Think of error handling as a safety net, not a primary control flow tool.

Most of the time, you should:

- Write code that avoids errors (by checking values)
- Use the console to debug when something goes wrong
- Add try/catch when you need to handle unexpected failures gracefully

As your programs grow, errors will become more subtle. Some will come from user input. Others will come from missing elements, timing issues, or unexpected data.

Being able to catch and handle errors means your code can respond intelligently instead of breaking in confusing ways. It also makes AI-generated code safer to test because you can isolate the part that may fail and inspect the actual error.

Putting it together with events

This section ties the basics together without going deep into the DOM yet. It uses variables, functions, conditionals, and event handlers.

In `index.html`, after the existing `<script>` elements, add a new `<script>` element to reference a new code file named `events.js`, as shown in the following code:

```
<script src="events.js"></script>
```

In the same folder as the HTML file, create the code file named `events.js`, and enter the following code:

```
const counterElement = document.querySelector("#counterValue");
const incrementBtn = document.querySelector("#incrementBtn");
const resetBtn = document.querySelector("#resetBtn");
```

```
statusElement.textContent = "Status: Putting it together.";

let counter = 0;

function renderCounter() {
  counterElement.textContent = String(counter);
  messageElement.textContent = `Message: Counter is now ${counter}.`;
}

incrementBtn.addEventListener("click", () => {
  counter = counter + 1;
  renderCounter();
});

resetBtn.addEventListener("click", () => {
  counter = 0;
  renderCounter();
});

// Initial render so the UI matches the variable.
renderCounter();
```

Refresh the web page and note that every time you click the **Increment counter** button, the counter increments by one. After clicking the button three times, the output is **Counter: 3**, as shown in *Figure 5.7*:

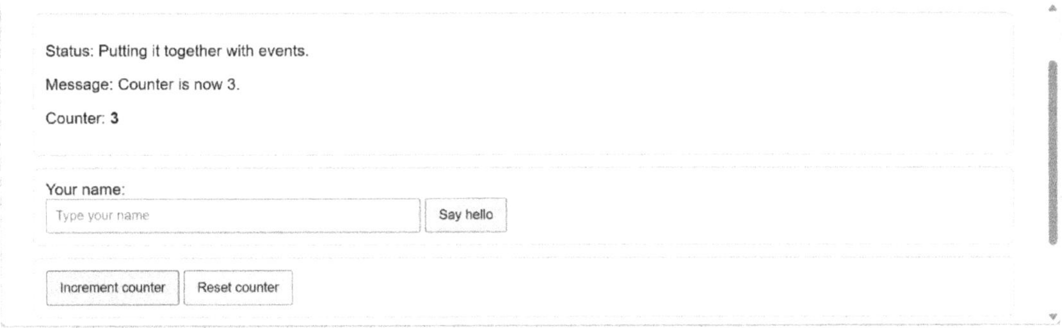

Figure 5.7: Incrementing a counter with button click events

This is the shape of most interactive web code. State lives in variables like `counter`, behavior lives in functions like `renderCounter`, and user actions on a web page trigger events.

AI can produce JavaScript quickly. That is not the difficult part. The difficult part is deciding what should happen when the user clicks, types, submits, or changes something. In the counter example, you need to know where the number is stored, which button changes it, and which part of the page must be updated afterward. That is the skill to practice: follow the moving parts, then decide whether the code matches the behavior you wanted.

Now that you've been introduced to JavaScript and the main components of the language, let's test what you've learned with a mini exercise.

Mini exercise and quiz

Use the same page and make some small modifications and additions:

- Change the counter step to add 5 each time
- Add a "Decrement" button
- Change the greeting to always use uppercase

Prompt: Please quiz me about JavaScript basics like declaring variables and writing simple functions. For example, "What does `const` vs `let` do?"

In the next section, we will connect these basics to the browser itself by looking at the DOM. That is where variables, functions, and events come together to change what the user sees and interacts with on the page.

DOM manipulation

In the `Chapter05` folder, create a folder named `DomManipulation`, and in it create a file named `index.html` with the following code:

You can download the source code for this web page from the following link: `https://github.com/markjprice/web-dev-ai/blob/main/Code/Chapter05/DomManipulation/index.html`

```
<!doctype html>
<html lang="en-US">
<head>
  <meta charset="utf-8" />
```

```
  <meta name="viewport"
        content="width=device-width, initial-scale=1" />
  <title>DOM Manipulation Playground</title>
  <link rel="stylesheet" href="styles.css" />
</head>
<body>
  <h1>DOM Manipulation Playground</h1>
  <p class="muted">Open Developer Tools Console. Reference one script
example at a time at the bottom.</p>

  <div class="grid">
    <section class="card" aria-labelledby="card-status">
      <h2 id="card-status">1) Status panel</h2>
      <p id="statusText">Status: Waiting…</p>
      <div class="row">
        <button id="btnSetStatus" type="button">
          Set status</button>
        <button id="btnClearStatus" type="button">
          Clear status</button>
      </div>
    </section>
    <section class="card" aria-labelledby="card-profile">
      <h2 id="card-profile">2) Profile editor</h2>
      <div class="row">
        <input id="nameInput" type="text" placeholder="Name" />
        <select id="moodSelect">
          <option value="neutral">Neutral</option>
          <option value="productive">Productive</option>
          <option value="sleepy">Sleepy</option>
          <option value="chaotic">Chaotic</option>
        </select>
        <button id="btnApplyProfile" type="button">Apply</button>
      </div>
      <p>Preview: <strong id="profilePreview">
        Anonymous (neutral)</strong></p>
    </section>
    <section class="card" aria-labelledby="card-todo">
```

```
      <h2 id="card-todo">3) Quick to-do list</h2>
      <div class="row">
        <input id="todoInput" type="text" placeholder=
          "Add a task (e.g., 'Refactor CSS')" />
        <button id="btnAddTodo" type="button">Add</button>
        <button id="btnClearDone" type="button">Clear done</button>
      </div>
      <ul id="todoList" class="muted">
        <li class="pill" data-done="false">
          <input type="checkbox" aria-label="Mark done" />
          <span>Write the first DOM example</span>
          <button type="button" data-action="remove">Remove</button>
        </li>
      </ul>
      <p class="muted" id="todoCount">0 items</p>
    </section>
    <section class="card" aria-labelledby="card-theme">
      <h2 id="card-theme">4) Theme + visibility</h2>
      <div class="row">
        <button id="btnToggleTheme" type="button">
          Toggle theme</button>
        <button id="btnToggleTodo" type="button">
          Show/Hide to-do card</button>
      </div>
      <p class="muted">This section is perfect for practicing class
toggling and attribute changes.</p>
    </section>
  </div>
  <script src="example1.js"></script>
</body>
</html>
```

Create a file named `styles.css`. To save space in this print book, you can download the source code for this web page from the following link: `https://github.com/markjprice/web-dev-ai/blob/main/Code/Chapter05/DomManipulation/styles.css`

Now let's see some *cool and practical* DOM manipulation examples that plug into that page. Use one example at a time: paste one block into the `<script>` tag, refresh, play with it, then replace it with the next block.

Example 1: Selecting elements and changing text

This code block teaches:

- DOM selection with `querySelector`
- Writing UI with `textContent`
- Responding to button clicks

Add the following code to a file named `example1.js`, which is referenced by the `<script>` element at the bottom of the web page:

```
const statusText = document.querySelector("#statusText");
const btnSetStatus = document.querySelector("#btnSetStatus");
const btnClearStatus = document.querySelector("#btnClearStatus");

btnSetStatus.addEventListener("click", () => {
  const now = new Date();
  statusText.textContent = `Status: Updated at ${now.
toLocaleTimeString("en-GB")}`;
});

btnClearStatus.addEventListener("click", () => {
  statusText.textContent = "Status: Waiting…";
});
```

Good practice: Use `textContent` (not `innerHTML`) to set text in the DOM. `textContent` treats everything as plain text, which is safe. `innerHTML` interprets strings as HTML so if that string comes from user input, an attacker could inject malicious code. Only use `innerHTML` when you fully control the content and understand the risks.

Prompt: Please explain the difference between `textContent`, `innerText`, and `innerHTML` with examples and security implications.

Refresh the web page and in the **1) Status panel** box, click the **Set status** and **Clear status** buttons and note the updated text as you click each one. For example, after clicking **Set status** you will see the current time, as shown in *Figure 5.8*:

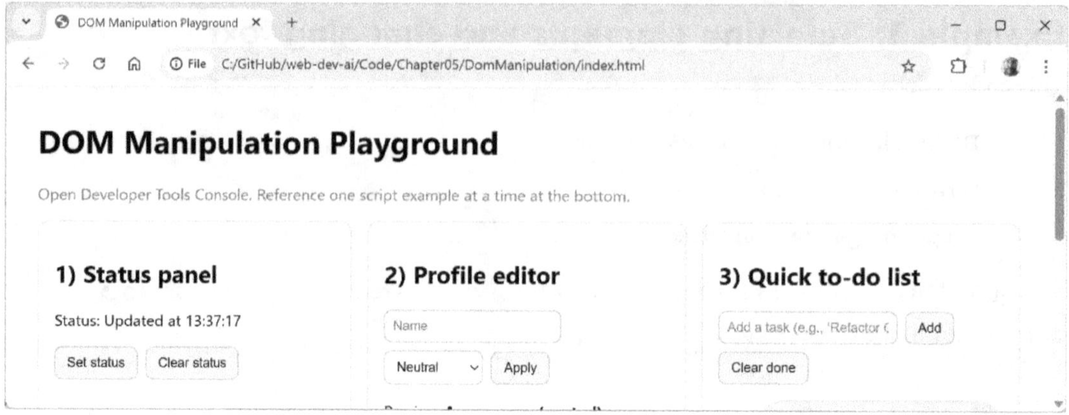

Figure 5.8: Updating text using the DOM

Handling missing values like null and undefined

As you start working with the DOM, you will occasionally run into situations where a value is missing. JavaScript represents this using two special values: `null` and `undefined`.

They look similar, but they mean slightly different things.

In the context of the DOM, `null` means nothing was found. `null` is an explicit "no value" result. It is often returned by APIs when something does not exist.

For example:

```
const element = document.querySelector("#doesNotExist");
console.log(element); // null
```

In this case, the browser searched the page for an element with that ID and did not find one, so it returned `null`. If you try to use that result as if it were a real element, your code will fail:

```
element.textContent = "Hello"; // Error
```

Beginners hit this DOM mistake often.

A safe pattern is to check for null before using the value:

```
if (element !== null) {
  element.textContent = "Hello";
}
```

Or more concisely:

```
if (element) {
  element.textContent = "Hello";
}
```

`undefined` means no value has been assigned. So `undefined` means a variable exists, but no value has been assigned to it:

```
let message;
console.log(message); // undefined
```

It can also appear when you access something that does not exist:

```
const user = { name: "Mark" };
console.log(user.age); // undefined
```

Here, the `user` object exists, but the age property does not, so JavaScript returns `undefined`.

The difference is subtle but useful:

- `null` usually comes from APIs or functions to indicate "nothing found."
- `undefined` usually means "this value was never set" or "does not exist."

In everyday code, you often treat them the same way: as signals that something is missing.

Good practice when working with the DOM

When you select elements from the page:

- Assume `querySelector` might return `null`
- Check before using the result if there is any doubt

For example:

```
const btn = document.querySelector("#myButton");

if (!btn) {
  console.warn("Button not found");
} else {
  btn.addEventListener("click", () => {
    console.log("Clicked");
  });
}
```

This kind of defensive check becomes more important as your pages grow and your JavaScript interacts with more dynamic content.

When something mysteriously breaks in JavaScript, it is often because a value was `null` or `undefined` and your code tried to use it anyway. Once you recognize those two values, these bugs become much easier to spot and fix.

With null and undefined covered, the next examples can focus on changing the page safely.

Example 2: Reading user input and updating the DOM

What this teaches:

- Reading values from input controls
- `trim()` function
- Conditionals
- Updating a single element

Add the following code block to a file named `example2.js` that the `<script>` element at the bottom of the web page references:

```
const nameInput = document.querySelector("#nameInput");
const moodSelect = document.querySelector("#moodSelect");
const btnApplyProfile = document.querySelector("#btnApplyProfile");
const profilePreview = document.querySelector("#profilePreview");

btnApplyProfile.addEventListener("click", () => {
  const name = nameInput.value.trim();
  const mood = moodSelect.value;

  const displayName = name === "" ? "Anonymous" : name;
  profilePreview.textContent = `${displayName} (${mood})`;
});
```

Refresh the web page and in the **2) Profile editor** box, enter a name including extra spaces before and after the name, select a mood option from the dropdown list, click the **Apply** button, and note a summary of your form edits appears after the **Preview** label, as shown in *Figure 5.9*:

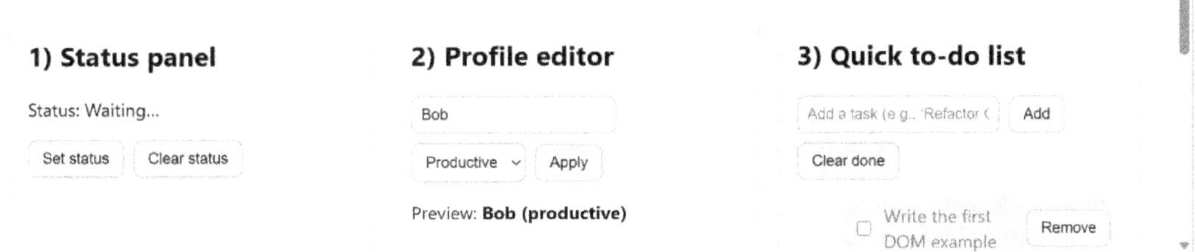

Figure 5.9: Selecting form options using the DOM

Example 3: Adding, removing, and counting list items

This section is about programmatically creating DOM elements. It teaches:

- Using `createElement` to create new HTML elements
- Using append to add an HTML element to an existing parent
- Using `dataset` to store custom data
- Simple UI bookkeeping

Add the following code block to a file named `example3.js` that the `<script>` element at the bottom of the web page references:

```
const todoInput = document.querySelector("#todoInput");
const btnAddTodo = document.querySelector("#btnAddTodo");
const todoList = document.querySelector("#todoList");
const todoCount = document.querySelector("#todoCount");

function updateCount() {
  const items = todoList.querySelectorAll("li");
  todoCount.textContent =
    `${items.length} item${items.length === 1 ? "" : "s"}`;
}

function makeTodoItem(text) {
  const li = document.createElement("li");
  li.className = "pill";
  li.dataset.done = "false";

  const checkbox = document.createElement("input");
  checkbox.type = "checkbox";
  checkbox.setAttribute("aria-label", "Mark done");
```

```
  const span = document.createElement("span");
  span.textContent = text;

  const removeBtn = document.createElement("button");
  removeBtn.type = "button";
  removeBtn.textContent = "Remove";
  removeBtn.dataset.action = "remove";

  li.append(checkbox, span, removeBtn);
  return li;
}

btnAddTodo.addEventListener("click", () => {
  const text = todoInput.value.trim();
  if (text === "") return;

  todoList.append(makeTodoItem(text));
  todoInput.value = "";
  todoInput.focus();
  updateCount();
});

updateCount();
```

Refresh the web page and in the **3) Quick to-do list** box, enter a task description like `Comment my code`, click the **Add** button, and note that a new item is dynamically added to the list of items, as shown in *Figure 5.10*:

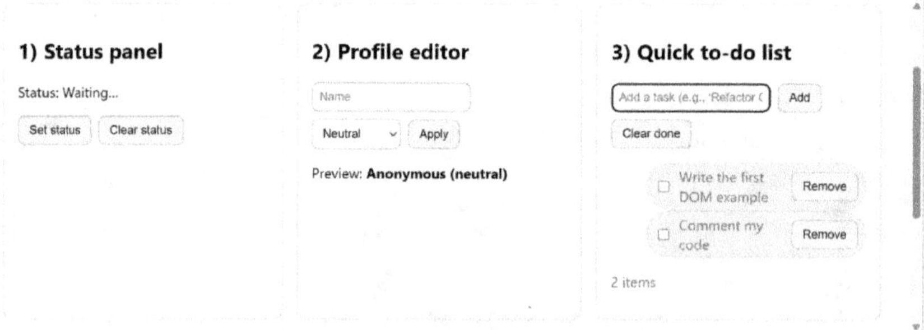

Figure 5.10: Adding items to a to-do list using the DOM

The **Remove** and **Clear done** buttons have not been implemented yet! You will do that in the next example.

Example 4: Event delegation

Event delegation means having one event handler for the whole list.

This is a common real-world technique. Instead of attaching listeners to every remove button and checkbox, you attach one listener to the parent unordered list element (`<ul>`) and inspect what was clicked.

This code example teaches:

- The concept of event bubbling
- Using `event.target` to identify the target of an event
- Using `closest`
- Class manipulation via `classList`

Add the following code block to a file named `example4.js` that the `<script>` element at the bottom of the web page references:

```
const btnClearDone = document.querySelector("#btnClearDone");

function updateCount() {
  const items = todoList.querySelectorAll("li");
  todoCount.textContent =
    `${items.length} item${items.length === 1 ? "" : "s"}`;
}

function syncDoneStyles(li) {
  const done = li.dataset.done === "true";
  li.classList.toggle("success", done);
}

todoList.addEventListener("click", (event) => {
  const target = event.target;

  if (target instanceof HTMLInputElement
    && target.type === "checkbox") {
```

```
    const li = target.closest("li");
    if (!li) return;

    li.dataset.done = String(target.checked);
    syncDoneStyles(li);
    return;
  }

  if (target instanceof HTMLButtonElement
    && target.dataset.action === "remove") {

    const li = target.closest("li");
    if (!li) return;

    li.remove();
    updateCount();
  }
});

btnClearDone.addEventListener("click", () => {
  const doneItems = todoList.querySelectorAll('li[data-done="true"]');
  for (const li of doneItems) {
    li.remove();
  }
  updateCount();
});

// Initialize styles for the starter item (if any)
for (const li of todoList.querySelectorAll("li")) {
  syncDoneStyles(li);
}
updateCount();
```

Refresh the web page and in the **3) Quick to-do list** box, remove the initial item, and then add three new items: `alpha`, `beta`, and `gamma`. Then select **alpha** and **beta** to show they are *done*, and click the **Clear done** button, as shown in *Figure 5.11*:

Figure 5.11: Selecting items as done in a to-do list using the DOM

Note the two *done* items are removed.

Next to the gamma item, click **Remove**, and note that the item is removed.

Prompt: When should I use event delegation instead of adding individual event listeners?

Example 5: Toggling classes and hiding sections

This code example teaches:

- Using `classList.toggle` to switch CSS classes on and off
- How to show or hide elements via CSS

Add the following code block to a file named `example5.js` that the `<script>` element at the bottom of the web page references:

```
const btnToggleTheme = document.querySelector("#btnToggleTheme");
const btnToggleTodo = document.querySelector("#btnToggleTodo");
const todoCard = document.querySelector("#card-todo").closest(".card");

btnToggleTheme.addEventListener("click", () => {
  document.body.classList.toggle("dark");
});
```

```
btnToggleTodo.addEventListener("click", () => {
  if (!todoCard) return;
  todoCard.classList.toggle("hidden");
});
```

Refresh the web page and in the **4) Theme + visibility** box, click the **Show/Hide the to-do list** button, and note that it disappears. Then click the **Toggle theme** button and note that the entire page switches between a normal and a dark theme, as shown in *Figure 5.12*:

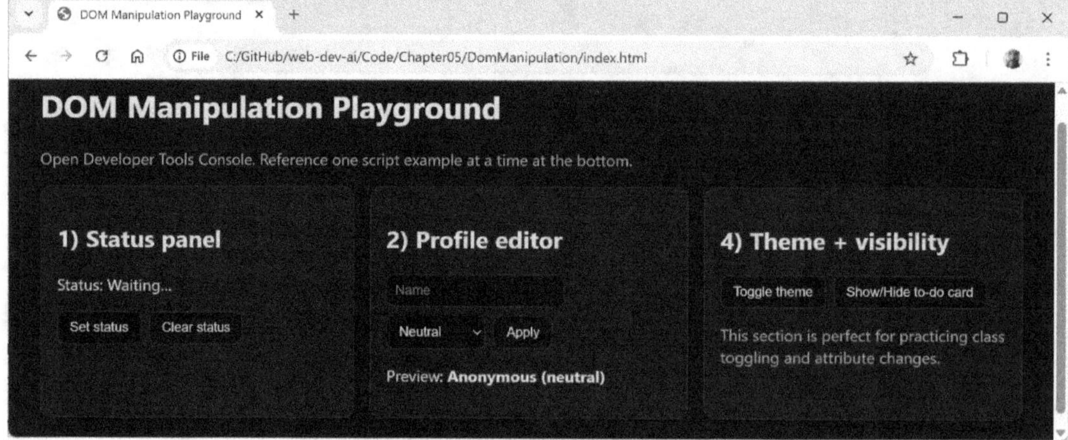

Figure 5.12: Selecting items as done in a to-do list using the DOM

The dark theme is defined in the styles.css file using a class named `.dark`. All the JavaScript needs to do is set the class on the `<body>` element, as shown in the following code: `document.body.classList.toggle("dark");`

Summary of DOM commands

Here is a concise reference summarizing the DOM methods, properties, and related APIs used across the DOM manipulation examples:

- `document.querySelector(selector)`: Returns the first element that matches a CSS selector, or `null` if none is found:

  ```
  document.querySelector("#statusText")
  ```

- `element.querySelector(selector)`: Searches only within that element's descendants for a match:

```
todoList.querySelectorAll("li")
```

- `element.querySelectorAll(selector)`: Returns a static list of all matching elements:

```
todoList.querySelectorAll('li[data-done="true"]')
```

- `element.textContent`: Gets or sets the plain text inside an element:

```
statusText.textContent = "Status: Waiting..."
```

- `element.value`: Gets or sets the current value of an input or select, for example, in a `<form>` element.
- `element.addEventListener(event, handler)`: Registers a function to run when an event occurs:

```
btnAddTodo.addEventListener("click", handler)
```

- `event.target`: The element that originally triggered the event.
- `element.closest(selector)`: Finds the nearest ancestor (or itself) matching a selector:

```
target.closest("li")
```

- `document.createElement(tagName)`: Creates a new element in memory (not yet in the DOM):

```
document.createElement("li")
```

- `element.append(...nodes)`: Appends one or more nodes as children.
- `element.remove()`: Removes the element from the DOM.
- `element.classList`: Read-only list of CSS classes on an element.
- `classList.toggle(className)`: Adds or removes a class depending on current state:

```
document.body.classList.toggle("dark")
```

- `element.dataset`: Accesses `data-*` attributes as a JavaScript object, for example, `<li data-done="true">`:

```
li.dataset.done = "true"
```

- `element.style.property`: Sets inline CSS styles directly on an element:

```
li.style.opacity = "0.75"
```

- `element.type`: Indicates the type of an input element:

```
target.type === "checkbox"
```

- `element.checked`: Boolean indicating whether a checkbox is checked.
- `element.setAttribute(name, value)`: Sets an HTML attribute on an element:

```
checkbox.setAttribute("aria-label", "Mark done")
```

- `element.focus()`: Moves keyboard focus to the element.
- `element.length`: Returns the number of items in a list or array.
- `Instanceof`: Checks whether a value is an instance of a given class:

```
target instanceof HTMLButtonElement
```

A useful tip to remember is that almost all DOM work follows the same pattern: select something, read or change a property, and react to events. Once you understand that pattern, the list above becomes a lookup rather than something to memorize.

Let's end with a quick practical test of what you've learned about JavaScript.

Prompt: Please generate a JavaScript snippet with errors for me to debug. How should I use AI tools to debug JavaScript errors without becoming dependent on them?

Practice, references, and resources

In this section, you will be tested on what you've learned in this chapter and be provided with useful links to reference materials and resources.

Check your understanding

Answer the following questions:

1. What happens if you try to use a variable before it is declared?
2. What is the difference between `let` and `const`?
3. What does `console.log(typeof age, age);` tell you?
4. What is a function and why are they useful?

5. Why does the code inside an event handler not run immediately?
6. What problem does === solve compared to ==?
7. What are the three common steps in DOM manipulation?
8. Why is `textContent` safer than `innerHTML`?
9. What is event delegation and why is it useful?
10. What does `document.querySelector("#id")` return?

Links

Here are the most authoritative and widely accepted JavaScript references you should know about. These are not blogs or opinion pieces. They are the sources that define how JavaScript actually works.

MDN JavaScript Guide

MDN Web Docs is the de facto standard documentation for JavaScript on the web. It is maintained by Mozilla with contributions from browser vendors and the wider web community.

`https://developer.mozilla.org/en-US/docs/Web/JavaScript/Guide`

This is the best starting point for learners. It explains JavaScript concepts progressively, with examples and clear language. It is especially strong on fundamentals like variables, functions, scope, objects, and the DOM.

MDN JavaScript Reference

This is the encyclopedic reference. Every global object, method, operator, and syntax form lives here. When you want to know exactly what something does, this is where you end up.

`https://developer.mozilla.org/en-US/docs/Web/JavaScript/Reference`

ECMAScript Language Specification

ECMAScript is the formal standard that defines JavaScript. It is maintained by Ecma International, specifically **Technical Committee 39 (TC39)**. Browsers implement this specification.

`https://tc39.es/ecma262/`

This document is precise, exhaustive, and not written for beginners. You do not read it cover to cover. You consult it when you want to understand edge cases, exact semantics, or why JavaScript behaves the way it does in strange situations.

For readers who are curious but not masochistic, MDN often links directly to relevant parts of the spec and explains them in human terms. That is the healthiest way to approach it.

MDN JavaScript Best Practices

This guide focuses on writing readable, maintainable JavaScript rather than clever code. It covers naming, structure, avoiding common mistakes, and writing code that ages well.

`https://developer.mozilla.org/en-US/docs/Learn/JavaScript/Best_practices`

MDN Using Strict Mode

Strict mode removes some of JavaScript's worst historical footguns and makes errors fail loudly instead of silently. Even if you do not introduce it formally yet, this page explains why JavaScript behaves the way it does.

`https://developer.mozilla.org/en-US/docs/Web/JavaScript/Reference/Strict_mode`

Airbnb JavaScript Style Guide

This is one of the most cited JavaScript style guides in the industry. You do not have to agree with every rule, but it strongly promotes consistency, clarity, and avoiding error-prone patterns. Many linters and tools are built around it. While not an official standards body, it is influential because large teams actually use it.

`https://github.com/airbnb/javascript`

Google JavaScript Style Guide

Another conservative, production-focused guide that emphasizes readability and long-term maintainability over cleverness.

`https://google.github.io/styleguide/jsguide.html`

Summary

In this chapter, you learned:

- What JavaScript is and why it is the piece that makes web pages interactive rather than static
- How to declare and use variables with `let` and `const`, and how JavaScript data types behave
- How to write and call functions to structure code and avoid repetition

- How to make decisions with `if` statements and how to repeat work using loops and work with lists of data
- How to use the browser console and `console.log` to inspect values and debug code
- How to respond to user actions by hooking up event handlers with `addEventListener`
- How to select elements, change text, read input values, and update the UI in real time
- How to create, insert, remove, and modify elements dynamically
- How to use classes and `data-*` attributes to connect JavaScript logic with CSS styling
- How event bubbling and event delegation simplify interactive code

JavaScript gives you a huge amount of flexibility. You can write code quickly, change it easily, and build interactive experiences with very little setup. But that flexibility comes at a cost. As your code grows, it becomes easier to introduce subtle bugs, pass the wrong data around, or break something without realizing it. So far, you have avoided those problems by being careful and checking your work. In the next chapter, you will see a different approach with TypeScript.

TypeScript builds on everything you have learned about JavaScript, but adds a system for describing your data and catching mistakes before your code runs. Instead of finding errors in the browser, you find them as you write the code.

6

TypeScript – Safer JavaScript

TypeScript is a programming language that builds on JavaScript by adding a static type system. TypeScript lets you describe what kind of data your variables, function parameters, and return values should have, and it checks that your code follows those rules before it runs.

The most important thing to understand is this: TypeScript is not a replacement for JavaScript. It is a layer on top of JavaScript. You write TypeScript, and a compiler turns it into plain JavaScript that browsers can run. The browser never sees TypeScript. It only ever runs JavaScript.

So why bother with TypeScript at all? Because once JavaScript projects get bigger, it becomes easier to pass the wrong data around, misspell a property name, or make a change that breaks something somewhere else without warning. TypeScript helps by making your assumptions explicit. It lets your editor and compiler catch more mistakes while you are writing the code, before those mistakes turn into runtime bugs.

By the end of this chapter, you will have a clear understanding of why TypeScript exists and when it is worth using. You will set up a basic TypeScript environment, write and compile some TypeScript code, and use common types and interfaces. You will also see how types make JavaScript code easier to change safely as a project grows.

Do not try to memorize every bit of syntax. Focus on why types are useful, what they can and cannot protect you from, and how they describe the data moving through your program.

In this chapter, we will cover the following topics:

- Why TypeScript?
- Setting up TypeScript
- Basic types and interfaces
- Hands-on exercise: making TypeScript work for you

Suggested chatbot prompts with example responses for this chapter can be found at the following link: `https://github.com/markjprice/web-dev-ai/blob/main/prompts/ch06-ts/readme.md`

Why TypeScript?

TypeScript exists because large JavaScript codebases get hard to trust.

Comparing JavaScript to TypeScript

JavaScript is dynamically typed. That means variables can hold any kind of value, and their type can change over time:

```
let value = 42;
value = "forty-two";
value = true;
```

The preceding code is perfectly valid JavaScript. Sometimes that flexibility is convenient. More often, especially in larger codebases, it becomes a source of bugs. You pass the wrong value to a function, mistype a property name, or misunderstand what a variable contains, and the error only shows up at runtime, possibly in a user's browser.

TypeScript addresses this by letting you say what you mean up front by suffixing a variable name with a colon `:` followed by a data type like `number`:

```
let value: number = 42;
value = "forty-two"; // Error
```

Now the mistake is caught immediately by your code editor or build process, as shown in *Figure 6.1* and in the following output:

```
Type 'string' is not assignable to type 'number'.
```

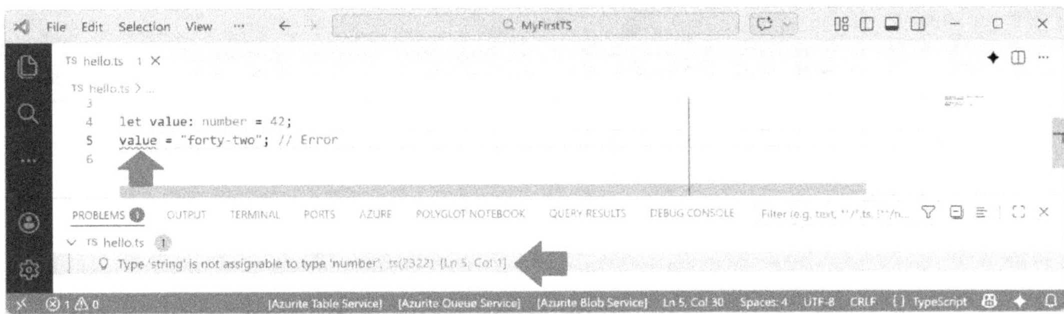

Figure 6.1: VS Code showing a type error using TypeScript

You see the mistake while writing the code, not later when you click through the app.

TypeScript tooling

Another reason TypeScript caught on is that the tooling is good. Because types describe what values are expected, editors can give far better autocomplete, inline documentation, and refactoring support.

A newer reason it matters is that it pairs well with AI coding tools. As developers rely more on AI to generate code, TypeScript acts as a safety net, catching incorrect assumptions, type mismatches, and incomplete logic early. AI-generated code often looks right before you notice the small but dangerous mistakes. TypeScript flags many of those mistakes while you are still editing the code.

If you rely heavily on AI and skip TypeScript, you are making life harder for yourself. TypeScript doesn't eliminate that risk, but it dramatically reduces the chance that bad AI output slips through unnoticed.

When you call a function in TypeScript, your editor can tell you:

- Which arguments are required
- Which are optional
- What type each argument expects
- What the function returns

In plain JavaScript, the editor often has to guess about data types. In TypeScript, it knows.

TypeScript is especially helpful when you are reading other people's code. JavaScript projects depend heavily on libraries and frameworks. With TypeScript, those libraries come with type definitions that describe their APIs precisely. You can explore how something works just by typing and reading hints, instead of constantly checking documentation or examples.

Prompt: How does TypeScript help when working with JSON data returned from an API?

Is TypeScript necessary?

Strictly speaking, it is not necessary. You can build entire websites and applications using only JavaScript, and many people do. However, once a project grows beyond a certain size, the lack of types starts to hurt. Bugs become harder to track down. Refactoring becomes risky. Making changes feels like defusing a bomb.

Refactoring is the process of improving the structure and readability of existing code without changing what it does. The goal is not to add new features or fix bugs, but to make the code easier to understand, maintain, and extend. This might include renaming variables for clarity, breaking large functions into smaller ones, removing duplication, or reorganizing files. Good refactoring keeps behavior the same while improving the design. In practice, this means you should always have tests or a way to verify that your code still works after changes. Tools like TypeScript and code editors make refactoring safer by highlighting where changes are needed and catching mistakes early.

TypeScript shifts that balance. It makes large codebases safer to change and easier to comprehend. It turns many runtime errors into compile-time errors. That tradeoff is why most frontend frameworks and many backend JavaScript projects now default to TypeScript.

One important reassurance for beginners: you do not need to master TypeScript on day one. Good JavaScript fundamentals still matter more. TypeScript makes JavaScript stricter and more explicit, but it does not replace understanding how the language works.

This is the same theme you saw in the JavaScript chapter. AI tools can produce code quickly, but they do not automatically know which values are allowed, which cases are missing, or which change might break another part of the program. TypeScript helps when you already have a clear idea of the data your code should accept and return. The types give that idea a written form. If your understanding is vague, TypeScript will not fix it. It will just give you more errors to read

A simple comparison: JavaScript lets values move freely;TypeScript asks you to describe those values before you pass them around. TypeScript makes more sense when you see it as part of the tooling around JavaScript, not just as extra syntax.

Prompt: Why doesn't TypeScript protect me from all runtime errors?

How TypeScript fits into the JavaScript toolchain

TypeScript adds a compile step to your workflow. You write `.ts` files, and the TypeScript compiler (`tsc`) checks types and outputs `.js` files. Those output files are what actually run in the browser or on the server:

```
TypeScript (.ts/.tsx) → TypeScript compiler or build tool → JavaScript
(.js) → Browser runs JavaScript
```

This sounds like extra work at first, but web development tooling usually hides most of it once the setup is done.

Prompt: Why do some developers use the term *transpile* about TypeScript?

What tools work best with TypeScript

VS Code is built by Microsoft, uses TypeScript internally, and has first-class TypeScript support out of the box. You get instant type checking, autocomplete, inline errors, and refactoring tools with zero configuration. This is not an accident. VS Code and TypeScript evolved together.

JetBrains IDEs like **WebStorm** also have excellent TypeScript support, especially for refactoring and navigation in large codebases. They tend to use more resources, but their navigation and refactoring tools are strong.

Linting and formatting tools matter more with TypeScript than with plain JavaScript. **ESLint** is commonly used alongside TypeScript to enforce consistent coding style and catch logic issues that are not strictly type errors. For example, it can warn if you declare a variable and never use it, forget to handle a case in a `switch` statement, or accidentally use == instead of ===. It can also enforce consistent patterns, such as always using `const` instead of `let` when a value does not change.

Prettier is often paired with it to keep formatting consistent and, frankly, boring. For example, automatically fixing indentation, spacing, and line breaks so that all code looks the same regardless of who wrote it.

Prompt: How does TypeScript handle existing JavaScript files in a project?

Why teams commit to TypeScript long-term

TypeScript pays off most clearly over time. The first few files may feel more verbose. After a few weeks or months, teams notice concrete benefits: safer refactoring, clearer APIs, fewer runtime surprises, and better onboarding for new developers. Types act as living documentation that cannot drift out of sync with the code.

That is why TypeScript has gone from optional to normal in much of professional JavaScript work. Not because JavaScript is bad, but because large systems need more guarantees than JavaScript alone was designed to provide.

JavaScript is what runs on the web. TypeScript is one of the main ways teams make larger JavaScript codebases safer to change.

Prompt: How do professional teams gradually introduce TypeScript into an existing JavaScript codebase?

Now let's set up TypeScript on your computer.

Which frameworks and libraries use TypeScript

TypeScript is now common in the web development world. Some frameworks use it by default, others strongly encourage it.

Angular is the most explicit example. Angular is written in TypeScript and expects application code to be written in TypeScript. The framework's design, decorators, and tooling assume types are present.

React is more flexible. React itself is written in JavaScript, but TypeScript is now the dominant choice for serious React projects. The React ecosystem has excellent type definitions, and most tutorials, templates, and professional codebases use React with TypeScript rather than plain JavaScript.

Vue sits somewhere in the middle. Vue.js started as a JavaScript-first framework, but Vue has first-class TypeScript support, and the core library itself is now written in TypeScript. For anything beyond small demos, TypeScript is increasingly the norm.

On the backend, TypeScript is extremely common with **Node.js** frameworks such as **NestJS** and is widely used with **Express**. Even though Node.js runs JavaScript, many teams prefer to write TypeScript and compile it before deployment.

In practice, frameworks aimed at bigger teams and bigger codebases usually expect TypeScript or strongly encourage it.

Declaration files and third-party libraries

One of the reasons TypeScript works so well in real projects is its support for declaration files. Declaration files describe the shape of existing JavaScript code so that TypeScript can type-check it, even when that code was never written in TypeScript.

A declaration file uses the `.d.ts` extension. It contains type information only. There is no executable code inside it. At runtime, JavaScript still runs exactly the same code it always did. The declaration file exists purely to help TypeScript understand what functions, objects, and classes are available, and how they are meant to be used.

For example, a JavaScript library might expose a function like this at runtime:

```
export function formatDate(date, format) {
  // implementation
}
```

A corresponding declaration file might describe it like this:

```
export function formatDate(date: Date, format: string): string;
```

With that declaration in place, your editor can now give accurate autocomplete, parameter hints, and error messages when you use the library from TypeScript.

Most popular JavaScript libraries already ship with their own declaration files, or they are available via the DefinitelyTyped repository and installed automatically using `npm` packages that start with `@types/`. When you install a library and TypeScript *just knows* how to use it, declaration files are the reason.

This also explains an important design decision in TypeScript: types are separate from implementation. You can add strong typing on top of existing JavaScript without rewriting it. That is why TypeScript was able to spread so quickly across the JavaScript ecosystem instead of requiring a clean break from the past.

Declaration files connect dynamic JavaScript libraries to TypeScript's static checks. They allow TypeScript to bring safety, tooling, and clarity to libraries that were never designed with types in mind, which is exactly why TypeScript integrates so smoothly into JavaScript development.

Who created TypeScript and why

TypeScript was created at Microsoft and first released in 2012. The lead architect was *Anders Hejlsberg*, an expert in programming language design. Before TypeScript, he was the chief designer of Turbo Pascal, Delphi, and later C#. TypeScript borrows many ideas from statically typed languages like C# while still respecting JavaScript's runtime model.

Microsoft's motivation was practical. They were building very large JavaScript applications, including complex web tooling, and found that JavaScript's dynamic nature made refactoring risky and bugs easy to introduce. TypeScript was designed to make JavaScript scale better without breaking compatibility with the web.

Why future TypeScript versions may break your code

TypeScript has historically been very careful about backward compatibility. Most upgrades have been smooth, and older code usually continues to work.

That is starting to change.

Recent versions, especially 5.9 and 6.0, are laying the groundwork for more disruptive changes in 7.0 and beyond. Microsoft and the TypeScript team have been unusually direct about this: they are actively warning developers to prepare.

The future changes are about cleaning up the past and tightening the rules.

You can think of the recent and upcoming versions like this:

- **TypeScript 5.9**: Still part of the stable and familiar TypeScript era. Improvements focus on performance, inference, and tooling.
- **TypeScript 6.0**: A transition release. Introduces deprecations and stricter defaults. Its main purpose is to prepare your codebase for breaking changes to come.

- **TypeScript 7.0**: A major shift. Expected to remove deprecated features and introduce deeper changes, including a new compiler implementation written in Go for performance.

To be blunt: 6.0 is the warning. 7.0 is the enforcement.

The big change coming in 7.0 is TypeScript is becoming less tolerant. For years, TypeScript tried to accommodate a wide range of JavaScript patterns, including older and loosely structured code. That flexibility made adoption easier, but it also created inconsistency and edge cases.

The future direction is:

- Remove legacy options
- Enforce stricter defaults
- Reduce ambiguity in module resolution and configuration
- Push developers toward modern JavaScript patterns

For example:

- Configuration options like baseUrl are being deprecated and scheduled for removal in TypeScript 7.0
- Older module systems and targets (such as AMD or ES5) are being phased out
- Compiler defaults are becoming stricter, sometimes without explicit opt-in

This reflects a deliberate decision: TypeScript is now prioritizing correctness and consistency over backward compatibility.

Preparing for the future with TypeScript 7

The TypeScript team is giving early warnings because these changes can break real projects. If you upgrade to version 7.0 blindly from an older setup, your build may fail due to deprecated options. Imports may stop resolving the way they used to, and previously working code may now produce errors.

To soften the transition, TypeScript introduced mechanisms like:

```
{
  "ignoreDeprecations": "6.0"
}
```

This lets you temporarily suppress warnings, but it is only a short-term escape hatch.

Older TypeScript versions often try to make things work but newer versions are more likely to say this is ambiguous or unsafe. That shift shows up in several ways:

- Stricter type checking becomes the default
- Fewer implicit behaviors
- Less tolerance for outdated configuration

TypeScript is becoming stricter because current JavaScript systems are larger, more complex, and increasingly assisted by AI-generated code. The language is shifting to match that reality.

And that connects directly to a broader change in development:

- Even the weakest AI can produce code that runs.
- The harder skill is keeping behavior correct as the project changes.

TypeScript's newer versions are pushing you in that direction, whether you like it or not.

Prompt: What deprecations or breaking changes should I check before upgrading my project to the latest TypeScript version?

Setting up TypeScript

TypeScript is not something the browser runs directly, so setting it up is really about preparing your development machine to write TypeScript, check it, and turn it into JavaScript. Once that pipeline exists, everything else builds on top of it.

Prerequisite: Node.js

TypeScript is distributed as a command-line tool and runs on Node.js. Even if your final code runs in the browser, Node.js is used during development.

On Windows, download the LTS (Long Term Support) version from the official Node.js website: `https://nodejs.org/en/download`, as shown in *Figure 6.2*:

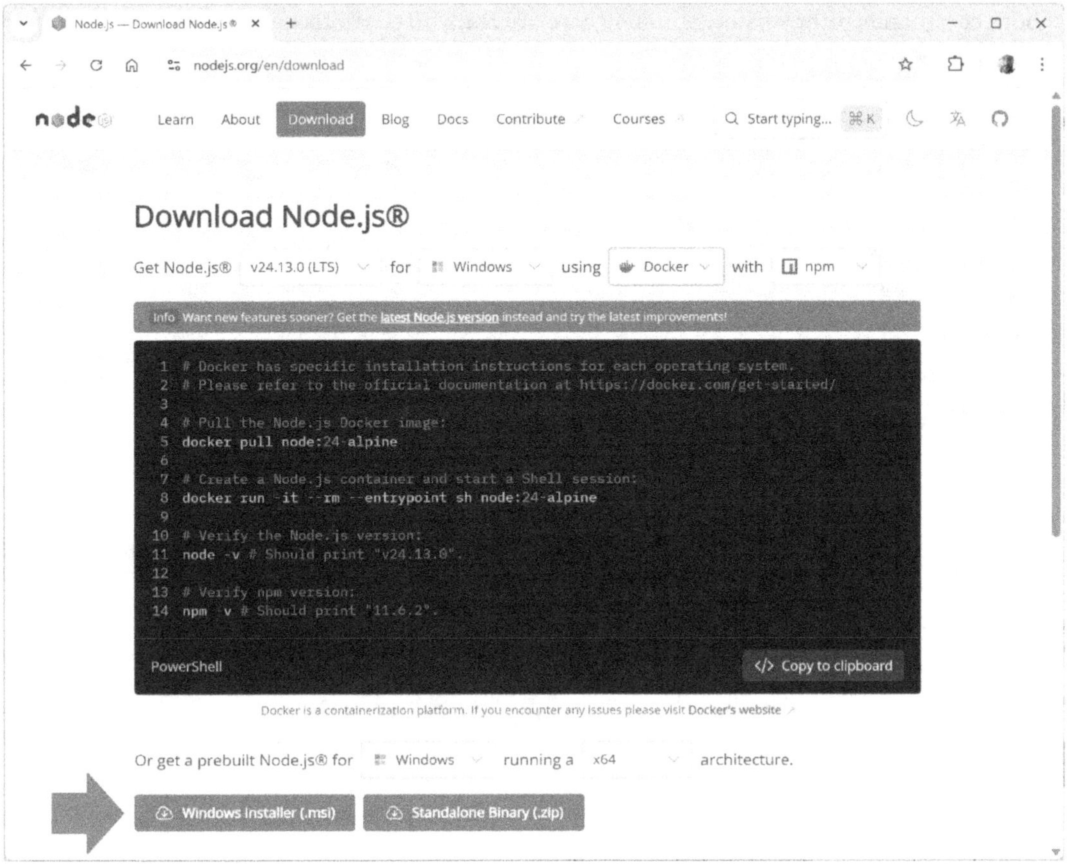

Figure 6.2: Downloading node.js LTS

Run the Windows installer for Node.js. Accept the defaults. This installs both `node` and `npm` (the **Node Package Manager**), which you will use constantly.

On macOS, you can either download the same installer or install Node via Homebrew. On Linux, most distributions provide Node via their package manager. The exact command varies by distro, but the goal is the same: get a recent LTS version.

To confirm installation on any platform, open a terminal or command prompt and run:

```
node --version
npm --version
```

If both commands print version numbers, you are ready to continue, as shown in the following output on February 1, 2026:

```
v24.13.0
11.6.2
```

The most recent LTS version at the time of writing in April 2026 is v24.14.1. The most recent Current version is v25.9.0. The exact version does not matter here. Any recent LTS version will do.

Installing the TypeScript compiler

TypeScript is installed via `npm`. You can install it globally so the `tsc` command is available everywhere:

```
npm install -g typescript
```

Warning! If `npm --version` prints a valid number but any other `npm` command including `npm install` crashes with the error `Class extends value undefined`..., this indicates `npm` is crashing while loading its own dependencies. That typically happens when `npm`'s installed files are inconsistent with the Node runtime or are partially corrupted. Issues around this error resolve via removing leftover Node/`npm` files and reinstalling Node LTS.

On macOS and Linux, you may need to prefix this with `sudo`, depending on how Node was installed.

Verify the installation:

```
tsc --version
```

The output on February 1, 2026:

```
Version 5.9.3
```

At this point, you have the TypeScript compiler installed. That alone is enough to write and compile TypeScript.

Editor support

TypeScript's real strength shows up inside your code editor.

If you are using VS Code, you already have excellent TypeScript support. There is nothing to install. As soon as you open a `.ts` file, you get inline errors, autocomplete, and type hints.

If you are using a JetBrains IDE such as WebStorm or Rider, TypeScript support is also built in and very strong.

Your first TypeScript project

Create a new folder named `Chapter06`, and a subfolder named `MyFirstTS`. Then change to the `MyFirstTS` directory:

```
cd MyFirstTS
```

In the `MyFirstTS` directory, create a file called `hello.ts`:

```
let message: string = "Hello, TypeScript";
console.log(message);
```

Now compile the TypeScript file:

```
tsc hello.ts
```

You should see a new file appear: `hello.js`. Open it, and you will notice something important. The types are gone:

```
var message = "Hello, TypeScript";
console.log(message);
```

This is the key idea to hold onto. TypeScript is a development-time tool. The output is plain JavaScript.

Good practice: Note the output uses `var` instead of `let`. That's because the TypeScript compiler transformed the TypeScript into an older version of JavaScript that more browsers can run. If you know that you do not need to support old browsers, then you can configure the TypeScript compiler to target `ES2020` or higher in a `tsconfig.json` file, and then the output will use `let` and `const` in its JavaScript. You will see how to do this later in this chapter.

You can now run the JavaScript file with Node:

```
node hello.js
```

The output should be:

```
Hello, TypeScript
```

If that works, your toolchain is functioning correctly.

When you call `console.log` in a browser, it writes to the **Console** tab in **Developer Tools**. When you call `console.log` in code run by Node.js, it writes to the standard output, like a command prompt or terminal window.

Introducing tsconfig.json

For anything beyond toy examples, you do not want to pass options to `tsc` every time. Instead, you create a configuration file called `tsconfig.json` at the root of your project.

In the `MyFirstTS` folder, generate a starter config:

```
tsc --init
```

This creates a file with many commented options:

```
{
  // Visit https://aka.ms/tsconfig to read more about this file
  "compilerOptions": {
    // File Layout
    // "rootDir": "./src",
    // "outDir": "./dist",

    // Environment Settings
    // See also https://aka.ms/tsconfig/module
    "module": "nodenext",
    "target": "esnext",
    "types": [],
    // For nodejs:
    // "lib": ["esnext"],
    // "types": ["node"],
    // and npm install -D @types/node
```

```
    // Other Outputs
    "sourceMap": true,
    "declaration": true,
    "declarationMap": true,

    // Stricter Typechecking Options
    "noUncheckedIndexedAccess": true,
    "exactOptionalPropertyTypes": true,

    // Style Options
    // "noImplicitReturns": true,
    // "noImplicitOverride": true,
    // "noUnusedLocals": true,
    // "noUnusedParameters": true,
    // "noFallthroughCasesInSwitch": true,
    // "noPropertyAccessFromIndexSignature": true,

    // Recommended Options
    "strict": true,
    "jsx": "react-jsx",
    "verbatimModuleSyntax": true,
    "isolatedModules": true,
    "noUncheckedSideEffectImports": true,
    "moduleDetection": "force",
    "skipLibCheck": true,
  }
}
```

You do not need to understand all of them yet. You only need the basics for now:

- `compilerOptions` control how strict TypeScript is and what kind of JavaScript it produces
- `target` controls which JavaScript features are allowed in the output
- `strict` enables safer type-checking rules
- `jsx` is for React projects, which we will not use in this book, so you can ignore or remove this option

Prompt: What does strict mode actually enable under the hood in TypeScript? What kinds of bugs TypeScript cannot catch, even with strict mode enabled?

A simple beginner-friendly setup looks like this:

```
{
  "compilerOptions": {
    "target": "ES2020",
    "strict": true,
    "outDir": "dist"
  }
}
```

Now, instead of compiling individual files, you can just run:

```
tsc
```

TypeScript will compile all `.ts` files in the project and place the output JavaScript in the `dist` folder.

The `target` setting controls which version of JavaScript TypeScript generates when it compiles your code. This affects which language features are allowed and how syntax is transformed. Common options include:

- `ES3`: This is a historical default dating back to early TypeScript versions, when supporting very old browsers (like Internet Explorer 8) was still common. In practice, almost no current project should rely on this default. ES3 lacks support for many standard JavaScript features, so TypeScript will aggressively transform your code, often producing verbose and harder-to-read output.
- `ES5`: Very old JavaScript, supported by almost all browsers. Only useful for legacy environments.
- `ES2015` (`ES6`): Introduces classes, arrow functions, and modules. A reasonable baseline for older but still widely supported environments.
- `ES2017` / `ES2018` / `ES2019`: Incremental improvements such as async/await (`ES2017`) and other modern features. Often used when targeting slightly older Node.js or browsers.
- `ES2020`: A popular baseline. Supports features like optional chaining and nullish coalescing with minimal transformation.
- `ES2022` and later (`ESNext`): Very up-to-date JavaScript with little or no down-level transformation. Best for current Node.js versions or recent browsers.

Good practice: Always set `target` yourself, to `ES2020` or later. The default exists for backward compatibility, not because it is a good choice today.

Prompt: Please explain the most important `tsconfig.json` options for beginners, and which ones are safe to ignore at first.

Platform notes (Windows vs macOS vs Linux)

From a TypeScript perspective, there are very few platform differences. It's good to note that:

- The TypeScript compiler behaves the same everywhere
- `.ts` files are portable across all operating systems
- The output `.js` files run the same in browsers

The main differences are:

- Command-line syntax for installing Node or global packages
- File system case sensitivity on Linux and macOS
- Path separators (\ vs /), which tooling usually handles for you

As long as you avoid hardcoding paths and rely on standard tools, your setup will work the same across platforms.

Setup summary

At this point, you should understand that setting up TypeScript really means three things:

1. Installing Node.js
2. Installing the TypeScript compiler
3. Creating a basic project with a config file

Everything else, frameworks, bundlers, and advanced build tools, builds on top of this foundation. Now that this setup is in place, you are ready to start learning types and interfaces.

Basic types and interfaces

This is where TypeScript starts to justify its existence. You already know how to write JavaScript. What TypeScript adds is the ability to describe your data in a precise, checkable way. Once you understand a small set of basic types and how interfaces work, the rest of the language becomes much easier to understand.

Basic types

TypeScript starts with the same primitive values you already use in JavaScript, but lets you be explicit about them.

A variable can be given a type using a **type annotation**. The annotation comes after the variable name, separated by a colon:

```
let count: number = 0;
let title: string = "Dashboard";
let isLoggedIn: boolean = false;
```

Here is what TypeScript is doing in the preceding code:

- `count` must always hold a number
- `title` must always hold a string
- `isLoggedIn` must always hold a boolean

If you later try to assign an incompatible value, TypeScript flags it immediately:

```
count = "zero";        // Error
isLoggedIn = "yes";    // Error
```

These errors appear in your editor as you type. The code may still compile depending on settings, but you are warned early instead of discovering the problem at runtime.

Prompt: How does TypeScript decide whether code compiles successfully even when there are type errors?

Strings deserve a quick special mention. TypeScript fully supports JavaScript template literals and infers their types correctly:

```
let userName: string = "Mark";
let message: string = `Hello, ${userName}`;
```

Prompt: What is the never type, and in what situations does it appear in real code?

Type inference

You do not always need to write type annotations. TypeScript is often smart enough to infer the type from the initial value:

```
let total = 100;        // Inferred as number
let label = "Total";    // Inferred as string
```

From this point on, `total` behaves as if you had written `: number`. If you later try to assign a `string`, TypeScript complains.

Good practice: Let TypeScript infer simple local variables, but be explicit at the boundaries of your program, such as function parameters and return values.

Arrays

Arrays are typed by describing the type of their elements followed by a pair of square brackets to indicate it is an array, like `number[]` for an array of `number` values:

```
let scores: number[] = [10, 20, 30];
let names: string[] = ["Alice", "Bob", "Charlie"];
```

This means every element in `scores` must be a `number`, and when calling the `push` method to add a new item, it must also therefore be a `number` value rather than another type like `string`:

```
scores.push(40);    // OK
scores.push("40");  // Error
```

Arrays are everywhere in DOM and API code, so this single rule pays off quickly.

Objects and inline types

You can describe the shape of an object directly:

```
let user: { name: string; age: number } = {
  name: "Mark",
  age: 42
};
```

This is fine for small, one-off objects, but it gets noisy and repetitive fast. That is where interfaces come in.

Interfaces

An **interface** is a named description of an object's shape. It does not exist at runtime. It is purely for TypeScript's type system:

```
interface User {
  name: string;
  age: number;
}
```

You can now use this interface anywhere you need a `User`:

```
let user: User = {
  name: "Mark",
  age: 42
};
```

If you forget a property or add one that does not belong, TypeScript catches it:

```
let user: User = {
  name: "Mark"
  // Error: age is missing
};
```

Interfaces are great when used with function parameters:

```
function formatUser(user: User): string {
  return `${user.name} (${user.age})`;
}
```

Prompt: Please explain function overloads in TypeScript and show a realistic example where they improve clarity.

Now the function clearly documents what it expects (a `User` object) and what it returns (a `string` value). If you pass the wrong shape, the error appears at the line where you call the function, not deep inside the function.

Prompt: What is the difference between an interface and a type alias in TypeScript, and when should I prefer one over the other?

The type keyword

The `type` keyword creates a type alias, meaning a name for any type expression. While `interface` describes the shape of objects, `type` can name any type, including unions, intersections, and primitives:

```
type Role = "admin" | "editor" | "viewer";
type ID = number | string;
```

Most TypeScript projects follow this convention: use `interface` for object shapes and `type` for everything else.

Structural typing vs nominal typing

TypeScript uses a **structural type system**. This means that compatibility between types is based on their shape, not on their name. If two values have the same structure, TypeScript considers them compatible, even if they come from different interfaces or type declarations.

For example:

```
interface User {
  name: string;
  age: number;
}
```

```
interface Person {
  name: string;
  age: number;
}

const u: User = { name: "Mark", age: 42 };
const p: Person = u; // OK
```

In the preceding code, even though `User` and `Person` are different interfaces, they describe the same shape. TypeScript allows the assignment because the required properties and their types match.

This is different from nominal typing, which is used by languages such as Java and C#. In a **nominal type system**, the name of the type matters. Two types with identical structure are still considered distinct unless there is an explicit relationship between them, such as inheritance or interface implementation.

Structural typing fits naturally with JavaScript, where objects are defined by the properties they have, not by explicit class declarations. It also makes TypeScript more flexible when working with plain objects, JSON data, and values returned from APIs.

However, this flexibility can sometimes be surprising. Because only the shape matters, TypeScript does not care where an object came from, only whether it has the right properties:

```
function printUser(user: User) {
  console.log(user.name);
}

printUser({ name: "Alice", age: 30 }); // OK
```

The object passed into the `printUser` function was never explicitly declared as a `User`, but it matches the required shape, so TypeScript accepts it.

The practical takeaway is that interfaces in TypeScript describe what a value must look like, not what it is called. That design choice keeps TypeScript lightweight and interoperable with JavaScript, while still providing strong guarantees about how data is used.

Literal types

So far, we have used types like `string`, `number`, and `boolean` to describe broad categories of values. Sometimes, that is still too loose. In real applications, a variable may only be allowed to hold one of a small, fixed set of specific values. This is where **literal types** come in.

A literal type says not just *this is a string*, but *this is this exact string*.

For example:

```
let status: "active" | "inactive";

status = "active";      // OK
status = "inactive";    // OK
status = "pending";     // Error
```

Here, `status` is still a string at runtime, but at development time TypeScript enforces that it can only be one of the two allowed values. Any typo or unexpected value is caught immediately by the editor or compiler.

Literal types are especially useful when modeling states, roles, or modes. For example:

```
type Role = "admin" | "editor" | "viewer";

interface User {
  name: string;
  role: Role;
}
```

Now the `role` property can only ever be one of those three values. This removes an entire class of bugs caused by misspellings or inconsistent conventions such as `"Admin"`, `"administrator"`, or `"user"`.

Literal types also work with numbers and Booleans, though string literals are the most common in everyday code. Here's how you might limit the possible values to represent the roll of a die:

```
type DieRoll = 1 | 2 | 3 | 4 | 5 | 6;
```

A useful way to think about literal types is that they sit between free-form values and enums. They give you strong guarantees and excellent editor support without introducing extra runtime constructs. As with interfaces, literal types exist only at development time. When your code runs, they disappear, leaving plain JavaScript behind.

TypeScript has the `enum` keyword that is a construct that defines a set of named constants. However, TypeScript projects often prefer literal union types because they're simpler and don't add runtime code. You may see enums used in older codebases and frameworks like Angular.

When a value must come from a short list, use a literal union type. It catches misspellings and makes the allowed values obvious.

Prompt: Please explain excess property checks in TypeScript and why object literals are treated differently from variables.

Union types

Sometimes a value is not limited to a single type, but it is still limited to a known set of possibilities. A **union type** lets you express exactly that. It says that a value can be one of several types, but not anything else.

You define a union type using the pipe character |, which you can read as *or*:

```
let id: number | string;

id = 42;          // OK
id = "42";        // OK
id = true;        // Error
```

In the preceding code example, `id` is allowed to be either a `number` or a `string`, but nothing else. This pattern is very common when working with APIs, user input, or database identifiers that may come in different forms.

Union types become even more useful when combined with control flow. TypeScript narrows the type based on checks you perform in your code:

```
function formatId(id: number | string): string {
  if (typeof id === "number") {
    return id.toFixed(0);
  }
  return id.toUpperCase();
}
```

Inside each branch, TypeScript understands exactly which type you are working with and allows only the appropriate operations. If you forget to handle one of the cases, the compiler can warn you.

Union types are also commonly used with literal types to describe fixed sets of values:

```
type Status = "active" | "inactive" | "pending";
```

This creates a union of string literal types, which is ideal for modeling states and modes in an application.

A useful way to remember it:

- Basic types describe categories of values
- Literal types describe exact values
- Union types describe a controlled choice between them.

Like interfaces and other types in TypeScript, union types exist only during development. They do not affect runtime behavior, but they dramatically reduce ambiguity while you are writing and changing code.

When a value can legitimately be more than one thing, union types let you say so explicitly, without falling back to overly permissive types like any.

Optional properties

Not every object has all properties all the time. Interfaces support optional properties using ?:

```
interface User {
  name: string;
  age?: number;
}
```

Now both of these are valid:

```
const a: User = { name: "Mark", age: 42 };
const b: User = { name: "Guest" };
```

When you use an optional property, TypeScript forces you to acknowledge that it might be missing:

```
function describe(user: User): string {
  if (user.age !== undefined) {
    return `${user.name} is ${user.age}`;
  }
  return `${user.name} (age unknown)`;
}
```

This prevents a large class of *cannot read property of undefined* errors.

Prompt: What are readonly properties in TypeScript, and how do they help prevent bugs?

Making absence explicit with null and undefined

In JavaScript, `null` and `undefined` are easy to ignore until they cause a runtime error. But in TypeScript, they are much harder to ignore because they become part of the stricter type system. This is one of the biggest practical differences between JavaScript and TypeScript.

With strict type checking enabled (which you should be using), `null` and `undefined` are not automatically allowed. You must explicitly say when a value can be missing (`undefined`).

For example:

```
let name: string = "Mark";
name = undefined; // Error
```

If a value really might be missing, you must say so:

```
let name: string | undefined;
```

Now TypeScript understands that `name` may or may not exist.

You already saw the ? syntax with optional properties:

```
interface User {
  name: string;
  age?: number;
}
```

Now I can explain that the ? does not just mean optional. It really means:

```
age: number | undefined
```

That is why TypeScript forces you to check:

```
if (user.age !== undefined) {
  console.log(user.age);
}
```

This is TypeScript forcing you to deal with reality: the value might not be there.

The distinction between `null` vs `undefined` in TypeScript still exists:

- `undefined` usually means "not provided" or "not set"
- `null` usually means "explicitly empty"

But in practice, many teams standardize on one (often `undefined`) to reduce confusion.

If you want to allow both, you must say so:

```
let value: string | null | undefined;
```

Most common JavaScript runtime errors look like this:

```
Cannot read property 'x' of undefined
```

TypeScript pushes those problems earlier. Instead of failing at runtime, you get an error while writing the code:

```
"Object is possibly undefined"
"Type 'undefined' is not assignable to type 'string'"
```

That forces you to stop assuming values exist and start handling the missing case explicitly.

Good practice: If a value might be missing, say so in the type. If it must exist, do not include `undefined` or `null`. Handle missing cases explicitly instead of hoping they never happen.

Optional parameters versus default parameter values

TypeScript supports two related but distinct ways of handling function parameters that may not always be provided: optional parameters and default parameter values. They solve similar problems, but they communicate slightly different meanings.

An optional parameter is marked with a question mark:

```
function greet(name?: string): string {
  if (name) {
    return `Hello, ${name}`;
  }
  return "Hello, guest";
}
```

In the preceding code, `name` may be omitted when the function is called. From TypeScript's point of view, an optional parameter is treated as a union with `undefined`. In other words, `name` has the type `string | undefined`. That is why TypeScript forces you to check that it exists before using it as a string.

Default parameter values look similar, but behave differently:

```
function greet(name: string = "guest"): string {
  return `Hello, ${name}`;
}
```

In this case, `name` is not optional from the type system's perspective. It is always a string inside the function body. If the caller omits the argument, JavaScript supplies the default value at runtime, and TypeScript reflects that behavior in its types.

This difference matters when you are writing function logic. With an optional parameter, you must handle the missing case explicitly. With a default value, TypeScript knows the parameter will never be undefined inside the function.

There is also a difference at the call site. Both of these calls are valid in both cases:

```
greet();
greet("Mark");
```

But defaults make the meaning clearer. Optional parameters say *this value might not exist*. Default parameters say *this value always exists but may fall back to a standard value.*

Good practice: Use optional parameters when the absence of a value is meaningful and must be handled explicitly. Use default parameter values when there is a sensible fallback and you want the rest of the function to work with a guaranteed, well-defined type.

Preventing errors instead of catching them

In JavaScript, error handling often means reacting after something goes wrong using `try` and `catch`. TypeScript shifts that balance. Many errors are prevented at compile time, before the code runs at all.

Consider this JavaScript example:

```
function formatName(user) {
  return user.name.toUpperCase();
}
```

If `user` is `null` or missing the `name` property, this fails at runtime.

In TypeScript, you would write:

```
function formatName(user: { name: string }): string {
  return user.name.toUpperCase();
}
```

Now the problem happens earlier:

- If you pass the wrong shape, TypeScript complains immediately
- The error appears when you call the function, not deep inside it

This is the main improvement to error handling in TypeScript compared to JavaScript: you prevent the error instead of catching it later.

TypeScript encourages you to design functions that make invalid states harder to represent.

For example:

```
function greet(name: string | undefined): string {
  if (!name) {
    return "Hello, guest";
  }
  return `Hello, ${name}`;
}
```

The type forces you to handle the missing case. Without TypeScript, it would be easy to forget that check.

But TypeScript does not eliminate runtime errors entirely. You still need `try` and `catch` for:

- Network requests
- File access
- JSON parsing
- Third-party libraries

Example:

```
try {
  const data = JSON.parse(input);
  console.log(data);
} catch (error) {
  console.error("Invalid JSON:", error);
}
```

TypeScript cannot guarantee that input is valid JSON. That is a runtime concern.

To summarize error handling:

- In JavaScript, you write code, you run it, but then you must handle errors when they happen
- In TypeScript, you describe your assumptions in types, many mistakes are caught before running anything, but you still handle truly unpredictable failures at runtime

Good practice: Use types to prevent predictable errors. Use `try` and `catch` for unpredictable ones. Do not use `try` and `catch` to hide type problems.

For example, this is a bad pattern:

```
try {
  user.name.toUpperCase();
} catch {}
```

The better fix is to design the type correctly:

```
if (user && user.name) {
  user.name.toUpperCase();
}
```

Or better yet:

```
function formatUser(user: { name: string }) {
  return user.name.toUpperCase();
}
```

TypeScript does not make your code error-free. It changes when and how errors show up:

- Predictable errors are caught early by types
- Unpredictable errors must be handled at runtime

Interfaces and the DOM

Interfaces become especially useful when dealing with structured data, such as form state or API responses:

```
interface TodoItem {
  id: number;
  text: string;
  done: boolean;
}

const todos: TodoItem[] = [];
```

From this point on, your editor knows exactly what a to-do item looks like. Autocomplete becomes accurate, and mistakes become harder to make.

Summary of basic types and interfaces

At this stage, the goal is not to memorize every possible type. It is to understand the mindset:

- Types describe intent
- Interfaces describe shape
- Errors move earlier in time

TypeScript does not change how your code runs. It changes how confidently you can change it. Once you internalize that, types and interfaces become useful checks while you edit your code.

Prompt: Please explain union types and intersection types in TypeScript with simple, real-world examples.

Now that you've seen the basic types and how to define your own interfaces for your custom types, let's practice what you've learned with some exercises.

Hands-on exercise: making TypeScript work for you

This exercise stays small so you can see how types and interfaces guide you while you edit.

Step 1: Initialize a TypeScript project

In the `Chapter06` folder, create a new folder named `TypesExercise`. In the folder, initialize a TypeScript project, as shown in the following command:

```
tsc --init
```

Step 2: Create a new TypeScript file

In the `Chapter06` folder, in the `TypesExercise` folder, create a file called `profile.ts`.

We will start with a simple interface that describes a user profile:

```
interface Profile {
  name: string;
  email: string;
  isActive: boolean;
}
```

This interface is your contract. Everything else in this file will revolve around it.

Step 3: Create a value that must match the interface

Add the following below the interface:

```
const profile: Profile = {
  name: "Mark",
  email: "mark@example.com",
  isActive: true
};
```

Now deliberately break it. For example, change the `isActive` property value to a string like `"true"`. Your editor should immediately complain, as shown in *Figure 6.3*:

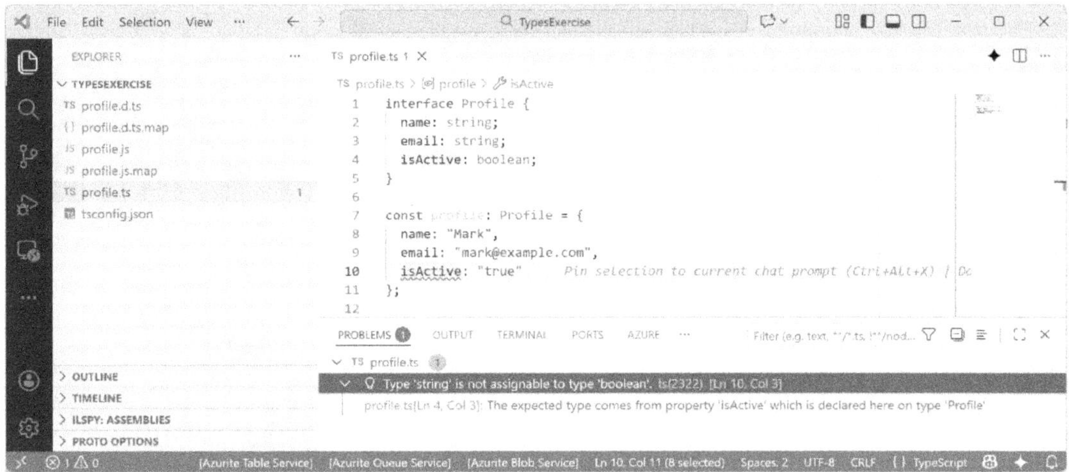

Figure 6.3: TypeScript in VS Code finding a type error

Fix the error and move on.

TypeScript is enforcing the shape of your data before the code ever runs.

Step 4: Add a function with typed parameters and a return value

Now write a function that works with a `Profile`:

```
function describeProfile(profile: Profile): string {
  const status = profile.isActive ? "active" : "inactive";
  return `${profile.name} (${profile.email}) is ${status}`;
}
```

Call the function and log the result:

```
console.log(describeProfile(profile));
```

Compile the project and then run it with Node.js, as shown in *Figure 6.4* and the following commands:

```
tsc
node profile.js
```

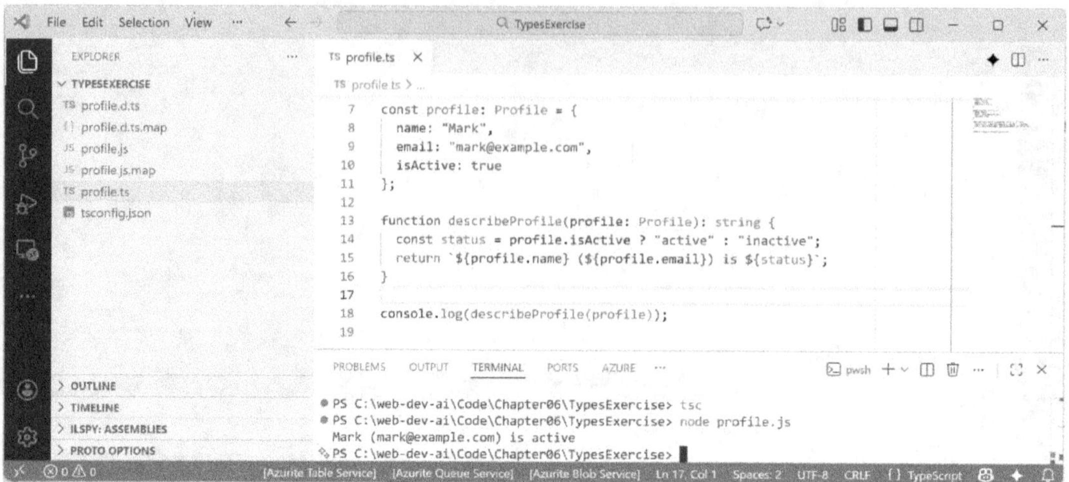

Figure 6.4: Successfully running the profile project

Open `profile.js` and confirm what you see. The interface is gone. The types are gone. Only JavaScript remains.

Good practice: Remember this: interfaces exist to help you write correct code, not to change runtime behavior.

Try passing a variable into `describeProfile` that does not match the interface, for example, a string. Watch where the error appears, as shown in *Figure 6.5*:

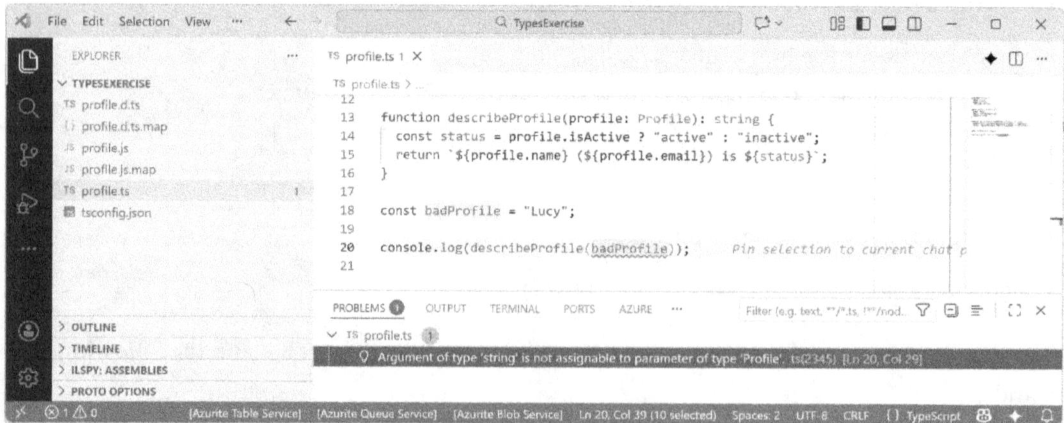

Figure 6.5: Error when passing a wrong data type to a function

Step 5: Introduce an optional property

Extend the interface to support an optional last login date, as highlighted in the following code:

```
interface Profile {
  name: string;
  email: string;
  isActive: boolean;
  lastLogin?: Date;
}
```

Update your data, as highlighted in the following code:

```
const profile: Profile = {
  name: "Mark",
  email: "mark@example.com",
  isActive: true,
  lastLogin: new Date()
};
```

Now update the function so it handles both cases, as highlighted in the following code:

```
function describeProfile(profile: Profile): string {
  const status = profile.isActive ? "active" : "inactive";

  if (profile.lastLogin) {
    return `${profile.name} (${profile.email}) is ${status}. Last login:
${profile.lastLogin.toDateString()}`;
  }

  return `${profile.name} (${profile.email}) is ${status}. Last login
unknown.`;
}
```

Warning! TypeScript forces you to handle the missing case explicitly by checking for the existence of the optional property.

Recompile the project and rerun it with Node.

Step 6: Work with arrays of typed objects

Now introduce a list of profiles, and then loop over the list and log descriptions:

```
const profiles: Profile[] = [
  {
    name: "Ilya",
    email: "ilya@boston-raiders.com",
    isActive: true
  },
  {
    name: "Shane",
    email: "shane@montreal-voyageurs.com",
    isActive: false
  }
];

for (const p of profiles) {
  console.log(describeProfile(p));
}
```

Try pushing an invalid object into the array and see what happens.

Optional challenges

If you want to go further, here are one or two small extensions for the profile project:

- Add a `role` field that only allows *admin*, *editor*, or *viewer*
- Write a function that filters only active profiles
- Change email to be optional and update the function accordingly

Each task makes you use the type system to describe the data more carefully. If you get stuck, ask your AI coach to explain the error before asking it to fix the code.

By the end of this exercise, you have:

- Defined and used basic types
- Created and enforced an interface
- Worked with optional properties
- Used typed functions and arrays
- Seen exactly what disappears when TypeScript compiles to JavaScript

By this point, TypeScript should look less abstract because you have seen it catch real mistakes.

Prompt: What are common mistakes beginners make when first using TypeScript?

Practice, references, and resources

In this section, you will be tested on what you've learned in this chapter and be provided with useful links to reference materials and resources.

Check your understanding

Answer the following questions:

1. What problem does TypeScript solve that JavaScript does not?
2. What does it mean that TypeScript is a development-time tool?
3. Why is TypeScript especially useful when working with AI-generated code?
4. What is type inference, and when should you rely on it?
5. Why is it recommended to be explicit with function parameters and return types?
6. What does it mean that interfaces describe the shape of data?
7. What is structural typing, and how is it different from nominal typing?
8. Why are literal union types often preferred over enums in modern TypeScript?
9. What does the target option in `tsconfig.json` control and why should you avoid relying on the default target?
10. Why do declaration files (`.d.ts`) matter when using third-party libraries?

Links

Here are the official, authoritative TypeScript resources you should know about. These are maintained by Microsoft and the TypeScript teams, so start with them before using blog posts or forum answers.

TypeScript handbook

This is the primary learning resource. It is structured, progressive, and written by the TypeScript team. The handbook explains not just syntax, but why features exist and how they are meant to be used. For most readers, this should be the first stop after this chapter.

`https://www.typescriptlang.org/docs/handbook/intro.html`

TypeScript documentation

This is the entry point for all official TypeScript documentation. From here, you can access the handbook, configuration options, compiler details, and guides for different environments.

`https://www.typescriptlang.org/docs/`

TypeScript playground

This is an interactive, browser-based editor that lets you experiment with TypeScript without installing anything. It shows TypeScript code on the left and the generated JavaScript on the right, which is excellent for reinforcing the "types disappear at runtime" concept.

`https://www.typescriptlang.org/play`

TypeScript compiler options

This page documents every compiler option in `tsconfig.json`. You do not need this immediately, but it becomes invaluable as soon as you want to tighten or relax rules in real projects.

`https://www.typescriptlang.org/tsconfig`

TypeScript GitHub Repository

This is the source of truth for the language itself. Issues, release notes, design discussions, and breaking changes all appear here first. Advanced readers will eventually end up here when they want to understand design decisions or track upcoming features.

`https://github.com/microsoft/TypeScript`

Release Notes (per TypeScript version)

This is useful for understanding how the language evolves. TypeScript moves quickly, and this page helps you see what changed and why.

`https://www.typescriptlang.org/docs/handbook/release-notes/overview.html`

Summary

In this chapter, you learned the following:

- What TypeScript is and how it builds on JavaScript rather than replacing it
- That browsers never run TypeScript directly and only ever execute the generated JavaScript
- How to set up a basic TypeScript environment using Node.js and the TypeScript compiler
- How the TypeScript compiler checks code at development time and then removes all types

- How type inference works and when to rely on it versus being explicit
- How interfaces describe the shape of objects and act as contracts within your code
- How optional properties work and how they force safer handling of missing data
- How typed functions and arrays reduce whole classes of runtime errors

In the next chapter, you will switch from types and toolchains to SQL, the language of relational databases. That is a good next step, because TypeScript is partly about making data shapes explicit, and SQL is about storing and querying structured data cleanly.

Get this book's PDF version and more

Part 2

Backend Web Development

In this second part of the book, you'll move behind the scenes to the part of the application that handles data, logic, and communication. You work with SQL, Python, and the Django framework to understand how requests are processed, how data is stored and retrieved, and how different parts of the system interact.

This part focuses on what happens after a browser request reaches the server. You see how small decisions in data modeling and application structure affect everything built on top. Instead of treating the backend as something abstract, you learn how requests, data, and code fit together, which makes debugging and extending applications much easier.

This part of the book includes the following chapters:

Part 2

Backend Web Development

7

SQL – Managing Data

Web pages can survive a bit of ugliness. Data models are less forgiving. Once your data is duplicated, inconsistent, or badly related, the whole application starts paying for it.

This chapter introduces SQL and relational databases using SQLite and a small sample database. The goal is not to turn you into a database administrator. It is to help you understand how structured data is stored, related, queried, and changed.

You will start with the basic ideas behind relational databases: tables, rows, columns, keys, relationships, `NULL`, and constraints. Then you will set up SQLite, inspect the sample database, and write real queries with `SELECT`, `WHERE`, `ORDER BY`, `JOIN`, `GROUP BY`, and `HAVING`. After that, you will modify data with `INSERT`, `UPDATE`, and `DELETE`, look at transactions, and finish with a practical introduction to indexes and performance.

By the end of this chapter, you should understand how relational databases store and connect related facts. Learning SQL syntax is important, but the bigger skill is learning to ask precise questions about data: what exists, how pieces relate, what must always be true, and what the application needs to answer.

In this chapter, we will cover the following topics:

- Introduction to SQL and databases
- Setting up SQLite and a sample database
- Writing queries and joining tables
- Modifying data
- Improving performance with indexes

Suggested chatbot prompts with example responses for this chapter can be found at the following link: `https://github.com/markjprice/web-dev-ai/blob/main/prompts/ch07-sql/readme.md`

Introduction to SQL and databases

We should start by answering the obvious question.

What is a database?

SQLite, PostgreSQL, MySQL, and SQL Server are database engines. SQL is the common language you use to talk to them. Each engine has its own extensions and quirks, but the core SQL concepts are shared.

A database is an organized system for storing data so it can be retrieved, updated, and kept consistent over time. In a relational database, data is stored in tables. Each table represents one kind of thing. For example, films, TV shows, actors, or episodes.

A table is made up of **rows** and **columns**. Each row represents a single record, such as one film or one person. Each column represents a single attribute of that record, such as a title, release year, or birth year. Every table has a **primary key**, which uniquely identifies each row. This is how the database keeps track of individual records without relying on names or other values that might change.

Relational databases are built around relationships between tables. Instead of duplicating data, tables reference each other using **foreign keys**. For example, an episode row does not repeat the show's name and release year. Instead, it stores a reference to the show's primary key. This keeps data consistent and avoids subtle bugs where the same fact exists in multiple places with slightly different values.

SQL is a language for asking for data and shaping the result. **SQL** stands for **Structured Query Language**, but the word *query* is a little too narrow. SQL is used not only to read data, but also to insert it, update it, delete it, and define the structure of the database itself. Subsets of SQL include the following:

- **Data Definition Language (DDL)**: This is used to define or modify the structure of your database. These commands deal with the containers (tables, views, indexes) rather than the actual data inside them. Key Commands: `CREATE`, `ALTER`, `DROP`, `TRUNCATE`. Analogy: Building the shelves in a library.

- **Data Manipulation Language (DML)**: This is the subset you likely use most often. It is used to add, modify, or delete the actual data records (rows) within the tables. Key commands: `INSERT`, `UPDATE`, `DELETE`. Analogy: Putting books onto the shelves or changing their covers.
- **Data Query Language (DQL)**: This is focused entirely on retrieving data. While some people group `SELECT` under DML, it is technically its own category because it doesn't manipulate the data, it only fetches it. Key command: `SELECT`. Analogy: Reading a book from the shelf.

There are more sub-languages like **Data Control Language (DCL)**, used for security and permissions with key commands like `GRANT` and `REVOKE`, and **Transaction Control Language (TCL)** that allows you to group multiple changes into a single transaction that either succeeds or fails as a whole. TCL has key commands like `COMMIT` and `ROLLBACK`. But I don't want to overwhelm you too soon!

Core SQL is not a programming language in the usual sense. The core SQL language has no loops, no if statements in the way Python or JavaScript does, and no concept of step-by-step control flow. You do not tell the database how to find the data. You describe the result you want, and the database engine decides the most efficient way to get there. That is why SQL is called declarative rather than procedural. You declare the outcome, not the procedure. You describe the result you want, not the steps to get there.

Good practice: Although SQL is primarily a declarative language, most real-world database systems also include procedural extensions. Procedural SQL exists because real applications sometimes need logic to do batch processing, data validation, and enforcement beyond simple constraints, and complex transformations during migrations or ETL processes. Procedural SQL keywords include: `DECLARE`, `SET`, `IF`, and `WHILE`. Use SQL the way it was intended: describe the result you want and let the database engine handle the details. Procedural features exist for edge cases, not as the default approach.

Prompt: I have been told that SQL has no loops, no `if`-statements in the way Python or JavaScript does, and no concept of step-by-step control flow. But I've seen that T-SQL does have those keywords. Why? Do all SQL dialects actually have flow control statements?

SQL dialects

While the ISO/ANSI SQL standard provides a blueprint for how SQL should work, almost every database company adds its own flavor or dialect. These dialects exist because different databases were built for different needs.

Here are a few important dialects and how they differ:

- **T-SQL (Transact-SQL)** is used by Microsoft SQL Server. T-SQL is SQL Server's procedural extension to SQL. It adds variables, control-flow statements, error handling, and stored procedure support, so database code can include more application-like logic. It focuses on high-performance business logic and deep integration with the Windows ecosystem.
- **PL/SQL (Procedural Language/SQL)** is used by Oracle Database. This dialect is widely considered the most sophisticated. It is heavily influenced by Ada (a strict programming language used in defense and aviation). It is built for massive, mission-critical enterprise systems where data integrity is the top priority.
- **PostgreSQL (PL/pgSQL)** is used by PostgreSQL. PostgreSQL is often favored by people who care about standards and advanced SQL features.

Prompt: How closely do modern databases actually follow the ISO SQL standard? Explain why SQL dialects diverged and why full portability is difficult in practice.

Why are there so many dialects of SQL? It's like how English has different accents and slang in London, New York, and Sydney. The core vocabulary is the same, but vendors also add features that make their systems more distinctive and less portable. Additionally, a database designed to run on a phone, such as SQLite, does not need the massive procedural overhead of an enterprise engine like Oracle. Also, many SQL dialects were invented before the official SQL standards were fully established.

How SQL is used to query data

Querying data means asking the database questions. SQL queries usually start with `SELECT`. A `SELECT` statement specifies:

- Which columns you want
- Which table or tables the data comes from
- Which rows should be included
- How the results should be sorted or grouped

For example, a simple query might say: *Give me the names and release years of all films released after 2000, sorted by year.* The SQL would look something like the following code:

```
SELECT title, year FROM films WHERE year > 2000 ORDER BY year
```

You are not telling the database how to scan the table, which index to use, or how to order operations. You are only describing the result set.

When a database receives a SQL query, it goes through several steps internally. It parses the SQL text, checks that the tables and columns exist, checks permissions, and then builds a query plan. The query plan is the strategy the database chooses to answer the query. Two identical queries can run very differently depending on indexes, data size, and the database engine, but the SQL you write does not change.

SQL is also used to modify data. `INSERT` adds new rows. `UPDATE` changes existing rows. `DELETE` removes rows. These statements follow the same declarative idea. You describe which data should be affected and what the new values should be, and the database handles the mechanics safely and consistently.

For example, to delete all films released before the year 2000, use the following code:

```
DELETE FROM films WHERE year < 2000
```

Why this separation matters

Because SQL describes the result rather than the step-by-step procedure, the same query can be used against a tiny table or a much larger one. Whether it performs well then depends on the schema, indexes, and the database engine's query plan. Poorly designed tables lead to awkward queries and performance problems, no matter how good your SQL looks.

SQL is a good place to repeat a theme from this book: typing the command is only part of the job. The harder part is deciding what the data should look like before the query exists. Which facts belong together? Which facts should never be repeated? Which values are optional? Which rules should the database enforce even if the application makes a mistake? Get those decisions wrong and every query becomes awkward. Get them right and most of the SQL becomes ordA database is the system that stores and protects your data. SQL is the language you use to ask questions of that system and to change what it contains. Learning SQL means getting used to thinking in sets and relationships, not lines of code executed one after another.

A database is the system that stores and protects your data. SQL is the language you use to ask questions of that system and to change what it contains. Learning SQL means getting used to thinking in sets and relationships, not lines of code executed one after another.

SQL data types

SQL data types define what kind of values a column can store and how the database interprets, compares, and stores those values. Choosing appropriate data types helps keep data valid and queries predictable.

Data types control:

- Which values are allowed
- How comparisons and sorting behave
- How indexes work
- How arithmetic and functions are applied

A poorly chosen data type can lead to confusing bugs, incorrect comparisons, and unnecessary complexity later.

Most relational databases group data types into a few broad categories.

Numeric types

These store numbers and allow arithmetic. Common examples include:

- `INTEGER` or `INT`: Whole numbers
- `REAL`, `FLOAT`, `DOUBLE`: Approximate decimal numbers
- `NUMERIC` or `DECIMAL`: Exact decimal numbers, often used for money

Good practice: Use integer types for counts, IDs, and years. Use exact decimal types for values where precision matters, such as money. Avoid floating-point types for currency.

Text types

These store strings of characters. Common examples include:

- `TEXT`: Prioritizes flexibility
- `VARCHAR(n)`: Expresses an expectation about maximum length (n)
- `CHAR(n)`: Fixed storage size (n)

For most application data, `TEXT` is sufficient unless you have a strong reason to enforce a length limit.

Date and time types

These store dates and timestamps. Common examples include:

- `DATE`
- `TIME`
- `TIMESTAMP`

Use date and time types instead of storing dates as text. They allow correct sorting, comparison, and date-based calculations.

Boolean types

These store true or false values. Common examples include:

- `BOOLEAN`
- `INTEGER` used as `0` or `1` in some systems

Use a Boolean type when available rather than an integer. It makes the meaning clear and avoids inconsistent conventions like mixing `0`, `1`, `true`, and `false`.

Binary types

These store raw binary data. Examples include:

- `BLOB`
- `BYTEA`

Binary types are used for files, images, or opaque data. They are rarely involved in filtering or joining and are often better stored outside the database unless transactional consistency is required.

SQLite and type affinity

SQLite is more flexible than most databases. It uses a system called **type affinity**, meaning columns have a preferred type, but the database does not strictly enforce it.

For example, a column declared as `INTEGER` can still store text. SQLite will try to convert values when possible, but it will not reject mismatched types in many cases.

This flexibility is convenient for learning and prototyping, but it means developer discipline matters more. Using appropriate types and constraints is still important, even if SQLite does not force them.

PostgreSQL and SQL Server, by contrast, enforce data types much more strictly.

Data types show what kind of data belongs in a column. They tell the database and future readers of your schema what kind of data belongs in each column. Choosing clear, appropriate types early makes queries simpler, prevents invalid data, and reduces surprises as your database grows.

Normalization is the next idea, and it is where many beginners first get stuck.

Database schema design

Database schema design is about deciding what data you store, how you structure it, and how pieces of data relate to each other. A well-designed schema makes queries simpler, data more consistent, and applications easier to change over time. A poorly designed one leads to duplication, bugs, and increasingly complex SQL.

Prompt: How do you safely change a database schema once real data exists? Please explain migrations and why they exist even when `ALTER TABLE` is available. Please include examples of schema design mistakes that are painful to fix later.

A table represents one kind of thing

In a relational database, each table models a single concept. Examples are a user, a film, an episode, or an order. A table should answer one clear question: *What is one row in this table?* If you cannot explain that in a short sentence, the table is probably doing too much.

A row represents one instance of that thing

Each row is a single record. One user, one film, one episode. Rows should be independent of each other. The database does not care about row order, and your design should not rely on it. Every row must be uniquely identifiable, which is why tables have a primary key. This is usually an integer ID or GUID that never changes, even if the data in the row does.

A column represents one attribute

Columns hold individual facts about the thing the table represents. A column should contain one value of one type. For example, a release year, an email address, or a duration in minutes. Mixing multiple facts into one column, such as storing a comma-separated list of actors in a single text field, makes querying harder and breaks the relational model.

What goes where

Good schema design starts by separating **entities** from **attributes**.

If a value describes the thing itself, it belongs in the table for that thing. A film's title and release year belong in the `titles` table. If a value describes a relationship between two things, it usually belongs in a separate table. A character name belongs to the relationship between an actor and a film, not to the actor or the film alone.

A useful rule of thumb is this: if a value would have to be repeated for multiple rows, stop and ask whether it should be stored somewhere else and referenced instead. Repeating the same data across multiple rows or tables seems harmless at first, especially in small examples. In real systems, it causes three classic classes of bugs known as anomalies:

- An **insertion anomaly** happens when you cannot add a piece of data without also adding unrelated data. For example, if a table mixes films and actors, you might not be able to add a new actor unless they are already linked to a film.
- An **update anomaly** occurs when the same value is stored in multiple places and must be changed everywhere. If you update it in one row but miss another, your data becomes inconsistent.
- A **deletion anomaly** happens when removing one piece of data accidentally deletes something else you wanted to keep. For instance, deleting the last film an actor appeared in might also remove the only record of that actor.

Normalization exists largely to prevent these problems. Normalization is a systematic way of structuring tables to reduce redundancy and dependency issues, typically by splitting data into related tables and linking them with keys.

You can learn more about the standard normal forms (1NF, 2NF, 3NF) and how they eliminate these anomalies at the following links: `https://www.guru99.com/database-normalization.html` and `https://en.wikipedia.org/wiki/Database_normalization`

Normalization: storing facts once

Normalization is the process of organizing data so that each fact is stored in exactly one place to provide a single source of truth. In practice, this usually means:

- Creating separate tables for separate concepts
- Using primary keys to identify rows
- Using foreign keys to reference related data
- Removing repeated or derived values

For example, instead of storing a person's name in every episode they appear in, you store the person once in a person table and reference them from an appearance or credit table. If the person's name changes, there is exactly one row to update.

Beginners often worry that splitting data into more tables makes querying harder. In reality, the opposite is true over time. Well-designed schemas lead to predictable joins and simpler logic. Poor schemas lead to string parsing, duplicated filters, and fragile assumptions.

Joins exist precisely to recombine normalized data at query time. That is the trade-off relational databases make: store data cleanly and consistently, then reconstruct the views you need using SQL.

Schema design decisions are hard to undo once data exists. Adding a new column is easy. Untangling duplicated data across millions of rows is not. That is why spending time on tables, rows, columns, and relationships early on pays off disproportionately later.

Good database schema design is about respecting what tables, rows, and columns are meant to represent, and resisting the temptation to repeat data for short-term convenience.

Prompt: Please explain normalization vs denormalization with a realistic example and show when denormalization is justified.

Primary and foreign keys

Primary keys and foreign keys are what give a relational database its identity and structure. They answer two fundamental questions: *Who is this row?* and *How does this row relate to others?*

Primary keys are for identity

A primary key uniquely identifies each row in a table. It is the database's notion of identity. No two rows in the same table can share the same primary key value, and a primary key cannot be `NULL` (meaning *unknown* or *not applicable*, which will be explained in more detail in a later section).

In practice, a primary key is usually a single column, often an auto-incrementing integer or a GUID. The actual value rarely matters to humans. What matters is that it is stable and unique. Titles can change, names can be corrected, and emails can be updated, but the primary key stays the same. This is why primary keys should never encode meaning or business logic.

For example, a person's name is a poor primary key. Names are not unique and they change. An internal `person_id` is a good primary key because it exists solely to identify the row.

Primary keys also serve as the target for relationships. Other tables point to them to say, *This row refers to that row.*

In SQLite, declaring a column as `INTEGER PRIMARY KEY` gives it a special role. The column becomes an alias for the internal `rowid`, and when you insert a row without providing a value, SQLite automatically assigns a unique integer. In practice, this behaves like an auto-incrementing ID, typically increasing by one each time a new row is added.

It is worth knowing that SQLite also supports an explicit `AUTOINCREMENT` keyword, but this is rarely needed. Without it, SQLite will usually pick the next highest unused value, which is fast and efficient. With `AUTOINCREMENT`, SQLite guarantees that it will never reuse a previously issued value, even if rows are deleted, but this comes with a small performance and storage cost. For most applications, `INTEGER PRIMARY KEY` on its own is the better choice.

Other database systems provide similar features, but with different syntax and behavior. In MySQL, you use the `AUTO_INCREMENT` attribute to achieve the same effect. In PostgreSQL, older code often uses `SERIAL`, while modern versions recommend `GENERATED AS IDENTITY`, which is more flexible and standards compliant. Although the goal is the same across all systems, which is to generate unique numeric identifiers automatically, the exact rules and guarantees can vary slightly, especially around gaps in sequences and reuse of deleted values.

Foreign keys are for relationships

A **foreign key** is a column in one table that references the primary key of another table. It represents a relationship between two entities.

For example, an episode belongs to a series. The episode table might contain a `series_id` column that references the primary key of the `series` table. That `series_id` is a foreign key.

Foreign keys let the database enforce rules about relationships. With a foreign key in place, the database can prevent:

- Inserting a row that refers to a non-existent parent
- Deleting a parent row that still has dependent rows
- Creating orphaned records that no longer make sense

This enforcement is a major advantage of relational databases over ad-hoc data storage.

One-to-many relationships

The most common relationship is one-to-many. One series has many episodes. One customer has many orders. One author has many books.

In a one-to-many relationship, the foreign key lives on the many side. Each episode row stores the `series_id` it belongs to. The `series` table does not need to know how many episodes it has. That information can always be derived by querying the `episodes` table.

Figure 7.1 shows a classic one-to-many relationship between the `people` table and the `emails` table. On the left, the `people` table stores one row per person, identified by a unique `id`. On the right, the `emails` table stores email addresses. Each email row includes a `person_id`, which links it back to the person it belongs to. The key idea is that one person can have many email addresses, but each email address belongs to only one person:

people (1)

id	full_name
1	John Doe
2	Jane Doe
3	Mika Jones

emails (M)

id	email	person_id
1	john_doe@gmail.com	1
2	jdoe@work.com	1
3	janed@msn.com	2
4	m_jones@gmail.com	3

Figure 7.1: One-to-many relationship

You can see this in the sample data:

- **John Doe** (id = 1) has two email addresses: `john_doe@gmail.com` and `jdoe@work.com`. Both rows in the `emails` table have `person_id = 1`.
- **Jane Doe** (id = 2) has one email: `janed@msn.com`
- **Mika Jones** (id = 3) also has one email: `m_jones@gmail.com`

So, the relationship works like this:

- `people.id` is the primary key
- `emails.person_id` is a foreign key
- The foreign key allows multiple rows in emails to point to the same row in people

The `1---M` notation in the diagram reinforces this: one row in people maps to many rows in emails. The duplication lives on the "many" side. The person_id value repeats in the emails table, and that repetition is what creates the relationship.

One-to-one relationship

Figure 7.2 shows a one-to-one relationship between the `people` table and the `notes` table.

Each person can have at most one note, and each note belongs to exactly one person. The relationship is shown as `1---1`, meaning there is no duplication on either side.

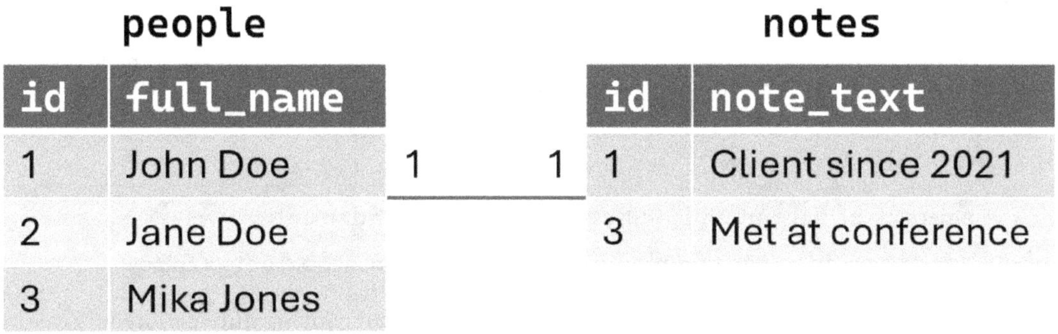

people

id	full_name
1	John Doe
2	Jane Doe
3	Mika Jones

1 — 1

notes

id	note_text
1	Client since 2021
3	Met at conference

Figure 7.2: One-to-one relationship

Looking at the data:

- **John Doe** (id = 1) is linked to a single note: "Client since 2021" (note id = 1)
- **Jane Doe** (id = 2) has no note in this example
- **Mika Jones** (id = 3) is linked to: "Met at conference" (note id = 3)

Even though not every person has a note, the rule still holds. No person has more than one note, and no note is shared between people.

In a real schema, this is usually enforced by placing a unique foreign key in the `notes` table, for example:

```
person_id INTEGER UNIQUE
```

That `UNIQUE` constraint is what turns a one-to-many structure into a true one-to-one relationship. The foreign key still lives on one side (for example, the `notes` table), but the uniqueness constraint prevents duplicates, so the relationship cannot expand into many.

Many-to-many relationships

Sometimes both sides can have many related rows. A film can have many actors, and an actor can appear in many films. This cannot be represented with a single foreign key.

Instead, you create a **junction table**, sometimes called a link table or join table. This table contains at least two foreign keys, one pointing to each side of the relationship. Each row represents one relationship instance.

For example, a `credits` table might contain `film_id` and `person_id` as foreign keys, plus extra columns such as `character_name` or `role`.

Figure 7.3 shows a many-to-many relationship between `people` and `addresses`, implemented using an intermediate table called `people_addresses`.

At a conceptual level:

- A person can have multiple addresses (home, work, and so on)
- An address can belong to multiple people (a shared household or workplace)

That means neither table can hold a simple foreign key without causing duplication or breaking the model. Instead, the relationship is handled through the `people_addresses` table.

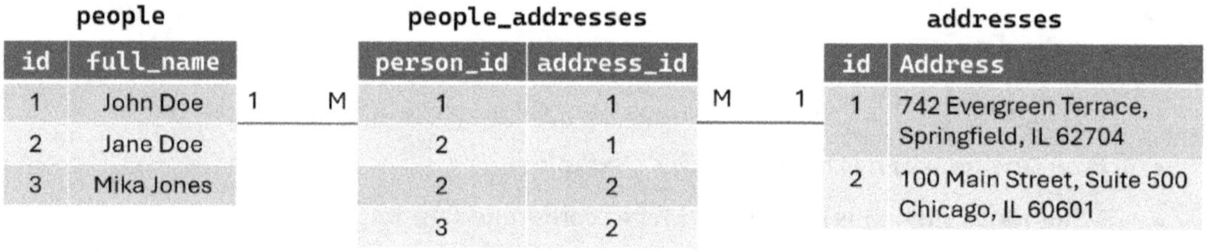

people

id	full_name
1	John Doe
2	Jane Doe
3	Mika Jones

1 — M

people_addresses

person_id	address_id
1	1
2	1
2	2
3	2

M — 1

addresses

id	Address
1	742 Evergreen Terrace, Springfield, IL 62704
2	100 Main Street, Suite 500 Chicago, IL 60601

Figure 7.3: Many-to-many relationship

How the data connects:

- `people.id` identifies each person
- `addresses.id` identifies each address
- `people_addresses` links them using pairs of IDs

Looking at the sample rows:

- **John Doe** (id = 1) resides at address 1: 742 Evergreen Terrace
- **Jane Doe** (id = 2) is linked to address 1 and address 2 so she shares the home address with John and works at address 2 (100 Main Street)
- **Mika Jones** (id = 3) works at address 2 with Jane

A many-to-many relationship cannot be represented directly with a single foreign key. To support many on both sides, you need a separate table that:

- Stores combinations of related rows
- Allows multiple entries per person and per address
- Keeps the schema normalized and avoids duplication

The intermediate table turns one complex many-to-many relationship into two simple one-to-many relationships:

- `people` is related to `people_addresses`
- `addresses` is related to `people_addresses`

This is the standard and correct way to model many-to-many relationships in relational databases.

Referential integrity and cascading rules

Foreign keys are usually defined with rules that say what happens when the referenced row changes. Common options include:

- `RESTRICT` or `NO ACTION`: prevent deletion if related rows exist
- `CASCADE`: automatically delete or update related rows
- `SET NULL`: keep the row but clear the foreign key

Choosing these rules is a design decision. Cascading deletes can be convenient, but they can also remove large amounts of data very quickly if used carelessly.

NULL values

`NULL` is one of the most misunderstood concepts in SQL, and many subtle bugs come from treating it like an ordinary value. In SQL, `NULL` does not mean zero, an empty string, or false. It means *unknown* or *not applicable*.

A `NULL` does not represent data that exists but happens to be blank. It represents the absence of a value. This distinction matters because SQL must account for uncertainty when comparing or filtering data.

Comparisons involving `NULL` do not behave the way most programmers expect. For example, the following expression is not `true`:

```
universe = NULL
```

But it is also not `false`! It is *unknown*. This is why SQL has special syntax for checking for `NULL`:

```
universe IS NULL
universe IS NOT NULL
```

Any time you want to test for missing data, you must use `IS NULL` or `IS NOT NULL`.

Three-valued logic

SQL uses three-valued logic, not two-valued logic. A condition can evaluate to: `TRUE`, `FALSE`, or `UNKNOWN`. Any comparison involving `NULL` produces `UNKNOWN`, not `TRUE` or `FALSE`. For example:

```
NULL = 'Star Trek'    evaluates to UNKNOWN
NULL <> 'Star Trek'   evaluates to UNKNOWN
NULL = NULL           evaluates to UNKNOWN
```

This has a practical consequence: the `WHERE` clause keeps only rows where the condition is `TRUE`. Rows where the condition is `FALSE` or `UNKNOWN` are excluded. This explains why queries sometimes lose rows unexpectedly when `NULL` values are involved.

`NULL` values can also affect joins in subtle ways. Join conditions that rely on equality will not match rows where the join key is `NULL`, because `NULL` never equals anything, including another `NULL`.

This is one reason why foreign key columns are often defined as `NOT NULL` unless there is a strong modeling reason to allow `NULL`.

Most `NULL` bugs come from forgetting that SQL has three truth states, not two, and that `UNKNOWN` is treated as *exclude this row* in filters.

Prompt: Please show me some common bugs caused by misunderstanding `NULL` and how to avoid them

Constraints

Constraints are rules enforced by the database to protect the integrity of your data. They act as a safety net that prevents invalid, inconsistent, or nonsensical values from ever being stored. Instead of relying on application code to *do the right thing*, constraints make the database itself responsible for guarding its own correctness.

Common constraints are shown in *Table 7.1*:

Constraint	Description
`NOT NULL`	Ensures that a column must always have a value. It prevents rows from being inserted or updated with missing data in fields that are required for the record to make sense. For example, a title name, an email address, or a release year usually cannot be `NULL`. Allowing `NULL` values in these columns forces every query and every application layer to constantly check for missing values. If a value is genuinely optional, allow `NULL`. If it is not, say so explicitly in the schema.
`UNIQUE`	Ensures that no two rows share the same value in a column, or in a combination of columns. It enforces logical uniqueness rather than identity. This is different from a primary key, which enforces row identity. For example, you might allow only one user account per email address, or only one episode number per season. In those cases, the values must be unique within a defined scope. They are especially important in multi-user systems, where two requests can arrive at nearly the same time.
`CHECK`	Restricts the range or format of values that can be stored in a column. It encodes simple business rules directly into the database. Examples include a release year must be greater than or equal to 1888, a rating must be between 1 and 5, and a status must be one of a fixed set of values. They are not meant to replace complex validation logic, but they are very effective for guarding basic invariants.
`FOREIGN KEY`	Enforces relationships between tables. It ensures that a value in one table refers to a valid row in another table. For example, an episode cannot reference a season that does not exist, and a credit cannot reference a person that is not in the person table. Foreign keys can also define what happens when related data changes. Common behaviors include preventing deletion, cascading deletes, or setting the reference to `NULL`.

Table 7.1: Common constraints

Each constraint type solves a different class of problem, but they work best together. `NOT NULL` ensures required data exists. `UNIQUE` ensures it is not duplicated. `CHECK` ensures it makes sense. `FOREIGN KEY` ensures it relates correctly to other data.

Without constraints, a database is just a passive storage system that accepts whatever it is given. With constraints, the database actively defends the assumptions your application is built on. This reduces bugs, simplifies queries, and makes long-term maintenance significantly easier. Constraints are about preventing bad data.

SQL naming conventions for database objects

Sticking to a consistent naming convention for your database objects will make it easier to maintain. Since most SQL dialects are case-insensitive but preserve case in display, a few conventions have become common to ensure your code remains readable and portable across different systems.

The most widely recommended convention, especially for PostgreSQL, MySQL, and SQLite, is **lower_snake_case**. For example:

- Table names: `user_accounts`, `order_items`, `product_categories`
- Column names: `first_name`, `created_at`, `email`

Why? Many SQL engines convert everything to lowercase internally. Using `lower_snake_case` ensures that your code looks the same in your editor as it does in the database logs.

Some guidelines for naming tables:

- Tables represent collections of things so use collective or plural names. For example, use a `users` table instead of a `user` table. A table is a container for many records.
- Avoid prefixes. Don't name tables `tbl_users`. Database tools already know it's a table.
- Be descriptive. If a table stores a relationship between users and groups, name it `user_groups` rather than `mapping_table_1`.
- Avoid SQL keywords. A table named `order` would conflict with `ORDER BY`, a table named `group` would conflict with `GROUP BY`, and USER is a keyword in PostgreSQL.

Good practice: Check your database's reserved words list when choosing table names. When in doubt, use more descriptive names like `user_accounts` or `customer_orders`.

Some guidelines for naming columns:

- For the column designated as the primary key (row unique identifier), there are two competing schools of thought. You can use the simple `id`, so every table has a column simply named `id`. But when joining users and orders, you end up with two columns named `id`, which can be confusing. Or you can use a prefix like `user_id` so the primary key column name includes the table name.
- Prefix Boolean column names with `is_`, `has_`, or `can_` to clarify that the value is `true` or `false`. For example, `is_active`, `has_discount`, and `can_post`.

- For dates and times, include a suffix to indicate if it is a date or a full timestamp. For example, `created_at` (timestamp), `birth_date` (date only).

Here are some names to always avoid:

- Never name a table `User`, `Order`, or `Group`. These are reserved keywords in some dialects of SQL and will require you to use annoying quotes like `"User"` or square brackets like `[User]` every time you write a query.
- Never use spaces in table or column names like `Order Date` because it will require you to use extra quotes like `"Order Date"` or square brackets like `[Order Date]` every time you write a query. Use underscores like `order_date`.
- Avoid abbreviations like `cust_addr_id`. Use `customer_address_id`. Space is cheap. Time spent decoding abbreviations is not.

Good practice: Using `UPPERCASE` for SQL keywords is the most widely accepted convention in the industry. While SQL is case-insensitive (meaning `select` works the same as `SELECT`), writing keywords in uppercase improves visual parsing.

Now, let's make sure that you have SQLite installed and then set up an example database.

Setting up SQLite and a sample database

SQLite is a small, fast, cross-platform, self-contained **Relational Database Management System (RDBMS)** that is available in the public domain. It's the most common RDBMS for mobile platforms such as iOS (iPhone and iPad) and Android. SQLite is the most used database engine in the world, and there are more than one trillion SQLite databases in active use. You can read more about this at `https://www.sqlite.org/mostdeployed.html`.

I am using SQLite here because it is cross-platform, easy to install, and more than enough for learning core SQL and database design.

Now let's install SQLite on your computer.

Setting up SQLite CLI tools for Windows

On Windows, we need to download SQLite CLI tools and add the folder for SQLite to the system path so it will be found when we enter commands at a command prompt or terminal:

1. Start your favorite browser and navigate to `https://www.sqlite.org/download.html`.
2. Scroll down the page to the **Precompiled Binaries for Windows** section.

3. Click **sqlite-tools-win-x64-3510200.zip** (the file will probably have a higher version number by the time you read this), as shown in *Figure 7.4*:

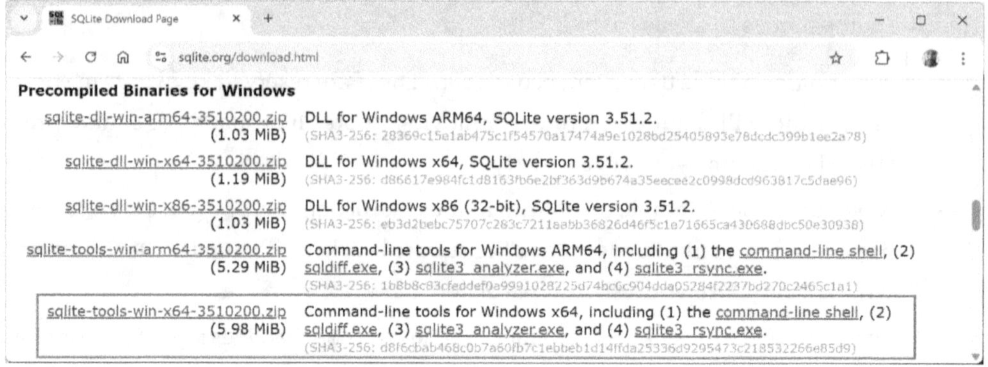

Figure 7.4: Downloading SQLite for Windows on Intel x64

4. Extract the ZIP file into a folder named `C:\Sqlite`. Make sure that the three extracted files, including `sqlite3.exe`, are directly inside the `C:\Sqlite` folder, or the executable will not be found later when you try to use it.
5. In the Windows **Start** menu, navigate to **Settings**.
6. Search for `environment` and choose **Edit the system environment variables.** On non-English versions of Windows, please search for the equivalent word in your local language to find the setting.
7. Click the **Environment Variables** button.
8. In **System variables**, select **Path** in the list, and then click **Edit...**.
9. If `C:\Sqlite` is not already in the path, then click **New**, enter `C:\Sqlite`, and press *Enter*.
10. Click **OK**, then **OK**, then **OK** again, and then close **Settings**.
11. To confirm that the path to SQLite has been configured correctly, at any command prompt or terminal, enter the following command to start SQLite:

```
sqlite3
```

12. Note the result, as shown in the following output:

```
SQLite version 3.51.2 2026-01-09 17:27:48
Enter ".help" for usage hints.
Connected to a transient in-memory database.
Use ".open FILENAME" to reopen on a persistent database.
sqlite>
```

13. To exit the SQLite command prompt, do the following:
    - On Windows, press *Ctrl* + *C* twice.
    - On macOS, press *Ctrl* + *D*.

Setting up SQLite for macOS and Linux

On macOS, SQLite is included in the `/usr/bin/` directory as a command-line application named `sqlite3`.

On Linux, you can get set up with SQLite using the following command:

```
sudo apt-get install sqlite3
```

SQLite can be downloaded and installed for other OSs from the following link:

`https://www.sqlite.org/download.html`.

Creating a Media sample database for SQLite

Now we can create a sample database for SQLite using a SQL script:

1. Create a folder named `Chapter07`.
2. Download the script to create a `Media` database for SQLite from the following link and save it to your local `Chapter07` folder: `https://github.com/markjprice/web-dev-ai/tree/main/Code/Chapter07/Media.sql`.
3. Start a command prompt or terminal in the `Chapter07` folder:
    - On Windows, start **File Explorer**, right-click the `Chapter07` folder, and select **New Command Prompt at Folder** or **Open in Terminal**.
    - On macOS, start **Finder**, right-click the `Chapter07` folder, and select **New Terminal at Folder**.
4. Execute the SQL script using SQLite to create a `Media.db` database file, as shown in the following command:

```
sqlite3 Media.db -init Media.sql
```

Warning! If you get the error `cannot open: "Media.sql"`, then you need to specify the path to the SQL script or copy it to the current directory because it is not being found in the current directory.

5. When the work is done, you will see the SQLite command prompt `sqlite>`, as shown in the following output:

```
-- Loading resources from Media.sql
SQLite version 3.51.2 2026-01-09 17:27:48
Enter ".help" for usage hints.
sqlite>
```

6. To exit the SQLite command prompt, do the following:
   - On Windows, press *Ctrl* + *C* twice.
   - On macOS or Linux, press *Ctrl* + *D*.
7. You can leave the command prompt or terminal window open because you will use it again soon.

Managing a SQLite database with SQLiteStudio

You can use a cross-platform graphical database manager named **SQLiteStudio** to easily manage SQLite databases. This is useful to review the data when fixing an issue, and when testing functionality. For example, you might want to add or modify some rows in some tables to test a feature.

Let's install SQLiteStudio now and use it to open and view the tables in the sample database:

1. Navigate to `https://sqlitestudio.pl` and then download and install the application.
2. Start **SQLiteStudio**.
3. Navigate to **Database** | **Add a database**.
4. In the **Database** dialog, in the **File** section, click on the yellow folder button to browse for an existing database file on the local computer, select the `Media.db` file in the `Chapter07` folder, and then click **OK**, as shown in *Figure 7.5*:

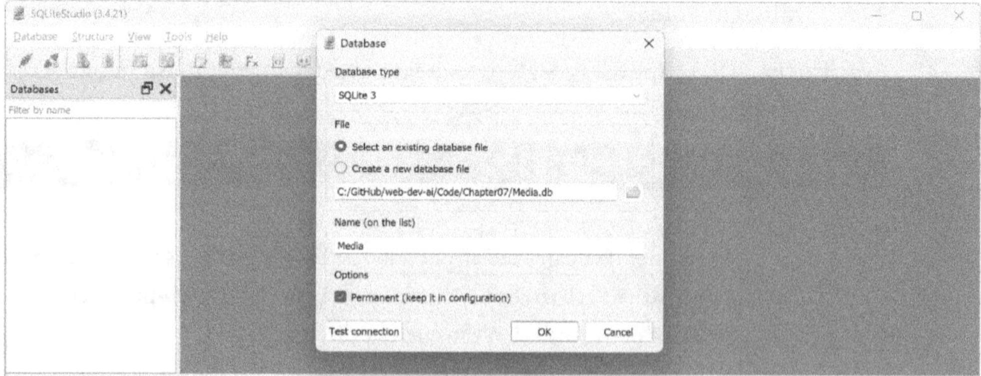

Figure 7.5: Adding the Media.db database file to SQLiteStudio

5. If you cannot see the **Media** database, then navigate to **View** | **Databases**.
6. In the **Databases** window, right-click on the **Media** database and choose **Connect to the database** (or just double-click **Media**). You will see the six tables that were created by the script: `credits`, `episodes`, `people`, `roles`, `seasons`, and `titles`.
7. Right-click on the **titles** table and choose **Edit the table** or just double-click the table.
8. In the table editor window, in the **Structure** tab, note the structure of the **titles** table, including:
   - Column names like `title_id`, `name`, `kind`, and `release_year`
   - Data types like `INTEGER` and `TEXT`
   - Primary key: `title_id`
   - Constraints like `UNIQUE (name, release_year)`, and `CHECK (kind IN('film', 'series'))` and `NOT NULL`, as shown in *Figure 7.6*:

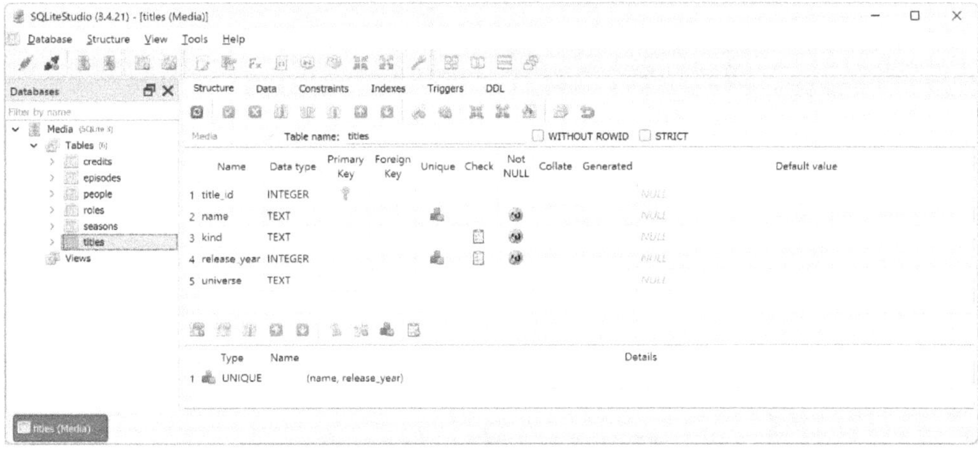

Figure 7.6: The table editor in SQLiteStudio showing the structure of the titles table

9. In the table editor window, click the **Data** tab, and you will see 5 rows in the **titles** table, as shown in *Figure 7.7*:

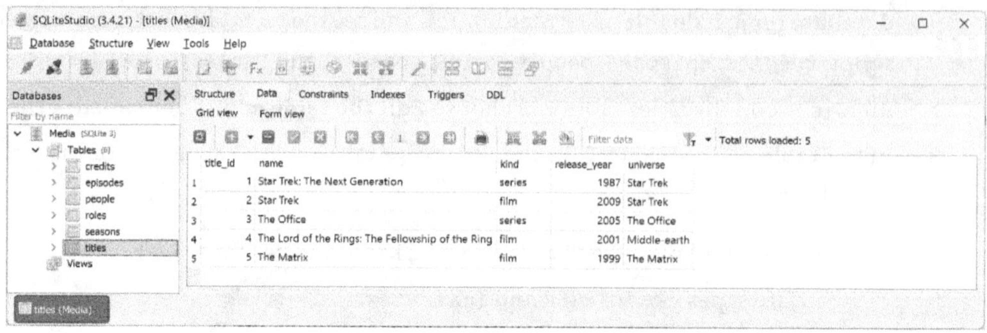

Figure 7.7: The Data tab showing the 5 rows in the titles table

10. Browse the other five tables to understand how they relate, as shown in *Figure 7.8*:

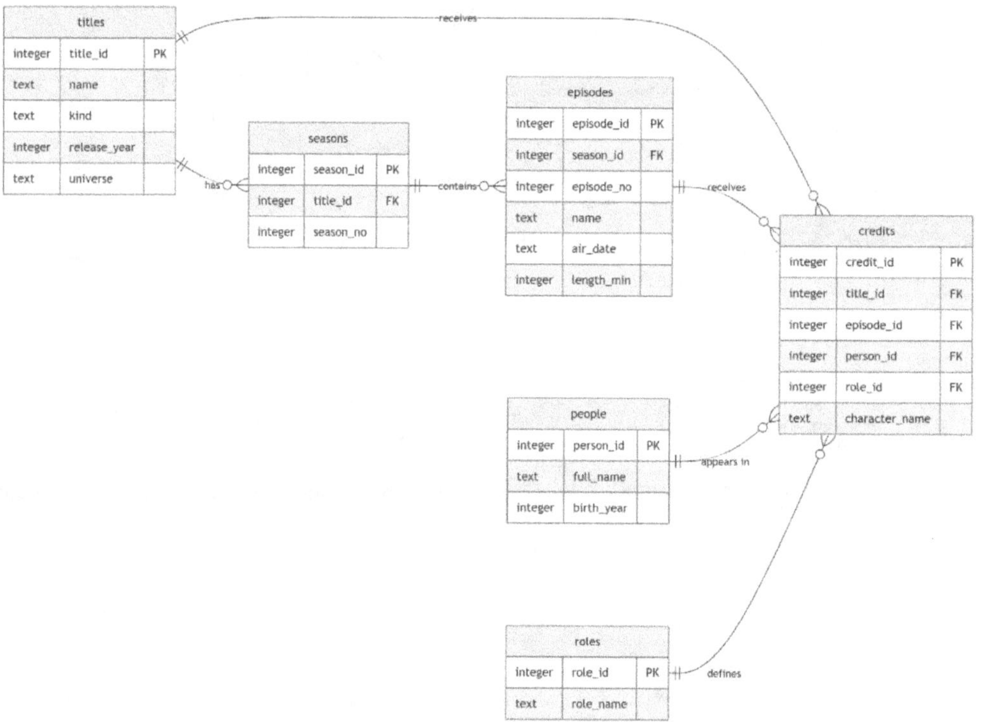

Figure 7.8: An entity-relationship diagram of the Media database

Prompt: Please create a Mermaid Entity-Relationship diagram drawn left-to-right for this database based on the attached SQL script.

Note the following about the preceding diagram:

- **Hierarchical chain**: There is a clear `titles` to `seasons` to `episodes` hierarchy.
- **Flexible credits**: The `credits` table allows for a person to be credited at the `title` level (like a movie star) or the episode level (like a guest star) by making `episode_id` nullable. The `credits` table acts as a many-to-many join table connecting `titles`, `people`, and `roles`.
- **Integrity rules**: The script uses `ON DELETE CASCADE` for all foreign keys, meaning if you delete a title, all associated seasons, episodes, and credits will be automatically removed.

11. In the **Database** window, right-click **Media** and select **Disconnect from the database**.
12. Quit SQLiteStudio.

Now we have a database, we are ready to write some queries and learn the syntax of SQL.

Writing queries and joining tables

This section focuses on reading data from one or more tables. Writing queries is about asking the database clear questions and getting back predictable, useful results. We will use the `Media` database you have already created.

Tools for running queries

SQLite has good tooling on every major platform, and you do not need much to get started. Below are the most practical cross-platform options, what they are good at, and when you would use each one.

SQLite command-line tool

The `sqlite3` CLI is the reference tool that ships with SQLite itself. It runs on macOS, Linux, and Windows, and it behaves consistently everywhere.

It is worth using because:

- Zero abstraction between you and SQL
- Excellent for learning, debugging, and scripting

- Good for running schema files and seed scripts
- Makes it very clear what SQL is doing, without UI noise

Typical usage looks like the following command:

```
sqlite3 media.db
```

Then, at the SQLite prompt `sqlite>`, you enter SQL statements and special commands like `.tables` (to list all the tables in the database) or like `.schema` to view schema/structure. For example, enter the following command:

```
.tables
```

You should see a list of the six tables, as shown in the following output:

```
credits   episodes  people    roles     seasons   titles
```

Now show the schema, aka the structure of the `titles` table, as shown in the following command:

```
.schema titles
```

You should see how the `titles` table was created, including column names and data types, the primary key, and constraints, as shown in the following output:

```
CREATE TABLE titles (
  title_id     INTEGER PRIMARY KEY,
  name         TEXT    NOT NULL,
  kind         TEXT    NOT NULL CHECK (kind IN ('film','series')),
  release_year INTEGER NOT NULL CHECK (release_year >= 1888),
  universe     TEXT    NULL,
  UNIQUE(name, release_year)
);
```

You can also enter just `.schema` without a table name to see the schemas of all the tables in the database.

Now enter a simple SQL query to return all columns of all rows in the `titles` table, as shown in the following command:

```
SELECT * FROM titles;
```

You should see the following results:

```
1|Star Trek: The Next Generation|series|1987|Star Trek
2|Star Trek|film|2009|Star Trek
3|The Office|series|2005|The Office
4|The Lord of the Rings: The Fellowship of the Ring|film|2001|Middle-earth
5|The Matrix|film|1999|The Matrix
```

Warning! If you see the SQLite prompt change to `...>` then it indicates that you have not completed the SQL statement with a semi-colon so SQLite expects you to continue entering more of SQL. Just enter the `;` and it will then run!

This CLI makes the mechanics visible: SQL is text sent to a database engine, and the engine returns rows or an error. For learning, that directness is useful.

SQLiteStudio

SQLiteStudio is a full graphical database browser and editor. It runs on all major platforms and is very beginner-friendly. It is useful early on because you can see the tables, rows, columns, and relationships while you write SQL.

Its main downside is that it can encourage clicking instead of writing SQL if overused. For learning SQL, you want to stay mostly in the query editor, not the table grid.

Let's explore some SQLiteStudio capabilities:

1. Start **SQLiteStudio**.
2. Navigate to **Tools** | **Open SQL Editor**.
3. In the **Query** tab editor, enter an example query, as shown in the following code, and then in the toolbar, click the **Execute query** button, as shown in *Figure 7.9*:

```
SELECT * FROM titles;
```

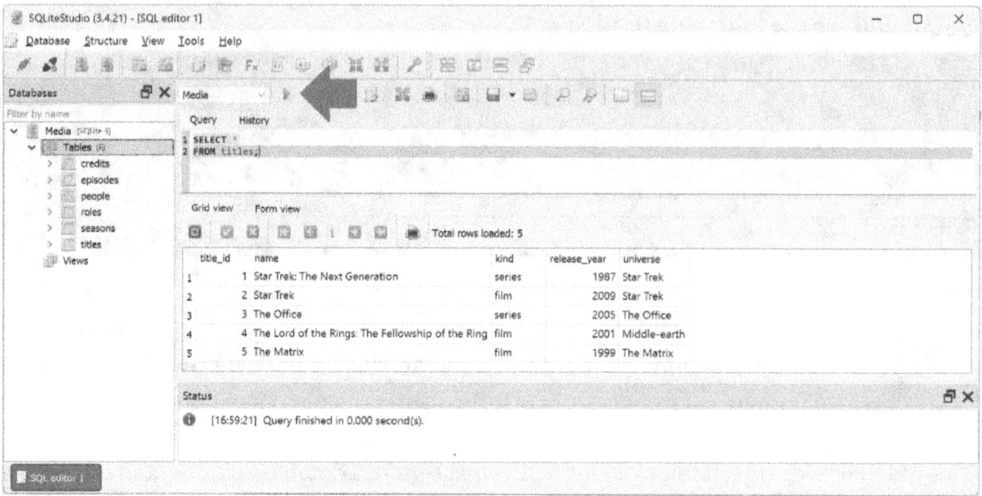

Figure 7.9: Running a SQL query using SQLiteStudio

SQLiteStudio is not as fussy as the SQLite CLI about terminating every SQL statement with a semi-colon. If you forget it, the query will still run.

VS Code and the SQLite extension

VS Code works well as a lightweight database client when paired with the right extension. Popular extensions allow you to open a SQLite database file directly, browse tables and schemas, run SQL queries inside the editor, and keep SQL files under version control.

This works well when SQL lives alongside application code, migrations, or exercises. It also mirrors how developers actually work in real projects.

The strengths include everything in one editor, SQL scripts saved as files, not ad-hoc queries, easy to rerun and modify queries, and it's a good fit if you later introduce Django or another backend.

Now let's make sure you can execute SQL statements using VS Code:

1. If you haven't installed the SQLite extension already, start VS Code, navigate to **Extensions**, search for `sqlite`, and then click **Install** on the **SQLite** extension (`alexcvzz.vscode-sqlite`).
2. In VS Code, navigate to **View** | **Command Palette...**, search for **Sqlite: New Query** and select it.

3. In the query editor, enter an example query, as shown in the following code:

```
SELECT * FROM titles;
```

4. Right-click in the query editor, select **Run Query**, select **Choose database from file**, and then browse to select the `Media.db` file. (You will only need to do this the first time you run the query so it connects to the database.)
5. The results will be shown in a second window pane, as shown in *Figure 7.10*:

Figure 7.10: Running a SQL query using the SQLite extension for VS Code

Next, we will introduce each important SQL keyword in turn. For any code examples, run them in your preferred tool: the SQLite CLI, SQLiteStudio, or VS Code and its SQLite extension. I recommend trying a mix of all three to see the pros and cons and which you prefer.

SELECT: the shape of a query

Every read query starts with `SELECT`. A `SELECT` statement answers four basic questions:

- What columns do I want? You can list the column names that you want, or use * to mean all of them.
- Where does the data come from? You must specify which table(s) you want to query.
- Which rows should be included? You can optionally filter which rows should be included using a `WHERE` clause.
- How should the results be ordered or grouped? You can optionally sort the results using an `ORDER BY` clause.

A minimal query looks like this:

```
SELECT name, release_year
FROM titles;
```

The preceding code asks the database to return two columns from every row in the `titles` table. The database does not guarantee the order of rows unless you explicitly ask for one.

Good practice: Start each SQL keyword on a new line to make the query easier to scan and understand.

Filtering rows with WHERE

Most queries care about only some rows. The `WHERE` clause filters the result set, as shown in the following code:

```
SELECT name, release_year
FROM titles
WHERE kind = 'film';
```

This returns only films, excluding TV series. The database evaluates the condition for every row and keeps only those that match.

You can combine conditions using `AND` and `OR`, as shown in the following code:

```
SELECT name, release_year
FROM titles
WHERE kind = 'film'
  AND release_year >= 2000;
```

This reads naturally: films released from 2000 onwards.

Sorting results with ORDER BY

If you care about order, you must say so explicitly, as shown in the following code:

```
SELECT name, release_year
FROM titles
ORDER BY release_year;
```

By default, ordering is ascending. You can reverse it, as shown in the following code:

```
SELECT name, release_year
FROM titles
ORDER BY release_year DESC;
```

You can also sort by multiple columns, as shown in the following code:

```
SELECT name, kind, release_year
FROM titles
ORDER BY kind, release_year DESC;
```

This groups films and series together and sorts each group by year.

Limiting the number of rows in the results

When exploring data, it is often useful to limit how many rows you see, as shown in the following code:

```
SELECT name, release_year
FROM titles
ORDER BY release_year DESC
LIMIT 3;
```

This returns only the three most recent titles. This is especially useful with large tables.

Good practice: If a query uses `LIMIT` and the result matters, it should almost always have an `ORDER BY` because without ORDER BY, LIMIT does not mean "the first N rows" in any meaningful sense. `LIMIT 3` does not mean *the first three titles you inserted* or *the oldest* or *the newest*. It means *any three rows*.

Selecting calculated values

SQL can return expressions, not just stored columns, as shown in the following code:

```
SELECT name,
       release_year,
       release_year + 10 AS ten_year_anniversary
FROM titles;
```

This does not modify the data. It simply shapes the output. Calculated columns are part of the result set, not the table.

Joining tables: bringing related data together

SQL becomes more useful when you combine data from multiple tables.

For example, episodes belong to seasons, and seasons belong to titles. To list episodes for a specific series, you join those tables together, as shown in the following code:

```
SELECT t.name AS series_name,
       s.season_no,
       e.episode_no,
       e.name AS episode_name
FROM titles t
JOIN seasons s  ON s.title_id = t.title_id
JOIN episodes e ON e.season_id = s.season_id
WHERE t.name = 'Star Trek: The Next Generation'
ORDER BY s.season_no, e.episode_no;
```

Each `JOIN` keyword connects tables using primary keys and foreign keys. You are not merging tables blindly. You are following relationships defined in the schema.

`titles t` and `seasons s` are examples of a table alias. It is shorthand that gives a table a temporary name for the duration of the query. `t` is an alias for the `titles` table. For the rest of the query, `t` and `titles` mean the same thing.

When queries involve joins, repeating full table names quickly becomes annoying. Also, when multiple tables have columns with the same name, aliases are required to disambiguate.

For example, both `titles` and `seasons` contain a `title_id` column. Without aliases, the database cannot know which one you mean, as shown in the following code:

```
SELECT title_id
FROM titles
JOIN seasons ON seasons.title_id = titles.title_id;
```

The preceding code is ambiguous and will fail.

We can clarify what we mean with table aliases, as shown in the following code:

```
SELECT t.title_id
FROM titles t
JOIN seasons s ON s.title_id = t.title_id;
```

Now the query is unambiguous.

Querying many-to-many relationships

Actors and titles have a many-to-many relationship through the credit table. This table is where the relationship lives.

To list the acting cast of a film we need to join four tables (`credits`, `titles`, `people`, and `roles`), as shown in the following code:

```
SELECT t.name AS title,
       p.full_name,
       c.character_name
FROM credits c
JOIN titles  t ON t.title_id = c.title_id
JOIN people  p ON p.person_id = c.person_id
JOIN roles   r ON r.role_id = c.role_id
WHERE t.name = 'The Matrix'
  AND r.role_name = 'actor'
ORDER BY p.full_name;
```

This query shows why junction tables matter. The character name belongs to the relationship between a person and a title, not to either table on its own.

Types of joins

Joins are how SQL recombines related data stored in separate tables. Each `JOIN` type answers a slightly different question about how rows from two tables should be matched. The differences matter, because they control which rows appear in the result and which are excluded.

INNER JOIN

An `INNER JOIN` returns only rows where a match exists in both tables. This is the most commonly used join and is often what people mean when they just say `JOIN`. In fact, you can just use `JOIN` instead of the full syntax `INNER JOIN`, as shown in the following code:

```
SELECT t.name, s.season_no
FROM titles t
JOIN season s ON s.title_id = t.title_id;
```

This returns only titles that actually have seasons. If a title has no seasons, it does not appear at all. Think of `INNER JOIN` as *only where both sides agree.*

Prompt: Please show me some examples where moving a condition from `WHERE` to `ON` changes the meaning of a `LEFT JOIN`.

LEFT JOIN (LEFT OUTER JOIN)

A `LEFT JOIN` returns all rows from the left table, and matching rows from the right table. If there is no match, the right-side columns are returned as `NULL`:

```
SELECT t.name, s.season_no
FROM titles t
LEFT JOIN seasons s ON s.title_id = t.title_id;
```

This returns every title, even films or series with no seasons. For those rows, `season_no` will be `NULL`. `LEFT JOIN` is used when the left table represents the thing you care about, and the right table is optional.

Good practice: A very common mistake is putting conditions on the right table in the `WHERE` clause, which turns a `LEFT JOIN` back into an `INNER JOIN`. Conditions that apply to the joined table should usually go in the `ON` clause instead.

RIGHT JOIN (RIGHT OUTER JOIN)

A `RIGHT JOIN` is the mirror image of a `LEFT JOIN`. It returns all rows from the right table, and matching rows from the left table:

```
SELECT t.name, s.season_no
FROM titles t
RIGHT JOIN seasons s ON s.title_id = t.title_id;
```

In practice, `RIGHT JOIN` is rarely needed. The same result can almost always be expressed more clearly by swapping table order and using `LEFT JOIN` instead. Many teams avoid `RIGHT JOIN` entirely for readability.

Warning! `RIGHT JOIN` was added to SQLite in version 3.39.0 back in 2022. If you're using an older SQLite version or certain tools that bundle older versions, `RIGHT JOIN` may not work. You can always rewrite a `RIGHT JOIN` as a `LEFT JOIN` by swapping the table order.

FULL JOIN (FULL OUTER JOIN)

A FULL JOIN returns:

- Rows that match on both sides
- Rows that exist only in the left table
- Rows that exist only in the right table

Where no match exists, columns from the missing side are NULL.

```
SELECT t.name, s.season_no
FROM titles t
FULL JOIN seasons s ON s.title_id = t.title_id;
```

This is useful for reconciliation and comparison queries, such as finding records that exist in one table but not the other.

Warning! SQLite does not support FULL JOIN directly. In SQLite, it must be simulated with a UNION of LEFT JOIN and RIGHT JOIN logic.

CROSS JOIN

A CROSS JOIN produces the Cartesian product of two tables. Every row from the first table is paired with every row from the second table.

```
SELECT t.name, r.role_name
FROM titles t
CROSS JOIN roles r;
```

If there are 5 titles and 3 roles, the result has 15 rows.

CROSS JOIN is rarely used accidentally, because the result size grows very quickly. When it is used deliberately, it is usually for generating combinations, test data, or reference matrices.

SELF JOIN

A SELF JOIN is not a separate join type, but a pattern. It is any join where a table is joined to itself using aliases.

```
SELECT t1.name, t2.name
FROM titles t1
JOIN titles t2
```

```
ON t1.universe = t2.universe
AND t1.title_id <> t2.title_id;
```

This compares rows within the same table. Self joins are common in hierarchies, comparisons, and graph-like relationships.

Prompt: Please explain `JOINs` visually using Venn diagrams and explain where those diagrams break down.

To summarize, `JOINs` reshape existing data by aligning rows across tables. Understanding which rows survive the join is far more important than memorizing syntax.

Now let's look at grouping and aggregates like `COUNT` and `SUM`.

Aggregates: asking summary questions

SQL is very good at answering questions about groups of rows. Some commonly used functions include the following:

- `COALESCE(expression1, expression2, ...)`: returns the first non-`NULL` value from a list of expressions. You give it two or more values or expressions, and it picks the first one that is not `NULL`. `COALESCE(universe, 'Standalone')` means, *if universe has a value, use it. If it is NULL, use 'Standalone' instead.*
- `COUNT(*)`: Returns the number of rows in the result set or in each group. It counts rows, not values, and it includes rows even if some columns contain `NULL`.

Prompt: Please explain why `COUNT(*)` and `COUNT(column)` produce different results with examples.

For example, how many titles exist per universe? We can use grouping with some functions, as shown in the following code:

```
SELECT COALESCE(universe, 'Standalone') AS universe,
       COUNT(*) AS title_count
FROM titles
GROUP BY COALESCE(universe, 'Standalone')
ORDER BY title_count DESC;
```

`GROUP BY` collects rows into groups. Aggregate functions like `COUNT`, `AVG`, `MIN`, and `MAX` operate on each group.

Another example: how many episodes does each series have? We can combine joining and grouping, as shown in the following code:

```
SELECT t.name,
       COUNT(e.episode_id) AS episode_count
FROM titles t
JOIN seasons s  ON s.title_id = t.title_id
JOIN episodes e ON e.season_id = s.season_id
WHERE t.kind = 'series'
GROUP BY t.title_id
ORDER BY episode_count DESC;
```

The rule to remember is that when you use `GROUP BY`, every selected column must either be grouped or aggregated.

Prompt: Why does `NULL` behave differently from other values in comparisons and aggregates?

Filtering groups with HAVING

`WHERE` filters rows before grouping. `HAVING` filters after grouping. Let's see an example that uses both, as shown in the following code:

```
SELECT t.name,
       COUNT(*) AS cast_size
FROM credits c
JOIN titles t ON t.title_id = c.title_id
JOIN roles  r ON r.role_id = c.role_id
WHERE r.role_name = 'actor'
GROUP BY t.title_id
HAVING COUNT(*) >= 2
ORDER BY cast_size DESC;
```

This returns only titles with two or more credited actors.

Prompt: Please show me some examples where `HAVING` is required and `WHERE` cannot be used.

A useful order for designing queries

When writing a query, design it in this order:

1. Start with the table and its columns that represent what you care most about with `SELECT` and `FROM`
2. Join outward to other tables to bring in related data with `JOIN`
3. Filter rows with `WHERE`
4. Group if you need summaries with `GROUP BY`
5. Filter groups with `HAVING`
6. Sort the final result with `ORDER BY`

SQL queries read top to bottom, but they make sense when designed inside out.

Syntax check: quick quiz

These questions catch mistakes beginners often make:

1. Which clause controls which rows are included in a result set?

   A) `SELECT` B) `WHERE` C) `ORDER BY` D) `GROUP BY`

2. Which clause guarantees the order of rows returned by a query?

   A) `WHERE` B) `LIMIT` C) `ORDER BY` D) `JOIN`

3. What does the following query return?

```
SELECT COUNT(*)
FROM titles
WHERE kind = 'series';
```

A) A list of TV series

B) The number of rows in the table

C) The number of TV series

D) One row per TV series

4. Which statement is true about `GROUP BY`?

   A) It filters rows before aggregation

   B) It sorts the result set

   C) Every selected column must be aggregated or grouped

   D) It can replace `JOIN`

5. What is the difference between `WHERE` and `HAVING`?

   A) `WHERE` filters columns, `HAVING` filters rows

   B) `WHERE` runs after `GROUP BY`

   C) `WHERE` filters rows before grouping, `HAVING` filters groups after grouping

   D) They are interchangeable

6. Which `JOIN` returns only rows that have matching values on both sides?

   A) `LEFT JOIN` B) `RIGHT JOIN` C) `FULL JOIN` D) `INNER JOIN`

7. Why is the following query invalid?

```
SELECT name, COUNT(*)
FROM titles;
```

   A) `COUNT` cannot be used with `SELECT`

   B) name must be part of a `GROUP BY` clause

   C) `titles` cannot be counted

   D) `COUNT(*)` requires a `WHERE` clause

Query exercises: write the SQL

For the exercises in *Table 7.2*, you should write the SQL yourself. Solutions should be runnable against the `Media` database schema used in this chapter.

Name	Description
Exercise 1: simple filtering	Write a query that lists the names and release years of all films, sorted from oldest to newest.
Exercise 2: limiting results	Write a query that returns the three most recent titles, regardless of whether they are films or series.
Exercise 3: joining tables	Write a query that lists all episodes for *Star Trek: The Next Generation*, showing the season number, episode number, and episode name, in broadcast order.
Exercise 4: many-to-many relationships	Write a query that lists all actors who appear in *The Matrix*, along with the character they played.
Exercise 5: aggregation	Write a query that shows how many titles exist in each universe. Treat titles with no universe as "Standalone".
Exercise 6: grouping and HAVING	Write a query that returns only titles that have two or more credited actors, along with the actor count.
Exercise 7: understanding joins	Write a query that lists all people in the database and the titles they are associated with. Include people even if they have only one credit.
Exercise 8: thinking in sets	Write a query that finds all people who appear in more than one title.

Table 7.2: Query exercises

A warning about SQL injection attacks

At this point, you are writing SQL by hand and running it directly against a database. That is safe because you control the input.

In real applications, SQL queries are often built using user input, such as form fields, query strings, or API parameters. If you insert that input directly into a SQL string, you create a serious security vulnerability called SQL injection.

For example, this kind of code is dangerous:

```
SELECT * FROM users WHERE email = '<user_input>';
```

If `<user_input>` is not handled safely, an attacker can change the meaning of the query. Instead of filtering rows, they can bypass checks or even modify data.

The rules to remember are simple:

- Never build SQL by concatenating user input into strings
- Always use parameterized queries (also called prepared statements)

You will see how to do this properly in *Chapter 9, Django – Web Development on the Backend*, where SQL is generated and executed by application code.

Good practice: If a value comes from a user, it must never be inserted directly into a SQL string.

Now that you have practiced reading, let's move on to modifying it. That means inserting new rows, updating existing rows, and deleting rows.

Modifying data

This section focuses on changing data. Until now, queries have been read-only. `INSERT`, `UPDATE`, and `DELETE` are the statements that modify what is stored in the database.

A good way to think about it is this: read queries are questions, write queries are decisions.

Start by making a backup copy of `Media.db` so that you can quickly reset if you make a mess of this section. Simply copy the file and name the copied file `Media_backup.db` or similar. (If you forget to make a backup then you can also just recreate the `Media.db` using the `Media.sql` script.)

For each subsection, run the SQL and note its effect on the data by running the following query on a table before and after each modification SQL statement, as shown in the following code:

```
SELECT * FROM <table_name>;
```

INSERT: adding new rows

`INSERT` creates new rows in a table. At a minimum, you must specify the table and the values for the required columns. Columns that allow `NULL` do not have to be supplied with values.

Inserting one row

The safest and most readable form explicitly names the columns, as shown in the following code:

```
INSERT INTO titles (name, kind, release_year, universe)
VALUES ('Arrival', 'film', 2016, NULL);
```

The preceding code says exactly what is being inserted and where. If the table later gains a new column, this statement will still behave correctly. In SQLite, a column declared as `title_id INTEGER PRIMARY KEY` is a special case because it becomes an alias for the internal `rowid`, and SQLite will automatically generate a value if you don't supply one.

Avoid relying on implicit column order, as shown in the following code:

```
INSERT INTO titles
VALUES ('Arrival', 'film', 2016, NULL);
```

This works only as long as the table definition never changes. That assumption rarely survives real projects.

Inserting multiple rows

You can insert more than one row at a time, as shown in the following code:

```
INSERT INTO roles (role_name)
VALUES ('producer'),
       ('composer');
```

This is clearer and more efficient than issuing multiple separate `INSERT` statements.

Inserting the result of a query

`INSERT` does not have to use literal values. You can insert the result of a query, as shown in the following code:

```
INSERT INTO credits (title_id, person_id, role_id, character_name)
SELECT t.title_id, p.person_id, r.role_id, 'Linguist'
FROM titles t, people p, roles r
WHERE t.name = 'Arrival'
  AND p.full_name = 'Amy Adams'
  AND r.role_name = 'actor';
```

This pattern is common when linking existing data together. It also avoids hard-coding IDs, which makes scripts safer and more portable.

UPDATE: changing existing rows

`UPDATE` modifies one or more existing rows. The `WHERE` clause is the most important part of an `UPDATE` statement because it prevents you from accidentally updating ALL rows in the table!

Updating a single column of a single row

For example, to ensure you only update the film named Arrival and not all the other films in the titles table, as shown in the following code:

```
UPDATE titles
SET universe = 'Standalone Sci-Fi'
WHERE name = 'Arrival';
```

This updates only the intended row. Without a `WHERE` clause, every row in the table is updated. This is where you will be especially glad you have database backups!

The following is valid SQL and a common source of accidental damage. A good habit is to always write the WHERE clause first, then add the SET clause:

```
UPDATE titles
SET universe = 'Standalone Sci-Fi';
```

Good practice: Always include a `WHERE` clause in `UPDATE` and `DELETE` statements.

Updating multiple columns

You can update several columns at once, as shown in the following code:

```
UPDATE episodes
SET length_min = 45,
    air_date = '1991-09-30'
WHERE name = 'Darmok';
```

Each affected row is updated as a single operation.

Updating with conditions and joins

Some databases allow `UPDATE` statements that reference other tables. Conceptually, you are still updating one table, but using related data to decide how. A subquery is a SELECT statement nested inside another SQL statement. The inner query runs first and its results are used by the outer query.

For example, updating all episodes for a specific series, as shown in the following code:

```
UPDATE episodes
SET length_min = 50
WHERE season_id IN (
  SELECT s.season_id
  FROM seasons s
  JOIN titles t ON t.title_id = s.title_id
  WHERE t.name = 'Star Trek: The Next Generation'
);
```

This reads as, *update episodes whose season belongs to this series.* The subquery finds all `season_id` values for a specific series, and the outer `UPDATE` uses those IDs to target the right episodes.

DELETE: removing rows

Be extremely careful with the `DELETE` statement. There is no undo.

Deleting just the rows you want to

`DELETE` removes rows from a table that match the `WHERE` clause, as shown in the following code:

```
DELETE FROM titles
WHERE name = 'Arrival';
```

The preceding code deletes only the matching row.

Warning! The following code deletes all rows in the table! The table structure remains, but the data is gone: `DELETE FROM titles;` There is no undo unless you've wrapped this statement in a transaction (you will learn about transactions in the next section). Always triple-check for a `WHERE` clause before running a `DELETE` statement.

Deleting with foreign keys

Foreign key constraints matter when deleting. If other tables reference the row you are deleting, the database may block the deletion, automatically delete dependent rows, or set foreign key values to `NULL`.

The behavior depends on how the foreign key was defined. This is deliberate protection, not an inconvenience.

Comparing deleting with dropping a table

`DELETE` removes rows but leaves the table structure intact. `DROP` removes the entire table, as shown in the following code:

```
DROP TABLE titles;
```

`DROP` is a schema change, not a data change. It is irreversible and should be treated with caution.

Now, let's see how we can add a sort of undo capability when we are modifying data.

Transactions

Transactions are how a database draws a hard line between *this change happened* and *this change did not happen*. They exist to prevent a system from ending up in a broken, half-updated state when something goes wrong.

Real database operations rarely involve a single statement. Even a simple user action can translate into multiple inserts, updates, or deletes. If one step succeeds and another fails, the database can be left in an inconsistent state.

Imagine adding a new order:

1. Insert the order
2. Insert the order items
3. Update inventory counts

If the order is inserted but updating inventory fails, did the operation work? From the user's point of view, no. From the database's point of view, half the changes were applied.

What a transaction is

A transaction is a group of database operations treated as a single unit of work. The database guarantees that either all the operations succeed together, or none of them take effect at all.

You explicitly control this with the following commands:

- `BEGIN` (or `START TRANSACTION`)
- `COMMIT`
- `ROLLBACK`

Until a transaction is committed, its changes are provisional. If something goes wrong, a rollback restores the database to exactly the state it was in before the transaction started.

Prompt: How do SQLite and PostgreSQL differ in transaction and locking behavior?

Atomicity in plain language

Transactions are often described using the ACID properties. The most important one for beginners is atomicity. Atomicity means *all or nothing*.

Either the entire transaction commits, or the database behaves as if it never happened. There is no in-between state that other users can see.

Prompt: Please explain the ACID properties in detail for a beginner with code examples using real-world failures like power loss or server crashes.

Why transactions matter even more with constraints

Constraints and transactions work together. If any statement inside a transaction violates a constraint, the database can abort the transaction. This prevents invalid data from leaking into the system.

For example, if one insert succeeds but a later insert violates a foreign key constraint, the entire transaction can be rolled back. The database does not leave behind partial results that break relationships.

Transactions are also about multiple users working at the same time. Without transactions, two users updating related data simultaneously can interfere with each other in unpredictable ways. Transactions define clear boundaries where changes begin and end, allowing the database to manage locking and isolation safely.

Good practice: Any time you have more than one statement that must succeed or fail together, you should be using a transaction. This includes creating related rows across multiple tables, updating totals or derived values, deleting data with dependent rows, and migrations and data fixes.

Single-statement operations are often implicitly transactional, but relying on that behavior is fragile and varies by database.

Prompt: What is isolation level, and why does it matter even for simple applications? Please explain lost updates, dirty reads, and phantom reads with simple examples.

Now that you know how to insert, update, and delete rows in tables, and how to manage multiple changes so they either all happen, or none of it happens, let's look at how to work with indexes.

Improving performance with indexes

You can write perfectly correct SQL that is painfully slow if the database has no efficient way to find the data. Indexes exist to solve that problem, and query plans explain how the database uses them.

What an index is

An **index** is a separate data structure that allows the database to find rows quickly without scanning an entire table. Conceptually, it is like the index in the back of a book. Instead of reading every page to find a name, you jump directly to the relevant pages.

In a database, an index stores selected column values in a structure optimized for lookup, along with references to the actual table rows. Most relational databases use variations of B-trees for indexes, which keep data sorted and allow fast searches, insertions, and range scans.

An important point is that an index is not the table itself. It is an additional structure that must be kept in sync with the table's data.

Why indexes make reads faster

Without an index, the database has no choice but to perform a **full table scan**. That means checking every row to see whether it matches your query. This is acceptable for small tables, but it becomes slow very quickly as the table grows.

With an index, the database can jump directly to the relevant rows. For example:

- Filtering with `WHERE` on indexed columns becomes much faster
- Joining tables on indexed keys becomes cheaper
- Sorting and grouping can often reuse the index order

Indexes are especially effective for selective queries, where only a small fraction of rows match the condition.

Prompt: Please explain how a database chooses between a table scan and an index scan.

Why indexes slow down writes

Every time you `INSERT`, `UPDATE`, or `DELETE` a row, the database must update not only the table, but also every index that involves the affected columns.

If a table has many indexes, each write operation has more work to do:

- New index entries must be created
- Existing entries may need to be reordered
- Deleted rows must be removed from indexes

This is why write-heavy workloads often have fewer indexes, while read-heavy workloads tend to have more. Indexes trade write speed and storage space for faster reads.

Prompt: Please show me some examples where adding an index makes a query slower, not faster.

How to choose effective indexes

A practical way to think about indexes is to start from your queries, not your tables. Ask:

- Which columns appear frequently in `WHERE` clauses?
- Which columns are used to join tables?
- Which columns are used to sort or group results?

These are prime candidates for indexes.

Also consider selectivity. Indexes are most useful when they significantly reduce the number of rows the database needs to examine. Indexing a column with only a few possible values, such as a Boolean flag, often provides little benefit on its own.

Prompt: Please explain index selectivity and why indexing Boolean columns is often useless.

Composite indexes, which cover multiple columns, can make specific queries much faster, but column order matters. An index on `(kind, release_year)` helps queries that filter by `kind`, or by `kind` and `release_year` together, but not queries that filter only by `release_year`.

When not to index

Not every column should be indexed. Indexes cost storage and slow down writes. Tables that are small, rarely queried, or frequently updated may not benefit from additional indexes.

A common beginner mistake is adding indexes just in case. A better approach is to add them in response to real queries and real performance problems.

Indexes do not make SQL faster in general. They make specific access patterns faster. Query plans are how the database explains which access pattern it chose and why.

Prompt: Please explain why `ORDER BY` can sometimes be satisfied by an index and sometimes cannot.

How to identify performance issues

Identifying performance issues in SQL is about understanding where time is being spent and why. Slow queries are rarely caused by SQL syntax itself. They are usually the result of how data is structured, how much data is involved, and how the database chooses to access it.

Start with symptoms, not guesses

Common signs of performance problems include:

- Queries that feel fast with small datasets but slow dramatically as data grows
- Reports or pages that hang or time out under load
- Queries that seem fine in development but struggle in production

The first mistake many developers make is trying to optimize blindly. Performance work should always start with observation.

Measure before you change

Before changing anything, establish what *slow* actually means. Run the query on realistic data and note how long it takes, how many rows it returns, and whether the time is consistent or varies wildly.

If a query returns thousands of rows when you expect tens, the problem is often logical, not technical.

Use EXPLAIN to see what the database is doing

Most databases provide `EXPLAIN` or `EXPLAIN ANALYZE` to show how a query will be executed. At a high level, look for:

- Full table scans on large tables
- Joins that process far more rows than expected
- Indexes not being used where you expected them to be
- Large differences between estimated row counts and actual row counts

You do not need to understand every detail of the plan. Even spotting a table scan versus an index scan is enough to explain many slow queries.

Check filtering and joins first

Performance problems often come from:

- Missing or incorrect `WHERE` conditions
- Joins that multiply rows unexpectedly
- Filtering after joining instead of before

A useful technique is to remove joins one by one and see how the query's behavior changes. This helps isolate where row counts explode.

Look at indexes last, not first

Indexes matter, but they are not a magic fix. Before adding an index, ask:

- Does the query filter or join on this column?
- Does the filter significantly reduce the number of rows?
- Is the data type and comparison correct?

Adding indexes to compensate for poor query logic usually leads to more complexity and slower writes without solving the real issue.

Performance issues are best approached systematically. Start by understanding what the query is doing, inspect the execution plan, verify row counts at each step, and only then consider indexing or refactoring.

Prompt: Please show me how to debug a slow SQL query step by step.

Practice, references, and resources

In this section, you will be tested on what you've learned in this chapter and be provided with useful links to reference materials and resources.

Check your understanding

Answer the following questions:

1. What does it mean that SQL is a declarative language?
2. What is the difference between a table, a row, and a column?
3. Why are primary keys important?
4. What is a foreign key, and what problem does it solve?
5. Why is normalization important in database design?
6. What is the purpose of the `WHERE` clause in a `SELECT` query?
7. What is the difference between `INNER JOIN` and `LEFT JOIN`?
8. What is the difference between `WHERE` and `HAVING`?
9. Why is it dangerous to run `UPDATE` or `DELETE` without a `WHERE` clause?
10. What is a transaction, and why is it important?

Links

SQL is standardized, but every database has extensions and edge cases. When in doubt, always check the official documentation for the database you are actually using. Trust vendor documentation first, blogs second, and copy-pasted snippets last.

Below are reliable, official SQL reference guides and documentation sites. They are maintained by the database vendors or core project teams and reflect actual behavior instead of myths propagated on sites like LinkedIn.

Cross-database and standards-oriented references

These are useful for readers who want a broader or more neutral view of SQL.

ISO SQL standard overview: `https://www.iso.org/standard/76583.html`

W3Schools SQL reference (non-official, but approachable and searchable): `https://www.w3schools.com/sql/`

MDN SQL overview: `https://developer.mozilla.org/en-US/docs/Glossary/SQL`

SQLite

SQLite is extremely well documented, and its docs are unusually readable.

Official SQLite documentation home: `https://www.sqlite.org/docs.html`

SQL language reference that is good for learning about SQLite-specific behavior and extensions: `https://www.sqlite.org/lang.html`

`SELECT` statement reference: `https://www.sqlite.org/lang_select.html`

Data types and type affinity which is important for understanding SQLite's flexibility: `https://www.sqlite.org/datatype3.html`

SQLite command-line tool documentation: `https://www.sqlite.org/cli.html`

PostgreSQL

PostgreSQL has one of the most comprehensive and rigorous SQL documentations available. It is verbose, but extremely precise.

PostgreSQL official documentation home: `https://www.postgresql.org/docs/`

PostgreSQL SQL command reference (alphabetical): `https://www.postgresql.org/docs/current/sql-commands.html`

Indexes and performance concepts: `https://www.postgresql.org/docs/current/indexes.html`

SQL Server (T-SQL)

Microsoft SQL Server uses Transact-SQL (T-SQL), which extends standard SQL with procedural features.

SQL Server documentation home: `https://learn.microsoft.com/sql/sql-server/`

T-SQL language reference: `https://learn.microsoft.com/sql/t-sql/language-reference`

Transactions and locking: `https://learn.microsoft.com/sql/t-sql/language-elements/transactions-transact-sql`

Summary

In this chapter, you learned that SQL is not mainly about clever syntax. It is about describing the data you want and relying on the database engine to work out how to retrieve or change it safely. That is why relational databases care so much about schema design, keys, constraints, and transactions. Good SQL starts with a good model.

You worked through the core pieces that make relational systems usable: tables, rows, columns, primary keys, foreign keys, normalization, NULL, and constraints. You then used those ideas in practice with SQLite, writing queries that filter, sort, join, group, and summarize data. You also saw how to change data safely and why transactions and indexes matter once a system becomes real rather than toy-sized.

Databases are unforgiving when the model is wrong. A confused schema leads to awkward queries, brittle joins, and performance work based on guesswork. A sound schema does not make every query easy, but it removes a lot of unnecessary difficulty. Start with the data model, then write the query that fits it.

Specifically, you learned:

- What SQL is and is not, including the idea that SQL is declarative and set-based rather than step-by-step
- How tables, rows, and columns model real-world concepts, and why repeating data leads to bugs and inconsistencies
- How primary keys give rows identity and foreign keys define and enforce relationships between tables
- How constraints such as `NOT NULL`, `UNIQUE`, `CHECK`, and foreign keys prevent invalid data from entering the database
- How to run SQL queries cross-platform using tools like SQLiteStudio, VS Code, and the SQLite command-line tool
- How to write `SELECT` queries to retrieve data, filter rows, sort results, and limit output predictably
- How to combine related data using different types of `JOIN`, and how to tell which rows appear in the result
- How to summarize data using `GROUP BY`, aggregate functions like `COUNT` and `AVG`, and filtering with `HAVING`
- How to insert new data, update existing data, and delete rows safely using `INSERT`, `UPDATE`, and `DELETE`

- Why transactions matter, and how they prevent databases from ending up in a "half-worked" state
- What indexes are, how they speed up reads while slowing writes, and how query plans explain database behavior

In the next chapter, you will learn about Python, a high-level, general-purpose programming language known for its readable syntax and large standard library, widely used for web development, data analysis, automation, and scripting. That is a good transition, because Python gives you a general-purpose language for building application logic, while this chapter has focused on the data layer that logic depends on.

Get this book's PDF version and more

Scan the QR code (or go to packtpub.com/unlock). Search for this book by name, confirm the edition, and then follow the steps on the page.

UNLOCK NOW

Note: Keep your invoice handy. Purchases made directly from Packt don't require an invoice.

8

Python – Programming on the Backend

Python is the language you will use for the backend side of this book, so this chapter is about getting comfortable with the parts of Python that matter most in real work. This chapter does not try to cover every corner of Python. It gives you enough fluency to read Python code, run it, change it, and understand what it is doing.

You will begin by installing Python and making sure it runs properly from the command line and inside VS Code. Then you will work through the basics: variables, values, conditions, loops, functions, and the built-in data structures that Python relies on heavily. After that, you will look at strings, debugging, exceptions, modules, packages, virtual environments, and file input and output (I/O). The chapter ends with a small command-line task tracker that pulls those ideas together into one working program.

Python syntax is only the starting point. You also need to see how Python programs are organized, how data moves through them, how they fail, and how to keep them understandable as they grow.

By the end of this chapter, you should understand Python's core syntax, know how to use its built-in data structures, and be able to write small but useful Python programs.

In this chapter, we will cover the following topics:

- Introducing Python
- Syntax and basics
- Data structures

- Strings in more depth
- Functions and classes
- Errors and debugging basics
- Modules, imports, and packages
- Virtual environments
- File input and output
- A small, cohesive mini-project

Suggested chatbot prompts with example responses for this chapter can be found at the following link: `https://github.com/markjprice/web-dev-ai/blob/main/prompts/ch08-python/readme.md`

Introducing Python

Python is a general-purpose language built around a simple idea: code should be readable.

It was created by Guido van Rossum and first released in 1991, which makes it older than Java, JavaScript, and even the web as we know it today. It feels modern because its design favors clarity over cleverness. That focus on readability is on purpose. Python assumes code will be read more often than it is written.

Clean syntax using indentation

One of the first things people notice about Python is how little visual noise there is. Python avoids excessive punctuation and boilerplate. Instead of braces or keywords to mark blocks of code, Python uses indentation. That means the structure of your program is visible at a glance:

- When something is nested, it is indented.
- When it ends, the indentation stops.

This forces consistency, but it also removes an entire category of errors that beginners often struggle with in other languages.

The official Python design philosophy, known as *The Zen of Python*, explicitly states that readability counts and that simple is better than complex. You can read it at the following link: `https://peps.python.org/pep-0020/`

Prompt: Why does Python use indentation instead of braces, and what trade-offs does this design make? How does Python's readability philosophy affect long-term maintenance of code? Please compare Python's design philosophy with JavaScript and C# in practical terms.

Professional Python

Python is often described as beginner-friendly, and that is true, but it leaves out something important. Python is not a beginner language that you leave behind later. It is used professionally across a wide range of industries, including web development, automation, scientific computing, data analysis, machine learning, game development, and system administration.

Companies such as Google, Netflix, and Spotify use Python extensively in production systems. That combination explains much of Python's appeal: it is easy to start with, but it does not trap you in beginner territory.

Prompt: What coding habits separate beginner Python developers from professionals?

A rich standard library

Another important aspect of Python is that it comes with a rich standard library. When you install Python, you already have access to tools for working with files, dates and times, text processing, networking, mathematics, and more. This is often summarized as "batteries included".

For beginners, this means you can do useful things quickly without installing extra packages. For experienced developers, it means fewer external dependencies and a more predictable development environment.

Python is interpreted, not compiled

Python is also an interpreted language, which affects how you work with it. You write Python code in plain text files, and the Python interpreter executes that code directly. There is no separate compilation step that turns your code into a standalone executable file, as happens in languages like C or C++, before you can run your program.

This gives you a quick feedback loop. You write a small piece of code, run it, see what happens, and adjust. That tight loop is especially valuable when learning, because experimentation becomes cheap and mistakes are easy to recover from.

A vast ecosystem

Python has a very large ecosystem. There are millions of Python developers worldwide, and an enormous amount of documentation, tutorials, libraries, and community support. If you encounter a problem, it is very likely that someone else has encountered it before and written about it. That support matters. Learning a language also means learning where to look things up, how to read documentation, and how to build confidence one small fix at a time. Python usually makes that learning process easier because it introduces complexity gradually.

Installing Python

Before diving into Python's syntax, you need a working Python installation. Python may already be installed on your computer, depending on your operating system:

- On Windows, Python is not reliably installed by default. Some newer Windows versions include a stub that launches the Microsoft Store, which often confuses beginners. The safest approach is to explicitly check.
- On macOS, Python is usually installed, but historically it was Python 2, which is no longer supported. Recent macOS versions may include Python 3, but you should still verify the version.
- On Linux, Python 3 is almost always installed because many system tools depend on it. Even so, checking is still necessary.

You can read the Python 2 end-of-life notice at the following link: `https://www.python.org/doc/sunset-python-2/`

Checking Python is done from the command line, because it is often run at the command line. Open a terminal or command prompt and run the following command:

```
python --version
```

If that does not work, try explicitly running Python 3, as shown in the following command:

```
python3 --version
```

You should see something like the following output:

```
Python 3.14.2
```

If so, then Python is installed correctly and you are ready to proceed.

What if Python is missing?

If you see an error such as `command not found` or a message pushing you to the Microsoft Store, then Python is either missing or not configured properly.

Warning! Python 3 is required for this book. Python 2 reached end of life in January 2020 and should not be used for new projects.

To manually install Python, for all platforms, the official source of truth is the Python website, maintained by the Python Software Foundation. You can download Python from the following link:

`https://www.python.org/downloads/`

Warning! For Windows, download the official installer from `python.org`, not the Microsoft Store, and during installation, make sure **Add Python to PATH** is checked. That checkbox is the single most common source of beginner frustration. If Python is not on the PATH, typing `python` will not work from the command line.

For macOS, downloading the macOS installer from `python.org` is the simplest option. Advanced users may prefer Homebrew, but beginners should not start there.

For Linux, Python 3 is usually already installed. If not, installation is done through the system package manager, such as `apt`, `dnf`, or `pacman`, depending on the distribution.

After installation, repeat the version check command to confirm success.

Python releases and lifecycle

Python releases go through five phases, as described in the following points:

1. **Early development (feature phase)**: Before the first beta, the next full release can accept new features, bug fixes, and security fixes.
2. **Pre-release (beta phase)**: After the first beta, no new features can go in, but feature fixes (including significant changes to new features), bug fixes, and security fixes are accepted for the upcoming feature release.

3. **Stable maintenance (bugfix phase):** Once a version has been fully released, bug fixes and security fixes are accepted. New binaries are built and released roughly every two months. This phase is also called maintenance mode or stable release.
4. **Security-only support:** After two years (18 months for versions before 3.13), only security fixes are accepted and no more binaries are released. New source-only versions can be released as needed.
5. **End-of-life:** Five years after a release, support ends. The release cycle is frozen; no further changes are allowed.

The descriptions come from the official Python release lifecycle page in the Python Developer Guide at the following link: `https://devguide.python.org/versions/`

At the time of writing in April 2026, as shown in *Figure 8.1* and explained in the following points:

- Python versions 2.6 to 3.9 have all reached their end-of-life and are therefore not supported
- Python versions 3.10 to 3.12 are all in their security phases meaning that although they are supported, they only get security fixes
- Python versions 3.13 and 3.14 are in their bugfix phase meaning they are actively supported with new binaries that you can download and install every two months

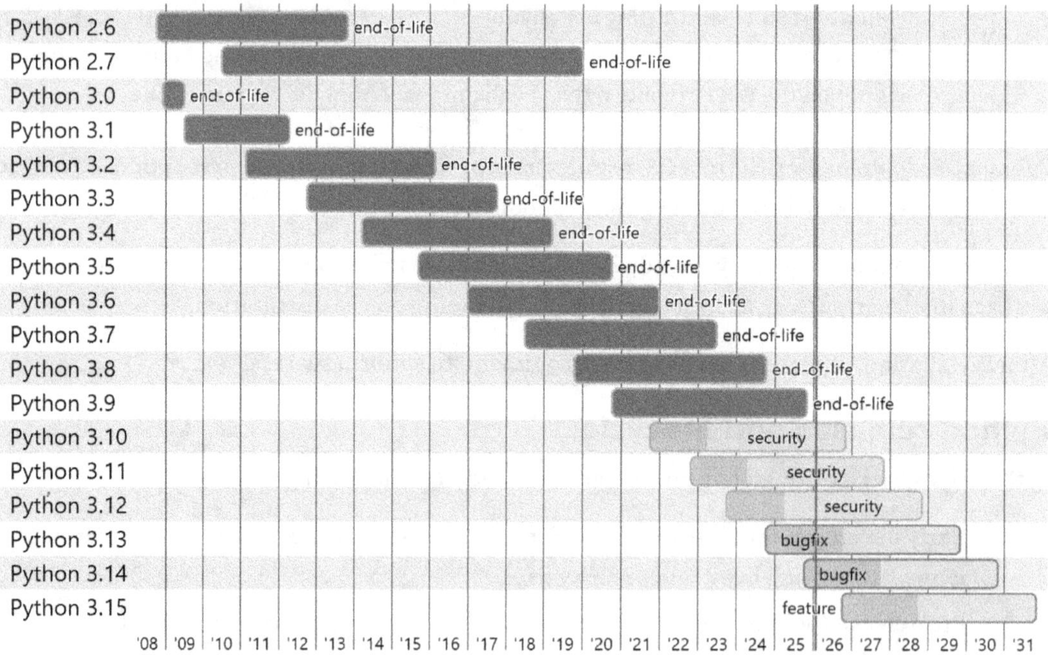

Figure 8.1: Python versions and their support phases

Good practice: Set bimonthly reminders in your calendar to check what the latest version of Python is and keep your installations updated.

Trying out the Python interactive shell

As a quick sanity check, let's try out the Python interactive shell.

At a command prompt or terminal, enter the following command:

```
python
```

Or:

```
python3
```

You should see the >>> prompt, which means that Python is running and ready. Try performing a simple calculation, as shown in the following command and output:

```
>>> 2+2
4
```

To exit the Python interactive shell, enter the following command:

```
>>> exit()
```

You can also press *Ctrl* + *D* on macOS and Linux, or *Ctrl* + *Z* then *Enter* on Windows.

A working Python installation is the first thing you need. Once Python runs reliably from the command line, the rest of the chapter can focus on learning the language itself, not fighting the environment.

In the rest of this chapter, you will move from understanding what Python is to actually using it. You will start with the basic rules and syntax that define how Python code works, and then you will explore Python's core data structures.

Syntax and basics

Python's syntax is purposely small. There are fewer rules to memorize than in most languages, but the rules that do exist matter a lot. This section focuses on the core building blocks you will use in almost every Python program: indentation, statements, variables, basic types, expressions, comments, and simple input and output.

Writing Python code files and running them

Python code is usually written in plain text files with a `.py` extension. Each file is a Python program, also called a script. VS Code is just an editor, but the Python extension connects it to the Python interpreter installed on the system.

Create a `Chapter08` folder, with a subfolder named `python-basics`. Open the `python-basics` folder in VS Code using **File** | **Open Folder**.

Opening a folder, rather than a single file, matters because VS Code uses the folder as the working context for running code and managing settings.

Next, in the `python-basics` folder, create a new file called `hello.py`.

Good practice: File names should be lowercase, use underscores instead of spaces, and avoid special characters. This convention is not enforced by Python, but it is widely followed and prevents subtle problems later.

In `hello.py`, write the simplest Python script, as shown in *Figure 8.2* and in the following code:

```
print("Hello, Python")
```

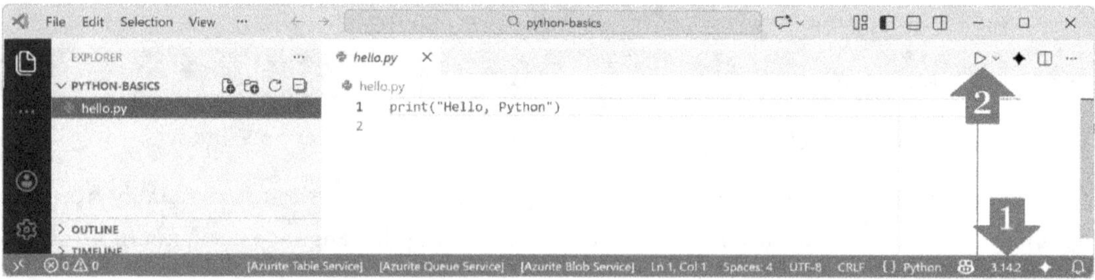

Figure 8.2: Writing Python code files in VS Code

You can (1) select the Python interpreter version by clicking in the status bar, and (2) run the code file by clicking the **Run Python File** button in the top-right of the code editor, as shown in *Figure 8.2*.

This file is not a project or an application. It is just a simple script. A sequence of instructions that Python will execute from top to bottom.

In VS Code, open the terminal with **Terminal** | **New Terminal**. This terminal opens in the folder you selected earlier. This is important because Python will look for files in the current directory.

In **Terminal**, enter the following command:

```
python hello.py
```

If that does not work, use:

```
python3 hello.py
```

The difference depends on how Python was installed, and both are normal. The result should appear immediately in the terminal, as shown in the following output:

```
Hello, Python
```

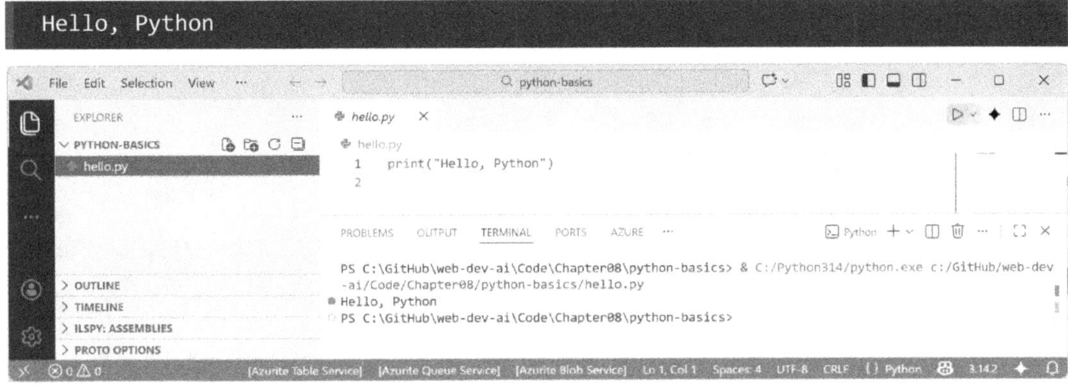

Figure 8.3: Viewing the output of running the Python code file in VS Code Terminal

VS Code did not run Python itself. It asked the operating system to run the Python interpreter, passed it the file name, and displayed the output. Remembering that chain will help later when debugging.

Running Python files with the UI

When a Python file is open, there is a ▶ button in the top-right corner of the code editor. Clicking it runs the current file using the selected Python interpreter and shows the output in the terminal. This button is doing the same thing as typing the command manually. It is not a different execution mode. If something fails here, it would also fail in the terminal.

In the bottom-right corner of VS Code, the Python version is shown in the status bar. If you click it, you can select which Python interpreter to use when you have multiple versions installed at the same time.

Python does not automatically re-run code when you save. The loop is always:

1. Edit the code file
2. Save the changes to the code file

3. Run the code file again

Modify the program slightly, as shown in the following code:

```
name = input("What is your name? ")
print("Hello,", name)
```

Run it again and show how input flows through the terminal, as shown in *Figure 8.4*:

Figure 8.4: Getting input from the user

Errors are normal and expected. If Python encounters something it cannot understand, it stops and prints a traceback. For now, the most important skill is reading the last line of the error message, which usually explains what went wrong and on which line.

You've now learned the basics of how to write Python code in `.py` files, how to edit those files in VS Code, and then run them using the Python interpreter via the terminal or the **Run Python File** button.

Now let's look more closely at how Python code is written.

The importance of indentation

The most important rule to understand first is **indentation**. In Python, indentation is not cosmetic. It defines structure. Blocks of code that belong together are indented by the same amount, usually four spaces. There are no braces to mark where a block starts or ends. When the indentation level increases, you are inside a block. When it decreases, you have left that block.

For example, indentation determines if a statement is inside a block or not, as shown in the following code:

```
if True:
    print("This line is inside the block")
    print("So is this one")
```

```
print("This line is outside the block")
```

The colon at the end of the `if` line tells Python that a block follows. The indentation tells Python which lines belong to that block. Mixing tabs and spaces is a common beginner mistake.

Good practice: The rule to adopt early is simple: always use spaces and always use the same number of spaces. For most code examples for languages like JavaScript or C#, I use two spaces to save horizontal space in my print books. In this book's Python examples, I use the traditional four spaces because indentation matters so much.

Python comments

Python supports **comments**, which are notes for humans that Python ignores. Comments start with a #, as shown in the following code:

```
# This is a comment
count = 10  # This comment is inline
```

Comments are useful for explaining why something is done, not what the code already clearly says. If the code is hard to explain without comments, that is often a sign the code itself should be simplified.

Python statements and variables

Python programs are made up of **statements**. A statement is a complete instruction that Python can execute. Some statements perform actions, like calling a function. Others define things, like variables or functions. Unlike some languages, Python usually uses one statement per line, which makes code easier to read and comprehend.

Next come **variables**. A variable is a name that refers to a value. In Python, you do not declare a variable's type explicitly. The type is inferred from the value you assign, as shown in the following code:

```
age = 42
name = "Mark"
pi = 3.14159
```

In the preceding code, age refers to an integer, `name` refers to a string, and `pi` refers to a floating-point number. Like JavaScript, Python is **dynamically typed**, which means the same variable name can later refer to a different type of value. That flexibility is useful, but it makes clear names and consistent use more important.

Prompt: Please explain dynamic typing in Python with examples of both its strengths and pitfalls.

Python data types

Python has a small set of built-in basic types that you will use constantly. The most common ones are integers (`int`), floating-point numbers (`float`), strings (`str`), and booleans (`bool`), as shown in the following code:

```
count = 10          # int
price = 9.99        # float
title = "Python"    # str
is_active = True    # bool
```

Strings in Python are enclosed in either single quotes or double quotes. Both are equivalent. Choose one style and be consistent. Strings can be combined using the + operator and repeated using *, as shown in the following code:

```
greeting = "Hello"
name = "World"
message = greeting + " " + name
print(message * 3)       # prints Hello WorldHello WorldHello World
```

Python expressions

Python supports **expressions**, which are combinations of values and operators that produce a result. Arithmetic expressions behave mostly as you would expect, as shown in the following code:

```
total = 10 + 3
difference = 10 - 3
product = 10 * 3
quotient = 10 / 3
modulus = 10 % 3

print(total, difference, product, quotient, modulus)
```

The / operator always produces a floating-point result. If you want integer division, use //, as shown in the following code:

```
result = 7 // 2   # result is 3
```

Python comparisons

Comparisons produce Boolean values. These are used heavily in decision-making, as shown in the following code:

```
x = 5
x > 3       # True
x == 5      # True
x != 10     # True
```

Note that == checks for equality. A single = is used only for assignment. Confusing these is a classic beginner error.

Conditional statements

To make decisions, Python uses **conditional statements**, most commonly `if`, `elif`, and `else`, as shown in the following code:

```
temperature = 18

if temperature > 20:
    print("It's warm")
elif temperature > 10:
    print("It's mild")
else:
    print("It's cold")
```

Only one branch runs. The first condition that evaluates to `True` wins. This structure reads top to bottom and closely mirrors how people explain decisions in plain language.

Comparison and logical operators

Conditions are built using comparison operators like:

- == equal to
- != not equal to
- <, <=, >, >=

Logical operators combine conditions:

- `and` requires both conditions to be `true`
- `or` requires at least one condition to be `true`
- `not` negates a condition

```
if rating >= 8 and rating <= 10:
    print("Positive")
```

Truthiness in Python

Python allows non-boolean values to be used in conditions. This is known as truthiness. For example:

- Empty lists, empty strings, and zero evaluate to `false`
- Non-empty collections and non-zero numbers evaluate to `true`
- `None` evaluates to `false`

```
if titles:
    print("There are titles to process")
```

This checks whether the list named `titles` is non-empty, without explicitly comparing lengths.

Structural pattern matching with match

Since Python 3.10, Python has **structural pattern matching**, introduced with the `match` statement. This fills the same role as a `switch` statement in JavaScript, but it is more flexible.

For example:

```
status = 404

match status:
    case 200:
        print("OK")
    case 404:
        print("Not found")
    case 500:
        print("Server error")
    case _:
        print("Unknown status")
```

In this simplest form, `match` behaves very much like a traditional `switch`. The underscore (_) is the default case.

Python's `match` is more flexible than a simple `switch` because it is based on pattern matching, not just value matching. It can match literal values, data structures, object attributes, type patterns, and combinations of patterns with guards. For example:

```
command = ("play", "Arrival")

match command:
    case ("play", title):
        print(f"Playing {title}")
    case ("stop", _):
        print("Stopping playback")
```

This is more flexible than a classic `switch` statement.

`("play", "Arrival")` is an example of a tuple. You will learn about tuples in the next section, *Data structures*.

Now let's move on to looping.

Looping statements

Looping statements let a Python program repeat work efficiently instead of writing the same code over and over. Python's looping model is simple, but it is built around a simple idea: you usually loop over things, not over numeric indexes.

The for loop

The `for` loop is the most commonly used loop in Python. It iterates over an iterable, like a list, tuple, string, dictionary, range, or any object that can produce values one at a time:

```
titles = ["Arrival", "The Matrix", "Star Trek"]

for title in titles:
    print(title)
```

This reads naturally: *for each title in titles*. You are not managing counters or indexes. Python handles iteration for you.

Looping with range

When you do need a sequence of numbers, `range` provides it:

```
for i in range(3):
    print(i)
```

This produces `0`, `1`, and `2`. `range` is commonly used when repeating an action a fixed number of times or when working with indexes.

The while loop

A `while` loop repeats as long as a condition remains `true`:

```
count = 0
while count < 3:
    print(count)
    count += 1
```

Unlike `for`, `while` loops require you to manage state explicitly. They are useful when you do not know in advance how many iterations are needed, but they are easier to misuse if the condition never becomes `false`.

Controlling loops with break and continue

`break` exits the loop immediately:

```
for title in titles:
    if title == "The Matrix":
        break
    print(title)
```

`continue` skips the rest of the current iteration and moves on to the next one:

```
for title in titles:
    if title.startswith("The"):
        continue
    print(title)
```

Both should be used sparingly. If a loop needs many breaks and continues, it often signals that the logic should be simplified or moved into a function.

Python loops are simple by design. The power comes from iterating over meaningful values instead of low-level mechanics, which keeps code readable as programs grow.

Prompt: Please explain `enumerate`, `range`, and `zip` with practical examples.

Python input and output

Finally, let's review basic input and output, which let programs interact with the outside world. The most common output function is `print`, as shown in the following code:

```
print("Hello, Python")
```

To get input from the user, Python provides the `input` function. It always returns a string, as shown in the following code:

```
name = input("What is your name? ")
print("Hello,", name)
```

If you need a number like an integer, then you must convert the input explicitly using the `int` or `float` functions, as shown in the following code:

```
age = int(input("How old are you? "))
```

This explicitness is intentional. Python prefers clarity over guessing what you meant.

At this point, you should understand how Python code is structured, how values are stored in variables, how basic types work, and how simple logic and interaction are expressed. These fundamentals will appear in every example that follows.

In the next section, data structures will build directly on these ideas and show how Python handles collections of information rather than single values. These data structures let you model real-world information directly in code, instead of juggling isolated values one at a time.

Data structures

So far, you have worked with single values stored in variables. That is useful, but real programs almost always deal with collections of data: a list of names, a set of options, a mapping from usernames to email addresses, or a sequence of values that changes over time.

Python's built-in data structures are one of the main reasons the language feels productive so quickly. They let you model real-world information directly, without ceremony.

Python's core built-in data structures are **lists, tuples, dictionaries**, and **sets**. You will use lists and dictionaries constantly, tuples occasionally, and sets when the problem fits.

We will start with lists, because they are the most familiar and the most flexible.

Lists

A **list** is an ordered collection of values. You create a list using square brackets, with items separated by commas, as shown in the following code:

```
numbers = [1, 2, 3, 4, 5]
names = ["Alice", "Bob", "Charlie"]
```

Lists can hold values of different types, although mixing types without a good reason is usually a bad idea, as shown in the following code:

```
mixed = [1, "two", 3.0]
```

Good practice: Python allows mixed types in a list by design, but doing so makes your code harder to understand, more error-prone, and less maintainable due to loss of predictability. When a list contains a single, consistent type, you can make assumptions about what operations are valid. For example, if a list contains only integers, you can safely add, compare, or sort them without extra checks. For most beginner-level and production code, a simple rule is that a list should contain items of the same kind, even if Python does not enforce it.

You access items in a list using an index. Python uses zero-based indexing, which means the first item is at position 0:

```
names[0]   # "Alice"
names[1]   # "Bob"
```

You can also use negative indexes to count from the end:

```
names[-1]  # "Charlie"
```

Lists are mutable, which means you can change them after creation. You can replace items, add new ones, or remove existing ones, as shown in the following code:

```
names.append("Diana")
names[1] = "Robert"
```

This mutability is why lists are often used to represent things that grow, shrink, or change over time.

Tuples

A **tuple** looks like a list, but it uses parentheses aka round brackets instead of square brackets, as shown in the following code:

```
coordinates = (51.5074, -0.1278)
```

Tuples are ordered collections like lists, but they are immutable. Once created, you cannot change their contents. This makes tuples useful for data that should not change, such as coordinates, configuration values, or fixed records.

To read an item from a tuple, you use the same syntax as with a list, as shown in the following code:

```
coordinates[0]  # 51.5074
```

If you try to assign a new value, Python will raise an error. This is a feature, not a limitation. It lets you express what the code should do clearly.

Prompt: Please explain why tuples exist when lists already work.

Dictionaries

The most important and distinctive data structure in Python is the **dictionary**. A dictionary stores key–value pairs like "age": 42, as shown in the following code:

```
user = {
    "name": "Mark",
    "age": 42,
    "is_admin": True
}
```

Instead of accessing values by position, you access them by key. Keys are usually strings, and values can be anything. You retrieve values using the key name, as shown in the following code:

```
user["name"]     # "Mark"
user["age"]      # 42
```

You can add or update entries by assignment, as shown in the following code:

```
user["email"] = "mark@example.com"
user["age"] = 43
```

Dictionaries are helpful because they map naturally to how we think about structured data. JSON, which is used everywhere on the web, maps almost directly to Python dictionaries and lists. If you understand dictionaries well, many web and data tasks suddenly become much easier.

Prompt: When should I choose a list versus a dictionary in real programs?

Sets

Then there are sets. A **set** is an unordered collection of unique values. You create a set using curly braces, like a dictionary but without key–value pairs, as shown in the following code:

```
tags = {"python", "web", "data"}
```

Sets automatically remove duplicates, as shown in the following code:

```
numbers = {1, 2, 2, 3}
# numbers is {1, 2, 3}
```

Sets are useful when you care about membership rather than order. For example, checking whether a value exists in a collection is fast and expressive with sets, as shown in the following code:

```
"python" in tags   # True
```

Across all these data structures, you will often use loops to process items one by one. The most common loop in Python is the `for` loop, as shown in the following code:

```
for name in names:
    print(name)
```

This reads almost like English. Python handles the indexing internally, which reduces errors and makes the code clearer.

Prompt: Please explain how Python's `for` loop works internally compared to index-based loops.

You will also frequently check conditions while working with collections, as shown in the following code:

```
if "email" in user:
    print("Email is set")
```

Prompt: Please explain sets with real-world use cases beyond removing duplicates.

Collections summary

At this stage, you do not need to memorize every method or operation. Focus on the role each structure plays:

- Lists are ordered and changeable
- Tuples are ordered and fixed
- Dictionaries map keys to values
- Sets store unique items with no guaranteed order

These four structures cover an enormous amount of everyday programming. As your programs grow, you will combine them freely: lists of dictionaries, dictionaries containing lists, sets derived from lists, and so on.

Prompt: Please show me some practical examples of nesting lists and dictionaries together.

In later chapters, you will see these same data structures appear everywhere: handling form data, processing files, working with databases, and exchanging data with web APIs. If you are comfortable with them here, everything that follows becomes easier to understand.

Prompt: Please explain common mistakes beginners make with mutable lists and dictionaries.

Now we've looked at collections, let's go deeper into `string` values.

Strings in more depth

Strings appear everywhere in Python programs. User input, file contents, URLs, JSON data, HTML, error messages, and configuration values are all strings. Because they are so common, Python provides a rich set of features for working with them. Understanding strings well pays off immediately, especially in web and data-related code.

A **string** in Python is an immutable sequence of characters. Immutable means that once a string is created, it cannot be changed in place. Any operation that appears to modify a string is actually creating a new one, as shown in the following code:

```
text = "hello"
text.upper()
print(text)
```

This prints `hello`, not `HELLO`, because `upper()` returns a new string and leaves the original unchanged. To change the original text, you must assign the result of calling the `upper()` function to the `text` variable, as shown in the following code:

```
text = text.upper()
print(text)
```

Now `text` refers to the new string. This immutability is a design choice that makes strings safer and more predictable.

Creating strings

Python provides several ways to create strings. You have already seen single-quoted and double-quoted strings, as shown in the following code:

```
name = "Alice"
city = 'London'
```

Both forms are equivalent. Use whichever makes the string easier to read, especially when it contains quotation marks.

For multi-line text, Python supports **triple-quoted strings**, as shown in the following code:

```
message = """Hello,
This is a multi-line string.
Goodbye."""
```

These are useful for long messages, documentation, or embedded text blocks.

F-strings

One of the most important Python features is **f-strings**. F-strings provide a clear and readable way to embed values directly into strings, as shown in the following code:

```
name = "Alice"
age = 30

message = f"{name} is {age} years old"
print(message)
```

The `f` prefix tells Python to evaluate expressions inside curly braces. This approach is clearer and less error-prone than string concatenation, especially as strings become more complex.

F-strings can include expressions, not just variable names, as shown in the following code:

```
price = 9.99
quantity = 3

total = f"Total: {price * quantity}"
```

String methods

Python strings come with many built-in methods for common tasks. You do not need to memorize them all, but a few are worth learning early.

The `lower()` and `upper()` methods change case:

```
text = "Python"
text.lower()   # "python"
text.upper()   # "PYTHON"
```

The `strip()` method removes whitespace from the start and end of a string:

```
raw = "  hello  "
clean = raw.strip()
```

This is especially useful when dealing with user input.

The `split()` method breaks a string into a list of substrings:

```
csv = "red,green,blue"
colors = csv.split(",")
```

The opposite operation is `join()`, which combines a list of strings into a single string, as shown in the following code:

```
colors = ["red", "green", "blue"]
result = ",".join(colors)
```

Indexing and slicing strings

Strings can be indexed and sliced, just like lists:

```
word = "Python"
word[0]       # "P"
word[1:4]     # "yth"
word[-1]      # "n"
```

Slicing creates new strings and never modifies the original.

Substrings

Another common task is checking whether a string contains a value or starts or ends in a particular way, as shown in the following code:

```
email = "user@example.com"

"@" in email
email.startswith("user")
email.endswith(".com")
```

These operations read cleanly and avoid fragile manual parsing.

User input starts as a string

It is also important to understand that input from the user always starts as a string:

```
age = input("How old are you? ")
```

If you need a number, you must convert it explicitly, as shown in the following code:

```
age = int(age)
```

Failing to do this is one of the most common beginner mistakes and a frequent source of `TypeError` and `ValueError` exceptions.

Strings are immutable

At this point, you should think of strings as immutable building blocks. You create them, transform them, combine them, and pass them around, but you never alter them in place. Python's string tools are designed to make these transformations readable and safe.

As you move into file handling, web development, and APIs, strings will dominate your code. Being comfortable with f-strings and a handful of core string methods will make that work feel straightforward rather than fiddly.

Now that we know how to handle string values in depth, let's see how you can break down a large, complex project into small functional units. This makes it easier to manage lots of code, and makes it easier to test and debug.

Functions and classes

As your programs grow beyond a few lines, repeating the same logic over and over quickly becomes painful. Functions solve this problem. A **function** is a named block of code that performs a specific task. Once defined, you can call it as many times as you like. This makes programs easier to read and easier to change.

Prompt: How do functions help programs scale beyond a few hundred lines? Please explain why small functions are easier to test and debug.

Defining functions

In Python, functions are defined using the `def` keyword, followed by the function name, a pair of parentheses, and a colon. The function body is indented, like any other block, as shown in the following code:

```
def greet():
    print("Hello, Python")
```

This code defines a function called `greet`. Nothing happens yet. Defining a function does not run it. To execute the code inside the function, you must call it by name, as shown in the following code:

```
greet()
```

When Python reaches this line, it jumps into the function, runs the indented block, and then returns to where it left off.

Function parameters

Most useful functions accept **parameters**. Parameters are variables that receive values from the caller. They let the function work with different data each time it is called, as shown in the following code:

```
def greet(name):
    print("Hello,", name)

greet("Alice")
greet("Bob")
```

In the preceding code, `name` is a parameter. When you call `greet("Alice")`, the value `"Alice"` is passed into the function and assigned to `name`.

Returning values from functions

Functions can also return values using the `return` statement. Returning a value sends data back to the caller and ends the function immediately, as shown in the following code:

```
def add(a, b):
    return a + b

result = add(3, 4)
print(result)
```

Functions do not only perform actions. They can compute a result and hand it back to the caller.

A function can have multiple `return` statements, but only one will run per call, as shown in the following code:

```
def check_age(age):
    if age >= 18:
        return "Adult"
    else:
        return "Minor"
```

As soon as `return` executes, the function exits.

Local variables and scope

Variables defined inside a function are local to that function. This means they exist only while the function is running and cannot be accessed from outside, as shown in the following code:

```
def example():
    x = 10
    print(x)

example()
# print(x)  # This would cause an error
```

This concept is called **scope**. Local variables help prevent accidental interference between different parts of a program. If everything were global, even small programs would become fragile very quickly.

Functions can call other functions, including ones you have written yourself, as shown in the following code:

```
def square(n):
    return n * n

def print_square(n):
    result = square(n)
    print(result)

print_square(5)
```

This kind of composition is normal in Python. Small functions that do one thing well are easier to test and easier to reuse than large functions that try to do everything at once.

Default parameter values

It is also worth noting that Python allows default parameter values, as shown in the following code:

```
def greet(name, greeting="Hello"):
    print(greeting, name)

greet("Alice")
greet("Bob", "Hi")
```

Defaults make functions flexible without making them complicated.

Grouping data and behavior with classes

So far, your Python code has been organized around variables and functions.

That works well for small scripts. But as programs grow, you often need a way to group related data and behavior together. That is what classes are for.

A **class** lets you define a new kind of object that has:

- **Data** (called attributes)
- **Behavior** (called methods)

Here is a basic class:

```
class Task:
    def __init__(self, title):
        self.title = title
        self.completed = False

    def mark_complete(self):
        self.completed = True
```

This class is a template for creating task objects.

Now you can create and use a task:

```
task = Task("Write Chapter 8")
print(task.title)         # Write Chapter 8
print(task.completed)     # False

task.mark_complete()
print(task.completed)     # True
```

The __init__ method

The `__init__` method runs when you create a new object:

```
task = Task("Write Chapter 8")
```

It is used to set up the initial state of the object:

- `self` refers to the current object
- `self.title` and `self.completed` are attributes stored on that object

The `__init__` method defines what data each instance of the class starts with. `self` is the object you are working with.

When you write:

```
task.mark_complete()
```

Python turns that into:

```
Task.mark_complete(task)
```

So `self` is the instance being passed in. You do not need to name it `self`, but you should. It is a strong convention and every Python developer expects it.

Making objects printable

By default, printing an object is not very helpful:

```
print(task)
```

You might see something like:

```
<__main__.Task object at 0x...>
```

You can improve this by defining a special method:

```
def __str__(self) -> str:
    status = "✓" if self.completed else "X"
    return f"{status} {self.title}"
```

Now:

```
print(task)
```

produces:

```
X Write Chapter 8
```

Let's break down the method:

- `__str__` is a special method name that Python calls when converting an object to a string
- `self` is the instance
- `-> str` is a type hint that says this method returns a string

So, whenever you see `def __str__(self) -> str:` in a class, it means, *When Python needs a string representation of this object, call this method and expect a string back.*

You will see this pattern often in real Python code, especially in frameworks like Django.

Methods are functions inside a class

A method is a function defined inside a class:

```
def mark_complete(self):
    self.completed = True
```

The only difference is that it operates on an instance (`self`).

This means everything you learned about functions still applies, including parameters, return values, and control flow. The difference is that methods usually work with the object's internal data.

Adding more structure

You can expand the class naturally:

```
class Task:
    def __init__(self, title, priority="medium"):
        self.title = title
        self.completed = False
        self.priority = priority

    def mark_complete(self):
        self.completed = True

    def is_high_priority(self):
        return self.priority == "high"

    def __str__(self) -> str:
        status = "✓" if self.completed else "X"
        return f"{status} [{self.priority}] {self.title}"
```

Now the object has multiple attributes, multiple methods, and a clear string representation.

Why classes matter for Django

You do not need classes for simple scripts.

But Django uses classes everywhere.

For example:

- Database models are classes
- Views are often classes
- Forms are classes

A Django model might look like this:

```
class Task(models.Model):
    title = models.CharField(max_length=200)
    completed = models.BooleanField(default=False)

    def __str__(self):
        return self.title
```

If you understand attributes, methods, `__init__`, and `__str__` then this code is not mysterious and scary. It is just a class with some framework-specific behavior.

Good practice: Use classes when you are modeling something with state (like a task, user, or order), you want to group related data and behavior, or you want multiple instances of the same kind of object. Avoid classes when a simple function or dictionary is enough or adding a class would make the code harder to follow.

Python's optional type hints

Type hints are optional annotations that describe the expected types of variables, parameters, and return values. They help with clarity and tooling, but they do not change how Python runs.

Type hints let you document purpose directly in the code:

```
def total_runtime(minutes: list[int]) -> int:
    return sum(minutes)
```

The preceding code says:

- `minutes` parameter is expected to be a list of integers
- `total_runtime` function is expected to return an integer

The code still runs exactly the same with or without the hints. Python does not enforce them at runtime. They are for humans and tools, not for the interpreter.

Type hints were added to address real problems in larger Python codebases. A function signature with type hints tells the reader how it is meant to be used without reading the implementation.

Code editors like VS Code can use type hints to:

- Provide more accurate autocomplete
- Highlight likely mistakes before you run the code
- Improve navigation and refactoring

Static type checkers can analyze your code and warn you about type mismatches that would otherwise only show up at runtime.

Type hints do not turn Python into a statically typed language. They are optional, gradual, and non-enforced by default. You can add type hints only where they help, mix typed and untyped code freely, and ignore them entirely if you choose.

This is called **gradual typing.** It lets teams add type information over time without rewriting everything.

Type hints are most valuable at boundaries:

- Function parameters and return values
- Public APIs
- Complex data structures
- Code that is reused by others

They are less useful for short-lived variables inside small functions, where the type is obvious.

Type hints are not required to learn Python. Beginners can write clean, correct code without them. However, understanding what they are and why they exist prepares readers for modern Python codebases, documentation, and frameworks like Django for web development.

Prompt: Please show me some examples where type hints prevent bugs without changing runtime behavior.

Decorators

Sooner or later, you will see Python code like this:

```
@something
def my_function():
    ...
```

That `@something` syntax is a **decorator**.

Decorators can look strange at first, but the core idea is simple: a decorator is a way to wrap one function with another function. This lets you add behavior without changing the original function body.

In other words, a decorator says, *before or after this function runs, do some extra work.*

This matters because Python treats functions as values. A function can be passed into another function, returned from a function, or replaced by another function.

Here is a very small example without using the @ syntax yet:

```
def say_hello():
    print("Hello")

def wrapper(func):
    def inner():
        print("Before the function runs")
        func()
        print("After the function runs")
    return inner

say_hello = wrapper(say_hello)
say_hello()
```

This prints:

```
Before the function runs
Hello
After the function runs
```

What happened?

1. `wrapper` takes a function as input
2. it defines a new function called `inner`
3. `inner` runs some extra code, then calls the original function
4. `wrapper` returns the new function
5. `say_hello` is replaced with that wrapped version

That is the essence of a decorator.

The @ syntax

Python provides a cleaner way to write the same idea:

```
def wrapper(func):
    def inner():
        print("Before the function runs")
        func()
        print("After the function runs")
    return inner

@wrapper
def say_hello():
    print("Hello")

say_hello()
```

This does the same thing as:

```
say_hello = wrapper(say_hello)
```

The `@wrapper` line is a more readable shortcut.

Why decorators exist

Decorators are useful when you want to add behavior to many functions in a consistent way. Common uses include logging, timing, access control, caching, and validation.

For example, instead of adding "print a log message" inside ten different functions, you can write one decorator and apply it to all ten. This keeps the core function focused on its real job.

Here is a simple decorator that logs when a function is called:

```
def log_call(func):
    def inner():
        print(f"Calling {func.__name__}")
        func()
    return inner

@log_call
def greet():
    print("Hi")

greet()
```

This prints:

```
Calling greet
Hi
```

The function greet still does its own job. The decorator adds extra behavior around it.

Decorators and function parameters

One complication is that real functions often take arguments. A decorator must usually accept those too.

Here is a version that handles any positional and keyword arguments:

```
def log_call(func):
    def inner(*args, **kwargs):
        print(f"Calling {func.__name__}")
        return func(*args, **kwargs)
    return inner

@log_call
def greet(name):
    print(f"Hello, {name}")

greet("Alice")
```

You do not need to master `*args` and `**kwargs` yet. For now, know that they allow the wrapper to pass through whatever arguments the original function expects.

Why beginners should care

You do not need decorators for everyday beginner Python scripts.

But you do need to recognize them, because they appear often in real Python codebases and web frameworks. Django uses decorators for tasks such as requiring login or restricting HTTP methods. Other libraries use them for caching, validation, and configuration.

At this stage, do not rush to write decorators. Make sure you can recognize what they do.

- A decorator wraps a function
- The `@name` syntax is shorthand
- Decorators add behavior without changing the original function body

Good practice: When first learning Python, use decorators sparingly. Read them often, recognize what they do, and only write your own when the benefit is obvious.

If a decorator hides simple logic that would be clearer written normally, it is probably making the code worse, not better.

That leads us neatly on to other guidance for writing functions.

Guidance for writing functions

At this stage, you should focus on writing clear, simple functions:

- Give them descriptive names
- Make them do one thing
- Pass data in using parameters
- Get results out using return values

Functions are the point where Python code starts to scale. Almost everything you do next, working with files, handling user input, processing data, or building web applications, will rely heavily on functions.

But before we go any deeper, let's get into handling errors and implementing strategies to debug problems.

Errors and debugging basics

Errors are a normal part of writing code. Every programmer, regardless of experience, sees error messages constantly. The difference between a beginner and an experienced developer is not how often errors happen, but how quickly they can understand and fix them. This section is about building that skill early.

When Python encounters a problem that it cannot recover from, it stops executing your program and prints an error message to the terminal. This message usually includes a **traceback**. A traceback is a report of what Python was doing when the error occurred.

Here is a simple example:

```
print(message)
```

If `message` has not been defined, Python will respond with something like the following:

```
Traceback (most recent call last):
  File "example.py", line 1, in <module>
    print(message)
NameError: name 'message' is not defined
```

The preceding output may look intimidating, but it follows a predictable structure. The most important rule is this: *read the last line first*. The final line tells you the type of error and usually explains the problem in plain language. In this case, Python is telling you that you tried to use a variable that does not exist.

The lines above the final message show where the error happened. They include the file name and line number. In small programs, this is often enough to locate and fix the issue immediately.

Common errors

There are a few error types that beginners encounter frequently. Learning to recognize them early will save a lot of time.

A `SyntaxError` means Python could not understand the structure of your code. This often happens because of a missing colon, unmatched parentheses, or incorrect indentation, as shown in the following code:

```
if x > 5
    print("Too big")
```

Here, the missing colon at the end of the `if` statement causes a syntax error before the program even runs.

An `IndentationError` is specific to Python and occurs when indentation is inconsistent or invalid, as shown in the following code:

```
if True:
print("Hello")
```

Python expects the indented block after the colon. Errors like this are common when copying and pasting code or mixing tabs and spaces.

A `TypeError` happens when you use a value in a way that does not make sense for its type, as shown in the following code:

```
age = "30"
age + 5
```

Python cannot add a string and an integer, so it raises a `TypeError`. The error message usually explains exactly what types were involved.

A `ValueError` occurs when a value is the right type but has an invalid value:

```
age = int("thirty")
```

Here, Python knows how to convert strings to integers, but "thirty" is not a valid number.

But what if your code runs without throwing an error and still gives results that you do not expect? That's where debugging skills become vital.

Debugging

Debugging starts with forming a simple hypothesis: what did I expect to happen, and what actually happened? Then you test that hypothesis by inspecting the program's state.

One of the simplest and most effective debugging tools is still the `print` function, as shown in the following code:

```
print(age)
print(type(age))
```

Printing values at key points in your program helps you confirm whether variables contain what you think they do. This approach is not elegant, but it is honest and effective, especially for beginners.

Make incremental changes

Another important habit is making small changes and re-running the program often. If you change ten things at once and something breaks, you do not know which change caused the problem. If you change one thing and re-run, the cause is obvious.

VS Code also provides basic debugging support through breakpoints and variable inspection, but you do not need to master the debugger yet. Understanding error messages and using simple print statements will take you surprisingly far.

Prompt: Please create a Python code file with a problem that needs debugging so that I can practice my debugging skills.

One final idea to internalize is that error messages are part of Python's documentation. They are written by humans and are meant to be read. When Python says something is not defined, incompatible, or invalid, it is almost always telling the truth. Your job is to connect that message to the code you wrote.

AI coding assistants can also help when debugging. You can paste an error message or traceback and ask for an explanation or suggested fix. This can be useful, especially when you are stuck. However, treat AI as a guide rather than an authority. Always read the error yourself first and try to understand what it is telling you before relying on a generated explanation.

If you can stay calm, read the last line, check the line number, and test small changes, debugging becomes a repeatable process instead of a source of frustration. That skill will serve you far longer than memorizing syntax rules.

Handling runtime errors safely

`try` / `except` blocks are how Python handles runtime errors safely. They let you protect parts of your program that might fail and decide what should happen instead of letting the program crash.

A `try` block contains code that might fail. When something goes wrong, Python does not continue. It raises an exception, which means it stops normal execution and signals that an error has occurred.

If an exception occurs, Python stops executing the `try` block immediately and looks for a matching `except` block to handle the problem:

```
try:
    age = int(input("How old are you? "))
except ValueError:
    print("Please enter a number.")
```

In the preceding code, if the age conversion succeeds, the `except` block is skipped. If it fails because the user enters something that cannot be converted to a number and the `int` function raises a `ValueError`, the program prints a friendly message instead of crashing.

User input is one of the most common sources of errors. Users type unexpected values, press *Enter*, or paste nonsense. We can handle this common issue easily:

```
try:
    quantity = int(input("Quantity: "))
    price = float(input("Price: "))
    total = quantity * price
    print(f"Total: {total}")
except ValueError:
    print("Invalid input. Please enter numbers only.")
```

Here, both conversions are protected. If either fails, the program handles it gracefully.

File operations fail for reasons outside your control: missing files, permissions, or disk issues. Again, we can handle these situations:

```
try:
    with open("config.txt", "r", encoding="utf-8") as file:
        text = file.read()
except OSError:
    print("Could not read configuration file.")
```

Without the `try` / `except`, the program would crash even though the error is not necessarily fatal.

Catching specific exception types is important. This avoids hiding unrelated bugs. Good practice is to specify which error type you expect:

```
try:
    result = 10 / value
```

```
except ZeroDivisionError:
    print("Cannot divide by zero.")
```

Other errors will still stop the program. Specific exceptions make error handling clearer and safer.

Good error handling anticipates what can go wrong, catches only what it understands, and leaves everything else visible so problems can be fixed properly.

Prompt: How should I decide whether to catch an exception or let it crash?

Now we will move on to structuring your code, which is especially important when you work on large Python projects.

Modules, imports, and packages

As programs grow, putting all your code into a single file quickly becomes unmanageable. Python solves this problem with **modules**. A module is simply a Python file. Any `.py` file can be used as a module, and modules let you organize code and reuse it across multiple programs.

Importing standard modules

At the most basic level, you make a module available in your current code file by *importing the module*, as shown in the following code:

```
import math
```

The preceding code tells Python to load another module and make its contents available to your program. In this case, `math` is part of Python's standard library, which means it ships with Python itself.

Once imported, you access names inside a module using dot notation, as shown in the following code:

```
import math

result = math.sqrt(16)
print(result)
```

Here, `math.sqrt` refers to the `sqrt` function defined inside the `math` module. This explicit naming is intentional. It avoids confusion about where functions come from and makes code easier to read.

Python also allows you to import specific names from a module:

```
from math import sqrt

result = sqrt(16)
```

This is shorter, but it comes with a trade-off. When you import names directly, it can be harder to tell where they originated, especially in larger programs. For beginners, using `import module_name` and dot notation is usually clearer.

Defining your own modules

Modules are not limited to the standard library. You can import your own Python files as well. Suppose you have two files in the same folder:

Here is a file named `helpers.py`:

```
def greet(name):
    print("Hello,", name)
```

Here is a file named `main.py`:

```
import helpers

helpers.greet("Alice")
```

When Python runs `main.py`, it looks for a file called `helpers.py` in the same directory and loads it as a module. This allows you to separate related code into logical units without any special configuration.

It is important to understand that when a module is imported, Python executes the code at the top level of that file once. This can lead to surprising behavior if a module contains code that runs immediately.

For example:

```
print("Loading helpers module")
```

If this line is at the top of `helpers.py`, it will run as soon as the module is imported. This is why modules usually contain only function definitions and constants, and not any executable logic.

Prompt: Please explain how Python decides where to look when importing a module.

Preventing execution in modules

There is a common Python pattern to control this behavior:

```
if __name__ == "__main__":
    print("This file is being run directly")
```

When a file is run directly, `__name__` is set to `"__main__"`. When it is imported, `__name__` is set to the module's name instead. This allows a file to behave both as a script and as an importable module.

Prompt: Why does Python execute module-level code on import? Please explain `__name__ == '__main__'` in more depth with real examples.

What's important for beginners about modules

At this stage, you do not need to memorize Python's full import system. What matters is understanding:

- A module is a `.py` file
- Importing a module makes its functions and constants available
- Python executes a module once when it is first imported
- Code meant for reuse should live inside functions

Modules are how Python scales from small scripts to real applications. They are also how you access the standard library and, later, third-party packages.

Prompt: Please show me some common mistakes with circular imports and how to avoid them.

Packages and how they relate to modules

At some point, you will want to use code that does not come with Python itself. Python solves this through **packages**. Understanding what a package is, how to install one, and how it relates to modules will remove a lot of mystery from Python development:

- A module is a single Python file. If you have a file called `utils.py` that contains utility function definitions, that file is a module.
- A package is a collection of one or more modules, usually organized into folders. Packages often provide a cohesive set of related functionality. For example, a package might include modules for HTTP requests, data parsing, and error handling, all grouped under one name.

From the developer's point of view, both modules and packages are accessed using `import`. Python does not care whether the name you import comes from a single file or a whole directory structure.

For example, you might import two modules from the standard library, as shown in the following code:

```
import math
import json
```

This works the same way for third-party packages once they are installed.

Installing packages

Python packages are installed using a tool called `pip`, which stands for **Python package installer**. Pip downloads packages from the Python Package Index, commonly called PyPI, which is the central repository for Python packages maintained by the community.

Installing a package is done from the command line, usually inside an activated virtual environment, as shown in the following command:

```
pip install requests
```

This command downloads the `requests` package and installs it into the active Python environment. Later in this chapter, you will learn about virtual environments. One of their benefits is that, if you are using a virtual environment, the package is installed only there, which avoids polluting your system with packages.

Once installed, you can import it into your code like a standard library module, as shown in the following code:

```
import requests

response = requests.get("https://example.com")
print(response.status_code)
```

Installing a package does not magically change Python's syntax or behavior. It simply makes additional modules available for import.

How packages work

Behind the scenes, Python searches a list of directories, known as `sys.path`, to find modules and packages. When you install a package with `pip`, it places files into one of these directories inside your environment. When you write `import requests`, Python looks through those locations until it finds a matching package.

You do not need to inspect `sys.path` or understand Python's full import algorithm at this stage. The important idea is that installation affects availability, not usage. Importing is how you actually use the code.

Package versions

It is also common to install a specific version of a package, as shown in the following command:

```
pip install requests==2.31.0
```

This matters because packages evolve. Code written against one version may not behave the same way against another. Virtual environments exist largely to manage this reality.

As projects grow, developers usually record installed packages in a file called `requirements.txt`:

```
requests==2.31.0
```

This file is not magic. It is simply a list of packages and versions. You can install all the packages listed, as shown in the following code:

```
pip install -r requirements.txt
```

The preceding command tells `pip` to install everything listed. This makes it easy to recreate the same environment on another machine or in a deployment system.

Prompt: Please explain `requirements.txt` vs tools like pip-tools or poetry

One final point that often trips up beginners: installing a package and importing it are separate steps. If you try to import a package that is not installed in the active environment, Python will raise a `ModuleNotFoundError`. When this happens, the fix is almost always to install the package into the environment you are currently using.

If you remember only one rule from this section, make it this:

- Pip installs packages into an environment
- Import uses those installed packages in your code

Once that distinction is clear, Python's packaging story becomes far less confusing and much more predictable.

We've mentioned virtual environments a few times while talking about packages. Let's look at them next.

Virtual environments

Sooner or later, every Python developer runs into a confusing situation: one project works, another suddenly breaks, and the error message mentions a package version you do not remember installing.

The problem

Virtual environments exist to prevent exactly this problem. They are not an advanced feature, but they are something you should understand conceptually early, even if you do not use them heavily yet.

By default, when you install a Python package, it is installed into a shared location associated with your Python interpreter. If all your projects share the same interpreter and the same installed packages, you can easily end up with conflicts. One project might need version 1 of a library, another might need version 2, and only one of them can win. This is not hypothetical. It happens a lot in real-world Python work.

Prompt: Please explain the difference between system Python and virtual environments.

The solution

A virtual environment is a self-contained Python environment that lives inside a project. It has its own Python interpreter and its own set of installed packages, isolated from everything else on your system. When you activate a virtual environment, Python commands and package installs apply only to that environment.

The basic rule is simple:

- One project equals one virtual environment
- Each environment has its own dependencies
- Projects do not interfere with each other

Python includes built-in support for virtual environments through the `venv` module, so no extra tools are required.

Prompt: Please show me what goes wrong when multiple projects share one environment.

Creating a virtual environment

Creating a virtual environment is usually done from the command line, inside your project folder, as shown in the following command:

```
python -m venv .venv
```

This creates a folder called `.venv` containing a copy of the Python interpreter and supporting files. The name `.venv` is a convention. The leading dot makes the folder less visually noisy, and many tools recognize it automatically.

Good practice: The dot prefix for the folder name is a convention. You can name the folder anything. Using `venv` is the older and still very common convention. Many tutorials and official examples use `venv`, so it aligns well with most learning materials. The downside is that the folder appears alongside your source code in alphabetical order, which some people find visually noisy, especially in larger projects.

Using `.venv` follows the Unix convention that directories starting with a dot are hidden by default on macOS and Linux. This keeps the project root visually cleaner and reinforces the idea that the virtual environment is an implementation detail rather than application code. Tools such as VS Code, Poetry, and some Python linters and formatters explicitly look for `.venv` and will auto-detect it without extra configuration. The trade-off is that hidden directories can be confusing for beginners. For professional projects, especially those using Python tooling and aiming for a tidy project root, `.venv` is increasingly popular.

Once created, the environment must be activated. Activating an environment is different depending on your OS:

- On Windows, enter the following command:

  ```
  .venv\Scripts\activate
  ```

- On macOS and Linux, enter the following command:

  ```
  source .venv/bin/activate
  ```

After activation, the terminal prompt usually changes to show the environment name. This is your visual cue that the environment is active. From this point on, running `python` or `pip` refers to the virtual environment, not the system-wide Python.

When you install packages inside an active environment, they are isolated to that project:

```
pip install requests
```

Another project, with a different environment, will not see that package unless it installs it explicitly.

VS Code and virtual environments

VS Code integrates well with virtual environments. When a `.venv` folder exists, the Python extension will usually detect it and offer to use it automatically. You can also select it manually using the Python interpreter selector in the bottom-right corner of the editor. Once selected, running Python files from VS Code uses the virtual environment interpreter behind the scenes.

Prompt: Please explain how VS Code detects and uses virtual environments.

At this stage, you do not need to know the advanced features. What matters is understanding why virtual environments exist and recognizing them when you see them.

You will often encounter files like `requirements.txt` or commands like:

```
pip install -r requirements.txt
```

These are simply ways to describe and reproduce the packages installed in a virtual environment. They make it possible for someone else, or a deployment system, to recreate the same setup reliably.

Good practice: Do not install project dependencies into your system Python once you start using virtual environments regularly. Mixing approaches leads to confusion very quickly.

In short, virtual environments allow many projects to coexist on the same machine without conflict. You do not need to use them for every tiny experiment, but for anything that matters or lasts longer than a single session, they are the correct default. Understanding this now will save you hours of frustration later.

Now let's look at how to read and write to the filesystem. This is where your Python projects "remember" previous work they've done.

File input and output

So far, most of your Python programs have lived entirely in memory. When the program ends, all its data disappears. File input and output, usually shortened to file I/O, is how programs read data from disk and write data back so it can be reused later.

At the most basic level, working with files involves three steps:

1. Open a file.
2. Read from it or write to it.
3. Close it.

Python hides much of this ceremony for you, but the underlying model is still the same.

Writing text to a file

The simplest way to write text to a file is to open it in *write* mode. If the file does not exist, Python creates it. If it does exist, Python overwrites it.

For example, to open or create a new file named `example.txt`, and write a short message to it, as shown in the following code:

```
with open("example.txt", "w", encoding="utf-8") as file:
    file.write("Hello, file")
```

Note the following about the preceding code:

- The `with` statement is important. It ensures the file is properly closed even if something goes wrong. You should treat with as the default way to work with files. The `with` statement isn't only for files, it's used for database connections, network requests, and any context manager, which is any object that can set up and tear down resources automatically.
- The `"w"` mode means write. There are other modes, but these are the most common:
    - `"w"` write, replacing the file
    - `"a"` append, adding to the end of the file
    - `"r"` read, which is the default

If you want to add content instead of replacing it, use append mode, as shown in the following code:

```
with open("example.txt", "a", encoding="utf-8") as file:
    file.write("\nAnother line")
```

Reading text from a file

Reading works the same way, but with the *read* mode, as shown in the following code:

```
with open("example.txt", "r", encoding="utf-8") as file:
    contents = file.read()

print(contents)
```

This reads the entire file into a single string. For small files like configuration files, logs, or simple data files, this is perfectly reasonable.

You can also read line by line, which is useful for larger files, as shown in the following code:

```
with open("example.txt", "r", encoding="utf-8") as file:
    for line in file:
        print(line.strip())
```

Each line includes a trailing newline character, which is why `strip()` is often used.

Files are just big strings

One important idea to internalize is that text files are just strings on disk. When you read a file, you get a string. When you write to a file, you are writing a string. Everything you learned in the strings section applies directly here.

That is why formats like CSV, JSON, and even HTML are approachable in Python. They are text first, structure second.

Prompt: Please explain why files are treated as strings in Python.

Using JSON for structured data

It is common to use JSON instead of inventing your own file format. JSON is a text-based format designed to represent structured data, and it maps cleanly onto Python's data structures:

- JSON objects map to Python dictionaries
- JSON arrays map to Python lists
- Strings, numbers, Booleans, and null map naturally

Instead of manually writing strings to a file, you can use the `json` module from the standard library, as shown in the following code:

```
import json

text = json.dumps(data, indent=2)
```

This converts Python data structures into a formatted string. Writing that string to disk is normal file I/O.

Reading JSON works in reverse, as shown in the following code:

```
data = json.loads(text)
```

The file itself is still plain text. JSON simply gives that text a predictable structure.

Paths and file locations

In small scripts, file names like `"tasks.json"` work because Python looks in the current working directory. In real programs, paths can get more complex. A commonly used module for handling paths is `pathlib`, as shown in the following code:

```
from pathlib import Path

DATA_FILE = Path("tasks.json")
```

Path objects make file operations clearer and safer than manipulating strings manually, as shown in the following code:

```
DATA_FILE.exists()
DATA_FILE.read_text(encoding="utf-8")
DATA_FILE.write_text(text, encoding="utf-8")
```

These are convenience methods built on top of normal file I/O. They still follow the same rules, but with less boilerplate.

Common file I/O errors

File operations can fail for reasons outside your program's control:

- The file does not exist.
- The file is locked or unreadable.
- The disk is full.
- The contents are not in the format you expect.

That is why file I/O is often wrapped in `try` and `except` blocks, as shown in the following code:

```
try:
    text = DATA_FILE.read_text(encoding="utf-8")
except OSError:
    print("Could not read file")
```

The preceding code prevents your program from crashing and lets you decide how to recover.

File I/O summary

File I/O is what gives a programming project permanence. Without it, tasks vanish when the program exits. With it, your program maintains state across runs.

The most important takeaway from this section is not the specific functions. It is this pattern:

- Convert in-memory data to text.
- Write that text to disk.
- Read it back later.
- Convert it back into Python data structures.

That pattern appears everywhere in Python development: configuration files, logs, caches, databases, and web APIs. If you understand file I/O at this level, nothing about saving and loading data later will feel mysterious.

Prompt: Please show me some common file I/O mistakes and how to avoid data loss.

Now let's build a complete mini-project using everything you've learned in this chapter.

A small, cohesive mini-project

In the final section of this chapter, we will build a small, cohesive mini-project: a Command-line Task Tracker.

This mini-project ties together everything you have learned so far: variables, conditionals, loops, data structures, functions, modules/imports, strings (including f-strings), file I/O, and basic error handling.

You will build a small command-line *task tracker* that can:

1. Add a task
2. List tasks
3. Mark a task as done
4. Delete a task
5. Save and load tasks from a JSON file so they persist between runs

You will keep the data model simple: a list of dictionaries. Each task will look like this:

```
{"title": "Buy milk", "done": False}
```

Writing the code

Create a new file in VS Code called `task_tracker.py` and paste the following code. Read it top-to-bottom first, then run it, then tweak it.

You can download this entire file from the following link: `https://github.com/markjprice/web-dev-ai/blob/main/Code/Chapter08/python-basics/task_tracker.py`

Good practice: If your code uses type hints, especially with classes or larger projects, add `from __future__ import annotations` at the top of the file and forget about it. It removes edge cases without adding complexity. For modern Python (3.10+), it is generally a good default to include this import at the top of your files if you are using type hints. It makes annotations more flexible and avoids subtle issues as your code grows. In newer Python versions (3.13+), this behavior is becoming the default, so this import will eventually no longer be necessary.

```
from __future__ import annotations

import json
from pathlib import Path

DATA_FILE = Path("tasks.json")

def load_tasks() -> list[dict]:
    """Load tasks from disk. If the file doesn't exist yet, return an
empty list."""
    if not DATA_FILE.exists():
        return []

    try:
        text = DATA_FILE.read_text(encoding="utf-8")
        data = json.loads(text)

        # Defensive check: ensure it's a list of dicts.
        if not isinstance(data, list):
            return []
        cleaned: list[dict] = []
        for item in data:
```

```
            if isinstance(item, dict) and "title" in item and "done" in
item:
                cleaned.append({"title": str(item["title"]), "done":
bool(item["done"])})
        return cleaned
    except (OSError, json.JSONDecodeError):
        # File can't be read or contains invalid JSON.
        return []

def save_tasks(tasks: list[dict]) -> None:
    """Save tasks to disk as JSON."""
    try:
        text = json.dumps(tasks, indent=2)
        DATA_FILE.write_text(text, encoding="utf-8")
    except OSError:
        print("Warning: could not save tasks to disk.")

def add_task(tasks: list[dict]) -> None:
    title = input("Task title: ").strip()
    if not title:
        print("Task title cannot be empty.")
        return

    tasks.append({"title": title, "done": False})
    save_tasks(tasks)
    print(f'Added: "{title}"')

def list_tasks(tasks: list[dict]) -> None:
    if not tasks:
        print("No tasks yet. Add one with: add")
        return

    for i, task in enumerate(tasks, start=1):
        status = "✓" if task["done"] else " "
        print(f"{i:>2}. [{status}] {task['title']}")

def mark_done(tasks: list[dict]) -> None:
    if not tasks:
```

```
        print("No tasks to mark as done.")
        return

    raw = input("Task number to mark done: ").strip()
    try:
        index = int(raw) - 1
    except ValueError:
        print("Please enter a valid number.")
        return

    if index < 0 or index >= len(tasks):
        print("That task number is out of range.")
        return

    tasks[index]["done"] = True
    save_tasks(tasks)
    print(f'Marked done: "{tasks[index]["title"]}"')

def delete_task(tasks: list[dict]) -> None:
    if not tasks:
        print("No tasks to delete.")
        return

    raw = input("Task number to delete: ").strip()
    try:
        index = int(raw) - 1
    except ValueError:
        print("Please enter a valid number.")
        return

    if index < 0 or index >= len(tasks):
        print("That task number is out of range.")
        return

    removed = tasks.pop(index)
    save_tasks(tasks)
    print(f'Deleted: "{removed["title"]}"')
```

```
def print_help() -> None:
    print("Commands:")
    print("  add     Add a new task")
    print("  list    List all tasks")
    print("  done    Mark a task as done")
    print("  delete  Delete a task")
    print("  help    Show this help")
    print("  quit    Exit the program")

def main() -> None:
    tasks = load_tasks()
    print("Task Tracker")
    print_help()

    while True:
        command = input("\n> ").strip().lower()

        if command == "add":
            add_task(tasks)
        elif command == "list":
            list_tasks(tasks)
        elif command == "done":
            mark_done(tasks)
        elif command == "delete":
            delete_task(tasks)
        elif command == "help":
            print_help()
        elif command in {"quit", "exit"}:
            print("Goodbye.")
            break
        elif command == "":
            continue
        else:
            print("Unknown command. Type: help")

if __name__ == "__main__":
    main()
```

Trying the project

Run the code file and try this quick session:

1. `add`: "Write 20 lines of Python"
2. `add`: "Make tea"
3. `list`
4. `done:2`
5. `list`
6. Quit and run it again. Your tasks should still be there, because they were saved to `tasks.json`.

What this mini-project reinforces

This mini-project applied the following knowledge:

- Data structures: a list of dictionaries is a very common Python pattern
- Functions: each command is implemented as a function that operates on the shared `tasks` list
- Modules/imports: you used `json` and `pathlib` from the standard library
- Strings: `strip()`, `lower()`, f-strings, and clean printing
- Errors and debugging: `try/except` prevents the program from crashing on invalid input or a bad JSON file

More mini-challenges to extend the project

If you are feeling inspired, try completing the following challenges:

1. Add a `due_date` field (using a string is fine) and display it in the list.
2. Add a `clear` command that deletes all tasks after a confirmation prompt.
3. Add a `search` command that lists tasks containing a keyword (case-insensitive).
4. Sort the list so undone tasks appear first, then done tasks.
5. Add a `rename` command to change a task title.

Prompt: How would this task tracker change if it used a database instead of JSON? What would it take to turn this script into a web application? Which parts of this project map directly to Django concepts?

The task tracker is small, but it already asks the questions real programs ask. Where should the data live? What happens when the user types rubbish? Which code should be split into a function? What would need to change if tasks moved from a JSON file into a database? AI can help write individual functions, but you still have to decide what the program is supposed to do and where each responsibility belongs.

Practice, references, and resources

In this section, you will be tested on what you've learned in this chapter and be provided with useful links to reference materials and resources.

Check your understanding

Answer the following questions:

1. What is the difference between a script and a module in Python?
2. Why does Python use indentation instead of braces?
3. What does it mean that Python is dynamically typed?
4. What is the difference between = and ==?
5. What happens when Python encounters an error while running a script?
6. Why is it important to read the last line of a traceback first?
7. Why is mixing types in a list usually a bad idea?
8. What is the difference between a list and a tuple?
9. What is the difference between a parameter and a return value?
10. What does it mean when Python raises an exception?
11. Why is catching specific exceptions better than catching all exceptions?
12. What is the difference between a module and a package?
13. Why are installing a package and importing it separate steps?
14. What problem do virtual environments solve?
15. What does activating a virtual environment change?
16. What are the three basic steps when working with files?
17. Why is the `with` statement recommended when working with files?

18. What is truthiness in Python? Give two examples.
19. Why are strings immutable? What practical effect does that have?
20. In the task tracker project, why is a list of dictionaries used instead of another structure?

Links

Here are the official Python documentation links you should reference, followed by a small set of high-quality, community-endorsed resources that are widely trusted and appropriate for beginners and professionals alike.

Official Python documentation at python.org

These links are maintained by the Python Software Foundation and are the canonical reference for Python behavior and features.

Python Tutorial: `https://docs.python.org/3/tutorial/`

Python Language Reference: `https://docs.python.org/3/reference/`

Python Standard Library documentation: `https://docs.python.org/3/library/`

Built-in Types: `https://docs.python.org/3/library/stdtypes.html`

venv documentation: `https://docs.python.org/3/library/venv.html`

Python installation guide: `https://www.python.org/downloads/`

Python FAQ: `https://docs.python.org/3/faq/`

PEP 8 – Python style guide: `https://peps.python.org/pep-0008/`

Prompt: How should I read Python documentation effectively?

Official packaging and dependency management resources

Python Packaging User Guide: `https://packaging.python.org/`

pip documentation: `https://pip.pypa.io/en/stable/`

Python Package Index (PyPI): `https://pypi.org/`

Community learning resources

Real Python: `https://realpython.com/`

Python Tutor: `https://pythontutor.com/`

Prompt: Which parts of Python should I master first for web development? What Python features should beginners ignore for now?

Summary

In this chapter, you learned the core pieces of Python that you will need for the rest of the book. You installed Python, ran scripts from the command line and in VS Code, and got used to Python's basic syntax, including indentation, variables, conditions, loops, and expressions. You also worked with the built-in data structures that make Python practical very quickly: lists, tuples, dictionaries, and sets.

You then moved into the parts of Python that matter once programs get a little larger: strings, functions, debugging, exceptions, modules, packages, virtual environments, and file I/O. Those topics matter because they are what turn a few lines of syntax into a program you can actually understand, organize, run, and maintain.

The task tracker at the end is the most important part of the chapter, because it shows how these ideas fit together. The program is still small, but it already has structure, persistent state, user input, error handling, and separate functions with clear jobs. That is the real bridge to the next chapter. Django will give you a web framework, but the habits that make Django code understandable start here, in plain Python.

Specifically, you learned:

- What Python is, where it is used, and why readability and simplicity are central to its design
- How to install Python, verify that it is working, and run Python code from the command line and from within VS Code
- How to write and execute Python scripts using .py files
- How Python syntax works, including indentation, statements, variables, and basic expressions
- How to use lists, tuples, dictionaries, and sets to model and manipulate collections of data
- How to write `if`, `elif`, and `else` blocks to make decisions in code

- How to write `for` loops to process items in a collection
- How to define and call functions, pass data using parameters, and return values
- How to read Python error messages and tracebacks, and how to debug common beginner mistakes
- How to organize code across multiple files using modules and imports
- How to install third-party Python packages using `pip` and understand the relationship between packages and modules
- What virtual environments are, why they exist, and how they prevent dependency conflicts
- How to work with strings effectively using f-strings and common string methods
- How to read from and write to files using file I/O, including safe patterns with `with`
- How to build a small but complete command-line program that ties together syntax, data structures, functions, file I/O, and basic error handling

In the next chapter, you will learn about Django, a high-level Python web framework for building database-driven websites. Django gives you a project structure, an object-relational mapper, routing, templates, forms, authentication, and an admin site, so you can spend more time on the application itself.

Learn more on Discord

To join the Discord community for this book – where you can share feedback, ask questions to the author, and learn about new releases – follow this QR code:

`https://discord.gg/rdEsrVbbC`

Django – Web Development on the Backend

This chapter introduces Django, a practical, opinionated web framework for building real applications without writing every piece of routing, forms, authentication, and database code yourself. You will see how Django fits into the broader web stack you have already learned, especially HTML, CSS, SQL, and Python, and why it includes common web features such as routing, forms, authentication, database migrations, and an admin interface instead of expecting you to assemble them yourself. You do not need to memorize every Django class, function, setting, and command. Focus on how Django structures a web project and why its conventions exist.

You will start by setting up a minimal Django project named *Scribble* for managing blog posts, and run it locally, then move through the core building blocks that make Django work, including the **Model-View-Template** (**MVT**) pattern:

- Models for cleanly mapping Python code to relational database tables
- Views for handling requests and passing data from the server to the browser
- Templates for rendering dynamic HTML without messily mixing logic and presentation

Along the way, you will explore the Django admin interface, which demonstrates how much functionality Django gives you for free once your models are defined.

By the end of the chapter, you should feel comfortable navigating a Django project and understand how its major parts cooperate to form a working web application. You will have a working Django project, a clear understanding of how models, views, and templates fit together, practical experience defining data and rendering dynamic pages, and confidence using the Django admin interface to inspect and manage your application's data.

In this chapter, we will cover the following topics:

- Introducing Django
- Setting up Django
- Django URL patterns and routing
- Django models
- Django views and templates
- Serving static files
- Django admin interface
- Django forms
- Django settings and configuration
- Error handling and debugging
- Authentication and authorization

Suggested chatbot prompts with example responses for this chapter can be found at the following link: `https://github.com/markjprice/web-dev-ai/blob/main/prompts/ch09-django/readme.md`

Introducing Django

Django is a high-level Python web framework for building websites that store and retrieve data. Its core idea is that most web applications share the same fundamental problems, so the framework should solve those problems once, in a consistent way, instead of forcing every developer to reinvent them. As a result, Django provides routing, database access, HTML templating, authentication, forms, security protections, and an admin interface out of the box.

MVT pattern

Architecturally, Django follows what it calls the **MVT pattern**: **Model, View, Template**. This is closely related to the more widely known **MVC pattern**: **Model, View, Controller**, but with slightly different naming that reflects Django's specific way of dividing responsibilities:

- Django's **Models** represent the data layer. They define your database schema using Python classes, and Django handles translating those definitions into SQL and database tables.
- Django's **Templates** are responsible for presentation. They generate HTML by combining static markup with dynamic data, while keeping most application logic out of the template itself.

- Django's **Views** coordinate the request. A view receives a **Hypertext Transfer Protocol (HTTP)** request, interacts with models if needed, and returns an HTTP response, often by rendering a template with some context data.

If you are used to MVC, Django's View roughly corresponds to a Controller, and Django's URL configuration and request handling cover work that some frameworks would put in a controller layer. **Uniform Resource Locator (URL)** configuration maps incoming requests to view functions or classes, which keeps request handling explicit and easy to follow. This separation of concerns makes Django applications easier to understand as they grow, because models hold data rules, views handle requests, and templates render HTML.

A summary comparison of the components of Django's MVT and MVC patterns is shown in *Table 9.1*:

Concept	**MVT**	**MVC**
Incoming request handled by:	URL configuration	Route
Logic executed by:	View	Controller
Data structure defined by:	Model	Model
Web page response generated by:	Template	View

Table 9.1: Comparing MVT and MVC design patterns

Prompt: Please explain Django's MVT architecture again, but this time trace a single HTTP request step by step from browser to database and back.

Opinionated and convention-driven

Django is popular partly because it gives you working features early. It is opinionated and convention-driven: follow Django's structure, and you get routing, database access, forms, authentication, and admin tools with little setup.

For example, defining a model automatically gives you database tables, a Python API for querying data, and an admin interface for managing records.

Common tasks like form validation, user authentication, and protection against common security issues are already solved, so you can spend time building features instead of infrastructure.

Django is especially well-suited to projects where correctness, maintainability, and development speed matter more than optimizing every performance detail from day one. Its design choices favor clarity and explicitness, which is why it is widely used for content-driven sites, internal tools, APIs, and data-heavy applications.

Prompt: What are the most common Django conventions that beginners try to fight, and why is it usually better to follow them?

Django projects versus Django apps

A useful concept to understand early is the difference between a Django project and a Django app:

- A **Django project** represents the entire website or system you are building.
- A **Django app** is a self-contained unit of functionality within that project. For example, a blog, a user accounts system, or a comments feature could each be separate apps.

A single Django project is made up of one or more apps, even if you only create one app to begin with. This structure encourages modular design and makes it easier to reuse or reorganize functionality as a project grows.

Prompt: Please show me a simple diagram of how Django projects and apps relate to each other in a real-world application.

What does batteries included mean?

Django is often described as "batteries included", and that phrase is worth unpacking. Django deliberately ships with solutions for common web development problems rather than leaving them as optional add-ons. Database migrations, authentication, form handling, security protections, and an administrative interface are all part of the core framework.

A **database migration** is a set of instructions that tells your database how to change its structure. Instead of directly editing the database, you write changes like adding a new column called `date_of_birth`, renaming that column, or creating a new table. Each of these changes is saved as a small file, usually in your project.

Where other web frameworks leave those features to additional layers on top of their framework, like a **content management system** (**CMS**), Django includes them.

This means Django projects tend to look similar to each other, which makes them easier to understand, maintain, and hand over to other developers.

The trade-off is that Django expects you to follow its conventions, but in return, you get routing, forms, authentication, migrations, static-file handling, and admin tools with little setup.

Request-response lifecycle

At a high level, Django applications follow a clear request–response lifecycle:

1. A browser sends an **HTTP** request to your web server.
2. Django matches that request against a set of URL patterns defined by `path()` to decide which view should handle it.
3. The view runs Python code, optionally queries the database through models like `Post.objects.filter()`, and produces an HTTP response. In many cases, that response is HTML generated by rendering a template, but it could also be JavaScript Object Notation (JSON), a redirect, or an error page.
4. This response is returned to the web browser to display to the user, or to the client app that made the request if it is just data.

Keeping this flow in mind makes it much easier to understand how the different Django components cooperate.

Django is a useful test of how well you understand a web application. An AI assistant can write a `path()` call or a `Post.objects.filter()` query quickly. The part you still have to judge is where that code belongs. Should this check live in the view, the model, the form, or middleware? What should happen if the post is missing, unpublished, or requested by the wrong user?

That is why Django is worth learning as a system, not as a pile of snippets. URLs choose views. Views make decisions. Models define and protect data. Templates render HTML. Middleware handles site-wide behavior. Settings describe the environment. When those pieces are clear in your head, generated code is much easier to review, debug, and reject when it puts logic in the wrong place.

Middleware

Before your view ever sees a request, Django runs it through a stack of **middleware**, which acts like a pipeline of processing steps. Each layer gets a chance to inspect or modify the request on the way in, and the response on the way out. This is how Django handles behavior that applies across the whole site without cluttering your view code.

Middleware is responsible for things that apply across your entire application, not just a single page. This includes session handling, security checks like **cross-site request forgery** (**CSRF**) protection, and user authentication. For example, when you access `request.user` in a view, that value has already been attached by Django's authentication middleware earlier in the pipeline.

This design keeps your views focused on your app's logic, while middleware handles the site-wide behavior around it. You are unlikely to write your own middleware at the start of learning Django, but understanding that it sits between the browser and your view helps explain how Django can provide so much functionality automatically, before your code even runs.

Beginner-friendly, but not only for small projects

Although Django is approachable for beginners, it is not a toy framework. It is designed to scale from small personal projects to large, long-lived applications. Many real-world systems start as simple Django projects and grow over time without changing frameworks.

Django's emphasis on explicit structure, clear separation of responsibilities, and predictable conventions helps keep complexity under control as applications evolve.

Django releases

Django has a very regular cadence for releases:

- Feature releases every eight months or so
- Every few releases, one is designated **long-term support** (**LTS**)
- LTS releases receive security and data-loss fixes for much longer than non-LTS releases

An LTS release is designed to be boring in the best sense. Many professional Django teams standardize on LTS releases only. If you want to target an LTS release, the latest at the time of publishing is Django 5.2, which will be supported until April 2028. Many professional Django teams standardize on LTS releases for that reason.

This book targets Django 6.0, which is a non-LTS release. It is supported until April 2027. Later versions will exist by the time you read this book, but the concepts and code shown here remain valid. For example, you should be able to target 6.1 when it releases in August 2026, or 6.2 in

April 2027, which is expected to be the next LTS release and will be supported until April 2030.

You can learn more about the current supported versions of Django at the following link: `https://www.djangoproject.com/download/#supported-versions`

Alternatives to Django

Although I chose Django for this book, it is not the only web framework for Python.

Flask is probably the most well-known alternative. It is much lighter than Django and gives you just the basics for handling HTTP requests and routing. You add other components yourself as needed. This makes Flask more flexible, but also means you need to make more decisions. You can learn more about Flask at the following link: `https://flask.palletsprojects.com/`

FastAPI is a newer framework that has become very popular for building APIs. It focuses on performance, modern Python features like type hints, and automatic documentation generation. It is widely used for backend services and AI-related applications. You can learn more about FastAPI at the following link: `https://fastapi.tiangolo.com/`

Pyramid sits somewhere in between Django and Flask. It allows you to start small and scale up in complexity, but it is less commonly used today than Flask or FastAPI. You can learn more about Pyramid at the following link: `https://docs.pylonsproject.org/projects/pyramid/`

In practice, most developers choose between three main options:

- Django for full-featured web applications
- Flask for simple or flexible projects
- FastAPI for APIs and high-performance services

For this book, Django is a sensible choice. It gives new web developers a structured environment with fewer decisions to make, which aligns well with your goal of teaching concepts rather than forcing readers to assemble a stack from scratch.

Expectations for this chapter

The focus in this chapter is on Django's core ideas: defining models, handling requests, rendering templates, and using the admin interface.

Django includes many other features, such as authentication systems and API tooling for building web services, but those build on the same foundations you will learn here.

Once you understand these basics, the rest of the framework becomes much easier to approach. With those ideas in place, you are ready to move on to creating your first Django project and seeing these ideas in action.

Setting up Django

Before writing any Django code, you need a working Python environment and a clean project setup. Django runs anywhere Python runs, so the steps are broadly the same on Windows, macOS, and Linux. The main differences are command syntax and file paths, which will be pointed out where relevant.

Creating and activating a virtual environment

Next, we will create a virtual environment for your Django project. This isolates your project's dependencies from the rest of your system and avoids version conflicts later.

Create a folder named `Chapter09`. Inside that folder, run the virtual environment command:

- On Windows, run: `python -m venv .venv`
- On macOS and Linux, run: `python3 -m venv .venv`

This creates a `.venv` folder containing a private Python installation for this project.

Now activate the virtual environment:

- On Windows, run: `.venv\Scripts\activate`
- On macOS and Linux, run: `source .venv/bin/activate`

When activation succeeds, your terminal prompt will usually change to show the virtual environment name:

```
(.venv) C:\web-dev-ai\Code\Chapter09>
```

From this point on, any Python packages you install will be limited to this project.

Installing Django

With the virtual environment active, install Django using `pip`:

```
pip install django
```

This downloads Django and its dependencies into the virtual environment:

```
Collecting django
  Using cached django-6.0.2-py3-none-any.whl.metadata (3.9 kB)
Collecting asgiref>=3.9.1 (from django)
  Using cached asgiref-3.11.1-py3-none-any.whl.metadata (9.3 kB)
Collecting sqlparse>=0.5.0 (from django)
  Using cached sqlparse-0.5.5-py3-none-any.whl.metadata (4.7 kB)
Collecting tzdata (from django)
  Using cached tzdata-2025.3-py2.py3-none-any.whl.metadata (1.4 kB)
Using cached django-6.0.2-py3-none-any.whl (8.3 MB)
Using cached asgiref-3.11.1-py3-none-any.whl (24 kB)
Using cached sqlparse-0.5.5-py3-none-any.whl (46 kB)
Using cached tzdata-2025.3-py2.py3-none-any.whl (348 kB)
Installing collected packages: tzdata, sqlparse, asgiref, django
Successfully installed asgiref-3.11.1 django-6.0.2 sqlparse-0.5.5
tzdata-2025.3
```

You can verify the installation by running `django-admin --version`, which should print a Django version number like `6.0.2`. If it does, Django is ready to use.

Using VS Code with Django

Open the `Chapter09` project folder in VS Code. VS Code should automatically detect the virtual environment and prompt you to select it as the interpreter.

If it does not, open the **Command Palette** and choose **Python: Select Interpreter**, then select the interpreter inside the `.venv` folder, as shown in *Figure 9.1*:

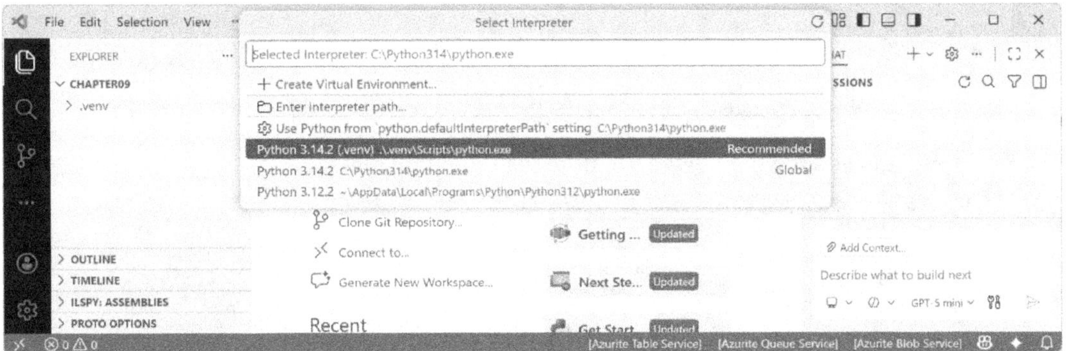

Figure 9.1: Selecting a Python interpreter for the Django virtual environment

Creating Django projects

At the command prompt or terminal, create your first Django project and name it `scribble` by running the following command:

```
django-admin startproject scribble
```

This creates a new folder called `scribble` with Python files like `manage.py` inside. The outer `scribble` folder is simply a container. The inner `scribble` folder holds the project configuration, including settings, URL configuration, and server startup code. At this stage, do not worry about memorizing these files. You will revisit them as they become relevant.

To confirm everything works, change into the outer `scribble` project directory using `cd scribble` and then run the development server using the following command:

```
python manage.py runserver
```

Django will start a local web server, usually at `http://127.0.0.1:8000/`, as shown in *Figure 9.2*:

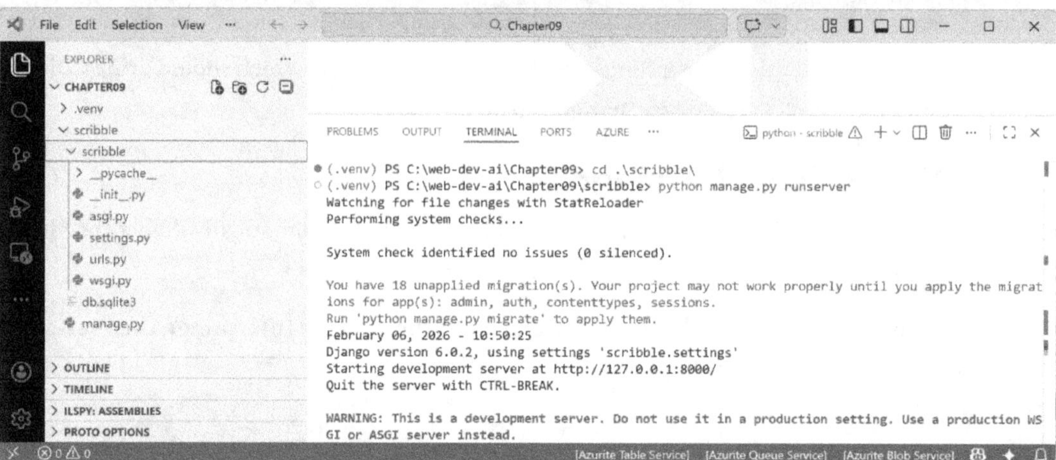

Figure 9.2: Running the Django project web server

In the output, and as shown in *Figure 9.2*, note the following message:

```
You have 18 unapplied migration(s). Your project may not work properly
until you apply the migrations for app(s): admin, auth, contenttypes,
sessions.
Run 'python manage.py migrate' to apply them.
```

You do not need to run the `python manage.py migrate` command yet. In the next section you will define some custom models for the blog feature of your Scribble project, and then you will run this command. At that point, both the system migrations mentioned in the preceding note and your custom model migrations will be applied.

Open that address in a browser. You can *Ctrl + Click* the link in the output rather than typing the URL manually. If you see the Django welcome page, your setup is correct, as shown in *Figure 9.3*:

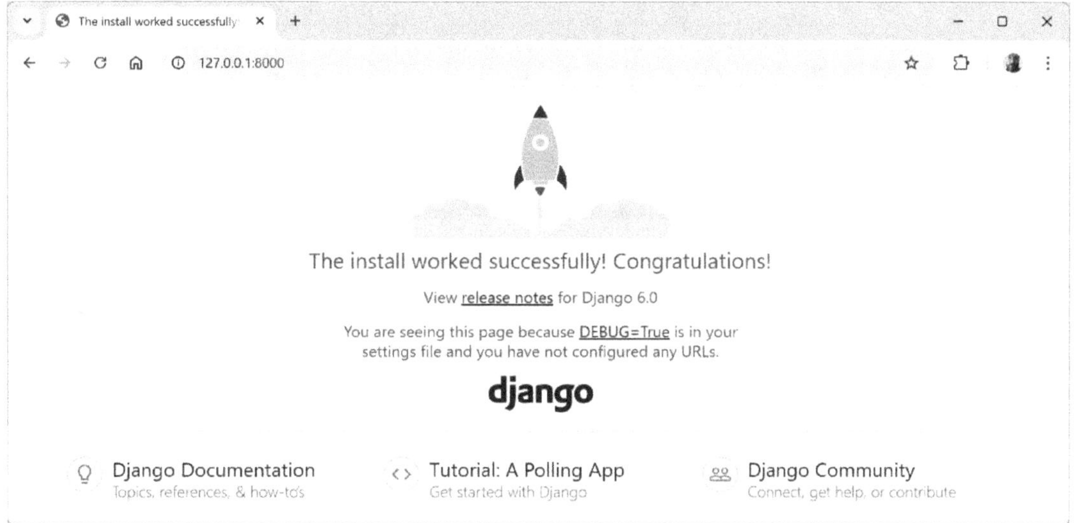

Figure 9.3: Django welcome page

Warning! This development server is designed for local use only, hence the message, as shown in *Figure 9.2*: **WARNING: This is a development server. Do not use it in a production setting. Use a production WSGI or ASGI server instead.** It automatically reloads when you change code and provides helpful error pages while you are learning. WSGI stands for Web Server Gateway Interface and ASGI stands for Asynchronous Server Gateway Interface.

In the terminal, press *Ctrl + C* to stop the web server.

Ctrl+Break is a legacy Windows term from older keyboards and console environments. Django's development server documentation historically used it, but in practice, *Ctrl+C* is the universal and correct instruction across all platforms today.

Good practice: A Django project contains generated files, local settings, cache folders, and sometimes secrets. When you use source control systems like Git, you should be careful not to blindly add everything in a Django project to the repository. For example, directories like `.venv` and `__pycache__`, database files like `db.sqlite3`, and secrets like passwords should be excluded. You will learn how to do this in *Chapter 11, Setting Up Your Project Environment*. In this chapter, we will not use source control, so we can focus on learning Django.

In the next sections, you will begin adding apps, models, and views to this project and see how Django's structure starts to make sense once real functionality is added.

Django URL patterns and routing

URLs are the entry point to every Django request. Before a view runs and before a template is rendered, Django must decide which piece of code should handle an incoming HTTP request. That decision is made by Django's URL routing system.

At a high level, Django works like this: a request arrives with a path such as `/posts/hello-django/`. Django compares that path against a list of URL patterns, from top to bottom, until it finds the first match. The matching pattern determines which view function or class is called and what data is passed into it.

URL patterns

URL patterns are defined using the `path()` function. A minimal example looks like this:

```
from django.urls import path
from .views import post_list

urlpatterns = [
    path("", post_list, name="post_list"),
]
```

Note the following about the preceding code:

- The empty string `""` represents the root of whatever URL prefix this file is included under.
- The `name` argument is more important than it first appears. It gives the URL a stable identifier that you can refer to elsewhere without hard-coding paths.

As projects grow, Django encourages you to split URLs by app. Each app defines its own `urls.py`, and the project-level `urls.py` includes them by calling the `include()` function, as shown highlighted in the following code:

```
from django.contrib import admin
from django.urls import path, include

urlpatterns = [
    path("admin/", admin.site.urls),
    path("", include("blog.urls")),
]
```

This keeps routing modular and mirrors Django's *project contains apps* philosophy. The project routes decide where an app lives in the URL space. The app routes decide what happens inside that space.

Prompt: Please show me some examples of `path()` vs `re_path()` and explain when regular expressions are necessary.

Dynamic segments in URLs

URL patterns often include dynamic segments. These are defined using path converters in angle brackets like this: `<path_converter_type:parameter_name>`.

For example, to show a single blog post by its slug:

```
path("<slug:slug>/", post_detail, name="post_detail"),
```

Here, `<slug:slug>` means *match a* `slug`*-shaped string and pass it into the view as a parameter named* `slug`. The view signature must match:

```
def post_detail(request, slug):
    ...
```

Common path converters include:

- `str` for any non-empty string
- `int` for integers
- `slug` for URL-friendly strings
- `uuid` for universally unique identifier (UUID) values

A URL-friendly string is a piece of text that is safe to use in a web address without causing ambiguity, encoding issues, or readability problems. In practice, a URL-friendly string has a few key characteristics: it uses lowercase letters only, it contains numbers if needed, words are separated with hyphens, not spaces or underscores, and it avoids punctuation, symbols, and non-ASCII characters. For example, if the title of a web page is *Hello, Django!*, its slug might be `hello-django`, or if the title is *C# & .NET Basics*, its slug might be `c-net-basics`.

Using converters keeps URLs readable and avoids manual parsing inside views.

Prompt: What are slugs really for, and why does Django treat them differently from normal text fields? How should I handle slug uniqueness and updates in real blog applications?

Named URLs

Instead of hard-coding links like `/posts/hello-django/`, templates should use the `{% url %}` tag, passing the name of the view that should process the request and the path defined by its slug. The contents of the `<a>` element should be whatever text you want to see in the link, like the title of the post:

```
<a href="{% url 'post_detail' slug=post.slug %}">
    {{ post.title }}
</a>
```

At this point, you do not need to understand the preceding template syntax. Template syntax is explained fully later in this chapter.

This does two important things.

1. It decouples templates from URL structure. You can change the URL pattern later without touching every template.
2. Django will raise an error if the URL name or arguments do not match, which catches mistakes early instead of silently producing broken links.

URL names also matter outside templates. Redirects and reverse lookups in views rely on them:

```
from django.shortcuts import redirect

return redirect("post_detail", slug=post.slug)
```

This is why naming URLs is a good practice.

Prompt: What problems do named URLs solve in large Django projects?

Ordering in URL patterns

Ordering matters in URL patterns. Django stops at the first match. This means more specific patterns should come before more general ones. For example, if you had both, as in this incorrect example:

```
path("<slug:slug>/", post_detail),
path("archive/", archive_view),
```

Then Django will treat `"archive"` as a slug and never reach the `archive/` view.

To fix this issue, `"archive/"` must appear before the slug pattern, as in this fixed example:

```
path("archive/", archive_view),
path("<slug:slug>/", post_detail),
```

Prompt: How does Django's URL resolver work internally, and why does URL order matter?

Routing and models

URL routing does not know or care about models. It simply matches strings and then calls views. Validation, database lookups, and `404 Missing resource` handling belong in the view layer. This separation keeps routing simple and predictable.

In practice, clean URL design pays off quickly. Readable paths, named routes, and consistent structure make templates easier to write and views easier to understand.

Now we are ready to learn about models, one of the best parts of Django because once you've defined the classes for your models, so much more happens for you. Django can create migrations, build database tables, generate admin forms, and give you a Python API for querying data.

Django models

In Django, a model is the single source of truth for your application's data. You define models as Python classes, and Django uses them to do three jobs at once:

- Describe the shape of your data
- Generate and evolve your database schema
- Provide a high-level API for creating, reading, updating, and deleting rows in the database

A model usually maps to a database table. Each attribute on the model maps to a column. Each instance of the model maps to a row. Django's **object-relational mapper (ORM)** sits between your Python code and the database, translating Python operations into SQL behind the scenes.

Creating your first app and model

Let's create a blog app with a model to represent posts:

1. Create an app feature named `blog`:

   ```
   python manage.py startapp blog
   ```

2. Register the `blog` app in `scribble/settings.py`, as shown in *Figure 9.4* and the following code:

   ```
   INSTALLED_APPS = [
       ...
       "blog",
   ]
   ```

Figure 9.4: Registering the blog app in settings.py

Warning! If you miss this step, the Scribble project will not know about the `blog` app and it won't scan the `blog` folder hierarchy to discover all its features and settings. A lot of problems are caused by forgetting to register an app after creating it.

3. You define models in `blog/models.py`. Add the highlighted code under the comment:

```
from django.db import models

# Create your models here.

class Post(models.Model):
    title = models.CharField(max_length=200)
    body = models.TextField()
    created_at = models.DateTimeField(auto_now_add=True)
    updated_at = models.DateTimeField(auto_now=True)
    is_published = models.BooleanField(default=False)

    def __str__(self) -> str:
        return self.title
```

Note the following about the preceding code:

- `CharField` is for short text and requires a `max_length` keyword argument or field option because the database needs a defined column size

`max_length` is a known as a **keyword argument** in Python, and more specifically a **field option** in Django.

- `TextField` i for longer free-form text
- `DateTimeField(auto_now_add=True)` sets the value once when the row is created
- `DateTimeField(auto_now=True)` updates the value every time the row is saved
- `BooleanField` stores `true` or `false`, with `default` used for new rows

Good practice: The `__str__` method is not required, but it is worth adding early. Django uses it in places like the admin UI, and a readable string makes debugging much nicer than seeing `Post object (3)` everywhere.

Applying migrations

Once you define or change a model, you need to apply the change to the database. Django does this using **migrations**. Think of migrations as version control for your schema.

Run the following command to create migration files that describe the schema change:

```
python manage.py makemigrations
```

Note the following output:

```
Migrations for 'blog':
  blog\migrations\0001_initial.py
    + Create model Post
```

Run the following command to apply those migrations to the database:

```
python manage.py migrate
```

Note the following output:

```
Operations to perform:
  Apply all migrations: admin, auth, blog, contenttypes, sessions
```

```
Running migrations:
  Applying contenttypes.0001_initial... OK
  Applying auth.0001_initial... OK
  Applying admin.0001_initial... OK
  Applying admin.0002_logentry_remove_auto_add... OK
  Applying admin.0003_logentry_add_action_flag_choices... OK
  Applying contenttypes.0002_remove_content_type_name... OK
  Applying auth.0002_alter_permission_name_max_length... OK
  Applying auth.0003_alter_user_email_max_length... OK
  Applying auth.0004_alter_user_username_opts... OK
  Applying auth.0005_alter_user_last_login_null... OK
  Applying auth.0006_require_contenttypes_0002... OK
  Applying auth.0007_alter_validators_add_error_messages... OK
  Applying auth.0008_alter_user_username_max_length... OK
  Applying auth.0009_alter_user_last_name_max_length... OK
  Applying auth.0010_alter_group_name_max_length... OK
  Applying auth.0011_update_proxy_permissions... OK
  Applying auth.0012_alter_user_first_name_max_length... OK
  Applying blog.0001_initial... OK
  Applying sessions.0001_initial... OK
```

Prompt: What exactly happens when I run `makemigrations` vs `migrate`?

If you are using the default SQLite database during learning, you will have a `db.sqlite3` file in your project folder. The same model code can later target PostgreSQL, SQL Server, and other supported databases by changing your database settings.

Prompt: How do I change the database system used in a Django project from SQLite to PostgreSQL or SQL Server?

Relationships

Relationships between models are one of Django's main strengths. Here are the three most common relationship types.

One-to-many relationships

One-to-many uses `ForeignKey`. For example, an author can have many posts:

```
class Author(models.Model):
    name = models.CharField(max_length=100)

    def __str__(self) -> str:
        return self.name

class Post(models.Model):
    author = models.ForeignKey(Author, on_delete=models.CASCADE, related_
name="posts")
    title = models.CharField(max_length=200)
    body = models.TextField()
    created_at = models.DateTimeField(auto_now_add=True)

    def __str__(self) -> str:
        return self.title
```

`on_delete=models.CASCADE` means if an author is deleted, their posts are deleted too. Django forces you to choose an `on_delete` behavior because databases need a clear rule for referential integrity.

One-to-one relationships

One-to-one uses `OneToOneField`. This is common for profile-style extensions, where each user has exactly one profile:

```
from django.contrib.auth.models import User

class Profile(models.Model):
    user = models.OneToOneField(User, on_delete=models.CASCADE)
    bio = models.TextField(blank=True)
```

Many-to-many relationships

Many-to-many uses `ManyToManyField`. For example, posts can have many tags and tags can belong to many posts:

```
class Tag(models.Model):
    name = models.CharField(max_length=50, unique=True)
```

```
    def __str__(self) -> str:
        return self.name

class Post(models.Model):
    title = models.CharField(max_length=200)
    tags = models.ManyToManyField(Tag, blank=True, related_name="posts")
```

You can download a complete `models.py` file for the `blog` app from the following link: `https://github.com/markjprice/web-dev-ai/blob/main/Code/Chapter09/scribble/blog/models.py`

Rerun the two migration steps to update the database with your latest changes:

```
python manage.py makemigrations
python manage.py migrate
```

Creating, updating, and deleting model data

Once you have defined some models, you can create, update, and delete instances of them using the following standard functions:

- `<model_name>.objects.create(<required_parameters>)`: Creates and returns a new instance (object) of the specified model
- `<model>.save()`: Save field changes to this model instance
- `<model>.delete()`: Delete this model instance

You can query a model using the following standard functions:

- `<model_name>.objects.filter(...)`: Returns a QuerySet with objects that match the criteria specified
- `<model_name>.objects.order_by(...)`: Returns a QuerySet with objects sorted by the field(s) specified

A **Django QuerySet** is a representation of a database *query*, not yet the results. Instead of immediately fetching data, a QuerySet describes what data you want, and Django only runs the actual SQL when the results are needed. This allows you to filter, sort, and combine queries incrementally while still producing a single efficient database query once you need the results.

Django QuerySets are lazy. Building a QuerySet does not hit the database until you actually evaluate it, for example, by iterating over it, slicing it, or converting it to a list. This is why you can chain filters without paying a cost for each step.

A common way to evaluate a QuerySet is to pass it to the `list` function:

```
list(<queryset>)
```

Prompt: What does it mean that Django QuerySets are lazy, and why is that important for performance?

Managing data with the Django shell

With models in place, Django gives you a Pythonic way to work with your data. Open the Django shell:

```
python manage.py shell
```

At the >>> prompt, try some basic operations:

1. Start by importing some classes:

```
from django.contrib.auth.models import User
from blog.models import Author, Post
from django.utils.text import slugify
```

2. Create a user (required for `Author`):

```
user = User.objects.create_user(
    username="mark",
    email="mark@example.com",
    password="testpassword123"
)
```

3. Create an author profile and reference the user you created:

```
author = Author.objects.create(
    user=user,
    display_name="Mark",
    bio="Author and Django enthusiast"
)
```

4. Create a blog post and reference the author:

```
post = Post.objects.create(
    author=author,
    title="Hello, Django",
    slug=slugify("Hello, Django"),
    body="This is my first post.",
    status="published"
)
```

Prompt: What is the `slugify` function and the `slug` class used for in Django?

5. Show the `post` object:

```
post
```

6. Query recent posts:

```
recent_posts = Post.objects.order_by("-created_at")[:5]
list(recent_posts) # convert the queryset to a list
```

7. Query published posts:

```
published_posts = Post.objects.filter(status="published")
list(published_posts)
```

8. Show the SQL that Django will run:

```
print(published_posts.query)
```

9. Update an existing post:

```
post.title = "Hello, Django (Edited)"
post.slug = slugify(post.title)
post.save()
```

10. Delete a post:

```
post.delete()
```

11. Exit the shell:

```
exit()
```

The `objects` attribute is Django's model manager. It provides query-building methods like `create`, `get`, `filter`, `exclude`, and `order_by`.

A few field options you will see constantly are shown in *Table 9.2*:

Field option	**Description**
`null=True`	The database column may store SQL `NULL`.
`blank=True`	Forms and validation allow an empty value.
`default=...`	Sets a default for newly created rows.
`unique=True`	Enforces uniqueness at the database level.
`choices=[(...), (...)]`	Constrains values to a fixed set, useful for status fields.

Table 9.2: Common field options and their descriptions

Warning! A common beginner pitfall is mixing up `null` and `blank`. As a rule of thumb: `blank` is about validation, especially when filling in forms, while `null` is about how the database stores the value. For text fields, Django often prefers empty strings rather than `NULL`, so you will frequently use `blank=True` without `null=True` on `CharField` and `TextField`.

By defining models first, you get a clean data layer that the rest of Django builds on.

Prompt: How does Django's ORM translate Python QuerySets into SQL, and when does it actually hit the database? Please show me the same Django ORM query and the SQL it generates, and explain each part.

SQL injection and how Django prevents it

SQL injection is one of the oldest and most damaging web application vulnerabilities. It happens when user input is treated as part of a SQL command instead of as data.

You already know how SQL queries work. The problem begins when an application builds those queries using strings.

Here is a simplified example in Python using raw SQL:

```
email = request.GET.get("email")
```

```
query = f"SELECT * FROM users WHERE email = '{email}'"
cursor.execute(query)
```

This looks harmless. But it is fundamentally unsafe.

If a user supplies this value:

```
' OR 1=1 --
```

The query becomes:

```
SELECT * FROM users WHERE email = '' OR 1=1 --'
```

That condition is always `true`. The query now returns every user in the database. The database is doing exactly what you asked. The problem is that you allowed the user to change the meaning of the query.

SQL does not distinguish between code (the structure of the query) and data (the values being compared). If you build SQL using string concatenation, you blur that boundary. The database cannot tell where your query ends and user input begins.

Instead of inserting values into SQL strings, you pass them separately:

```
cursor.execute(
    "SELECT * FROM users WHERE email = %s",
    [email]
)
```

Now the SQL query structure is fixed, and the value is treated strictly as data. Even if the user enters malicious input, it cannot change the query's meaning.

The good news is that Django's ORM protects you automatically when used correctly.

For example:

```
User.objects.filter(email=email)
```

Django generates SQL internally and safely binds parameters. The input is never treated as executable SQL. This is one of the main reasons to use an ORM. It removes an entire class of security bugs by design.

But even in Django, SQL injection is still possible if you step outside the ORM.

For example:

```
cursor.execute(f"SELECT * FROM users WHERE email = '{email}'")
```

or:

```
User.objects.raw(
    f"SELECT * FROM users WHERE email = '{email}'"
)
```

Both reintroduce the same vulnerability. Remember: you also need to review code written by an AI. That means recognizing dangerous patterns such as raw SQL built from user input.

Good practice: Django ORM queries are safe by default. Raw SQL is safe only if you use parameters. String concatenation is always unsafe. If you remember nothing else, remember this: Never mix user input directly into a SQL string.

In web development, especially with AI-assisted coding, it is very easy to generate working code quickly. It is also very easy to generate insecure code quickly.

SQL injection is a good example of the difference between code that works and code that is safe. The database will happily execute whatever valid SQL it receives. It is your responsibility to make sure that SQL cannot be manipulated by users.

In the next section, you will see how views and templates use the ORM to fetch model data and turn it into dynamic pages.

Django views and templates

Views and templates are the point where your data becomes something a user can actually see. Models define what the data looks like, but views decide which data is used for a request, and templates decide how that data is presented as HTML.

Views

A Django view is a Python function or class that takes an HTTP request and returns an HTTP response. Most views follow the same basic shape: fetch some data using models, then return a rendered template.

In your `blog` app, in `views.py`, import your `Post` model and add code to define a `post_list` function, as shown highlighted in the following code:

```
from django.shortcuts import render
from blog.models import Post
```

```
# Create your views here.

def post_list(request):
    posts = (
        Post.objects
        .filter(status="published")
        .order_by("-created_at")
    )
    return render(request, "blog/post_list.html", {"posts": posts})
```

The `render` helper function combines three things into a single response: the incoming request, a template name, and a context dictionary. The context dictionary is how you pass Python objects into the template.

To make this view callable from a web browser, you map it to a URL. In your `blog` app, create `urls.py`:

```
from django.urls import path
from .views import post_list

urlpatterns = [
    path("", post_list, name="post_list"),
]
```

Then include the app's URLs in the project's main `urls.py` by importing the `include` function and adding an entry for an empty path `""` to `urlpatterns`, as shown highlighted in the following code:

```
from django.contrib import admin
from django.urls import path, include

urlpatterns = [
    path("admin/", admin.site.urls),
    path("", include("blog.urls")),
]
```

At this point, a request to / will call `post_list`, fetch published posts from the database, and render a template.

Improving performance by prefetching related data

When your template accesses related objects such as `post.author` or `post.tags`, Django may run additional database queries for each post. This can quickly become inefficient as the number of posts grows.

The `select_related()` method tells Django to fetch related objects, like `author`, in the same database query using a SQL join. The `prefetch_related()` method handles relationships like tags by running a second query and combining the results in Python.

Using these methods avoids the common N+1 query problem, where one query for a list of objects triggers many additional queries for related data.

An improved version of the `post_list(request)` method would add calls to both methods, as shown highlighted in the following code:

```
def post_list(request):
    posts = (
        Post.objects
        .filter(status="published")
        .select_related("author")
        .prefetch_related("tags")
        .order_by("-created_at")
    )
    return render(request, "blog/post_list.html", {"posts": posts})
```

Before optimizing a view, check what the template will access, how that translates into database queries, and where performance problems actually come from. An AI can generate a working `post_list()` function in seconds, but it may not reliably predict what data you will use in your template or the best way to optimize database access.

You must make judgments about behavior, not just writing code.

Templates

Templates live in a dedicated directory, usually `<app_name>/templates/<app_name>/`, for example `blog/templates/blog/`. The nested folder structure is deliberate. It avoids name clashes when multiple apps define templates with the same filename.

You can define the whole template in one file like `post_list.html`:

```
<!DOCTYPE html>
<html>
<head>
    <title>Blog</title>
</head>
<body>
    <h1>Latest posts</h1>

    {% for post in posts %}
        <article>
            <h2>{{ post.title }}</h2>
            <p>{{ post.body|truncatewords:30 }}</p>
        </article>
    {% empty %}
        <p>No posts yet.</p>
    {% endfor %}
</body>
</html>
```

Django's template language is intentionally limited. You can use variable interpolation with `{{ ... }}`, simple control flow with `{% for ... %}` and `{% if ... %}`, and filters like `truncatewords`.

Warning! You cannot write arbitrary Python code in templates, and that is a feature. It enforces a clean separation between logic and presentation.

Prompt: Why does Django deliberately limit logic in templates, and how does this compare to template systems that allow full programming logic?

Inheriting templates

Templates become more reusable when you introduce inheritance. A base template defines the shared structure (stored in `<app_name>/templates`), and child templates override specific blocks (stored in `<app_name>/templates/<app_name>`).

In the base template, you define replaceable blocks using the following syntax: {% block <block_name> %}<default_block_content>{% endblock %}. For example, to define a block named title with a default content of My Site, use {% block title %}My Site{% endblock %}. You can define as many replaceable blocks with unique names as you like.

Then in an inherited template, you define the contents for each named block using the following syntax: {% block <block_name> %}<block_content>{% endblock %}. For example, to provide the content for a block named title with Blog as its content, use {% block title %}Blog{% endblock %}.

In the blog folder, create a folder named templates.

In the blog/templates folder, create a file named base.html:

```
<!DOCTYPE html>
<html>
<head>
    <title>{% block title %}My Site{% endblock %}</title>
</head>
<body>
    <header>
        <h1>My Django Site</h1>
    </header>

    <main>
        {% block content %}{% endblock %}
    </main>
</body>
</html>
```

Note that the content block does not provide any default content, so if a template does not supply any content, it will remain empty.

In the blog/templates folder, create a folder named blog.

In the blog/templates/blog folder, create a file named post_list.html:

```
{% extends "base.html" %}

{% block title %}Blog{% endblock %}
```

```
{% block content %}
    <h2>Latest posts</h2>

    {% for post in posts %}
        <article>
            <h3>{{ post.title }}</h3>
            <p>{{ post.body|truncatewords:30 }}</p>
        </article>
    {% empty %}
        <p class="no-posts">No posts yet. Check back soon.</p>
    {% endfor %}
{% endblock %}
```

This pattern keeps HTML consistent across pages and reduces duplication, which matters as soon as a site grows beyond a single view.

Prompt: Please explain Django template inheritance using a real multi-page website layout example.

Returning response status codes

Views are also responsible for returning responses that are not HTML. Redirects, 404 errors, JSON responses, and form submissions all live in views.

For example, a detail view for a single post might look up an object by slug and return a 404 `Missing resource` status code if it does not exist:

```
from django.shortcuts import get_object_or_404, render

def post_detail(request, slug):
    post = get_object_or_404(Post, slug=slug, status="published")
    return render(request, "blog/post_detail.html", {"post": post})
```

This illustrates an important design principle: views handle decisions and error conditions, templates assume they have valid data and focus only on rendering.

Class-based and function-based views

Django also supports class-based views, which reduce repetition for common patterns like list and detail pages. They are powerful, but harder to read when you are new.

For learning purposes, function-based views as you've seen so far are often clearer because you can see the full request–response flow in one place. Once that understanding is solid, class-based views make much more sense.

Prompt: Please show me examples of function-based views and compare them to class-based views with concrete examples of the same page implemented both ways. When do class-based views reduce complexity, and when do they make code harder to understand?

Trying out your view and template for listing posts

Now we can try out our view and template for listing posts.

At a command prompt or terminal, enter the command to start the web server:

```
python manage.py runserver
```

Start your web browser and navigate to the following link: `http://127.0.0.1:8000/`

If the latest posts list is empty, then use the shell to add some posts as you learned to do in the models section earlier.

You will need to get the existing author with a primary key of 1 using the following code:

```
author = Author.objects.get(pk=1)
```

Then you can add more posts using the following code:

```
post = Post.objects.create(
    author=author,
    title="<type a title>",
    slug=slugify("<type a title>"),
    body="<type a body>",
    status="published"
)
```

In short, views decide what happens for a request, templates decide what the user sees, and models supply the data. Keeping those responsibilities separate is one of the reasons Django applications remain understandable as they grow.

Now let's see how we can support static files like CSS files and images in our website.

Serving static files

Static files are assets that are sent to the browser exactly as they are, without being generated dynamically. This includes CSS stylesheets, JavaScript files, images, fonts, and icons. Django treats these very differently from templates, and understanding that distinction early prevents a lot of confusion.

Templates are rendered on the server and can contain logic and placeholders. Static files are not rendered at all. Django never opens a CSS file to inspect it or modify it. It simply sends the file to the browser when asked.

Where static files are stored

Django expects static files to live in a folder named `static`. In an app-based project, with an app name of `blog`, the usual layout would look like this:

```
blog/
  static/
    blog/
      style.css
      logo.png
```

The nested `blog` folder is deliberate. Just like templates, this avoids name collisions when multiple apps define files with the same name, such as `style.css`.

To use a static file in a template, you must first load Django's `static` template tag:

```
{% load static %}
```

Then you can reference static files using the `{% static ... %}` helper and pass the `static`-folder relative path to the file:

```
<link rel="stylesheet" href="{% static 'blog/style.css' %}">
<img src="{% static 'blog/logo.png' %}" alt="Logo">
```

This is important. You should never hard-code paths like `/static/blog/style.css`. Using `{% static ... %}` allows Django to change how static files are served without breaking your templates.

Configuring the static files folder

Static files are configured in `settings.py` using `STATIC_URL`:

```
STATIC_URL = "static/"
```

During development, when `DEBUG=True`, Django automatically finds static files inside each installed app's `static` directory and serves them for you. This is why you can start using CSS immediately without any extra setup.

In production, this changes. Django does not serve static files itself. Instead, static files are collected into a single directory and served by a web server such as Nginx or a **content delivery network (CDN)**. The key takeaway for now is that Django's static file system is designed to support that transition without changing your templates.

A CDN is a distributed network of servers that delivers static content to users from a location geographically close to them. Instead of every request for images, CSS, JavaScript, or videos going back to a single origin server, a CDN caches those files on many edge servers around the world. When a browser requests a static asset, the CDN serves it from the nearest available location, which reduces latency, lowers load on the origin server, and improves reliability.

Common beginner mistakes with static files

A common beginner mistake is confusing static files with templates. If you put CSS inside a templates directory, Django will not find it as a static file. If you try to put template logic inside a CSS file, Django will ignore it. Templates and static files live in parallel worlds and serve different purposes.

Another common mistake is forgetting to load the `static` tag in a template. If `{% static %}` is used without `{% load static %}`, Django will raise a clear error when `DEBUG=True`.

From a mental-model perspective, static files are part of the presentation assets of your site, not part of request handling or data flow. Templates simply reference them.

Adding a stylesheet to improve the post list page

Right now, the blog post list is functional, but it looks plain and boring. Let's add a CSS stylesheet to make it feel more like a real website and, in the process, reinforce how Django handles static files.

Let's add a stylesheet to improve the look of the template for rendering a list of posts:

1. Inside your `blog` app folder, create the following directories:

   ```
   blog/
     static/
       blog/
   ```

2. Inside the `blog/static/blog` folder, create a file named `style.css`.
3. Add the following CSS to `blog/static/blog/style.css` that keeps things simple with neutral colors, readable typography, and card-style posts:

   ```
   /* Base page styling */
   body {
       font-family: system-ui, Helvetica, Arial, sans-serif;
       background-color: #f5f7fa;
       margin: 0;
       padding: 0;
       color: #222;
   }

   /* Page Layout */
   main {
       max-width: 800px;
       margin: 3rem auto;
       padding: 0 1rem;
   }

   /* Header */
   header {
       background-color: #2d3748;
       color: #ffffff;
       padding: 1.5rem 1rem;
       text-align: center;
   }
   ```

```
header h1 {
    margin: 0;
    font-weight: 600;
}

/* Blog posts */
article {
    background-color: #ffffff;
    border-radius: 8px;
    padding: 1.5rem;
    margin-bottom: 1.5rem;
    box-shadow: 0 8px 20px rgba(0, 0, 0, 0.05);
}

article h3 {
    margin-top: 0;
    margin-bottom: 0.5rem;
    color: #2b6cb0;
}

article p {
    line-height: 1.6;
    margin: 0;
}

/* Empty state */
.no-posts {
    text-align: center;
    color: #666;
    font-style: italic;
    margin-top: 3rem;
}
```

4. In `blog/templates/base.html`, add support for static files. At the top of the file, load the `static` template tag:

```
{% load static %}
```

5. In `blog/templates/base.html`, link the stylesheet inside the `<head>` section:

```
<link rel="stylesheet" href="{% static 'blog/style.css' %}">
```

Because `post_list.html` extends `base.html`, it will automatically pick up the stylesheet.

6. Start the development server if it is not already running:

```
python manage.py runserver
```

7. Open a browser and navigate to: `http://127.0.0.1:8000/`.

You should now see a clean, styled list of blog posts with a proper layout, spacing, and typography, as shown in *Figure 9.5*:

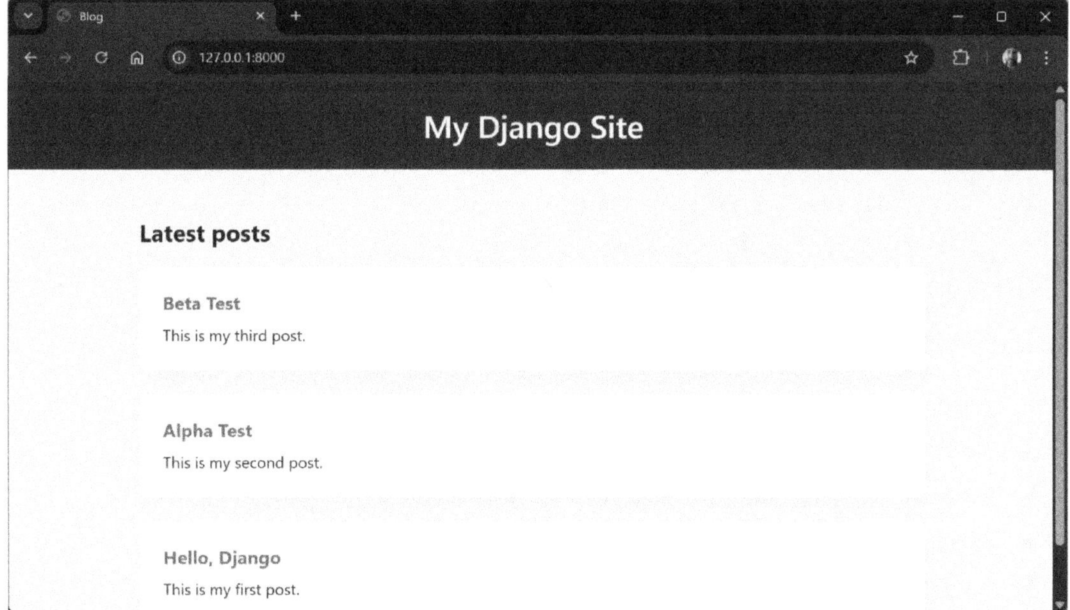

Figure 9.5: styled blog post list page

Now let's see how you can use a built-in admin user interface for managing data in your website.

Django admin interface

One of Django's most distinctive features is the built-in admin interface. It is a working data-management interface that is generated automatically from your models. As soon as your models exist, Django can give you a working interface for creating, editing, and deleting data.

Registering your models for administration

By default, Django only shows models that have been explicitly registered. To make your blog models appear, open `blog/admin.py` and register them:

```
from django.contrib import admin
from .models import Author, Post, Tag, Comment

admin.site.register(Author)
admin.site.register(Post)
admin.site.register(Tag)
admin.site.register(Comment)
```

Django's admin becomes even more useful when you customize it. Customization is done by defining `ModelAdmin` classes. Here is a more realistic configuration for the `Post` model:

```
@admin.register(Post)
class PostAdmin(admin.ModelAdmin):
    list_display = ("title", "author", "status", "created_at")
    list_filter = ("status", "created_at", "author")
    search_fields = ("title", "body")
    prepopulated_fields = {"slug": ("title",)}
    ordering = ("-created_at",)
```

Note the following about the preceding code:

- `list_display` controls which columns appear in the list view
- `list_filter` adds a filter sidebar for common fields
- `search_fields` enables full-text search over selected fields
- `prepopulated_fields` automatically generates slugs from titles
- `ordering` defines the default sort order

Prompt: What's the difference between using `admin.site.register(Post)` and using `@admin.register(Post)` with a `class PostAdmin(admin.ModelAdmin)` and attributes like `list_display` to register a Django model?

You can also edit related objects inline. For example, comments are usually managed alongside posts rather than separately:

```
class CommentInline(admin.TabularInline):
    model = Comment
    extra = 0

@admin.register(Post)
class PostAdmin(admin.ModelAdmin):
    list_display = ("title", "author", "status", "created_at")
    inlines = [CommentInline]
```

This allows an editor to manage comments directly on the post edit page, which matches how many editorial teams work.

The admin respects all the rules defined in your models. Field validation, required fields, choices, relationships, and permissions are enforced automatically. If you mark a field as read-only or restrict who can edit a model, the admin reflects that immediately. This tight integration is one of Django's strengths.

Logging into the admin site as a superuser

The admin site is enabled by default when you create a Django project. To use it, you first need a superuser, also known as an administrator account. Create one from the command line:

```
python manage.py createsuperuser
```

Follow the prompts to set a username, email address, and password.

Then start the development server and visit the following link:

`http://127.0.0.1:8000/admin/`

Log in with the superuser credentials.

You will see the Django admin dashboard, which lists all registered models grouped by app, as shown in *Figure 9.6*:

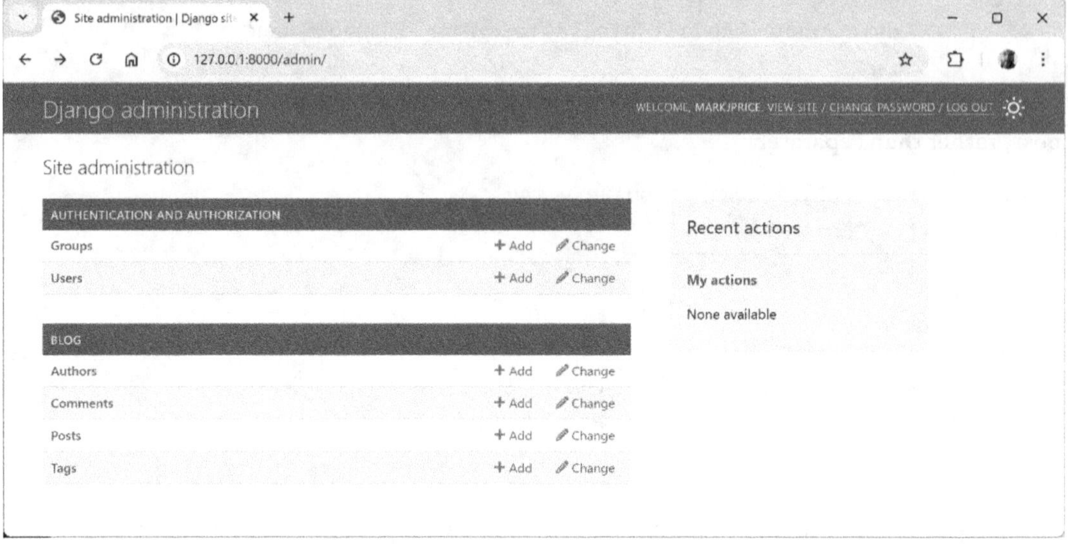

Figure 9.6: Django admin dashboard

Clicking a model shows a list view of existing records.

Click **Users**, and note the user that you added programmatically using the shell to add users, authors, and posts, and the superuser (**STAFF STATUS** enabled) that you added using the command line, as shown in *Figure 9.7*:

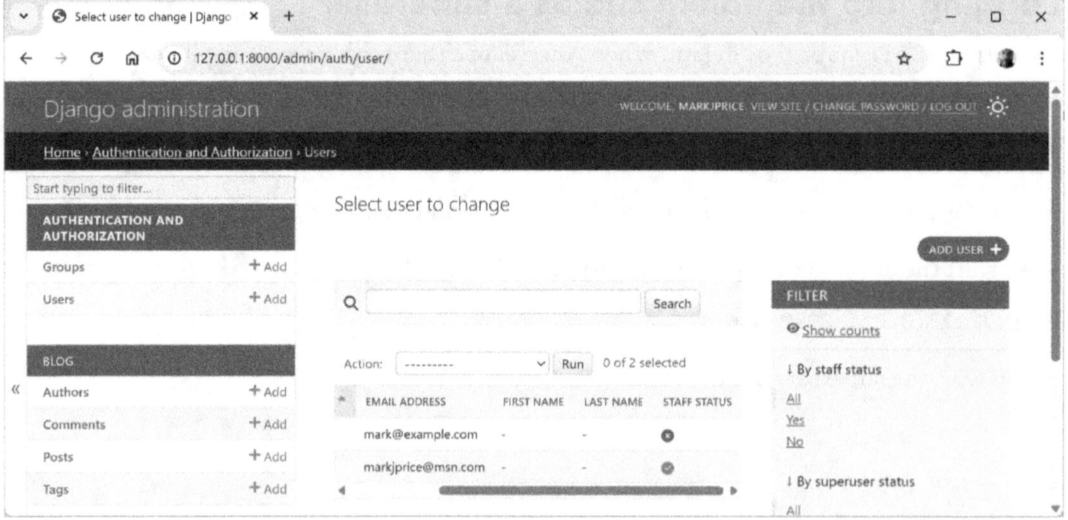

Figure 9.7: Users

Click **Posts**, and note the existing posts are listed in a filterable table, as shown in *Figure 9.8*:

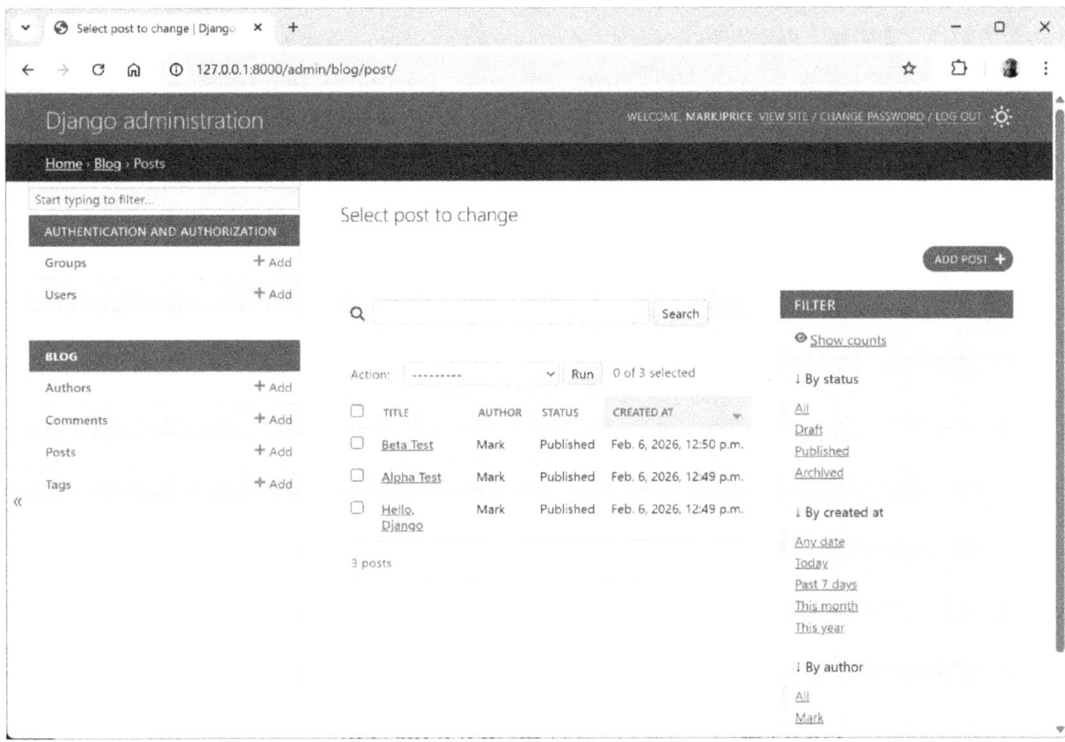

Figure 9.8: Posts

Clicking an individual blog post record opens a form for editing it, as shown in *Figure 9.9*:

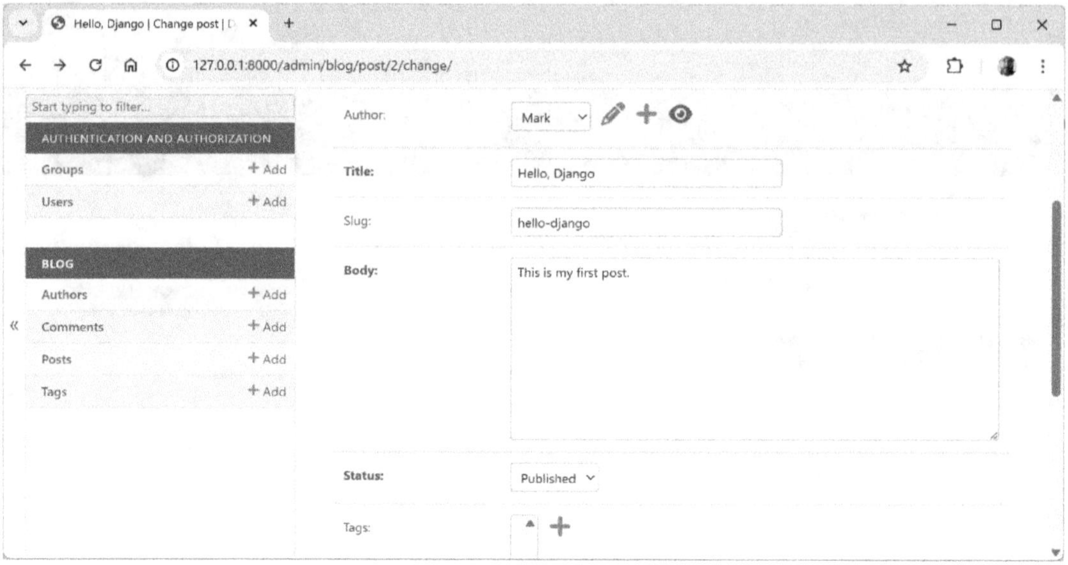

Figure 9.9: Editing an individual blog post

It is important to understand what the admin is and is not for. The admin is designed for trusted users managing internal data. It is not intended to be a public-facing UI, and you should not treat it as one. For editors, moderators, and internal tools, it is often more than sufficient. For end users, you usually build custom views and templates instead.

Prompt: What are the limits of the Django admin, and when should you stop using it and build custom views?

For learning, the admin is especially useful. It gives you instant feedback that your models are correct, your relationships work, and your migrations ran successfully. Many experienced Django developers use the admin as a diagnostic tool long after a project ships.

Prompt: How does the Django admin interface infer so much functionality from just model definitions?

Now that you've seen the admin interface and how it provides automatic forms to modify model data, let's see how you can build your own forms to show to website visitors.

Django forms

Almost every interactive website needs to accept user input, validate it, and either save it to the database or act on it safely. Django's forms system solves this problem end to end, using Python code instead of hand-written validation logic scattered across views.

At the highest level, a Django form is defined using a Python class that does three things. It defines what input is expected, it validates that input, and it provides cleaned, trustworthy data back to your view. Django keeps this logic out of templates and largely out of views.

There are two main kinds of forms in Django that derive from built-in classes: `Form` and `ModelForm`.

Plain forms

A plain `Form`-based class is useful when you want input that is not directly tied to a database model, such as a contact form or a search box.

A minimal example of a contact form looks like this:

```
from django import forms

class ContactForm(forms.Form):
    name = forms.CharField(max_length=100)
    email = forms.EmailField()
    message = forms.CharField(widget=forms.Textarea)
```

This single class definition gives you HTML form fields, validation rules, and error messages. Django already knows how to validate email addresses, required fields, and maximum lengths.

Model-based forms

A `ModelForm`-based class goes further. It connects a form directly to a model and handles saving data for you. This is the most common pattern in Django applications.

For example, a form for creating blog posts:

```
from django import forms
from .models import Post

class PostForm(forms.ModelForm):
    class Meta:
        model = Post
        fields = ["title", "slug", "body", "status", "tags"]
```

Django inspects the model and automatically creates form fields with the correct types, validation rules, and widgets. If you later change the model, the form updates automatically.

Using a form in a view follows a standard pattern that you will see everywhere in Django codebases. The view handles two cases: displaying the form in response to a `GET` request, and processing submitted data in response to a `POST` request triggered when the form is filled in and then submitted:

```
from django.shortcuts import render, redirect
from .forms import PostForm

def create_post(request):
    if request.method == "POST":
        form = PostForm(request.POST)
        if form.is_valid():
            form.save()
            return redirect("post_list")
    else:
        form = PostForm()

    return render(request, "blog/post_form.html", {"form": form})
```

Note the following about the preceding code:

- `request.POST` contains submitted form data
- `is_valid()` runs all validation rules and returns a Boolean
- Cleaned, validated data is available via `form.cleaned_data`
- `form.save()` creates or updates the database row for a `ModelForm`

If validation fails, Django automatically attaches error messages to the form. You do not need to write error-handling logic yourself.

Prompt: Why does Django separate forms from models instead of just using HTML forms directly?

Rendering forms

Rendering the form in a template is straightforward:

```
<form method="post">
    {% csrf_token %}
    {{ form.as_p }}
    <button type="submit">Save</button>
</form>
```

The `{% csrf_token %}` tag is required for security. Django protects against cross-site request forgery by default, and forms are where this protection matters most.

Prompt: Please explain CSRF protection in Django in simple terms with an example attack scenario.

`form.as_p` is a convenience for learning and prototyping. It renders each field wrapped in a paragraph. For real projects, you usually render fields individually so you can control layout and styling:

```
{{ form.title.label_tag }}
{{ form.title }}
{{ form.title.errors }}
```

One useful feature of Django forms is that validation happens before your view logic continues. This means your views can assume they are working with cleaned and validated data. You do not have to check whether an email is valid or whether a required field is missing. Django already did that work.

Prompt: What security problems does Django's forms system solve automatically?

Integrating forms with other Django components

Forms also integrate cleanly with models, admin, and templates. The same validation rules apply whether data comes from a public form or the admin interface.

It is worth being explicit about what forms are not. They are not just HTML generators. They are a validation and data-cleaning layer that sits between untrusted user input and your application logic. That design is why Django forms feel slightly heavier at first, but save a lot of time and mistakes as applications grow.

Once you understand forms, a large class of Django features suddenly makes sense: authentication views, comment systems, admin pages, and APIs all build on the same underlying ideas.

Now let's look at settings and configuration.

Django settings and configuration

Every Django project is driven by a single configuration module, usually called `settings.py`. This file answers a simple question: how should this project behave in this environment? Understanding settings is less about memorizing options and more about knowing where Django looks for answers.

When you run `python manage.py runserver`, Django loads the settings module defined by the `DJANGO_SETTINGS_MODULE` environment variable. In a default project, this points at `mysite.settings`. Everything from database connections to installed apps flows from this file.

Debug mode

One of the first settings you will encounter is `DEBUG`:

```
DEBUG = True
```

When `DEBUG` is on, Django shows detailed error pages, auto-reloads code changes, and serves static files for you. This is exactly what you want while learning and developing.

In production, `DEBUG` must be turned off, because those error pages expose sensitive information. Even without covering deployment yet, it is worth knowing that `DEBUG` changes Django's behavior in fundamental ways.

Prompt: Why is `DEBUG=True` so useful for learning Django, and what exactly changes when `DEBUG=False`?

Installed apps

INSTALLED_APPS is the setting that controls which parts of Django are active:

```
INSTALLED_APPS = [
    "django.contrib.admin",
    "django.contrib.auth",
    "django.contrib.contenttypes",
    "django.contrib.sessions",
    "django.contrib.messages",
    "django.contrib.staticfiles",
    "blog",
]
```

If an app is not listed here, Django ignores it. Models are not loaded, admin registrations do not run, templates are not discovered, and migrations are skipped. Many mysterious Django problems turn out to be missing entries in INSTALLED_APPS.

Database configuration

Database configuration lives in DATABASES. By default, Django uses SQLite, which is file-based and requires no setup:

```
DATABASES = {
    "default": {
        "ENGINE": "django.db.backends.sqlite3",
        "NAME": BASE_DIR / "db.sqlite3",
    }
}
```

This is ideal for learning and small projects. The important takeaway is that your models do not change when you switch databases. You update settings, run migrations, and Django's ORM handles the rest.

Template configuration

Templates are configured via the TEMPLATES setting:

```
TEMPLATES = [
    {
        "BACKEND": "django.template.backends.django.DjangoTemplates",
        "DIRS": [],
        "APP_DIRS": True,
        "OPTIONS": {
            "context_processors": [
                "django.template.context_processors.debug",
                "django.template.context_processors.request",
                "django.contrib.auth.context_processors.auth",
                "django.contrib.messages.context_processors.messages",
            ],
        },
    },
]
```

`APP_DIRS: True` tells Django to look for templates inside each installed app's `templates` directory. If you later add a project-level templates folder, you list it in `DIRS`. Understanding this distinction helps avoid template-loading errors that otherwise feel opaque.

Static files

Static files are configured separately from templates:

```
STATIC_URL = "static/"
```

During development, Django collects static files from each app's `static` directory and serves them automatically. In production, this is handled differently, but the key point is that static files are discovered through configuration, not hard-coded paths.

Hosts

Another setting worth noticing early is `ALLOWED_HOSTS`. When `DEBUG` is off, Django refuses to serve requests for unknown hostnames. This is a security measure that prevents certain classes of attack. While it may seem irrelevant during development, it explains errors that appear the first time a project is deployed.

Settings are code

A recurring theme in Django is that settings are Python code, not a declarative format like YAML or JSON. This allows you to compute values, import environment variables, and share logic.

For example, advanced projects often split settings into multiple files or read secrets from the environment instead of hard-coding them. You do not need that complexity yet, but it helps to know that Django expects settings to grow with the project.

Settings are global, but not magical. When something behaves unexpectedly, ask yourself which setting controls it. Once you know where to look, most configuration problems become straightforward.

By the time you finish this chapter, you should not aim to memorize `settings.py`. Instead, you should feel comfortable opening it, recognizing the major sections, and knowing which parts to change when Django's behavior needs to be adjusted.

Prompt: What settings cause the most confusion for beginners, and why?

Settings define how the project behaves: which apps are installed, which database is used, where templates are loaded from, and how security checks are applied. Even then, things will go wrong. A URL name will not match. A template will be in the wrong folder. A model field will be misspelled. The next section shows how to read Django's errors and find the line that caused the problem.

Error handling and debugging

Errors are not a sign that something has gone wrong with Django. They are Django doing its job and telling you precisely where your assumptions do not match reality. Learning how to read and react to Django errors is one of the fastest ways to become productive with the framework.

Detailed error message when debug is enabled

When `DEBUG` is set to `True`, Django shows a detailed error page whenever an exception occurs. This page is verbose on purpose. It includes the exception type, the error message, a stack trace, local variables, and often a clear hint about what Django was trying to do at the time. Beginners often skim past this information, but almost everything you need is already on that page.

Prompt: Please walk through a real Django error page and explain how to read the traceback from bottom to top.

Traceback

The most important part of the debug page is the **traceback**. It shows the chain of function calls that led to the error, with the most recent call at the bottom. Start there. That is usually where your code appears. Click through to see the exact line that triggered the exception and the values of local variables at that moment.

You learned about traceback in more detail in *Chapter 8, Python – Programming on the Backend.*

Prompt: Why does Django prefer raising errors loudly instead of failing silently?

Common errors

Some common errors you will encounter early on:

- `TemplateDoesNotExist` usually means the template path is wrong or the app is not in `INSTALLED_APPS`
- `NoReverseMatch` means Django could not find a URL with the name or parameters you specified. This almost always points to a mismatch between URL names and `{% url %}` usage
- `IntegrityError` often appears after changing models. It indicates a database constraint was violated, such as a missing foreign key or duplicate value in a unique field
- `FieldError` typically means a typo in a model field name inside a QuerySet

Understanding the category of error already narrows the search dramatically.

Development server error logs

The Django development server logs errors to the terminal as well. Always check the console where `runserver` is running. Import errors, syntax errors, and startup problems appear there before a request is even handled. If the server will not start, the terminal output is the first place to look.

Shell debugging

The Django shell is an underrated debugging tool. If something fails in a view, reproduce it step by step in the shell. First, start the shell:

```
python manage.py shell
```

Next, execute statements to identify issues with your models:

```
from blog.models import Post

Post.objects.filter(status="published")
```

If the query fails in the shell, the problem is not your view or template. This isolates issues quickly and removes the browser from the equation.

Printing as debugging

Printing is still useful. Strategic `print()` statements inside views can confirm which code paths are running and what data looks like at runtime. In development, this output appears directly in the terminal. For more complex projects, Python's logging system integrates cleanly with Django, but `print()` is perfectly acceptable while learning.

HTTP errors

It is also worth understanding Django's philosophy around HTTP errors. Not all errors are bugs. A missing web resource should usually return a 404, not crash the application. Django provides helper functions like `get_object_or_404()` to make this explicit:

```
from django.shortcuts import get_object_or_404

post = get_object_or_404(Post, slug=slug, status="published")
```

This raises an exception internally, but Django catches it and returns a proper `404` response. This is an example of Django encouraging correct error handling rather than defensive programming everywhere.

Good practice: read error messages

One important habit to build early is reading error messages in full. Django's errors are rarely vague. They often tell you exactly what setting, field, or file caused the issue. Skipping ahead to fixing without understanding usually leads to a second error rather than a solution.

Remember that DEBUG=True is a development tool, not a crutch. It is designed to teach you how Django works by showing its internals when something breaks. If you learn to trust and interpret these error pages, debugging Django applications becomes a methodical process rather than guesswork.

Once you are comfortable with Django's error messages and tools, you will find that many problems are resolved faster than in lighter frameworks, precisely because Django refuses to fail silently.

Now let's end this chapter by reviewing security topics like authentication.

Authentication and authorization

Authentication is one of the areas where Django's batteries included philosophy is most obvious. Django ships with a complete authentication system that handles users, passwords, sessions, permissions, and login state without requiring third-party libraries or custom database tables.

Prompt: Please explain Django's authentication system as part of the request-response lifecycle.

The built-in User model

At the center of this system is the User model, provided by django.contrib.auth. A user represents an authenticated identity, not a profile or a person's extended details. It stores usernames, hashed passwords, email addresses, and flags such as whether the user is active, staff, or a superuser. You have already interacted with this model indirectly when creating a superuser for the admin interface.

Authentication in Django answers two related but distinct questions:

1. Who is this user? This is authentication.
2. What is this user allowed to do? This is authorization.

Django keeps track of whether a user is logged in by using something called a session, which is a small piece of data stored between requests. When a user logs in, Django stores their user ID in that session. On each new request, Django reads this session data and looks up the corresponding user, then attaches it to the request object. That is why you can write code like:

```
def some_view(request):
    if request.user.is_authenticated:
        ...
```

The `request.user` value is always available. If the user is logged in, it represents the user. If the user is not logged in, Django provides an `AnonymousUser` object. It behaves enough like a user object for common checks, but it represents "no logged-in user." This means you do not need to check for missing values, and your authentication checks stay simple and consistent.

Built-in views for logging in and out

Django includes ready-made views for logging in and out. To use them, you add URL patterns like this:

```
from django.contrib.auth import views as auth_views

urlpatterns = [
    path("login/", auth_views.LoginView.as_view(), name="login"),
    path("logout/", auth_views.LogoutView.as_view(), name="logout"),
]
```

You then create a `registration/login.html` template, and Django handles the rest. This is a good example of Django's philosophy: common problems should not require custom code unless you want custom behavior.

Protecting views

Protecting views is straightforward. If a page should only be accessible to logged-in users, use the `login_required` decorator:

```
from django.contrib.auth.decorators import login_required

@login_required
def create_post(request):
    ...
```

If an anonymous user tries to access this view, Django automatically redirects them to the login page. This is controlled by the `LOGIN_URL` setting.

Permissions and groups

Permissions and **groups** provide a higher-level authorization system. Every model automatically gets basic permissions such as *add*, *change*, *delete*, and *view*. These permissions are enforced in the admin interface and can also be checked in code:

```
if request.user.has_perm("blog.change_post"):
    ...
```

Groups allow you to bundle permissions together and assign them to users. This is how Django supports roles like editor, moderator, or administrator without hard-coding logic into views.

Prompt: What is the difference between authentication and authorization in Django, with concrete examples? How do permissions and groups actually work under the hood?

User-related data

A common beginner question is where user-related data should live. The rule of thumb is simple: authentication data belongs on `User`, domain-specific data belongs elsewhere. That is why it is common to create a one-to-one profile model linked to `User`, as you did with `Author` for tracking who wrote a blog post. This keeps the authentication system clean while still allowing rich application-specific behavior.

Integrated but optional

One important point to emphasize is that Django's authentication system is optional but the admin, forms, permissions, sessions, middleware, views, and templates all know how to work with it. You can ignore it entirely for public-only sites, or you can lean on it heavily for internal tools, content management, and role-based systems. The admin interface, forms, permissions, and middleware all speak the same authentication language, which reduces the amount of glue code you must write.

For this chapter, you only need the main idea: authentication is already wired into Django's request lifecycle. Once you recognize that `request.user` is just another piece of data flowing through views and templates, Django's approach to security becomes easier to understand and extend.

Prompt: How would this Django blog project evolve if I wanted to add comments, pagination, or an API later? What parts of Django stay the same when moving from a small personal project to a large production system?

Practice, references, and resources

In this section, you will be tested on what you've learned in this chapter and be provided with useful links to reference materials and resources.

Check your understanding

Answer the following questions:

1. What problem is Django designed to solve?
2. What does *batteries included* mean in Django?
3. What are the three parts of Django's MVT pattern?
4. How does Django's MVT differ from MVC?
5. What is the request–response lifecycle in Django?
6. What is the difference between a Django project and an app?
7. What is the purpose of URL routing in Django?
8. Why does the order of URL patterns matter?
9. What is a Django model and what does it represent?
10. What is the difference between `makemigrations` and `migrate`?
11. What is a QuerySet and what does it mean that it is lazy?
12. What is the role of a Django view?
13. Why does Django limit logic in templates?
14. What is the difference between templates and static files?
15. What is the purpose of the Django admin interface?

Scenario-based questions

Now answer the following deeper questions:

1. You create a new Django app but your models do not appear in the admin. What is the most likely cause?
2. You visit a URL and get a `NoReverseMatch` error. What does this usually mean?
3. A URL like `/archive/` is being handled by a slug route instead of the intended view. Why?
4. You define a new field on a model but do not run any commands. What happens?
5. You chain multiple filters on a QuerySet. Does this hit the database multiple times? Why or why not?
6. You try to write Python logic inside a template and it fails. Why?
7. You hard-code `/static/style.css` in your template, and later static files break in production. Why?
8. A form submission sends invalid data. Where should validation happen in Django?

9. You want to create a form tied directly to a model. Which approach should you use?
10. A view tries to fetch a database object that does not exist. What is the correct Django approach?
11. You see a detailed error page with a traceback. Where should you look first and why?
12. You log in as a user and then access another page. How does Django know who you are?
13. You want to restrict a view to logged-in users only. What is the simplest way?
14. You are building a public-facing UI. Should you rely on the Django admin interface? Why or why not?
15. You switch from SQLite to PostgreSQL. Do you need to rewrite your models? Why?

Links

Below are the official Django documentation links for the topics covered in this chapter. These are the canonical references and are kept up to date by the Django project itself. All links point to the latest stable documentation on the official Django site.

Core Django documentation

Django documentation home: `https://docs.djangoproject.com/`

Tutorial: `https://docs.djangoproject.com/en/stable/intro/tutorial01/`

Models and the ORM

Models: `https://docs.djangoproject.com/en/stable/topics/db/models/`

Field reference: `https://docs.djangoproject.com/en/stable/ref/models/fields/`

Relationships: `https://docs.djangoproject.com/en/stable/topics/db/examples/`

QuerySets: `https://docs.djangoproject.com/en/stable/topics/db/queries/`

Migrations: `https://docs.djangoproject.com/en/stable/topics/migrations/`

Views, request handling, URLs and routing

Views: `https://docs.djangoproject.com/en/stable/topics/http/views/`

Class-based views: `https://docs.djangoproject.com/en/stable/topics/class-based-views/`

Shortcuts aka Helper functions: `https://docs.djangoproject.com/en/stable/topics/http/shortcuts/`

URLs: `https://docs.djangoproject.com/en/stable/topics/http/urls/`

URL resolvers: `https://docs.djangoproject.com/en/stable/ref/urlresolvers/`

Templates and forms

Templates: `https://docs.djangoproject.com/en/stable/topics/templates/`

Reference: `https://docs.djangoproject.com/en/stable/ref/templates/language/`

Built-in template tags and filters: `https://docs.djangoproject.com/en/stable/ref/templates/builtins/`

Forms: `https://docs.djangoproject.com/en/stable/topics/forms/`

Fields: `https://docs.djangoproject.com/en/stable/ref/forms/fields/`

ModelForm: `https://docs.djangoproject.com/en/stable/topics/forms/modelforms/`

Admin, authentication and authorization

Admin: `https://docs.djangoproject.com/en/stable/ref/contrib/admin/`

Admin actions and customization: `https://docs.djangoproject.com/en/stable/ref/contrib/admin/actions/`

Authentication: `https://docs.djangoproject.com/en/stable/topics/auth/`

Login and logout views: `https://docs.djangoproject.com/en/stable/topics/auth/default/`

Settings and configuration

Settings: `https://docs.djangoproject.com/en/stable/topics/settings/`

Reference: `https://docs.djangoproject.com/en/stable/ref/settings/`

Static files: `https://docs.djangoproject.com/en/stable/howto/static-files/`

Error reporting: `https://docs.djangoproject.com/en/stable/howto/error-reporting/`

Summary

In this chapter, we learned the following:

- What Django is, how it fits into the web stack, and why it is designed for rapid, maintainable development
- How Django's MVT architecture relates to the more familiar MVC pattern and how responsibilities are divided between models, views, and templates

- How to create and configure a Django project and app using a virtual environment and VS Code on Windows, macOS, or Linux
- How to define models, relationships, and field types, and how Django's ORM maps Python code to relational databases
- How migrations work, why they exist, and how to evolve a database schema safely as models change
- How to write views that handle HTTP requests, query data, and return responses
- How to build templates using Django's template language, including loops, filters, and template inheritance
- How Django's URL routing system maps paths to views and why named URLs matter
- How to work with forms and `ModelForm` to validate user input and save data securely
- How to use and customize the Django admin interface to create, edit, filter, and search application data
- How Django's authentication system works and how users, sessions, permissions, and access control fit together
- How to configure core settings such as installed apps, databases, templates, and static files
- How to interpret Django error messages, use the debug tools, and troubleshoot common development issues

Django does remove a lot of repetitive work, but its bigger value is structure. Once you know where URLs, views, models, templates, forms, middleware, settings, and authentication fit, you can write better code, review AI-generated code more safely, and debug problems with less guesswork.

In the next chapter, you will move from Django's web framework structure to the command line environment that supports everyday development work. You will learn how Bash and other shells provide a way to interact with your operating system through commands, letting you run programs, automate repetitive tasks, and understand what tools like Python, Git, and Django are really doing when they run commands.

Get this book's PDF version and more

Scan the QR code (or go to packtpub.com/unlock). Search for this book by name, confirm the edition, and then follow the steps on the page.

Note: Keep your invoice handy. Purchases made directly from Packt don't require an invoice.

10

Bash/Shell – Command-Line Skills for Developers

Scripting with Bash or a similar shell may seem separate from web development, but it is never far away. Whether you are creating a new project, installing dependencies, running a development server, managing files, or deploying code, you will repeatedly find yourself typing commands into a terminal.

Shells like **Bourne Again Shell** (**Bash**) and **Z Shell** (**Zsh**) let you turn one-off commands into repeatable steps that you can save, edit, and run again later.

Remember that in Stack Overflow's 2025 survey of 31,771 developers, 48.7% said they have done extensive development work with Bash/Shell. That makes shell scripting worth learning even if you mainly think of yourself as a web developer.

Bash is the default shell on most Linux systems and has long been central to macOS and server environments. Even on Windows, modern development environments expose Bash through tools like Windows Subsystem for Linux and Git Bash. As a result, Bash has become a common language across platforms.

Since macOS Catalina in 2019, the default shell on Macs is Zsh, not Bash. The basic commands in this chapter work identically in both shells. macOS also ships with a rather old version of Bash. To install an updated Bash on macOS, use the following Homebrew command: `brew install bash`. Alternatively, you can use Zsh because the differences won't matter for this chapter's content.

This chapter deliberately keeps Bash grounded in everyday developer tasks rather than treating it as a full programming language to be mastered in isolation. You will learn what Bash is and how it fits into the wider idea of a shell, practice the core commands used to navigate and manipulate files and then write a small script that automates a real task. You should finish the chapter feeling comfortable reading and adapting shell commands, even if you never write complex scripts entirely on your own.

Because the command line can feel unforgiving, we will also look at how AI tools can help you check your understanding. Used well, they can explain unfamiliar commands, suggest safer alternatives, and help you understand why something failed rather than just pasting in a fix you do not understand.

By the end of this chapter, you will understand what Bash does, navigate the file system, run common commands, write a simple Bash script, and use AI tools to check unfamiliar commands before you run them.

In this chapter, we will cover the following topics:

- Introducing Bash
- Setting up Bash on Windows
- Basic commands
- Writing a simple script
- Automating your Django development
- Using AI for shell help

Suggested chatbot prompts with example responses for this chapter can be found at the following link: `https://github.com/markjprice/web-dev-ai/blob/main/prompts/ch10-bash/readme.md`

Introducing Bash

Bash stands for **Bourne Again Shell**, and it is both a Unix shell and a command language. In simple terms, Bash is the program that sits between you and the operating system, reading the commands you type and turning them into actions.

When you open a terminal window and type something like `python manage.py runserver` or `npm install`, you are not talking directly to Python or Node. You are talking to Bash, and Bash is responsible for launching those programs, passing arguments to them, and handling their output.

Prompt: Please explain the difference between Bash, a shell, and a terminal, with concrete examples.

Shell scripting

A shell is a user interface for the operating system, just not a graphical one. Instead of clicking icons or menus, you issue text commands. Unix systems have always treated this text-based interface as a normal way of working, which is why shells like Bash became so scriptable and expressive. Over time, Bash also became a programming language, with variables, conditionals, loops, and functions. This allows you to move beyond individual commands and start automating sequences of tasks.

Bash is especially useful in development because so many tools are designed around it. Running a local development server, starting and stopping background processes, cleaning build directories, or chaining together multiple tools are all straightforward in Bash.

Deployment scripts are almost always written as shell scripts. Continuous integration systems execute Bash commands to build, test, and deploy applications. Dockerfiles rely heavily on shell commands to assemble images. Even when you are using other development tools, Bash is often the glue holding everything together.

Script portability

Another reason Bash matters is portability. A Bash script written on your machine will usually run unchanged on a Linux server in the cloud. This shared environment is one of the reasons cloud infrastructure, DevOps practices, and containerization took off so quickly. When documentation says *run the following commands*, it is almost always assuming a Bash-like shell, even if it does not say so explicitly.

Terminals and shells

It is also worth separating Bash from the terminal itself. The terminal is just the window or application that displays text and accepts input. Bash is the program running inside that terminal. Other shells exist, such as `zsh` or `fish`, but Bash remains the common baseline. Even if your system uses a different default shell, Bash is usually installed and widely supported, which is why it is still taught and referenced so often.

At the outermost layer is the terminal window. This is just a user interface. On Windows, it might be **Windows Terminal**, on macOS **Terminal.app**, and on Linux, one of many terminal emulators. Its job is simple: display text and send your keystrokes somewhere. The terminal does not understand commands.

Running inside the terminal is the shell, in this case, Bash. Bash is a program. It reads the text you type, interprets it, keeps track of state such as the current directory and environment variables, and decides what to do next. When you press *Enter*, Bash parses the command line, expands variables, applies quoting rules, and resolves what should be executed.

When Bash recognizes a command like `ls`, `python`, or `docker`, it then launches an external program. These programs are separate executables provided by the operating system or installed tools. Bash starts them as child processes, passes arguments to them, and waits for them to finish. Their output flows back through Bash and is displayed by the terminal.

So, the flow is always:

```
You type text → the terminal sends it to Bash → Bash interprets it → Bash
runs programs → output flows back up to the terminal.
```

This flow explains several beginner confusions:

- Why changing shells does not change the terminal window
- Why Bash scripts can run Python, Docker, Git, or any other tool
- Why errors often come from the program you launched, not from Bash itself
- Why the same Bash command behaves the same on macOS, Linux, WSL, and servers

Bash gives you direct, scriptable control over your development environment. You do not need to know everything it can do, but understanding the basics will make many everyday tasks faster, clearer, and less mysterious.

To summarize:

- **Terminal**: window (just input/output)
- **Shell (Bash)**: interpreter (understands commands)
- **Programs**: actual tools (`ls`, `python`, `docker`)

Prompt: Why is Bash still widely used when alternative shells like `zsh` and `fish` exist?

Common syntax across commands

Bash commands usually follow a predictable shape: a **command name**, followed by **options** (sometimes called flags), followed by arguments. Making this clear early helps you recognize patterns without needing to memorize everything.

For example:

```
ls -l src
```

- `ls` is the command (to list files)
- `-l` is an option (to use long, detailed format)
- `src` is an argument (the name of a folder to list)

```
docker run -p 8000:8000 image-name
```

- `docker` is the command (to use Docker)
- `run` is a subcommand (what you want Docker to do)
- `-p` is an option (publish a port)
- `8000:8000` is an argument (map local port to container port)
- `image-name` is an argument (the name of an image to run)

You do not need to memorize all the options yet. Focus on recognizing this space-delimited structure, as it will make new commands much easier to understand later.

Prompt: Please explain the general structure of a Bash command: command name, options, and arguments.

Stateful commands

Bash is stateful, meaning that when you type commands, Bash maintains context. Your current working directory, environment variables, and command history all persist from one command to the next.

This is why `cd` (change directory) matters, why a command can work one moment and fail the next, and why restarting a terminal sometimes fixes things. New developers often assume each command runs in isolation. It does not.

Prompt: What does it mean that Bash is stateful, and how does that affect scripts?

Command history and editing

One useful result of Bash being stateful is that it remembers what you have done. Every command you type is stored in your command history, which means you rarely need to retype long or complex commands.

Repeat previous commands

Press the ↑ (up arrow) key to cycle backward through previous commands:

```
docker run -p 8000:8000 my-image
```

If you just ran this command and want to run it again, press ↑ and press *Enter*. This is especially helpful when working with long commands or when you are experimenting and need to retry something.

Search your command history

Instead of scrolling back line by line, you can search your command history:

1. Press *Ctrl* + *R*
2. Start typing part of a previous command, for example `docker`
3. Bash will show the most recent matching command

Press *Enter* to run it, or keep pressing *Ctrl* + *R* to cycle through matches.

Edit commands before running them

When you recall a command using ↑ or *Ctrl* + *R*, you can edit it before pressing *Enter*. Developers do this constantly:

```
docker run -p 8000:8000 my-image
```

You might change just the port:

```
docker run -p 5000:5000 my-image
```

This is much faster and less error-prone than typing the whole command again.

Why this helps

Beginners often think they need to type every command from scratch. In practice, experienced developers rely heavily on command history to:

- Retry commands after fixing an error
- Make small adjustments to previous commands
- Explore and experiment more quickly

This is another example of how Bash maintains state between commands. Your history, current directory, and environment all persist, which is why the terminal becomes more useful the longer you use it.

You do not need to memorize every command. Focus on understanding what commands do, and let the *history* feature help you reuse them efficiently.

Tab completion

Tab completion is a feature provided by the shell, not the terminal. When you press *Tab*, the shell tries to autocomplete what you're typing, based on context:

- File and folder names
- Command names
- Options and flags (for some tools)

With Bash, basic completion works out of the box (files, folders, commands), but more advanced completion (like Git branches, Docker options) depends on `bash-completion` being installed.

Zsh is much more full featured by default, with better suggestions, sometimes menu-style completion. Zsh is often enhanced further with frameworks like Oh My Zsh.

Across Bash, Zsh, and most environments, you can usually press *Tab* to complete file and folder names, and press *Tab* twice to show available options, and completion based on the current directory.

Splitting long commands across lines

Some commands can become long and difficult to read, especially when they include multiple options or arguments. Instead of writing everything on one line, you can split a command across multiple lines using a backslash (\).

The backslash tells Bash that the command continues on the next line.

For example, instead of writing:

```
docker run -p 8000:8000 -v $(pwd):/app -e DEBUG=true my-image
```

You can write it like this:

```
docker run \
  -p 8000:8000 \
  -v $(pwd):/app \
  -e DEBUG=true \
  my-image
```

This makes the command easier to read and modify, especially when copying from documentation or working with complex setups.

Important rules:

- The backslash must be the very last character on the line
- Do not add spaces after the backslash
- Bash treats all lines as one continuous command

If you forget the backslash, Bash will try to run each line as a separate command, which usually leads to errors.

Many real-world commands, especially with tools like Docker, Git, or cloud CLIs, can become long and hard to manage. Splitting them across lines helps you:

- Understand each part of the command
- Avoid mistakes when editing
- Copy and paste commands more safely

You will often see this style in documentation and scripts. Even though it looks like multiple lines, Bash still runs it as a single command.

Commands can be combined

Bash works especially well with text. Everything is text in and text out. Commands write to standard output, errors go to standard error, and those streams can be redirected or connected together. The **pipe operator** | sends one command's output to another command's input:

```
ls -la | grep ".py"  # List only Python files
cat log.txt | wc -l  # Count lines in a file
```

Redirection using > or >> sends output to a file:

```
echo "Hello" > file.txt   # Write (overwrites)
echo "World" >> file.txt  # Append
```

These two operators let small commands work together.

You do not need to learn pipes and redirection in depth yet, but keep in mind that commands can be chained together, which is why the shell feels composable rather than monolithic.

Creating shortcuts with aliases

As you start using the command line more often, you will notice that you type the same long commands repeatedly. Bash provides a simple way to create shortcuts for these commands using something called an alias.

An **alias** is just a short name that expands into a longer command.

In a Django project, you often run:

```
python manage.py runserver
```

You can shorten this to a single word:

```
alias serve="python manage.py runserver"
```

Now you can start the development server by typing:

```
serve
```

This does the same thing as the full command, but it is faster to type and easier to remember.

When you type a command, Bash first checks:

1. Is this an alias?
2. If so, replace it with the full command
3. Then execute the result

So:

```
serve
```

becomes:

```
python manage.py runserver
```

before anything is run.

Aliases are most helpful for long or repetitive commands and commands with flags you always use. For example:

```
alias ll="ls -la"
alias migrate="python manage.py migrate"
alias test="python manage.py test"
```

Now your workflow becomes:

```
serve
migrate
test
```

Temporary vs permanent aliases

If you define an alias in the terminal, it only lasts for that session. If you close the terminal, it disappears.

To make aliases permanent, add them to your shell configuration file:

- Bash: `~/.bashrc` or `~/.bash_profile`
- Zsh: `~/.zshrc`

For example, open your config file and add:

```
alias serve="python manage.py runserver"
```

Then reload it:

```
source ~/.bashrc
```

Now the alias will be available every time you open a new terminal.

Aliases are simple text replacements. They are great for shortcuts but limited because they cannot easily handle arguments, so they are not ideal for multi-step routines. They can also make commands less obvious to other developers because they are not standard.

If a shortcut becomes complex or needs logic, it is usually better to turn it into a script instead.

Aliases are one of the fastest ways to make the command line feel less repetitive. Think of aliases as quick shortcuts and scripts as repeatable processes.

Commands are unforgiving

Bash is powerful but not forgiving. A graphical file manager usually asks before deleting things. Bash often does exactly what you asked, immediately. The point is not to scare you, just to encourage a habit of reading commands carefully before pressing *Enter*, especially when copying from documentation or AI output.

Bash is not being introduced so you become a shell expert. It is being introduced so you can follow instructions, understand what tools are doing, and write small scripts when repetition becomes annoying.

Bash is a good place to slow down before accepting an AI-generated answer. A command such as `rm`, `chmod`, or `docker` run can change files, permissions, processes, or network access. Before running it, check what it will touch and whether it depends on your current directory.

Before you run a command, ask: Where am I in the file system? What files will this touch? Does it create something, delete something, change permissions, start a process, or send data over the network? That kind of thinking matters more than typing the command from memory. The command line rewards developers who understand behavior.

Many readers will be using Windows, which is a problem since Bash (or an alternative Bash-like shell like Zsh on Macs) is not a standard component of Windows. If you are using Windows and don't have Bash or similar, in the next section you will learn how to install it. If you're not using Windows, you can skip the next section and continue with the section titled *Basic commands*.

Setting up Bash on Windows

To use Bash on Windows, install **Windows Subsystem for Linux** (**WSL**).

WSL 2 is supported on Windows 11 and on Windows 10 version 1903 (build 18362) or later.

Install WSL from an elevated terminal

Open PowerShell as Administrator, then run:

```
wsl --install
```

Alternatively, to install a specific Linux distribution like Ubuntu, run: `wsl --install -d Ubuntu`. To list available distributions, run: `wsl --list --online`

This installs WSL and typically installs a default Linux distribution (often Ubuntu) depending on your Windows version and configuration, as shown in the following output:

```
Downloading: Ubuntu
[==========================53.5%                              ]
```

If you already have WSL installed, check what you have:

```
wsl -l -v
```

This lists installed distributions and whether each is WSL 1 or WSL 2, as shown in the following output:

```
  NAME              STATE           VERSION
* docker-desktop    Stopped         2
  Ubuntu            Running         2
```

Launch your Linux distribution and complete first-time setup

Open the **Start** menu, run your distro, for example, **Ubuntu**, and follow the prompts to create a Linux username and password. This is separate from your Windows login.

From now on, when you start **Ubuntu**, you should see the Bash prompt, as shown in *Figure 10.1*:

Figure 10.1: Ubuntu Bash prompt and terminal window

Update packages inside Linux

In the WSL terminal, run:

```
sudo apt update
sudo apt upgrade -y
```

This keeps the environment current and avoids confusing install issues.

Good practice: sudo runs a command with administrator (root) privileges. When you use it, the system asks for your Linux password to confirm the action. This level of access should be used carefully and only for system-level tasks, such as installing software with apt. For everyday development commands like pip install, python, or npm, you should not need sudo. If those tools only work when run with elevated privileges, it usually means your environment or permissions are set up incorrectly and should be fixed rather than bypassed.

Confirm Bash is running

In the WSL terminal, run:

```
echo "$SHELL"
```

You should see a path like /bin/bash (or similar).

In the WSL terminal, run:

```
bash --version
```

You should see a version output (with copyright and license information):

```
GNU bash, version 5.2.21(1)-release (x86_64-pc-linux-gnu)
```

Create a practice folder for the chapter

In the WSL terminal, run:

```
mkdir -p ~/bash-chapter
cd ~/bash-chapter
```

In the WSL terminal, check where you are:

```
pwd
```

You should see that you are in home, then your username like mine markjprice, and then the new directory that you just created:

```
/home/markjprice/bash-chapter
```

In the WSL terminal, run:

```
ls -la
```

If you are done with Bash, in the WSL terminal, you can run:

```
exit
```

In Windows File Explorer, you can use the Linux node to view your WSL installations, as shown in *Figure 10.2*:

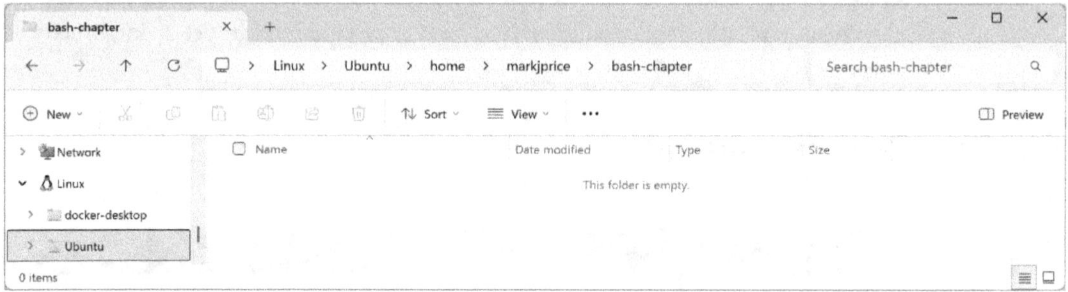

Figure 10.2: Windows File Explorer and its WSL integration

These commands behave exactly as described in the chapter.

Now let's put this background into practice by learning some common basic commands.

Basic commands

Before writing scripts or automating anything, you need a small vocabulary of everyday commands. These are the commands you will use constantly when working on projects, following tutorials, or debugging issues from the terminal. You do not need to memorize every option. Knowing what each command is for is far more important than knowing every flag it supports.

The core commands we will use in this chapter are:

- `pwd` – prints the current working directory
- `ls` – lists files and directories
- `cd` – changes the current directory
- `mkdir` – creates a new directory
- `touch` – creates an empty file
- `cp` – copies files and directories
- `mv` – moves or renames files and directories
- `rm` – deletes files and directories
- `cat` – prints the contents of a file
- `echo` – outputs text to the terminal

Navigation commands

Let's start by focusing on just `pwd`, `ls`, and `cd` first. The rest will make more sense once navigation feels natural.

pwd – print working directory

`pwd` tells you where you are in the file system. This matters because most commands operate relative to the current directory:

```
pwd
```

Typical output would be something like:

```
/Users/mark/projects/my-site
```

Whenever a command fails with *file not found*, `pwd` is often the first thing to check. Many problems turn out to be caused by running a command in the wrong directory.

ls – list directory contents

`ls` shows you what files and folders exist in the current directory. Common options include `-l` for a detailed listing and `-a` to show hidden files:

```
ls -la
```

Prompt: What happens step by step when I type a command like `ls -la` into a terminal?

Hidden files often start with a dot, such as `.git` or `.env`, and are common in development projects.

Prompt: What are hidden files in Unix systems, and why do they start with a dot?

cd – change directory

`cd` changes your current working directory. For example, to move into a folder called `src`:

```
cd src
```

To go up one level, use:

```
cd ..
```

To return to your home directory:

```
cd ~
```

Getting comfortable with cd is essential, because almost everything else depends on being in the right place.

Prompt: Please explain relative vs absolute paths in Bash using a directory tree example.

Creating things

Now let's see two commands to make a directory or a file.

mkdir – make directory

mkdir creates a new directory:

```
mkdir scripts
```

You can create nested directories in one step using -p:

```
mkdir -p app/static/css
```

This is common when setting up project structures.

touch – create a file

touch creates an empty file if it does not already exist:

```
touch app.py
```

If the file already exists, touch simply updates its timestamp. Developers often use it to quickly create placeholder files.

Moving, copying, and deleting

You often need to move, copy, or delete filesystem items.

cp – copy files and directories

cp copies files from one location to another:

```
cp settings.example.json settings.json
```

To copy a directory and its contents, use the -r (recursive) option:

```
cp -r templates templates_backup
```

mv – move or rename files

mv moves files or directories. It is also used for renaming:

```
mv old_name.py new_name.py
```

or:

```
mv build/ dist/
```

There is no separate rename command. Renaming is just a move within the same directory.

rm – remove files and directories

rm deletes files:

```
rm debug.log
```

To remove a directory and everything inside it, use -r:

```
rm -r temp/
```

This command does not send files to a recycle bin. Once deleted, they are usually gone. This is one of the reasons developers treat rm -r with respect.

Prompt: Why does rm not ask for confirmation by default, and how do experienced developers stay safe?

Showing text

Lastly, let's see how to output a file or a string to the console.

cat – display file contents

cat prints the contents of a file to the terminal:

```
cat README.md
```

It is useful for quickly inspecting small text files, configuration files, or logs without opening an editor.

echo – print text

echo outputs text to the terminal:

```
echo "Hello, Bash"
```

It is often used in scripts to show progress messages or to test variables and command output.

These commands form the foundation of almost everything you will do in Bash. Once they feel familiar, reading shell-based instructions becomes much easier, and writing simple scripts starts to feel natural.

Working with web resources

Now let's see some network commands.

curl – transfer data from or to a server

`curl` is used to make HTTP requests from the command line. It is commonly used to download data, test APIs, or interact with web services:

```
curl https://example.com
```

This fetches the content of the URL and prints it to the terminal.

To save the response to a file, use the `-o` option:

```
curl -o index.html https://example.com
```

You can also send data, for example when working with APIs:

```
curl -X POST -d "name=Mark" https://example.com/api
```

Developers often use `curl` to debug APIs, check responses, or automate requests in scripts.

wget – download files from the web

`wget` is designed for downloading files from the internet. It is especially useful for saving files directly to disk:

```
wget https://example.com/file.zip
```

This downloads the file and saves it with its original name.

To save it with a different name, use `-O`:

```
wget -O archive.zip https://example.com/file.zip
```

Unlike `curl`, `wget` is focused on downloading and can resume interrupted downloads, which is useful for large files.

Let's put it all together by writing a simple script.

Writing a simple script

So far, you have been typing one command at a time into the terminal. A Bash script is simply a way to save a sequence of commands into a file and run them together. This is useful whenever you notice yourself repeating the same steps over and over, or when you want to document a process in a form that the computer can execute.

For example, let's say you've been working with Django and you find yourself repeating the same three commands in order, over and over again:

1. Change to the project directory:

   ```
   cd project
   ```

2. Activate the virtual environment:

   ```
   source .venv/bin/activate
   ```

3. Run the web server:

   ```
   python manage.py runserver
   ```

If you create a script file named `run_dev.sh` that contains these three commands, then three steps become one:

- Run the script:

  ```
  ./run_dev.sh
  ```

A script replaces repeated typing with a single command.

Script files

A Bash script is just a plain text file. By convention, it usually has a `.sh` extension, although the extension itself is not technically required. Let's start with a minimal example.

Create a new file called `run_dev.sh`:

```
touch run_dev.sh
```

Open it in VS Code and add the following commands:

```
#!/usr/bin/env bash

echo "Starting development environment..."
python manage.py runserver
```

The first line is called the **shebang**. It tells the operating system which program should be used to run the file. In this case, it says *use Bash*. The `env` form is preferred because it works across different systems where Bash might live in slightly different locations.

The remaining lines are just normal Bash commands, exactly the same as if you had typed them into the terminal by hand.

Prompt: Please explain the shebang line in Bash scripts and why `/usr/bin/env bash` is recommended.

Making script file executable

Before you can run the script, you need to make it executable:

```
chmod +x run_dev.sh
```

If you forget this step and try to run the script, you will typically see an error like:

```
$ ./run_dev.sh
bash: ./run_dev.sh: Permission denied
```

This happens because the file exists, but the operating system does not have permission to execute it as a program. Adding the execute permission with `chmod +x` resolves this.

Now you can run it like this:

```
./run_dev.sh
```

The `./` path prefix matters. It tells Bash to look for the script in the current directory rather than searching for a system command with the same name.

Prompt: What does `chmod +x` actually change at the operating system level?

At this point, you have already learned something important: scripts run in the same shell environment you have been using interactively. If your script fails, the commands inside it would probably fail if you typed them manually as well. This makes debugging much less mysterious.

Adding logic to scripts

You can add simple logic to make scripts more useful. For example, variables let you avoid hard-coding values, like setting a `PORT` variable to `8000` and then referencing it with `$PORT` in a command:

```
#!/usr/bin/env bash

PORT=8000
echo "Starting server on port $PORT"
python manage.py runserver "$PORT"
```

On some systems, you may need to use `python3` instead of `python`.

You can also stop a script when something goes wrong. The following line tells Bash to exit immediately if any command fails:

```
set -e
```

Placed near the top of the script, this prevents later commands from running in a broken state, which is especially useful in build or deployment scripts.

For safer scripts, use the full safety preamble:

```
set -euo pipefail
```

Note the following about the preceding command:

- `-e`: Exit immediately if any command fails
- `-u`: Exit if you use an undefined variable (this catches typos)
- `-o pipefail`: A pipeline fails if any command in it fails

This combination prevents entire categories of subtle bugs. Place it near the top of every script.

Prompt: Why does my Bash script exit early when I use `set -e`?

A simple but realistic script might combine several tasks:

```
#!/usr/bin/env bash
set -e

echo "Cleaning old files..."
rm -rf dist/

echo "Running tests..."
python manage.py test

echo "Starting server..."
python manage.py runserver
```

Nothing here is complicated, but putting these steps into a script means they always run in the same order, the same way, every time. That consistency is the real value of shell scripts.

You do not need to turn Bash into your primary programming language. Think of scripts as glue. They connect tools, enforce routines, and save mental effort.

Always quote variables

Unquoted variables in Bash can cause bugs and security issues:

```
# If NAME contains spaces:
NAME="John Smith"
echo Hello, $NAME      # Bash sees: echo Hello, John Smith (3 args)
echo "Hello, $NAME"    # Bash sees: echo "Hello, John Smith" (1 arg)
```

In Bash, $VAR without quotes is subject to word splitting. If the value contains spaces, Bash splits it into multiple arguments. Good practice is to use "$VAR" to prevent this:

```
FILE="my document.txt"
rm "$FILE"    # Correct: deletes "my document.txt"
rm $FILE      # Bug: tries to delete "my" and "document.txt"
```

This is the single most common source of bugs in Bash scripts.

Script arguments

So far, the scripts you have seen do exactly one thing in exactly one way. Bash scripts become much more useful when they can accept input from the command line.

Arguments passed to a script are available as numbered variables. `$1` refers to the first argument, `$2` to the second, and so on.

Create a file called `hello.sh`:

```
#!/usr/bin/env bash

NAME="$1"
echo "Hello, $NAME"
```

Make it executable and run it:

```
chmod +x hello.sh
./hello.sh Mark
```

This pattern shows up everywhere, from small utility scripts to large deployment tools. It allows one script to handle many similar tasks without modification.

Relative and absolute paths

Paths inside a Bash script work the same way they do in the terminal. Relative paths are resolved from the current working directory, not from the location of the script itself.

This means the following script can behave differently depending on where it is run from:

```
rm data/output.txt
```

If you want predictable behavior, either use absolute paths or explicitly change the directory at the start of the script:

```
cd /Users/mark/projects/my-site
```

Understanding this early avoids a common class of bugs where scripts work for one person but fail for another.

Prompt: Why does running the same Bash command sometimes work in one directory but fail in another?

Comments in scripts

Bash scripts support comments using the # character. Anything after # on a line is ignored by Bash:

```
# Clean old build files
rm -rf dist/
```

Comments explain intent, which is often more important than explaining syntax. A script you understand today may be confusing in six months without comments.

Bash as glue

Bash does not replace other languages or tools. It connects them.

A single script might call Git, Docker, Python, and a web server in sequence. Bash does not care what language a tool is written in. If it can be run from the command line, Bash can orchestrate it.

This is why Bash remains relevant even as new languages and frameworks appear. It sits at the boundary between tools and lets them work together.

A note on safety

Bash scripts can change or delete files, stop services, and deploy code. They usually do exactly what they are told, without asking for confirmation.

Before running a script that you did not write yourself, read it. This is especially important for scripts copied from the internet or generated by AI tools. Treat shell scripts with the same caution you would give to executable files from an unknown source.

Prompt: What are common beginner mistakes in Bash scripts, and how can I spot them?

Automating your Django development

So far, the examples have been small and focused. Now let's connect Bash directly to something you have already done: running a Django project.

In the previous chapter, you repeatedly ran a sequence of commands:

1. Create or activate a virtual environment
2. Install dependencies
3. Apply database migrations
4. Start the development server

Typing these every time is repetitive and easy to get wrong. This is exactly the kind of task Bash scripts are meant to simplify.

The problem is repetition

A typical Django setup session might look like this:

```
python -m venv .venv
source .venv/bin/activate
pip install -r requirements.txt
python manage.py migrate
python manage.py runserver
```

There is nothing complicated here. But you run this sequence often enough that it becomes friction.

The solution is a shell script

Create a new file in your Django project root:

```
touch run_dev.sh
```

Open it in your code editor and add the following:

```
#!/usr/bin/env bash
set -euo pipefail

echo "Setting up Django development environment..."

# Create virtual environment if it does not exist
if [ ! -d ".venv" ]; then
  echo "Creating virtual environment..."
  python -m venv .venv
fi

# Activate virtual environment
echo "Activating virtual environment..."
source .venv/bin/activate

# Install dependencies
if [ -f "requirements.txt" ]; then
  echo "Installing dependencies..."
  pip install -r requirements.txt
```

```
else
  echo "No requirements.txt found, skipping install"
fi

# Apply database migrations
echo "Running migrations..."
python manage.py migrate

# Start development server
echo "Starting Django development server..."
python manage.py runserver
```

Make the script executable:

```
chmod +x run_dev.sh
```

Now, instead of running five commands, you run one:

```
./run_dev.sh
```

This script is not doing anything new. It is just making your routine explicit and repeatable:

1. It checks if `.venv` exists before creating it
2. It activates the environment
3. It installs dependencies only if a `requirements.txt` file exists
4. It applies migrations every time
5. It starts the server

Each step is something you were already doing manually.

Why automation scripts matter

You are not writing code for its own sake. You are capturing a process: *This is how this project should be started.* That has a few benefits:

- You do not forget the steps
- You avoid subtle environment issues
- You reduce typing and small mistakes
- You make the workflow obvious to someone else reading the project

If someone else clones your repository, they do not need instructions like "run these five commands." They can just run:

```
./run_dev.sh
```

Adding a configurable port for the server

You can make the script slightly more flexible by accepting a port number:

```
PORT="${1:-8000}"
echo "Starting server on port $PORT..."
python manage.py runserver "$PORT"
```

Now you can run:

```
./run_dev.sh 5000
```

or fall back to the default:

```
./run_dev.sh
```

This is a typical use for Bash in a project: take a setup routine you already know and save it as a script.

Good practice: This script assumes a Unix-like environment (Linux, macOS, or WSL on Windows). On native Windows without WSL, activation uses a different path (`.venv\Scripts\activate`). In real projects, teams often provide separate scripts or use tools that handle cross-platform differences.

Now, let's see how AI can help you learn and use shell scripts.

Using AI for shell help

The command line has a reputation for being hostile, largely because error messages can be terse and documentation often assumes prior knowledge. AI tools can make the command line easier to learn. Used properly, they act like an on-demand explainer rather than a magical command generator.

A sensible way to use AI with Bash is to ask why something works or fails, not just what to type. For example, if you see a command in documentation that you do not understand, you can ask:

- Please explain what this Bash command does, piece by piece:

  ```
  docker run -p 8000:8000 -v $(pwd):/app my-image
  ```

A good AI response will break the command into flags, arguments, and substitutions, helping you build intuition rather than encouraging blind copying.

Help with syntax

AI is also helpful for syntax reminders. Bash has many small rules that are easy to forget, such as spacing around brackets or how variables are expanded. Instead of searching through man pages, you can ask targeted questions like:

- How do I loop over all `.txt` files in Bash and print their names?
- What does `set -e` do in a Bash script, and when should I avoid it?

Help with errors

When a script fails at the command prompt, pasting the error message and a small, relevant snippet of the script often leads to useful explanations:

- This Bash script exits immediately with `permission denied`. Why?
- Here is my script and the error output. What is wrong with it?

This works particularly well because Bash errors are often indirect. The line that fails is not always the line that caused the problem, and AI tools are good at spotting those patterns.

If you're trying out your scripts in a code editor like VS Code, then you don't even have to copy and paste into your preferred chatbot. GitHub Copilot Chat will inspect your active terminal session automatically, as the terminal context is included as part of your conversation. It shows the last command, working directory, and exit code for each open terminal.

Prompt: Please explain common Bash error messages like `permission denied` or `command not found`.

Beware that AI has limited context

That said, there are limits. AI chatbots like ChatGPT and Gemini that run in a web browser do not see your file system, environment variables, or installed software. If a suggested command deletes files or modifies system state, it will do so just as eagerly as if a human had written it. Treat AI output as advice, not authority.

VS Code with GitHub Copilot, Rider with its AI Assistant, and CLI tools like Claude Code and OpenAI Codex do have lots of tools to gather context so are much better at providing dynamic relevant help. You will work with these more in later chapters.

Before running an AI-suggested command, make sure you can say what it reads, what it writes, and what it might delete or change. If you cannot explain that much, ask the AI to break the command down first.

That makes AI most useful as a command explainer, not as a source of commands to paste blindly.

Prompt: How can I safely debug a Bash script step by step?

Practice, references, and resources

In this section, you will be tested on what you've learned in this chapter and be provided with useful links to reference materials and resources.

Check your understanding

Answer the following questions that are deliberately conceptual rather than rote, encouraging explanation over memorization:

1. What role does Bash play between you and the operating system?
2. Why is Bash described as stateful, and how does that affect everyday command usage?
3. Explain the difference between a terminal application and the Bash shell.
4. Why might a command work in one directory but fail in another?
5. What problem does a Bash script solve that typing commands manually does not?
6. What is the purpose of the shebang line at the top of a script?
7. Why must a script be marked as executable before it can be run?
8. What risks are associated with `rm -r`, and how can developers reduce them?
9. How does allowing scripts to accept arguments make them more flexible?
10. What are the benefits and limitations of using AI tools for Bash help?

Answers can be found in Appendix A: `https://github.com/markjprice/web-dev-ai/blob/main/docs/appendix_a.pdf`

Practical exercise

Write a Bash script that creates a directory, creates a file inside it, writes a line of text to the file, and prints the file contents to the terminal. Then explain each line in your own words.

Solution can be found in Appendix A: `https://github.com/markjprice/web-dev-ai/blob/main/docs/appendix_a.pdf`

References

Bash has been around for decades, and its documentation reflects that maturity. Some resources are reference-heavy, others are more tutorial-oriented. It is useful to know which to reach for depending on whether you are learning or troubleshooting.

GNU Bash Reference Manual

The authoritative source is the GNU Bash Reference Manual. This is the specification-level documentation for Bash and is maintained as part of the GNU Project. You can read it online at the following link:

`https://www.gnu.org/software/bash/manual/bash.html`

This manual is exhaustive. It explains Bash syntax, built-in commands, variables, quoting rules, redirection, job control, and scripting features in precise terms. You would not normally read it cover to cover, but it is excellent when you need to understand exactly how something behaves.

Bash man page

Closely related is the Bash `man` page, which is what you see when you type:

```
man bash
```

This is more concise and is often quicker when you just need a reminder about syntax or options. For `man` pages on specific commands, enter `man <command>`, for example:

```
man ls
man cd
man rm
```

The preceding commands will give you detailed, authoritative information about individual commands. These `man` pages are not always friendly, but they are accurate and ubiquitous.

The Bash Guide for Beginners

This guide focuses on fundamentals and common patterns, making it a good complement to the reference manual:

`https://tldp.org/LDP/Bash-Beginners-Guide/html/`

Advanced Bash-Scripting Guide

Despite the name, this is widely used as a reference for real-world scripting patterns. It is opinionated in places, but extremely thorough:

`https://tldp.org/LDP/abs/html/`

Explainshell

This tool lets you paste a shell command and see each part explained inline. It is particularly helpful when reading unfamiliar commands in documentation or CI logs: `https://explainshell.com/`

ShellCheck

ShellCheck is a static analysis tool for shell scripts. It highlights common mistakes, unsafe patterns, and portability issues. Even experienced shell users rely on it:
`https://www.shellcheck.net/`

Summary

In this chapter, you learned how Bash fits into a developer's daily routine. Specifically:

- What Bash is, and how it functions as a Unix shell and command language
- How to navigate the file system from the command line using core commands such as `cd`, `ls`, and `pwd`
- How to create, copy, move, and delete files and directories safely from the terminal
- How to inspect file contents and produce output using commands like `cat` and `echo`
- How to write a simple Bash script to automate a sequence of commands
- How to use variables and command-line arguments inside Bash scripts
- How to use AI tools to understand shell commands and debug scripts rather than blindly copying them

The main lesson is that Bash gives you a way to control your development environment. The commands matter, but what matters more is knowing what they will do before you run them.

In the next chapter, you will use these command-line skills to set up a complete web development project and the environment needed to work on it.

Get this book's PDF version and more

Scan the QR code (or go to packtpub.com/unlock). Search for this book by name, confirm the edition, and then follow the steps on the page.

UNLOCK NOW

Note: Keep your invoice handy. Purchases made directly from Packt don't require an invoice.

Part 3

Survey Project

In this third part of the book, you'll bring everything together in a single, complete project. You build a survey application that includes a frontend interface, backend logic, and a working database. The goal is to move beyond isolated examples and see how a real system behaves when all the pieces are connected.

AI is used throughout the build, helping generate code, suggest approaches, and speed up repetitive tasks. At the same time, you are expected to read, question, and refine what it produces. By the end of this part, you will have a working application and more practice deciding when AI output is useful, wrong, or needs changing.

This part of the book includes the following chapters:

- *Chapter 11, Setting Up Your Project Environment*
- *Chapter 12, Unit, Integration, and End-to-End Testing*
- *Chapter 13, Specifying and Building the Initial Project*
- *Chapter 14, Adding Project Features Using Spec-Driven Development*
- *Chapter 15, Deploying to Public Servers*

11

Setting Up Your Project Environment

The last part of this book shifts from learning individual technologies for frontend and backend web development to applying them in one realistic project. Rather than isolated examples, you will design and build a complete web application named **TallyApp**, a small survey and polling application.

This project is deliberately scoped to be small enough to understand end to end, but rich enough to feel like something you could plausibly extend or deploy. In this chapter, we kick off the TallyApp project by installing and configuring your development tools.

As a noun, a *tally* is a running count or record of items, events, or votes. It often refers to the total reached by incrementing the count step by step. For example, *the final tally of votes* means the completed count. As a verb, to *tally* means to count or to add items to a running total. It can also mean to agree or correspond. For example, *the numbers do not tally* means they do not match.

By the end of this chapter, you will have configured your development environment with GitHub Copilot, set up a consistent and repeatable environment using Docker, and learned how to place code under version control using Git so you are ready to start building features with confidence.

This chapter is about knowing which tool solves which problem. Copilot helps while you write and review code. Docker gives everyone the same runtime. Git records the history of the project so you can try changes without fear. You will use all three before adding TallyApp features.

In this chapter, we will cover the following topics:

- Introducing TallyApp
- Configuring GitHub Copilot as your coding assistant
- Docker for consistent server setup
- Source code version control using Git

Suggested chatbot prompts with example responses for this chapter can be found at the following link: `https://github.com/markjprice/web-dev-ai/blob/main/prompts/ch11-env/readme.md`

Introducing TallyApp

TallyApp is a survey and polling application with three clear areas of functionality.

1. First, it allows an authenticated user to design and publish surveys. This includes defining different types of questions, such as multiple choice and free-text responses, and generating a public link that can be shared with respondents.
2. Second, it provides a clean, focused experience for people taking a survey, where they can follow a link, answer questions, and submit their responses without needing an account.
3. Third, it gives the survey creator tools to analyze results, using charts and structured data views to explore trends and individual answers.

Across the upcoming chapters, you will incrementally set up your development environment with an AI coding assistant, and then specify, build, and refine TallyApp. Just as importantly, these chapters model how real web projects are developed. You will make design decisions, revisit earlier choices, and see how backend logic, frontend presentation, and data analysis fit together.

By the end of the TallyApp project, you will not just have learned individual features of web frameworks and languages. You will have built and understood a complete, working web application, and you will be in a much better position to design one of your own.

A warning about leaning on AI

A warning comes from Anthropic in their article, *How AI assistance impacts the formation of coding skills*: `https://www.anthropic.com/research/AI-assistance-coding-skills`.

Anthropic researchers conducted a randomized controlled trial involving 52 software developers.

All participants had regular experience with Python but were unfamiliar with a specific async library called Trio. They were randomly assigned to two groups:

- **AI-assisted group**: Participants could use an AI coding assistant during the task.
- **Control group**: Participants did not have AI assistance but could use documentation and web search.

Each participant completed two feature-building tasks using Trio. After finishing, they all took a quiz designed to measure mastery of the concepts they had just worked with. The quiz covered debugging, code reading, code writing, and conceptual understanding.

Here is what the study found:

- On average, developers who used AI scored significantly lower on the post-task quiz (about 50 percent) compared to those who coded without AI (about 67 percent). This represented a 17 percent gap, roughly equivalent to two letter grades in a typical academic setting.
- The biggest differences were observed on debugging and conceptual understanding questions, indicating that AI use was associated with weaker mastery of those skills.
- The AI-assisted group finished the coding tasks only slightly faster, but this time difference was not statistically significant.
- Qualitative analysis showed that some participants spent substantial time composing AI prompts (up to 30 percent of total time in some cases), which ate into potential efficiency gains.

The researchers concluded that:

- AI assistance can undermine learning when people are acquiring a new, unfamiliar skill. Relying on the assistant to generate and debug code appears to reduce the cognitive effort that builds deep understanding.
- Not all AI use is the same. Some participants who used AI mainly to ask conceptual questions or request explanations alongside generated code performed much closer to the control group. Those who offloaded thinking and delegated work to the AI tended to score lowest.
- The study suggests that AI does not automatically speed learning, especially on unfamiliar tasks, and may even impede skill formation if developers use it as a shortcut rather than as a learning tool.

The study's warning is simple: AI can help you finish a task without helping you learn the material. The way you use the assistant matters. Asking for explanations is different from letting it do the work.

Good practice: Always ask the AI to explain the code it writes while you are learning a new topic. Ask conceptual questions or request explanations alongside generated code. Avoid delegating work to the AI; stay in control.

Prompt: Please explain the risks of over-relying on AI during early learning. Design a learning plan that balances AI use with deep skill formation.

Before we dive into building a project, there are some tools that we need to configure and learn about, including GitHub Copilot and the models it will use, Docker and its containers, and Git for version control.

Configuring GitHub Copilot as your coding assistant

First, let's explain why this book uses VS Code and its GitHub Copilot extension.

Your choice of AI coding tool

A summary of the most popular companies' AI chatbots and coding tools is shown in *Table 11.1*:

Company	**Product**	**Use case**
Microsoft	GitHub Copilot	Popular AI coding tool embedded in IDEs like VS Code, JetBrains, and so on; suggests code completions and refactorings; agent mode; GitHub Copilot CLI; highly adopted by engineering teams
OpenAI	ChatGPT	Conversational AI, productivity, research assistance, ideation, coding help
OpenAI	Codex	LLM tailored for coding; powers GitHub Copilot and other coding integrations; supports multi-language code generation and completion

Company	Product	Use case
Anthropic	Claude, Claude Code	Agentic harness and a family of models (Haiku, Sonnet, Opus, Mythos) optimized for reasoning, long-context understanding and coding; increasingly popular in enterprise and coding workflows
Google	Gemini	General-purpose AI integrated with Google products; strong at multimodal tasks (text, image, voice) and integrated search
Google	Code Assist, Gemini CLI	Coding-focused variants of Gemini tailored to assist developers within the Google ecosystem tools
Perplexity Labs	Perplexity AI	Search-grounded chatbot emphasizing factual answers with cited sources; strong at research and knowledge exploration
Anysphere	Cursor	Coding tool with deep codebase understanding; positioned as a competitor in the developer workflow with strong contextual coding aids
X	Grok	Focuses on real-time responses and trending info pulled from social feeds; often associated with memes

Table 11.1: Various companies' AI chatbots and coding tools

Chatbots like ChatGPT, Gemini, Claude, Perplexity, or Grok focus mainly on natural language interaction. They handle writing, summarizing, general research, and can also support coding queries, but coding assistance is just one of many tasks. They are best used as code and framework learning mentors.

AI coding assistants such as GitHub Copilot, Codex, or Cursor are optimized for developer workflows. They integrate with code editors and IDEs, suggest completions, generate project-specific code, and can assist with debugging and tests.

GitHub Copilot lets you choose between multiple coding AI models. For example, Copilot itself, Anthropic's Claude, and OpenAI's Codex. This means you're not locked into a single model; you can pick whichever agent best fits your task.

Ollama and similar local LLM frameworks let you run a wide variety of LLMs on local desktop or server hardware. Models like `Qwen3-Coder`, `StarCode2`, `Codestral`, `Devastral`, and so on are open source and optimized for coding tasks. You can run them locally through Ollama without ever sending data to the cloud.

If you care about data privacy, offline use, full control, and avoiding cloud APIs, then you want local LLM frameworks like Ollama with open-source coding models. **Bring Your Own Key** (**BYOK**) model support is a fast-moving feature set, and some capabilities may differ between chat, inline chat, and completions.

If you want the easiest start, use Copilot Free (cloud). You get a monthly allowance without configuring any keys.

If you want the best quality and do not mind API spend, keep Copilot models for day-to-day coding and optionally add your OpenAI API key so you can use specific provider models when needed.

If you want to avoid per-request costs and keep data local, run Ollama and select it via VS Code's model management so Copilot Chat can use a local model for many tasks.

I have written an online-only article to cover use of local models in detail: `https://github.com/markjprice/markjprice/blob/main/with-ai/local-models.md`

Local setups are better in specific areas:

- **Privacy**: No code leaves your machine. Useful for proprietary or sensitive work
- **Cost (long-term)**: No per-token billing. Heavy usage becomes cheaper over time
- **Latency**: Instant response for small models. No network dependency
- **Control**: You can fine-tune. You can customize behavior

A practical setup is to use both cloud and local models, but for different jobs:

- Use cloud models when you need stronger reasoning, larger context, or help comparing design options
- Use local models when the task is small, private, or repetitive: explaining syntax, drafting a helper function, refactoring one file, or sketching tests

Good practice: If the task requires judgment, not just generation, use a cloud model.

Configuring GitHub Copilot

At the end of this section, you will have GitHub Copilot running in VS Code for inline completions and chat. You will also have a second path configured so Copilot Chat can use either:

- The built-in Copilot models (including the free plan if you qualify)
- Your own model provider, including a local Ollama model, to avoid per-request API costs

VS Code's **BYOK** model support is part of how Copilot Chat can be powered by third-party providers (including Ollama for local models).

Prerequisites are:

- VS Code installed
- A GitHub account you can sign into from VS Code. You can sign up at the following link: `https://docs.github.com/en/get-started/start-your-journey/creating-an-account-on-github`
- Pick one of the following options:
    - GitHub Copilot Free plan (no API key required)
    - An OpenAI API key or another supported provider key for BYOK
    - A local model runtime like Ollama for local inference

Warning! GitHub Copilot inline suggestions (the autocomplete you accept with *Tab*) are not the same thing as **Copilot Chat**. VS Code's BYOK model system is primarily about powering chat and editing experiences with different model providers. Some BYOK capabilities may not apply to completions in the same way. Treat local-model support as a chat-first (and edit-first) path, not a guaranteed replacement for every Copilot feature.

Install and sign in to Copilot in VS Code:

1. Open VS Code and trigger Copilot setup by clicking the Copilot icon in the status bar.
2. Sign in with GitHub. Follow the sign-in prompts. If your GitHub account already has Copilot access, VS Code uses it. If you do not have a subscription, VS Code can enroll you into the Copilot Free plan (with monthly usage limits).
3. Verify Copilot is active. Open any code file, type a few characters, and pause. If Copilot is active, you should see gray *ghost text* suggestions you can accept (usually *Tab*).

4. Open the **Copilot Chat** view and confirm it responds. In VS Code, Copilot Chat uses a model picker in the chat input area as shown in *Figure 11.1*:

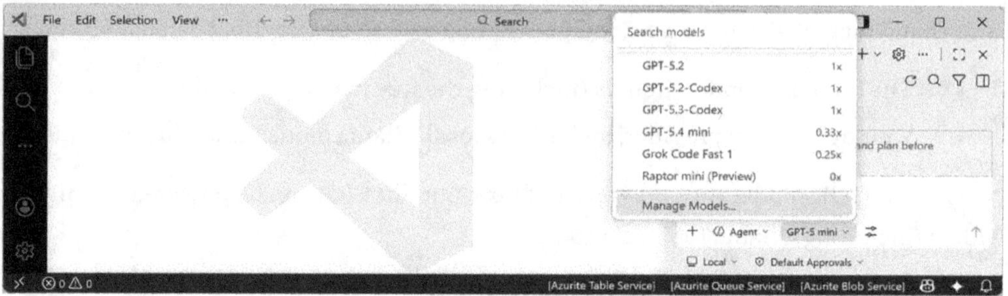

Figure 11.1: Selecting a model in GitHub Copilot Chat

5. Confirm your plan and limits (especially on Free). If you're using Copilot Free, expect monthly caps such as a limit on inline suggestions and a smaller number of premium requests (used by newer or more expensive models). For current limits, see Copilot plans at the following link: `https://github.com/features/copilot/plans`

Prompt: Please explain how token limits and context windows affect AI coding assistants when working with a large Django codebase.

GitHub Copilot tips

Here are some tips to improve your experience with GitHub Copilot:

- **Use the model picker intentionally in Chat.** Copilot supports multiple models, and the model you pick affects latency, accuracy, and cost multipliers (premium requests). For quick Q&A or lightweight edits, a faster model is often enough. For complex refactors or reasoning-heavy debugging, switch to a stronger model when you need it.
- **Know what burns premium requests.** On plans that include premium requests, the newest frontier models often cost more per request (Copilot documents this as multipliers). If you're on Free, be conservative: do exploration with cheaper models, then spend premium calls on the final *do it right* pass.
- **Ask for structured outputs to reduce token churn.** Copilot Chat gets better (and cheaper) when you constrain it. Examples:

    - "List three approaches and recommend one."
    - "Give a patch-style diff for these two files."
    - "Only change the methods touched by this failing test."

- **Watch your privacy knobs in VS Code.** If you're writing proprietary code, review Copilot settings in VS Code and tighten anything you are not comfortable with.

Ensure you have an OpenAI API key available

This section is for readers who want to use their own provider key from OpenAI or another supported provider to power chat and coding experiences in VS Code:

1. Create and store your OpenAI API key. Create an API key in your OpenAI account and store it in a password manager. Do not hardcode it into source control.
2. Open VS Code's language model management UI by running the command to manage models. For example, in the Command Palette, select the menu item **Chat: Manage Language Models**.
3. Add your provider key like OpenAI. Choose **Bring your own language model key**. Select **OpenAI** or another provider and then paste the key.

Warning! VS Code's BYOK is not available for Copilot Business or Copilot Enterprise accounts (it is for individual plans like Free/Pro/Pro+).

4. Select the provider-backed model in Copilot Chat. In Copilot Chat, use the model picker to choose the model you just added.
5. Do a quick smoke test:

```
Summarize this file and suggest two refactoring steps.
```

Now that you've configured VS Code and GitHub Copilot to be your coding assistant, let's see how Docker is useful for making a consistent development setup.

Docker for consistent server setup

Docker is a way to package an application and everything it needs including runtime, OS libraries, dependencies, and configuration defaults into a repeatable unit called an **image**. You then run that image as a **container**.

The practical benefit for TallyApp is consistency: developers on Windows, macOS, and Linux can run the same Django stack with the same versions and the same behavior, without spending hours fighting local setup differences.

Important concepts

Here are the important concepts that you need to know about Docker:

- **Images:** A built, immutable template. You typically build one for your Django app. Prebuilt images are used for common services like database engines and management software.
- **Containers:** A running instance of an image. Containers can be started, stopped, and replaced easily.
- **Dockerfile:** A text file describing how to build an image. It contains layer-by-layer instructions to choose the base image, install dependencies, copy code, and how to start the process.
- **Docker Compose:** A way to define and run a multi-container application with a single command. For example, the web container might be your Django project, a `db` container might host the PostgreSQL database engine, and so on.
- **Volumes:** Persistent storage managed by Docker. This matters most for databases. If you do not use a volume for PostgreSQL, your data disappears when the database container is replaced.
- **Networks:** Compose automatically creates a private network so containers can talk to each other by service name. For example, the Django container can reach the database at hostname `db`.
- **Ports:** The doorways you expose to your host machine. You might map container port 8000 to host port 8000 so you can open the site in your browser.

Prompt: What is the difference between Docker volumes and bind mounts? Please explain why bind mounts are ideal for development but risky in production.

Downloading and installing Docker

Even if you deploy TallyApp with SQLite first, it is still useful to learn Docker using PostgreSQL because it demonstrates a realistic multi-service setup. It also provides a clean upgrade path for you when you want fewer SQLite concurrency limits later.

Prompt: Please explain the concurrency limitations of SQLite in Django applications. What isolation levels does PostgreSQL use and how do they compare to SQLite? When should a Django project move from SQLite to PostgreSQL?

To use Docker, you will need the following:

- **Docker Desktop** on Windows or Mac or **Docker Engine** on Linux
- A Django project with a `manage.py`

Install Docker for your operating system from the following link: `https://www.docker.com/products/docker-desktop/`.

Setting up a basic TallyApp project

Now we can build the simplest Django project before containerizing it:

1. Create a folder named `Chapter11`. Inside that folder, run the virtual environment command that will create a `.venv` folder containing a private Python installation for this project:
    - On Windows, run: `python -m venv .venv`
    - On macOS and Linux, run: `python3 -m venv .venv`
2. Activate the virtual environment:
    - On Windows, run: `.venv\Scripts\activate`
    - On macOS and Linux, run: `source .venv/bin/activate`
3. When activation succeeds, your terminal prompt will usually change to show the virtual environment name:

```
(.venv) C:\web-dev-ai\Chapter11>
```

4. With the virtual environment active, install Django using pip:

```
pip install django
```

5. Verify the installation:

```
django-admin --version
```

6. You should see the Django version number like `6.0.2`. If so, Django is ready to use.
7. At the command prompt or terminal, create a Django project and name it `tallyapp`:

```
django-admin startproject tallyapp
```

8. Change to the `tallyapp` project directory:

```
cd tallyapp
```

9. Apply migrations to the local SQLite database:

```
python manage.py migrate
```

10. Create an administrator account and then follow the prompts to set a username, email address, and password:

```
python manage.py createsuperuser
```

11. Run the Django development server:

```
python manage.py runserver
```

12. Start your preferred browser and navigate to `http://127.0.0.1:8000/`.

You can *Ctrl* + *Click* the link in the output rather than typing the URL manually. If you see the Django welcome page, your setup is correct.

To view the admin site, navigate to `http://127.0.0.1:8000/admin/`.

Setting up Docker to host the project

Now we can create files to configure this project to be hosted in a Docker container and talk to PostgreSQL in another container to use as its database.

You will create three files:

- `Dockerfile` defines how to build one container for the Django project web app and is about creation
- `.dockerignore` defines what files and folders to exclude from the image
- `docker-compose.yml` defines how to run multiple containers together and is about co-ordination between containers

Creating a Dockerfile

We will start by defining a `Dockerfile` that tells Docker how to build an image for a container. You can think of the `Dockerfile` as a recipe. It answers the following questions:

- What base system do we start from?
- What dependencies do we install?
- What code do we copy in?
- What command runs when the container starts?

For the TallyApp project, the `Dockerfile` will:

- Start from `python:3.12-slim` because it is a stable, lightweight official Python base image that works well for a Django 6 project, but it is not the newest Python image available
- Install dependencies from `requirements.txt`
- Copy your TallyApp Django project into `/app`
- Run `python manage.py runserver`

The `Dockerfile` produces a reusable image like `tallyapp-web-image`. That image will be a self-contained unit, and you can run it anywhere.

In the `Chapter11\tallyapp` folder, create a file named `Dockerfile` with the following content:

```
# Use an official Python image as the base
FROM python:3.12-slim

# Prevents Python from writing .pyc files and
# buffers to stdout/stderr
ENV PYTHONDONTWRITEBYTECODE=1
ENV PYTHONUNBUFFERED=1

# Set a working directory inside the container
WORKDIR /app

# System deps (optional but common): build tools
# for some Python packages
RUN apt-get update \
    && apt-get install -y --no-install-recommends build-essential \
    && rm -rf /var/lib/apt/lists/*

# Install Python dependencies first
# (for better layer caching)
COPY requirements.txt /app/
RUN pip install --no-cache-dir -r requirements.txt
```

```
# Copy the rest of the project
COPY . /app/

# Default command for the container (development-friendly)
CMD ["python", "manage.py", "runserver", "0.0.0.0:8000"]
```

Note the following about the preceding code:

- We start the image with `python:3.12-slim` to get a stable, widely supported Python runtime with a minimal base system, avoiding the unpredictability of `latest` while keeping images small and reproducible.

Prompt: Is `python:3.12-slim` the latest and best Python image for a Docker container?

- It installs dependencies from `requirements.txt`.
- It copies your code into the image.

Prompt: Why is `COPY requirements.txt` done before `COPY .`.?

- It runs Django's development server bound to `0.0.0.0` so it is reachable from outside the container.

Warning! For a production container you must replace `runserver` with `Gunicorn`, but for now, this is a clear first step. You will learn about `Gunicorn` in *Chapter 13, Specifying and Building the Initial Project.*

Creating a Docker Ignore file

When you build a Docker image, Docker sends the entire project folder (called the build context) to the Docker daemon. By default, that means everything in your project directory is included, even files you do not want in your image. This is where a `.dockerignore` file helps.

Just like `.gitignore` tells Git which files to skip (you will see this in the next section), `.dockerignore` tells Docker which files to exclude from the image build process. This keeps your images smaller, faster to build, and avoids accidentally including sensitive or unnecessary files.

Create a file named `.dockerignore` in the same folder as your Dockerfile, and add the following:

```
# .dockerignore
.venv/
__pycache__/
*.pyc
.git/
.gitignore
db.sqlite3
.env
*.sqlite3
docker-compose.yml
Dockerfile
.DS_Store
```

The benefits include:

- **Smaller images**: Virtual environments, cache files, and local databases can be large. Excluding them reduces image size significantly.
- **Faster builds**: Docker uploads the build context before building. Fewer files means faster builds, especially as your project grows.
- **Stronger security**: Files like `.env` may contain secrets such as API keys or database passwords. If included in an image layer, they can be very difficult to remove later.
- **Cleaner environments**: Your container should contain only what it needs to run. Development artifacts like `.venv` or `.git` are irrelevant inside the container.

Even though the `Dockerfile` uses `COPY . /app/`, the `.dockerignore` file ensures that excluded files are never copied in the first place. This keeps your image clean without needing complex `COPY` rules.

Good practice: Keep your `.dockerignore` file aligned with your `.gitignore` file, but do not assume they should be identical. Docker cares about build context and image contents, while Git cares about version control. Some files, like `Dockerfile` or `docker-compose.yml`, are tracked by Git but usually do not belong inside the final image.

Creating a Docker Compose file

Next, we will define a `docker-compose.yml` file. While a `Dockerfile` defines how to build a single image, and a `.dockerignore` file excludes files and folders from an image, a `docker-compose.yml` file defines how to run multiple containers together.

You could run your Django container manually with docker run, but it would get messy fast. You would need to start PostgreSQL separately, link containers manually, pass environment variables by hand, and manage ports and volumes yourself. Docker Compose replaces all of that with one command and a single config file.

The `docker-compose.yml` file is **orchestration**. It answers:

- What containers do we need?
- How do they connect?
- What environment variables do they use?
- What ports are exposed?
- What volumes persist data?

For our TallyApp project, Docker Compose will define two services:

- `web` is the Django app container (built from the `Dockerfile`)
- `db` is a PostgreSQL container

It will also:

- Connect the two containers via a network
- Map ports (`8000`, `5432`)
- Set environment variables for the Django project
- Create a volume for database persistence

Running a single command, `docker compose up`, will start the entire system, not just one container.

In the `Chapter11\tallyapp` folder, create a `docker-compose.yml` file for Django and PostgreSQL:

```
services:
  db:
    image: postgres:16
    environment:
      POSTGRES_DB: tallyapp
      POSTGRES_USER: tallyapp
```

```
      POSTGRES_PASSWORD: tallyapp_password_change_me
    volumes:
      - tallyapp_postgres_data:/var/lib/postgresql/data
    ports:
      - "5432:5432"
    healthcheck:
      test: ["CMD-SHELL", "pg_isready -U tallyapp -d tallyapp"]
      interval: 5s
      timeout: 5s
      retries: 5

  web:
    build:
      context: .
    depends_on:
      db:
        condition: service_healthy
    environment:
      # Django will read these to build DATABASES config (you wire this up
in settings.py)
      DJANGO_DB_NAME: tallyapp
      DJANGO_DB_USER: tallyapp
      DJANGO_DB_PASSWORD: tallyapp_password_change_me
      DJANGO_DB_HOST: db
      DJANGO_DB_PORT: "5432"
      DJANGO_SECRET_KEY: dev-only-change-me
      DJANGO_DEBUG: "1"
    ports:
      - "8000:8000"
    volumes:
      - .:/app

volumes:
  tallyapp_postgres_data:
```

Note the following about the preceding code:

- `db` uses the official PostgreSQL image and initializes a database using environment variables documented for that image.
- `db` has a `healthcheck`, and `web` depends on `db` being `service_healthy`, not merely started.
- The `tallyapp_postgres_data` volume is what keeps database data persistent across container restarts.
- The `web` service builds from your `Dockerfile`
- The `volumes: - .:/app` bind-mount means code changes on the host instantly appear inside the container, which is ideal for a Docker-based dev environment.
- `depends_on` starts the database container before the web container, but by itself it does not guarantee that PostgreSQL is ready to accept connections. To make startup more reliable, we defined a PostgreSQL `healthcheck` and set `depends_on` to wait for condition: `service_healthy`. Then Docker Compose waits until the database reports that it is ready before starting Django.

Switching from SQLite to PostgreSQL

Now we can configure project files like the Python dependencies and Django project settings so that the project uses PostgreSQL instead of SQLite:

1. In the `Chapter11\tallyapp` folder, create a `requirements.txt` file to configure Django 6 to use PostgreSQL in Docker:

   ```
   Django>=6.0,<7.0
   psycopg[binary]>=3.1
   ```

2. In `settings.py`, you can switch database config based on environment variables. A simple pattern is:

   - If `DJANGO_DB_HOST` is set, use PostgreSQL
   - Otherwise, fall back to SQLite for local non-Docker runs

   ```
   import os

   DJANGO_DB_HOST = os.environ.get("DJANGO_DB_HOST")

   if DJANGO_DB_HOST:
       # PostgreSQL configuration
   ```

```
    DATABASES = {
        "default": {
            "ENGINE": "django.db.backends.postgresql",
            "NAME": os.environ.get("DJANGO_DB_NAME", "tallyapp"),
            "USER": os.environ.get("DJANGO_DB_USER", "tallyapp"),
            "PASSWORD": os.environ.get("DJANGO_DB_PASSWORD", ""),
            "HOST": DJANGO_DB_HOST,
            "PORT": os.environ.get("DJANGO_DB_PORT", "5432"),
            "CONN_MAX_AGE": 60,  # persistent connections (good for
production)
        }
    }
else:
    # SQLite fallback (default for local development)
    DATABASES = {
        "default": {
            "ENGINE": "django.db.backends.sqlite3",
            "NAME": BASE_DIR / "db.sqlite3",
            "OPTIONS": {
                "timeout": 20,  # helps reduce "database is locked"
errors
            },
        }
    }
```

Build and run the Docker system

Now we can build the Docker image and start the containers using Docker Compose:

1. Build images:

```
docker compose build
```

2. Start containers:

```
docker compose up
```

3. At this point PostgreSQL is running in one container, and Django is running in another container, exposed on `http://localhost:8000`, as shown in *Figure 11.2*:

```
Developer Command Prompt for VS 2022 - docker compose up
db-1  | 2026-02-22 14:11:12.265 UTC [1] LOG:  starting PostgreSQL 16.12 (Debian 16.12-1.pgdg13+1) on x86_64-pc
-linux-gnu, compiled by gcc (Debian 14.2.0-19) 14.2.0, 64-bit
db-1  | 2026-02-22 14:11:12.265 UTC [1] LOG:  listening on IPv4 address "0.0.0.0", port 5432
db-1  | 2026-02-22 14:11:12.265 UTC [1] LOG:  listening on IPv6 address "::", port 5432
db-1  | 2026-02-22 14:11:12.276 UTC [1] LOG:  listening on Unix socket "/var/run/postgresql/.s.PGSQL.5432"
db-1  | 2026-02-22 14:11:12.284 UTC [64] LOG:  database system was shut down at 2026-02-22 14:11:12 UTC
db-1  | 2026-02-22 14:11:12.292 UTC [1] LOG:  database system is ready to accept connections
web-1 | Watching for file changes with StatReloader
web-1 | Performing system checks...
web-1 |
web-1 | System check identified no issues (0 silenced).
web-1 |
web-1 | You have 18 unapplied migration(s). Your project may not work properly until you apply the migrations
 for app(s): admin, auth, contenttypes, sessions.
web-1 | Run 'python manage.py migrate' to apply them.
web-1 | February 22, 2026 - 14:11:13
web-1 | Django version 6.0.2, using settings 'tallyapp.settings'
web-1 | Starting development server at http://0.0.0.0:8000/
web-1 | Quit the server with CONTROL-C.
web-1 |
web-1 | WARNING: This is a development server. Do not use it in a production setting. Use a production WSGI o
r ASGI server instead.
web-1 | For more information on production servers see: https://docs.djangoproject.com/en/6.0/howto/deploymen
```

Figure 11.2: Two containers running in Docker Compose

Prompt: What actually happens under the hood when I run `docker compose up`?

4. In **Docker Desktop**, expand the **tallyapp** entry to see its two containers for the PostgreSQL database and the **tallyapp-web** Django host, as shown in *Figure 11.3*:

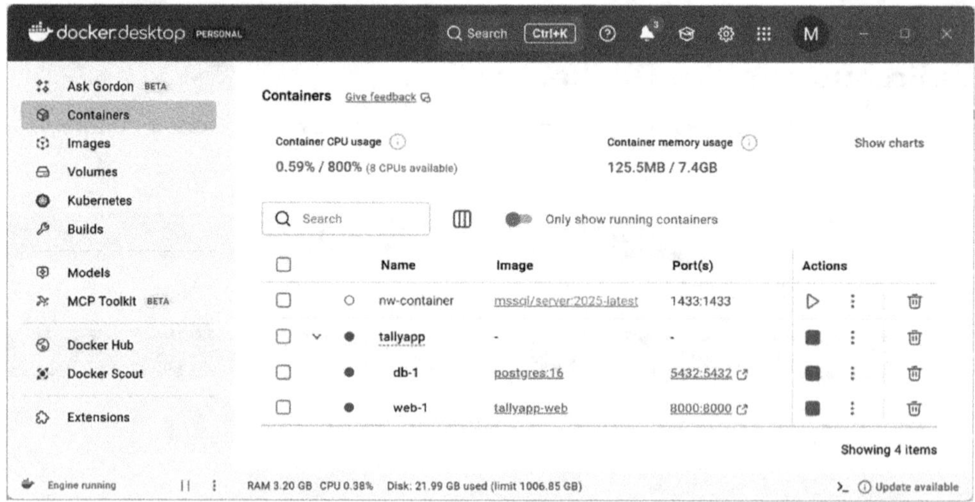

Figure 11.3: Two containers running in Docker Desktop

5. In a new terminal window, run migrations and create an admin user inside the `web` container:

```
docker compose exec web python manage.py migrate
docker compose exec web python manage.py createsuperuser
```

Docker changes where you run commands and where you look for errors. You usually do not SSH into a server. You run commands inside the container that already has your app and dependencies. You also read the container logs, because that is where the app is running.

6. Start your preferred browser and navigate to the admin site: `http://localhost:8000/admin/`
7. Log in with the administrator account that you previously created and view the list of users, as shown in *Figure 11.4*:

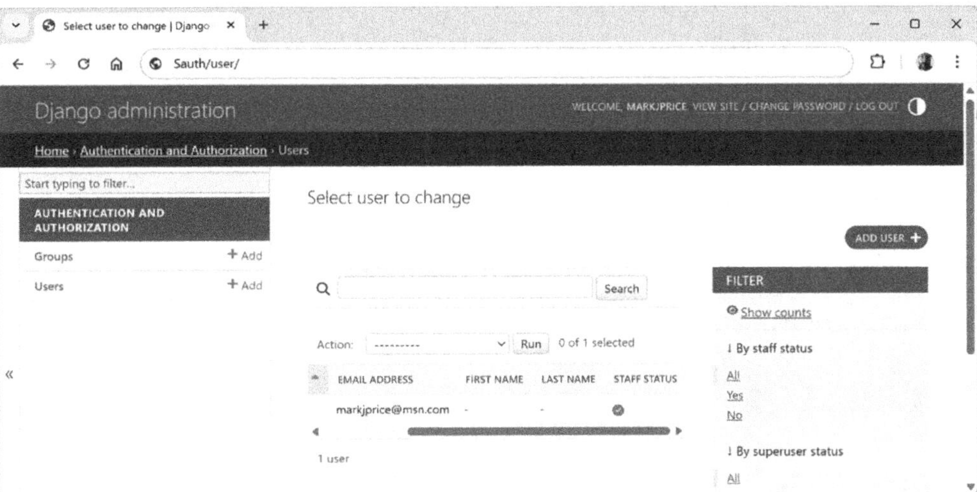

Figure 11.4: Administrator accounts

8. Close the browser.
9. At the command prompt or terminal, stop the containers:

```
docker compose down
```

To stop containers and remove volumes (this wipes the database) use the `-v` switch: `docker compose down -v`. This reinforces why volumes matter. Without a volume, a database container is disposable, and so is its data.

Reducing image size with multi-stage builds

The `Dockerfile` shown earlier is simple and easy to understand, but it includes tools that are only needed during installation, such as compilers. These tools increase the size of the final image and are not required when the application is running.

The current Docker image includes compilers (`gcc`, `make`), package manager cache, and build dependencies. Those are not needed at runtime and increase both the image size and potential attack surface.

A more advanced technique called a **multi-stage build** separates the build environment from the runtime environment. The first stage installs dependencies, and the second stage copies only the results into a clean image.

A multi-stage build separates:

1. **Build stage**: Install dependencies, compile anything needed
2. **Runtime stage**: Copy only what is needed to run the app

This avoids shipping unnecessary tools like compilers into your final image.

Here is a rewritten version of your `Dockerfile` using a multi-stage build:

```
# ---- Stage 1: Build dependencies ----
FROM python:3.12-slim AS builder

WORKDIR /app

RUN apt-get update \
 && apt-get install -y --no-install-recommends build-essential \
 && rm -rf /var/lib/apt/lists/*

COPY requirements.txt .

RUN pip install --upgrade pip \
 && pip install --prefix=/install --no-cache-dir -r requirements.txt
```

```
# ---- Stage 2: Runtime image ----
FROM python:3.12-slim

WORKDIR /app

ENV PYTHONDONTWRITEBYTECODE=1
ENV PYTHONUNBUFFERED=1

# Copy installed packages from builder
COPY --from=builder /install /usr/local

# Copy project code
COPY . /app/

CMD ["python", "manage.py", "runserver", "0.0.0.0:8000"]
```

This produces smaller images, faster downloads, and a reduced attack surface. The final image only contains a Python runtime, your dependencies, and your app. Multi-stage builds are common in production setups, but optional for learning projects.

Viewing logs to debug container issues

When something goes wrong in a Docker-based setup, the first place to look is the container logs.

If you ran your containers with:

```
docker compose up
```

You will already see logs in that terminal window.

However, if you run containers in the background or open a new terminal, you can view logs using:

```
docker compose logs
```

This shows the combined output of all services, including your Django app and PostgreSQL database. For example, you might see Django startup messages, database connection errors, migration warnings, and Python exceptions.

You can focus on just one container:

```
docker compose logs web
```

Or:

```
docker compose logs db
```

This is useful when you want to separate Django errors from database output.

To watch logs as they happen:

```
docker compose logs -f
```

This is like running `docker compose up`, but works even if the containers are already running in the background.

Viewing logs is important because Docker changes how you debug problems. You are no longer running everything directly on your machine. Your app runs inside containers, so errors show up there, not in your editor or terminal history.

If the app fails to start, or cannot connect to the database, the logs will usually tell you why.

For example:

- "could not connect to server" tells you that PostgreSQL is not ready
- "no such table" tells you that database migrations were not applied
- Python traceback tells you that there is a bug in your code

Common mistakes and quick fixes

If Django starts before PostgreSQL is accepting connections, you might see connection errors on first startup. The simplest fix for a learning project is to rerun `docker compose up` or retry migrations. In more advanced setups you add a *wait for DB* script.

Prompt: Please show me a wait-for-database script for Django containers.

Docker reduces *works on my machine* problems by giving everyone the same Dockerfile and Compose services. That is why teams use it.

During learning, keep credentials clearly marked as development-only when using secrets in compose files. In real deployments, you would use environment injection, secret managers, or Docker secrets rather than committing passwords.

Prompt: Please explain the difference between environment variables, .env files, and Docker secrets. What are best practices for managing secrets in Docker Compose?

Where this fits in TallyApp's overall deployment story

This Docker setup is primarily a development environment, but it teaches patterns that carry into production: immutable builds, multi-service composition, and persistent data via volumes.

It also sets up an easy database upgrade path: you can develop locally with PostgreSQL in containers, then later deploy with PostgreSQL on a VPS or managed PostgreSQL without changing your application logic, only its configuration.

While Docker focuses on packaging applications into consistent, portable environments, it does not address how code itself is tracked, shared, and evolved over time. That is where Git comes in. If Docker ensures that software runs the same way everywhere, Git ensures that teams (including human and AI programmers) can collaborate on that software without losing track of changes or overwriting each other's work. Together, Docker and Git form a natural pairing in web development workflows, but before combining them, it is important to understand how Git manages version control so each change can be saved, reviewed, and, if necessary, undone.

Source code version control using Git

Before you add features to TallyApp, you need protection against your own mistakes. Git gives you a complete history of your project, lets you experiment safely, and makes collaboration and deployment straightforward.

This section teaches a focused, practical subset of Git using VS Code's built-in Git integration. You will learn how to initialize a repository, make meaningful commits, create branches, connect to a remote, and recover from common mistakes.

What Git does

Git is a distributed version control system. It records snapshots of your project over time.

A few terms matter, as summarized in *Table 11.2*:

Term	Definition
Repository	A folder that Git tracks. It contains a hidden `.git` directory that stores the project history.
Commit	A saved snapshot of your project at a specific moment, along with a message explaining the change.
Working branch	The files you are currently editing.
Staging area	The set of changes you intend to include in the next commit.
Branch	A parallel line of development. You can experiment on a branch without affecting `main`.
Remote	A hosted copy of your repository, typically on GitHub, GitLab, or Bitbucket.

Table 11.2: Common Git terms

Git runs locally on your machine. Services such as GitHub host a remote copy so you can back up and share your work.

Prompt: Please explain Git's staging area in detail using a step-by-step explanation.

Initializing Git for TallyApp in VS Code

After creating your TallyApp Django project, initialize Git immediately:

1. Open the `TallyApp` folder in VS Code.
2. Click the **Source Control** icon in the left sidebar.
3. Click **Initialize Repository**, as shown in *Figure 11.5*:

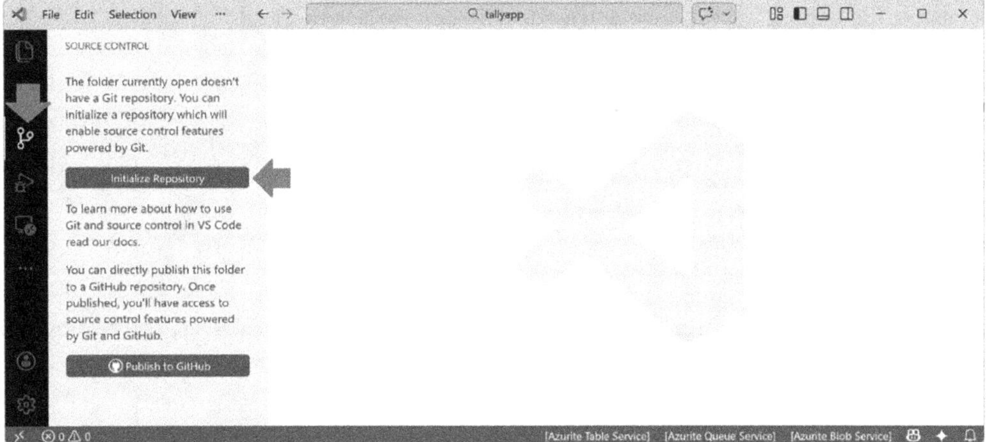

Figure 11.5: VS Code Source Control view

4. You now have a local Git repository, as shown in *Figure 11.6*:

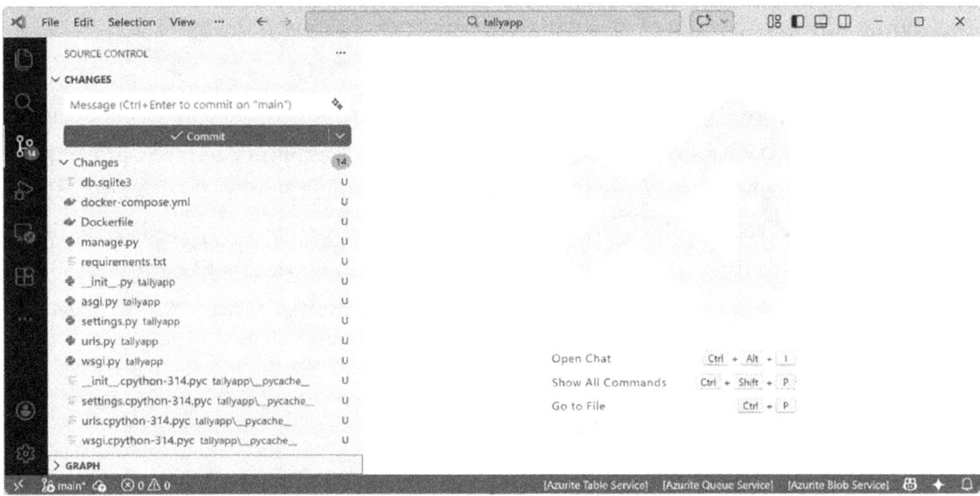

Figure 11.6: VS Code Source Control view

Creating a .gitignore for Django

A Django project generates files that should not be committed. You want to track source code, not machine-specific artifacts or secrets.

Create a file named `.gitignore` at the root of your project and add:

```
.venv/
__pycache__/
*.py[cod]
*.sqlite3
.env
.DS_Store
```

This ignores virtual environments, Python bytecode, SQLite databases, environment variable files, and operating system clutter.

Good practice: If you use SQLite for development, ignoring `db.sqlite3` is recommended. Your database state should be reproducible from migrations, not committed as a binary file.

You should now see that fewer files will be committed, as shown in *Figure 11.7*.

Warning! Do not ignore `*.md` files. Markdown files are often used for documentation, README files, architecture notes, and even AI prompts. In many projects, they are part of the source of truth, not generated output. Ignoring them would mean losing important context and documentation from your repository. A good rule of thumb is this: only ignore files that can be recreated automatically (like virtual environments, caches, or compiled files). If a file contains human-written knowledge, it should almost always be committed.

Making Your First Commit

Once Git is initialized:

1. Navigate to **Source Control** where you will see a list of untracked files.
2. Click the + icon next to **Changes** to stage everything, as shown in *Figure 11.7*:

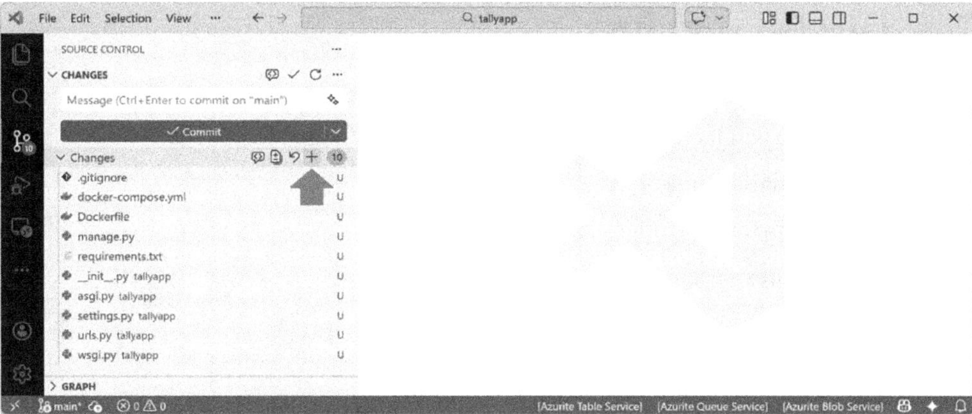

Figure 11.7: Stage All Files

3. Enter a commit message like: `Initial TallyApp project scaffolding`, and then click **Commit**, as shown in Figure *11.8*:

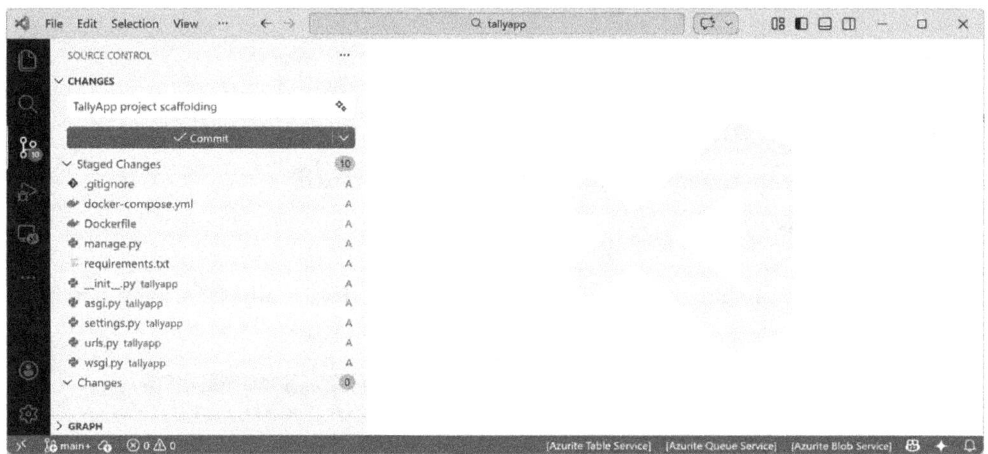

Figure 11.8: Source Control panel showing 0 Changes, 10 Staged Changes, and the commit message box

Good practice: A commit should describe intent, not mechanics. Good messages explain what changed and why. Examples for TallyApp: Add Survey model and admin registration, Create survey CRUD views and templates, Add login protection to survey pages, Improve styling of survey list.

The daily Git workflow

As you build TallyApp, follow this loop:

1. Make sure you have no changed files.
2. Make a small change.
3. Run the app and verify it works.
4. Stage all files.
5. Write a clear commit message.
6. Commit.

This discipline makes your history readable and makes debugging easier later.

In Source Control:

- Files under **Changes** are modified but not staged
- Files under **Staged Changes** will be included in the next commit

You can stage individual files using the + icon.

Creating a branch for a feature

Branches let you experiment without risking the `main` branch.

To create a branch:

1. Click the branch name in the bottom-left of VS Code, usually `main`, as shown in *Figure 11.9*:

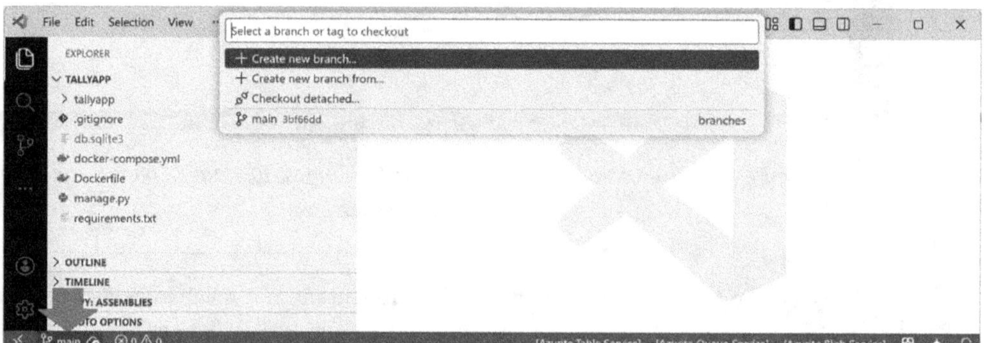

Figure 11.9: Creating a new Git branch

2. Select **Create new branch**, and type a name like: `feature/home-page`, and then press *Enter*.

3. At the command prompt or terminal, create a new feature:

```
python manage.py startapp homepage
```

4. In `tallyapp/settings.py`, add the app, as shown highlighted in the following code:

```
INSTALLED_APPS = [
    'django.contrib.admin',
    'django.contrib.auth',
    'django.contrib.contenttypes',
    'django.contrib.sessions',
    'django.contrib.messages',
    'django.contrib.staticfiles',
    "homepage",
]
```

5. In `homepage/views.py`, add statements to import some types, and define two functions, as shown highlighted in the following code:

```
from django.contrib.auth.decorators import login_required
from django.contrib.sessions.models import Session
from django.shortcuts import render
from django.utils import timezone

# Create your views here.

def _active_authenticated_user_count() -> int:
    """
    Approximation: count non-expired sessions that have an
authenticated user id.
    This counts sessions, not unique users. One user on two devices
counts twice.
    """
    now = timezone.now()
    active_sessions = Session.objects.filter(expire_date__gt=now)

    count = 0
    for s in active_sessions:
        data = s.get_decoded()
        if data.get("_auth_user_id"):
```

```
            count += 1

    return count


def home(request):
    context = {
        "active_user_count": _active_authenticated_user_count(),
    }
    return render(request, "homepage/home.html", context)
```

What this *signed-in users* number really means: It counts users with a valid, unexpired session. It does not guarantee they are actively using the site this second. It may count the same person multiple times (phone + laptop). It can stay non-zero for a while even if people close the browser, because sessions often expire hours or days later. This approach loads all sessions from the database, which works fine for a small project but would be too slow for a production site with thousands of sessions. The leading underscore in the function name `_active_authenticated_user_count` is a Python convention that signals that this function is an internal helper, not part of the public API.

6. In the homepage folder, create a `urls.py` file:

```
from django.urls import path
from .views import home

urlpatterns = [
    path("", home, name="home"),
]
```

7. In `tallyapp\urls.py`, add a reference to the new feature, as shown highlighted in the following code:

```
from django.contrib import admin
from django.urls import path, include

urlpatterns = [
```

```
    path('admin/', admin.site.urls),
    path("", include("homepage.urls")),
]
```

8. Create `templates/base.html`:

```
<!DOCTYPE html>
<html>
<head>
    <title>{% block title %}My Django Site{% endblock %}</title>
</head>
<body>
    <header>
        <h1>My Django Site</h1>
    </header>

    <main>
        {% block content %}{% endblock %}
    </main>
</body>
</html>
```

9. Create `templates/homepage/home.html`:

```
{% extends "base.html" %}
{% block title %}Home · TallyApp{% endblock %}

{% block content %}
<div class="card">
  {% if user.is_authenticated %}
    <p class="muted">Hi {{ user.username }}. You're signed in.</p>
  {% else %}
    <p class="muted">You're not signed in yet. Log in to admin.</p>
    <div class="card-actions">
      <a class="btn primary" href="/admin">Log in</a>
    </div>
  {% endif %}

  <hr style="border:0;border-top:1px solid rgba(255,255,255,0.14);
```

```
margin:16px 0;">

  <p class="muted">
    Signed-in users right now (approx): <strong>{{ active_user_count
}}</strong>
  </p>
</div>
{% endblock %}
```

10. Now commit as before.

Your work on the home-page feature is isolated and you can switch between it and the main branch at will.

Merging a branch

To merge back into main:

1. Switch back to main.
2. 2. Open the **Command Palette** and choose **Git: Merge Branch**.
3. Select your feature branch.

If no conflicts exist, Git creates a merge commit.

Prompt: Show a realistic Git branching strategy for a small Django team.

Connecting to a remote Git server

A remote Git server provides backup and enables collaboration:

1. In **Source Control**, click **Publish Branch**, as shown in *Figure 11.10*:

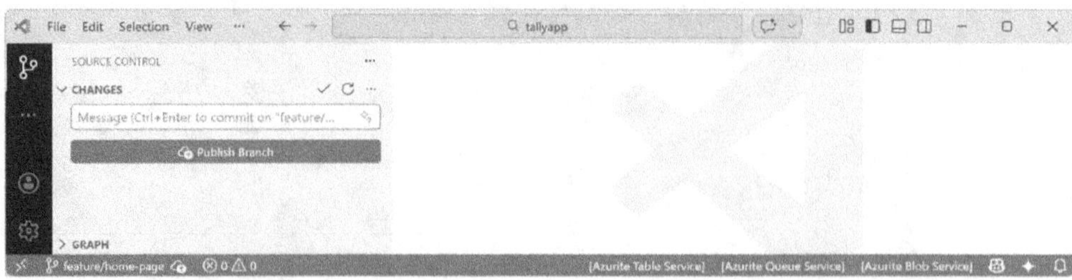

Figure 11.10: VS Code showing the "Publish Branch" button

2. Sign in when prompted, and then select the **public TallyApp** repository.
3. After publishing, your commits are pushed to GitHub.

Warning! When you publish to a public GitHub repository, anyone can see the files. Be careful that .gitignore excludes secrets such as passwords, API keys, and local environment files. You can also use a private repository while learning.

From this point forward:

- Use **Commit** to save locally
- Use **Sync Changes** to push to GitHub

Working with pull requests and code review

So far, you have created branches and merged them locally. That works when you are working alone, but most real projects use a slightly different process.

Instead of merging directly into the main branch, developers open a pull request.

A **pull request** is a way to propose a change, review it, and discuss it before merging.

Here is the standard process used by most teams:

1. Create a feature branch:

   ```
   git checkout -b feature/home-page
   ```

2. Make changes and commit them:

   ```
   git add .
   git commit -m "Add home page view and template"
   ```

3. Push the branch to GitHub:

   ```
   git push origin feature/home-page
   ```

4. Open a pull request in GitHub:
   - Compare your branch to main
   - Add a description of what changed and why

5. Review the changes:
   - You (and others) can comment on specific lines
   - You can suggest improvements or fixes
6. Make updates if needed:

```
git add .
git commit -m "Fix feedback from review"
git push
```

7. Once approved, merge the pull request into `main`.

A pull request is not just a button in GitHub. It serves three important purposes:

- **Review**: someone checks the code before it becomes part of the main project
- **Discussion**: design decisions can be questioned and improved
- **History**: the project records not just what changed, but why

Even if you are working alone, opening a pull request for your own work is useful. It gives you a chance to review your changes before merging. The pull request step slows you down slightly, but that is the point. It forces you to think before code becomes permanent.

This is especially important when using AI-generated code. It is easy to accept code that "looks right" but has subtle issues. A pull request creates a natural checkpoint for review. AI makes it easier to produce code quickly. Pull requests are where you apply human judgment to decide whether that code is actually good.

Many teams protect the `main` branch so it cannot be changed directly. All changes must go through a pull request. This prevents accidental mistakes and ensures every change is reviewed.

Pulling changes and handling conflicts

If you work on multiple machines or collaborate, you will need to pull changes:

1. Click **Sync Changes** or run **Pull**.

   If conflicts occur, VS Code opens a merge editor.

2. Choose one of: **Accept Current Change**, **Accept Incoming Change**, or **Accept Both Changes**.
3. Edit if necessary. What should be edited is entirely dependent on the specific conflict scenario.

4. Save, stage, and commit the resolved file.

A conflict does not mean corruption. It means Git needs help deciding between two edits.

Undoing common mistakes

You only need three recovery tools at this stage.

- **Discard local edits**: Right-click a modified file in **Source Control** and choose **Discard Changes**.
- **Unstage a file**: Right-click a staged file and choose **Unstage Changes**.
- **Amend the last commit**: If you forgot a file:
    1. Stage the file.
    2. Open the **Source Control** menu **...**.
    3. Choose **Commit** | **Amend Commit**.

  Amend rewrites the last commit. Only use it if you have not pushed yet.

Prompt: Please demonstrate how to undo a bad commit safely.

Where Git fits in this book's project

From this point onward:

- Every meaningful change to TallyApp should be committed
- Each new feature should live on a branch
- Each chapter section should end with a commit

By the time you deploy TallyApp, committing, branching, and reviewing changes should feel like the normal rhythm of the project.

Prompt: Please explain how Docker, Git, and AI coding assistants fit together in a web development workflow.

Practice, references, and resources

In this section, you will be tested on what you've learned in this chapter and be provided with useful links to reference materials and resources.

Programming languages and human languages

I have written an online article about programming languages and human languages:

`https://github.com/markjprice/markjprice/blob/main/with-ai/languages.md`

Check your understanding

Answer the following questions about the topics we covered in this chapter:

1. What is the main goal of the TallyApp project introduced in this chapter?
2. What does it mean to treat prompts as programs when using AI tools?
3. Why is it risky to rely too heavily on AI when learning to code?
4. What is the difference between an AI chatbot and an AI coding assistant?
5. What problem does Docker solve in development?
6. What is the difference between a Docker image and a container?
7. Why are Docker volumes important when using databases?
8. What is the purpose of `docker-compose.yml`?
9. What is the main benefit of using Git in a project like TallyApp?
10. Why is it important to commit small, meaningful changes in Git?

Answers are found in the GitHub repository for this book at the following link:

`https://github.com/markjprice/web-dev-ai/blob/main/docs/Appendix-A.pdf`

Links

Here are some useful links related to the technologies covered in this chapter.

GitHub Copilot

Quickstart: `https://docs.github.com/en/copilot/get-started/quickstart`

GitHub Copilot official docs: `https://docs.github.com/en/copilot`

GitHub Copilot reference: `https://docs.github.com/en/copilot/reference`

GitHub Copilot in VS Code: `https://code.visualstudio.com/docs/copilot/overview`

Customize AI in VS Code: `https://code.visualstudio.com/docs/copilot/customization/overview`

Docker

Dockerfile reference: `https://docs.docker.com/reference/dockerfile/`

Compose file reference: `https://docs.docker.com/reference/compose-file/`

PostgreSQL - Official Image: `https://hub.docker.com/_/postgres`

Psycopg: `https://www.psycopg.org/docs/`

Git

Official Git documentation: `https://git-scm.com/docs`

VS Code Git: `https://code.visualstudio.com/docs/sourcecontrol/overview`

Pro Git (free online book): `https://git-scm.com/book/en/v2`

GitHub Git Guides: `https://docs.github.com/en/get-started/using-git`

Summary

In this chapter, we learned the following:

- The overall purpose and scope of the TallyApp project, including its three functional areas: survey creation, survey participation, and results analysis
- How AI tools change the way beginners should practice, review code, and avoid offloading too much thinking
- Practical guidance on how to use AI responsibly while learning, including asking for explanations and avoiding full delegation of thinking
- How to choose and configure AI coding tools, including GitHub Copilot in VS Code, model selection and premium request awareness, **Bring Your Own Key** (**BYOK**) model configuration, and trade-offs between cloud-hosted and local models
- An introduction to Docker concepts, how to install Docker Desktop, and create a containerized Django development environment
- How to configure a `docker-compose.yml` with Django and PostgreSQL and persist database data using volumes

- How to switch Django's database configuration dynamically between SQLite and PostgreSQL using environment variables
- Core Git concepts, including repository, commit, branch, staging area, and remote
- How to initialize a Git repository in VS Code, create a proper `.gitignore` for Django projects, make meaningful commits, and create and then merge feature branches
- How Copilot, Docker, and Git support the TallyApp project before you start adding application features

From this point forward, TallyApp has a foundation: an AI coding assistant, a repeatable runtime environment, and version control. In the next chapter, you will start using that foundation to test the application properly. You will learn about multiple types of testing, from unit testing small components to end-to-end testing by simulating a user visiting the website and interacting with its user interface.

12

Unit, Integration, and End-to-End Testing

Do not leave testing until the end. It is how you turn a working prototype into dependable software. In a real project like TallyApp, features interact, users do things you did not expect, and small changes break code that looked unrelated. A good test suite lets you refactor, extend, and deploy with fewer nasty surprises.

A view might return the wrong survey. A permission check might let one user edit another user's data. A form might accept invalid input. A JavaScript or template change might make a button disappear. You might fix one bug and accidentally reintroduce an older one.

Tests are how you make those risks visible. A good test suite does not prove your application is perfect. It gives you fast, repeatable feedback about the behavior you care about most.

This chapter explores testing at three different levels:

- Small, fast unit tests that validate isolated pieces of logic
- Broader integration and user interface tests that verify components work together
- Using AI tools to draft, review, and improve tests

You will see how these layers catch different kinds of mistakes. When combined thoughtfully, they give you a safety net, so you can change code without guessing whether the project still works.

You will start with unit tests for small pieces of logic, then move into Django integration tests that exercise views, Uniform Resource Locators (URLs), authentication, forms, and the database. After that, you will use Playwright to automate a few browser-level user journeys. You will also learn how to manage test data, run tests in continuous integration, and use AI tools without letting them generate shallow tests that only look useful.

The main habit to build is simple: before you ask whether the code works, ask what behavior the system is supposed to guarantee.

By the end of this chapter, you will have designed and implemented a layered testing strategy for TallyApp, written meaningful unit and integration tests in Django, automated real browser interactions with end-to-end tests, and learned how to use AI tools to accelerate test creation without handing over engineering judgment.

In this chapter, we will cover the following topics:

- The testing pyramid and testing philosophy
- Unit testing Python and Django
- Integration testing Django applications
- End-to-end web user interface testing
- Managing test data and fixtures
- Continuous integration and automated test pipelines
- Asking an AI to write tests

Suggested chatbot prompts with example responses for this chapter can be found at the following link: `https://github.com/markjprice/web-dev-ai/blob/main/prompts/ch12-test/readme.md`

The testing pyramid and testing philosophy

Before you write many tests, it helps to know where each kind of test belongs. That model is usually described as the testing pyramid.

The testing pyramid

The **testing pyramid** describes the ideal distribution of tests in a healthy application, as shown in *Figure 12.1* and described in the following list:

- At the base are unit tests
- In the middle are integration tests
- At the top are end-to-end or UI tests

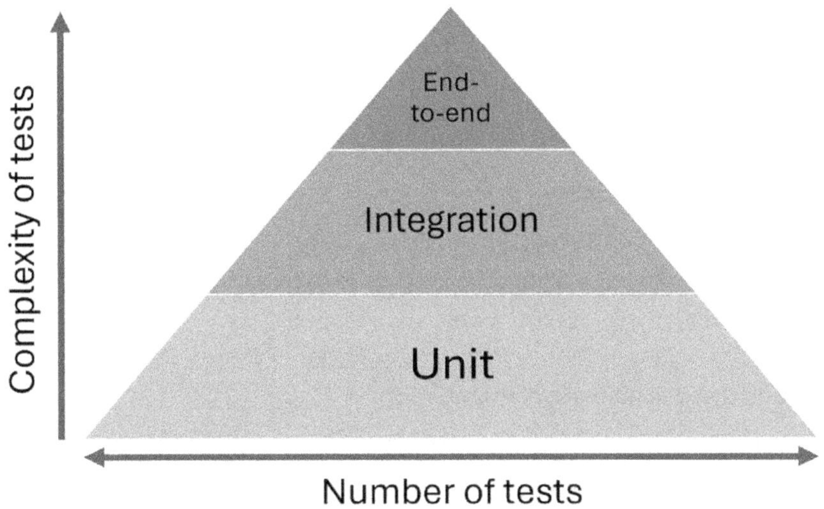

Figure 12.1: The testing pyramid

The basic idea is:

- You should have many fast, isolated unit tests
- Fewer integration tests that exercise multiple components together
- Very few slow, browser-level tests

Why put more tests at the bottom?

- Unit tests are fast, deterministic, easy to debug, and cheap to run in large numbers
- UI tests are slower, more fragile, and more complex to debug

If most of your tests are UI tests, the suite soon becomes slow, fragile, and annoying to debug. If you rely mostly on unit tests, you get fast feedback and can run tests constantly while developing.

Prompt: Please explain the historical origins of the testing pyramid and how it differs from the testing trophy model. What are real-world examples of teams that inverted the testing pyramid and what problems did they face?

In this section, we focus on the base of the pyramid: unit and server-side integration testing in Python and Django. Browser automation will be covered in the next section.

What counts as a unit?

A *unit* is usually a small, self-contained piece of logic:

- A function
- A method
- A class
- A small module

A **unit test** verifies that one piece of logic behaves as expected for given inputs.

For example:

- A function that calculates survey statistics
- A model method that determines whether a survey is published
- A form validation rule that rejects empty titles

Small, focused tests are easier to understand when they fail.

Arrange, act, assert

Most tests follow this structure:

1. **Arrange**: Set up the data and environment.
2. **Act**: Call the function or method under test.
3. **Assert**: Verify the result.

Example in plain terms:

1. **Arrange**: Create a `Survey` object.
2. **Act**: Call `survey.is_open()`.
3. **Assert**: Confirm it returns `True`.

This pattern helps future you and other test readers understand the test quickly by keeping tests readable and consistent.

Prompt: What makes a good unit test beyond Arrange–Act–Assert? Give examples of bad but syntactically correct tests.

Determinism and isolation

Good unit tests are:

- **Deterministic**: They always produce the same result given the same inputs
- **Isolated**: They do not depend on external systems such as the real database (unless intentionally testing DB behavior), network calls, current time (unless controlled), or random values

Good practice: For testing time-dependent logic, you can use `freezegun` (`https://github.com/spulec/freezegun`) or `time_machine` (`https://github.com/adamchainz/time-machine`) to freeze the clock at a specific moment. This makes tests deterministic regardless of when they run. `freezegun` is older and very popular. `time_machine` is newer, faster, and it is a good default for many current Python projects.

A test that randomly fails is often worse than no test because flaky tests erode trust. Once people stop trusting test failures, they stop reading them carefully.

Prompt: Please explain the difference between confidence, coverage, and correctness in software testing.

Now let's look at unit testing in more depth.

Unit testing Python and Django

Unit tests are where you check small pieces of logic before they disappear inside views, forms, and templates. At this level, you focus on small, self-contained pieces of logic such as functions, model methods, validation rules, and permission checks, and verify that they behave correctly for specific inputs.

In a Django project like TallyApp, this means testing pure Python utilities as well as model behavior, form validation, and custom business rules using Django's TestCase and its built-in test database. These tests should be fast, deterministic, and isolated, so you find mistakes while the code is still fresh in your head. When your unit tests are strong, they form a stable base for everything else in your test suite.

Prompt: How does Django's test runner create and destroy the test database internally?

Django's test base classes

Django provides several base test classes, each designed for a slightly different purpose. Choosing the right base class avoids slow tests and misleading tests.

Table 12.1 is a compact summary of the most commonly used test base classes:

Test Base Class	Transactions Rolled Back Per Test	Typical Use Case
`SimpleTestCase`	Not applicable	Pure logic tests that do not touch the database or Django models. Useful for utility functions and simple view logic with `RequestFactory`.
`TestCase`	Yes (fast transactional rollback)	Most model, form, and integration tests. Default choice for Django apps. Fast and isolated.
`TransactionTestCase`	No (flushes DB between tests)	When you need to test real transaction behavior, such as commit/rollback effects or database constraints that require an actual commit. Slower than `TestCase`.
`LiveServerTestCase`	Yes	End-to-end tests that require a real HTTP server, often used with Selenium or Playwright in integration mode. Spins up a live test server.
`StaticLiveServerTestCase`	Yes	Same as `LiveServerTestCase`, but also serves static files during tests. Useful for full browser-based UI testing.

Table 12.1: Most commonly used test base classes

Practical guidance:

- Use `TestCase` by default. It is optimized for speed and isolation and covers most scenarios in a Django project like TallyApp.
- Use `SimpleTestCase` when no database is needed. This keeps tests faster and makes intent explicit.
- Use `TransactionTestCase` only when you truly need to test behavior that depends on committed transactions.
- Use `LiveServerTestCase` or `StaticLiveServerTestCase` when driving a real browser for end-to-end tests.

In many Django projects, most tests will use `TestCase`, with the others reserved for specialized scenarios.

Python unit testing basics

Python ships with a built-in testing framework called `unittest`. Django builds on top of it.

A minimal `unittest`-style test looks like this:

```
import unittest

def add(a, b):
    return a + b

class AddTests(unittest.TestCase):

    def test_adds_two_numbers(self):
        result = add(2, 3)
        self.assertEqual(result, 5)
```

You run tests with:

```
python -m unittest
```

In Django projects, you usually run:

```
python manage.py test
```

Django automatically discovers tests inside files named `tests.py` or inside `tests/` packages.

Django's TestCase and the Test database

Django provides its own `TestCase` class, which extends `unittest.TestCase`.

Key features:

- Automatic test database. Django creates a temporary test database before running tests and destroys it afterward.
- Transaction isolation. Each test runs in a transaction that is rolled back, ensuring a clean state.
- Client for simulating HTTP requests. Django includes a test client for making fake `GET` and `POST` requests without a real browser.

Example model test:

```
from django.test import TestCase
from .models import Survey
from django.contrib.auth.models import User

class SurveyModelTests(TestCase):

    def test_survey_string_representation(self):
        user = User.objects.create_user(
            username="mark",
            password="password123"
        )

        survey = Survey.objects.create(
            title="Favorite Sci-Fi Series",
            owner=user
        )

        self.assertEqual(str(survey), "Favorite Sci-Fi Series")
```

This test:

- Uses the test database
- Creates real model instances
- Verifies model behavior
- Leaves the database clean afterward

This is the everyday shape of many Django tests.

Prompt: Please explain the difference between `TestCase`, `TransactionTestCase`, `SimpleTestCase`, and `LiveServerTestCase` in Django.

Testing views with the Django test client

There are two useful ways to test Django views.

Use `RequestFactory` when you want to call a view directly in isolation. This bypasses URL routing and middleware, so it behaves more like a traditional unit test of the view function itself. If the view depends on authentication, session data, or other middleware behavior, you must provide that manually. Django's documentation describes `RequestFactory` as a way to generate a request object and test a view like any other function.

Use `self.client` when you want to test the full Django request pipeline without launching a real browser. This includes URL routing and more of the framework behavior, so these tests are broader than isolated unit tests, but they are still fast and very useful in everyday Django projects. Django describes the test client as a way to simulate a user interacting with the application at the view level.

Example using `RequestFactory`:

```
from django.test import RequestFactory, TestCase
from django.contrib.auth.models import User
from surveys.views import survey_list

class SurveyViewUnitTests(TestCase):
    def setUp(self):
        self.factory = RequestFactory()
        self.user = User.objects.create_user(
            username="alice",
            password="example123"
        )

    def test_survey_list_with_authenticated_user(self):
        request = self.factory.get("/surveys/")
        request.user = self.user
```

```
        response = survey_list(request)

        self.assertEqual(response.status_code, 200)
```

Example using the Django test client:

```
from django.urls import reverse
from django.test import TestCase
from django.contrib.auth.models import User

class SurveyViewTests(TestCase):

    def test_login_required_for_survey_list(self):
        response = self.client.get(reverse("survey_list"))
        self.assertEqual(response.status_code, 302)
```

This verifies:

- An anonymous user is redirected
- The URL configuration is correct
- The view enforces authentication

You can also test `POST` submissions:

```
def test_create_survey(self):
    user = User.objects.create_user(
        username="mark",
        password="password123"
    )

    self.client.login(username="mark", password="password123")

    response = self.client.post(reverse("survey_create"), {
        "title": "Best Programming Language"
    })

    self.assertEqual(response.status_code, 302)
    self.assertTrue(
        Survey.objects.filter(title="Best Programming Language").exists()
    )
```

The preceding code covers the server-side behavior of the form without opening a browser.

Testing models, forms, and business logic

In a Django app like TallyApp, your tests should cover:

- **Model logic**: Custom methods such as `is_open()`, `can_edit(user)`, or computed properties
- **Form validation**: Ensure invalid data is rejected and correct error messages appear
- **Permission logic**: Confirm that only owners can edit or delete their surveys
- **Utility functions**: Pure Python functions for calculating statistics or transforming data

A useful rule is, *if it contains logic, test it, and test behavior, not boilerplate.* But if it is just a template rendering static content, unit tests are usually unnecessary.

The test examples in this chapter use a `Survey` model that you'll create in the next chapter. For now, read and understand the patterns, and your AI will implement them once the model exists.

Prompt: What is parametrized testing in `pytest` and when is it useful?

Property-based testing with Hypothesis

Most tests you have seen so far are example-based. You choose specific inputs, call a function, and assert the expected result. **Property-based testing** takes a different approach. Instead of writing many individual examples, you describe a general property that should always be true, and a tool generates a wide range of inputs automatically to try to break it.

In Python, the most popular property-based testing library is **Hypothesis**. Rather than testing only a few handpicked values, Hypothesis generates dozens or hundreds of inputs, including edge cases you might not think of, such as empty strings, extremely large numbers, unusual Unicode characters, or boundary values.

For example, suppose you have a simple utility function in TallyApp that calculates the percentage of responses:

```
def percentage(part, total):
    if total == 0:
        return 0
    return round((part / total) * 100, 2)
```

A traditional test might look like this:

```
def test_percentage_basic():
    assert percentage(1, 4) == 25.0
```

That is fine, but it only tests one example. With Hypothesis, you can define properties that should hold for many inputs:

```
from hypothesis import given
from hypothesis import strategies as st

@given(
    part=st.integers(min_value=0, max_value=10_000),
    total=st.integers(min_value=0, max_value=10_000),
)
def test_percentage_is_between_0_and_100(part, total):
    result = percentage(part, total)
    assert 0 <= result <= 100
```

Now Hypothesis will generate many combinations of `part` and `total` and verify that the result always falls within a valid range. If it finds a failing case, it will shrink the input to the smallest example that still breaks the property, which makes debugging easier.

When you run this, Hypothesis will find cases where `part > total`, producing results above 100%. This is the point of property-based testing because it found a bug we didn't anticipate. Then you'd need to decide how to handle the discovered bug: should the function clamp the result to 100%, or should the property allow values above 100%? To fix the function, you could use the following code:

```
def percentage(part, total):
    if total == 0:
        return 0
    return min(round((part / total) * 100, 2), 100.0)
```

Property-based testing is especially useful for:

- Pure functions with mathematical or logical invariants
- Data transformations
- Validation logic
- Parsers and formatters
- Anything that should behave consistently across a wide input space

It is less useful for complex integration tests that depend heavily on databases, HTTP calls, or external systems.

With property-based tests, the question changes from *What example should I test?*, you ask, *What must always be true?* For business logic in TallyApp like score calculations, survey statistics, or normalization rules, that perspective can uncover edge cases that example-based tests miss.

Measuring coverage

Testing is also about knowing where the blind spots are. The `coverage.py` tool measures how much of your code runs during tests.

You typically:

1. Run tests with coverage enabled.
2. Generate an HTML report.
3. Inspect which lines were never executed.

High coverage does not guarantee correctness, but low coverage almost guarantees blind spots.

Prompt: What does 100 percent code coverage fail to tell you? What is branch coverage versus line coverage? How does `coverage.py` work internally?

A sensible testing strategy for TallyApp

For a project like TallyApp:

- Write unit tests for model methods and validation logic
- Use Django's test client for authentication and create, read, update, and delete (CRUD) flows
- Keep tests small and focused
- Avoid testing trivial getters or Django internals

Different kinds of tests exercise different parts of the system. Use the lightest tool that still gives you confidence in the behavior you care about, as shown in *Figure 12.2*:

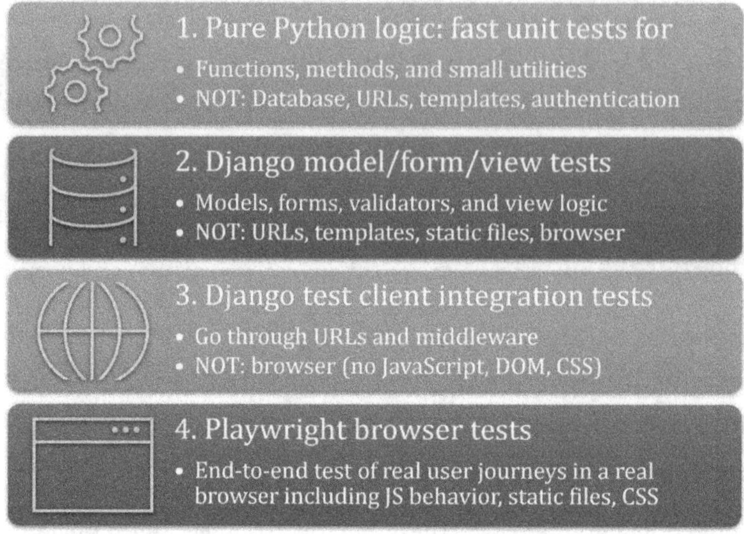

Figure 12.2: Testing layers in TallyApp

Start with the cheapest layer that can prove the behavior. If a pure Python unit test can prove it, do not use a browser test. It will be faster, simpler to maintain, and easier to debug.

Aim for:

- Fast test runs
- Clear failures
- Confidence when refactoring

The goal is to catch most bugs with layers 1 to 3. Reserve Playwright tests in layer 4 for the flows that matter most to real users. When unit tests and server-side integration tests are strong, UI testing becomes a thin safety layer rather than your only defense. That keeps browser tests valuable without letting them dominate the suite.

Testing is where you decide what the application is allowed to do. An AI assistant can write another `assertEqual` line, but it cannot decide whether an unpublished survey should be invisible, whether a creator can edit a survey after responses exist, or whether a duplicate submission should leave the database unchanged. Those decisions belong to the developer. Once you make them explicit as tests, the code has something concrete to satisfy.

pytest and pytest-django

Many Django projects use `pytest` instead of `unittest`-style classes. But you should verify that `pytest-django` supports your Django version before assuming that you can use it. You can check for the latest compatibility information at the following link: `https://github.com/pytest-dev/pytest-django`

Why developers prefer `pytest`:

- Simpler syntax (plain functions instead of classes)
- Powerful fixture system
- Better error output
- More flexible test organization

A `pytest`-style test might look like this:

```
def test_survey_str(db, django_user_model):
    user = django_user_model.objects.create_user(
        username="mark",
        password="password123"
    )

    survey = Survey.objects.create(
        title="Favorite Editor",
        owner=user
    )

    assert str(survey) == "Favorite Editor"
```

Note the following about the preceding code:

- `db` is a fixture that enables database access
- Assertions use plain `assert` instead of `self.assertEqual`

`pytest-django` integrates `pytest` with Django's settings and test database.

Many Django teams use `pytest` with `pytest-django`.

Prompt: Why do many professional Django teams prefer `pytest` over `unittest`? Please include a comparison of the same Django test written in `unittest` style and `pytest` style.

Now let's move on from unit testing to integration testing.

Integration testing Django applications

Integration tests sit in the middle of your test suite. They are not trying to prove every micro-detail of a function (unit tests), and they are not trying to drive a real browser (end-to-end UI tests). Instead, they verify that multiple Django layers cooperate correctly: URL routing, view logic, templates, middleware, authentication, sessions, and database reads and writes.

Django makes this style of testing fairly painless because the built-in test runner automatically creates a temporary test database, wraps each test in a transaction, and provides a test client that can make request-like calls against your Django project without starting a browser.

What you test at the integration level

A good integration test suite answers questions like these:

- If I request a named URL, do I hit the expected view and get the correct HTTP response? (URLs + views)
- If I am not logged in, do protected pages redirect me to the login page? If I am logged in, do I get access? (authentication flow)
- Do middleware hooks actually run and alter requests or responses the way the live site will? (middleware in the request/response pipeline)
- Do views correctly create, update, and query database rows, and does the response reflect those changes? (database interactions)

Prompt: What are the most common mistakes developers make when writing integration tests?

TestCase and the test client

Django's `django.test.TestCase` gives you a database that is set up for each test run, and it provides a `self.client` attribute you can use to perform requests like GET and POST. The client can also follow redirects and record the redirect chain when you pass `follow=True`.

A typical pattern is:

1. Create the database state you need (users, surveys, questions, responses).
2. Make an HTTP request with `self.client.get(...)` or `self.client.post(...)`.

3. Assert status codes, redirects, context data, and database effects.

When you call `self.client.get()` in a Django `TestCase`, Django's test client simulates an HTTP request and runs it through (almost) the entire Django stack without a real browser, as shown in *Figure 12.3*:

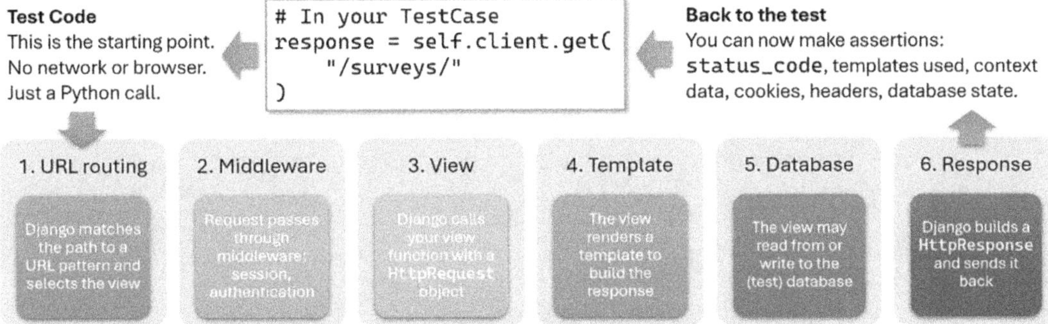

Figure 12.3: Django integration test request path

`self.client` runs a request through Django's real request/response cycle including routing, middleware, templates, and the database, all without a browser.

Example: testing URL routing and a view together

This example assumes you have a survey detail page that shows a published survey.

In the file `tests/test_surveys_integration.py`:

```
from django.test import TestCase
from django.urls import reverse, resolve

from surveys.views import survey_detail
from surveys.models import Survey


class SurveyDetailIntegrationTests(TestCase):
    @classmethod
    def setUpTestData(cls):
        # setUpTestData runs once for the class (faster than setUp per
test)
        cls.survey = Survey.objects.create(
            title="Customer Satisfaction",
            slug="customer-satisfaction",
```

```
            is_published=True,
        )

    def test_url_resolves_to_expected_view(self):
        url = reverse("surveys:detail", kwargs={"slug": self.survey.slug})
        match = resolve(url)
        self.assertEqual(match.func, survey_detail)

    def test_detail_page_returns_200_and_includes_title(self):
        url = reverse("surveys:detail", kwargs={"slug": self.survey.slug})
        response = self.client.get(url)

        self.assertEqual(response.status_code, 200)
        self.assertContains(response, "Customer Satisfaction")
```

Note the following about the preceding code:

- `reverse()` ensures you are testing the named route rather than hardcoding URLs, so refactors are safer.
- `resolve()` verifies your `URLconf` points at the correct view.
- `self.client.get()` exercises URL routing + middleware stack + view + template rendering together.

Warning! Objects created in `setUpTestData` are shared across all tests in the class. If a test modifies and saves the object, subsequent tests see the modified version. Use `setUpTestData` only for data that tests read but don't change. For mutable test data, use `setUp` instead.

Example: testing a login-required view

For creator-only pages in TallyApp, a typical rule is: if you are not authenticated, you should be redirected to the login page. Once logged in, you should see the page.

MDN's Django testing tutorial shows this exact pattern with `assertRedirects` for *redirect if not logged in*:

```
from django.contrib.auth import get_user_model
from django.test import TestCase
from django.urls import reverse
```

```
User = get_user_model()


class SurveyCreateAuthIntegrationTests(TestCase):
    @classmethod
    def setUpTestData(cls):
        cls.user = User.objects.create_user(
            username="mark",
            email="mark@example.com",
            password="pass12345",
        )

    def test_redirects_to_login_when_not_authenticated(self):
        url = reverse("surveys:create")
        response = self.client.get(url)

        # If you use Django's login_required decorator, this is the
default behavior:
        # redirect to settings.LOGIN_URL with ?next=<original_url>.
        login_url = reverse("login")
        self.assertRedirects(
            response,
            f"{login_url}?next={url}",
            fetch_redirect_response=False,  # avoids making a second
request
        )

    def test_returns_200_when_authenticated(self):
        self.client.force_login(self.user)
        url = reverse("surveys:create")
        response = self.client.get(url)

        self.assertEqual(response.status_code, 200)
        self.assertContains(response, "Create survey")
```

Note the following about the preceding code:

- `force_login` is ideal when you are not testing the login form itself, only the access control and behavior once authenticated.
- `assertRedirects` is the most direct way to test redirects in Django's test client.

Example: testing a full "POST creates rows" flow

Now let's test something closer to real behavior: submit a POST that creates a survey, confirm you are redirected to the new survey page, and confirm the survey exists in the database:

```
from django.contrib.auth import get_user_model
from django.test import TestCase
from django.urls import reverse

from surveys.models import Survey


User = get_user_model()


class SurveyCreatePostIntegrationTests(TestCase):
    @classmethod
    def setUpTestData(cls):
        cls.user = User.objects.create_user(
            username="creator",
            email="creator@example.com",
            password="pass12345",
        )

    def test_post_creates_survey_and_redirects(self):
        self.client.force_login(self.user)

        url = reverse("surveys:create")
        response = self.client.post(
            url,
            data={
                "title": "Conference Feedback",
                "slug": "conference-feedback",
```

```
                "is_published": False,
            },
            follow=False,
        )

        self.assertEqual(response.status_code, 302)

        created = Survey.objects.get(slug="conference-feedback")
        self.assertEqual(created.title, "Conference Feedback")
        self.assertFalse(created.is_published)

        # Optionally verify where we redirect to
        expected = reverse("surveys:detail", kwargs={"slug": created.
slug})
        self.assertRedirects(
            response,
            expected,
            fetch_redirect_response=False,
        )
```

If you want to validate the final page content after redirects, pass `follow=True` and assert on the final response. Django's docs describe `follow=True` and the `redirect_chain` attribute:

```
response = self.client.post(url, data=payload, follow=True)
self.assertEqual(response.status_code, 200)
self.assertGreaterEqual(len(response.redirect_chain), 1)
self.assertContains(response, "Conference Feedback")
```

Practical guidance

Keep integration tests stable:

- Prefer named URLs (`reverse()`) over hardcoded paths. It reduces brittleness during refactors.
- Use `setUpTestData` for expensive setup shared across tests; use `setUp` for per-test state you intend to mutate.
- Assert the minimum that proves the behavior. For example, assert a redirect and a database row exists, rather than asserting the entire HTML output.

- If a test fails, diagnose in this order:
    1. Did you hit the right URL name and arguments?
    2. Did you get redirected (`302`) when you expected a `200`?
    3. Did authentication state exist (`force_login` or `login`)?
    4. Did your database setup match what the view expects?

Prompt: Please explain how to test database constraints and unique indexes, and race conditions or concurrency issues properly in Django.

Where integration tests end and end-to-end tests begin

The test client will never run JavaScript, it will never validate that a button is clickable in a real browser, and it will not find layout issues. That is the job of Playwright-based end-to-end tests. But for most server-side workflows in Django, integration tests give you the best feedback for the time they take.

Now let's move on to end-to-end testing, also known as user interface testing.

End-to-end web user interface testing

Unit tests and Django's test client give you fast feedback, but they still do not prove that TallyApp works in a real browser. Web UI tests sit at the top of the testing pyramid: you run the application, open a real browser engine, and automate the same actions a user performs like clicking links, filling forms, submitting, and verifying what appears on screen.

This section uses Playwright, a browser automation tool that is fast, reliable, and supports Chromium, Firefox, and WebKit. We'll use it to test a small number of important end-to-end user journeys for TallyApp.

What UI tests are for

UI tests are best used for critical flows that must not break:

- Authentication flow:
    - A logged-out user is redirected to login for protected pages
    - A user can log in and log out

- Core product flow:
    - A logged-in user can create a survey
    - The new survey appears in the survey list
    - A user can edit and delete their survey
- Authorization boundaries:
    - User A cannot edit or delete User B's surveys (tested by attempting direct navigation)

Avoid using UI tests for everything. They are slower than unit tests and take more work to keep stable. Your goal is a small suite that proves the app works from the user's point of view.

Why Playwright instead of Selenium

Historically, Selenium has been the most popular web UI testing framework. Selenium can work, but Playwright is usually a better fit for modern projects because:

- **Auto-waiting is built in.** It waits for elements to be ready, which reduces flaky tests.
- **Locators are resilient.** They re-query and track elements rather than finding once and praying.
- **Great debugging.** It can record screenshots, videos, and traces.
- **Cross-browser.** One **application programming interface** (**API**) drives Chromium, Firefox, and WebKit consistently.
- **Plays nicer with AI coding agents.** The Playwright **Model Context Protocol** (**MCP**) server (`playwright-mcp`) integrates well with GitHub Copilot.

Prompt: Please compare Playwright and Selenium in terms of architecture and reliability.

Make your UI easy to test

UI tests get dramatically more reliable if you adopt two habits:

- **Prefer accessible selectors**: Playwright can locate elements by role, label, and visible text. This encourages good HTML and makes tests less brittle.
- **Use test IDs sparingly**: For a few key elements, add `data-testid="..."` attributes. This prevents styling changes from breaking tests.

Example in a Django template:

```
<button type="submit" data-testid="save-survey">Save</button>
```

Use this sparingly. Most of the time, prefer labels and roles.

Choosing the Playwright style for a Django project

Playwright supports two common approaches:

1. Python + `pytest`. Fits naturally in a Django/Python repo. Tests look like Python tests and can run alongside your other test tooling.
2. TypeScript runner (Playwright Test). Excellent if your team is already TypeScript-heavy. Not required for TallyApp.

For this Django-first book project, Python with `pytest` is the simplest and most consistent choice.

Installing Playwright

You need two things:

- The Python Playwright package
- The actual browser binaries Playwright uses

Typical setup commands (run in your virtual environment):

```
python -m pip install playwright pytest
python -m playwright install
```

Optional but recommended for better assertions and waiting helpers:

```
python -m pip install pytest-playwright
```

If you already use `pytest` for unit tests, this fits nicely. If not, you can still run Playwright tests separately, but `pytest` keeps things tidy.

Organizing UI tests in the Git repository

A clean structure is to keep UI tests separate from Django unit tests:

- `tests/` for unit and integration tests
- e2e/ for web user interface tests

Example:

- `e2e/test_auth_flow.py`: a test of the website's authentication

- `e2e/test_surveys_crud.py`: a test of the database CRUD operations for surveys

This prevents confusion about which tests require a running server and a browser.

Running Django for UI tests

UI tests need a running server.

You have two reasonable approaches:

1. Run the Django dev server manually. Start the server in one terminal, and then run Playwright tests in another terminal:

   ```
   python manage.py runserver
   ```

   This setup works, but it requires coordination. The server must already be running before the tests start, and if it is not, the failures can be confusing because Playwright will simply fail to connect. In automated environments such as CI, you would not rely on two manual terminals. Instead, you would start Django as part of the test run itself, either by using a test server (such as Django's `LiveServerTestCase`) or by using a test runner that launches and tears down the server automatically. That leads us to the second option.

2. Start a test server from `pytest`. This is cleaner for CI, but a little more setup.

   For this book, starting the dev server manually is often easier, and then you can implement the automated approach later. A simple improvement, even during development, is to script both steps together. For example, you can use a shell script or task runner that starts Django and then runs Playwright tests once the server is ready. This removes the need to manually coordinate two terminals:

   ```
   # Example (Unix-like systems)
   python manage.py runserver &
   pytest e2e
   ```

   This is a simple approach for learning, but in real projects, you would use a more robust process that waits for the server to be ready before running tests.

   When beginners run Playwright tests without a running server, they see connection refused errors, timeouts, and `page.goto failed` messages. None of those errors clearly say: "you forgot to start Django."

   In the examples below, assume the server is running at: `http://127.0.0.1:8000`.

A first Playwright test: Login Required Redirect

Create `e2e/test_auth_flow.py`:

```
import re
from playwright.sync_api import Page, expect

BASE_URL = "http://127.0.0.1:8000"


def test_protected_page_redirects_to_login(page: Page) -> None:
    page.goto(f"{BASE_URL}/surveys/")

    # Expect we end up on the login page (URL patterns vary by project).
    expect(page).to_have_url(re.compile(r".*/login/?(\?.*)?$"))

    # And the login form should be visible (adjust label/text to your
templates).
    expect(page.get_by_label("Username")).to_be_visible()
    expect(page.get_by_label("Password")).to_be_visible()
```

Notes:

- `expect` provides automatic waiting and clearer failures than manual sleeps.
- Use labels where possible. If your form fields do not have labels, add them. It improves accessibility and testability.

Prompt: What is the Page Object Model and should I use it with Playwright?

Testing a real user journey: Create a Survey

UI tests should exercise the same steps a user takes. For that, you need a known user account.

You can create test users in a few ways:

- Create a dedicated user in your dev database
- Use a setup script/fixture to create a user automatically
- Use the Django admin to create a user once

The simplest is: create a user once (for example, `mark` / `password123`) and use that in early UI tests, then later evolve into an automated setup. For learning, creating a test user manually is fine. In a real project, E2E tests should create their own data programmatically. Django's `StaticLiveServerTestCase` provides a test server with a clean test database, or you can write a setup script that creates the required test user before each test run.

Create `e2e/test_surveys_crud.py`:

```
import os
from playwright.sync_api import Page, expect

# Read base URL from an environment variable with a default.
BASE_URL = os.environ.get("BASE_URL", "http://127.0.0.1:8000")
USERNAME = "mark"
PASSWORD = "password123"

def login(page: Page) -> None:
    page.goto(f"{BASE_URL}/login/")
    page.get_by_label("Username").fill(USERNAME)
    page.get_by_label("Password").fill(PASSWORD)
    page.get_by_role("button", name="Log in").click()
    expect(page).to_have_url(f"{BASE_URL}/surveys/")

def test_create_survey(page: Page) -> None:
    login(page)

    page.get_by_role("link", name="New survey").click()
    expect(page).to_have_url(f"{BASE_URL}/surveys/new/")

    page.get_by_label("Title").fill("Best Star Trek Captain")
    page.get_by_role("button", name="Save").click()

    # Back on list page, new survey should appear.
    expect(page).to_have_url(f"{BASE_URL}/surveys/")
    expect(page.get_by_text("Best Star Trek Captain")).to_be_visible()
```

This test proves:

- Authentication works
- Navigation works
- Forms render and submit
- Data appears in the UI

Adjust the link text, button text, and URLs to match your templates.

Edit and delete tests

Once you have created a working test, edit and delete follow the same pattern. Keep them short:

```
def test_edit_survey_title(page: Page) -> None:
    login(page)

    page.get_by_text("Best Star Trek Captain").click()  # or click an
"Edit" link
    page.get_by_label("Title").fill("Best Star Trek Series")
    page.get_by_role("button", name="Save").click()

    expect(page.get_by_text("Best Star Trek Series")).to_be_visible()

def test_delete_survey(page: Page) -> None:
    login(page)

    page.get_by_text("Best Star Trek Series").click()
    page.get_by_role("button", name="Delete").click()

    expect(page.get_by_text("Best Star Trek Series")).not_to_be_visible()
```

If your UI uses confirmation dialogs, Playwright can handle them, but a beginner-friendly approach is to implement a simple confirmation page in Django rather than a browser modal.

Keeping UI tests reliable

Most flaky UI tests come from two causes: unstable selectors and timing assumptions.

- Use stable selectors:
    - Prefer `get_by_role`, `get_by_label`, and visible button/link names
    - Use `data-testid` only for a handful of key controls

- Never use sleeps:
    - Avoid `time.sleep(...)`
    - Use `expect(...)` which waits until the condition is `true` or times out
- Reset state. UI tests should not depend on the previous test order. If your tests create surveys, either:
    - Create unique titles per test, or
    - Clean up after the test, or
    - Reset the database between UI runs (best for CI)

Debugging failures: headed mode, screenshots, and traces

When a UI test fails, you want evidence. Unlike unit tests, browser tests involve timing, rendering, and user interaction, so failures are not always obvious from the test output alone.

One of the most important concepts to understand is the difference between headless and headed browser modes:

- **Headless mode (default)**: The browser runs without a visible window. This is faster and is typically used in CI pipelines and automated runs.
- **Headed mode**: The browser window is shown on screen. You can watch the test interact with the page in real time, which is extremely useful when debugging.

Good practice: Use headless for speed and automation. Use headed when something is failing and you need to see what is happening.

Run tests in headed mode (visible browser) while developing or debugging tests:

```
pytest -s e2e --headed
```

You can also slow down interactions to make them easier to follow:

```
pytest -s e2e --headed --slowmo 200
```

The preceding code adds a delay (in milliseconds) between actions so you can visually track what the test is doing.

Even with the headed mode, you often want a record of what went wrong, especially in CI where no screen is visible. A simple pattern is to capture a screenshot when a test fails:

```
def test_something(page: Page) -> None:
    try:
        # test steps...
        pass
    except Exception:
        page.screenshot(path="e2e_failure.png", full_page=True)
        raise
```

For more complex failures, Playwright also supports tracing, which records:

- Screenshots at each step
- Document Object Model (DOM) snapshots
- Network activity

Traces let you replay the test step-by-step after it fails, which is often more useful than a single screenshot.

Running UI tests from VS Code

The recommended workflow for running UI tests from within VS Code is the following:

1. Open the integrated terminal.
2. Start Django in one terminal:

   ```
   python manage.py runserver
   ```

3. Run UI tests in another terminal:

   ```
   pytest e2e
   ```

If you add the Python extension, you can also run individual tests from the editor using the *Run Test* code lens.

What to aim for in TallyApp

A sensible Playwright suite for TallyApp is small and boring:

- Login required redirect
- Login/logout
- Create survey

- Edit survey
- Delete survey
- User A cannot edit User B's survey

That's enough to catch most *I broke the UI* regressions without turning your test suite into a slow, flaky monster.

Once you can simulate real user interactions in the browser, the next challenge is controlling the data those tests depend on so they remain reliable and repeatable.

Managing test data and fixtures

Most flaky or painful Django tests are not caused by Django. They are caused by messy test data. If the test setup is slow, confusing, or tightly coupled to unrelated details, tests become hard to write and easy to break. Good test data management keeps tests fast, readable, and independent.

The goal is simple: each test should set up only the data it needs, create it in a predictable way, and never depend on data created by some other test.

Fixtures, factories, and why factories usually win

Django supports *fixtures*, usually JSON/YAML/XML files you load into the test database. They are tempting because you can create data once and reuse it. In practice, they often become brittle: a fixture file grows over time, contains irrelevant objects, and breaks whenever you change models. Django documents fixtures and how they are loaded via the `loaddata` management command. For example:

```
python manage.py loaddata initial_data
```

Django will look for files named `initial_data.json`, `initial_data.yaml`, or `initial_data.xml` in known fixture locations. Django searches in:

- A `fixtures/` folder inside each app
- Any directories listed in `FIXTURE_DIRS` in `settings.py`
- The current working directory

Factories (created in code) are usually a better default. They produce the exact objects a test needs, right where the test can see them, with sane defaults and explicit overrides. Factories also make refactors easier because model changes tend to cause clear Python errors instead of mysterious fixture load failures.

Good practice: Use factories for most tests. Use fixtures only for small, stable reference data (for example, a short list of countries, or a couple of static *question types*) and only if that data truly is stable.

Django fixtures in tests

Django's TestCase can load fixtures automatically by declaring a fixtures attribute on the test class. This is convenient, but you should keep fixture files small and focused. For example:

```
from django.test import TestCase


class SurveyListFixtureTests(TestCase):
    fixtures = ["surveys_small.json"]

    def test_list_page_shows_published_surveys(self):
        response = self.client.get("/surveys/")
        self.assertEqual(response.status_code, 200)
```

Problems you tend to hit with fixtures:

- **Hidden coupling**: Tests depend on fixture IDs, ordering, or assumptions about what's inside the file.
- **Hard to read**: The data is not near the assertion, so you mentally jump between files.
- **Refactor pain**: Renaming a field or changing a constraint can break fixture loading across many tests at once.
- **Slow growth**: One fixture becomes "the fixture" and accumulates unrelated objects.

If you do use fixtures, keep them small, and name them after the specific scenario they support.

Prompt: What are the risks of overusing shared fixtures in large projects?

Factories in plain Django

You do not need a library to use factories. A simple approach is to write helper functions that create objects with defaults, and override with parameters. The defaults should be realistic, and they should always create valid objects.

Example helpers:

```
from django.contrib.auth import get_user_model
from surveys.models import Survey

User = get_user_model()

def make_user(**kwargs):
    defaults = {
        "username": "user1",
        "email": "user1@example.com",
        "password": "pass12345",  # note: create_user will hash it
    }
    defaults.update(kwargs)
    return User.objects.create_user(
        username=defaults["username"],
        email=defaults["email"],
        password=defaults["password"],
    )

def make_survey(**kwargs):
    defaults = {
        "title": "Sample Survey",
        "slug": "sample-survey",
        "is_published": True,
    }
    defaults.update(kwargs)
    return Survey.objects.create(**defaults)
```

Then in a test:

```
from django.test import TestCase
from django.urls import reverse

class SurveyListFactoryTests(TestCase):
    def test_list_shows_only_published(self):
        make_survey(title="Published A", slug="a", is_published=True)
        make_survey(title="Draft B", slug="b", is_published=False)

        response = self.client.get(reverse("surveys:list"))
        self.assertContains(response, "Published A")
        self.assertNotContains(response, "Draft B")
```

Factories with factory_boy

If you want a more scalable factory approach, the most common Django-friendly library is `factory_boy`, which provides declarative factories and handy features like sequences and subfactories. In a book context, it's worth mentioning as an option, even if you keep the core examples library-free.

A typical pattern with `factory_boy` is:

- Use `Sequence` for unique slugs/usernames.
- Use `SubFactory` for related models.
- Keep the default state valid and minimal.

Prompt: Please compare `factory_boy`, `pytest` fixtures, and Django fixtures with pros and cons.

Database transactions and test isolation in Django

Django's TestCase isolates tests using database transactions. At a high level:

- Django creates a test database (or reuses one, depending on settings) for the test run.
- Each `TestCase` runs inside a transaction and is rolled back so the next test starts clean.

This is why you can safely create objects in one test without them leaking into another.

`TransactionTestCase` is a lower-level base class that does not wrap each test in the same fast transactional approach, and is used when you need to test behavior that depends on real transaction commits. This is less common for typical web app tests, but matters if you test transaction hooks or some concurrency behavior.

Practical implications:

- Use `TestCase` for most integration and model tests.
- Use `TransactionTestCase` only when you have a specific reason.
- Keep tests deterministic. Do not depend on implicit ordering from the database unless you specify ordering.

Avoiding brittle shared state

Brittle shared state is anything global that tests accidentally depend on. It causes failures that appear random, especially when you run tests in a different order or run a single test file in isolation.

Common sources of brittleness and how to avoid them are shown in *Table 12.2*:

Problem	**Solution**
Relying on hardcoded primary keys "Assume the first survey has id=1."	Retrieve the object you just created, or query by a stable field (slug), or store the returned object and use its id.
Relying on queryset default ordering "The first item in Survey.objects.all() is the newest."	Use explicit ordering in queries or in the model Meta ordering, and assert based on content rather than position.
Sharing module-level objects across tests. For example, you create a Survey at import time in the test module. This will run once when the test module is imported, which makes ordering and isolation unpredictable.	Always create objects inside setUp, setUpTestData, or the test method.
Leaking external state: caches, emails, files, time	If your code touches Django cache, email outbox, file storage, the current time, or environment variables, make sure your tests control it.

Table 12.2: Common sources of test brittleness and how to avoid them

Now let's look at continuous integration and automated test pipelines.

Continuous integration and automated test pipelines

A test suite only changes your day-to-day behavior if it runs automatically, every time. That is what **continuous integration** (**CI**) does: whenever code is pushed or a pull request is opened, the CI system creates a clean environment, installs dependencies, and runs your tests. If anything fails, you find out immediately, before the change is merged or deployed.

GitHub Actions is the default choice for many Django projects because it is built into GitHub, supports Linux runners, and is easy to express as a YAML workflow that runs on `push` and `pull_request`.

Discipline is the point

CI is a team rule enforced by a machine.

Disciplined CI usually means:

- Every push and pull request runs the test suite, not just when someone remembers to do it.
- The `main` branch stays green. Broken builds are treated as stop-the-line events.
- Pull requests are not merged if CI fails. This can be enforced with branch protection rules in GitHub.
- Flaky tests are fixed or removed quickly. A flaky test is worse than no test because it trains everyone to ignore failures.
- CI runs in a clean environment, so it catches *works on my machine* bugs.

Prompt: Why do some teams resist writing tests? How do you introduce testing discipline into a team that has none? Please explain the economic argument for automated testing.

A minimal Django CI workflow with SQLite

This workflow runs on every push and pull request, sets up Python, installs dependencies, and runs Django's test runner with warnings enabled, which is useful for catching deprecations early. Django itself recommends running tests with Python warnings enabled using `python -Wa manage.py test`.

You do not need to add this workflow to TallyApp now, but this is what a minimal workflow looks like.

Warning! Never store secrets (API keys, passwords, secret keys) directly in your repository or in `ci.yml`. Use environment variables and GitHub Actions Secrets instead. If a repository is public, anything committed to it is visible to everyone.

Create: `.github/workflows/ci.yml`:

```
name: CI

on:
  push:
    branches: [ "main" ]
  pull_request:

jobs:
  test:
    runs-on: ubuntu-latest

    strategy:
      fail-fast: false
      matrix:
        python-version: [ "3.14", "3.13", "3.12" ]

    steps:
      - name: Checkout
        uses: actions/checkout@v4

      - name: Set up Python
        uses: actions/setup-python@v5
        with:
          python-version: ${{ matrix.python-version }}
          cache: "pip"

      - name: Install dependencies
        run: |
          python -m pip install --upgrade pip
          pip install -r requirements.txt
```

```
      - name: Run tests
        env:
          DJANGO_SETTINGS_MODULE: tallyapp.settings
          # If you use environment variables in settings.py, set them here
too.
          # DJANGO_SECRET_KEY: "ci-only-not-secret"
        run: |
          python -Wa manage.py test
```

Note the following about the preceding code:

- It runs on `push` and `pull_request`, meaning every change is tested automatically.
- It uses `actions/setup-python` to install a specific Python version consistently across runs, and can cache pip dependencies to keep CI fast.
- A small Python version matrix catches compatibility issues early, especially if your readers might use different Python versions.

This section about CI is to raise your awareness about the technique, but we won't implement it in this book because it overcomplicates the project when you're first learning.

Prompt: What is the difference between continuous integration, continuous delivery, and continuous deployment?

Now let's see how AI can help you write tests.

Asking an AI to write tests

AI tools are very good at producing plausible-looking tests very quickly. They are not good at knowing whether those tests are meaningful. Used properly, an AI assistant can help you draft and revise tests faster. Used carelessly, it will generate a large volume of shallow tests that assert almost nothing.

The difference comes down to how you prompt, how you review, and whether you treat AI as a junior engineer or as an oracle.

The best way to use AI for testing is to start with a good walking skeleton: a project that already has a working test suite, a sensible structure, and examples at the right layers of the test pyramid. For example, if your project already has a few clear unit tests, a small number of integration tests, and perhaps one end-to-end test, the AI can usually extend those patterns effectively. Without that foundation, it is much more likely to generate inconsistent, redundant, or low-value tests.

Establish the testing strategy first. Then use AI to extend it.

Using AI to draft initial test cases

AI is most helpful when you give it:

- The model or view code.
- A clear description of expected behavior.
- Constraints and edge cases you care about.
- The testing style you want, such as Django `TestCase` or `pytest`.

Example prompt:

```
Here is my Django model for Survey. Write unit tests that verify
validation rules, default values, and any constraints. Use Django TestCase
and avoid relying on primary key values.
```

The output will usually:

- Create a `TestCase` subclass.
- Instantiate a model instance.
- Call `full_clean()` to test validation.
- Assert defaults and field behavior.

This gives you a first draft. You still need to ask: are these the tests I would have written? Or did the AI simply test that objects can be saved?

Prompt: What are the research findings about AI-generated tests and their reliability?

Using AI to generate edge cases

AI is often better at brainstorming edge cases than at writing elegant production code. That makes it particularly useful for negative and boundary tests.

Example prompt:

```
Given this Django form for creating a survey, list edge cases I should
test. Focus on boundary values, invalid combinations, and security-related
inputs.
```

A good answer might suggest:

- Empty title
- Overly long title exceeding `max_length`
- Slug collision
- Invalid characters in slug
- Duplicate submission
- User not approved by admin
- Attempt to publish without required questions
- Extremely long text input

Once you see the list, you can either write the tests yourself or ask the AI to generate tests for specific edge cases, as in this example prompt:

```
Write a test that verifies creating a survey fails when the user is
not approved. Use self.client and assert the correct redirect or error
message.
```

This shifts the AI from hallucinating behavior to implementing a behavior you have already defined.

Using AI to explain failing tests

When a test fails in CI, pasting the failure output into an AI assistant can be surprisingly effective.

Example prompt:

```
Here is the traceback from my Django test run. Explain what is happening
and suggest likely causes. Do not rewrite my code, just diagnose.
```

The AI can often:

- Identify that a redirect is happening instead of a `200`.
- Notice that an object does not exist because setup data was incomplete.
- Spot a mismatch between URL names and `reverse()` usage.
- Recognize a validation error triggered by new model constraints.

This is especially helpful for beginners, who often struggle to interpret multi-layered Django tracebacks involving middleware, URL resolution, and database errors.

Using AI to refactor brittle tests

AI is also useful for cleaning up overly verbose or fragile tests.

Suppose you show it a test like this:

- Hardcoded URL paths.
- Repeated user creation boilerplate.
- Manual login logic.
- Repeated model setup across many tests.

Example prompt when using agent mode in a code editor:

```
Refactor these Django integration tests to reduce duplication. Extract
factories or helper methods. Avoid relying on hardcoded URLs.
```

The AI can:

- Replace literal paths with `reverse()`.
- Introduce a `make_user` helper.
- Use `force_login` instead of manual `POST` login in tests that do not test the login view.
- Consolidate repeated setup into `setUp` or `setUpTestData`.

AI is useful here because the task is mechanical: reduce duplication without changing behavior.

The risks of shallow AI-generated tests

The biggest danger is not incorrect syntax. It is false confidence.

Common problems with AI-generated tests are shown in *Table 12.3*:

Problem	**Explanation**
They only assert `status_code == 200`.	A page can return `200` and still be wrong.
They assert the presence of text that is unrelated to the business rule.	For example, asserting `Survey` appears on a page, rather than verifying that the correct survey title appears and the incorrect one does not.
They mirror the implementation rather than the test behavior.	If your view calls `Survey.objects.filter(is_published=True)`, an AI may generate a test that asserts the exact same query, rather than asserting that unpublished surveys are not visible.

Problem	Explanation
They ignore negative cases.	AI tends to produce happy-path tests unless you explicitly ask for failure modes.
They rely on brittle details.	Hardcoded primary keys, implicit ordering, or assumptions about IDs starting at 1.
They overfit to the current code.	If you later refactor internal logic but preserve behavior, shallow tests may break unnecessarily because they were testing implementation details.

Table 12.3: Common problems with AI-generated tests

Prompt: Please show examples of weak AI-generated tests and how to improve them.

How to review AI-generated tests critically

Treat AI output as a pull request from an enthusiastic but inexperienced developer. Review it with the same skepticism.

Ask these questions:

1. What behavior does this test prove?
2. Would this test fail if the business rule were broken?
3. Is this asserting meaningful outcomes, or just that the page loads?
4. Is it testing implementation details rather than observable behavior?
5. Does it cover both success and failure paths?
6. Does it rely on fragile assumptions about IDs or ordering?
7. Is setup minimal and clear?

If the test would still pass after you deliberately break the intended behavior, it is not a good test.

A useful discipline exercise is this:

1. Accept the AI-generated test.
2. Temporarily break the feature intentionally.
3. Run the test.
4. Confirm that it fails for the right reason.

If it does not fail, the test is weak.

When AI is most valuable in testing

AI is most helpful for:

- Generating edge-case lists
- Drafting repetitive scaffolding
- Suggesting additional assertions you may have missed
- Explaining complex tracebacks
- Refactoring test duplication

It is least reliable when:

- Interpreting ambiguous requirements
- Inferring security rules
- Guessing business logic
- Designing a test strategy from scratch without clear constraints

Tests are executable specifications. AI can help you write them faster, but it cannot decide what your system should guarantee.

AI-generated tests can look impressive, run green, and still assert nothing that matters.

Used carefully, AI helps. Used lazily, it gives you more code to review. The difference is not in the model. It is in you, the human reviewer.

Prompt: Please explain how to design prompts that generate higher-quality automated tests.

Practice, references, and resources

In this section, you will be tested on what you've learned in this chapter and be provided with useful links to reference materials and resources.

Check your understanding

Answer the following questions about the topics we covered in this chapter:

1. What is the purpose of the testing pyramid?
2. What makes a good unit test?

3. What does the Arrange–Act–Assert pattern describe?
4. Why are flaky tests considered worse than no tests?
5. What is the role of Django's `TestCase` class?
6. What is the difference between unit tests and integration tests in Django?
7. Why should UI (end-to-end) tests be used sparingly?
8. What is the main advantage of using factories over fixtures?
9. What does continuous integration (CI) do for a project?
10. What is the biggest risk of AI-generated tests?

Answers are found in the GitHub repository for this book at the following link:

`https://github.com/markjprice/web-dev-ai/blob/main/docs/Appendix-A.pdf`

Links

Martin Fowler – Test Pyramid. A modern articulation of the testing pyramid and tradeoffs between unit, integration, and UI tests. Essential conceptual grounding:

`https://martinfowler.com/articles/practical-test-pyramid.html`

Google Testing Blog – Testing on the Toilet and Testing Strategy. Practical guidance from large-scale engineering teams. Strong perspective on flakiness and CI discipline:

`https://testing.googleblog.com/`

Django Testing Overview. Django's testing documentation is unusually strong:

`https://docs.djangoproject.com/en/6.0/topics/testing/overview/`

`pytest` documentation: `https://docs.pytest.org/`

`pytest-django` documentation: `https://pytest-django.readthedocs.io/`

Playwright documentation: `https://playwright.dev/python/docs/intro`

Summary

In this chapter, you built a practical testing strategy for TallyApp. You learned why the testing pyramid favors many fast unit tests, fewer integration tests, and only a small number of browser-level end-to-end tests.

You learned the following:

- The practical difference between unit tests, integration tests, and end-to-end browser tests, and where each fits in a Django application
- How to write unit tests for Python functions, Django models, forms, and business logic using Django's TestCase and the built-in test database
- How to implement high-value end-to-end UI tests with Playwright to verify real user journeys such as login, create, edit, and delete flows
- How to manage test data using factories instead of brittle fixtures, and how to avoid fragile shared state and hidden coupling
- How continuous integration runs your tests automatically on every push or pull request, enforcing discipline and keeping the main branch stable
- How to use AI tools to draft tests, generate edge cases, explain failures, and refactor repetitive test code
- How to critically review AI-generated tests to avoid shallow assertions and false confidence, treating tests as executable specifications rather than decorative code

The most important idea is that tests are executable decisions about behavior. AI can help write the code, but you still have to decide what the application must guarantee.

In the next chapter, you will learn how to specify the TallyApp project and write a one-shot prompt to build the initial project.

Learn more on Discord

To join the Discord community for this book – where you can share feedback, ask questions to the author, and learn about new releases – follow this QR code:

`https://discord.gg/rdEsrVbbC`

13

Specifying and Building the Initial Project

A good software project starts before anyone writes code. It starts with understanding the goal. What are you building? Who is it for? What problem is it meant to solve? And just as important, what are you choosing not to build?

In this chapter, we move from isolated examples to the first working version of TallyApp. It is realistic enough to teach planning, structure, data modeling, permissions, forms, and testing, but still small enough to finish.

TallyApp is a survey platform. Approved users can create and publish surveys. Members of the public can complete them anonymously. Survey creators can review both individual responses and aggregated results. This type of website is familiar, practical, and large enough to force real design decisions without overwhelming you with unnecessary complexity or turning into a product you could spend a year building.

This chapter is about thinking before building. You will define the scope before implementation. You will set constraints before you let the tools lead you. You will use a lightweight, AI-assisted planning process to translate a structured project brief into a working Django application. Along the way, you will see how a clear brief reduces guessing, limits feature creep, and makes technical decisions less arbitrary.

Those questions matter more than the first lines of code. If you ask an AI assistant to build the project before you define the main decisions, you will probably get a pile of code that looks impressive but makes assumptions you did not choose. So, before building, you will write a short project brief. The brief describes the goal, users, features, non-goals, constraints, and definition of done.

This is a simplified version of how real projects work. You will build an extensible survey system with authentication, permissions, data modeling, testing, and a clean user interface.

By the end of this chapter, you will have defined a clear project brief for TallyApp, translated that brief into an actionable development plan, scaffolded a Django 6 project with appropriate apps and models, implemented core authentication and survey functionality, and established a small project that you can extend in the next chapter.

In this chapter, we will cover the following topics:

- Defining the scope and goals of the project
- Creating the TallyApp project
- Reviewing the AI-created project
- Using the Codex App for interactive development

Suggested chatbot prompts with example responses for this chapter can be found at the following link: `https://github.com/markjprice/web-dev-ai/blob/main/prompts/ch13-project/readme.md`

Defining the scope and goals of the project

Before installing anything or writing code, be explicit about what you are building and, just as importantly, what you are not. A clear scope makes technical decisions easier and keeps the project focused as it grows.

The project you will build is a web project called TallyApp. At a high level, TallyApp allows people to create surveys, share them publicly, collect responses, and analyze the results. This is similar to many real-world applications and gives us plenty of opportunities to explore backend logic, frontend presentation, data modeling, and visualization without drifting into unnecessary complexity.

User journeys

TallyApp supports three main user journeys.

User journey 1: Create and publish a survey

An authenticated user can create a survey with a title and description, add questions, and choose different question types such as multiple choice and free-form text answers. Once the survey is ready, it can be published and given a public link that can be shared with others. This part teaches data modelling, forms, validation, and permissions.

User journey 2: Take a survey

Anyone with the public link can view the survey and submit responses without needing an account. The interface is intentionally simple and task-focused. Respondents answer questions and submit the form, and their responses are stored reliably. This part of the project highlights URL design, templates, form handling, and protecting against invalid or duplicate submissions.

User journey 3: View and analyze results

The survey creator can view aggregated results, such as counts and percentages for multiple-choice questions, as well as individual responses for free-text questions. Results are presented using tables and charts, so patterns are easy to spot. This part of the application introduces reporting queries, basic analytics, and data visualization.

Project limits

It is also important to define boundaries. TallyApp is not a full enterprise survey platform. We are not building user billing, team collaboration, advanced permissions, or complex branching logic between questions. These omissions are deliberate. They keep the focus on learning how to design and build a complete web application rather than chasing more features or building something we can monetize.

Why a survey project?

The best way to learn web development is to work on real projects that you would use yourself or that at least spark an interest in you.

If you are a student or a professional developer who has no choice over the projects or technologies that you implement, how can you work on a real project that needs the technologies you are interested in learning about?

Attributes of a good learning project

To help us learn all the different technologies that web developers need to know these days, we need a project that:

- Genuinely needs a mix of technologies and skills.
- Is cool, fun, and practical, so it will stretch our skills both from an engineering perspective as well as creatively.
- Is as real as possible, and that we would use ourselves.

- Has already been implemented by others with public products that we can draw inspiration from, preferably with some open-source examples so we can review code implementations. Even if not, a product with feature screenshots would help us draft a **product requirements document** (PRD).

A PRD lists the features for a product to allow someone to understand what it should do. It does not say how it should do it. That would be defined in a functional specification that is more detailed.

- Has a small enough **minimum viable product (MVP)** that we have an achievable short-term goal to aim for.
- Has a large enough potential that it stretches to something much more complex long-term.

When you're struggling with a bug, you need to stay motivated. The best way to stay motivated is to work on a project that you will use yourself. Eat your own dog food, as they say.

Prompt: Please explain the difference between a product requirements document and a functional specification with examples from a Django web app.

Features of survey and polling tools

Personally, I have used survey and polling software to gain insight into my students and readers. For example, the most popular survey product is probably Google Forms, although there are dozens of alternatives, as shown in the following list:

- Google Forms: `https://workspace.google.com/forms/about/`
- Microsoft Forms: `https://www.microsoft.com/en-us/microsoft-365/online-surveys-polls-quizzes`
- Poll Everywhere: `https://www.polleverywhere.com/`
- TechRadar's best list: `https://www.techradar.com/best/best-survey-tools`

Most survey tools have a free tier, so you can try them out. We are looking at these products for inspiration, not trying to copy them.

After exploring the core features that define survey and polling tools, the next step is to look more closely at the building blocks of any survey: the different types of questions you can ask and how each one shapes the data you collect.

Question types

There are dozens of question types, from multiple choice to scale selection via matrix and freeform text, as shown in *Figure 13.1*:

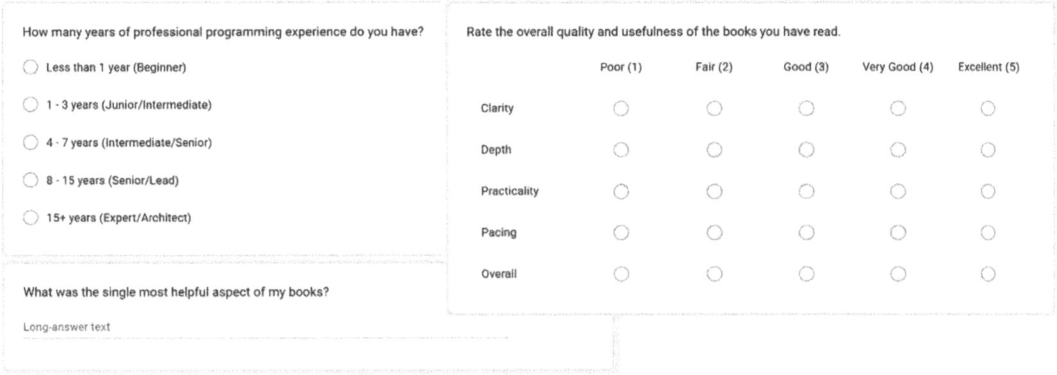

Figure 13.1: Types of survey questions in Google Forms

Some of these question types should be easy enough to implement, like the plain text response or selecting one option from many. Others are likely to be harder to implement once you think about all the potential possibilities.

Polling and quizzes

Survey tools have similar features to other tools, like live polling and quiz builders. They all need some way to build the survey, poll, and quiz, and some way to take it, and finally, ways to analyze the results.

I often deliver live training sessions and webinars. It is useful to ask the audience a bit about themselves, like where in the world they are, what their current experience is, and what they expect to get out of the session. The main difference between a survey and a live poll is the duration that question items are available to answer. The main difference with a quiz is the concept of a correct answer and scoring at the end.

Quizzes also share a lot of similarities. The main difference is the breadth of question item types. You can imagine that a quiz builder for learning mathematics or physics could have some quite elaborate components with complex implementations.

Analyzing the responses

Another major feature of survey tools is the ability to analyze the results using everything from basic charts to complex machine learning algorithms to spot unusual patterns.

What are the product requirements?

A product requirements document is the result of analyzing a business problem. It defines a set of suggested features that solve the problems that the software is supposed to address.

Minimal requirements overview

A minimal viable product for a survey tool would include:

- A website to take a survey anonymously
- A website to view the survey results
- Data storage for the survey question items and responses

Minimal website requirements

To take a survey, the solution should provide a website. This is to make the surveys accessible to as many people as possible. Every device has a web browser, so a website will have the broadest reach. We can also easily share surveys using hyperlinks.

The website should respond to a request to take a survey identified by a unique value, as shown in the following link:

```
https://www.tallyapp.net/123456
```

The website should allow anonymous visitors, present the question items to them, and record their responses. To keep it simple, there could be no restrictions on taking the survey multiple times. There would be no user registration required or authentication checks.

Prompt: What security risks exist in anonymous survey submissions? What other vulnerabilities should I watch for in a survey web application?

Minimal question item types

The website should support the following question types:

- Single line plain text
- Multi-line plain text
- Rating (1-10)
- Multiple choice (one selection). Shows radio buttons

Each item type should allow a plain text question.

Minimal data storage requirements

How should a survey and its responses be stored? It needs to be simple At first, it is tempting to think a document database would be simpler because a survey looks like a nested document: survey, questions, choices, responses. But TallyApp also needs permissions, reporting, filtering, and aggregation. For this book, a relational database is the better teaching choice because it makes those relationships explicit.

Minimal analysis app requirements

The analysis app should show a list of all surveys and their status, for example, if they are active, if they are complete, how many have taken them, the details of their answers, and summaries of the results. Numeric results should appear as tabular data as well as charts.

Prompt: What mistakes do beginners make when defining the scope for their first web app?

Ideas for extended requirements

One of my favorite aspects of a survey tool is that there are many areas where you can choose to extend the minimal product:

- A website that a visitor can register with and track the surveys they have completed
- Dozens of different question types
- Dozens of ways to analyze the results
- Multiple ways to store the questions and results, from a fully normalized database to document-based cloud storages
- Multiple ways to process the results and provide a service layer above the data stores

I have put more ideas for extending a survey project online. You can read them at the following link: `https://github.com/markjprice/web-dev-ai/blob/main/docs/extending-ideas.md`

Now let's create the TallyApp project.

Creating the TallyApp project

This section creates the first working version of TallyApp. It is deliberately small: one `Survey` model, plus create, edit, and delete screens restricted to logged-in users. It also includes register, log in, and log out. The UI uses clean, simple styling with plain CSS, and includes SVG assets for a logo and a *survey sketch* illustration used on editing pages.

Assumptions for this section:

- Django 6
- Python 3.14
- A local virtual environment
- SQLite database (we can swap to PostgreSQL later)

Practical AI-assisted project planning

Formal spec-driven development that you will learn about in the next chapter can be useful, but for a beginner-friendly process, it is often excessive. Full spec systems involve structured requirement documents, traceability, staged refinement loops, and sometimes dedicated command sets or multi-agent AI workflows. That is valuable in large teams building regulated or mission-critical systems. It is not necessary for learning how to design and build a clean Django application.

Instead, you can use a lightweight approach. The idea is to write a short, structured project brief in Markdown, then use a carefully written one-shot prompt to guide the AI.

Prompt: Show me an example of a bad one-shot prompt for TallyApp and how to improve it.

For example, before building TallyApp, create a file named `project-brief.md` with clearly defined sections such as:

- Goal
- Target users
- Core features
- Non-goals
- Technical constraints
- Definition of done

This forces you to define scope before writing code. Including a *Non-goals* section prevents accidental feature creep, which is one of the most common problems in both human-led and AI-assisted development.

Once the brief is written, you can prompt your AI assistant along the following lines:

```
I am building a Django 6 project called TallyApp. The attached Markdown
file describes the requirements. Please:
- Break the project into implementation phases.
- Propose Django models and relationships.
- Suggest URL patterns and app structure.
- Provide initial scaffolding for models, views, and templates.
- Restate the requirements in your own words before generating code and
identify any ambiguities.
```

That final instruction is important because it forces the AI to review the requirements before coding. This reduces hallucinations and makes assumptions visible. It also models a good professional habit to clarify before you implement.

This is why the brief matters. Codex or Claude Code can create Django files in seconds, but they will still make product decisions unless you make them first. Should TallyApp allow someone to submit the same survey twice? Should a survey become locked after it is published? Should results be stored for easy reporting later, or only for simple display now? Those are not coding questions. They are design decisions. Write them down before asking the AI to build anything. The better your brief, the better the code has a chance of being.

Prompt: Why does asking the AI to restate requirements before generating code reduce hallucinations? Please explain the psychology behind structured prompting and why it improves code quality.

Review the AI's work before running it

After receiving the output, you do not blindly paste it into your editor. You review it. Here's a checklist:

- Review the model relationships.
- Confirm the field data types.
- Look out for unnecessary complexity.
- Run database migrations and tests.

It is particularly important to look out for security issues:

- Every form template should include `{% csrf_token %}`
- Protected views should use `@login_required` or `LoginRequiredMixin`
- Watch out for raw SQL queries that could allow SQL injection attacks so the code should use the Django object-relational mapper (ORM) exclusively
- User input should never be rendered unescaped, for example `{{ variable }}` will automatically escape the output
- Make sure that `SECRET_KEY` is not hardcoded in any committed file
- Survey submission views should validate ownership and permissions

The AI produces a draft, but you remain the software engineer who applies human judgment to the generated code.

This approach captures many of the benefits of spec-driven thinking:

- Explicit scope
- Defined constraints
- Clear success criteria
- Reduced ambiguity
- Structured planning before coding

But it avoids the overhead of formal specification frameworks.

As your skills grow and your projects become more complex, you can adopt more formal spec-driven approaches, as you will see in the next chapter. But for building TallyApp and mastering web development fundamentals, a clear project brief plus a well-crafted prompt is the right balance of structure and simplicity.

Prompt: Compare one-shot prompting with iterative refinement prompting for building a Django project.

Choosing a Django version

Although Django 5.2 is the only active **Long-Term Support (LTS)** release (supported until April 2028), we will target Django 6.0 because the 6 versions will have an LTS version 6.2 starting in April 2027 during the expected lifetime of this book, as shown in *Figure 13.2* and at the following link: `https://www.djangoproject.com/download/`

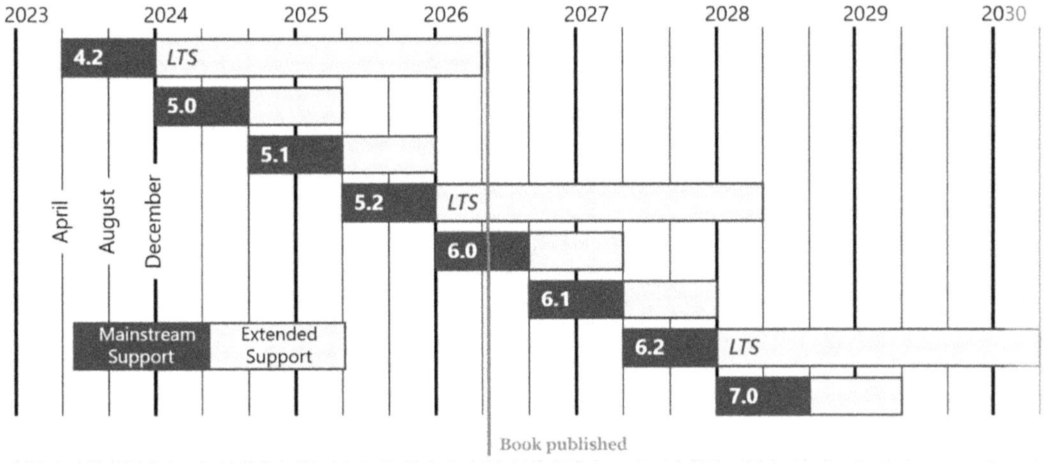

Release Series	Latest Release	End of mainstream support[1]	End of extended support[2]
4.2 LTS	4.2.28	December 4, 2023	April 2026
5.2 LTS	5.2.11	December 3, 2025	April 2028
6.0	6.0.2	August 2026	April 2027

Figure 13.2: Django supported releases

Now that we've chosen to target Django 6.0 or later, let's write the project brief.

AI project brief for TallyApp

Create a file named `project-brief.md` in the root of your project containing the following Markdown code:

This project brief can be downloaded from the following link: `https://github.com/markjprice/web-dev-ai/blob/main/Code/TallyProject/project-brief.md`

```
# TallyApp - Project Brief

## 1. Overview

### Project Goal
```

```
TallyApp is a web application that allows approved users to create surveys
and publish them publicly. Members of the public can take surveys without
registering. Survey creators can view both individual responses and
aggregated results.

### Problem It Solves

TallyApp allows individuals or organizations to quickly gather structured
feedback using multiple types of survey questions without building custom
software.

---

## 2. Target Users

### Survey Creators
- Must register for an account with a valid email address.
- Must be approved by an administrator before creating surveys.
- Can create, publish, and end surveys.
- Can view results (individual and aggregated).

### Survey Takers
- Do not need to register.
- Can submit responses anonymously.

### Home Page for Target Users
- Describes functionality of website.
- Two large buttons to:
    1. Create a Survey (Register or Log In)
    2. Take a Survey

---

## 3. Core Features (Version 1 Scope)

### Authentication & Authorization
- Define a custom group named SurveyCreators whose membership authorizes
```

```
survey creation functionality.
- Survey Creator registration.
- Admin approval required before users can create surveys; users are added
to SurveyCreators group when approved.
- Login and logout.
- Only members of SurveyCreators group can create surveys.

### Survey Creation
- Create or edit a survey with:
  - Title
  - Description
  - Start date
  - Optional end date
  - Publish status
  - "Show on homepage" flag (default: true)

- Unpublished surveys do not have results.
- Surveys cannot be edited after publishing.
- Surveys cannot be unpublished.
- Surveys can be ended early. This cannot be reversed.
- Surveys may be open-ended (no end date).
- Once ended a survey cannot be taken by users.
- Surveys consist of zero, one or more question items that can be added,
edited, or removed via the survey edit page.
- Surveys each have a unique public URL shown on the survey edit page as
soon as they are created.
- Published survey with start_date in future cannot be taken and show a
warning page with the start date shown.

### Question Types
Each survey can contain multiple questions of the following types:

1. Multiple choice - single answer
2. Multiple choice - multiple answers
3. Text input (free-form)
4. Matrix ratings with range of ratings e.g. 1 to 5 for one or more items

Question/choice authoring UI must be fully implemented.
```

```
- Dynamic form handling for mixed question types.

### Public Survey Access
- Public homepage lists published surveys (if "Show on homepage" is true) with a public URL to take the survey.
- Surveys support pagination on list views.
- Public users can submit responses.
- Surveys may display results "to date."

### Results
Survey creators can:
- View aggregated results.
- View individual responses.
- View responses even while survey is still open.
- View pie and bar charts for suitable results.
- View report of any duplicate submissions per email/IP/session.

### Graphics, styling and branding
- SVG assets for a logo and a survey sketch illustration used on editing pages.
- The UI uses CSS and SVG files to give TallyApp a subtle brand: gradient header or navbar, colorful logo SVG, light tinted background sections.

### Data Storage
- SQLite database.
- Relational model with clear foreign key relationships.

### Testing
- Basic unit tests for:
  - Model behavior
  - Permissions
  - Publishing rules
  - Survey response submission
- End-to-end tests using Playwright for:
  - Each user story.

---
```

```
## 4. Non-Goals (Out of Scope)

- No payments.
- No social authentication.
- No real-time updates (no WebSockets).
- No advanced analytics.
- No export to CSV.
- No REST API.
- No role system beyond admin approval and standard user.

---

## 5. User Stories

1. As a user, I want to register so that I can create surveys.
2. As an admin, I want to approve users before they create surveys.
3. As an approved user, I want to create and publish a survey.
4. As a survey creator, I want to end a survey early.
5. As a public visitor, I want to complete a survey without registering.
6. As a survey creator, I want to see both aggregated results and
individual responses.

---

## 6. Data Model (High-Level)

### User
- Extends Django's built-in User model.
- Has a custom group named SurveyCreators whose membership gives access to
create, edit and delete survey features.

### Survey
- Creator (ForeignKey to User)
- Title
- Description
- Start date
- Optional end date
- Published flag
```

```
- Show on homepage flag
- Created timestamp
- Ended early flag (optional)

### Question
- Survey (ForeignKey)
- Text
- Question type (single choice, multiple choice, text)
- Order field

### Choice
- Question (ForeignKey)
- Text
- Order field

### Response
- Survey (ForeignKey)
- Optional email identifier
- Submitted timestamp

### Answer
- Response (ForeignKey)
- Question (ForeignKey)
- Selected choice(s) (ManyToMany or intermediate model as appropriate)
- Text answer (for text questions)

---

## 7. Technical Constraints

- Python 3.14
- Django 6.x
- SQLite database
- Clean, modern, mobile-friendly responsive UI
- Server-rendered templates
- No JavaScript frameworks required

---
```

```
## 8. Security & Permissions

- Only approved users can create surveys.
- Only survey creators (and administrators) can view the results of their
own surveys.
- Public users can submit responses.
- Surveys cannot be modified after publishing.
- Only admins can approve users to create surveys.

---

## 9. Definition of Done

- Users can register and log in.
- Admin can approve users.
- Approved users can create and publish surveys.
- Public users can submit responses.
- Survey creators can view results.
- Pagination works.
- Basic unit tests pass.
- Application runs locally using SQLite without errors.

---

## 10. Future Enhancements (Not Version 1)

- CSV export
- Charts and visual analytics
- Survey scheduling automation
- Email invitations
- API endpoints
- Role-based permissions beyond basic approval
```

A blank project brief template can be downloaded from the following link: `https://github.com/markjprice/web-dev-ai/blob/main/Code/TallyProject/project-brief-template.md`

Reviewing the full steps

Before we ask an AI to generate code, it helps to see the full steps from idea to working application. The prompt is only one step in that process, as shown in *Figure 13.3*:

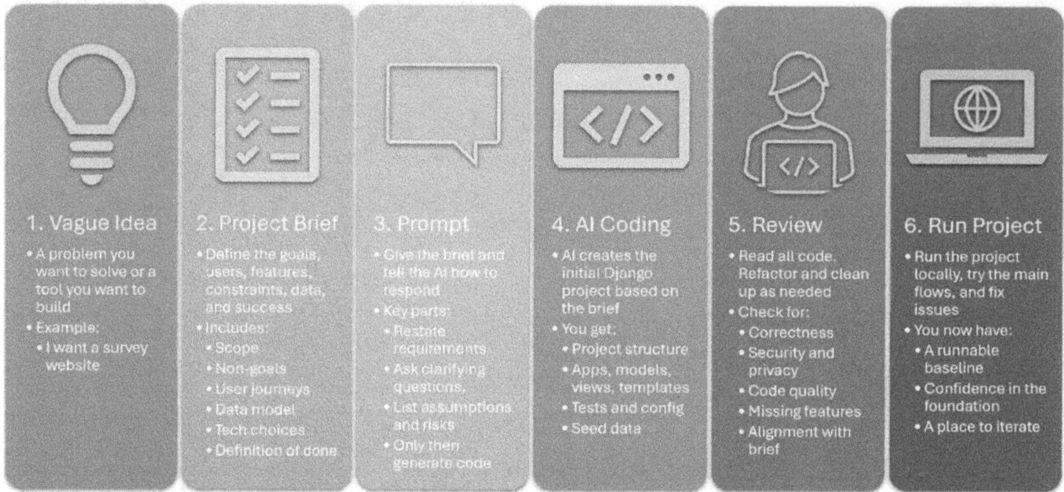

Figure 13.3: From idea to working project with AI assistance

A project brief guides the AI, but human review and iteration are what turn generated code into a usable application. Human judgment is the difference. AI writes code. You decide what should be built.

To summarize: Think clearly ⟶ Write a solid brief ⟶ Guide the AI ⟶ Review everything → Fix what is wrong ⟶ Iterate. Good results come from a good brief and careful review, not from a magic prompt.

Improving your project briefs

Before asking an AI to build a new project by following your project brief, it's good practice to ask your AI to review it. For example:

```
Read project-brief.md and act as a senior engineer reviewing a new project
before implementation.

Your job is to find everything that is missing, unclear, or risky.

Work in phases:
```

```
# Phase 1: Gap analysis
Identify missing or weak areas across:

- Requirements clarity and scope boundaries
- User journeys and edge cases
- Data model assumptions
- Permissions and security
- Validation and error handling
- Performance and scalability risks
- Testing strategy
- Operational concerns (deployment, configuration, secrets)

Do not suggest solutions yet. Just list gaps and ambiguities.

# Phase 2: Targeted interview
Ask me focused questions to resolve those gaps.
- Skip obvious or already well-defined areas
- Prioritize high-impact uncertainties
- Ask one topic at a time, not a long list
- Push for concrete decisions, not vague preferences

Continue until there are no meaningful unknowns left.

# Phase 3: Trade-offs and assumptions
For any remaining open decisions, propose 2–3 options with clear trade-
offs.

# Phase 4: Update the brief
Produce an improved version of the file named project-brief-ai-enhanced.md
that:
- Preserves all correct existing content
- Clarifies ambiguous sections
- Adds missing constraints and edge cases
- Makes assumptions explicit

Show the updated file in full. Do not remove sections unless clearly
incorrect.

Be concise, direct, and practical. Avoid generic advice.
```

This will enhance your project brief because doing a gap analysis stops the AI from immediately asking weak questions like: *Who are your users?* Instead, it has to think first, then ask.

This makes the AI slow down and inspect the brief before jumping into code. That is closer to how an experienced developer reviews a feature request before implementation.

If you prefer a more compact version of the prompt:

```
Read project-brief.md and review it like a senior engineer before
implementation.

1. List missing or unclear areas (requirements, edge cases, data model,
permissions, validation, performance, testing).
2. Interview me with focused questions to resolve the most important gaps.
Ask one topic at a time.
3. For unresolved decisions, propose options with trade-offs.
4. Produce an improved version of the brief, preserving correct content
and making assumptions explicit.

Skip obvious points. Be direct and practical.
```

Prompt: What are the risks of blindly trusting AI-generated scaffolding code?

Now let's look at the visual design of a website.

Guiding AI with a design.md

The project brief defines what the system should do. It only briefly defines how the system should look, feel, or behave from a user interface perspective. If you skip that step, the AI will make those decisions for you. Often, you need to be more specific, especially when creating a public website for an organization with a strong brand.

A simple way to avoid this is to create a second document alongside your project brief: `design.md`.

This file captures your design decisions in plain language so that both you and your AI assistant follow the same rules.

Why a separate design document?

Separating design from the project brief keeps concerns clear:

- The project brief defines behavior, features, and constraints
- The design document defines layout, interaction, and visual consistency

This mirrors how real projects are often structured. Product and engineering define behavior. Design defines how that behavior is presented.

For a learning project like TallyApp, pixel-perfect design is unnecessary. Consistency is enough.

What goes into design.md?

A useful `design.md` does not need to be long; it should answer a few practical questions:

1. **Layout and structure**: Describe the overall page structure:
    - Header with navigation (**Home**, **My Surveys**, **Login/Register**)
    - Main content area with a fixed-width container
    - Footer (optional)

    ```
    Pages use a simple layout: a top navigation bar, a centered content
    column, and minimal distractions. Avoid complex multi-column
    layouts.
    ```

2. **Navigation and flow**: Explain how users move through the app:
    - Where users land after login
    - How they access survey creation
    - How they return to previous pages

    ```
    After logging in, users are redirected to "My Surveys." Primary
    actions should be visible without scrolling.
    ```

3. **Forms and interaction patterns**: Define how forms behave:
    - Labels above inputs
    - Clear validation messages
    - Submit buttons at the bottom

    ```
    All forms use server-side validation with clear error messages shown
    above each field. Avoid JavaScript-heavy form logic.
    ```

4. **Styling approach**: Set constraints on styling:
   - Use plain CSS
   - Avoid heavy frameworks unless needed
   - Prefer simple color palette

   ```
   Use a minimal CSS approach. No CSS frameworks. Keep colors neutral
   with one accent color for actions.
   ```

5. **Components and reuse.** Encourage consistency:
   - Buttons look the same everywhere
   - Tables follow a consistent structure
   - Messages use a shared style

   ```
   Use reusable CSS classes for buttons, alerts, and tables. Do not
   redefine styles per page.
   ```

6. **Accessibility and clarity.** Even at a basic level:
   - Use semantic HTML
   - Ensure readable text
   - Avoid hidden interactions

   ```
   Prefer semantic HTML elements. Buttons should be <button>, not
   clickable <div> elements.
   ```

Using a design file with AI tools

Once you have both `project-brief.md` and `design.md`, you can include both in your prompt:

```
The project-brief.md file defines functionality. The design.md file
defines layout, styling, and interaction rules. Follow both.
```

This reduces a common problem where AI-generated code mixes styling approaches or creates inconsistent UI patterns.

Some tools are starting to formalize this idea. For example, Anthropic's Claude Design encourages separating design intent from implementation so the model can generate more consistent user interfaces.

Introducing Claude Design by Anthropic Labs: `https://www.anthropic.com/news/claude-design-anthropic-labs`

You do not need a special tool like Claude Design to apply the same idea. A simple `design.md` file achieves most of the benefit.

Good practice: Do not turn `design.md` into a full design system. For TallyApp, a single page of guidelines is enough. The purpose is not to design a production UI. The purpose is to stop the AI from inventing one.

The more clearly you define behavior and design upfront, the less time you spend fixing code later.

Now let's move into the step where most people jump too early: writing the prompt.

A one-shot prompt for applying your project brief

You can paste the following into your AI assistant after attaching or pasting the project brief:

```
I am building a Django 6 web application called TallyApp.

The project-brief.md file in the current directory contains the full
project brief. The design.md file defines layout, styling, and interaction
rules. Follow both.

Before generating any code:

1. Restate the project requirements in your own words.
2. Identify any ambiguities or design decisions that need clarification.
3. List assumptions you will make.
4. Highlight potential complexity risks.

Then:

5. Break the implementation into logical development phases.
6. Propose a Django app structure.
7. Design the data models with fields and relationships.
8. Suggest URL patterns.
9. Outline views and their responsibilities.
10. Define permission rules and enforcement strategy.
11. Explain how surveys become immutable after publishing.
12. Explain aggregation logic for multi-select answers.
```

```
Only after completing the above analysis, generate beginner-friendly
scaffolding code for:

- models.py
- basic forms
- views
- urls.py
- minimal templates
- static files including CSS and SVG
- basic unit tests
- E2E tests using Playwright

Keep the implementation simple.
Avoid advanced patterns unless clearly justified.
Explain why you choose particular modeling decisions, especially for
multiple-choice answers and text responses.
```

Prompt: How would you modify the TallyApp one-shot prompt to enforce stricter architectural constraints?

Since we are using this simple technique, a Markdown file for the spec and a single prompt, we don't need the interactivity of a tool like GitHub Copilot in a code editor or **integrated development environment** (**IDE**). We can use an AI **command-line interface** (**CLI**) like Codex or Claude Code. Since it is common for developers to switch between the two main competitors in this space due to model capability fluctuations and cost spikes, we will look at both CLI tools.

One-shot prompt using OpenAI Codex

Let's see how to do this using OpenAI Codex:

1. In your `web-dev-ai` folder, create a folder named `TallyProject`.
2. In the `TallyProject` folder, in a terminal, start OpenAI Codex:

   ```
   codex
   ```

3. Select **Yes, continue** and press *Enter*, as shown in *Figure 13.4*:

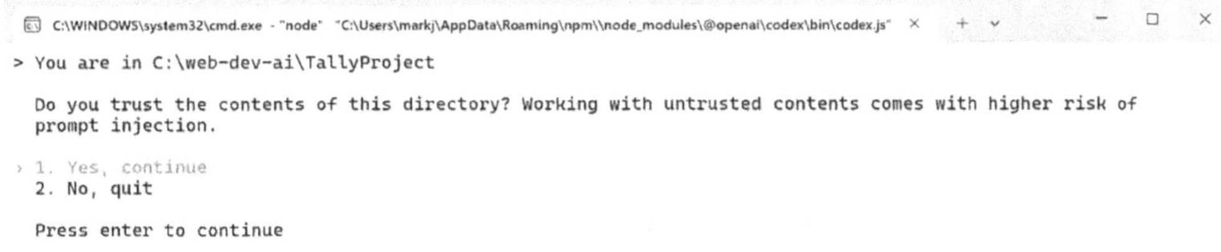

Figure 13.4: Trusting the project directory in OpenAI Codex

4. Note that you can change the model by typing `/model`. I have set my model to the latest at the time of writing (`gpt-5.5-codex`) with `medium` thinking time. Note the context window has 100% left (this will drop as Codex works on our project), as shown in *Figure 13.5*:

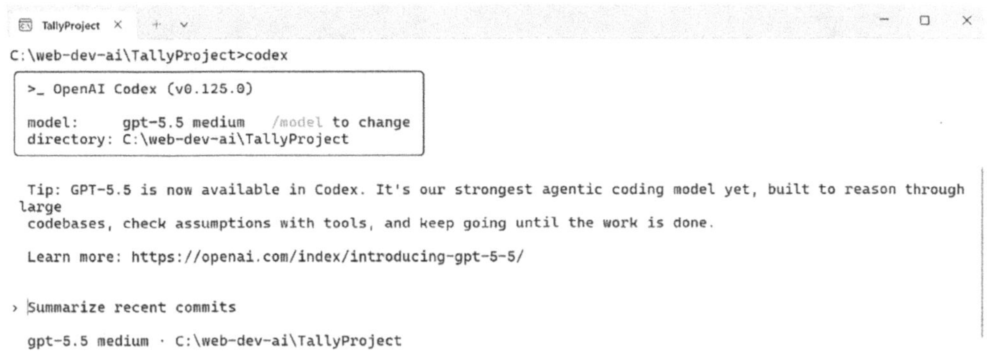

Figure 13.5: OpenAI Codex configured to use the gpt-5.5-codex model with medium thinking

5. Copy and paste the one-shot prompt into the prompt.
6. When you see the following response, press *Enter* to accept:

```
[Pasted Content 1207 chars]
```

7. Note that Codex will start creating files and running checks. Let it work, but read what it says as it goes:

```
• I have the brief parsed and there's no existing code yet, so I'll scaffold a single Django app (surveys)
  with beginner-friendly function-based views, model-level safeguards, and templates/static/test files.
  Plan: (1) create models and forms that encode publish immutability + mixed-question responses, (2) wire
  views/URLs/templates for creator and public flows, (3) add CSS/SVG assets, (4) add unit + Playwright E2E
```

```
  scaffolds and summarize decisions.

• I'm starting file creation now, beginning with models.py and
forms.py so the permission, immutability, and
  answer-shape rules are encoded before wiring the UI.

...

• I'm now wiring the core application flow (views.py, urls.py,
templates, tests) around the models/forms
  already created, keeping everything function-based and explicit
for beginner readability.

...

• Core Python files are in place; next I'm adding minimal templates
and static assets so the scaffold is
  runnable and visually aligned with the brief (Pico baseline +
small brand overrides + SVGs).

...

• I'm writing tests now (unit + Playwright scaffold) and then I'll
run a quick syntax/import check; I also
  need one small template fix ({% load static %}) before validation.

...
```

8. You will occasionally be prompted to accept some work:

```
Would you like to run the following command?

  $ Get-ChildItem -Recurse -Directory -Filter __pycache__ | Remove-
Item -Recurse -Force

' 1. Yes, proceed (y)
  2. Yes, and don't ask again for commands that start with `Get-
```

```
ChildItem -Recurse -Directory -Filter
     __pycache__ | Remove-Item -Recurse -Force` (p)
  3. No, and tell Codex what to do differently (esc)

  Press enter to confirm or esc to cancel
```

9. You will have to explicitly tell it to complete other steps, as shown in *Figure 13.6*:

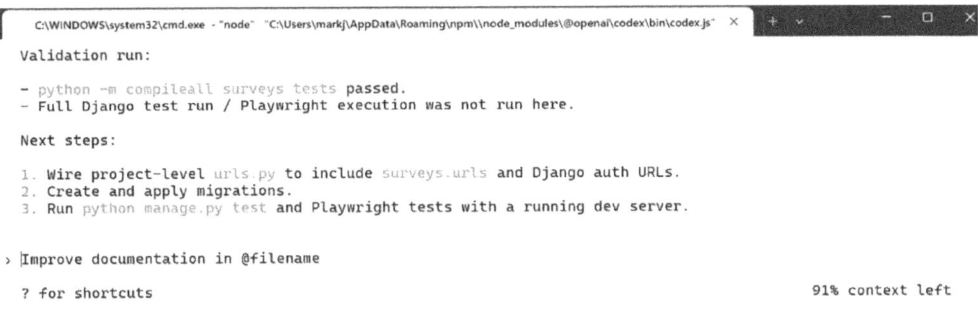

Figure 13.6: Codex showing next steps

10. Tell it to continue with the next steps:

```
Please complete those three next steps.
```

11. If any step requires additional permissions, you will be prompted to agree:

```
Would you like to run the following command?

  Reason: Do you want to allow running Playwright tests with
unrestricted npm/network access so E2E
  dependencies can be resolved?

  $ npx playwright test

' 1. Yes, proceed (y)
  2. Yes, and don't ask again for commands that start with `npx
playwright test` (p)
  3. No, and tell Codex what to do differently (esc)

  Press enter to confirm or esc to cancel
```

12. Run the database migrations:

```
python manage.py migrate
```

13. Create a superuser:

```
python manage.py createsuperuser
```

14. Start the website:

```
python manage.py runserver
```

15. Start your preferred browser and navigate to the website hosted at `http://127.0.0.1:8000`, as shown in *Figure 13.7*:

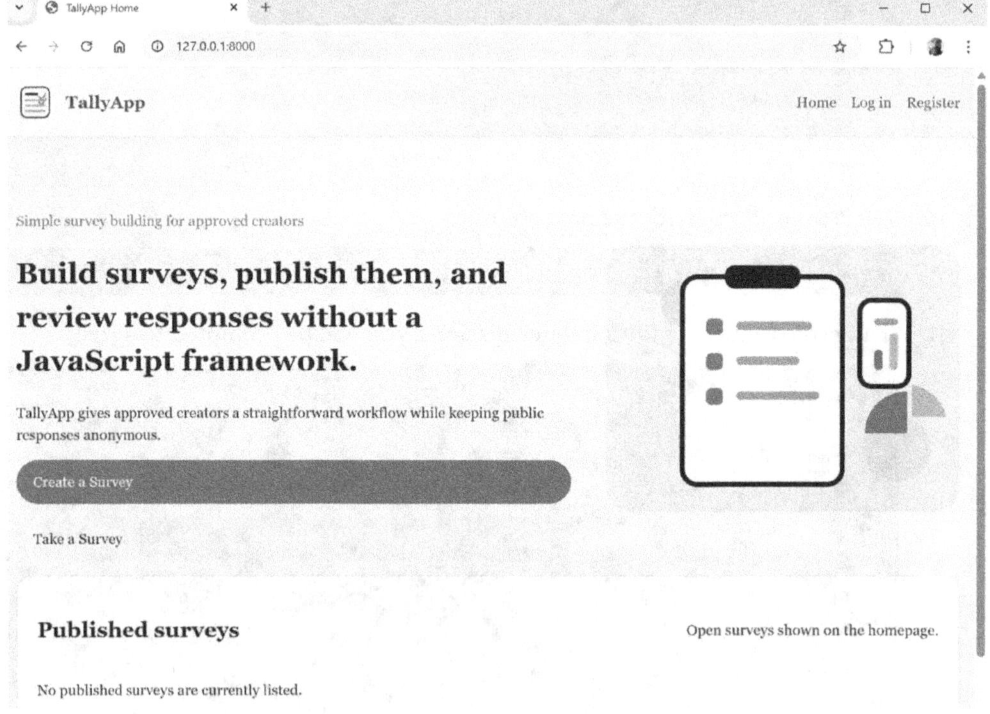

Figure 13.7: The final website

Now we can try out the website's functionality.

Complete the following tasks using the website:

1. Registering as a new user
2. Logging in as a new user

3. Logging out
4. Logging in as the superuser that you created
5. Approving a user as a survey creator
6. Logging in as the new user and creating a survey
7. Adding a question to a survey
8. Publishing the survey
9. Logging out and then taking a survey anonymously

If you want to build the project using Claude Code, you can follow the steps in the next section, or skip it to the next section where you will review the code written by your AI sidekick.

One-shot prompt using Claude Code

Let's see how to do this using Claude Code:

1. In your `web-dev-ai` folder, create a folder named `TallyProject-Claude`.
2. In the `TallyProject-Claude` folder, in a terminal, start Claude Code:

```
claude
```

3. Select **Yes, continue** and press *Enter*, as shown in *Figure 13.8*:

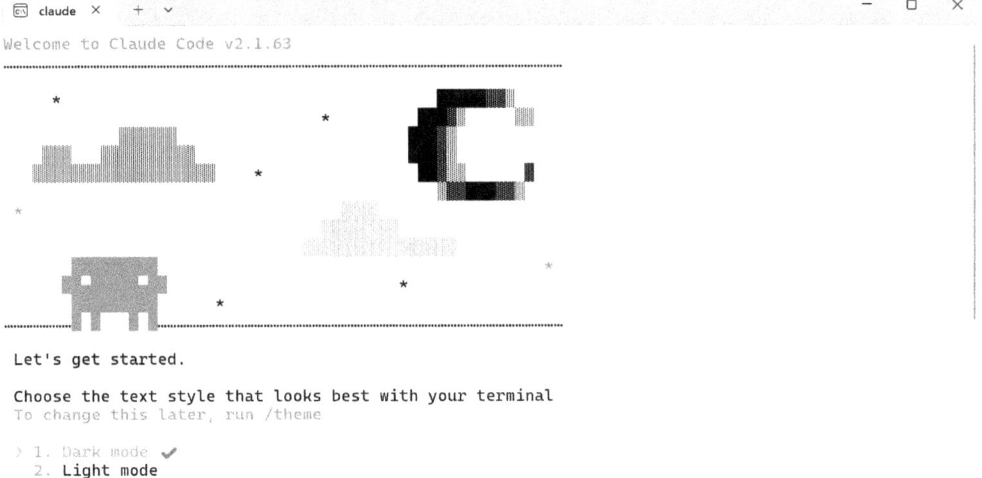

Figure 13.8: Choosing a text style in Claude Code

4. Choose how you want to pay for the service, as shown in *Figure 13.9*:

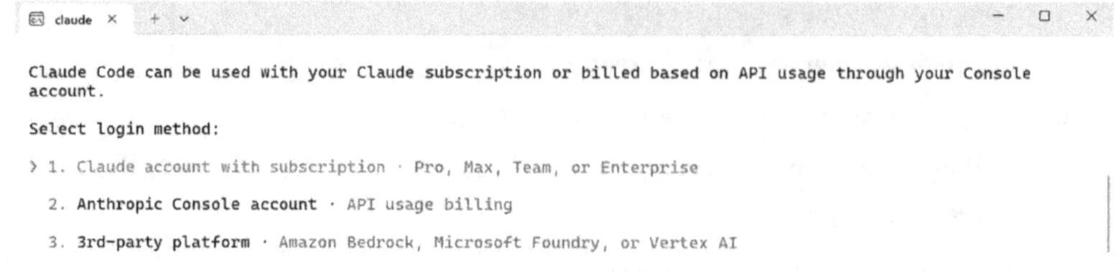

Figure 13.9: Choosing your billing in Claude Code

5. Copy and paste the one-shot prompt into the prompt.
6. When you see the following response, press *Enter* to accept:

```
[Pasted Content 1207 chars]
```

7. Note that Claude Code starts working. Be patient and watch it work.

Prompt: Please explain how AI tools like Codex and Claude Code differ in workflow philosophy.

Avoiding AI usage limits

AI tools often impose usage limits, especially on free or lower-tier plans. A few habits reduce wasted prompts and help you avoid running out halfway through a task.

First, be deliberate with your prompts. Instead of sending multiple small, vague requests, combine them into a single, clear and well-structured prompt. This reduces back-and-forth and gets you closer to a useful result in one response. (In a distributed architecture, this principle is known as: *Be chunky, not chatty*.)

Second, iterate efficiently. Rather than restarting from scratch, refine previous prompts or ask the AI to improve its own answer. Building on existing context uses fewer requests and produces better results.

Third, avoid unnecessary experimentation when working on real tasks. It's easy to burn through usage by trying many variations. When you have a clear goal, stay focused and direct.

Finally, switch tools or modes when appropriate. Some platforms offer different models, free tiers, or fallback options. Knowing when to use a lighter model versus a more advanced one can help you stay within limits.

The key idea is to treat AI interactions as a resource. Thoughtful, well-structured prompts not only improve quality but also help you stay productive without running into caps.

With the initial project now generated, the next step is to step back and examine what the AI has actually produced before making any changes.

Reviewing the AI-created project

Use VS Code to open the root project folder, as shown in *Figure 13.10*:

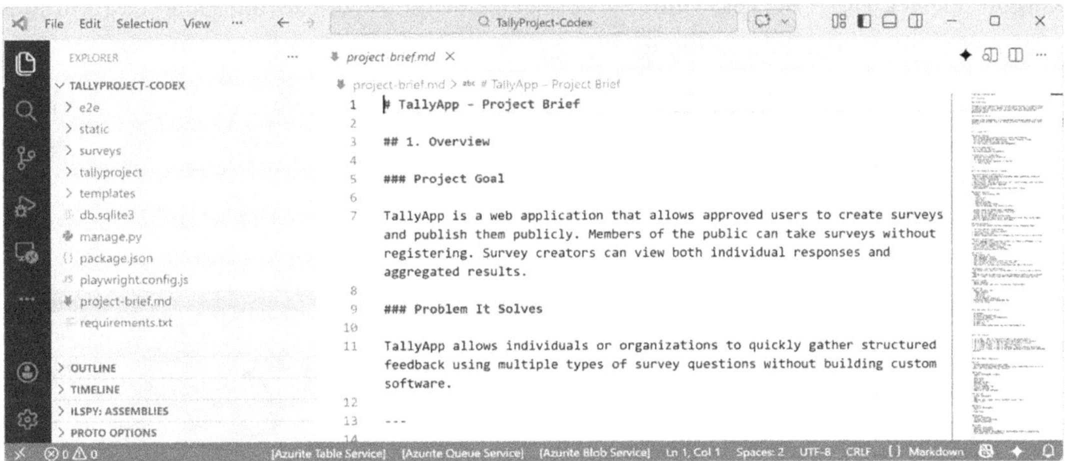

Figure 13.10: VS Code showing the TallyApp project folder

Browse the folder structure and note the following:

- `tallyproject/` is the project that holds global configuration like `settings.py` and `urls.py`
- `surveys/` is an app that contains actual functionality like models, views, and business logic
- `templates/` is for shared layouts and base templates
- `static/` is for CSS, JS, and images used across the site
- `db.sqlite3` is the SQLite database in the project root

- `manage.py` is the main way you interact with the project, for example:

```
python manage.py runserver
python manage.py migrate
```

- `requirements.txt` defines the Python dependencies and allows the project to be recreated with: `pip install -r requirements.txt`
- `package.json`, `playwright.config.js`, and `e2e` are JavaScript-based end-to-end web UI configuration and folders, with `app.spec.js` containing the actual Playwright tests

Asking the AI to explain its work

For each file, review its contents and understand what it is doing. If you don't understand, ask your AI sidekick, either by typing into the Copilot chat window, or copying some code into your preferred browser-based chat interface.

For example, I asked Gemini to explain the Playwright tests, as shown in *Figure 13.11* and its response can be read at the following link: `https://github.com/markjprice/web-dev-ai/blob/main/docs/gemini-tests.md`

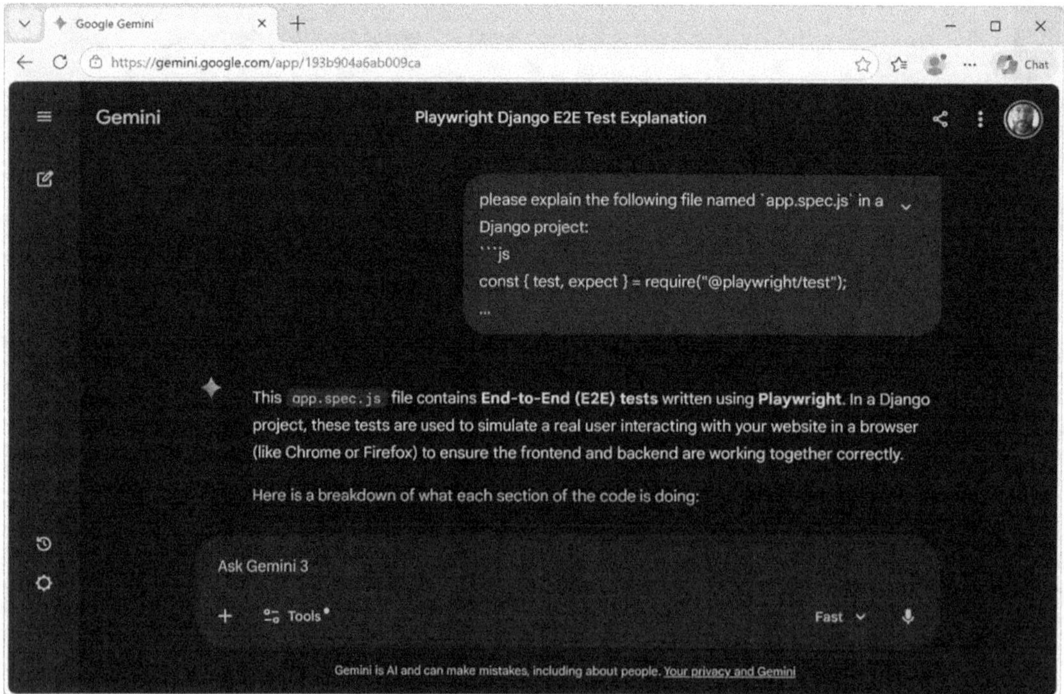

Figure 13.11: Asking Gemini to explain Playwright tests

Prompt: How do environment variables improve E2E test reliability? Please explain how `test.skip()` works in Playwright and when it should be used.

I also used Copilot in VS Code, as shown in *Figure 13.12*:

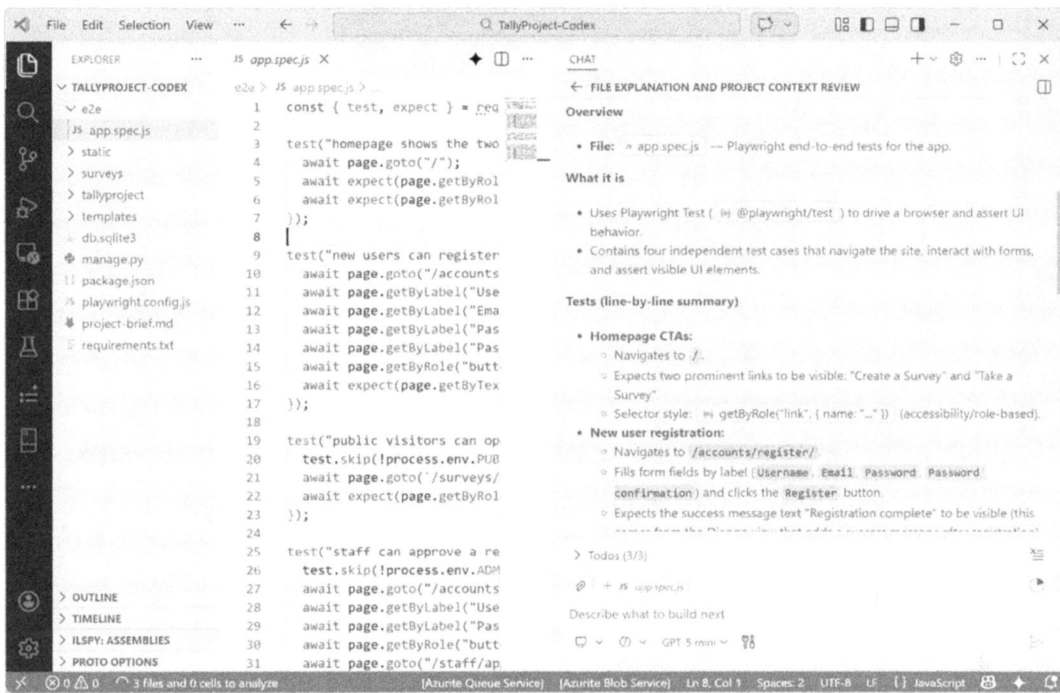

Figure 13.12: Asking Copilot in VS Code to explain Playwright tests

And note that Copilot provides direct links to Django files to explain the tests, as shown in *Figure 13.13*:

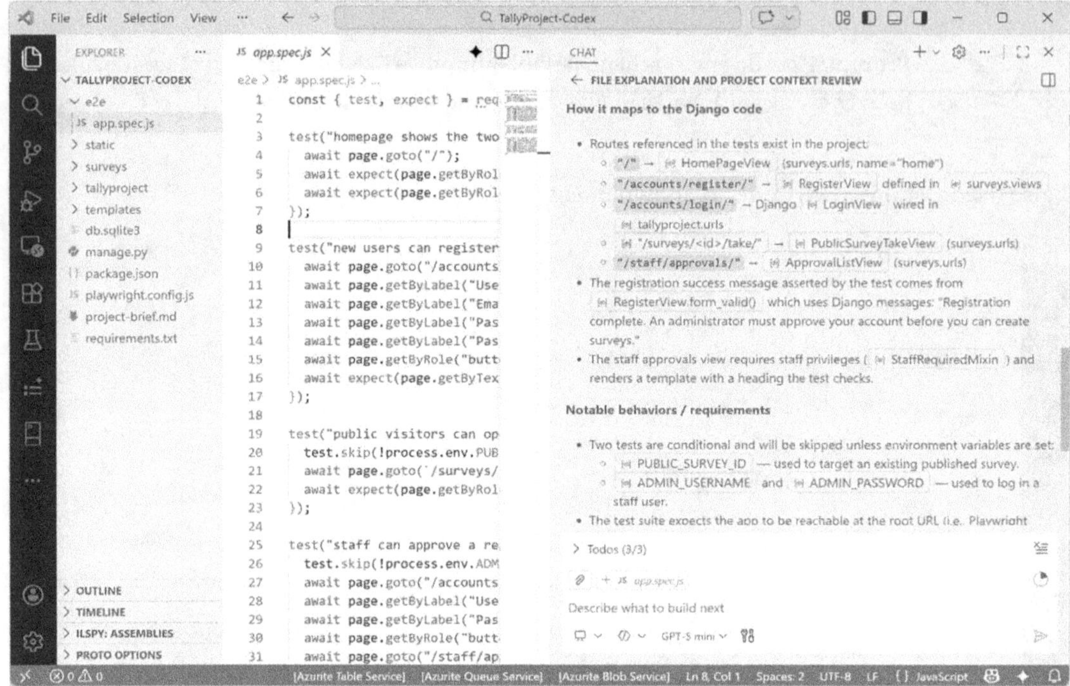

Figure 13.13: Copilot with links to Django code files tested by Playwright

Reviewing stylesheets and graphics

In the `static` folder, open the files in the `css` and `img` folders:

- `site.css` contains CSS styles for the whole website. Do you understand how the rules work? Go back to *Chapter 3, CSS – Styling Your Web Pages*, and review what you learned. Ask your AI sidekick to explain anything that you don't understand.

Prompt: How should I structure prompts when asking AI to explain unfamiliar code?

- `logo.svg` defines an icon for the website. When you open this file with VS Code, by default it will show the image, but you can right-click the file and choose **Open With...** to open it with a **Text Editor** side-by-side, as shown in *Figure 13.14*:

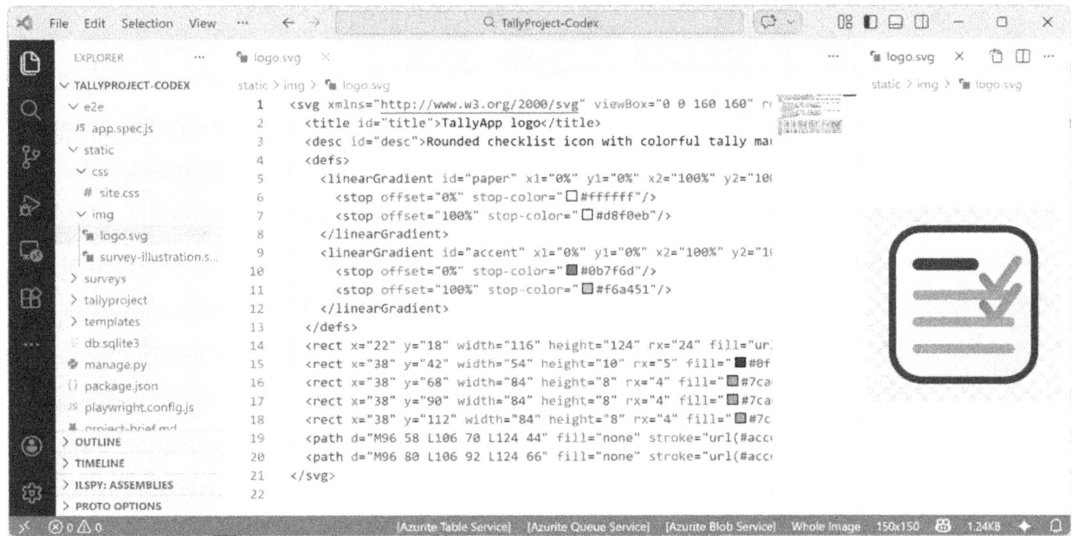

Figure 13.14: An SVG file open in image viewer and text viewer

- `surveys` folder is an app feature for managing surveys, where `urls.py` defines all the URL patterns:

```
urlpatterns = [
    path("", HomePageView.as_view(), name="home"),
    path("creator/", SurveyListView.as_view(), name="survey_list"),
    path("creator/surveys/new/", SurveyCreateView.as_view(),
name="survey_create"),
    path("creator/surveys/<int:pk>/", SurveyDetailView.as_view(),
name="survey_detail"),
    path("creator/surveys/<int:pk>/edit/", SurveyUpdateView.as_
view(), name="survey_update"),
    path("creator/surveys/<int:pk>/publish/", SurveyPublishView.
as_view(), name="survey_publish"),
    path("creator/surveys/<int:pk>/clone/", SurveyCloneView.as_
view(), name="survey_clone"),
    path("creator/surveys/<int:pk>/end/", SurveyEndView.as_view(),
name="survey_end"),
    path("creator/surveys/<int:pk>/results/", SurveyResultsView.
as_view(), name="survey_results"),
    path("creator/surveys/<int:pk>/responses/", SurveyResponsesView.
as_view(), name="survey_responses"),
    path("creator/surveys/<int:survey_pk>/questions/new/",
```

```
QuestionCreateView.as_view(), name="question_create"),
    path("creator/questions/<int:pk>/edit/", QuestionUpdateView.
as_view(), name="question_update"),
    path("creator/questions/<int:pk>/delete/", QuestionDeleteView.
as_view(), name="question_delete"),
    path("staff/approvals/", ApprovalListView.as_view(),
name="approval_list"),
    path("staff/approvals/<int:user_pk>/approve/", ApproveUserView.
as_view(), name="approve_user"),
    path("surveys/<int:pk>/take/", PublicSurveyTakeView.as_view(),
name="take_survey"),
]
```

- `templates` folder contains the HTML for the website:
    - `base.html` contains the template for all web pages. Review it and make sure that you understand all the HTML tags used in it. Ask your AI sidekick if there is anything that you do not understand.

```
{% load static %}
<!DOCTYPE html>
<html lang="en">
<head>
    <meta charset="utf-8">
    <meta name="viewport" content="width=device-width, initial-
scale=1">
    <title>{% block title %}TallyApp{% endblock %}</title>
    <link rel="stylesheet" href="{% static 'css/site.css' %}">
</head>
<body>
    <header class="site-header">
        <div class="wrap nav-shell">
            <a href="{% url 'home' %}" class="brand">
                <img src="{% static 'img/logo.svg' %}" alt="TallyApp
logo" class="brand-logo">
                <span>TallyApp</span>
            </a>
            <nav class="site-nav">
                <a href="{% url 'home' %}">Home</a>
```

```
                {% if request.user.is_authenticated %}
                    <a href="{% url 'survey_list' %}">My Surveys</a>
                    {% if request.user.is_staff %}
                        <a href="{% url 'approval_list'
%}">Approvals</a>
                    {% endif %}
                    <form method="post" action="{% url 'logout' %}">
                        {% csrf_token %}
                        <button type="submit" class="link-
button">Log out</button>
                    </form>
                {% else %}
                    <a href="{% url 'login' %}">Log in</a>
                    <a href="{% url 'register' %}">Register</a>
                {% endif %}
            </nav>
        </div>
    </header>
    <main class="wrap page-shell">
        {% if messages %}
            <ul class="messages">
                {% for message in messages %}
                    <li class="message {{ message.tags }}">{{
message }}</li>
                {% endfor %}
            </ul>
        {% endif %}
        {% block content %}{% endblock %}
    </main>
</body>
</html>
```

- `registration` folder contains two web pages for logging in and registering.
- `surveys` folder contains web pages for approving creators, managing surveys, and so on.

Prompt: If TallyApp grew to 1 million responses per survey, what architectural changes would be needed? How would I evolve TallyApp into a multi-tenant SaaS product?

The most interesting design decision in TallyApp

If there is one part of TallyApp where database design really matters, it is how survey answers are modeled. Everything else in the system is fairly straightforward.

The difficulty comes from one simple fact: not all questions are the same.

TallyApp currently supports three question types:

- Multiple choice, single answer
- Multiple choice, multiple answers
- Free-form text

At first glance, it might seem tempting to store everything in one flexible `Answer` model with a few nullable fields. For example:

- A `selected_choice` field for single-answer questions
- A `selected_choices` many-to-many field for multi-answer questions
- A `text_value` field for text questions

That works, but it forces you to think carefully about data integrity. You must ensure:

- Single-answer questions never store multiple choices
- Multiple-answer questions can store multiple choices
- Text questions never reference a choice
- Choice-based questions never store free-form text in place of a choice

The model must encode rules that reflect the business logic of your application.

This is where the relational thinking that you learned about in *Chapter 7, SQL – Managing Data,* becomes interesting. One common and clean approach is:

- A `Response` model representing one user's submission
- An `Answer` model representing a response to a single question
- A foreign key from `Answer` to `Question`
- A foreign key from `Answer` to `Response`
- A nullable foreign key to `Choice` for single-answer questions
- A many-to-many relationship to `Choice` for multi-answer questions
- A text field for text responses

Then you enforce rules at the form or model validation level based on `question.question_type`.

This design teaches three useful ideas:

1. First, it shows how relational databases model variability. Instead of creating three separate tables for three question types, you create one flexible structure and constrain it logically.
2. Second, it teaches normalization. A survey response is not a flat blob of JSON. It is a structured set of answers, each tied to a question. That makes aggregation, filtering, and reporting dramatically easier.
3. Third, it highlights future extensibility. If you later decide to add rating-scale questions or numeric inputs, your model already has a clear extension point.

There is also an important architectural lesson here. The data model defines what is possible. If you or your AI model answers carelessly, you will struggle later when implementing features like aggregated counts, filtering by question, validation rules, export features, and performance optimization.

In fact, many real-world systems that outgrow themselves do so because their early data models were too simplistic.

Prompt: Please explain in depth why modeling survey answers is the most important architectural decision in TallyApp. Show three different database designs for handling single-choice, multi-choice, and text answers, and compare trade-offs. How would a senior engineer review AI-generated Django models?

Lastly in this chapter, we will look at Codex's GUI app, released in February 2026 for Mac and March 2026 for Windows.

Using the Codex App for interactive development

So far in this chapter, you have used a one-shot prompt to generate a complete project scaffold. That technique is efficient but it is still mostly text-based. You describe what you want, the AI generates code, and then you review it.

The **Codex App** introduces a different way of working. Instead of only describing the system in text, you can interact with a running application and give feedback directly against what you see.

This is especially useful once TallyApp is running locally and you move from *build the structure* to *refine the behavior and interface.*

You can learn more about the Codex App at the official documentation: `https://developers.openai.com/codex/app`

What the Codex App adds

The Codex App is a graphical interface for working with AI-assisted development. It sits alongside your editor and local development environment and allows you to:

- Chat with a model about your codebase
- Run commands and inspect outputs
- Work with files and generated code
- Interact with a live preview of your application

The key difference from earlier workflows in this chapter is that the AI is no longer working from descriptions alone. It can be guided using the actual running UI.

This reduces a common problem with AI-assisted development: vague instructions such as *make this look better* or *fix the layout*, which often produce inconsistent results.

Browser-based interaction for UI work

One of the most useful features of the Codex App is its ability to interact directly with a running web application through a built-in browser panel. This turns web UI work into something much closer to pointing at the screen and saying, "Change this."

Once your Django development server is running, you can connect the Codex App to your local site:

1. Start a chat with your preferred model
2. Start your Django dev server (for example, `python manage.py runserver`)
3. Open the browser panel in the Codex App
4. Navigate to your local site (for example, `http://127.0.0.1:8000`)
5. Use the browser tools to inspect and annotate the UI

The browser panel includes features such as:

- Taking screenshots of the current page
- Adding annotations to specific UI elements
- Sending those annotated screenshots directly into the chat

When you click on a button, form, or layout element and attach a comment, the model receives both the visual context (screenshot) and your instruction tied to a specific part of the UI.

For example:

```
This button is too small and blends into the background. Make it more
prominent and consistent with the primary action style.
```

This is far more precise than describing the problem in text alone.

In earlier sections, you saw how important it is to define behavior and structure before generating code. UI refinement has a similar challenge: describing visual issues in words is often imprecise.

The browser interaction feature improves this in three ways:

1. **Shared context**: The AI sees exactly what you see, instead of inferring layout from templates and CSS.
2. **Targeted changes**: Feedback is attached to a specific element, not a vague description of a page.
3. **Faster iteration**: You can quickly try changes, review them, and refine again without rewriting long prompts.

This saves you from describing layout problems from memory.

Example steps with TallyApp

Once your TallyApp project is running locally, you might use these steps:

1. Open the homepage in the Codex browser panel.
2. Click the **Create a Survey** button.
3. Add an annotation, as shown in *Figure 13.15*:

    ```
    This should be the primary action. Increase contrast and add more
    padding.
    ```

4. Let Codex propose changes to your CSS and templates.
5. Review the changes before applying them.

6. Reload and repeat.

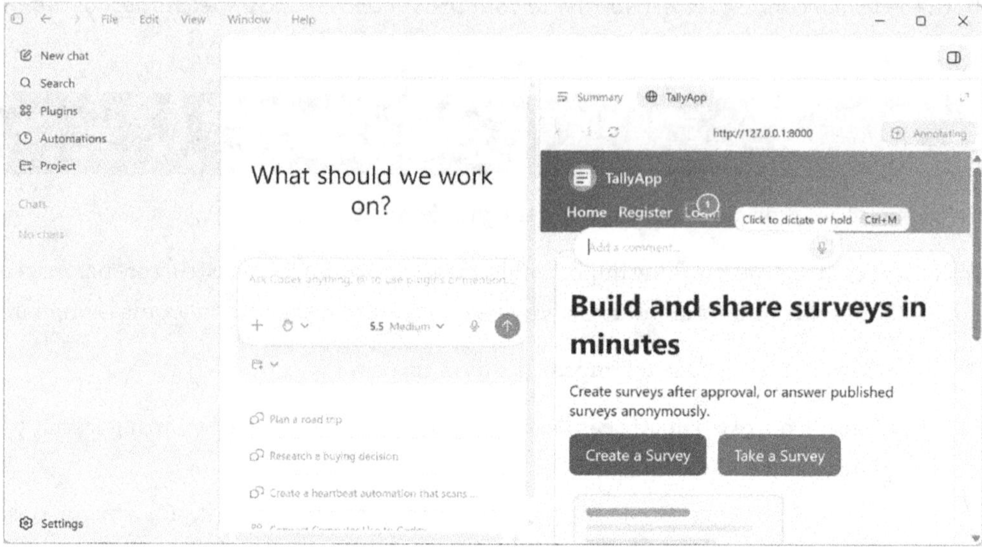

Figure 13.15: Annotating the TallyApp home page with a comment using Codex App

You can follow a similar process for form layouts, navigation structure, error messages, spacing, and alignment issues.

Limitations and good habits

This feature is useful, but it should still be used with the same discipline as the rest of your workflow.

Keep these points in mind:

- Do not accept UI changes blindly. Always review generated CSS and templates.
- Keep your `design.md` in sync with changes, so you do not drift into inconsistent styles.
- Avoid making many small, uncoordinated tweaks. Prefer grouped, intentional changes.
- Use this for refinement, not initial architecture.

Also note that interaction is currently element-by-element. If you want to change multiple components consistently, you should describe the pattern, not just individual elements.

Use the Codex browser interaction when:

- The application is already running
- You are refining layout, styling, or usability
- You can point to specific issues on the screen

Do not rely on it for:

- Initial project design
- Data modeling decisions
- Security or permission logic

Those still belong in your project brief and design thinking earlier in the chapter.

Practice, references, and resources

In this section, you will be tested on what you've learned in this chapter and be provided with useful links to reference materials and resources.

Check your understanding

1. Why is defining the scope before writing code important?
2. What is the purpose of a project brief in this chapter's workflow?
3. What is the difference between a **Product Requirements Document** (**PRD**) and a functional specification?
4. What are the three main user journeys in TallyApp?
5. Why are non-goals explicitly defined in the project brief?
6. What is a **Minimal Viable Product** (**MVP**), and why is it important here?
7. Why is a lightweight AI-assisted planning approach used instead of full spec-driven development?
8. Why should you ask the AI to restate requirements before generating code?
9. Why is reviewing AI-generated code an essential step?
10. Why is modeling survey answers considered the most important design decision in TallyApp?
11. You start building features before defining the scope and later feel overwhelmed. What went wrong?
12. Your AI generates a large, complex Django project with features you did not ask for. Why did this happen?
13. You ask an AI to generate code immediately without clarifying requirements first. What risk does this introduce?
14. You define a feature but do not specify that it is out of scope for MVP. What is the likely outcome?

15. You build survey answers as a single unstructured JSON blob. What problems might you face later?

Answers are found in the GitHub repository for this book at the following link:

`https://github.com/markjprice/web-dev-ai/blob/main/docs/Appendix-A.pdf`

Links

OpenAI Codex Documentation: `https://platform.openai.com/docs`

OpenAI CLI Tools Overview: `https://platform.openai.com/docs/guides/tools`

Claude Code Overview: `https://www.anthropic.com/claude-code`

Anthropic Claude Documentation: `https://docs.anthropic.com/`

Anthropic Console: `https://console.anthropic.com/`

Anthropic Claude certification community-created information: `https://github.com/paullarionov/claude-certified-architect/blob/main/guide_en.MD`

Copilot CLI course: `https://github.com/github/copilot-cli-for-beginners`

Summary

In this chapter, you moved from learning separate web development skills to building the first version of TallyApp.

You learned the following:

- Defined a clear scope for a real-world web application, including explicit goals, target users, and non-goals to prevent feature creep
- Understood how to translate high-level product ideas into a structured PRD-style brief
- Identified core user journeys: creating surveys, taking surveys anonymously, and reviewing aggregated and individual results
- Distinguished between MVP scope and extended features, and understood why deliberate constraints improve learning and execution
- Practiced lightweight AI-assisted project planning using a structured Markdown project brief and used a one-shot prompt that forces an AI assistant to restate requirements, identify ambiguities, list assumptions, and highlight risks

- Scaffolded a Django 6 project using AI assistance via OpenAI Codex CLI and Claude Code.
- Inspected generated Django project structure, including apps, templates, static assets, and URL configurations, and used AI tools (Gemini, Copilot) to explain and explore unfamiliar code
- Reviewed static files, base templates, URL patterns, and Django template logic to deepen understanding of server-rendered applications

In the next chapter, you will learn about spec-driven development for adding new features to an existing project like TallyApp.

Get this book's PDF version and more

Scan the QR code (or go to packtpub.com/unlock). Search for this book by name, confirm the edition, and then follow the steps on the page.

Note: Keep your invoice handy. Purchases made directly from Packt don't require an invoice.

14

Adding Project Features Using Spec-Driven Development

In the previous chapter, you used a large prompt and a product requirements document to generate the first working version of TallyApp. That approach demonstrated how AI tools can scaffold an entire project quickly. However, real software projects rarely stop after the first implementation. New features are added, behavior is refined, and edge cases are discovered as the system evolves.

For the next feature, do not start by asking the AI to "add something useful." Start by writing down the feature. Say what it should do, who can use it, what should happen when it fails, and how you will check that it works.

This style of working is often called **Spec-Driven Development**. The specification becomes the agreed description of the feature, and the code becomes its implementation. When AI coding assistants are involved, this discipline is particularly important because they tend to fill in missing details by inventing behavior based on unvalidated assumptions. A clear specification leaves fewer gaps for the AI to fill and gives the AI less room to invent behavior you did not ask for.

In this chapter, you will apply this approach to the existing TallyApp Django project. Instead of generating a brand new application, you will extend the current codebase by designing and implementing a small but realistic feature.

By the end of this chapter, you will have written a structured feature specification, used an AI coding assistant to implement it inside an existing Django project, and verified that the implementation satisfies clearly defined acceptance criteria.

In this chapter, we will cover the following topics:

- Spec-driven development
- Using Spec Kit to structure specifications
- Adding a URL shortener feature to TallyApp
- Ideas for extending TallyApp

Suggested chatbot prompts with example responses for this chapter can be found at the following link: `https://github.com/markjprice/web-dev-ai/blob/main/prompts/ch14-spec/readme.md`

Spec-driven development

In Spec-Driven Development, you begin with a written description of what the system should do. Instead of starting with code and hoping the design sorts itself out, write down the feature first: the problem, what is in scope, what is out of scope, and what must be true when the work is finished. Then you implement.

This idea is not new. Good engineers have always written requirements, user stories, and acceptance criteria. What is new is the presence of AI coding assistants. Tools such as GitHub Copilot, OpenAI Codex, and Claude Code can generate large amounts of code quickly. They can scaffold projects, refactor modules, and even propose architectural changes. That can help, but it also introduces risk. Without a clear specification, AI tools will confidently implement assumptions you did not intend. They will fill in gaps you did not know existed. They will optimize for plausibility rather than correctness. That is dangerous because plausible code is often harder to spot than obviously broken code.

Spec-Driven Development brings discipline to AI-assisted coding. The specification becomes the reference document. It defines the scope of the feature, the non-goals, the data model, the behavior of the user interface, and the error conditions. The AI is not asked to *build an app*. It is asked to satisfy explicit acceptance criteria. Each requirement must be traceable to code. Each behavior must be verifiable.

This is why the specification matters. Codex or Claude Code can write a lot of Django code, but it will not know whether a feature is finished unless you define finished. For the URL shortener, that means writing rules such as: who can create links, how codes are generated, what happens for an unknown code, and which tests must pass.

Prompt: Why do AI coding assistants tend to make incorrect assumptions when specifications are incomplete? Describe the risks of vague requirements when using AI coding assistants.

Tests turn a specification from a document into something enforceable. A spec that cannot be verified is simply documentation. A spec backed by automated tests becomes enforceable. In a Python web project, this usually means mapping acceptance criteria to unit tests with `pytest` and, where appropriate, browser-level tests. The test suite becomes the referee. When AI generates code, the tests decide whether that code is acceptable. If it fails, the implementation is wrong, regardless of how polished it looks.

What a good specification contains

A useful web feature spec should be short, but not vague. For TallyApp, a typical feature spec might include the following sections:

- **Goal:** A short paragraph describing what this feature enables. Example: *Allow authenticated users to create, edit, and delete surveys.*
- **Non-Goals:** List what you are deliberately not building. Example: *No public survey sharing in this iteration.*

Prompt: Please explain why "non-goals" are important in software specifications and give examples from real-world projects.

- **User Stories:** Write the main interactions from the user's perspective:
  - As a logged-in user, I can create a new survey
  - As a logged-in user, I can edit the title of an existing survey
  - As a logged-in user, I can delete my own survey

- **Acceptance Criteria**: These are precise, testable conditions. Acceptance criteria should be written so they can become tests without reinterpretation. Avoid vague statements like *the UI should be clean*. They should be observable facts:
    - When a valid survey form is submitted, the survey is saved in the database
    - When an invalid form is submitted, validation errors are displayed
    - A user cannot edit another user's survey
    - After deletion, the survey no longer appears in the list view

Prompt: Please show me some examples of poorly written acceptance criteria and how to rewrite them into clear, testable requirements.

- **Data model changes**: Define fields, relationships, and constraints. For example:
    - Survey: `id` (primary key), `owner` (foreign key to user), `title` (string, max length 200), `created_at` (timestamp). If a field has constraints, write them down. If a relationship has cascading behavior, specify it.
- **Error handling and edge cases**:
    - What happens if a user attempts to edit a survey that does not exist?
    - What happens if required data is missing?
    - What HTTP status codes should be returned for forbidden access?

Prompt: Please give examples of edge cases developers often forget when writing specifications. Please explain how to identify hidden assumptions in a software specification.

- **Verification commands**: Write down how you will check the feature later:
    - Run unit tests
    - Run integration tests
    - Start the development server and confirm behavior manually if needed

Prompt: Please explain how spec-driven development differs from **test-driven development (TDD)** and **behavior-driven development (BDD)**. Include a side-by-side comparison of spec-driven development, TDD, and BDD, including strengths and weaknesses of each approach.

Tools for Spec-Driven Development

There is not one standard way to do spec-driven work. Different teams structure their specifications differently, use different terminology, and automate different parts of the process. Some developers prefer lightweight Markdown documents stored alongside the source code. Others use structured templates that resemble traditional requirements documents. Some processes emphasize automated tests as the executable form of the specification, while others focus on planning artifacts that guide AI tools through staged implementation.

A small ecosystem of tools has begun to appear to support this style of development. One example is **Spec Kit**, an open-source project from GitHub that provides templates and commands for writing specifications, generating implementation plans, and breaking features into tasks. Another tool is **OpenSpec**, which aims to standardize machine-readable software specifications that can be interpreted by AI agents. Some developers are also experimenting with specification-first workflows built into AI coding environments such as Cursor, Continue, and Claude Code, where structured prompts and planning steps guide the model through feature development.

Warning! Because GitHub Spec Kit, OpenAI Codex, Anthropic Claude Code, and other AI tools are evolving quickly, treat exact prompts and small setup details as likely to drift over time.

Now that you've been introduced to some spec-driven development tools, let's look in more detail at one practical option.

Using Spec Kit to structure specifications

One practical tool that supports Spec-Driven Development is **Spec Kit**, an open-source project published by GitHub. It provides a structured workflow and templates for writing specifications, planning implementations, and coordinating AI-assisted development.

Spec Kit is not a framework or library. Instead, it is a lightweight system that helps developers organize their specifications so that both humans and AI assistants can understand them clearly.

The Spec Kit workflow

Spec Kit organizes development into a sequence of stages. Each stage produces a document that clarifies the system before moving on to the next step.

A typical workflow looks like this:

1. Project principles, also called the constitution

A document that defines the high-level rules and philosophy of the project. These might include conventions such as coding standards, architectural constraints, or testing requirements.

Example questions addressed in this stage:

- Should the system prioritize simplicity or extensibility?
- What testing practices are required?
- What technologies are allowed or forbidden?

This document sets the rules the AI should follow when it changes the project.

2. Feature specification

The specification describes the feature that will be built.

It typically includes:

- The goal of the feature
- Non-goals and constraints
- User stories
- Acceptance criteria
- Data model changes
- Error handling and edge cases

This is the stage where you define exactly what the feature must do.

3. Implementation plan

Once the specification is approved, the next document describes how the feature will be implemented.

The plan usually includes:

- Architecture changes

- New modules or services
- Database migrations
- Testing strategy
- Deployment considerations

AI tools are particularly useful in this stage because they can suggest implementation approaches based on the specification.

4. Task breakdown

The implementation plan is then converted into a list of concrete development tasks.

For example:

- Create ShortLink Django model
- Add redirect view
- Create form for generating short links
- Write unit tests

These tasks can be executed sequentially, often with AI assistance.

5. Implementation

Only after the specification, plan, and tasks are defined does the actual coding begin.

At this stage, the AI assistant is given clear instructions and constraints. Instead of inventing behavior, it simply implements what has already been described.

Prompt: Please explain how tools like Spec Kit and OpenSpec help prevent AI coding assistants from introducing unintended features.

Structure helps, but it has a cost. Before using Spec Kit for every change, it is worth knowing when a lighter approach is enough.

When is Spec Kit overkill?

Spec Kit can help keep AI-generated work on track, but it can be too much for small changes. You are trading some coding time for more planning and review time.

Let's understand when Spec Kit is likely overkill or unnecessary.

When a lighter prompt is enough

If you are in the exploratory phase, for example, prototyping a UI or testing a basic concept, Spec Kit's rigid flow (`/constitution` → `/specify` → `/plan` → `/tasks`) can slow you down.

Small projects often benefit from vibe coding, where you give a high-level prompt and iterate on the code directly. Setting up a Constitution for a weekend hobby project is overkill.

High context-to-code ratio

Spec Kit can generate hundreds of lines of Markdown for a single feature. For a small project (like a basic URL shortener with two views), the documentation can be longer than the code. The exception is when learning because a smaller project is easier to understand.

The risk is that you spend more time reading and correcting the AI's plans and specs than it would take to simply write the code or review a single-shot AI output.

Minor tweaks and one-off bug fixes

If you're just changing a button color, updating a regex, or fixing a simple logic error, just prompt your AI coding tool directly. Running a full `/specify` and `/plan` cycle for a 5-line change is inefficient and adds unnecessary files to your repository.

Token cost and speed

Each step in the Spec Kit workflow involves significant back-and-forth with the LLM, consuming thousands of tokens and taking several minutes of processing time.

For a small project, you want the result in 10 seconds. Spec Kit makes you wait for the AI to think through the architecture, which is often unnecessary for well-trodden paths (like a basic Django app).

Birgitta Böckeler's taxonomy

Spec-Driven Development is best understood as a spectrum. At one end, you might write a short prompt that captures intent. At the other, you might produce a full specification with acceptance criteria and validation steps. *Birgitta Böckeler* describes spec-driven work as a spectrum rather than a single rigid process.

Birgitta Böckeler's taxonomy of Spec-Driven Development is not a formal standard like a published specification. It is a practical way of describing how it shows up at different levels of rigor when working with AI.

Lightweight

You still think before you code, but the spec is minimal. It might be a short paragraph, a checklist, or even a well-crafted prompt. Typical characteristics:

- A brief description of the goal
- Maybe a couple of constraints or edge cases
- Often embedded directly in the AI prompt
- Little or no separate artifact

Use this for small features, bug fixes, and exploratory work where you are iterating quickly. The key idea is that you are guiding the AI, but not formalizing everything. This still counts as SDD because you describe the change before coding.

Structured

This is closer to what we will see in this chapter. Typical characteristics:

- A clearly written specification
- Defined behavior and user interactions
- Data model considerations
- Acceptance criteria or test cases
- Separate from the implementation step

Use this for medium-sized features, changes with multiple moving parts, and where correctness matters more than speed. The key idea is that the spec becomes a reference point.

Formal or end-to-end

This is the full version, often associated with frameworks like Spec Kit. Typical characteristics:

- Multiple structured artifacts (spec, plan, tasks, validation steps)
- Traceability from requirements to implementation
- Iterative refinement of the spec itself
- Strong alignment between humans and AI over longer workflows

Use this for large features or systems, high-risk or high-complexity work, and team environments where coordination matters. The key idea is that the specification drives the entire lifecycle, not just the initial prompt.

You can learn more about Birgitta Böckeler and watch some of her conference talks at the following link: `https://gotopia.tech/experts/1305/birgitta-boeckeler`

Alternatives to Spec Kit

Structured AI development workflows are not one-size-fits-all. Heavier frameworks, such as Spec Kit, can work well when you need strong guardrails, explicit planning, and traceable handoffs across a larger or riskier project.

For smaller features or solo work, a lighter approach such as **OpenSpec** may be a better fit because it preserves the habit of writing down intent without turning the process into a document factory. The goal is to give the AI enough clear context to produce better code.

For readers exploring spec-driven AI workflows, there is a spectrum. Spec Kit is more structured and stage-oriented. OpenSpec is lighter and less stage-oriented. Beginners should be wary of any method that produces lots of planning documents without clearly improving implementation, testing, or review.

You can learn more about OpenSpec as an alternative to Spec Kit at the following link: `https://github.com/Fission-AI/OpenSpec`

Spec Kit commands

Spec Kit includes helper scripts that automate parts of this process. After initializing the project, you can run commands that guide the development process:

1. `/speckit.constitution` – define project principles
2. `/speckit.specify` – create a baseline specification
3. `/speckit.plan` – generate an implementation plan
4. `/speckit.tasks` – break the plan into tasks
5. `/speckit.implement` – execute the implementation

Additional commands help refine the specification or check consistency between artifacts.

Warning! GitHub's current Spec Kit README notes that most agents expose /`speckit.*` slash commands, but Codex CLI in skills mode uses `$speckit-*` instead. Skills mode is behind a feature flag, so if you didn't explicitly enable it, you're not using it. To enable skills mode, you should have started Codex like this: `codex --enable skills`. If you didn't pass that flag (or configure it in your setup), then skills are off.

These commands do not generate production code themselves. Instead, they structure the conversation with the AI so that each step builds on the previous one.

AI coding tools are good at filling gaps. That is useful when the gap is obvious, but risky when the missing detail is a product decision. If the spec does not say whether short links are public, private, expiring, or trackable, the tool may choose for you.

Spec Kit reduces this problem by making the specification explicit and structured. Because the specification, plan, and tasks all live in the repository, they can be reviewed, versioned, and improved over time.

For teams experimenting with AI-assisted development, this approach provides a useful balance: the speed of AI-generated code combined with the discipline of traditional software engineering.

Install the Specify CLI

For this chapter, install the GitHub SpecKit **Specify CLI** with `uv`, as shown in the following command:

```
uv tool install specify-cli --from git+https://github.com/github/spec-kit.
git
```

`uv` is a fast Python package manager from Astral. We use it here because Spec Kit's installation from a Git repository works more reliably with `uv tool install`. If you prefer, you can also clone the repository and install with `pip install -e`.

If `uv` is not installed yet, install `uv` first, then run the command above. You can install `uv` from the following link: `https://docs.astral.sh/uv/getting-started/installation/`.

After installation, confirm that the Specify CLI and its dependencies are available:

```
specify check
```

With the process in place, let's apply it to a small feature that fits naturally into a survey application.

Adding a URL shortener feature to TallyApp

A useful way to learn how to do Spec-Driven Development is to add a feature to an existing system. In this section, you will add a URL shortener to TallyApp.

Why a URL shortener?

A URL shortener might seem unrelated to surveys. But survey creators often want to share their survey links in emails, presentations, or printed materials. A long URL such as `https://tallyapp.example.com/surveys/8e5a4c39-2f4d-4b9e-bbfa-2c10a96d21fd/take/` is inconvenient to share. A short link such as `https://tallyapp.example.com/s/abc123` is easier to remember and distribute.

The goal of this feature is to allow survey creators to generate a short link that redirects to their survey.

Prompt: Please explain how URL shorteners work internally. Describe the algorithms commonly used to generate short URL codes and compare random code generation with hash-based URL shortening.

Writing the feature specification

Before writing any code, define the behavior of the feature.

A typical feature specification includes the following sections.

Goal

Allow authenticated users to create short URLs that redirect to longer links inside TallyApp.

The most common use case will be generating short links for surveys.

Non-Goals

To keep the feature small and focused, we explicitly exclude several capabilities:

- No analytics tracking in the first version
- No expiration dates for links
- No custom aliases (users cannot choose the short code)
- Only authenticated users can create short links

These restrictions prevent the feature from expanding into a full commercial-style service.

User stories

Describe the interactions from the user's perspective:

- As a logged-in user, I can create a short link for a survey URL
- As a logged-in user, I can view a list of the short links I created
- As any visitor, I can visit a short URL and be redirected to the target page

Figure 14.1 shows what happens when someone visits a short link like `/s/abc123`:

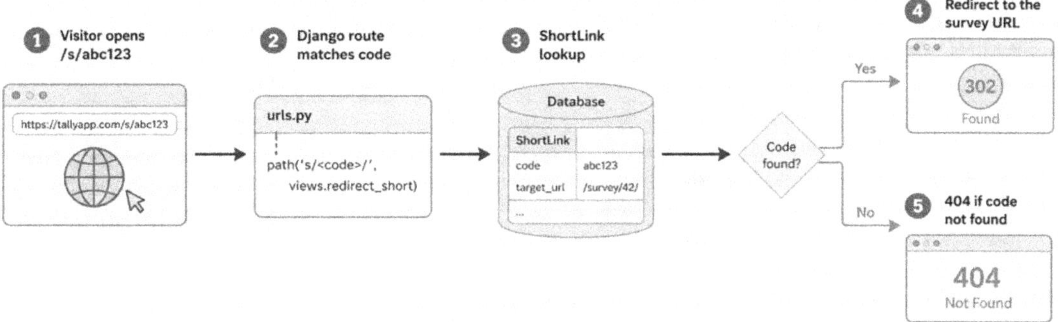

Figure 14.1: URL shortener request flow

The URL shortener request flow:

1. The browser requests the short URL from your site.
2. Django matches the `/s/<code>/` pattern and calls the view `redirect_short`.
3. The view looks up the code in the ShortLink table.
4. Django returns an HTTP 302 redirect to the original survey URL for the browser to request.
5. Django returns a `404 Not Found` response if the code does not exist.

Acceptance criteria

These criteria define observable behavior:

- When a valid URL is submitted, a short code is generated
- The short code is unique
- Visiting `/s/<code>` redirects to the stored target URL

- A user can only see short links they created
- If a short code does not exist, a `404 Not Found` response is returned

These conditions are specific enough to be turned into automated tests.

Data model

Add a new Django model named `ShortLink`. Its fields are shown in *Table 14.1*:

Field	Type	Description
`id`	primary key	internal identifier
`owner`	`ForeignKey(User)`	creator of the short link
`target_url`	`URLField`	the original URL
`code`	`CharField(10)`	unique short identifier
`created_at`	`DateTimeField`	timestamp

Table 14.1: Fields for the ShortLink model

Model constraints are:

- code values must be unique and have a maximum of ten characters
- code values should be randomly generated from URL-safe characters

Verification steps

The feature can be verified by:

1. Running unit tests
2. Visiting a generated short link in the browser
3. Confirming the redirect behavior

Ask the AI to generate an implementation plan

Once the specification exists, you can give it to an AI coding assistant and ask for a plan.

Example prompt:

```
You are helping extend an existing Django project named TallyApp.

Implement the following feature according to the specification below.
```

```
[Paste spec]

First generate an implementation plan. Do not write code yet.
```

A good plan should suggest steps like these:

1. Create a new Django app named `shortlinks`
2. Define the `ShortLink` model
3. Add migrations
4. Create views for:
    - creating short links
    - redirecting short links
5. Add URL routes
6. Create a basic HTML form
7. Add unit tests

Review the plan before asking the AI to implement it.

Plan and implement the URL shortener feature using Specify and Codex

First, a note on the moving parts. GitHub's Spec Kit and its Specify CLI can initialize an existing project, install templates, and generate agent-specific command files. Spec Kit supports Codex CLI as a first-class agent option, and it specifically documents `specify init . --ai codex` and `specify init --here --ai codex` for existing projects.

OpenAI's current Codex setup flow is: sign in, select the folder or repository you want Codex to work on, and then start a task.

Let's use SpecKit with Codex step-by-step:

1. Start in the root folder of your existing Django project, the same folder that contains `manage.py` and your app folders.
2. Initialize Spec Kit in the current folder instead of creating a new folder:

    ```
    specify init . --ai codex
    ```

Spec Kit also supports `--script ps` if you want PowerShell-oriented scripts, which is a sensible choice on Windows: `specify init . --ai codex --script ps`

3. You will be warned about existing files, as shown in *Figure 14.2*:

Figure 14.2: Initializing Specify in a project folder

4. Press *Y* to continue.
5. Select if you want Bash/shell or PowerShell scripts. Either will work on Windows as long as you have installed **Windows Subsystem for Linux 2 (WSL2)**. On Mac or Linux, select Bash.

Prompt: Please explain how GitHub Spec Kit works internally and what files it generates in a project repository. Show the directory structure created by Spec Kit and explain the purpose of each file.

6. Set an environment variable for Codex configuration for this project:

```
setx CODEX_HOME "C:\web-dev-ai\TallyProject\.codex"
```

7. Start Codex with the latest GPT model, for example, 5.5 in April 2026:

```
codex --model gpt-5.5
```

At the time of writing in April 2026, OpenAI also says GPT-5.5 is now available in Codex and is the recommended choice for most Codex tasks; in the CLI you can start a session with `codex --model gpt-5.5`. You can check the latest OpenAI Codex model at the following link: `https://developers.openai.com/codex/models`

8. In Codex, create a constitution file, as shown in *Figure 14.3* and the following output:

```
/speckit.constitution
This is an existing Django project named TallyApp.

Project principles:
1. Keep the architecture simple and beginner-friendly.
2. Prefer Django built-ins over third-party packages unless there is
a strong reason.
3. Write code that is readable for learners new to Django.
4. Use pytest or Django tests to verify acceptance criteria.
5. Add small, incremental features instead of broad architectural
rewrites.
6. Preserve existing behavior unless the spec explicitly changes it.
7. Use server-rendered Django templates unless a richer client-side
experience is clearly justified.
8. Avoid over-engineering.
```

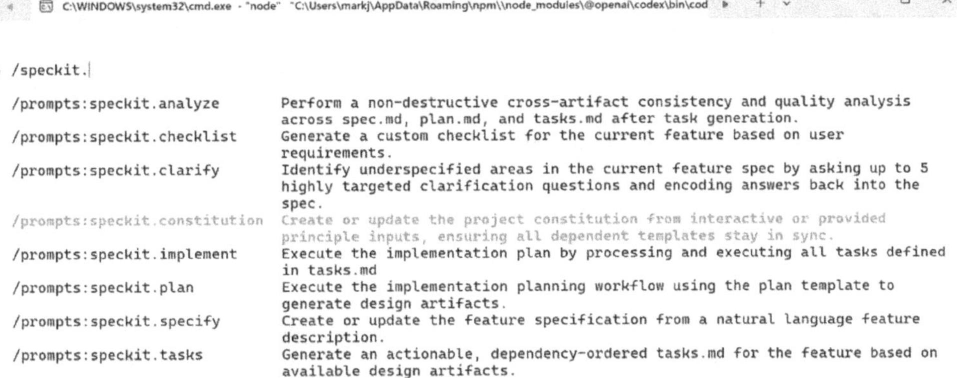

Figure 14.3: Creating a constitution file

Create the URL shortener specification

Next, run the Spec Kit specification step. The documented command is `/speckit.specify`.

In Codex, run:

```
/speckit.specify
```

Then paste a focused prompt like this:

```
Create a feature specification for adding a URL shortener to the existing
TallyApp Django project.

Goal:
Allow authenticated users to create short URLs that redirect to longer
links inside TallyApp. The main use case is generating short links for
surveys so they are easier to share.

Non-goals:
- No click analytics in this version
- No expiration dates
- No custom aliases
- Only authenticated users can create short links

User stories:
- As a logged-in user, I can create a short link for a survey URL
- As a logged-in user, I can view a list of short links I created
- As any visitor, I can visit a short URL and be redirected to the target
page

Acceptance criteria:
- When a valid URL is submitted, a short code is generated
- The short code is unique
- Visiting /s/<code> redirects to the stored target URL
- A user can only see short links they created
- If a short code does not exist, return 404 Not Found

Data model:
ShortLink
- owner: ForeignKey(User)
- target_url: URLField
- code: CharField(max_length=10, unique=True)
- created_at: DateTimeField(auto_now_add=True)

Constraints:
- code must be unique
```

```
- codes should be randomly generated
- deleting the owning user deletes the link

Please generate a spec that matches the existing Django codebase and keeps
the implementation small and teachable.
```

When Codex generates the spec, read it carefully. This is the point where you should correct anything too clever, too broad, or inconsistent with the existing TallyApp design.

It is fine to make changes to any of the files that Specify creates for you.

Should Spec Kit files be committed to Git?

In most teaching and team projects, yes: commit the specification artifacts that explain the feature, especially the `specs/` folder and files such as `spec.md`, `plan.md`, `tasks.md`, and `quickstart.md`. These files are part of the project's design history. They explain what you asked the AI to build, what was accepted, and how the feature should be verified.

Treat the `.specify/` folder more carefully. It can contain project-level Spec Kit configuration, templates, scripts, and agent command files. For a team project, commit it if you want everyone to use the same Spec Kit workflow. For a solo experiment, you can keep it local if it only contains generated helper files that can be recreated.

Do not blindly commit everything. Before committing, run `git status` and inspect the changed files. Do not commit secrets, personal machine paths, API keys, temporary output, caches, `__pycache__/`, virtual environments, or agent logs. If Spec Kit creates files that define the shared workflow, commit them. If files are only the local tool state, ignore them.

Here's a small `.gitignore` example:

```
# Python
__pycache__/
*.py[cod]
.venv/
.env

# Local tool output
out/
*.log

# Keep Markdown specs and project documentation tracked.
# Do not ignore *.md.
```

Generating the spec is not the same as approving it. This is the first point where your judgment matters more than the AI's fluency.

Review the generated spec file

Spec Kit stores specs as repository artifacts. For example, a feature folder under `specs/` containing `spec.md` and related planning documents.

Open the new spec file and check for five things:

- The goal is clear.
- Non-goals really limit scope.
- Acceptance criteria are testable.
- The data model is small and fits Django.
- The feature does not add extras like dashboards, analytics, **Quick Response** (**QR**) codes, or admin processes you did not request.

This review matters because the rest of the steps will build on this file.

Ask Codex to produce the implementation plan

Once the specification looks right, move to the planning phase with:

```
/speckit.plan
```

Use a prompt like this:

```
Create an implementation plan for the URL shortener feature in TallyApp.

Constraints:
- Existing Django project
- Keep the code simple and suitable for a teaching project
- Prefer one new app named shortlinks unless there is a compelling reason
not to
- Use Django templates and standard views
- Include tests for redirect behavior, permissions, and 404 handling
- Do not introduce background jobs, analytics, or external services
```

Then inspect the plan. A good plan should mention creating the app, model, migration, form, views, routes, template, and tests, without wandering into unnecessary abstractions.

Prompt: How should developers structure prompts when asking AI to generate an implementation plan?

Ask Codex to break the plan into tasks

Next, run:

```
/speckit.tasks
```

Prompt it like this:

```
Break the URL shortener implementation plan into a sequence of small,
reviewable tasks.

Each task should be concrete and produce a visible result.
Include tasks for:
- model creation
- migrations
- creation form
- list page for a user's links
- redirect route
- tests
- brief documentation update
```

Keep the work small at this stage. If Codex creates a giant single task called *Implement URL shortener*, push back and ask it to split the work more finely.

Have Codex implement the feature

Now run:

```
/speckit.implement
```

Give Codex a strict prompt such as:

```
Implement the URL shortener feature according to the approved
specification, plan, and task list.

Requirements:
- Follow the project principles
```

```
- Keep the implementation minimal and readable
- Do not add features not in the spec
- Update URLs, templates, models, and tests as needed
- Run the test suite and report any failures clearly
- Show me the diff or summarize changed files before any large refactor
```

OpenAI Codex is a coding agent that works on project folders and repositories, and GitHub Spec Kit is designed to supply the staged artifacts Codex can act on. That combination is exactly what you want here: the spec constrains the agent, and the agent writes the code.

Codex will output a summary:

```
Implemented the URL shortener feature and kept it within the approved
scope: one new shortlinks app, standard Django views/templates, no
analytics, no background jobs, no external services.

  What Changed
  Core feature:

  - Added shortlinks/models.py, shortlinks/forms.py, shortlinks/views.py,
shortlinks/urls.py, shortlinks/admin.py, and shortlinks/migrations/0001_
initial.py.
  - Added the create/list templates at shortlinks/templates/shortlinks/
shortlink_form.html and shortlinks/
    templates/shortlinks/shortlink_list.html.
  - Wired the app into tallyapp/settings.py and tallyapp/urls.py.
  - Added a simple navigation entry in surveys/templates/surveys/base.html
and a dashboard button in surveys/
    templates/surveys/dashboard.html.

  Verification and docs:

  - Added feature tests in shortlinks/tests.py and a regression check in
surveys/tests.py.
  - Updated project-brief.md, quickstart.md, and marked all tasks complete
in tasks.md.
```

```
  - Added a minimal .gitignore for Python/Django and local Node artifacts.

Tests
  Ran python manage.py test shortlinks surveys

  Result: 17 tests run, all passed.

  Notes
  All URL shortener tasks are now marked complete. The working tree
also contains pre-existing planning/spec changes under .specify/ plus
generated __pycache__ updates from test execution; I did not revert those
automatically.
```

According to the output, all URL shortener tasks are now marked complete, so the next step is to review the implementation and then if we are happy, to accept it. Passing tests are encouraging, but they are not permission to stop thinking.

Review the implementation before accepting it

Do not trust the first pass blindly. Read every changed file. I would specifically inspect:

- `shortlinks/models.py`
- `shortlinks/views.py`
- `shortlinks/forms.py` if one was added
- `shortlinks/urls.py`
- The project `urls.py`
- Templates for create/list pages
- Test files
- Any migration files

Pay attention to whether Codex followed the spec literally. AI coding agents can produce working code, but they still have a habit of adding helpful things nobody asked for.

Prompt: Please explain how developers can review AI-generated code effectively.

Run Django locally and verify the feature manually

From the TallyApp root, run the usual Django commands:

1. Codex may already have created the migration, but this command is harmless if there are no model changes. Make the migrations:

   ```
   python manage.py makemigrations
   ```

2. Perform the migrations:

   ```
   python manage.py migrate
   ```

3. Run the tests:

   ```
   python manage.py test
   ```

4. Start the web project:

   ```
   python manage.py runserver
   ```

5. Then manually verify the acceptance criteria in the browser:

   - create a short link as a logged-in user
   - confirm the code is generated
   - visit `/s/<code>` and confirm redirect behavior
   - try a non-existent code and confirm 404
   - confirm one user cannot see another user's short links

This manual pass is still worth doing even when the tests are green.

Optional refinement pass

A good final Codex prompt is:

```
Review the implemented URL shortener feature against the specification and
acceptance criteria.

Identify:
- any missing behavior
- any unnecessary complexity
- any code that should be simplified for teaching purposes
- any tests that are missing
```

The preceding review prompt is where the workflow often pays off. It asks Codex to review the code against the agreed spec.

So we've now added a new feature, reviewed it, and if needed, refined it. The URL shortener is only one example. The same steps become more useful as the feature becomes more ambiguous or touches more parts of the system.

For the last section of this chapter, let's think of some other features that could extend the capabilities of our project.

Ideas for extending TallyApp

At this point, the TallyApp project has authentication, survey creation, response collection, analytics, testing infrastructure, and now an additional feature built using Spec-Driven Development.

However, many interesting directions remain for expanding the application.

The best way to practice spec-driven workflows is to keep adding small, clearly defined features.

Here are several ideas that would make engaging exercises.

Interactive map location questions

Instead of selecting a country from a dropdown list, respondents could choose their location on a map.

Imagine a question such as: *Where are you participating from?*

The interface could display a globe or world map where users click their location.

The response would store latitude and longitude coordinates. Survey analytics could then display responses geographically, showing clusters of participation across different regions.

Prompt: Design a specification for geographic survey responses using a map interface.

Drag-and-drop ranking questions

Some surveys ask users to rank items in order of preference.

For example: *Rank these programming languages by how much you enjoy using them.*

A drag-and-drop interface could allow respondents to reorder items visually:

1. Python
2. JavaScript
3. Go
4. Rust

The result would store the ranking order in the database.

This kind of question type introduces interesting data modeling challenges.

Prompt: Design a specification for drag-and-drop ranking questions in a survey app and explain the data modeling challenges involved in ranking questions.

Survey branching logic

More advanced surveys show different questions depending on earlier answers.

Example: *Do you own a car?*

Yes → show questions about driving habits

No → skip to public transport questions

This feature introduces conditional logic in the survey engine and forces you to think carefully about how questions and responses are structured.

Prompt: Design a specification for adding branching logic to a survey system.

Real-time response dashboards

Survey creators might want to see responses updating live while participants are answering.

This could be implemented using WebSockets, Django Channels, or live updating charts.

Watching responses accumulate in real time makes the application feel much more dynamic.

Prompt: Explain how WebSockets could be used to create real-time survey response dashboards.

Survey themes and styling

Another visual improvement would allow survey creators to customize the appearance of their surveys.

Possible features include:

- Color themes
- Custom logos
- Light and dark modes

This would give you a reason to practice CSS custom properties, theme classes, and light/dark styling.

Prompt: Please show me how to add theming support to a Django web application.

Practice, references, and resources

In this section, you will be tested on what you've learned in this chapter and be provided with useful links to reference materials and resources.

Check your understanding

Answer the following questions:

1. What is Spec-Driven Development, and why is it useful when working with AI coding assistants?
2. Why is writing a specification before coding more important when using AI tools than when coding manually?
3. What are the key sections of a good feature specification?
4. Why are non-goals an important part of a specification?
5. What makes acceptance criteria effective?
6. How do tests turn a specification into an executable contract?

7. What is the role of Spec Kit in this workflow?
8. What are the main stages in the Spec Kit workflow?
9. Why can Spec-Driven Development be considered overkill for small changes?
10. Why should you review AI-generated code even after tests pass?
11. You ask an AI tool to "add a useful feature" without a specification. The result includes extra functionality you did not want. Why did this happen?
12. You write a specification but skip the non-goals section. The implementation becomes overly complex. What went wrong?
13. Your acceptance criteria say "the UI should be user-friendly." Why is this a problem?
14. A task list contains one large item: "Implement URL shortener." Why is this a problem?
15. You run `/speckit.implement` without reviewing the spec or plan. What is the likely outcome?
16. You complete the implementation and tests pass, but you skip manual testing. What risk remains?

Answers are found in the GitHub repository for this book at the following link:

`https://github.com/markjprice/web-dev-ai/blob/main/docs/Appendix-A.pdf`

Links

Here are some useful links.

Spec-Driven Development guide: `https://github.com/github/spec-kit/blob/main/spec-driven.md`

GitHub Engineering Blog: Spec-Driven Development with AI

`https://github.blog/ai-and-ml/generative-ai/spec-driven-development-with-ai-get-started-with-a-new-open-source-toolkit/`

Spec-Driven Development using Markdown as a programming interface

`https://github.blog/ai-and-ml/generative-ai/spec-driven-development-using-markdown-as-a-programming-language-when-building-with-ai/`

Martin Fowler: Exploring Spec-Driven Development

`https://martinfowler.com/articles/exploring-gen-ai/sdd-3-tools.html`

Django redirect shortcut documentation

`https://docs.djangoproject.com/en/stable/topics/http/shortcuts/#redirect`

Django Redirects Guide

`https://realpython.com/django-redirects/`

Summary

In this chapter, you used Spec-Driven Development to add a new feature to an existing Django project. You saw how a written specification gives an AI coding assistant clearer boundaries, especially when the feature affects models, views, routes, templates, and tests.

You learned how to define goals, non-goals, user stories, acceptance criteria, data model changes, and verification steps. You also saw how tools such as Spec Kit can turn that specification into a staged process: project principles, feature spec, implementation plan, task list, implementation, review, and refinement.

Most importantly, you practiced the part of development that AI cannot do for you: deciding what behavior is wanted, what behavior is out of scope, and how you will prove that the system works.

Specifically, you learned the following:

- What Spec-Driven Development is and why it is useful with AI coding assistants
- How to structure a feature specification
- How to extend an existing Django project using a written specification
- How to add a URL shortener feature to TallyApp
- How to verify that an implementation satisfies defined acceptance criteria
- How small, well-defined features make large systems easier to evolve

In the next chapter, you will learn how to deploy your web project to a host server so that it becomes available publicly, so other people can reach it.

Get this book's PDF version and more

Scan the QR code (or go to packtpub.com/unlock). Search for this book by name, confirm the edition, and then follow the steps on the page.

Note: Keep your invoice handy. Purchases made directly from Packt don't require an invoice.

15

Deploying to Public Servers

In the previous chapters, you built TallyApp as a local Django project. That was enough while you were designing features, writing tests, and learning how the pieces fit together. But a web application is not really finished until someone else can use it.

In this chapter, you will deploy TallyApp to a server so other people can use it over the internet. That means moving from a development setup on your own machine to a production-style setup that keeps running, accepts requests from the internet, protects user data, serves static files, stores a real database, and rebuilding the server by hand each time.

This chapter gives you a working deployment path for a small Django app. You will see each major piece, configure it yourself, and keep the setup simple enough to understand.

We will use a deliberately simple stack: a small **Virtual Private Server** (**VPS**), Ubuntu, Nginx, Gunicorn, Django, and SQLite. This is not the only way to deploy Django, but it is a good learning setup because you can see every major part of the system. Later, the same architecture can grow by replacing SQLite with PostgreSQL, adding Cloudflare, using managed backups, or automating deployment with **Continuous Integration and Continuous Deployment** (**CI/CD**).

By the end of this chapter, you will have deployed TallyApp to a publicly accessible server, understand how requests flow through a production Django stack, know how to preserve and back up user data across deployments, and understand which parts of the stack need to change as traffic grows.

In this chapter, we will cover the following topics:

- Deployment options for a Django website
- Protecting a Django website from common attacks
- Deploying TallyApp
- Final thoughts

Deployment options for a Django website

When you have been working locally, running the site just meant starting Django's development server and opening a browser on your own machine. Deployment replaces that temporary set-up with a system that keeps running, can accept requests from the public internet, and survive reboots and crashes.

In practical terms, deployment involves:

- A server that is always on and reachable from the internet
- A web server that listens on standard HTTP ports
- An application server that runs Django as a long-lived process
- A database that persists data independently of your code
- A repeatable process for updating code and applying migrations

None of this is specific to TallyApp. These are the same building blocks used by Django sites of all sizes.

A production architecture for TallyApp

At a high level, TallyApp will run in production using a common, deliberately boring architecture, as shown in *Figure 15.1*:

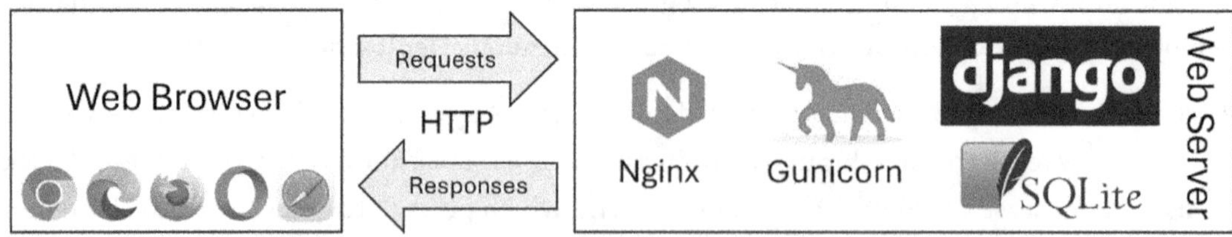

Figure 15.1: A simple production architecture for TallyApp

The components have clear responsibilities:

- **Nginx** receives public web traffic, serves static files, and helps handle **Transport Layer Security (TLS)**, a cryptographic protocol that secures data sent over a network (TLS is often terminated by Nginx, Cloudflare, or both). When you visit a site using `https://`, TLS ensures three things: (1) Encryption: data is unreadable to anyone intercepting it. (2) Authentication: the server proves it really is who it claims to be. (3) Integrity: data cannot be silently altered in transit.
- **Gunicorn** runs Django as a production application server.
- **Django** processes requests and talks to the database.
- **SQLite** stores survey data on disk as a persistent file.

Keeping these jobs separate makes later changes less painful. You can move from SQLite to PostgreSQL, or put Cloudflare in front of Nginx, without rewriting your views and models.

Prompt: Please explain the difference between a web server, application server, and database in a Django deployment, with a real-world analogy.

Why a production Django site needs Gunicorn and Nginx

Django's built-in development server is not designed for production use. Instead, Django applications are typically run behind a **Web Server Gateway Interface (WSGI)** server. WSGI is a specification, not a library. Gunicorn is one of the common WSGI implementations used with Django.

Gunicorn runs your Django project as a long-lived Python process. It does not listen directly on the public internet. Instead, it listens on a local socket and waits for Nginx to forward requests to it:

1. A browser sends an HTTP request.
2. Nginx receives it first.
3. That server calls your Django application using the WSGI interface.
4. Django returns a response object.
5. The server sends the HTTP response back to the browser.

WSGI exists so that Django (and other web frameworks) do not need to know or care which web server is in front of them. As long as the server speaks WSGI, Django can run behind it.

Key points about WSGI:

- It is synchronous and request–response based, meaning each request is handled in a blocking way. The server passes a request to your Django app, and that worker is tied up until the response is fully generated. If your code waits on something slow, like a database query or an API call, that worker just sits there waiting. It cannot do anything else in the meantime. Request–response based means a connection is not kept open to send multiple messages back and forth over time.
- In practice, this means WSGI works very well for traditional web pages and APIs, but it is not designed for things like real-time updates, chat systems, or live notifications where long-lived connections are needed.
- Django is a WSGI application, and Gunicorn is a WSGI server.

Gunicorn loads your Django project and calls it for each incoming request using the WSGI protocol.

Prompt: What is WSGI and how does it compare to ASGI in Python web apps? When would I choose ASGI (e.g. Daphne/Uvicorn) instead of Gunicorn?

Gunicorn configuration

For TallyApp, we will intentionally keep Gunicorn's configuration conservative. It will have a single worker process and optionally a small number of threads. It will be managed by the operating system's service manager, so it starts automatically on boot.

This configuration works particularly well with SQLite, which prefers limited write concurrency.

Using Nginx as a reverse proxy

A reverse proxy receives the public request and forwards it to another service behind the scenes. Nginx sits in front of Gunicorn and acts as the public-facing web server. Its responsibilities include:

- Listening on ports 80 and 443
- Serving static files such as CSS and images
- Forwarding dynamic requests to Gunicorn

Nginx handles slow clients efficiently so your Django app does not have to.

This division of labor is one of the reasons Django applications perform well even on modest hardware.

Prompt: Please explain reverse proxies in simple terms and why Nginx is used in front of Gunicorn and include a request flow diagram showing how Nginx, Gunicorn, and Django interact.

Choosing between shared hosting, VPS, and cloud platforms

For this book, a VPS is the best place to start. A VPS gives you a full Linux machine with root access at a low monthly cost. You install exactly what you need and nothing more.

You should also note that other options exist:

- Shared hosting is cheaper but usually unsuitable for Django deployments
- Platform-as-a-service (PaaS) offerings handle more for you, but you learn less about the moving parts
- Large cloud providers offer enormous flexibility, but also complexity that is unnecessary at this stage

A small VPS lets you see how the pieces fit together without overwhelming you.

The monthly cost mostly depends on the amount of CPU, memory, storage, and bandwidth you choose, as shown in *Figure 15.2*:

Figure 15.2: Typical monthly costs for a VPS

You should be able to find a VPS hosting provider for about US$5-10 per month, which will be enough to have a proper web server to host your Django projects. But to get lower costs, you often have to commit to one or more years of hosting, so expect to pay $60-$120 for a year of hosting. Many readers may prefer just to host locally and never actually deploy to a public server.

Prompt: What are the trade-offs between VPS, PaaS, and serverless for a Django app?

SQLite as the database

People often say SQLite is not suitable for production, but that is too broad. SQLite is a file-based database that excels at simplicity and reliability, but it has limits around concurrent writes.

For TallyApp, SQLite is a reasonable choice if:

- Traffic is modest
- Database writes are short-lived
- The application runs with a small number of worker processes
- **Write-ahead logging** (WAL) is enabled

The database itself is just a file on disk. Django reads and writes it using the SQLite library. There is no database server to install or manage.

Prompt: Please explain **write-ahead logging** (WAL) in SQLite and why it matters for concurrency. At what point does SQLite become a bottleneck in a production Django app?

Database persistence and migrations

One of the most important deployment rules is this: *never treat your database as disposable.*

Your application code can be replaced at any time. Your database must survive deployments.

To achieve this:

- Store the SQLite database file outside the application code directory
- Update code separately from data
- Use Django migrations to evolve the database schema

When you deploy a new version of TallyApp, you run migrations against the existing database. Data remains intact while the schema changes incrementally. This mirrors how migrations work with larger databases such as PostgreSQL. The commands are similar even though the database engine is different.

Backing up your data

Even for a learning project, backups matter. Users will assume their survey responses persist.

SQLite provides built-in mechanisms for creating consistent backups of a live database. A typical approach is:

- Create a snapshot using SQLite's backup facilities
- Store the snapshot in a dated backup directory
- Optionally copy it off the server

This can be automated with a daily scheduled task. The key idea is consistency. Always use SQLite's own tools to create backups rather than copying the database file blindly, especially if the application may be running while the backup is taken.

Updating the site safely

A typical update cycle for TallyApp looks like this:

1. Upload or pull the latest code
2. Install or update dependencies
3. Apply migrations
4. Collect static files
5. Restart the application service

Because data lives outside the code directory, updates are routine and low-risk. This is an important mental shift from local development, where deleting and recreating databases is common.

When to move to PostgreSQL

When traffic grows or writes become frequent and unpredictable, SQLite will start to show its limits. This is not a failure. It is simply the point at which the application has outgrown a file-based database.

The next step is usually PostgreSQL running on the same VPS. The architecture remains almost identical. Nginx and Gunicorn stay the same. Django stays the same. Only the database backend changes.

This is one of Django's strengths. Database backends are swappable with minimal application changes if you have followed best practices.

Prompt: Please walk me through migrating a Django project from SQLite to PostgreSQL safely.

Scaling further with a managed database

Beyond a single VPS, databases are often moved to managed services. At that point:

- Application servers can be scaled horizontally
- Databases gain automated backups and replication
- Operational complexity shifts from you to the provider

TallyApp does not need this level of infrastructure, but understanding the path matters. Your Django project can grow with your needs.

Summary of deployment options

Deploying TallyApp to the internet does not require exotic tools or complex cloud services. A small VPS, a conventional web stack, and a disciplined approach to data persistence are enough.

More importantly, this chapter establishes patterns that will serve you well beyond this project. The same principles apply whether you are deploying a learning app, a startup prototype, or a production service with real users and real expectations.

With a clear deployment approach in place, the next step is to ensure that your application remains secure and resilient once it is exposed to the unpredictable environment of the public internet.

Protecting a Django website from common attacks

Once your site is live on the public internet, it will start receiving traffic from sources you did not invite. Some will be legitimate users. Many will be automated bots scanning for weaknesses. This is normal.

For a beginner Django project like TallyApp, the goal is not to eliminate all risk. That is unrealistic. The goal is to avoid obvious mistakes, reduce the impact of common attacks, and make the site resilient enough that it keeps working even under nuisance traffic.

Django already includes many built-in protections, but they only help if you use them correctly and deploy your application with care.

You might make the following assumptions:

- **People will try to bring your site down**: Partly true, but not in a targeted way. Most traffic will be automated bots. The architecture above handles that well.
- **A single server might be fragile**: Correct. A single Droplet is a single point of failure. But for a demo site, that is acceptable if you have backups and can redeploy quickly.
- **You need strong protections from day one**: Not really. You need basic Django settings and server protections, not heavy infrastructure. The combination of Django best practices + Cloudflare + basic server hardening covers most real risks.

Understanding the most common attacks

Most attacks against small web applications are not sophisticated. They are automated and repetitive, looking for easy wins.

The most relevant categories for a Django app are shown in *Table 15.1*:

Name	Description
Cross-site scripting (XSS)	Attackers try to inject malicious JavaScript into pages viewed by other users. Django templates escape output by default, which blocks most simple cases. Problems usually arise when developers deliberately bypass escaping.
Cross-site request forgery (CSRF)	A user is tricked into submitting a request they did not intend, such as changing account details. Django includes CSRF protection middleware, but it must be enabled and used correctly in forms.
SQL injection	Malicious input attempts to alter database queries. Django's **object-relational mapper** (**ORM**) protects against this by using parameterized queries, but unsafe raw SQL can reintroduce the risk.
Authentication abuse	Bots attempt to guess passwords or reuse leaked credentials. Login pages are a common target.
Security misconfiguration	This is one of the most common problems. Leaving `DEBUG = True`, exposing secrets, or failing to restrict allowed hosts can leak sensitive information or open the door to attacks.
File upload abuse	If your app allows uploads, attackers may try to upload malicious files or extremely large files to exhaust resources.
Denial of service (DoS)	Rather than hacking the site, attackers overwhelm it with traffic or expensive requests. For small apps, this is usually application-level abuse, not large-scale network flooding.

Table 15.1: Common types of website attack

The **Open Worldwide Application Security Project (OWASP) Top 10** is a widely recognized list of the most common and impactful security risks affecting web applications. Maintained by a global community of security professionals, it highlights patterns seen in actual breaches. Rather than being an exhaustive list, it serves as a practical guide to the kinds of vulnerabilities developers are most likely to encounter, helping teams prioritize the issues that matter most when building and deploying secure applications.

The OWASP Top 10 continues to highlight issues like broken access control, injection, and misconfiguration as leading causes of vulnerabilities in web applications: `https://owasp.org/Top10/2025/`

Prompt: Please give some examples of XSS, CSRF, and SQL injection in Django apps.

A practical security baseline for beginners

You do not need expensive tools to protect a small Django application. A simple, well-configured setup goes a long way.

Start with Django's deployment checklist:

1. Set `DEBUG = False`
2. Define `ALLOWED_HOSTS`
3. Keep your `SECRET_KEY` private
4. Run `python manage.py check --deploy`

Django explicitly warns that running with `DEBUG = True` in production can expose stack traces, settings, and sensitive internal details.

Prompt: What does Django's `check --deploy` command actually validate internally?

Enforcing HTTPS and secure cookies

Django recommends enforcing HTTPS across the entire site, not just login pages, because session cookies are shared across requests. Always serve your site over HTTPS. This protects login sessions and user data.

In your Django settings you should enable the following options:

```
if not DEBUG: # Only enabled in a production environment.
    SECURE_SSL_REDIRECT = True
    SESSION_COOKIE_SECURE = True
    CSRF_COOKIE_SECURE = True
    SECURE_HSTS_SECONDS = 31536000  # 1 year
    SECURE_HSTS_INCLUDE_SUBDOMAINS = True
    X_FRAME_OPTIONS = "DENY"
    SECURE_CONTENT_TYPE_NOSNIFF = True
```

Note the following about the preceding settings:

- `SECURE_SSL_REDIRECT = True`: Forces all HTTP requests to be redirected to HTTPS. If a user visits `http://your-site.com`, Django will automatically redirect them to `https://your-site.com`. This ensures all communication is encrypted. Without this, users might access your site over plain HTTP, which allows attackers to intercept or modify traffic (man-in-the-middle attacks).
- `SESSION_COOKIE_SECURE = True`: Ensures that session cookies are only sent over HTTPS. Browsers will not include the session cookie in HTTP requests. Session cookies identify logged-in users. If sent over HTTP, they can be intercepted and used to hijack sessions.
- `CSRF_COOKIE_SECURE = True`: Ensures that the CSRF protection cookie is only sent over HTTPS. Similar to session cookies, but specifically for CSRF tokens. CSRF protection depends on a secret token. If that token is exposed over HTTP, an attacker could potentially bypass CSRF protections.
- `SECURE_HSTS_SECONDS = 31536000` (1 year in seconds): Enables **HTTP Strict Transport Security (HSTS)** and tells browsers to always use HTTPS for your site for the next year. After visiting your site once over HTTPS, the browser will refuse to connect over HTTP for the specified duration. It prevents downgrade attacks where an attacker tries to force a user back to HTTP.

Warning! You should only enable this once you are confident HTTPS is working correctly everywhere.

- `SECURE_HSTS_INCLUDE_SUBDOMAINS = True`: Extends HSTS to all subdomains. For example: api.your-site.com, admin.your-site.com, and so on. Attackers often target weaker subdomains. This ensures the entire domain is HTTPS-only.

- `X_FRAME_OPTIONS = "DENY"`: Prevents your site from being embedded inside an `<iframe>`. The browser will block any attempt to load your pages in a frame on another site. Protects against clickjacking attacks, where a malicious site tricks users into clicking hidden elements from your site.
- `SECURE_CONTENT_TYPE_NOSNIFF = True`: This tells browsers not to guess (or "sniff") the content type of a response. The browser must respect the `Content-Type` header sent by the server. Prevents certain attacks where a file is disguised as one type (e.g., text) but executed as another (e.g., JavaScript).

Taken as a group, these settings enforce HTTPS everywhere, protect sensitive cookies, prevent common browser-based attacks (clickjacking, MIME sniffing), and reduce the risk of interception and manipulation of traffic.

They are part of Django's built-in *secure by default in production* approach, but they only work correctly when your app is properly deployed behind HTTPS (for example, using Nginx or a cloud platform that terminates TLS).

Warning! Do not enable these blindly in development because HTTPS is often not configured locally, and redirects and secure cookies can break your dev workflow.

Protecting against XSS and CSRF

Django helps here, but only if you follow its conventions:

- Use Django templates rather than building HTML strings manually
- Avoid marking user input as safe unless absolutely necessary
- Ensure all forms include CSRF tokens, as shown in the following form:

```
<form method="post">
    {% csrf_token %}
    <!-- form fields -->
</form>
```

For additional protection, consider enabling a **Content Security Policy** (**CSP**), which restricts where scripts can be loaded from. Django 6 includes built-in support for CSP configuration, for example settings like `SECURE_CSP`, but earlier Django versions, like the current LTS version 5.2, do not.

A CSP is a browser-enforced security mechanism that controls which resources a web page is allowed to load and execute. It is defined by the server (usually via an HTTP response header) and tells the browser things like which domains JavaScript can be loaded from, whether inline scripts are allowed, and where images, stylesheets, fonts, and other assets can come from.

The goal is to reduce the impact of attacks such as **cross-site scripting (XSS)**. Even if an attacker manages to inject malicious code into your page, a well-configured CSP can prevent that code from running because it is not from an approved source.

A simple example might look like this:

```
Content-Security-Policy: default-src 'self'; script-src 'self' https://trusted.cdn.com;
```

The preceding HTTP header tells the browser to only load resources from your own site by default, and only allow scripts from your site and a trusted **Content Delivery Network** (**CDN**).

CSP works best as an additional layer of defense. It does not replace secure coding practices, but it makes exploitation significantly harder when something goes wrong.

You can learn more about CSP at the following link: `https://developer.mozilla.org/en-US/docs/Web/HTTP/Guides/CSP`

Avoiding SQL injection

The safest approach is simple: use Django's ORM:

```
# Safe
User.objects.filter(username=username)
```

Avoid constructing SQL queries manually using string concatenation. If you must use raw SQL, use parameterized queries.

Django's documentation emphasizes that its ORM protects against SQL injection by default, but only when used properly.

Securing authentication

Login endpoints are a favorite target for bots.

Basic protections include:

- Enforce strong passwords
- Add rate limiting to login attempts
- Consider adding a human-verification challenge after repeated failures
- Avoid exposing the Django admin at predictable URLs without additional protection

A simple rate-limiting approach can dramatically reduce brute-force attempts.

Handling file uploads safely

If your app allows file uploads:

- Limit file size
- Validate file types
- Never execute uploaded files
- Store uploads outside your main application domain

Django recommends serving uploaded files from a separate domain or storage system to reduce risk.

Defending against denial-of-service

For a small project, most DoS attempts are actually abusive usage patterns.

Common examples:

- Repeated login attempts
- Large file uploads
- Expensive database queries
- Aggressive crawling

Low-cost defenses include:

- Rate limiting key endpoints
- Limiting upload size
- Using caching where appropriate
- Moving static files to a CDN

Using a service like Cloudflare can provide free or low-cost protection, including basic **Distributed Denial of Service** (**DDoS**) mitigation and request filtering.

Prompt: Please show me how to implement rate limiting in Django using middleware or third-party packages. Please explain how Cloudflare protects a small website from bots and attacks.

Protecting secrets and configuration

Never store secrets in your source code repository.

Use environment variables instead:

```
import os

SECRET_KEY = os.environ["DJANGO_SECRET_KEY"]
```

Django's deployment guidance stresses that sensitive settings must remain confidential.

Logging, monitoring, and backups

Security is not just about prevention. You must also detect and recover.

At a minimum:

- Enable logging for errors and suspicious activity
- Monitor failed login attempts
- Keep regular database backups
- Test restoring from backups

For example, add the following code to your `settings.py`:

```
import os

LOG_DIR = os.path.join(BASE_DIR, "logs")
os.makedirs(LOG_DIR, exist_ok=True)

LOGGING = {
    "version": 1,
    "disable_existing_loggers": False,
    "formatters": {
        "verbose": {
            "format": "{asctime} {levelname} {name} {message}",
            "style": "{",
```

```
        },
    },
    "handlers": {
        "file": {
            "level": "WARNING",
            "class": "logging.FileHandler",
            "filename": os.path.join(LOG_DIR, "django.log"),
            "formatter": "verbose",
        },
    },
    "loggers": {
        "django": {
            "handlers": ["file"],
            "level": "WARNING",
            "propagate": True,
        },
    },
}
```

The preceding code:

- Logs warnings, errors, and exceptions
- Writes to `logs/django.log`
- Captures suspicious activity like bad requests or errors

To check the server logs, use the following Bash/shell commands:

```
sudo journalctl -u gunicorn -f
sudo tail -f /var/log/nginx/error.log
```

To log failed logins, add the following code to your login view:

```
import logging
logger = logging.getLogger(__name__)

def login_view(request):
    if request.method == "POST":
        username = request.POST.get("username")
        password = request.POST.get("password")
```

```
        user = authenticate(request, username=username, password=password)

        if user is None:
            logger.warning(f"Failed login attempt for username:
{username}")
        else:
            login(request, user)
```

OWASP highlights that failures in logging and monitoring can allow attacks to go unnoticed for long periods.

Use a ready-made package to track logins

To track failed login attempts, temporarily block brute-force attacks, and store attempts in the database, you can install a Django middleware package named Axes:

```
pip install django-axes
```

Then enable the package in `settings.py`:

```
INSTALLED_APPS += ["axes"]
MIDDLEWARE += ["axes.middleware.AxesMiddleware"]

AUTHENTICATION_BACKENDS = [
    "axes.backends.AxesBackend",
    "django.contrib.auth.backends.ModelBackend",
]

AXES_FAILURE_LIMIT = 5
AXES_COOLOFF_TIME = 1  # hours
```

This package logs to permanent tables so you must then run database migrations:

```
python manage.py migrate
```

It is reasonable to expect that a public demo site like TallyApp will receive unwanted traffic. However, this will mostly come from automated bots, not targeted human attackers.

Summary checklist

For a beginner-friendly deployment, aim for the following:

- Disable debug mode

- Enforce HTTPS everywhere
- Use secure cookies
- Configure `ALLOWED_HOSTS`
- Keep secrets out of source control
- Use Django's ORM and built-in protections
- Add rate limiting to login and public endpoints
- Limit and validate file uploads
- Put a CDN or proxy in front of your site
- Enable logging and maintain backups

Each of the preceding points is covered in detail in either this chapter or *Chapter 9, Django – Web Development on the Backend.*

This does not make your application invulnerable. It makes it robust enough for production use, which is exactly what you need for a public-facing example like TallyApp.

With these security fundamentals in place, we can now move on to deploying TallyApp to a public server, applying these practices in a real, working environment.

Deploying TallyApp

The first step is to pick a host server provider. This is the machine that will run your application continuously and make it accessible to users over the internet. Unlike your local development environment, this server must be reliable, reachable at all times, and capable of handling requests from unknown users and automated systems.

There are several categories of hosting to choose from, each with different trade-offs. Shared hosting is inexpensive but too restrictive for most Django applications. Platform-as-a-service options remove much of the operational burden, but they also hide how deployment actually works. At the other end of the spectrum, large cloud providers offer enormous flexibility, but can introduce unnecessary complexity for a small project. For a project like TallyApp, a VPS strikes the right balance. It gives you full control over a Linux machine at a low cost, while still being simple enough to understand how all the pieces fit together.

Choosing a VPS also aligns well with the architecture introduced earlier in this chapter. You will install and configure each component yourself: the web server, the application server, and the database. This might sound like extra work, but it is where much of the learning happens. Instead of relying on a black-box platform, you will see exactly how requests flow through your system and how your application behaves in a real environment.

In the next section, we will use DigitalOcean as our hosting provider. It offers a straightforward way to create and manage virtual servers, with predictable pricing and strong documentation. More importantly, it allows us to focus on understanding deployment rather than wrestling with infrastructure complexity.

Why DigitalOcean is a good fit for TallyApp

I chose to use **DigitalOcean** as my host provider because it sits in a useful middle ground between too abstract platforms that hide everything and hyperscale clouds that overwhelm beginners with options and pricing complexity.

For a project like TallyApp, it is arguably useful for learning because it forces you to understand what is happening during deployment, without drowning you in enterprise concerns.

The biggest advantage is simplicity. You can go from zero to a public server in minutes using a **Droplet**, which is just a virtual machine. That maps nicely to how Django is traditionally deployed, using tools like Gunicorn and Nginx.

The documentation is strong and beginner-friendly. DigitalOcean has spent years building tutorials specifically for common stacks like Django, including step-by-step guides for Ubuntu, Gunicorn, and Nginx. You can read the DigitalOcean documentation tutorials at the following link: `https://www.digitalocean.com/community/tutorials`.

DigitalOcean VPS also gives you full control. You will learn how web servers, reverse proxies, and application servers fit together, rather than relying on a black-box platform.

The downsides you should be aware of

The trade-off for simplicity is that you are responsible for more things yourself.

You are managing a server. That means:

- Applying security updates
- Configuring firewalls
- Managing processes and services
- Handling scaling manually

There is no automatic scaling. If your site suddenly gets popular or attacked, a single Droplet can become overwhelmed.

You still own application security because it is not fully managed. Unlike platforms such as Heroku or Vercel, DigitalOcean does not automatically handle many application-level protections. You need to configure them.

Backups and monitoring are optional add-ons. They are not fully integrated by default unless you enable them.

Is it suitable for a public demo like TallyApp?

Yes, with one condition: you must add a thin layer of protection in front of it. A single low-cost Droplet is perfectly capable of running a Django app with light to moderate traffic. For a book companion site, that is usually more than enough.

However, exposing a raw server directly to the internet is not ideal. Without additional protection, it will quickly receive:

- Bot traffic scanning for vulnerabilities
- Login brute-force attempts
- Crawlers and scrapers
- Occasional traffic spikes

This is where combining DigitalOcean with a proxy layer becomes important.

What protection DigitalOcean provides

DigitalOcean gives you infrastructure-level security, but not full application protection.

Included protections:

- Basic network isolation through virtual private networking
- Cloud firewalls to restrict inbound traffic by port and IP
- Secure Shell (SSH) key authentication instead of passwords
- Datacenter-level physical security
- DDoS protection at the infrastructure level (limited and not deeply configurable)

These are useful server-level protections, but they do not protect against:

- Application-layer attacks (for example, login abuse)
- XSS or CSRF issues
- Misconfigured Django settings
- Bot traffic targeting your endpoints

Some useful features are available but require enabling or additional cost, as shown in *Table 15.2*:

Feature	Description
Backups	Automatic backups typically cost around 20% of the Droplet price.
Monitoring and alerts	Basic monitoring is available, but you need to configure alerts yourself.
Load balancers	Start at around $12 per month. Useful if you scale beyond a single server.
Managed databases	More expensive than self-hosting PostgreSQL, but reduce operational risk.

Table 15.2: DigitalOcean features that can be enabled

The missing piece: edge protection

DigitalOcean gives you the server, but it does not filter every bad request before it reaches your app. This is where adding Cloudflare (or a similar service) in front of your Droplet enhances your protection.

With even a free Cloudflare plan, you get:

- CDN caching for static content like CSS stylesheets and images
- Basic DDoS protection
- Bot filtering
- TLS termination (HTTPS handled at the edge)

At a low cost, you can add:

- Rate limiting (for login and forms)
- Web Application Firewall (WAF) rules

When paired with a simple edge service like Cloudflare and good Django configuration, DigitalOcean plus Cloudflare and correct Django settings is enough for a small public TallyApp deployment.

Deploying step-by-step

You will benefit more from understanding deployment than from taking the shortest path to a working server.

We will standardize on the following target stack: a small Droplet for the app server, Ubuntu LTS, SQLite for database simplicity, Nginx as reverse proxy, Gunicorn for Django, **Uncomplicated Firewall (UFW)**, and optional backups. That is suitable for a public demo app with modest traffic.

Create a DigitalOcean Droplet

Now we can create a Droplet to host our website project:

1. Register a DigitalOcean account at the following link: `https://cloud.digitalocean.com/`
2. On your account's **Projects** page, you will already have a default project, often named **first-project**. We can leave this as-is.
3. Click **Create**, and then click **Droplets**, as shown in *Figure 15.3*:

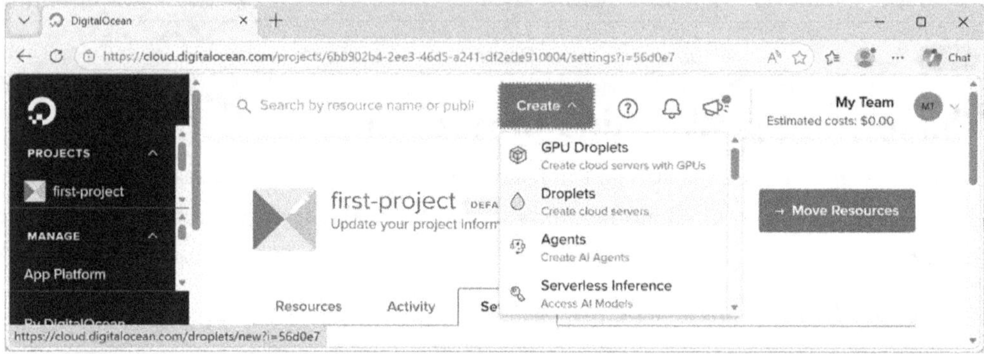

Figure 15.3: Creating a Droplet

4. Select a region, either close to most of your expected visitors, or close to you. I chose **New York**.
5. Select an image for your operating system. I chose **Ubuntu 24.04 (LTS) x64**.
6. Select the Droplet size. I chose:
    - Basic (shared CPU)
    - Regular SSD
    - $12 per month
    - 2 GB / 1 CPU
    - 50 GB SSD Disk
    - 2 TB transfer
7. Optionally, enable an automated backup plan. I chose **Daily Backups** at a cost of $3.60 per month. Backups are kept for one week. For the time window, I chose midnight to 4 a.m. in the Eastern US time zone.

8. Select an authentication method. I chose **SSH**. Click **Add SSH Key** and follow the instructions. You must name the SSH key (I used `tallyapp-sshkey`) and it will create two files. The file without `.pub` is your private key. Keep it private. The `.pub` file is the public key you copy to DigitalOcean.

You can learn more about how to connect to Droplets using SSH at the following link: `https://docs.digitalocean.com/products/droplets/how-to/connect-with-ssh/`

9. Click **Create Droplet**.
10. Note the IP address assigned to your server, as shown in *Figure 15.4*:

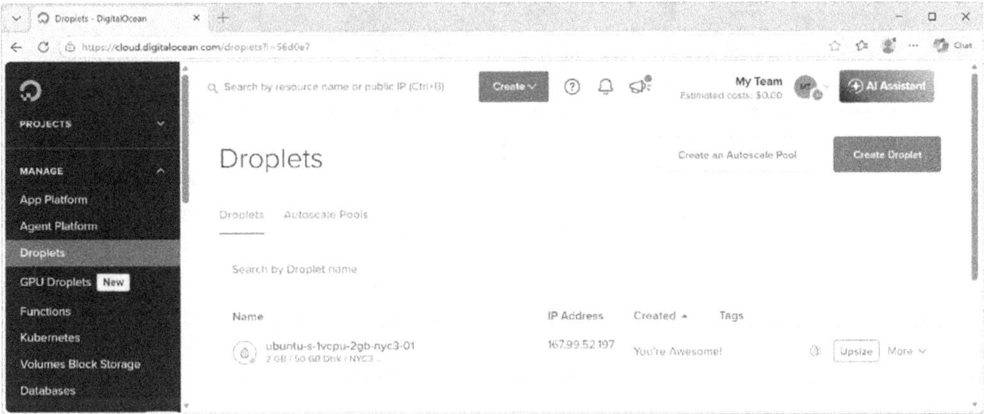

Figure 15.4: Your server's IP address

11. At the command prompt or terminal, enter the command to connect to your remote server using the private SSH key file you created earlier, the default `root` user account, and the IP address of the remote server:

```
ssh -i tallyapp-sshkey root@167.99.52.197
```

The default username on initial creation is `root` on most operating systems, like Ubuntu and CentOS. If you add another user, you can use that username instead.

12. Enter the passphrase for the SSH key.

13. You will now be connected to the remote server host, as shown in the following lightly edited output:

```
Welcome to Ubuntu 24.04.3 LTS (GNU/Linux 6.8.0-71-generic x86_64)

System information as of Tue Mar 24 16:46:12 UTC 2026

  System load:           0.01
  Usage of /:            4.0% of 47.39GB
  Memory usage:          10%
  Swap usage:            0%
  Processes:             99
  Users logged in:       0
  IPv4 address for eth0: 167.99.52.197
  IPv4 address for eth0: 10.17.0.5
  IPv6 address for eth0: 2604:a880:800:14:0:2:b6e3:6000

...
```

Initial remote server set up

You are about to enter commands to update OS packages, add yourself as a Linux user, enable the firewall, and so on:

1. Update packages and be patient for a few minutes while this happens:

```
apt update && apt upgrade -y
```

2. Add a user named tallyapp:

```
adduser tallyapp
```

3. Give yourself admin rights:

```
usermod -aG sudo tallyapp
```

4. Switch to your account:

```
su - tallyapp
```

5. Allow SSH through the firewall:

```
sudo ufw allow OpenSSH
```

6. Enable firewall:

```
sudo ufw enable
```

7. Install system dependencies (Python pip, virtual environment support, Sqlite, Nginx, and Git):

```
sudo apt install -y python3-pip python3-venv nginx git sqlite3
```

8. Clone your project from its public GitHub repository:

```
git clone https://github.com/yourusername/tallyapp.git
```

Alternatively, you can clone my TallyApp source code repository, found at the following link: https://github.com/markjprice/tallyapp

9. Change to the app folder:

```
cd tallyapp
```

10. Create a virtual environment:

```
python3 -m venv .venv
```

11. Activate the virtual environment:

```
source .venv/bin/activate
```

12. Install Python dependencies:

```
pip install -r requirements.txt
```

13. Install Gunicorn:

```
pip install gunicorn
```

14. Create a .env file:

```
nano .env
```

15. Define some environment variables:

```
DEBUG=False
SECRET_KEY=your_secret_key
ALLOWED_HOSTS=your_domain,your_server_ip
```

16. Apply migrations (this will create the SQLite database file `db.sqlite3`) and collect static files:

```
python manage.py migrate
python manage.py collectstatic
python manage.py createsuperuser
```

17. Test Gunicorn by entering the following at the terminal or command prompt:

```
gunicorn --bind 0.0.0.0:8000 tallyapp.wsgi:application
```

18. Enter the following link at the terminal or command prompt:

```
http://your_server_ip:8000
```

19. Stop Gunicorn by pressing *Ctrl* + *C*.
20. Configure Gunicorn as a service by creating a configuration file:

```
sudo nano /etc/systemd/system/gunicorn.service
```

21. Modify the contents of the `gunicorn.service` file:

```
[Unit]
Description=gunicorn daemon
After=network.target

[Service]
EnvironmentFile=/home/tallyapp/tallyapp/.env
User=tallyapp
Group=www-data
WorkingDirectory=/home/tallyapp/tallyapp
ExecStart=/home/tallyapp/tallyapp/.venv/bin/gunicorn \
    --workers 1 \
    --bind unix:/home/tallyapp/tallyapp/gunicorn.sock \
    tallyapp.wsgi:application

[Install]
WantedBy=multi-user.target
```

22. Start and enable Gunicorn:

```
sudo systemctl start gunicorn
```

```
sudo systemctl enable gunicorn
```

23. Configure Nginx:

```
sudo nano /etc/nginx/sites-available/tallyapp
```

24. Modify the file:

```
server {
    listen 80;
    server_name your_domain your_server_ip;

    location /static/ {
        root /home/tallyapp/tallyapp;
    }

    location / {
        include proxy_params;
        proxy_pass http://unix:/home/tallyapp/tallyapp/gunicorn.
sock;
    }
}
```

25. Enable Nginx:

```
sudo ln -s /etc/nginx/sites-available/tallyapp /etc/nginx/sites-
enabled
sudo nginx -t
sudo systemctl restart nginx
```

26. Configure firewall for web traffic:

```
sudo ufw allow 'Nginx Full'
```

27. Enable HTTPS:

```
sudo apt install certbot python3-certbot-nginx
sudo certbot --nginx -d your_domain
```

Prompt: Please write a bash script to deploy a Django app safely with zero downtime.

At this point, the application can run, but the most valuable part of the system is not the code. It is the data users create after the site goes live.

Now let's review the steps to back up the SQLite database.

Backing up your SQLite database

With SQLite, your entire database is a single file at the following location on the host server:

```
/home/tallyapp/tallyapp/db.sqlite3
```

If this file is lost or corrupted, your data is gone, so backups are essential.

You can back up the database file using the following command:

```
sqlite3 db.sqlite3 ".backup 'db-backup.sqlite3'"
```

Warning! Do not use a simple copy (`cp`) command. Copying the file may be acceptable only when the app is stopped or quiet. Use SQLite's `.backup` command or Online Backup API for a live database. SQLite documents its Online Backup API for copying a live database at the following link: `https://sqlite.org/backup.html`

You could create a `backups` directory:

```
mkdir -p ~/backups
```

Then perform a backup with timestamp:

```
sqlite3 /home/tallyapp/db.sqlite3 \
  ".backup /home/tallyapp/backups/db-$(date +%F-%H-%M).sqlite3"
```

Example output:

```
db-2026-03-24-14-30.sqlite3
```

Automating backups with cron

So far, you have created backups manually. That is fine for testing, but in a real deployment, you need backups to happen automatically and consistently. This is where `cron` comes in.

`cron` is a built-in Linux scheduler that runs commands at specified times. It is extremely reliable and widely used for routine maintenance tasks like backups, log rotation, and cleanup.

To edit your scheduled tasks, run:

```
crontab -e
```

If this is your first time using it, you may be asked to choose an editor (select nano for simplicity). This opens your personal crontab file.

Each line in a crontab file has five time fields followed by the command:

```
* * * * * command
| | | | |
| | | | └── Day of week (0-7, where 0 and 7 = Sunday)
| | | └──── Month (1-12)
| | └────── Day of month (1-31)
| └──────── Hour (0-23)
└────────── Minute (0-59)
```

This matters because small mistakes here can mean backups never run or run too often.

To add a job every 6 hours, add the following line:

```
0 */6 * * * sqlite3 /home/tallyapp/db.sqlite3 ".backup /home/tallyapp/
backups/db-$(date +%F-%H-%M).sqlite3"
```

The preceding code works as follows:

- `0 */6 * * *`: Runs at minute 0, every 6 hours (midnight, 6am, 12pm, 6pm).
- `sqlite3 /home/tallyapp/db.sqlite3`: Works with your SQLite database file.
- `".backup /home/tallyapp/backups/db-$(date +\%F-\%H-\%M).sqlite3"`: Backs up the database file with a timestamp like: `db-2026-04-02-12-00.sqlite3`. The `%` characters are escaped (`\%`) because `cron` treats `%` specially. Without escaping, the command will break.

Before relying on this, make sure the backups directory exists:

```
mkdir -p /home/tallyapp/backups
```

Limiting backup size

If you never delete old backups, they will eventually fill your disk. This is one of the most common failures on small servers.

To delete backups older than 7 days, you can run:

```
find /home/tallyapp/backups -type f -mtime +7 -delete
```

The preceding code works as follows:

- `-type f`: only applies to files
- `-mtime +7`: modified more than 7 days ago
- `-delete`: remove them

To automate cleanup, add a second scheduled task to `cron`:

```
30 2 * * * find /home/tallyapp/backups -type f -mtime +7 -delete
```

This runs every day at 02:30 a.m..

Good practice: It is best to do cleanup as a separate job because that keeps backup creation simple and fast, cleanup happens during low-traffic hours, and you avoid mixing responsibilities in one command.

Off-server backups

For better protection, copy backups off the server:

- Use `scp` to download locally
- Sync to cloud storage (for example, object storage or a backup service)

Prompt: How can I automate backups and test restoring a SQLite database?

What you have built

You now have a complete deployment:

- Django running via Gunicorn
- Nginx serving requests
- SQLite database stored locally
- Automated backups protecting your data

This setup is intentionally simple and cost-effective, making it ideal for a public demo project while still following standard deployment practices.

Prompt: How would I monitor a small Django app in production without expensive tools?

The manual process is worth doing once because it teaches you what deployment really does. Once you understand the steps, automation starts to make sense.

Continuous Integration (CI) and Continuous Deployment (CD)

As your project grows, manually copying files to a server and restarting services becomes tedious and error-prone. CI/CD replaces that manual process with an automated pipeline that builds, tests, and deploys your application in a consistent way.

CI focuses on validating changes. Every time you push code to your repository, an automated process runs tasks such as installing dependencies, running tests, and checking code quality. The pipeline should catch problems early, before they reach your server.

CD takes the next step. Once changes pass validation, they are automatically deployed to your server. Instead of logging into your VPS and running commands by hand, the pipeline performs the same steps every time in a predictable sequence.

A typical CI/CD pipeline for a Django project

For a Django project like TallyApp, a typical CI/CD pipeline looks like this:

1. A developer pushes code to a Git repository (for example, GitHub).
2. A CI service (such as GitHub Actions) starts a workflow.
3. The workflow installs dependencies and runs tests.
4. If the checks pass, the CD stage connects to your server.
5. The server pulls the latest code.
6. Migrations are applied.
7. Static files are collected.
8. The application service (Gunicorn) is restarted.

This mirrors the manual deployment steps you followed earlier, but removes the risk of forgetting a step or introducing inconsistencies.

GitHub Actions

A minimal example using GitHub Actions might:

- Trigger on every push to the main branch
- Run `pip install -r requirements.txt` and `python manage.py test`
- Use SSH to connect to your server and execute deployment commands

The benefits are immediate:

- Deployments become repeatable and reliable
- Errors are caught before they affect users
- You spend less time managing servers and more time improving your application

There are trade-offs. CI/CD adds some initial complexity, and mistakes in your pipeline can deploy broken code quickly. For that reason, many teams start with continuous integration only and add automated deployment once they are confident in their tests.

For a small project like TallyApp, CI/CD is not required. But even a simple pipeline gives you a taste of how software is built and maintained, and prepares you for larger projects where manual deployment is no longer practical.

Prompt: Please show me a beginner-friendly CI/CD pipeline for deploying Django automatically.

You now have more than a Django project. You have a small public system with moving parts, user data, security settings, and an update process.

Final thoughts

You have now done something that many people who learn web development never actually do: you have taken an idea, built it into a working application, and deployed it to the public internet.

Deployment changes the nature of the project. On your own machine, the app is an experiment. On a public server, it has users, data, expectations, and consequences. It needs to stay up, respond quickly, and behave predictably even when things go wrong.

What you have built in this chapter is intentionally simple, but it is not a toy. The architecture you used is the same pattern that underpins a large number of real-world Django applications. The difference between a learning project and a production system is not the tools. It is how carefully those tools are used.

Deployment makes the book's main point concrete. It is not enough to generate a settings file or copy a shell command. You need to know where requests go, where data lives, which files must survive an update, and what you will do when something fails. AI can help write configuration files and shell commands, but it cannot decide what risks your system should accept. That judgment is still yours.

Throughout this book, you have worked alongside an AI sidekick. You have used it to generate ideas, explain concepts, write code, debug problems, and explore alternatives. That is not a shortcut. It is a new way of working.

Who will win?

The developers who will thrive over the next decade are not the ones who memorize the most syntax. They are the ones who can:

- Ask good questions
- Break problems into smaller pieces
- Evaluate generated solutions critically
- Understand what their code is actually doing
- Adapt quickly as tools evolve

AI can accelerate you, but it cannot replace understanding. If anything, it raises the bar. It becomes easier to produce code, which means it becomes more important to recognize when that code is wrong, insecure, or inefficient.

A project like TallyApp is your starting point, not your destination.

From here, you might:

- Add new features and refine the user experience
- Replace SQLite with PostgreSQL and explore scaling
- Introduce background tasks and asynchronous processing
- Set up automated deployments and monitoring
- Build entirely new projects using the same patterns

The key idea to take away is this: modern web development is no longer about working alone. It is about working effectively with tools that help you write, check, deploy, and maintain software. Your AI sidekick is one of those tools. Used well, it makes you faster. Used poorly, it makes you dependent.

This project has given you a place to keep practicing that understanding.

Practice, references, and resources

In this section, you will be tested on what you've learned in this chapter and be provided with useful links to reference materials and resources.

Check your understanding

Answer the following questions about the topics we covered in this chapter:

1. Why is Django's development server not suitable for production use?
2. What role does Gunicorn play in a Django deployment?
3. What responsibilities does Nginx handle in your architecture?
4. Why is SQLite acceptable for TallyApp, and what are its limitations?
5. Why must your database be stored separately from your application code?
6. Why should `DEBUG` be set to `False` in production?
7. What problem does HTTPS solve, and how is it enforced in Django?
8. Why is rate limiting important for login endpoints?
9. What is the purpose of a reverse proxy?
10. How does Cloudflare improve the resilience of a small web application?

Answers are found in the GitHub repository for this book at the following link:

`https://github.com/markjprice/web-dev-ai/blob/main/docs/Appendix-A.pdf`

Links

Security in Django:

`https://docs.djangoproject.com/en/stable/topics/security/`

How to deploy Django:

`https://docs.djangoproject.com/en/stable/howto/deployment/`

Gunicorn documentation: `https://docs.gunicorn.org/en/stable/`

Nginx documentation: `https://nginx.org/en/docs/`

Web security guidelines: `https://infosec.mozilla.org/guidelines/web_security`

Let's Encrypt Certbot documentation: `https://certbot.eff.org/docs/`

DigitalOcean, How to deploy Django with Gunicorn and Nginx:

`https://www.digitalocean.com/community/tutorials/how-to-set-up-django-with-postgres-nginx-and-gunicorn-on-ubuntu`

Cloudflare Learning Center: `https://www.cloudflare.com/learning/`

Martin Fowler's Continuous Integration:

`https://martinfowler.com/articles/continuousIntegration.html`

Summary

In this chapter, you deployed TallyApp as a public web application instead of a local development project. You saw how a production Django stack separates responsibilities: Nginx receives public traffic and serves static files, Gunicorn runs Django, Django handles application behavior, and the database stores user data.

You also learned why deployment is not just copying code to a server. A real deployment needs secure settings, environment variables, HTTPS, firewall rules, process management, migrations, static file collection, logging, and backups. Even a small demo site needs these habits because public servers attract bots, mistakes, and unexpected traffic.

The setup in this chapter is intentionally modest. A single VPS with Django, Gunicorn, Nginx, and SQLite is enough for a public learning project. As the project grows, you can move to PostgreSQL, add Cloudflare, improve monitoring, and automate deployment with CI/CD.

Specifically, you learned the following:

- Deployment turns a local Django app into a continuously running public service
- A production stack separates concerns: Nginx (web), Gunicorn (app), Django (logic), database (data)
- WSGI allows Django to run behind different web servers without modification
- A small VPS provides the best balance of control, cost, and learning value for beginners
- SQLite is acceptable for low-traffic apps but has limits around concurrent writes
- Data must persist independently of application code and be protected with regular backups
- Safe deployments follow a repeatable process: update code, apply migrations, collect static files, restart services
- Django includes strong built-in protections, but only when configured correctly, and the most common risks come from misconfiguration, not sophisticated attacks

- A simple security baseline plus an edge service like Cloudflare is enough for most small apps
- A host like DigitalOcean provides infrastructure, but application-level protection is the developer's responsibility
- Scaling a Django app usually means swapping components, not rewriting the application

In the *Epilogue*, you will learn about the next steps on your web development learning journey.

Get this book's PDF version and more

Scan the QR code (or go to packtpub.com/unlock). Search for this book by name, confirm the edition, and then follow the steps on the page.

Note: Keep your invoice handy. Purchases made directly from Packt don't require an invoice.

16

Unlock Your Exclusive Benefits

Your copy of this book includes the following exclusive benefits:

Follow the guide below to unlock them. The process takes only a few minutes and needs to be completed once.

Unlock this Book's Free Benefits in 3 Easy Steps

Step 1

Keep your purchase invoice ready for *Step 3*. If you have a physical copy, scan it using your phone and save it as a PDF, JPG, or PNG.

For more help on finding your invoice, visit `https://www.packtpub.com/en-us/unlock?step=1`.

Note: If you bought this book directly from Packt, no invoice is required. After *Step 2*, you can access your exclusive content right away.

Step 2

Scan the QR code or go to `packtpub.com/unlock`.

On the page that opens (similar to *Figure 16.1* on desktop), search for this book by name and select the correct edition.

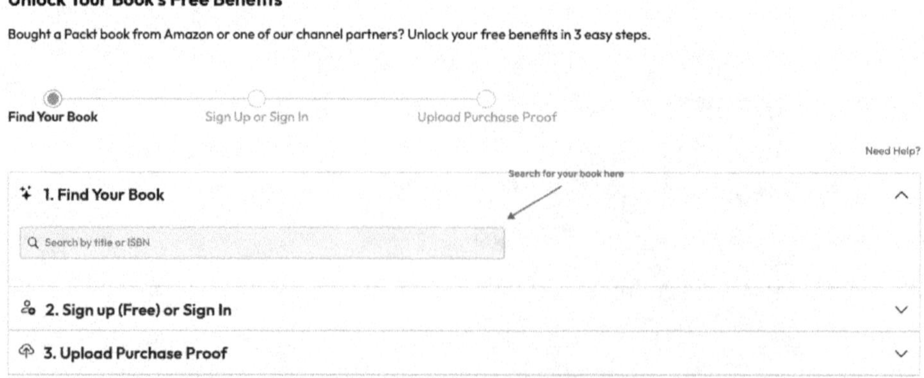

Figure 16.1: Packt unlock landing page on desktop

Step 3

After selecting your book, sign in to your Packt account or create one for free. Then upload your invoice (PDF, PNG, or JPG, up to 10 MB). Follow the on-screen instructions to finish the process.

Need Help

If you get stuck and need help, visit `https://www.packtpub.com/unlock-benefits/help` for a detailed FAQ on how to find your invoices and more. This QR code will take you to the help page.

Note: If you are still facing issues, reach out to `customercare@packt.com`.

Epilogue

I wanted this book to be different from most web development books. I hope you found it practical, hands-on, and worth the time you spent with it.

This epilogue contains the following short sections:

- What you've learned
- What to do next
- Next steps for learning web development with Packt
- Good luck!

What you've learned

You started with basic HTML and ended with a deployed web app with a real database.

Along the way, you learned nine languages and technologies (HTML, CSS, SVG, JavaScript, TypeScript, SQL, Python, Django, and Bash/Shell), built and styled interactive web pages, designed relational database schemas, created a full Django application with authentication, forms, and admin, wrote unit, integration, and end-to-end tests, containerized your app with Docker, managed your code with Git, and deployed to a production server with Nginx and Gunicorn.

That's a lot to cover. I hope you feel proud of what you've accomplished.

You also practiced using AI tools for more than code generation:

- Ask better questions
- Evaluate AI-generated output
- Debug and refine solutions
- Think about systems, behavior, and syntax together

The individual tools will change, but the habit you have practiced here will last: looking at a feature as a whole system. Where does the data come from? Where is it stored? Who is allowed to change it? What happens when something fails? Once you can answer those questions, the code becomes easier to write, review, and fix.

Most importantly, you've practiced a way of learning that will continue to serve you as tools evolve. The specific frameworks and models will change. What will last is your ability to understand a problem, break it into pieces, and use AI without letting it do your thinking for you.

Finishing the book is not the end. It is the point where you have enough pieces to start building something that is yours.

What to do next

If frontend interests you:

- Build a small portfolio site
- Learn a framework (React, Vue)
- Explore accessibility and performance

If backend interests you:

- Build APIs with Django REST Framework
- Learn authentication and security in depth
- Deploy a real project with users

If full-stack and deployment interest you:

- Extend TallyApp with analytics, authentication, and payments
- Add tests and CI/CD
- Explore scaling and caching

If AI-assisted development interests you:

- Try agent workflows
- Compare models deliberately
- Build a tool that uses AI APIs

Before moving on to another book or course, build something of your own. It doesn't need to be large or complicated. It just needs to be real and relevant to *you*:

- A personal website
- A simple tool you would use
- A variation of TallyApp with new features

You will learn more from one small project you finish than from three larger projects you abandon.

If you want to go deeper into specific areas, here are some books that will give you a structured path you can follow.

Next steps for learning web development with Packt

A printed book always runs out of room before a subject runs out of interesting corners. For subjects that you want to learn more about, I hope that the notes, good practice tips, and links in the GitHub repository point you in the right direction: `https://github.com/markjprice/web-dev-ai/blob/main/docs/book-links.md`.

If you are looking for other books from my publisher that cover related programming subjects, there are many to choose from, as shown in *Figure E.1*:

Figure E.1: Packt books to take your web development learning further

Here are short descriptions of each of these five programming books:

1. *Responsive Web Design with HTML5 and CSS, Fifth Edition*, covers HTML5 and CSS techniques for building responsive websites and web applications. It includes practical examples and updated guidance for modern browser-based development. `https://www.amazon.com/dp/1837028230/`
2. *JavaScript from Beginner to Professional* introduces JavaScript for web application development. It combines explanations, code exercises, and projects for readers building their first JavaScript skills. `https://www.amazon.com/dp/1800562527/`

3. *Learn Python Programming, Fourth Edition* introduces Python programming fundamentals and practical applications. It covers features from Python 3.9 to 3.12, including type hints, command-line applications, and examples related to Python web development. `https://www.amazon.com/dp/B0DC6DYPV2/`
4. *Django 5 By Example, Fifth Edition* teaches Django through four projects: a blog application, a social website, an e-commerce application, and an e-learning platform. It covers planning, implementation, common problems, and Django development practices. `https://www.amazon.com/dp/1805125451/`
5. *Hands-On Automated Testing with Playwright* introduces Playwright for end-to-end testing. It covers setup, dynamic content, accessibility testing, parallel execution, AI-generated test scripts, and examples for e-commerce and single-page applications. `https://www.amazon.com/dp/1806106477/`

Good practice: Before investing in any book, check which versions of the language or framework it covers. The core concepts will be the same, but some newer features (like Django 6's template partials or Python 3.14's performance improvements) might not be covered. Always cross-reference with the official documentation for the version you want to learn about.

If you are looking for other books from my publisher that cover related AI subjects, there are many to choose from, as shown in *Figure E.2*:

Figure E.2: Packt books to take your AI learning further

Here are short descriptions of each of these five AI books:

1. *Practical Generative AI with ChatGPT* introduces practical uses of ChatGPT, including prompt writing, AI assistants, document and image analysis, and code generation. It is aimed at readers who want to apply generative AI to everyday tasks. `https://www.amazon.com/dp/1836647859/`
2. *The GitHub Copilot Handbook* explains how to use GitHub Copilot across the software development lifecycle. It covers coding assistance, code review, team workflows, and the AI-powered features available in GitHub Copilot. `https://www.amazon.com/dp/1806116634/`
3. *Agentic Coding with Claude Code* introduces Claude Code for AI-assisted software development. It covers agent-based workflows, project design, and building full-stack applications with Claude Code. `https://www.amazon.com/dp/1806022591/`
4. *Learn Model Context Protocol with Python* explains the Model Context Protocol (MCP) and how it can be used to build AI-enabled applications in Python. It covers MCP concepts, implementation patterns, and examples for connecting AI systems to tools and data. `https://www.amazon.com/dp/1806103230/`
5. *Building AI Agents with LLMs, RAG, and Knowledge Graphs* covers the design and implementation of AI agents using large language models, retrieval-augmented generation, and knowledge graphs. It introduces core concepts and techniques for building systems that retrieve information and take actions. `https://www.amazon.com/dp/183508706X/`

To see a list of all the books that I have published with Packt, you can use the following link: `https://subscription.packtpub.com/search?query=mark+j.+price`.

Good luck!

I wish you the best of luck with all your web development projects. AI tools will continue to evolve, but your ability to think clearly, design systems, and evaluate solutions will remain the foundation of your skill as a developer.

Use AI as a helper while you learn, not as a substitute for learning. Ask it to explain, compare, test, and challenge your work. Let it save you time on boilerplate. Do not let it decide what you are trying to build or whether the result is good enough. That judgment is still yours.

So build something else. Keep it small. Keep it real. And keep asking how and why it works.

That's how you get better.

Learn more on Discord

To join the Discord community for this book – where you can share feedback, ask questions to the author, and learn about new releases – follow this QR code:

`https://discord.gg/rdEsrVbbC`

Index

Symbols

B

C

D

J

L

M

N

O

Q

R

W

X

Z

www.ingramcontent.com/pod-product-compliance
Lightning Source LLC
LaVergne TN
LVHW081255100826
845148LV00005B/883

* 9 7 8 1 8 0 6 1 1 1 2 5 1 *